1993

MEDICAL
AND
HEALTH ANNUAL

Encylopædia Britannica, Inc.

CHICAGO
AUCKLAND · GENEVA · LONDON · MADRID · MANILA · PARIS · ROME · SEOUL · SYDNEY · TOKYO · TORONTO

1993 Medical and Health Annual

Editor	Ellen Bernstein
Senior Editor	Linda Tomchuck
Contributing Editors	David Calhoun, Charles Cegielski

Editorial Advisers

Stephen Lock, M.D.
Editor Emeritus
British Medical Journal
London

Drummond Rennie, M.D.
Professor of Medicine
Institute for Health Policy Studies
University of California at San Francisco;
Deputy Editor (West), *Journal
of the American Medical Association*

Creative Director, Art	Cynthia Peterson
Operations Manager, Art	Marsha Mackenzie
Senior Picture Editor	Holly Harrington
Picture Editors	Kathy Creech, Harriett Hiland
Art Production Supervisor	Stephanie Motz
Illustrators/Layout Artists	Kay Diffley, John L. Draves, Steven N. Kapusta, James I. Montes
Art Staff	Patricia A. Henle, Sandra M. Kieffer, Diana M. Pitstick

Manager, Copy Department	Anita Wolff
Copy Supervisor	Barbara Whitney
Copy Staff	Ellen Finkelstein, John Mathews, Deirdre McAllister, Letricia Riley

Manager, Production Control	Mary C. Srodon
Production Control Staff	Marilyn L. Barton, Stephanie A. Green, Lee Anne Wiggins

Manager, Composition/Page Makeup	Melvin Stagner
Supervisor, Composition/Page Makeup	Michael Born, Jr.
Coordinator, Composition/Page Makeup	Danette Wetterer
Composition/Page Makeup Staff	Griselda Cháidez, Duangnetra Debhavalya, Carol A. Gaines, Vertreasa Hunt, John Krom, Jr., Thomas J. Mulligan, Arnell Reed, Gwen E. Rosenberg, Tammy Yu-chu Wang

Director, Management Information Systems	Michelle J. Brandhorst
Management Information Systems Staff	Steven Bosco, Ronald Pihlgren, Philip Rehmer, Vincent Star

Manager, Index Department	Carmen-Maria Hetrea
Index Supervisor	Edward Paul Moragne
Index Staff	Manal Salah Issa, Beverly E. Sorkin

Librarian	Terry Passaro
Associate Librarian	Shantha Uddin
Curator/Geography	David W. Foster
Assistant Librarian	Robert M. Lewis

Yearbook Secretarial Staff	Dorothy Hagen, Catherine E. Johnson

Editorial Administration

Robert McHenry, General Editor
Robert F. Rauch, Director of Yearbooks
Karen M. Barch, Vice President, Editorial Development
Elizabeth P. O'Connor, Director, Editorial Financial Planning

Encyclopædia Britannica, Inc.
Robert P. Gwinn, Chairman of the Board
Peter B. Norton, President

Library of Congress Catalog Card Number: 77-649875
International Standard Book Number: 0-85229-570-7
International Standard Serial Number: 0363-0366

Foreword

We are especially pleased to offer as the opening **Feature** article in the 1993 *Medical and Health Annual* a report on the state of the art of organ transplantation by world-renowned transplant surgeon Sir Roy Calne. Not only is Sir Roy a pioneer of one of the most complex and daring types of surgery, he also happens to be an accomplished artist. Appropriately, "Scalpel and Brush" (pages 6–19) is illustrated with a selection of his paintings—dramatic scenes of the operating theater and compassionate portraits that reflect both the suffering and the remarkable courage of transplant recipients.

The political and military aspects of the Persian Gulf war and its aftermath have been exhaustively examined in the mass media. Considerably less attention has been focused on the enormous public health consequences of the war and continuing economic sanctions against Iraq. Those consequences are the subject of "Persian Gulf War: The Human Tragedy" (pages 20–41). Although the war itself officially lasted only six weeks, it resulted in hundreds of thousands of military and civilian casualties, unprecedented numbers of refugees, massive infrastructural and environmental damage throughout the Gulf region, major food shortages and consequent high rates of malnutrition, and—perhaps most tragic of all—widespread emotional disturbances in innocent children.

A disease with a well-deserved reputation as a fierce and unrelenting killer is the subject of "In the Time of Cholera" (pages 72–95). In January 1991, after a 100-year absence, cholera made a dramatic and unexpected appearance in the Americas. The first confirmed cases occurred in Peru; some six weeks later an estimated 10,-000 were falling ill weekly; by the end of the year, some 300,000 people in Latin America had been infected and more than 3,000 had died. Although effective interventions are now at hand, cholera is still proving that it cannot be stopped in parts of the world where poverty forces people to live without adequate sanitation or clean water.

Although the stereotype of the British may be that they revere tradition and staunchly refuse to change their time-honored habits, a noted British physician informs us that this is no longer the case, at least when it comes to diet and life-style. In "Pursuing Health—the British Way" (pages 96–113), he describes the many public health efforts that *are* clearly having an impact. One of these is the campaign against smoking—a leading crusader against cigarettes being the princess of Wales.

Food is the focus of two **Feature** articles in this volume. Medical scientists have been gathering evidence for several decades that what people eat—particularly the amount of fat in their diets—is directly linked to their risk of developing heart disease. In "A Look at Eating Habits and Heart Disease Around the World" (pages 42–61), an internationally known cardiologist and his dietitian colleagues survey the cuisines of China, Japan, Italy, France, Russia, Mexico, India, and the Middle East in order to answer the questions: Do some countries have particularly "heart-healthy" cuisines? If so, which foods and what cooking methods make them so? After assessing these very different native diets, the authors then offer tips for American diners who want to make heart-smart choices when sampling the fare in their own country's many ethnic restaurants.

"Eat, Drink, and Be Healthy!" (pages 62–71) presents an exciting new lifetime eating plan for Americans, conceived by leading health and nutrition experts along with some of the country's most celebrated chefs and gas-tronomists—the grande dame of gastronomy, Julia Child, among them. In fact, it was Child's contention that Americans had developed an unwarranted "fear of food" that inspired this meeting of minds. The plan that the taste and health professionals came up with aims to help people rediscover the *pleasures* of the table and proposes that eating a healthful diet and enjoying delicious foods need *not* be mutually exclusive.

And two **Features** focus on drink. "Advertising Alcohol: This Brew's for You" (pages 152–167) is a probing look at the strategies behind the alcoholic beverage industry's tremendously successful efforts to convince people that drinking is safe, sexy, and sophisticated. Some readers may be amazed—even shocked—to learn of some of the tactics used by the industry to promote its products—especially those that target young people and minorities.

"Alcohol Warning Labels: Are They Working?" (pages 168–171) examines the labels that must, by law, inform drinkers of the health risks of consuming alcohol. Specifically, are the warnings noticed? If so, are they read and understood? And, most important, does the message have an impact—*i.e.*, does it affect drinking behavior?

The above are just a few of this *Annual*'s **Features**—lavishly illustrated articles that strive to convey the excitement and challenge in the broad fields of medicine and health.

* * *

Unquestionably, the number one medical story of the 1990s continues to be AIDS. As it has since the first few cases of this baffling new disease were identified in the early 1980s, the *Annual* continues to report on the many facets of the epidemic, whose pace has been stunning. The volume's coverage of AIDS is by no means confined to a single article or a single section of the book. **Feature** articles look at the instrumental role that AIDS posters are playing in the global campaign to inform the public about this deadly disease ("Sexually Transmitted Disease: Keeping the Public Posted"—pages 114–129) and at the search for potential new AIDS drugs in the plant world ("Drugs: Some Do Grow on Trees"—pages 130–151). In the **World of Medicine** (pages 224–414) the impact of AIDS is considered in no fewer than a dozen reports—among them "AIDS," "Disabilty," "Eye Diseases and Visual Disorders," "Obstetrics," "Pharmaceuticals," "Women's Health," and the Special Report "TB: The Captain of All These Men of Death Returns." In **HealthWise**, the last section of the book, an internationally recognized authority on human sexuality addresses "Sex Education in the Age of AIDS" (pages 451–455). Finally, a selection that merits special mention is the one we have called **Editors' Choice**. In observance of World AIDS Day (Dec. 2, 1991), U.S. Surgeon General Antonia C. Novello delivered a speech to a large audience in Washington, D.C.; her remarks were addressed primarily to young people. The editors felt that Novello's message was an especially compelling one that deserved a wider audience. On pages 208–212 we present highlights of that speech.

* * *

The editors have attempted to prepare an authoritative resource that is timely, stimulating, and informative—one that addresses matters of health that are on the minds of our readers. We hope we have succeeded.

Ellen Bernstein

—Editor

Contents

Scalpel
and
Brush

by Sir Roy Calne

Liver transplantation is a relatively new form of treatment for patients with fatal liver disease, for whom previously there was no hope. The surgical technique was developed by Francis D. Moore and Thomas Starzl, working independently in Boston and Denver, Colorado, respectively, in the early 1960s. The procedure was formidable when first undertaken in healthy animals, and when Starzl did the first human liver transplant in 1963, it was clear that in the sick patient this operation was among the most major yet devised.

A formidable operation

The liver lies at the center of the body and has multiple connections to vital structures, particularly the major blood vessels. Many of the functions of the liver are not known. It is a complicated organ that produces the clotting factors and many other vital substances in the blood and removes many wastes and poisons from the circulation. Removing the diseased liver in a very frail, chronically ill patient is dangerous for the patient and an exacting and difficult task for the surgeon. Patients with end-stage liver disease are often emaciated, and their ability to tolerate anesthesia and surgery is poor; they tend to bleed catastrophically because they are deficient in clotting factors. Furthermore, the veins in the abdominal cavity may be under great pressure due to internal hemorrhage or the blockage of the main drainage vein within the liver. Not surprisingly, the early clinical results of liver transplants were appalling, and only a few such operations were attempted in the 1960s.

In 1968 a liver transplantation program was begun at the University of Cambridge, where animal studies had led to an interesting finding: that the liver is less likely to be rejected than other grafted organs. Extensive studies of liver grafts in pigs had demonstrated that the animals could survive for many years without any immunosuppressive treatment. This was the first demonstration of immunologic tolerance produced without drugs in an immunologically mature animal.

Sir Roy Calne is Professor of Surgery at the University of Cambridge and has served as President of the International Transplantation Society and Vice President of the Royal College of Surgeons. In 1984 he established the University of Cambridge Children's Liver Fund after he performed the U.K.'s first liver transplant in a child. In 1991–92 an exhibition of his paintings, "The Gift of Life," was shown in London; Basel, Switzerland; and New York City.

(Opposite page) "Child After a Liver Graft" (1990) by Roy Calne

6

The author is a pioneer of organ transplantation. In recent years he has also recorded on canvas the difficulties and achievements of this relatively new surgical specialty. (Right) The artist captures the drama of the moment in the operating theater as surgeons remove a patient's diseased liver. In the photograph the author (center) and his assistants carry out the highly complex and delicate operation of transplanting a liver. Since 1968 surgeons at Addenbrooke's Hospital, Cambridge, have performed over a thousand liver transplants.

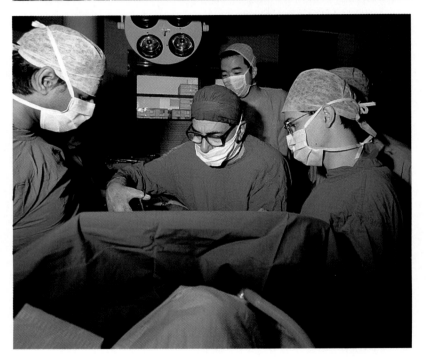

Unfortunately, in humans immunosuppressive treatment with potent medications *is* necessary but, once established, a liver graft is less likely to be rejected than grafts of other organs. Moreover, when other organs from the same donor are transplanted along with the liver, there is evidence— both in animals and in humans—that these grafts will survive with less rejection than when grafted without the liver.

Although the early results of liver transplantation were disappointing, there were occasional outstanding successes, which prompted Starzl in the U.S. and this author and colleagues in England to persevere. Then in 1980 a new immunosuppressive drug, cyclosporine A, produced far

8

better results in all types of organ transplants and enabled liver transplantation to become an acceptable form of treatment. It was Jean F. Borel, a scientist working at the Sandoz laboratories in Basel, Switzerland, who discovered that cyclosporine, a substance derived from an earth fungus, would suppress the immune system in a way that no other compound had. This author was privileged to work with Borel in the 1970s, studying cyclosporine's effects in experimental animals.

There are now approximately 140 liver transplant centers in the world—half in North America and most of the rest in Europe. Approximately 85% of children and 70% of adults are well one year after liver transplantation. Moreover, the indications for the surgery have widened. They include: chronic, end-stage liver disease, such as cirrhosis due to hepatitis viruses, autoimmune disorders, or alcoholic liver disease; acute liver failure caused by poisoning, viral disease, or drug reactions; and a variety of metabolic diseases, such as alpha-1 antitrypsin deficiency and Wilson's disease, some of which lead to cirrhosis.

Liver transplantation is also the best available treatment for certain rare diseases in which the liver itself functions normally but fails to produce one vital enzyme. In some patients the liver does not produce the enzyme that metabolizes oxalates in the body. Oxalate crystals thus accumulate, first in the kidney, causing kidney failure, and then in other tissues throughout the body. Owing to the failure of renal function, a kidney transplant is necessary, and a liver graft is needed to provide the missing enzyme. A kidney graft alone would be destroyed by excess oxalate deposits.

In children the most common indication for liver grafting is the condition biliary atresia (sometimes called neonatal hepatitis). In this disease the child's bile ducts are blocked, usually at birth, causing jaundice and leading to cirrhosis. A surgical procedure is usually carried out to construct a new exit for bile by joining the intestine to the liver, an operation known as the Kasai procedure. Often this is unsuccessful, and most of these children die from cirrhosis. Certain other metabolic and viral diseases can also damage or destroy the livers of children, who then require liver grafts.

It is now evident that the long-term results of liver transplantation can be excellent. The longest survivor to date is a patient of Starzl's, who received a new liver in 1969 and has needed no antirejection drugs since 1981. The longest survivor of the liver transplantation program at Cambridge was operated on in 1973. Indeed, after liver grafting, patients can lead normal lives, indulge in vigorous sport, and have children.

Procuring livers for transplant

Most organs for transplantation are from cadavers. A worldwide problem that has yet to be overcome is a chronic shortage of organ donors. In the United States, for example, there are generally about 1,600 patients on waiting lists for new livers. In the United Kingdom there are sufficient livers for adults since liver disease is less common there than in most other countries. However, for children there are not enough donors.

In children it is essential that a donor liver not be too large; if it is, the transplant will fail. But most donor livers are from adults. To overcome this,

Jean F. Borel discovered the immunosuppressive drug cyclosporine, or cyclosporin, a proteinlike substance derived from an earth fungus. The drug, which has unique anti-graft-rejection properties, improved the outcome of all types of organ transplants and enabled liver transplantation to become a successful treatment for end-stage liver disease. In the 1970s the author worked with Borel, studying the drug's effects in animals, and was the first to use it in patients with organ grafts.

"Jean Borel, Discoverer of Cyclosporin" (1988) by Roy Calne

9

The author was inspired by and has followed in the footsteps of the British surgeon-artist Charles Bell (1774–1842), whose paintings and drawings showed great compassion for the suffering of patients. The work at right is Bell's painting of a soldier dying from tetanus, an acute infection characterized by prolonged contraction of muscles, for which there was no effective treatment at the time.

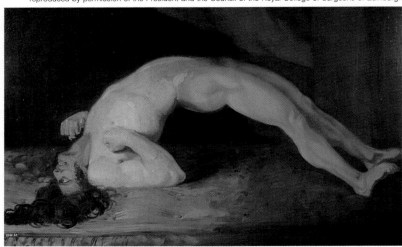

frequently a lobe, or portion, of an adult's liver is used. Success with this approach has led to the use of lobes of livers from living donors, usually from a parent of the sick child (called a live-donor segmental transplant). In Japan, where it had not been permitted to remove organs from brain-dead patients, this became a common procedure. Also, live-donor segmental transplants have been performed routinely for the past several years by surgeons at Wyler Children's Hospital at the University of Chicago.

Procuring a single vital organ from a dead donor for transplant necessarily involves tragedy; the relatives of the deceased must authorize the removal of organs at a time when they are acutely bereaved. For the recipient of a transplant to survive, the grafted organ must function immediately; thus, the cells of the organ itself must be alive, although the person from whom it came is dead. Organs for transplantation are therefore usually removed from victims of brain death due to internal hemorrhage or sudden

Rembrandt had a keen interest in both the scientific and aesthetic aspects of anatomy. The artist's esteem for the surgeon's vocation is reflected in his painting of the eminent 17th-century Dutch anatomist Nicolaes Tulp lecturing to members of the Amsterdam Guild of Surgeons.

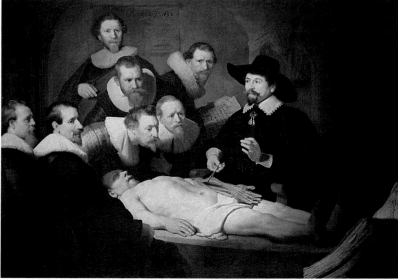

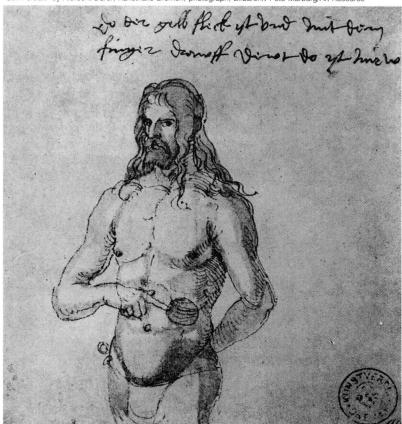

Albrecht Dürer's profound comprehension of human anatomy is combined with his artistic proficiency in this sketch of himself, which he sent to his doctor with a request for medicine to cure his pain. The artist's message, translated from the German, reads: "Where the yellow patch is with the finger pointing, that is where it hurts me."

trauma to the brain—for example, from one who has been killed in an automobile accident.

The diagnosis of brain death, or more accurately brain-stem death, is made when brain damage is complete and there is swelling of the brain, which closes off its blood supply. (The patient in this state is comatose, and the heart, lungs, and homeostatic functions of the body can no longer function spontaneously.) For it to be established that loss of brain-stem function is irreversible, there must be a rigorous assessment of numerous criteria— criteria that have been agreed upon by neurologists and neurosurgeons worldwide. The determination of brain death is made by doctors (usually neurologists, anesthetists, or specialists in intensive care) who are uninvolved with any transplant operations that may be performed subsequently.

Once brain-stem death has been established, since there is no chance of the patient's recovery, the next of kin will generally agree to have mechanical ventilation stopped. It is under these circumstances that relatives are asked if organs of the deceased can be removed and used for transplantation. Of course, many patients who die in hospitals are unsuitable as donors because they have suffered from infection or cancer, which could be transferred along with the graft.

Transplantation of parts of vital organs from living donors (such as the lobes of a parent's liver for a child) or of a single organ of a pair (such

11

as a kidney) is regarded as an ethical procedure if the donor is closely related. Moreover, the results of such transplants tend to be better than those from unrelated donors because there is a much greater likelihood of a tissue match. In fact, among brothers and sisters there is a one-in-four chance of a close match of the main tissue groups and therefore an excellent prospect of long-term success of a transplant. However, when a close blood relative is not available, the use of organs from unrelated living donors raises very serious ethical and moral concerns. Most national and international transplant societies regard the buying and selling of organs as unacceptable. There is similar concern about using organs from executed criminals. Nonetheless, these practices have occurred, particularly in less developed countries.

Because there is a universal shortage of organs for transplantation, transplant specialists are investigating so-called xenografts—transplantation of tissues from one species to another. At present, the immunologic barrier is much greater than that encountered within a species, but there is hope that one day transplants from animals—for example, from pigs to humans—will be possible.

Once removed from the body, an organ must be kept in perfect condition while awaiting transplantation. Without a blood supply, organs deteriorate rapidly. This process can be slowed (but not stopped) by cooling. Infusing

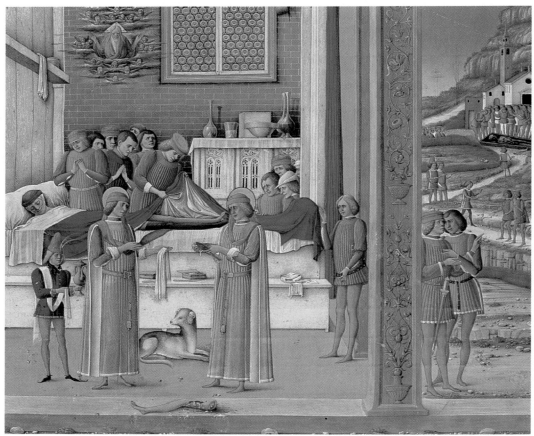

"The Legend of Saints Cosmas and Damian," attributed to Andrea Mantegna; photograph, Society of Antiquaries of London

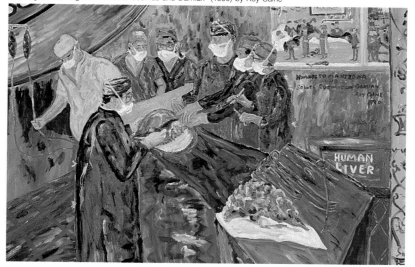
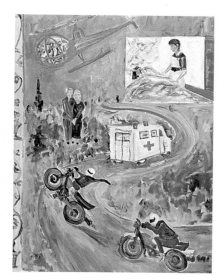

the blood vessels within an organ with protective fluids prolongs the permissible period during which it can be stored without deterioration. During this preservation period tissue typing can be done and organs transferred from one hospital center to another—often from one country to another—to achieve the best match in a suitable patient. In the U.K. most livers come from within the British Isles, but every year a few are sent from continental Europe, and vice versa. With modern preservation methods, the liver can be kept refrigerated safely for around 20 hours, although the organ should be grafted as soon as possible to avoid deterioration.

In North America and Europe there are well-developed organ-distribution networks, which keep up-to-date records of patients waiting for transplants. These networks then arrange for the distribution of organs that become available on a fair-sharing basis to recipients who are appropriate in terms of organ size and tissue type.

The ordeals of patients

At the University of Cambridge's Addenbrooke's Hospital, nearly 1,000 liver transplants have been performed since 1968, and in the course of that time, many aspects of the operation itself and of the care and treatment of patients have changed. The improvement in results is clear, but along the way there have also been tragedies. Patients who have had great expectations and have placed their trust in the surgical team to give them a new chance of life have had fatal complications.

In addition to performing a highly complicated operation, the transplant surgeon necessarily becomes involved in the emotional life of his patients and develops close ties with patients' families, especially with the parents of children requiring liver grafts. The relationships with patients, many of whom have traveled great distances for their operations, often continue long after the transplant. Certainly this author's life has been deeply affected by the individual ordeals of many of his patients. One of my patients became not only a friend but a mentor.

Saints Cosmas and Damian, twin-brother physicians who lived in the 3rd century AD, are said to have transplanted the leg of a corpse to a patient with cancer of the leg. The miraculous operation was the subject of several paintings by Renaissance artists; the diptych (opposite page) is attributed to Andrea Mantegna. The two panels show stages in the transplantation process—from the exhumation of a black Moor to the grafting of his leg to the patient to God's blessing of the operation. (Above) The author pays tribute to the artist Mantegna and to the surgeons Damian and Cosmas in his own two-panel painting showing the stages of a modern-day transplant—from the tragic death of a motorcyclist through the dramatic rescue of another patient, who is the fortunate recipient of the young accident victim's liver.

13

A patient and a painter

In 1988 the Scottish artist John Bellany, who was suffering grievously from alcoholic liver disease, which had resulted in cirrhosis and hemorrhage, came to Cambridge for a liver transplant. He approached his own operation with enormous courage—a feature that is remarkable in many transplant patients. Bellany, however, was unique in that immediately upon leaving the intensive care unit he called for paints and paper. Lying on his back, too weak to raise his head, he drew and painted a series of self-portraits, with the aid of a shaving mirror. During his three-week hospital convalescence he produced some 60 drawings and paintings—not just of himself but of the surgery, the staff, and the hospital milieu.

This author, who had always enjoyed drawing and painting, was extremely moved by those works. My own artwork, however, had been purely a hobby—that is, until I met Bellany. In the course of his recovery Bellany gave me some lessons. One assignment was to paint a portrait of him. That lesson showed me how different my concept of him as a patient was from his own. I saw him from the point of view of a surgeon—as a very sick man who had been through a huge operation. I did a watercolor of Bellany convalescing that shows the artist in his physically weak state—just able to sit up in a chair and hold a glass of milk. By contrast, Bellany portrayed himself as one surviving the indignities and pain of a dreadful operation and the frustration of being unable to do even simple things for himself.

I am indebted to John Bellany for showing all of us on the surgical team the patient's side of liver transplantation in a manner much more eloquent than words. As a consequence of my personal relationship with Bellany, my painting is no longer just a weekend hobby. I have attempted to capture on canvas many aspects of the world in which I am daily involved. My paintings are an attempt to show the drama that transpires in the operating theater, the intimacies of patient care, and, above all, the bravery of individual patients.

Painting had been merely a hobby for the author until he met the Scottish artist John Bellany. In 1988 Bellany had a liver transplant at Addenbrooke's Hospital, Cambridge. During his convalescence Bellany not only produced some 60 drawings and paintings, including the self-portrait below, but also gave lessons to the author, whose portrait of Bellany (below right) shows the patient just strong enough to sit up and drink a glass of milk. The artist and surgeon-artist became and remain close friends.

(Left) "Bonjour Professor Calne" (1988) by John Bellany; (right) "John Bellany Recovering from His Liver Transplant Operation" (1988) by Roy Calne

"Child with Liver Graft Treated with FK-506" (1990) by Roy Calne

The first child in Europe to receive the experimental immunosuppressive drug FK-506 was a patient of the author's. The drug was discovered in Japan and is produced by the Fujisawa Pharmaceutical Co. The author's painting of this young patient, who responded well to the new drug, shows Mt. Fuji in the background.

Painting the portraits of patients enables me to know them better, and it often makes them feel more at ease about their own struggles. Painting has also been a way for me to pay tribute to my colleagues—the physicians and nurses who play a vital role in the care of transplant patients—and to some of the medical pioneers who have made liver transplantation possible.

Artists and surgeons

Artistic endeavors by surgeons are not really new or unusual. Surgeons have always needed to understand anatomy and to communicate their knowledge to colleagues; the visual image was, and still is, an important way of achieving this end. In school I had used drawing to learn anatomy and biology.

Just one of the great surgeon-artists whose work has inspired me is Charles Bell (1774–1842). Bell showed extraordinary compassion for his fellow humans. One of his most poignant paintings is that of a soldier of the Crimean War in the grips of fatal attack of tetanus—for whom no treatment could be of any help.

There have also been many great artists with extraordinary comprehension of human anatomy. Leonardo da Vinci was master of both the aesthetic and scientific aspects of human anatomy. With no texts to guide him, Leonardo performed approximately 30 dissections of human cadavers in his lifetime. He sought to know not only the precise location of anatomic structures but their functions as well.

Rembrandt, too, had a keen interest in anatomy. He captured the atmosphere of the anatomic dissection in two notable works, both portraying renowned Dutch anatomists of his day: "Doctor Nicolaes Tulp Demonstrating the Anatomy of the Arm" (1632) and "The Anatomy Lesson of Doctor Joan Deyman" (1656), in which the doctor performs a brain dissection on a corpse.

Albrecht Dürer (1471–1528) used his knowledge of anatomy in a unique

15

self-portrait in which he indicated the precise location of a pain in his abdomen. He then sent his drawing to his doctor with a request for appropriate medicine.

Gift of life: a selection of paintings

The idea of transplanting an organ from a dead person to treat somebody with a disease is by no means new. It was recorded in the early history of the Christian Church in the legend of Saints Cosmas and Damian, who were twin-brother physicians. There are many paintings of their miraculous transplantation of a leg from the exhumed corpse of a black Moor to a church member who had cancer of the leg. One of these is attributed to Andrea Mantegna, the Italian painter and engraver who lived from 1431 to 1506. The painting is divided into two panels, showing various stages of the miraculous operation performed by the legendary saints.

Tribute to a master. Mantegna's work served as a model for my own painting "Homage to Mantegna and Saints Cosmas and Damian" (1990). In one panel I have attempted to show all the stages of a contemporary transplant drama: A motorcyclist dies suddenly and violently in a road accident. He is rushed in an ambulance to the intensive care unit, attended by a watchful and compassionate nurse. The grieving parents allow the removal of their son's liver, which is flown by helicopter to another hospital to save the life of a severely ill patient. A second panel focuses on the drama in the operating theater—the transplant team at work rescuing the dying patient. A miniature replica of Mantegna's work in the upper right-hand corner links the contemporary surgeons to their legendary predecessors.

A unique couple. In 1989 my colleagues and I performed a liver transplant on an Italian patient. After his surgery he allowed me to do his portrait; he was a man with very classical features. Two years later he came

Many children have been patients in the University of Cambridge liver transplantation program—some as young as just three months of age. Although the operation is both complex and risky for these young patients, it is also highly successful; about 85% of children who receive new livers are well one year after their grafts. Both children below showed great bravery. The girl is pictured recovering after her third transplant, having rejected two previous livers. When the author painted the portrait of the young boy, he was still in intensive care and receiving oxygen.

(Left) "Girl with Green Teddy Bear After Three Liver Grafts" (1992); (right) "Boy After Liver Graft" (1991), both by Roy Calne

(Left) "Eileen O'Shea After Three Liver Transplants, Awaiting Her Fourth" (1991);
(right) "Yeoman Warder—'Beefeater' from the Tower of London After Two Liver Grafts" (1991), both by Roy Calne

to see me, and he looked very worried. Although he was well himself, his wife was very ill, and she now needed a liver transplant, though for a completely different illness from the one her husband had suffered from. She, too, received a successful liver graft at our institution and allowed me to paint her portrait.

Tiniest patients. The situation of children needing liver transplants is particularly distressing since the nature of the operation cannot be explained to them. Often the parents will clutch at any straw, no matter how unlikely are the chances of success. Many children have received new livers at the University of Cambridge—some as early as the first three months of life. I have tried to depict the helplessness of several of our youngest patients. In one of these a baby boy who had suffered from biliary atresia recovers from his surgery with monitoring lines and catheters in place—a minute creature in relation to the nurse and doctor caring for him. Another tiny child with the same condition is shown clinging—as if for dear life—to the thumb of the nursing sister.

An experimental drug. Transplant surgeons still cannot always control rejection of a graft, and better immunosuppressive drugs are needed. A new drug that is currently under investigation is derived from a fungus that was discovered in Japanese soil and is produced by the Japanese pharmaceutical company Fujisawa. The first child in Europe treated with this drug, known as FK-506, was a patient of ours for whom the usual medications did not prevent graft rejection. He responded well to FK-506, which he first received in 1989. I painted him sitting on the floor playing with a toy; Mount Fuji rises in the background.

The remarkably courageous patient shown above left is a nurse who had rejection episodes after three liver transplants. She then went through the ordeal of having a fourth—successful—graft. The author painted her after each of her operations. The author went to London to paint the above portrait of his former patient, a yeoman warder, who had resumed full duty at the Tower of London after undergoing two liver transplants.

17

The problem of graft rejection. Some patients have had more than one liver transplant. A yeoman warder (beefeater) now on full duty at the Tower of London needed a second transplant after his first was rejected. Yet another of our patients, a nurse, had four liver transplants. After the first she developed gas gangrene, an extremely rare and lethal complication, which meant that her liver had to be taken out. Her condition was then very precarious. The next day transplant surgeons from Germany generously sent a liver for her, which, though it saved her life, was of the wrong blood group and was rapidly rejected. While sitting for a portrait after her third transplant, she asked whether she could have still another operation because it was clear that she was jaundiced and that the new liver was slowly being rejected. What extraordinary courage! This patient is now well after four transplants—all performed in the course of a single year. Her remarkable fortitude has had a profound effect on all of us who perform liver transplantation.

A tragic case. Despite many advances, not all patients survive liver transplantation. A young Irish boy born with Wilson's disease, a metabolic disorder that causes excessive copper to accumulate in the liver and other body tissues, was in a coma when he became our patient. When he woke up following a liver graft, he was in a terribly poor state, requiring mechanical ventilation through a tracheostomy. Although he could not speak to me, he was able to write. I did a portrait of him in the intensive care unit, in the course of which we became friends. I told him I would draw him again when he had recovered and was much stronger, but sadly he developed an infection and died shortly afterward. Nonetheless, his parents wished to see the painting and felt comforted that their son's courage had been portrayed.

"Combined Heart, Lungs, and Liver Graft—Mr. Wallwork Operating" (1991) by Roy Calne

In the catalog to the author's recent exhibition of paintings, the chief executive of the Sandoz pharmaceutical company in Basel, Switzerland, wrote: "I recognise in Sir Roy an outstanding spirit of curiosity and boldness which has been matched with patience and faith in order to discover and develop new dimensions in science and now art."

A long and difficult multiorgan transplant. Some patients suffer an even greater ordeal than transplantation of the liver; two of our patients have had combined transplants of heart, both lungs, and liver. I did a sketch of one of these operations at four o'clock in the morning, after I had just completed the liver dissection and my colleague John Wallwork was doing the delicate replacement of the heart and lungs. Ten days later I painted a portrait of the patient, who was recovering well.

A still-evolving procedure

For a surgeon working in a new field, performing an operation that is dangerous for the patient and carries a significant mortality, the daily challenges and emotional involvement are great. Over the next several decades there will be important advances that will make liver transplantation not only safer but eventually a routine operation. Future surgeons will undoubtedly look back on the present era and wonder why we had so much trouble. I hope that my paintings will provide a partial answer.

Persian Gulf War

The Human Tragedy

by Andrew Haines, M.D., and Ian Lee Doucet

For both medical and moral reasons, it is important to count the public health costs of the Persian Gulf war of January–February 1991. These *human* costs extend far beyond the immediate military and civilian casualties to include the consequences of Iraq's shattered infrastructure and the polluted environment of the Gulf as well as wider effects in the Third World.

Public health conditions in Iraq during 1991 provide a clear example of the impact that a high-technology war can have on a complex, urbanized society when civilian infrastructure becomes a target of military action. These conditions also demonstrate that the effects of modern warfare are not confined to the time of battle but are suffered substantially long after the war has "ended." The latest marvels of precision weaponry did little to confine the destruction to the armed antagonists. Thus, while the winning side boasted of the greatest use yet of state-of-the-art arms, those weapons caused the death of many of the most vulnerable members of civilian society: the ill and the elderly, pregnant and nursing women, and babies and children. Further, the social debilitation caused by the war has continued through international sanctions and trade embargoes, resulting in many more deaths. Ultimately, the civilian casualties may considerably exceed military casualties.

Iraq before the Gulf war

Public health in Iraq after the Gulf war can best be seen against the situation before the war and in comparison with the effects of the Iran-Iraq war that had ended two years earlier. Before the Gulf crisis started, with Iraq's invasion of Kuwait on Aug. 2, 1990, Iraq was a middle-range developing country with a modern social infrastructure. Among many other recent achievements, its medical facilities and public health system were well developed.

Between 1965 and 1990 Iraq evolved from a largely rural and agricultural society to an urbanized nation, with a service-based economy. In 1965, 50% of employment was in agriculture; by 1988 the proportion had fallen to about 12%, and 80% of employment was in the service sector. The country's population grew substantially, from 6.8 million in 1960 to 18.3

Andrew Haines, M.D., is Professor of Primary Health Care, University College and Middlesex School of Medicine, Whittington Hospital, London. Ian Lee Doucet is Research Officer, Medical Educational Trust, London.

(Opposite page) In April 1991, two months after the end of the Persian Gulf war, a Kurdish man and his child were new arrivals at the Isikveren refugee camp in the mountainous southeastern region of Turkey, where they would attempt to survive without adequate food, shelter, or medicine and with little hope in sight for resettlement.
Photograph, Patrick Robert—Sygma

20

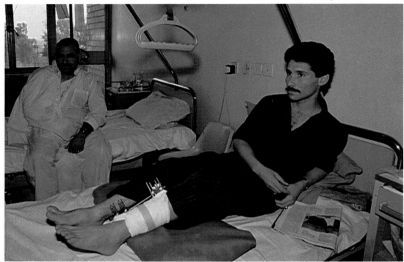

Wounded soldiers who served in Iraq's army during the eight-year Iran-Iraq war recuperate in a hospital in Baghdad in 1988. The number of Iraqis injured in the war placed a huge burden on the country's medical services.

The helmets of dead soldiers lie in rows along the Iraqi front in February 1984. An estimated 150,000 Iraqi men who fought in the war with Iran were killed.

million in 1990, with about 70% living in towns or cities. The predominantly young population was mixed ethnically and religiously: 53.5% Shi'ite Muslim, 42.3% Sunni Muslim, 3.5% Christian, and 0.7% other.

Indexes of public health showed dramatic improvement between 1960 and 1990. Of urban dwellers, 97% had access to health facilities, as did 70% of rural dwellers. There were some 130 hospitals and 850 community health centers, providing 28,000 public hospital beds and 9,000 private beds. Hospital facilities were modern and generally well equipped; many of the country's medical personnel had been trained in Europe and the United States. Clinics were dependent for supplies on a well-developed and lengthy road-distribution system.

With the start of the Iran-Iraq war in 1980, military expenditure increased dramatically from its already high level of 8.7% of gross national product (GNP) in 1960 to 32% in 1986 (compared with the average of 4.2% for the 126 less developed countries). At the same time, oil revenues and financial reserves were hit severely by the war. Health expenditure was reduced to 0.8% of GNP, which is below the average for less developed countries, and education expenditure was cut to 3.7%, about equal to that of most less developed countries.

Despite these cutbacks and other exigencies of the Iran-Iraq war, the previous trend of improvements in health seems to have continued during 1980–88. The proportion of one-year-olds immunized in Iraq increased dramatically during that time, from 35% in 1981 to 86% in 1988–89 (compared with 24 and 70%, respectively, for all less developed countries). By 1990 immunization coverage was 95%.

Although Iraq survived the Iran-Iraq war with much of its public health achievement intact, other war-related changes had had a profound impact—notably on its labor force and its economic strength. Out of a population of 13.5 million in 1981 and a labor force of about 4 million, the army removed 550,000 men. By 1986 this had increased to about one million, mainly by forced conscription—including those as young as 16 years. After eight years of war, most of these men did not return to civilian life. Probably 150,000 were killed, 70,000 captured, and many wounded. Most of the survivors were not demobilized at the end of the war.

The number of wounded Iraqi troops put a huge burden on the country's medical services. To redress the effects on the labor market, in May 1987 trade unions were abolished, as were regulated working hours and conditions. Further, unknown numbers of civilians, particularly in Iraq's easternmost areas—notably Basra—were killed or injured or lost their means of livelihood as a result of Iranian shelling and Iraqi military responses. Then, between the time Iraq invaded Kuwait and the beginning of the Persian Gulf war, vast numbers of immigrant workers—mainly from Egypt, The Sudan, and the Indian subcontinent—fled Iraq.

Economically, too, Iraq ended its eight-year war with Iran with huge losses. Annual oil revenue had plunged from $26.1 billion in 1980 to $5 billion–$8 billion in 1986, while military expenditures had risen hugely. In 1986 Iraq's war costs were estimated at $600,000 to $1 billion per month. Its foreign exchange reserves of $35 billion were exhausted, and foreign debts of about $85 billion had been incurred. Throughout the Iran-Iraq war,

Saddam Hussein had sought to insulate the civilian population, particularly the large middle class, from economic losses, and so a minimum of imports for civilian needs—$7 billion–$8 billion per year—was maintained.

The January–February toll: Iraqi deaths

The death toll of the anti-Iraq coalition (allied forces) is thought to be 343, but the number of Iraqi military dead has not been made public. The most common estimate is 100,000-plus. That Iraqi military casualties were substantial may be inferred from the ferocity of the allied air attack, from the lack of resistance to its ground attack, from the nature of the weapons used by the allies (including weapons of mass destruction, such as fuel-air explosives that destroy life over an area of many hectares and have been likened to small nuclear weapons), and from an allied policy that included what many believe was militarily needless slaughter. According to one report, which described the routing of Iraqi troops caught in disorderly retreat: "For a 50 or 60 mile stretch from just north of Jahra to the Iraqi border, the road was littered with exploded and roasted vehicles, charred and blown up bodies."

An estimate of 25,000 deaths from the above action alone circulated among the allied forces. In addition, 2,000 Iraqi soldiers died in one post-cease-fire attack on a large retreating Iraqi convoy, which had fired rockets at a platoon of the 24th Infantry Division. Pentagon officials were quoted as saying that on the main battlefront, "heaps of Iraqi corpses are being buried in mass graves across the desert." As allied ground forces advanced, they used bulldozers to bury thousands of enemy dead in trenches. Also, many injured and uninjured Iraqi soldiers were buried *alive* in trenches, according to members of the U.S. 1st (Mechanized) Infantry Division, a fact the Pentagon has confirmed.

Precise numbers of civilians killed during the six weeks of fighting are not known either. One survey based on extensive interviews estimated 5,000 to 15,000 Iraqi civilian deaths as a direct result of the allied attacks.

On the night of Feb. 26, 1991, an allied air attack killed masses of fleeing Iraqi soldiers and civilians along a 90-kilometer (56-mile) stretch of highway in Kuwait; many were literally incinerated in their vehicles. The scene witnessed by reporters was appropriately dubbed "the highway to hell." A former U.S. admiral described the post-cease-fire slaughter as "just sickening. . . . The senseless killing of fleeing troops does not contribute in any way to the successful conclusion of this war."

The notorious air attacks in the first two weeks of the war alone were later estimated to have caused 2,500 to 5,000 civilian deaths. The second phase of the air attack specifically targeted elements of the civilian infrastructure, such as bridges, electricity plants, and other essential services.

There are many reasons to suspect substantial civilian casualties. For one thing, the war was taken into the cities rather than being confined to the desert battlefront. A quarter of the population lived in Baghdad, where one district had 40,000 inhabitants per square kilometer. Basra was described in many reports as looking as if it had been hit by a nuclear bomb. A UN report of March 20, 1991, estimated that 9,000 homes throughout the country were destroyed or damaged beyond repair during the war. The Kurdish rebel commander Masoud Barzani instanced 3,000 civilian casualties in the northern town of Kirkuk alone.

In the first 19 days of the war, the TNT tonnage of bombs dropped on Iraqi soil was three times that dropped in all of World War II. The monthly tonnage dropped was nearly twice that of the war in Vietnam and three times that of the Korean War. The great majority of this bombing was less discriminate than the "surgical strikes" described by the media suggested. About 90,000 tons of explosives were dropped by allied air forces, of which only 7,400 tons (7%) were the so-called smart weapons. Indeed, at least 20% of the smart weapons missed their target, as did 50 to 70% of all other weapons. In addition, artillery and multiple rocket launchers delivered another 20,000–30,000 tons of ordnance.

Unprecedented uprooting of people

The Gulf war was preceded by one of the world's largest population dislocations. It was followed by a second major dislocation, which one year later remained unresolved.

Immigrant workers. Prewar Iraq and Kuwait were host to 2.8 million workers from other countries. The great majority of them, employed in the most menial jobs and desperately poor, had been driven from their own countries by poverty and oppression. More than two million immigrant workers fled Iraq and Kuwait between August 1990 and the war's end. Of these, 850,000 fled via Jordan, placing a huge burden on that country's population of three million.

Such a mass movement of refugees in such a short period had no precedent and exceeded the capacity of relief agencies. Many returned to conditions of poverty and disease in their countries of origin. Although the impact of such events on the future health of these people is impossible to quantify, it is sure to be immense.

Kurdish refugees in the north. After the war, from March to May 1991, approximately 1.9 million, mostly Kurdish, refugees fled to inhospitable camps on the Iranian and Turkish borders; most (1.4 million) went to Iran. After the rigors of the war itself, the desperate conditions of the Kurds' exodus, then of the mountain camps in which they sought refuge, greatly increased the incidence of death and disease. More than 1.1 million of the total 1.9 million refugees were women and children. Not only were they exposed to extremely harsh weather, they had neither clean

Residents mourn their losses the morning after a February 1991 bombing raid destroyed homes, injured 20 civilians, and killed 8 in the Azimer district of Baghdad. The impact of the six weeks' war on the lives of civilians was enormous; the social debilitation that resulted would endure long after the fighting stopped.

water nor adequate shelter, food, or health services. In April 1991 the UN Disaster Relief Organization and the UN High Commissioner for Refugees (UNHCR) reported: "According to [Iranian] government officials, the infant mortality rate among the refugees is extremely high with nearly 1,000 babies dying each day from exposure." In late April the UNHCR stated that on the Turkish border "respiratory and intestinal diseases as well as exposure are mainly responsible for a mortality rate estimated at between 7 and 12 per 10,000 per day. The population is estimated to include over 50 percent young children (less than 12 years)." In many of the refugee camps there was no proper mortality surveillance. The U.S. Centers for Disease Control (CDC) reported crude mortality rates during April in three camps as ranging from 4 to 10.4 per 10,000 people daily, but in another camp the toll was known to be 380 deaths per 10,000 per day.

In May and June 1991 many of the surviving Kurdish refugees trekked to new camps that were being set up in northern Iraq under allied forces and UN protection. These "safe havens" and "autonomous areas" had their own health hazards. A British doctor visiting hospitals in Dyanah, Shaqlawa, and Rania in May and June reported that 30 to 40% of a total 1,000 hospital outpatient cases per week were typhoid fever. This was attributed to poor sanitation and lack of clean drinking water. Diarrhea and dehydration were also common, causing the death of many young children.

The scale of the resettlement problem was huge: by August 1991, 450,000 refugees had returned from Turkey and 1,280,000 from Iran. By late 1991 this large population of refugees was still far from resettled. The protective allied forces, which had earlier created the "safe havens," had largely disappeared. Few towns and villages destroyed by Saddam Hussein's forces had been rebuilt. Many Kurds were living in hastily constructed mud and brick huts, not in their original villages but in centers to which Hussein's forces had compelled them before the war for easy control. Preparations for the approaching winter started late, and the UNHCR admitted that its aim of "winterizing" the displaced population by Novem-

An estimated 850,000 foreign workers in Iraq and Kuwait fled to Jordan between the start of the Gulf crisis in early August 1990 and the war's end in February 1991. Jordan was ill-equipped to accommodate such a huge number of displaced persons, and relief assistance was sorely inadequate.

Dominique Aubert—Sygma

ber could not be achieved. Disruption was also caused by Iraqi military forces, which were blockading fuel and other supplies, launching small-scale attacks, and maneuvering as if about to attack. Owing to this disruption and to the failure of aid agencies to supply seeds and fertilizers, the sowing of winter crops was abandoned in many areas. Further, Saddam Hussein refused to pay the salaries of government employees, teachers, health workers, and others in the Kurdish areas. In late November 1991 Hussein's forces started construction of a fortified line isolating Kurdistan

In April 1991 Kurdish refugees, a large majority of them women and children, crossed over rugged, snow-covered mountains into Turkey. They were exposed to harsh weather and conditions for which they were little prepared, only to arrive at inhospitable, overcrowded, and unsanitary camps such as the Silopi Transit Camp (above).

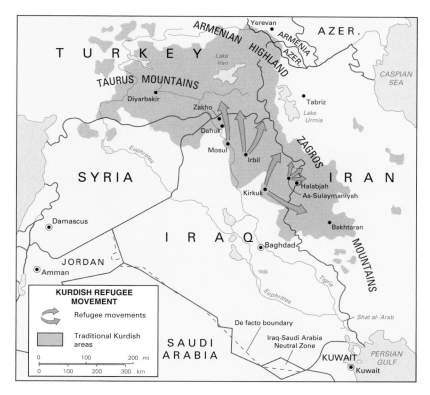

Refugee children are treated for dysentery at a clinic run by Médicins sans Frontières (Doctors Without Borders) in Cukurca, Turkey.

from the rest of Iraq. UNHCR estimated in February 1992 that only about 25% of the required fuel supplies and less than 40% of food supplies were entering Kurdistan.

As a result, by December 1991 many Kurds had returned to the unsanitary camps on the Turkish border; many were suffering severely from the previous year's deprivations. The UN estimated that 350,000 would try to pass the winter of 1991–92 in Turkish mountain camps, while a total of 640,000 were living in parts of Iraq that were not controlled by the government but were dependent on international aid. From the start, food supplies were inadequate. Then heavy snows in December and January 1992 halted all major food shipments, and in early January many children in the higher camps were reported ill and suffering from malnutrition. The death toll among the vast population of uprooted Kurds, who were lacking proper shelter, food, and medicine, would surely surge.

Shi'ites' plight in the south. In the spring of 1991, international media attention focused largely on the refugee problem in the Kurdish north of Iraq, but a similar human tragedy was unfolding in the south. When after the war Saddam Hussein's troops put down Shi'ite uprisings, many of the survivors fled into the large marshy areas around the Tigris and Euphrates rivers. Towns in the south, which had borne the brunt of the allied attack, were further damaged in the uprising; in Basra one in three buildings was destroyed. The UN estimated that there were 50,000 Shi'ite refugees in September 1991. And considering the destruction they had suffered by allied forces, the attacks by Iraqi forces, the number of people displaced, the inadequate food supplies, the extreme summer heat, and the lack of access to clean water, sanitation, and medical care, extremely high mortality in this group would be expected.

Others uprooted. Other refugees after the war included some 90,000–100,000 Iraqis, mostly of the Christian minority, who sought asylum in Jordan. Many were turned away and have since returned to Iraq. There were additionally some 23,000 Shi'ites from southern Iraq who fled the

The incidence of respiratory and intestinal illness among refugee populations far exceeded the capacity of relief workers. Many refugees—both young and old—died of exposure before receiving medical attention of any kind.

Shi'ite refugees flee to Kuwait to escape the fierce fighting raging between supporters and enemies of Saddam Hussein in the southern Iraqi city of Basra in March 1991.

country, settling in a camp in Saudi Arabia. Another camp in Saudi Arabia held 13,000 Iraqi former prisoners of war. Human rights organizations have voiced concern that "perhaps as many as 283" Iraqis in Saudi Arabia were coerced into signing "voluntary" repatriation papers and that many were arrested or executed upon returning to Iraq. Further, some 850,000 Yemeni immigrant workers in Saudi Arabia were driven out of that country, adding 7% to the population of the newly formed Republic of Yemen. These Yemenis were said to suffer harassment, including rape and torture.

Displaced within Iraq. For people who did not attempt to flee Iraq, the public health situation seems to have been little better than that of the refugees. Many were displaced from their homes (one estimate is that before the start of the war half a million Baghdad residents alone fled the city). These internally displaced people were often removed from family, work, and financial sources of support and had poor or no health care. Although the internally displaced were recipients of international aid, it

Witnesses to Saddam Hussein's army's attacks on uprisings in the largely Shi'ite southern regions of Iraq reported the use of napalm and chemical weapons and told of such atrocities as civilians being hanged from electricity poles, dead bodies being dragged through the streets behind tanks, and patients and medical staff being slain in hospitals.

At a food-distribution site operated by the Turkish army, Kurdish refugees fight for meager rations of bread. Two months after the fighting had stopped, Iraqis uprooted by the war still struggled for survival in the most inhospitable of circumstances.

was estimated that 4,000 to 6,000 Iraqi nonrefugee civilians had died of starvation and disease by May 1991. This level of mortality and morbidity immediately after the war continued for the remainder of 1991 and into 1992 as sanctions prevented the restoration of the social fabric.

International aid: inadequate at best

Many international aid and relief agencies have been involved in the Gulf area since the crisis began in August 1990. Huge efforts have gone into ameliorating the public health consequences of the war. This has taken away from these agencies' existing commitments in other areas of humanitarian need in the world, notably in sub-Saharan Africa, which has meanwhile suffered major famine. Nonetheless, a full year after the cease-fire, there was unanimity among those providing aid that—despite their best efforts—the public health catastrophe in Iraq was continuing. For one thing, the funds needed for rebuilding the civilian infrastructure were far beyond the available resources. And most important, sanctions imposed by the United Nations prevented Iraq itself from undertaking the national reconstruction necessary to return to prewar standards of public health. In July 1991 the UN estimated that the country needed $22 billion over one year to restore essential services and provide the Iraqi people with adequate food and health care.

The quality of international aid in the Persian Gulf was variable. The relief effort that was focused on the 500,000 Kurdish refugees fleeing to Turkey in March–May 1991 was described by a senior manager of the Save the Children Fund as a disgraceful shambles. Though it was obvious that the Kurds' desperate flight in harsh conditions would have grave consequences, relief came late, was often inappropriate, and was, for the most part, ill-coordinated. At the same time, little assistance came from Turkey, which, although it has a generally good record in disaster management, in this case was of little help and actually obstructed the provision of aid. For example, a medical team that did not know the basics of rehydration therapy was reported to have been sent to aid a refugee population suffering from diarrhea. Military teams dropped often inappropriate supplies literally on top of some of the camps—in several instances actually killing or injuring refugees for whom the supplies were meant!

In contrast, the 1.4 million Kurdish refugees reaching Iran, although they had considerably less in terms of international aid or media attention, received far better treatment, principally from the Iranian government. Iran had a broad and competent policy that appropriately reflected the refugees' needs. Moreover, foreign groups worked within that policy and were accountable for their actions.

Although incompetence and wastefulness characterized many of the aid efforts, at least some of the problems were attributable to the limitations under which the agencies operated. All agencies of the United Nations were required to respect the country's "sovereignty, territorial integrity, political independence, and security" and to exhibit "non-interference in the internal affairs of Iraq." An exception was made to allow the allied military action against Iraq, but no such exception was made to save the Kurdish, Shi'ite, and other civilians suffering the consequences of the war and sanctions.

Non-UN and nongovernmental relief agencies, on the other hand, have trodden a more independent path. For example, the medical relief group Médecins sans Frontières (Doctors Without Borders) operates on the belief that "assistance to individuals in danger is above the rule of non-interference into the affairs of a country." But such relief groups tend to be small and have quite limited resources. Nevertheless, the presence of these groups in postwar Iraq has provided a valuable witness to the population's suffering and has probably deterred the worst depredations of Saddam Hussein.

Infrastructural damage: life rendered tenuous

Allied bombing and shelling destroyed much of the civilian infrastructure of Iraq: roads, communications, electricity supplies, water and sewerage

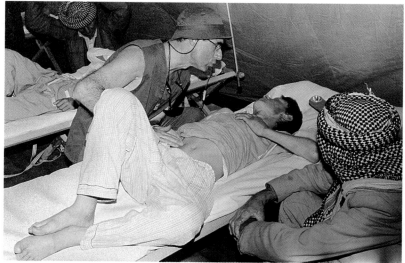

Zafer—Sipa Press

A French doctor examines an ailing Kurdish man in Kasork, part of an allied security zone set up in northern Iraq to encourage refugees in Turkey and Iran to return. Although the capacity of voluntary relief organizations in postwar Iraq has been limited, the very presence of these agencies serves as a testament to the ongoing suffering of civilians.

In February 1991 a UNICEF-World Health Organization team found that even before the end of the fighting, virtually all of Iraq's fuel refineries and storage facilities had been demolished. The refinery above, in Baghdad, was bombed in an allied air attack. Meanwhile, trade embargoes prevented the importation of alternative fuel supplies.

systems, and, of course, health care facilities. Some of this destruction was added to by the subsequent suppression of local uprisings in the Kurdish north and Shi'ite south. A UN fact-finding mission to Iraq in March 1991 (predating much of the civil strife) revealed the extent of the infrastructural destruction due to the war itself.

The recent conflict has wrought near-apocalyptic results upon the economic infrastructure of what had been, until January 1991, a rather highly urbanized and mechanized society. Now, most means of modern life support have been destroyed or rendered tenuous. Iraq has, for some time to come, been relegated to a pre-industrial age, but with all the disabilities of post-industrial dependency on an intensive use of energy and technology . . . as a result of war, virtually all previously viable sources of fuel and power . . . and modern means of communication are now, essentially, defunct.

Richard Reid of UNICEF described the infrastructural damage to Baghdad by comparing the city to "a body . . . with every main bone broken and with its joints and tendons cut."

Electricity, water, and sanitation. The infrastructural devastation was cumulative in its effects. For example, destruction of power plants and electricity-supply systems meant that water plants could not purify and pump clean drinking water, nor could sewage plants function or crops be irrigated. Without electricity, hospitals and laboratories were unable to keep blood preservatives, sensitive drugs, vaccines, and reagents properly refrigerated. Moreover, alternative resources were unavailable owing to the UN-imposed embargo on fuel imports.

In February 1991 a team from the World Health Organization (WHO) and UNICEF reported, "All significant electrical power generating plants in Iraq have now been destroyed, and similarly the refineries and main fuel storage facilities." In Baghdad, which is a flat city requiring constant pumping of sewage to prevent backup and overflow, "members of the team saw that the sanitation status of the city is critically deteriorating." One month later a joint Oxfam-Save the Children Fund mission reported that as little as 4% of electricity-generating equipment was operational.

In March, Martti Ahtisaari, UN under secretary-general for administration and management, led a mission to assess humanitarian needs in Kuwait and Iraq in the immediate postcrisis period. Ahtisaari's comprehensive report described the sanitary conditions that his team found.

With the destruction of power-plants, oil refineries, main oil storage facilities and water-related chemical plants . . . [the] supply of water in Baghdad dropped to . . . less than 10 per cent of the overall previous use . . . untreated sewage has now to be dumped directly into the river. . . . water plants . . . are using river water with high sewage contamination. . . . no bacteriological testing and control is possible. . . . the population draws its water directly from polluted rivers and trenches. A further major problem, now imminent, is the climate. Iraq has long and extremely hot summers, the temperature often reaching 50 degrees Celsius [122° F]. . . . the quantity of water must be increased . . . and the heat will accelerate the incubation of bacteria, and thus the health risks ascribable to the water quality . . . will be further exacerbated— especially viewed in the overall circumstances which have already led to a fourfold increase in diarrhoeal disease incidence among children under five years of age, and the impact of this on their precarious nutritional status.

Sound water supply and energy for pumping are essential in Iraq not only to immediate human and industrial needs but also for future food supply, as Iraqi agriculture relies heavily on irrigation. Thus, the 1991 summer harvest was seriously compromised by total crop failures in many areas, and yields were extremely low elsewhere.

In August an international study team reported that as a result of war destruction and sanctions, electricity, water, and sanitation systems would deteriorate to the point of collapse if trends continued. In southern Iraq 30% of hospital water sources were contaminated with fecal organisms. In hospitals in northern Kurdish areas, water was found to be polluted, and in several hospitals raw sewage backed up into the patient wards.

Such a situation continuing for many months would have profound implications for public health. Before the war over 90% of Iraq's population had access to safe water supplies, and efficient surveillance ensured high-quality drinking water. Moreover, the use of larvicides to eliminate the parasites that cause malaria, leishmaniasis, and other waterborne diseases had saved Iraq from the epidemics found in many other less developed countries. This destruction of a vital part of Iraq's infrastructure and the prevention of its speedy repair have taken a significant toll on the health of the civilian population.

Food. In February, only days after the cease-fire, the WHO-UNICEF mission reported food rations of 750–1,000 kilocalories per person per day, describing this as less than half the daily requirement of a five-year-old child and less than one-third the caloric requirement of a pregnant woman. Later the mission saw strong signs of further decreases in food availability, due to the destruction of food supplies and new crops, hyperinflated prices, and the UN embargo on food imports. The UN embargo (from August 1990) had a profound effect on a country that normally produced only 30% and imported 70% of its food but in wartime conditions was producing probably less than 15%. Even though the embargo on food was technically lifted in late March, one year later aid agencies were still complaining

Françoise DeMulder—Sipa Press

In October 1991 Iraqi citizens signed a petition demanding the lifting of the international sanctions and trade embargoes that had prolonged their suffering long beyond the cease-fire.

of bureaucratic delays in providing the limited food and medical aid they were capable of delivering. Other restrictions remained, not allowing the Iraqi government and private companies to resume importation of food and medical supplies.

In mid-March 1991 the report prepared by Ahtisaari attested to the scarcity of food:

Flour is at a critically low level, and . . . supplies of sugar, rice, tea, vegetable oil, powdered milk and pulses [edible seeds from plants] are currently at critically low levels or have been exhausted. . . . Livestock farming has been seriously affected by sanctions. . . . The sole laboratory producing veterinary vaccines was destroyed during the conflict. . . . The country has had a particular dependence upon foreign vegetable seeds, and the mission was able to inspect destroyed seed warehouses . . . all stocks of potatoes and vegetable seeds had been exhausted.

By early 1991 food prices had increased dramatically, while workers' earnings had plummeted. Real earnings in mid-1991 were less than 7% of their precrisis level in terms of food-purchasing power. Food-price indexes rose on average between 1,500 and 2,000%. Poverty, measured in terms of private incomes, rose to a level greater than that in India. Although the effects of this dire situation were moderated somewhat by Iraq's food-distribution-and-rationing system, which many observers have described as equitable and efficient, for most of 1991 that system provided less than half of nutritional needs. Unable to import food, the government reduced allocations of staple foods from 343,000 metric tons per month in September 1990 to 135,000 tons in January 1991.

In July 1991 a UN mission reported, "The rapidly deteriorating food supply situation has brought the Iraqi population to the brink of a severe famine. The nutritional situation of the population continues to deteriorate." The UN estimated that Iraq needed to import 7.5 million tons of food at a

Food price increases* in Iraq after sanctions			
food item (per kilogram unless stated)	price per unit (Iraqi dinars)† Aug. '90	Aug. '91	percentage increase
wheat flour	0.05	2.42	4,531
powdered milk	0.75	27.33	3,661
bread (piece)	0.01	0.33	2,857
baby formula (450 grams)	0.45	10.00	2,222
sugar	0.20	4.42	2,208
cooking oil	0.48	10.33	2,138
rice	0.23	4.08	1,801
tea	1.70	23.67	1,392
tomato	0.27	1.25	469
chick-peas	0.65	2.92	449
potatoes	0.45	1.92	426
eggs (carton of 30)	3.83	12.50	350
onions	0.37	1.25	341
dates	0.52	1.75	339
lamb	7.00	16.33	233
beef	6.83	16.90	247

*prices are averages reported in Mosul (northern Iraq), Baghdad (central Iraq), and Basra (southern Iraq)
†one dinar = $3.23
Adapted from *Hunger and Poverty in Iraq 1991* by Jean Dreze and Haris Gazdar, London School of Economics, September 1991

cost of $2.6 billion to cover the year July 1991–June 1992. That amount could not possibly be funded by the international community and sanctions still forbade Iraq to resume oil exportations as a source of revenue.

Health and health care. The consequences for civilian health of these breakdowns in essential services have been catastrophic. After August 1990 less than one-thirtieth of Iraq's normal medical services were provided, and stocks of basic drugs were reduced to one-sixth of normal. In February 1991 WHO and UNICEF found that primary health care and preventive services had suffered most. During the air attacks the headquarters of Iraq's Ministry of Health was directly hit, and all telecommunications were lost. Subsequently, the ministry's capacity for distributing supplies to clinics was reduced to 10% of what it had been before the war. During the war prenatal care, mother-and-child health clinics, child growth monitoring, laboratory services, and all epidemiological surveillance and reporting of communicable diseases ceased. Oxfam reported that the "excellent system of disease and health status monitoring" and the previous 95% immunization coverage had become impossible to maintain.

There was no quick recovery from this immediate postwar situation. Six months after the cease-fire, a major UN survey described in detail a health care system shattered first by war and then by international sanctions. Less than half the diagnostic and medical equipment was operable. Two-thirds of hospital power generators were out of order. Hemodialysis units, dependent on electric power, closed; 28 kidney disease patients in the northern city of Mosul and 17 in Basra died because they could not be dialyzed. In 1989 Iraq had purchased $360 million in drugs and medical appliances; in 1991 relief agencies supplied only $50 million of these essential items.

Registers of clinics revealed that by mid-February 1991 the incidences of diarrhea and acute respiratory infections had increased fourfold since the war's end. In April Eric Hoskins, who coordinated the Medical Aid for Iraq relief team, reported: "Throughout the country, critical shortages of clean drinking water have led to epidemics of gastro-enteritis. Thousands have died. In Nasiriyah . . . 98 per cent of admissions to the town's pediatric hospital are children with diarrhoea. Infants as young as two months old are admitted badly nourished, dehydrated and dying."

In April and May a group from the Harvard School of Public Health visited Iraq to assess the medical situation. It predicted that 170,000 children under the age of five years would die in the coming year as a result of the Gulf war—a figure that was later reduced to 100,000. In July 1991 Prince Sadruddin Aga Khan, executive delegate of the secretary-general of the UN, reporting on humanitarian needs in Iraq, found that "all the indicators, testimonies, anthropometric measurements, mortality and morbidity data collected consistently pointed to widespread and severe malnutrition in Iraq. The children examined by qualified investigators appeared to be at the lowest limit of adaptation to a reduced dietary intake."

The previously mentioned international study team undertook a household survey in order to avoid the uncertainties of estimating ill health from hospital data alone. From a sample of 9,034 households interviewed, the investigators estimated that mortality of children under five years had in-

In July 1991 a UN fact-finding mission reported that "the rapidly deteriorating food supply situtation [had] brought the Iraqi population to the brink of a severe famine" and that the nutritional status of the people was continuing to deteriorate. By August the cost of a carton of 30 eggs had risen to over $40, with food-price increases on staple items averaging about 1,500%.

35

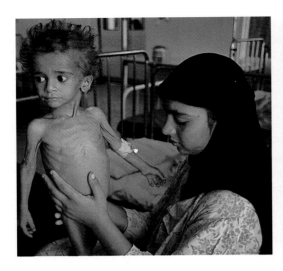 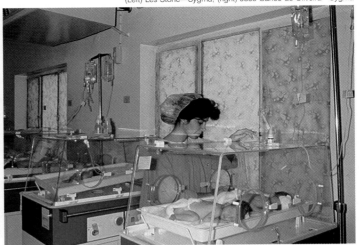

A special care unit for babies in a Baghdad hospital (above right) was typical of the modern, well-equipped, and competently staffed health care facilities that Iraq had before the Gulf war. By contrast, the severely malnourished child above was in a hospital facility after the war; power had been destroyed, trained staff were lacking, and essential drugs and equipment were in short supply. The demise of the health care system combined with the scarcity of food and other severe deprivations meant that the very survival of an estimated 900,000 malnourished Iraqi children under the age of five was threatened.

creased nearly fourfold in the months January to August 1991 compared with the same period the previous year. Additionally, of 2,902 children examined, 29% were found to be malnourished, suggesting that 900,000 of the 3.6 million Iraqi children under five were malnourished.

This team also surveyed 29 hospitals and 17 community health centers throughout Iraq, finding wide variations in child mortality. During the hot summer months, mortality and morbidity—most often resulting from malnutrition—were worse in the south than in the north. In many cases either parents did not take sick children to hospitals or doctors refused to admit them because, as one doctor at Ibn Baladi Hospital in Baghdad said, if all malnourished children were admitted, "the hospitals would be full in one day." Malnourishment in mothers was also evident and was reflected in the increased number of low-birth-weight babies. In Kut, for example, low-birth-weight infants represented 30–50% of all live births in 1991, compared with 12–14% in 1990.

Other surveys of health conditions in postwar Iraq found that in children and adults waterborne diseases including typhoid, gastroenteritis, and cholera were at epidemic levels, and hepatitis, meningitis, and malaria were widespread. Moreover, with the curtailment of the child-vaccination program, preventable diseases such as measles and polio were resurgent. In all hospitals and clinics, drugs were in very short supply, affecting the outcome of curable diseases and affecting people with chronic diseases. For example, heart attacks increased in the absence of antiangina drugs; teenagers with diabetes, lacking insulin, died; and leukemia patients were unable to continue lifesaving chemotherapy regimens.

Environmental disaster: yet-unknown health costs

In the April–May 1991 issue of *The New Economy*, Michael Renner gave a detailed account of the "environmental aftershock" of the war. In mid-March satellite pictures showed that "thick clouds of toxic smoke were extending for many hundreds of miles, stretching from Romania and Bulgaria to Afghanistan and Pakistan." Renner also described "the presence of more than one million soldiers with their immense arsenals" as having "placed severe strains on the already fragile desert ecology of Kuwait, Saudi Arabia and Iraq." Many others have documented extensive war and postwar damage to the environment of the Gulf region.

Oil and pollution. During the Iraqi occupation, much of Kuwait's petroleum industry was pillaged and sabotaged, which had effects throughout the Persian Gulf region and beyond. Iraq mined the majority of Kuwait's wellheads, and allied bombing and shelling caused many fires and oil spills, including those of the vast northern oil fields near Kirkuk and Ba'iji. When a UN mission arrived to assess the damage in March 1991, it found that of 1,330 active wells, about 650 were ablaze and many others were gushing oil. Between four million and eight million barrels of oil a day were thus lost. According to the U.S. Environmental Protection Agency (EPA), the oil fires, which released vast amounts of hydrocarbons, sulfur dioxide, and nitrogen oxide into the atmosphere, were producing about 10 times as much air pollution as all U.S. industrial and power plants combined.

Although the last oil fire was extinguished early in November 1991—sooner than most predictions—unburned oil continued to pour into the desert. The U.S. Army Corps of Engineers estimated that up to 150 million barrels had spilt, creating large "black lakes" of oil. Burning wells actually cause less pollution damage than nonburning wells gushing oil. The Kuwaiti Institute for Scientific Research feared that groundwater would become contaminated by oil or toxic heavy metals leaching out of it.

Atmospherically, the effects seem to have been neither as small as many officials anticipated nor as global as some had predicted before the start of the war. Toxic particulate matter was deposited heavily over Kuwait and southern Iraq, adversely affecting crops and livestock. In November 1991, nine months after the war's end, levels of carcinogenic and mutagenic gases tens of times higher than those established as safe by WHO and the EPA were found; these high levels occurred repeatedly for short periods, against a more constant background of increased atmospheric pollution.

Allan Tannenbaum—Sygma

An environmentalist takes samples from amid the smoke and flames of Kuwait's burning oil wells to test for toxins. It was impossible to predict precisely what the long-term health effects would be of Saddam Hussein's torching of over 700 wells in an attempt to destroy Kuwait's oil industry. However, it was evident that in the short term smoke would pollute the air over an extensive area and that the massive "black lakes" of unignited oil would seep into the land, contaminating already scarce food and water supplies.

Pollution from the smoke and the soaking of unignited oil into land can be expected to have many cumulative and prolonged effects on animal, plant, and human health—directly, as short-term pollution of food, water, and air, and indirectly, by contaminating and reducing food and water supplies and increasing malnutrition and susceptibility to disease.

Ordnance. Unexploded and spent ammunition littering the desert and many civilian areas poses a further health hazard. During the war Iraq placed about half a million mines. Many of the 90,000 tons of bombs dropped by the allied forces were cluster bombs, which disperse into hundreds of bomblets, not all of which exploded. "At least 600 bombs, rockets, and artillery shells dropped or fired every day of the war will have failed to explode and thus constitute a continuing hazard," stated one U.S. expert. In addition, unburned oil had in some cases engulfed ordnance and mines, further complicating its cleanup.

The limitations of ordnance-clearance efforts have been illustrated in various reports. In Kuwait City a French team removed 15,000 mines from a 6.4-kilometer (four-mile) stretch of beach but expected to miss 2%, which left 300 mines in a small area. As of October 1991, 44 Americans had been killed by unexploded ordnance. On average, in the year following the war, six people were killed every day by picking up or standing on unexploded ordnance. In the Basra area alone it was reported that approximately 100 civilians a month had lost their life as a result of inadvertent contact with an antipersonnel mine.

In addition to killing, unexploded ordnance and mines maim and cause lifelong disability. An editorial in the *British Medical Journal* described the kinds of physical harm that such ammunition can cause: "They drive dirt, bacteria, clothing and metal and plastic fragments into the tissue, causing secondary infections. The shock wave from an exploding mine can destroy blood vessels well up the leg, forcing surgeons to amputate much higher than the site of the primary wound." The editorial called on doctors world-wide to work for a ban on these indiscriminate weapons.

French troops clear land mines from a stretch of beach in Kuwait City. What makes these weapons so abhorrent is that they lie dormant until an unsuspecting person, vehicle, or animal triggers their detonating mechanism. Physicians have called for an international ban on these indiscriminate weapons that are most likely to kill or maim innocent civilians, often months or years after a war has ended.

But spent as well as unexploded ammunition poses hazards. Allied forces left at least 40 tons of depleted uranium shells on the battlefields—material that is chemically toxic and radioactive and threatens to pass into food chains and water supplies, as well as directly endangering cleanup teams. An appraisal by the Atomic Energy Authority in the U.K. calculated that there was enough uranium in southern Iraq and Kuwait as a result of the Gulf war to cause 500,000 deaths if all of it were absorbed.

Politics and prognosis. In the early months following the Gulf war, plans were made for comprehensive investigations of the environmental situation and the public health threat, but later many of these were canceled or curtailed. Official pronouncements in early 1992 gave an optimistic picture, minimizing any substantial health consequences of environmental damage, despite the lack of data. The Kuwaiti government became reticent and obstructive of independent surveys, such as one conducted by Greenpeace in November 1991, and has restricted access to baseline data. Probably the only ongoing study of the long-term human effects of the damaged environment is one funded by the European Communities and being conducted by a single scientist.

Quantifying the human impact of these dramatic environmental changes is necessarily a complex undertaking, and the chaotic aftermath of war makes precise measurement and surveillance difficult, especially where the political will is lacking. The human effects occurring now are part of a developing long-term process whose true impact may not be evident for years. Whatever the long-term effects turn out to be, pollution and ordnance are both adding to the current public health crisis—by killing or injuring a substantial number of victims, adding to the burden on health facilities, and delaying the return to a normally functioning infrastructure and productive economy.

The war's psychological toll

The psychological effects of war and deprivation are debilitating in a way that makes recovery from disaster conditions much harder to achieve. Children and pregnant or nursing mothers are the groups most vulnerable to psychological disturbance in this context. Throughout 1991 reports by the agencies providing aid in the Gulf noted widespread psychological disturbances in children—whether or not they were physically injured—and the inability of some nursing mothers to lactate even when receiving apparently adequate nutrition.

In August the international study team included an assessment of children's mental health in its comprehensive survey of conditions in postwar Iraq. Child psychologists reported that the levels of anxiety, stress, and pathological behavior they saw in Iraqi children were unprecedented in their collective experience (which had included study of the effects of war on children in Mozambique, The Sudan, and Uganda). Of 214 primary school children interviewed six months after the war, nearly two-thirds believed that they would not survive to become adults. The psychologists wrote:

The most significant impression from the interviews . . . was their lack of life, their deep depression, sad appearance, tiredness, and lack of joy. . . . They are deeply disturbed.

39

QUESTION	PERCENTAGE ANSWERING YES
Do you often think about the event now?	86.7
Do you often get scared or upset when you think about the event?	79.4
Do you often go over in your mind what happened, like seeing pictures or hearing sounds of what happened?	77.6
Do you often dream about the event?	50.0
Do you sometimes feel as if the event is happening all over again?	48.9
Do you stay away from situations or activities that make you remember what happened?	55.2
Do you try not to think about what happened?	73.5
Do thoughts or feelings about the event make it hard for you to remember things well, like remembering what you have learned in class?	56.3
Since the event happened, do you feel more alone inside, as if your friends or parents do not really understand how you feel?	57.4
Since the event happened, do you worry that you may not live to become an adult?	62.2
Since the event happened, do you enjoy playing with friends or participating in sports or other activities less than before?	74.7

Adapted from Atle Dyregrov, M.D., and Magne Rauladen, M.D., "The Impact of the Gulf Crisis on Children in Iraq," *Health and Welfare in Iraq After the Gulf Crisis: An In-Depth Assessment,* International Study Team, October 1991

Child psychologists and international agencies that provided aid in the Gulf reported widespread emotional disturbances—including high levels of anxiety, stress, and pathological behavior—in children, whether or not they had been physically injured. The responses of 107 primary school children in a Baghdad suburb and 117 children in Basra to a Post-Traumatic Stress Reaction Checklist (above) administered in August–September 1991 is a reflection of the war's psychological impact on innocent youngsters. ("Event" refers to the Persian Gulf crisis beginning on Aug. 2, 1990.)

For some children, these problems may endure for their entire lifetime . . . haunted by the smell of gunfire, fuel from planes, fires and burned flesh. Many children are still struggling with the memories of what they touched: remains of planes, blood, dead bodies and wounded relatives.

Grim conclusions

As a result of the Gulf war, at least 40 low- and middle-income developing countries faced the economic equivalent of a natural disaster; some saw their GNP fall by 25%. Direct losses to them were conservatively estimated at $12 billion. Oil prices rose sharply, while income fell owing to reduced demand for exports and loss of migrant workers' remittances. These economic factors will undoubtedly have an adverse impact on health in these already impoverished countries.

The public health effects on Iraq's civilian population of the eight-year Iran-Iraq war stand in stark contrast to the six-week Persian Gulf war. Both wars caused similar numbers of Iraqi military deaths, but civilian deaths were substantial during the Gulf war and greater still after it. The Gulf war simply shattered the social fabric of Iraq and the remarkable improvements in public health it had made over the previous decades.

One year later Kuwait still did not have a democratically elected government. Far from correcting or curbing Saddam Hussein's long record of persecution of Kurds and Shi'ites, the Gulf war provided further opportunities for human rights violations. Iraqi violations against Kuwaitis during the occupation of Kuwait were replaced by Kuwaiti maltreatment, torture, and murder of Palestinians, Jordanians, and others, including Kurds, seeking safety from Hussein. Despite his defeat by allied forces, Saddam Hussein was left with military means to renew his terrorization of Kurds and Shi'ites, which prompted massive refugee movements. The huge refugee problem continued unresolved into the winter of 1991–92; meanwhile, media interest in the plight of the refugees waned, as did evidence of concern and responsibility on the part of the international community.

One year after the Persian Gulf war, Palestinian women in the Hawali district, a ghettolike slum in Kuwait City, were homeless, stateless, and at the mercy of the vindictive Kuwaiti government. Many of the estimated 150,000 remaining Palestinians of the 450,000 who made their homes in that country before the war had been tortured, imprisoned, or murderered, while those who had been forced out or escaped during the Iraqi occupation were unwelcome in the Middle Eastern countries to which they fled.

While the centers of Baghdad and Basra have been rebuilt with modern shopping facilities, the country's population as a whole suffers increasing pauperization as a combined result of international sanctions, the Iraqi regime, and massive war damage. Sanctions were rejected as an effective means of forcing Saddam Hussein to leave Kuwait, but they continued to be used after the war despite the fact that their principal impact was on the most vulnerable groups of society.

On a fact-finding mission to Iraq with the voluntary group Physicians for Human Rights, H. Jack Geiger, professor of community medicine at the City University of New York and a specialist in the study of war, described the Gulf war as "a bomb now, die later, kind of war" and summed up the human consequences as "a slow-moving catastrophe of immense proportions." Simply put, the Gulf war of January–February 1991 resulted in a public health disaster for Iraqi civilians, an environmental disaster for the region, and a personal disaster for millions of refugees and displaced persons.

Although the actual fighting lasted only six weeks, the Gulf war's toll on the lives of people has been astutely described as "a slow-moving catastrophe of immense proportions." The human costs will be felt for years to come.

A Look
at Eating Habits and
Heart Disease Around the World

by Antonio M. Gotto, Jr., M.D., D. Phil., Lynne W. Scott, M.A., R.D./L.D., and Mary Carole McMann, M.P.H., R.D./L.D.

Cardiovascular disease—which encompasses coronary heart disease (CHD), stroke, and other disorders of the heart and blood vessels—accounts for about one of every four deaths worldwide, more than any other single cause. The toll varies widely, from almost 50% of deaths in developed nations to as little as 16% in some less developed countries. Many factors account for the higher incidence of cardiovascular disease, and especially CHD, in developed countries. Richer diets that are higher in fat and calories are partly responsible. In addition, people in developed countries live longer than their counterparts in nonindustrialized nations, and since CHD—like other chronic diseases—is usually a disease of adults, it is more prevalent in countries where life expectancy is longer.

The diet and heart disease connection

For nearly half a century, medical scientists have been working to identify the differences between populations that have high and low rates of heart disease. Early on, it became clear that what people eat has a major effect on their chances of developing CHD, and investigators began focusing on dietary differences between populations with widely varying CHD rates.

The first comprehensive study of CHD rates in different areas of the world was undertaken in the 1950s. Researchers found that among industrialized nations, Japan had the lowest and Finland the highest reported rates of CHD. Between 1956 and 1964 the landmark Seven Countries Study was conducted by a group of investigators seeking to learn more about the worldwide incidence of CHD. They examined CHD rates, diet, and other factors affecting the health of men in Finland, Greece, Italy, Japan, The Netherlands, the United States, and Yugoslavia. At the end of a five-year period, it was found that Italy and Japan had the lowest death rates from CHD: 7 deaths per 10,000 people per year in Italy and 9 in Japan (although Japan had the lowest incidence of CHD). Finland and the U.S. had the highest rates (47 deaths per 10,000 each), followed by The Netherlands (35 deaths per 10,000).

Of the seven countries in the study, the percentage of calories derived from fat was highest in the U.S., on the Greek island of Crete, and in The

Antonio M. Gotto, Jr., M.D., D.Phil., *is Chairman, Department of Medicine, Baylor College of Medicine, and Chief, Internal Medicine Service, the Methodist Hospital, Houston, Texas. A past President of the American Heart Society, he is coauthor of* The Living Heart Diet, The Living Heart Brand Name Shopper's Guide, *and* The Chez Eddy Living Heart Cookbook. *He is also the founder of the Methodist Hospital's critically acclaimed Chez Eddy Restaurant, where elegant gourmet meals are also "heart healthy."*

Lynne W. Scott, M.A., R.D./L.D., *is Assistant Professor, Department of Medicine, Baylor College of Medicine, and coauthor of* The Living Heart Diet *and* The Living Heart Brand Name Shopper's Guide.

Mary Carole McMann, M.P.H., R.D./ L.D., *is a Research Dietitian at Baylor and editor of* The Living Heart Brand Name Shopper's Guide.

(Opposite page) "Spaghetti Meets Tomato in the Collision of the Continental Plates" by Roark Gourley; photographed by Laurie M. Penland at the National Museum of Natural History

A Japanese youngster devours a traditional meal in a Tokyo noodle shop. Noodles of many kinds, a valuable source of complex carbohydrates, enjoy a prominent place in the diet of Japan. (Below) At a produce stand in a village in the Campania region of Italy, women choose from an abundant supply of fresh, locally grown vegetables and fruits. Of several industrial countries studied in the 1960s, Japan and Italy had the lowest rates of death from coronary heart disease. Medical scientists attributed this finding largely to the healthy diets— high in fruits, vegetables, and complex carbohydrates and low in saturated fats—of these two nations.

Netherlands (40% each), followed by Finland (35–39%). Countries with the lowest fat intake were Japan (9%) and Italy (25–27%). In further analyzing dietary differences, the researchers found that data correlating *saturated fat* intake with CHD were even more impressive than those for the total amount of fat in the diet. The percentage of calories derived from saturated fat in Finland ranged from 19% in the western part of the country to 22% in the east; in the U.S. the intake of saturated fat ranged from 17 to 18%. The Japanese diet, however, derived only 3% of calories from saturated fat, the Cretan diet 8%, and the Italian diet 9 to 10%. The Seven Countries data demonstrated quite clearly that the CHD death rate is more closely related to the level of saturated fat in the diet than to total fat or any other dietary factor.

A closer look at the Finnish diet revealed that men in Finland drank large amounts of whole milk with a very high fat content (4–5% fat), and this was their primary fat source. (Whole milk in the U.S., by comparison, has 3.5% fat.) Meat, especially beef and sausage, and butter were other major sources of fat and saturated fat for the Finnish men. Meat and various dairy products were the primary sources of saturated fat in the diets of men in the U.S.

A lesson from the Eskimos

A further link between diet and heart disease was established in the mid-1970s, when Danish researchers noted an association between high fish consumption and a lower death rate from heart disease among Eskimos (Inuit) in Greenland. Despite the fact that their diet was as high in fat and cholesterol as that of Danes or North Americans, the Greenland Eskimos had one-tenth the death rate from heart disease. The most striking difference between the diet of the Eskimos and that of the Danes and North Americans was in the types of fat consumed: the Eskimo diet was high in total fat but low in saturated fat; the Danish diet, in contrast, contained twice the saturated fat of the Eskimo diet. The Eskimos have traditionally

eaten large amounts of seal, whale, and fish. Although meat from these animals is high in fat and cholesterol, it is unique in containing large quantities of highly polyunsaturated omega-3 fatty acids and low levels of saturated fat. The omega-3 fatty acids enter the food chain when fish eat marine plant life (phytoplankton); the fish then are consumed by seals, walrus, and whales. The fish with the highest levels of omega-3 fatty acids are usually those that inhabit colder waters, where the omega-3 fatty acids act much like antifreeze, keeping their bodies pliable in the frigid environment.

Studies of the Eskimo diet alerted researchers to the fact that not all unsaturated fats are alike in their effects on the body. This prompted further studies comparing fish intakes in countries with high and low rates of CHD. Interestingly, in Japan, where the overall diet is characterized by a relatively high level of omega-3 fatty acids obtained from fish and other sea life, there were some fairly significant differences in fish consumption among the various geographic areas. On the island of Okinawa, for example, the amount of fish eaten was found to be twice that of mainland Japan, and the death rate of Okinawans was the lowest in the country. Western populations, such as those of the U.S. and the United Kingdom, tend to consume less fish—and to have higher CHD death rates. A retrospective study reported in The Netherlands in the 1980s showed that eating as little as one or two fish dishes per week may help to prevent CHD. In several studies subjects who were fed large amounts of either fish or fish oil rich in omega-3 fatty acids had favorable changes in cholesterol levels and, more especially, levels of triglyceride in the blood.

Regional trends in CHD

About 20 years after the completion of the Seven Countries Study, the Inter-Society Commission for Heart Disease Resources reported additional data showing that CHD death rates were still highest in Finland and in the U.S. and other English-speaking countries. While Italy and Japan continued to have low rates, both the incidence of CHD and the CHD death rate in these two countries increased between the 1960s and 1980s, a period during which the average intake of saturated fat in the Italian and Japanese diets also increased. Statistics from Japan showed that the CHD death rate per

Trends in fat consumption (numbers represent percentage of calories from fat)						
	Japan		Italy		U.S.	
	1960s*	1980s†	1960s*	1980s‡	1960s*	1980s§
fat	11	25	25–27	36	40	37
saturated fat	3	8	9–10	13	17–18	14
monounsaturated fat	4	9	13–14	14	17–18	15
polyunsaturated fat	4	8	3	6	4–6	8

*adapted from Seven Countries Study
†adapted from Ministry of Welfare, Japan
‡adapted from Household Survey on Food and Nutrient Intakes
§adapted from U.S. Surgeon General's Report

100,000 population had risen from 36 in 1960 to 41 in 1985 (compared with the U.S. rate of 193 in 1985). In both Italy and Japan the trend over time toward a diet higher in fat and saturated fat has corresponded to an increased incidence of CHD.

An ongoing World Health Organization project—known as MONICA (an acronym derived from the words *monitoring* and *cardiovascular*)—is currently collecting data on patterns of CHD in 26 countries of Europe, North America, and the western Pacific. The objectives of MONICA are to measure trends in incidence of and deaths from CHD and to assess the extent to which these are related to changes in known risk factors in different countries. Data collected in 1984 showed that women aged 35 to 64 had about half the death rate from heart disease as men the same age and that women living in France, Spain, and Switzerland had the lowest rates. The highest death rates for women were observed in Russia (Siberia), Scotland, and Yugoslavia. Among men, the highest heart disease rates were found in Siberia, Yugoslavia, and Finland and the lowest in Spain, France, and China. (Japan was not included in the 1984 data.)

The MONICA data seem to confirm a phenomenon noted in several earlier studies conducted in the Northern Hemisphere—namely, a trend toward higher heart disease mortality rates in northern countries than in southern. Medical scientists believe that this trend, which has been observed on the European continent as well as regionally in Mexico, may be associated with dietary differences among the different geographic areas. Heart disease mortality rates in Russia (Siberia) and in northern Europe (Scotland, Finland, Northern Ireland) are among the highest in the world; however, Czechoslovakia and Yugoslavia—in central Europe—also have exhibited high death rates from heart disease.

Fish should certainly be on the menu of those seeking a "heart-healthy" diet. Most fish is low in fat. Only a few varieties, such as salmon and mackerel, are high in fat, but these contain omega-3 fatty acids, which are beneficial.

In Mexico, for example, deaths from heart disease among males vary from approximately 70 per 100,000 in the south to 173 in the north; among females the respective rates are 54 and 96 per 100,000. People in northern Mexico consume more meat (predominantly beef, pork, and sausage), eggs, and whole milk—foods high in saturated fat and cholesterol—than their neighbors in the south. The northerners also use lard in cooking. In the south more corn (primarily in tortillas), beans, lentils, and fresh fruits and vegetables are eaten, and eggs are less available. Tortillas and beans are staples of the southern diet.

In Europe death rates from CHD are lower near the Mediterranean—for example, in Greece and southern Italy—than in northern countries. Notably, the traditional diet in southern Italy and Greece is relatively high in total fat—but the primary source of fat is olive oil, which is high in monounsaturated fat. Research has shown that people who replace the saturated fat in their diet with monounsaturates lower their blood cholesterol level, which, in turn, helps reduce the risk of heart disease. In general, people in Mediterranean countries also eat more fruits and vegetables and less saturated fat than do those in northern or central Europe or the U.S. The French, however, are an interesting exception, since they have a low rate of heart disease but resemble northern Europeans and Americans in their intake of animal fats. This phenomenon has been called the "French paradox" (discussed in detail below).

Hazards of affluence and westernization

Researchers have considered the possibility that genetic factors may play a role in predisposing some groups to higher rates of CHD. However, studies of immigrant populations have confirmed that diet, especially saturated fat intake, is an even better predictor of CHD rates than are racial and ethnic background. Research has shown that as people from countries with a low incidence of CHD move to countries with a higher incidence and adopt the local dietary habits, they soon begin to exhibit the higher incidence. In one such investigation (known as the Ni-Hon-San Study) scientists looked at one group of Japanese men living in Japan (Nippon), a second group of Japanese who had immigrated to Hawaii (Honolulu), and a third group living in San Francisco. The rate of CHD was twice as high among the Japanese men living in Hawaii and three times as high among those in California as it was among the men living in Japan.

In another investigation of the effect of switching from a low-fat diet to one more characteristic of affluent, Western countries, a team from the Oregon Health Sciences University (Portland) recruited 13 men and women from a Tarahumara Indian community in the Sierra Madre Mountains of northern Mexico to participate in a short-term dietary study. The normal diet of these people consists of large quantities of corn and beans and other vegetables and fruits; they also consume small amounts of fish, game, and eggs. The Tarahumara diet is low in fat and cholesterol. High blood pressure, elevated cholesterol levels, and CHD are rare among the Tarahumara. They live in rugged terrain, have a high level of physical activity, and in general are in excellent physical condition. After five weeks of

Corn tortillas and beans, foods that are rich in complex carbohydrates and low in fat, are staples of the diet in the south of Mexico, where the rate of death from heart disease is lower than in the north. The northern diet, on the other hand, includes more meat, milk, and eggs, all of which are important sources of saturated fat and cholesterol.

47

Will these Japanese teens eating hot dogs at a fast-food establishment in the port city of Kobe be more likely than their forebears to suffer from obesity, elevated cholesterol levels, and other CHD risk factors associated with Western eating habits? Probably yes. The typical Japanese diet of rice and noodles, seafood, and vegetables is being forsaken by the younger generation, who prefer frankfurters, French fries, and hamburgers to traditional fare.

eating a diet extremely high in calories (4,100 calories per day, compared with their usual 2,700 calories), study participants had increased blood levels of total cholesterol, low-density lipoprotein cholesterol (the so-called bad cholesterol), and triglyceride, and all had gained weight, thus altering their risk of developing heart disease—and all within a very short time. The effects on CHD risk of such dietary trends in large populations over prolonged periods of time are likely to be significant.

Eating around the world

What foods do people around the world eat, and how "heart healthy" are these native diets? The eating pattern in any given region depends on a number of variables, including the kinds of food available, whether locally grown or imported, the existence of food storage and processing facilities, and prevailing cultural patterns. In countries that cover a vast area with widely differing climatic conditions (*e.g.,* China), there are likely to be a number of regional cuisines. Likewise, where the population has much ethnic and religious diversity, many different styles of cooking may coexist. In addition to regional and cultural differences, socioeconomic conditions are influential and may account for considerable variations in the diet even in a small, culturally homogeneous population. The following is a brief survey that examines the "heart healthfulness" of some distinctive cuisines from different countries around the world.

Japan. Ever since researchers discovered that the Japanese had an extremely low rate of death from heart disease, there has been considerable scientific interest in the Japanese diet. Although, as noted above, Japanese cuisine has become increasingly westernized in recent decades, much is known about their traditional eating habits. In many areas of Japan it is possible to find some people eating the traditional Japanese diet alongside others whose eating habits are more typically Western.

Rice has long been the staple of Japanese cuisine, whether eaten plain or flavored. Noodles, another source of complex carbohydrates (starch), are also widely used in Japanese cooking. Products made from soybeans, a good source of vegetable protein, are important; miso, tofu, and shoyu (soy sauce) are common ingredients in many Japanese dishes. Fish of all types—eaten raw, broiled, boiled, steamed, panfried, or deep-fried—are the main source of animal protein in the diet of this island nation. Most Japanese eat some food obtained from the ocean—seaweed, fish, shellfish, marine mammals, and other sea creatures—at least every day and often at every meal. Tea is the universal beverage, and the possible health benefit from drinking green tea is a subject of current scientific scrutiny. Pickled vegetables and fruits add piquancy to Japanese meals. As a rule, the Japanese prefer to eat foods fresh and in their "proper' seasons, rather than depending on canned and frozen foods.

Since the end of World War II, the people of Japan have adopted many Western eating habits. Although the consumption of chicken, pork, and beef has become more common, and eggs have grown in popularity, cost has helped limit use of these items. American-style fast-food restaurants are proliferating and are especially popular with young people, a trend viewed with alarm by many Japanese health authorities. According to a report in the Oct. 14, 1990, issue of the *Chicago Tribune,* when a study of eating habits was conducted by a Japanese food industry organization, not a single traditional dish was ranked among the 10 favorite foods of junior-high students. French fries led the list.

Italy. Italian cuisine must be viewed as a collection of regional eating patterns. Pasta of all types and shapes is the basis of the Italian diet; people in southern Italy favor the tubular eggless pasta, while flat, ribbonlike egg noodles predominate in the north. Other important sources of starch include cornmeal, bread, and, especially in northern Italy, rice. Fruits and vegetables play an important role in Italian cooking; tomatoes and tomato paste are essential ingredients in many dishes. Traditionally, butter has been the most popular cooking fat in northern Italy, while olive oil has dominated in the kitchens of the south.

Italians love cheese; they eat it by itself or in salads, pasta, and meat dishes. About half the milk produced in Italy is consumed as cheese. Fish and shellfish, second in importance only to pasta in coastal areas, are often eaten in soups or chowders or may be canned in oil or fried. Popular meats, including veal, pork, poultry, lamb, beef, organ meats, and game, are often sautéed. Italians also enjoy high-fat, highly seasoned meats, such as bologna and salami. Eggs may be incorporated into omelets and main dishes. Ice cream is very popular in Italy; gelato is a milk-based frozen dessert, and granita, which is like sherbet, is made of flavored syrup and finely shaved ice.

France. French cuisine has presented medical scientists with an intriguing puzzle, the so-called French paradox: although the French eat slightly more fat than Americans do, they have fewer heart attacks. As in other countries with lower heart attack rates, the diet in France contains an abundance of fruits, vegetables, and complex-carbohydrate foods, such as bread. At the same time, however, the intake of foods higher in saturated

John Dominis

From the simplest of ingredients—wheat, water, and, in some varieties, eggs—come the myriad kinds of pasta, the basis of much Italian cuisine. The average Italian eats about 27 kilograms (60 pounds) per year of this nutritious high-carbohydrate, low-fat staple, compared with the 8.5 kilograms (19 pounds) of pasta per capita consumed in the U.S.

fat and cholesterol surpasses that of other countries having a low incidence of heart attack. The French have a fondness for butter, cream sauces, pâtés, an enormous variety of cheeses, and rich, buttery baked goods such as croissants. Even more puzzling, the death rate from heart disease in southwestern France—where foie gras (the enlarged livers of force-fed ducks and geese) is commonly eaten and the intake of saturated fat is said to be the highest in the industrialized world—is even lower than in other parts of France. Duck and goose fat are used in French cooking as well as in pâté. It is of note that goose fat has about half the saturated fat, twice the monounsaturated fat, and almost four times the polyunsaturated fat of butter, making it closer in chemical composition to vegetable fat than to animal fat. Furthermore, while research has shown a correlation between heart disease incidence and intake of whole milk—as was found in Finland, for example—there appears to be no link between heart disease and the liberal consumption of cheese, as in France. Some experts have speculated that the calcium in cheese somehow binds to the fat, thus preventing the fat from being absorbed. However, this has not been proved.

How is it then that the French seem to be able to break all the dietary "rules" that have emerged from years of epidemiological study? The answer may be that the French consume more red wine than does any other nationality, averaging almost 99 bottles per person per year, compared with only 9 bottles in the United States. It has been suggested that red wine may actually confer some sort of protection against heart disease—perhaps by reducing the stickiness of blood platelets (which, in turn, reduces the potential for artery-blocking clots). However, because of the risk of alcohol abuse, most authorities are understandably hesitant about recommending alcohol consumption as a means of preventing heart disease. Indeed, France has a high rate of alcoholism, and death rates from alcohol-induced diseases (cirrhosis and other liver disease) are about double those of the U.S. Perhaps new studies will eventually shed light on the paradox of the French diet. In the meantime, no one is recommending that

"A votre santé!" Drinking a toast to health may have concrete benefits beyond those conferred by a friend's good wishes. In exploring the relationship between diet and heart disease in France, researchers have been perplexed by the finding that the French, with their well-known predilection for rich, fatty foods, have a comparatively low rate of CHD. Some experts believe that the substantial consumption of red wine by the French may have a cardioprotective effect. This theory awaits proof, however.

Jean-Marie Truchet—Tony Stone Worldwide

Assailed by food shortages brought on by political and economic upheaval, these Russian consumers find little besides cabbage at the state store in St. Petersburg. With the exception of such traditional staples as cabbage and potatoes, fresh produce of any kind has been scarce in Russia in recent times.

people in other parts of the world increase their consumption of cheese, butter, and foie gras.

Russia. In prerevolutionary times the cuisine of Russia varied from opulent to extremely plain. While the upper classes were likely to dine on a wide variety of foods, many of them rich and lavishly decorated, the peasant diet consisted primarily of whole grain bread, kasha (groats), and soups based on beets, cabbage, or fish. After the revolution of 1917, however, Russian cuisine underwent years of drastic change. And with the political changes of the early 1990s have come severe food shortages, which have had a considerable impact on the diet of the average Russian.

Data collected in the mid-1970s showed that Russians were eating a diet that provided about 40% of calories from fat; of these, 17% were from saturated fat, butter and beef being the primary sources. Daily cholesterol intake ranged from about 300 to 600 milligrams. Bread, butter, sugar, beef, potatoes, and milk provided about half the total calories in the Russian diet, and butter was the largest source of saturated fat.

The Russians are fond of pies, and they make them from fruits (cranberries, apples), vegetables (cabbage, potatoes), beef, or fish. Cabbage, which is abundant during the summer, is preserved for winter consumption by the addition of salt; potatoes are plentiful all year. Fish, other than salted herring, is not widely available, and fresh fruit has been scarce in recent times. Before the political upheaval of the '90s, a meal in one of the fancier Russian restaurants might have included a wide variety of zakuski (hors d'oeuvres), such as blini—thin buckwheat pancakes—with sour cream and caviar, and a main course of fish.

A vendor selling blini—thin buckwheat pancakes that are served with a variety of fillings—attracts eager customers on a street in Donetsk, Ukraine.

India. The foods available to Indian families differ radically in both quantity and variety on the basis of socioeconomic circumstances. There are also regional and religious differences in cuisine. The starchy mainstay of the Indian diet differs by the area of the country. Unleavened whole wheat bread, called chapati, dal (lentils), and legumes predominate in the north; rice and dosa (a sort of crepe, made from ground lentils and rice powder)

51

in the south; wheat and millet with lentils and legumes in the west and northwest; and rice with lentils or legumes in the east.

Hinduism is the predominant religion of India, and those Hindus who are strict vegetarians get much of their protein from lentils. Vegetables include potatoes, onions, beans, and split peas. Although Hindus who do eat meat prefer chicken, goat, or lamb, pork is often the most affordable for poorer Indians; Hindus do not eat beef. Muslims are allowed to eat most meats, but pork is prohibited. Fish is eaten in the south and east; it is usually prepared in a curry with rice or deep-fried. Fresh fruits—including mangoes, guavas, and bananas—are prized in the Indian diet but are more readily available to those in the middle and upper socioeconomic groups than to the poorer classes. The consumption of vegetables, cheese, milk, yogurt (often used in cooking or diluted in drinks called lassi), and eggs is also limited by their costliness. Less well-to-do Indians use very small amounts of fat, usually peanut or cottonseed oil, in cooking; middle- and upper-class Indians may eat a number of deep-fried dishes, such as the fritterlike pakora. The use of ghee (clarified butter) in Indian cooking, which used to be synonymous with wealth, is now less popular because of its cost and health concerns about saturated fat; lard is never used in Indian cuisine.

A woman in the northwestern Indian state of Gujarat prepares chapatis on a cast-iron griddle. These delicate crepelike whole wheat breads are a mainstay of the northern Indian diet.

Henry Wilson

Turkey. Many varieties of vegetables, fresh and dried fruits, fish, and cheese—especially goat's milk cheese—are commonly eaten in Turkey. Breakfast usually consists of cheese, bread, and fruit. Generous amounts of butter or lamb fat are used in preparation of vegetable and meat dishes, the latter consisting mainly of veal, lamb, beef, and pork. Although margarine is available, butter is served with most meals. Most brands of margarine in Turkey are made with a combination of palm-kernel oil and sunflower and cottonseed oils; palm-kernel oil is highly saturated, while sunflower and cottonseed oils are unsaturated. Common Turkish snack foods include chocolate, pistachio nuts, and roasted chick-peas.

Ethnic dining in the U.S.

The contemporary diet in the United States is about as diverse as the country's population. It is certainly possible to speak of typical "American" food—southern fried chicken, Yankee pot roast, Virginia ham, Manhattan (or New England) clam chowder, for example; however, many of the dishes eaten every day by people in the U.S., like most of the people themselves, had their origins somewhere else. Moreover, sampling the cuisines of the world is quite a popular American pastime. In restaurants all over the country, at virtually every meal, Americans can be found enjoying the foods of other lands.

According to a National Restaurant Association Survey in 1989, the three favorite ethnic cuisines in the U.S. are Chinese, Italian, and Mexican. More than 70% of those surveyed said they had dined in restaurants featuring these cuisines. Other ethnic cooking styles mentioned included French (which had been tried by 45% of those surveyed), Spanish (39%), German (38%), Japanese (36%), and Greek (35%).

How heart healthy is ethnic dining in the United States? It must be noted that many of the dishes that are served in ethnic restaurants are not exactly "authentic." American versions often differ from the native dishes because certain exotic ingredients are unavailable or would be too costly. Then again, recipes may be modified to appeal to local tastes; they may be made less salty than they would be in Japan, for example, or not as spicy as they would be if served in India. More important from the standpoint of heart health, the American adaptations often contain more meat, cheese, butter, and other fats and fewer grains, legumes, and vegetables than the recipes after which they are modeled, making them higher in calories, total fat, and saturated fat than the originals. However, by becoming aware of the ingredients and cooking methods used in different ethnic dishes, diners who are trying to limit their fat intake can enjoy an enormous variety of cuisines and still eat a heart-healthy diet—one that follows the dietary recommendations of the American Heart Association and other major health organizations, namely, to consume 30% or less of total calories as fat, less than 10% of total calories as saturated fat, and less than 300 milligrams of cholesterol per day.

The following sections describe the Americanized versions of several popular ethnic cuisines. Some guidelines are given to help diners make heart-healthy choices when ordering from a restaurant menu.

Chinese cuisine. One of the greatest differences between the typical Chinese and American diets is in the amount of fat consumed. Rural Chinese eat a diet that derives about 15% of calories from fat—compared with nearly 36–37% in the U.S. diet. The Chinese also get less of their protein from animal sources. A meal in a Chinese restaurant in the U.S. that serves the popular Cantonese-style cuisine might consist of egg rolls fried in deep fat, barbecued pork ribs, chow mein with crispy (fried) noodles, and fried rice. Such a meal is very high in fat. Clearly, this is not how the Chinese manage to have extremely low rates of heart disease! If restaurant diners make wise choices, though, they can enjoy some of the delights of Chinese cuisine without sacrificing the health benefits.

Because Chinese cooking styles are regional, the various dishes on the restaurant menu may be quite different from one another, depending on the origin of the recipe. Food from the north and northeast (Beijing [Peking]) is likely to be flavored with garlic, leeks, and onions and served with noodles and dumplings. Rice is the staple in the eastern and coastal regions of China (Shanghai), and the more highly seasoned, saltier foods from this area may contain a lot of soy sauce and sugar. The hotter, spicier dishes served in western and central China (Sichuan [Szechwan] and Hunan) often contain chili peppers and may be higher in fat than other regional fare. Foods eaten in the south (Guangzhou [Canton]) probably most closely resemble the dishes offered in the large majority of Chinese restaurants in the U.S.; Cantonese dishes tend to be steamed or stir-fried and may contain sugar and a sauce made with chicken broth.

The foods commonly served in most Chinese restaurants range from heart-healthy low-fat dishes, such as steamed whole fish and vegetable dumplings, to high-fat fare containing meats and vegetables that have been deep-fried, stir-fried, or both (*e.g.,* sweet-and-sour dishes). The steamed white rice that accompanies many Chinese dishes is fat free; however, fried rice, a favorite of U.S. restaurant-goers, is quite high in fat (especially if it contains beef or pork). Most Chinese vegetables, such as Chinese

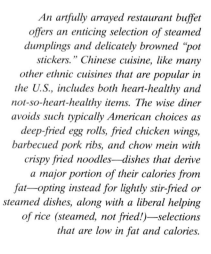

An artfully arrayed restaurant buffet offers an enticing selection of steamed dumplings and delicately browned "pot stickers." Chinese cuisine, like many other ethnic cuisines that are popular in the U.S., includes both heart-healthy and not-so-heart-healthy items. The wise diner avoids such typically American choices as deep-fried egg rolls, fried chicken wings, barbecued pork ribs, and chow mein with crispy fried noodles—dishes that derive a major portion of their calories from fat—opting instead for lightly stir-fried or steamed dishes, along with a liberal helping of rice (steamed, not fried!)—selections that are low in fat and calories.

Stock, Boston

A delicious-looking plateful of rotini and fresh vegetables flavored with garlic and herbs fulfills all the requirements of the diner seeking an entree that is nutritious as well as low in saturated fat and cholesterol. Pasta and other kinds of noodles are, in fact, integral to two of the world's most heart-healthy cuisines—Italian and Japanese.

cabbage, bamboo shoots, water chestnuts, and snow peas, are very low in both calories and fat—unless, of course, they are stir-fried. The egg rolls, fried chicken wings, and fortune cookies offered in many Chinese restaurants are not part of the traditional Chinese cuisine but were developed for American restaurants.

Many Chinese dishes—for example, the dried and pickled items—are high in sodium, which can contribute to high blood pressure. Although sweet-and-sour sauce and duck sauce (or plum sauce) are fairly low in sodium, others such as bean paste and soy, oyster, and hoisin sauces have a higher sodium content. Monosodium glutamate (MSG), which contains about one-third the sodium of salt, is a flavor enhancer often used in Chinese food. People who are sensitive to MSG (symptoms of "Chinese restaurant syndrome" include warmth, headache, and pressure in the face and upper chest muscles) should request that their meal be prepared with no MSG.

Italian cuisine. Most dishes served in Italian restaurants are based on pasta. The type of sauce and amount of cheese served with the pasta determine its "richness." For example, fettuccine Alfredo has a creamy sauce made with butter, eggs, cheese, and cream and is very high in fat and saturated fat; on the other hand, marinara sauce, a tomato sauce flavored with garlic and herbs that is commonly served with spaghetti, is much lower in fat and saturated fat. When eating in an Italian restaurant, it is wise to avoid dishes that are fried, contain cheese or sausage or have a creamy sauce. Pizza can be made with a fraction of the usual amount of cheese (or no cheese) and topped with grilled fresh vegetables and Canadian bacon instead of fatty sausage and pepperoni. A slice of crusty Italian bread is delicious, even without butter. A trend in some Italian restaurants is to offer olive oil, in which diners may dip their bread, on the theory that, as an unsaturated vegetable oil, it is a "heart-healthier" choice than butter. However, since olive oil is as high in fat and calories as all other vegetable oils, it should be eaten in moderation.

Another way to control the fat content of the meal is to request that salad dressing be served on the side instead of on the salad, thus allowing the diner to control the amount used. For dessert the person who is limiting fat intake might choose a fruit-flavored Italian ice, or granita, instead of the richer spumoni and gelati.

Mexican cuisine. Although much of the food served in Mexican restaurants is high in fat, it is possible to limit the amount of fat in the meal by ordering wisely. Tortillas form the basis for many dishes; corn tortillas—made with masa harina (ground corn), lime, and water—are low in fat; flour tortillas—which are usually made with lard—can contain more than four times as much fat. When corn tortillas are fried to make crispy tacos, tostadas, and tortilla chips, however, they have six to seven times the fat and saturated fat of soft or steamed tortillas. Upon request, restaurants will usually substitute soft or steamed corn tortillas for fried ones in most dishes.

Mexican foods that are typically low in fat include chicken fajitas, salsa, the marinated seafood dish called ceviche, soft (*i.e.,* not fried) corn tacos, grilled fish, and grilled chicken breast without the skin. Typical high-fat foods include refried beans (traditionally made with lard), chorizo (sausage), and anything that is fried. Pico de gallo, the spicy relish served as an appetizer, is a low-fat choice, but the crunchy tortilla chips usually eaten with it are high in fat. Requesting that cheese and sour cream be served on the side or omitted from dishes helps decrease saturated fat. Guacamole, although high in fat, is low in saturated fat.

Japanese cuisine. Japanese restaurants offer many selections that are low in fat and saturated fat. In fact, with the exception of deep-fried specialties such as tempura, most Japanese food contains little added fat. Japanese dishes typically consist of large amounts of steamed rice—or sometimes noodles—and vegetables, combined with morsels of meat,

Diners may be sorely tempted by this heaping plate of nachos—golden fried tortilla chips covered with layers of refried beans (probably cooked with lard) and cheese and topped off with a generous dollop of sour cream—a dish that bears little resemblance to authentic Mexican cooking.

fish, and poultry. Seafood, which is very low in saturated fat, plays a key role in Japanese cuisine. Low-fat choices on the Japanese menu include soups, nabemono (Japanese casseroles), chicken teriyaki, menrui (noodles), sashimi, and sushi; *yakimono,* which means "broiled," is a good word to look for on the menu. Perhaps the greatest concern for Americans indulging in Japanese cuisine is the liberal use of salty foods and sauces. Japanese food is often seasoned with soy sauce or has another high-sodium sauce added. Pickled vegetables, also very high in sodium, are popular but should be eaten sparingly.

French cuisine. French cuisine is celebrated for its rich, creamy sauces: hollandaise, béarnaise, Mornay, espagnole, béchamel. Wine sauces, such as bordelaise, tend to be lower in fat and cholesterol and are a better choice for diners trying to reduce their fat intake. Au gratin dishes, which are topped with butter and cheese, should probably be avoided. When dining in an establishment that offers nouvelle cuisine, it is a good idea to ask about cooking methods and the ingredients in the sauces; some of these dishes are not as low in fat and cholesterol as this style of cooking suggests. When a dish is prepared with a sauce, requesting that the sauce be served on the side allows the diner to control the amount of fat, calories, and salt added to the meal by this typically high-fat, high-sodium accompaniment. Plain breads are a better selection than croissants and other high-fat baked goods. Choosing the simplest dishes on the menu— fresh vegetable salads (with vinegar-based dressings, served on the side); steamed or grilled vegetables; grilled, broiled, or roasted meat, fish, and poultry (sauces on the side); and fresh fruit for dessert—helps assure diners of a heart-healthy meal while allowing them to enjoy the unique flavors of French cuisine.

Greek and Middle Eastern cuisine. Greek food can be high in fat if a lot of olive oil is used in preparation or added on the top of a dish after preparation. When ordering a dish that customarily has added oil, it is a good practice to ask that this be omitted. Because lamb—which is very popular in Greek cuisine—is higher in saturated fat than beef, diners should take care to order a lean cut, such as leg of lamb (with the fat trimmed off). Flaky phyllo dough is often used as the basis of both entrées and sweets, many of which contain cheese, nuts, and other high-fat ingredients; these pastry-wrapped dishes should be eaten in only limited amounts. When ordering a Greek salad, it is wise to request that the feta cheese, olives, and anchovies be served on the side. A tasty lower-fat meal might include an appetizer such as tzatziki (a dish made of yogurt and cucumbers), pita bread, plain rice, and a fish or chicken dish.

Middle Eastern cuisine is similar to that of Greece in many ways: it features meats (often lamb); a variety of vegetables, legumes, and grain products; the distinctive flat bread called pita; green and black olives; and olive oil. Appetizers such as baked stuffed eggplant and stuffed grape leaves are low in fat. Someone interested in a heart-healthy meal might request that visible fat be removed from meat before cooking and that butter not be used to baste shish kebab. Popular grain dishes include rice pilaf, couscous (which may be combined with vegetables or chicken and served

A waitress at a Japanese restaurant in Philadelphia displays a delectable plate of sushi—vinegared rice combined with morsels of raw fish and garnished with a variety of vegetables. Sushi and sashimi dishes are increasingly popular in the U.S. and offer diners a low-fat feast for the eyes as well as the stomach!

For the average consumer, confused by the plethora of dietary recommendations and exasperated with continually changing advice from the experts, making choices at the grocery store is no simple task!

as an entrée or side dish), and tabbouleh (which may be high in olive oil). Chick-peas (garbanzos) are often pureed with fava beans to make the crispy, deep-fried patties called falafel or mashed with tahini (sesame-seed paste) and lemon juice to make the dip known as hummus; while tasty, both dishes are high in fat. Fresh fruit is a lower-fat choice for dessert than baklava or the other very sweet pastries commonly served at the end of a Middle Eastern meal.

Indian cuisine. Indian cuisine features a number of foods that are low in calories, fat, saturated fat, and cholesterol. Vegetable salads are often served with a dressing of fresh lemon juice, making them a heart-healthy choice. People watching their fat intake should ask if the yogurt—which is commonly used in vegetable salads and to make sauces—is low fat and request that margarine be used instead of butter to baste tandoori fish and chicken (roasted in a clay pot, or tandoor). Lentils and rice, which are important in Indian cuisine, are low in fat unless butter has been added, and breads—except those that are fried—are healthful. High-fat choices on the Indian menu include deep-fried appetizers, sautéed meats, and foods to which coconut milk or high-fat sauces have been added. Sesame oil (unsaturated) and coconut oil (highly saturated) are commonly used in Indian cooking; diners would be wise to ask which oil is used before ordering a dish.

What to eat: some answers and more questions

Over the past 50 years, the epidemiological data linking diet and heart disease have continued to mount. Of course, data in themselves, while interesting and useful, can do nothing to directly alter behavior. They cannot cause people to exercise more, eat better, or stop smoking. For changes in eating habits to occur, research data must be translated into specific dietary recommendations, which are then converted into practical guidelines for food selection, such as limiting foods high in saturated fat. In fact, since the late 1960s public health organizations in 11 countries have been issuing dietary recommendations for the general population aimed at preventing CHD. These guidelines are periodically revised or modified as additional findings throw new light on the complex interactions of diet and disease.

As knowledge about the association of diet and CHD grows, dietary recommendations are likely to change still more. Although the link between saturated fat intake and CHD is well established, researchers now believe that the specific fatty acids that make up saturated, polyunsaturated, and monounsaturated fat may have different effects on the development of CHD. For example, researchers have found that stearic acid, a common saturated fatty acid that is found in beef and chocolate, does not raise blood cholesterol. However, saturated fatty acids known to increase cholesterol are found along with the stearic acid in both of these foods. What impact, if any, should this knowledge have on the food choices people make? Likewise, researchers do not know precisely why eating fish helps prevent CHD, only that it does. Some researchers have asked: Is it specific types of fatty acids, such as the omega-3 fatty acids, or other, as-yet-unidentified constituents of fish that provide protection against CHD? For the present, most authorities feel confident in advising people to include more fish in their diets.

Are the amounts of *trans* fatty acids (polyunsaturated fats formed during the hydrogenation, or hardening, process) found in margarines and vegetable shortenings likely to increase blood cholesterol levels? Although a 1990 study in which people consumed approximately nine times the amount of *trans* fatty acids in the typical American diet indicated that this is true, most health experts in the U.S. feel that normal consumption of *trans* fatty acids does not pose a risk.

What effects do specific foods and beverages that are popular in the American diet—for example, beef and coffee—have on blood cholesterol? Some people who are watching their cholesterol insist on avoiding beef altogether. Yet research has shown that a diet low in fat and saturated fat with lean beef as the only entrée does not raise blood cholesterol levels compared with a similar diet containing chicken and fish as the only entrées. After years of debate on coffee, recent research demonstrated that drinking moderate amounts of brewed and filtered coffee (not coffee prepared by boiling coffee grounds in water) does not raise cholesterol levels. And, of course, medical scientists are continuing to try to unravel the intricacies of the French paradox.

Meanwhile, researchers in a variety of settings around the world continue to gather facts and analyze data. Eventually they may uncover answers to these and other lingering questions about the number one killer—coronary heart disease.

Sidney Harris

ON THE MENU
a glossary for diners

Chinese

bok choy—a variety of Chinese cabbage

cellophane noodle—thin, translucent noodle made from mung beans; used in soup or stir-fried with meat

dim sum—Cantonese brunch or luncheon meal that features dumplings, steamed or deep-fried, stuffed with pork, shrimp, beef, sweet paste, or preserves

glutinous rice—short-grained, opaque, white rice that is sticky when cooked

hoisin sauce—sauce made from soybeans that are mashed, fermented, and seasoned with salt, sugar, and garlic

lychee—fruit of a Chinese evergreen, consisting of a sweet, edible, raisinlike pulp around a single seed

mango—pear-shaped tropical fruit, usually deep orange

mooncake—festive pastry made with lard and stuffed with a sweet filling

tofu—a smooth, custardlike curd made by pureeing soybeans and coagulating soybean milk

water chestnut—small tuber with tough brown outer skin and crisp white flesh

Italian

Alfredo—rich sauce with butter, cream, egg, and cheese; served with pasta

antipasto—literally "before the pasta"; an appetizer

Bel Paese—semisoft, mild, uncooked whole-milk cheese

Bolognese, alla—meat sauce (containing ground beef and pork or ham, chopped vegetables, milk, white wine, and tomatoes) often used for pasta

canneloni—thin, rectangular sheets of dough rolled and stuffed with meat filling

gelato—milk-based Italian ice cream

gnocchi—pastalike dumplings, made of farina, semolina, potatoes, and/or flour

granita—grainy-textured fruit ice or sherbet

marinara—tomato sauce flavored with garlic and herbs; served with pasta

minestrone—hearty vegetable and pasta soup

mozzarella—pleasant, slightly sour cheese made from cow's or water buffalo's milk

Parmesan—pale yellow, cooked, pressed cheese made from partially skimmed cow's milk; it is often grated

parmigiana—dishes in which meat or vegetable is floured, sautéed, and covered with melted Parmesan cheese

pesto—sauce (basil, garlic, pine nuts, and Parmesan or Romano cheese in olive oil) used in minestrone and on pasta

polenta—cornmeal pudding, which is often cooled and sliced before being fried, baked, or grilled with various other foods

prosciutto—fresh ham cured by salting and air-drying but not generally by smoking

provolone—cheese that is delicate and creamy for two to three months and then becomes spicy and sharp

ricotta—fresh, moist, unsalted variety of cottage cheese

risotto—rice cooked with butter, chopped onion, and stock to which savory foods can be added

Romano—round white or very pale yellow cheese made by cooking and pressing whole milk from ewes

scampi—large shrimp or prawn; found in Italian waters

spumoni—frozen dessert made of several layers of variously colored and flavored ice cream, often containing pistachio nuts and candied fruit

tortellini—rings of dough stuffed with items such as chopped pork, turkey, prosciutto and sausage, cheese, egg yolks, and nutmeg, which are boiled and served in consommé or with butter

zabaglione—frothy dessert custard flavored with marsala wine

ziti—large tube pasta cut into short segments

Mexican

arroz con pollo—rice cooked with chicken

buñuelo—unsweetened dough rolled into flat circles, deep-fried, and sprinkled with cinnamon-sugar or honey

burrito—flour tortilla wrapped around meat or beans; may be served with lettuce, tomato, sour cream, and avocado

cabrito—baby goat meat or kid

caldo de pollo—chicken soup; boiled whole pieces of chicken and vegetables

caldo de rez—beef soup; usually made from beef bones and beef shank meat with vegetables

ceviche (also seviche)—marinated raw fish and shellfish

chicharrones—pork cracklings, also refers to fried pork rinds

chili con carne—beef seasoned with garlic and chili peppers and served with beans

chili relleno—pepper stuffed with cheese or meat and dipped in egg batter and fried

chimichanga—flour tortilla filled with meat and fried; may be served with a chili sauce

chorizo—a highly seasoned sausage of chopped pork

empanada—fried or baked turnover filled with meat or with sweetened apples, pineapple, or pumpkin; a type of pan dulce

enchilada—tortilla dipped in hot fat and filled with beef, pork, chicken, or cheese and served with enchilada sauce

fajita—beef or chicken cut in strips, marinated and seasoned with peppers, herbs, and spices and cooked with onion and bell peppers; eaten with a soft tortilla

flan—caramelized custard made with milk, sugar, and eggs

flauta—rolled corn tortilla filled with chicken or beef and deep-fried

frijoles—beans; frijoles negros are black beans

frijoles a la charra or "borracho beans"—boiled beans seasoned with tomatoes, onions, bacon, beer, and cilantro; other meats such as pork skins, chorizo, or ham may be added

guacamole—mashed avocado mixed with chopped onion, chilies, tomatoes, and lime juice; served as a dip, salad, or sauce

huevos rancheros—fried eggs smothered with salsa

menudo—soup made from beef tripe and spices that may contain hominy

mole—red chili sauce made from dried chilies, chocolate, sesame seeds, and chicken broth; served with meat

nacho—tortilla chip topped with cheese, refried beans, and jalapeño peppers

pan dulce—sweet bread prepared with lard or vegetable shortening; usually dry and very light textured

pico de gallo—relish of tomatoes, cilantro, onions, and chopped serrano or jalapeño peppers, seasoned with garlic and lemon juice

quesadilla—flour or corn tortilla filled with meat or cheese and fried

refried beans—frijoles, or beans, mashed and cooked with fat, usually lard

salsa—hot sauce made from tomatoes, onions, chilies, and Mexican seasonings

sopaipilla—puff of deep-fried dough sprinkled with powdered sugar; served with syrup or honey (eaten as a bread or dessert)

taco—tortilla (often fried) filled with seasoned ground meat, lettuce, and tomato and served with chili sauce

tamale—dough of ground corn (masa) and lard or shortening filled with ground beef, chicken, or pork; wrapped in corn husk or banana leaf and steamed

tortilla—Mexican bread; corn tortillas are made with cornmeal, salt, and water; flour tortillas are often made with lard

tostada—fried tortilla topped with beans or meat, cheese, lettuce, tomato, sour cream, and avocado; also known as chalupa

Japanese

harusame—cellophane or transparent noodles

katsuobushi—dried bonito, used as an ingredient in many foods

kombu—dried kelp (seaweed)

kome—Japanese rice

laver—a type of seaweed

menrui—noodles often used in soups

miso—soybean paste made from fermented cooked soybeans, wheat or rice, and salt

mochi—rice cake

sake—an alcoholic beverage made from fermented rice

sashimi—slices of raw fish, often dipped in soy sauce and horseradish

shiitake—Japanese mushroom, available dried in the U.S.

shoga—ginger root

shoyu—all-purpose soy sauce, made of soybeans, wheat or barley, and malt

soba—thin noodles made of buckwheat flour

somen—thin wheat noodles, usually eaten cold

sukiyaki—a beef dish, cooked at the table by simmering meat in seasoned liquids

sushi—vinegared rice garnished with raw fish and/or wrapped in laver; rice mixture may also be garnished with cooked shrimp, fish, vegetables, seaweed, or egg

tempura—food coated in a thin batter and fried in deep fat

teriyaki—grilled poultry, fish, or meat that has been marinated in a sweet, spicy soy sauce mixture

French

au gratin—indicates foods topped with cheese and, sometimes, butter

béarnaise—classic sauce containing butter, egg yolk, wine vinegar, shallots, and spices

béchamel—basic white sauce containing milk and roux and flavored with onion

bordelaise—sauce of red or white wine with bone marrow and chopped parsley

café au lait—coffee with hot milk

croissant—yeast-leavened, crescent-shaped, flaky pastry

crème brûlée—rich custard topped with a layer of sugar that is caramelized under the broiler just prior to serving

escargot—snail

espagnole—basic brown sauce made from roux, brown stock, diced vegetables, tomato puree, and herbs

foie gras—enlarged livers of force-fed geese and ducks (especially those found in the cities of Toulouse and Strasbourg, France) that are often used to make a smooth, rich, seasoned pâté

hollandaise—thick sauce containing vinegar, egg yolk, and butter, flavored with lemon juice

hors d'oeuvre—appetizer; a light, finger food eaten before the meal

Mornay—classic sauce made by using butter and adding grated Parmesan and Gruyère cheeses and, possibly, egg yolk to béchamel sauce

pâté—rich mixture or spread made of meat, poultry, game, fish, or vegetables

quiche—open-faced pie filled with a savory custard mixture; term is often used to mean quiche Lorraine, which contains eggs, cream, bacon, and, often, Swiss cheese

roux—mixture of equal amounts of flour and butter or other fat that is used as a thickener

sorbet—"water ice" flavored with fruit juice or puree or other flavoring and containing beaten egg white to prevent ice crystals from forming; sherbet

Greek and Middle Eastern

baba ghanoush—appetizer of pureed eggplant, tahini, lemon juice, olive oil, and garlic

baklava—sweet dessert made of phyllo dough, honey, butter, and nuts

chick-pea—round legume, often used dried; garbanzo

couscous—cooked cracked wheat, usually combined with vegetables or meat and served with a sauce

falafel (also falafil, felafel)—patty made of minced chick-peas and/or fava beans that is deep-fried

feta—salty, white, high-fat Greek cheese with a crumbly texture made from goat's or ewe's milk; when made outside Greece, it may be made from cow's milk or a combination of cow's and goat's milk

gyros—pressed beef or lamb roasted on a vertical spit, thinly sliced, and usually served on pita bread

halvah—candy made of tahini and honey

hummus (also hommos)—mashed chick-peas with lemon, garlic, and tahini

phyllo—dough that can be made of only flour and water or can also contain egg and fat; it is rolled very thin and layered before being filled with sweets or other ingredients such as cheese, meat, or vegetables

plaki—fish cooked with tomatoes, onion, and garlic

pita—round, flat, hollow bread that is low in fat

rice pilaf—rice that has been sautéed, steamed in stock, seasoned, and cooked with vegetables; it is often served with meat, fish, or poultry

shish kebab—entrée made of cubes of meat, often lamb, and vegetables placed on a skewer and broiled

tabouli (also tabbouleh)—dish containing cracked wheat, parsley, onion, tomato, olive oil, lemon, and mint

tahini—paste of crushed raw sesame seeds seasoned with lemon juice and spices that is used in many Middle Eastern dishes; high in fat

tzateki—spicy flavored sauce made from yogurt

tzatziki—appetizer made with yogurt and cucumbers

Indian

aviyal—vegetable curry

balushahi—sweet pastry, deep-fried in ghee and dipped in syrup

barfi—sweet made from cooked, thickened milk flavored with coconut, cocoa, or nuts

chapati (also chapatti)—fried pancakelike bread made of whole wheat flour

chatni (also chutney)—a highly seasoned relish made of fruit or vegetables; originally eaten with Indian curries

dal (also dall, daal, or dahl)—lentil dish, usually pureed

dosa—pancake or crepe of rice powder

ghee—clarified butter

halva—sweet milk pudding flavored with fruits or vegetables, such as carrots or pumpkin

idli—steamed dumpling of ground lentils and rice powder

kari—Tamil word for a seasoned sauce; source of the word *curry*

khir—dessert pudding of milk and cream of rice; served chilled

naan—flat bread made of white flour and shaped like a leaf

rayta (also raita)—combination of yogurt and raw or cooked vegetables with herbs and spices

roti—bread

tandoor—cylindrical clay oven used for baking and roasting

uppama—wheat cereal cooked with vegetables

EAT, DRINK, AND BE HEALTHY!

by C. Wayne Callaway, M.D.

Eating a healthful diet and eating delicious food seem the ultimate in contradictions to many Americans. Although taste is the number one motivator for food selection, many people perceive an inverse relationship between taste and health: the better a food tastes, the less likely it is to be good for their health. More often than not, the foods touted by the nutrition community—fruits, vegetables, breads, and cereals—are not the ones relished by a public whose preferences, in the main, are for foods containing fat, sugar, and salt.

Fear of food

Over the past two decades, the focus of dietary recommendations for the American public has shifted from the prevention of deficiency diseases to the prevention of chronic diseases such as coronary heart disease, stroke, and cancer, all of which are associated to some extent with dietary excesses. There is widespread agreement in the scientific community that changes in the diet can improve the health of the general population and help prevent chronic disease. Four major U.S. reports on diet and health published in the years 1988–90 recommended reducing consumption of dietary fat and increasing consumption of complex carbohydrates and fiber.

But how does the public view these recommendations? Consider the results of a 1990 Gallup survey commissioned by the American Dietetic Association. Nearly half of the Americans polled said they believe the foods they like are not good for them; 36% said they feel guilty about eating the foods they like; and more than half indicated they are eliminating foods from their diet. The foods that those who "feel guilty" are eliminating most often are meat and dairy products, major sources of iron and calcium. Ironically, most American women fail to get enough of these essential nutrients. Furthermore, excluding favorite foods often leads to feelings of deprivation, which in turn may lead to binge eating.

"I've never known so many people to be so worried about what they eat or so many who think of the dinner table as a trap that's killing them with

C. Wayne Callaway, M.D., is Associate Clinical Professor of Medicine, George Washington University, Washington, D.C. He has served as the medical consultant to the project "Resetting the American Table: Creating a New Alliance of Taste & Health" since its inception.

(Overleaf) Culinary maven Julia Child believes that Americans have become altogether too worried about what they eat. She particularly laments that people are no longer partaking of the pleasures of the table. In her words: "We must never lose sight of a beautifully conceived meal." Child was the catalyst for a new dietary approach that aims to bring the joy of eating back to the American table. Photograph, John Dominis

chemicals or butter," said Julia Child, the grande dame of gastronomy, in a recent newspaper interview. Fearing the demise of the art of good eating and the loss of important cultural traditions, Child voiced her concern that in its campaign to promote better health, the nutrition community was overlooking the multitude of reasons why people eat (other than to meet nutritional needs). She lamented the fact that fewer and fewer Americans were experiencing the simple pleasures of the table. Was it possible that the seemingly divergent views of health promoters and gastronomists could coexist, let alone become part of a collaborative effort?

Taste and health: necessarily at odds?

It was Child's keen observation that a great many Americans seemed to suffer from an unwarranted "fear of food" that served as a catalyst to an exciting new approach to American eating, an approach that casts taste and health as equals in the equation of good health. In an effort to help Americans rediscover the joys of eating while moving toward a healthier diet, the American Institute of Wine & Food, a nonprofit educational organization that was founded in 1981 by Child, Robert Mondavi (chairman of the Robert Mondavi Winery), and others to advance the understanding, appreciation, and quality of what Americans eat and drink, took on the challenge of bringing together noted culinary and health leaders to explore whether a healthful diet and life-style could, in fact, incorporate the pleasures of the table.

A core group of 13 advisers from these two communities met in June 1990 and agreed on a platform of issues for the project known as "Resetting the American Table: Creating a New Alliance of Taste & Health." Subsequently, 50 prominent taste and health professionals were invited to attend a consensus conference in Boston, cosponsored by Tufts University School of Nutrition and the Frances Stern Nutrition Center, New England Medical Center Hospitals. Those who were invited were viewed as influential, forward-thinking leaders who would be willing to listen with an open mind to what the "other side" had to say. Chefs, food and health writers, public health policymakers, nutrition and exercise scientists, physicians, registered dietitians, anthropologists, psychologists, education specialists, and food marketers and retailers from around the country converged for this two-day, history-making meeting to address the issues, air differences, and, most importantly, search for common ground.

Some issues brought on heated arguments. On the other hand, the two contingents found there were quite a few issues upon which they readily reached agreement. Ultimately, willingness on both sides to compromise resulted in the creation of a consensus document that established a common vision, a common language, and common values and standards for the taste and health communities. This document, *Standards for Food and Diet Quality,* provided something tangible for the meeting participants to share with their professional peers, who in turn could use the document's tenets to enlighten their colleagues and ultimately to bring the messages home to consumers.

Eating for health and pleasure

"In matters of taste consider nutrition and in matters of nutrition consider taste. And in all cases consider individual needs and preferences." This is the umbrella tenet of the consensus document. The document was formulated with the healthy general population in mind. However, its tenets could apply even to those with certain medically diagnosed conditions such as hypercholesterolemia (elevated blood cholesterol). The major point of difference is that such persons may require a lower overall fat intake than the 30% of calories recommended in the federal government's 1990 *Dietary Guidelines for Americans,* issued jointly by the Department of Agriculture and the Department of Health and Human Services.

Four core values are at the heart of *Standards for Food and Diet Quality:*
- Taste is the first determinant of American consumers' food choices. In addition to taste, a multitude of psychological, physiological, social, cultural, ethnic, and economic factors contribute to shaping people's food preferences.
- Dietary recommendations should respect culinary traditions that reflect and support the cultural and ethnic heritages of Americans. At the same time, they must recognize individual needs to achieve nutritional adequacy and a sense of well-being.

In 1990 the American Institute of Wine & Food, cofounded by Julia Child, brought together a select group of noted health professionals and culinary experts to explore whether good food and good health are necessarily mutually exclusive. What emerged from this historic meeting of minds was the "Resetting the American Table" project. What makes the approach so appealing is that it enables people to enjoy their favorite foods and not feel guilty about doing so.

Taste and health professionals unanimously agree that meals should not be a hit-or-miss proposition. Indeed, too many Americans today eat on the run. Anthropologists point out that it is at the family dinner table that many important cultural and social rituals are shared and passed along from one generation to another.

● Nutrition and good health, as well as the cultural importance of food preparation and the enjoyment of eating, depend upon a healthy, positive atmosphere around the table at home.

● There are no "good" or "bad" foods in isolation. It is the overall diet that counts.

Starting with these basic premises, the health and taste leaders addressed the specific issues of nutrition; physical activity; food availability, quality, and preparation; food safety; and education.

A healthful diet can include *all* foods. The nutrition component of the *Standards* document endorses the principles of moderation, variety, balance, and choice delineated in the 1990 *Dietary Guidelines for Americans*: (1) eat a variety of foods, (2) maintain healthy weight, (3) choose a diet that is low in fat, saturated fat, and cholesterol, (4) choose a diet with plenty of vegetables, fruits, and grain products, (5) use sugars only in moderation, (6) use salt and sodium only in moderation, and (7) if one drinks alcoholic beverages, one should do so in moderation. The taste and health leaders went further, however, proposing that (1) all foods can be part of a healthful diet when considered over time and (2) with a little planning, a diet can include foods of high as well as moderate or low fat content and still meet dietary guidelines. These two concepts have proved particularly compelling. Evaluating diet quality over a period of several days, rather than by individual foods or meals, enables people to enjoy favorite foods, such as a special dessert, or to eat a big meal without the guilt that is so often associated with such an indulgence. The concept takes into account individual needs and differences in food choices and acknowledges that different people can achieve their nutritional needs in different ways. Balancing over time allows people either to plan ahead for or to make up after special occasions—to balance higher fat food choices with lower fat selections. The caveat is that when making higher fat choices, it is important to consider how often a food is eaten and in what quantity.

66

Exercise expands food choices. The key message regarding physical activity that emerged from the meeting of experts is that a moderate amount is a critical component of a healthy life-style. Exercise should be pursued for both well-being and health as well as for the flexibility it allows in the amounts and kinds of foods that can be eaten and enjoyed. Many studies have shown that physically active people can and do eat more than less active, overweight individuals—without gaining weight.

One of the participants at the Boston meeting was Steven N. Blair, director of epidemiology at the Institute for Aerobics Research, Dallas, Texas. A recent landmark study conducted by Blair and colleagues found that even moderate amounts of exercise on a regular basis afford substantial health benefits. Those who are "modestly fit" enjoy lower rates of heart disease, cancer, and other chronic diseases and have lower mortality rates than those who are essentially sedentary. Blair and other exercise authorities believe that the pursuit of adequate fitness and the enjoyment of food *are* mutually compatible.

Making the most of the best foods. In considering food availability, quality, and preparation, the formulators of the new approach to taste and health emphasized that by preparing more foods at home from basic ingredients, people can gain greater control over the quality and composition of their diets. They also emphasized using high-quality raw materials and ingredients in peak condition to achieve maximum flavor and nutritive value.

Although the visual appeal of fresh foods can contribute to the pleasure of the meal, flavor and texture were deemed more important. Culinary experts stress that when foods taste good, people are more apt to enjoy them as they are. For example, a flavorful fresh vegetable dish prepared with a few herbs and not overcooked is likely to be enjoyed without fat-laden sauces. The experts recommend reserving the use of fat for preparations

Theo Westenberger

Experts agree that even a moderate amount of exercise on a regular basis offers substantial health benefits for most people. Being physically active also allows people considerable choice and flexibility in the types and amounts of foods they can consume and, most importantly, enjoy!

"Tonight, I feel like eating something controversial."

Drawing by Wm. Hamilton; © 1990 The New Yorker Magazine, Inc.

American cuisine is a remarkable mixture of foods from around the world—many of which were introduced by immigrants.

Many traditional ethnic dishes can be prepared in ways that maximize both flavor and nutritional value and at the same time spare fat and calories. Those who prepare foods at home from fresh ingredients have the greatest control over the quality and the composition of their diets.

where its presence makes a considerable difference in flavor and texture.

Good food must be "safe" food. Nutrition and culinary authorities stress the importance of a safe food supply. They have called for careful handling and preparation and efficient storage of foods throughout the food-distribution chain and in both home and commercial kitchens in order to minimize the potential for food-borne illnesses. They also see the need to reduce undesirable drug and pesticide residues on foods.

Educating professionals and the public. Finally, *Standards for Food and Diet Quality* emphasizes that consumers and commercial food preparers alike need to be educated; they need to learn how to identify affordable, high-quality ingredients and learn the cooking skills necessary for preparation of healthful, flavorful dishes practically, easily, and safely.

The "new alliance of taste and health" places great value on traditional and ethnic foods in American society. By no means is the concept elitist or limited to certain population groups. The participants at the Boston meeting paid special attention to the fact that American cuisine is a remarkable mixture of regional dishes and foods from around the world, many of which were introduced by immigrants. Indeed, many ethnic groups still consider the act of gathering around the family table to share a meal and the preparation of traditional dishes as ways of upholding their cultural heritage. Because fresh vegetables, grains, and other unprocessed ingredients are inherent in many ethnic cuisines, education efforts can emphasize cooking methods that take advantage of low-fat ways of preparing these ingredients.

Spreading the word

The *Standards* document conceived in Boston was meant to be a starting point for further discussions. Review and acceptance of the document and strategies for implementing it have been the focus of four subsequent meetings with an expanded audience of taste and health leaders. These took place in San Francisco and Los Angeles in the spring of 1991 and in Washington, D.C., and New York City a few months later. A similar meeting was slated for Chicago in the fall of 1992.

Creative tips for reducing fat in menus

- substitute fruit juices or wine for part of the oil in dressings and marinades
- when making a sauce, add butter last, whisking in a tablespoon or less to add smoothness and buttery flavor
- if a recipe calls for "drizzling" on butter, brush it on lightly instead
- grill meats in the broiler or a cast-iron skillet on top of the stove as alternatives to sautéing or frying in fat
- if a recipe uses hard cheese, grate it instead of slicing it to use less
- make double portions of vegetables for dinner so there will be leftovers for snacks
- refrigerate stews and soups overnight before eating, then skim off the solidified fat
- rely on mustards and greens rather than fat-laden spreads to add moisture to sandwiches

Source: *Resetting the American Table*, © 1992 The American Institute of Wine & Food

The need to educate children was cited as the number one priority by participants nationwide. If children learn from the start to eat and enjoy foods that are both healthful and tasty, those good habits are likely to be maintained for life. The experts felt that children need to develop "culinary literacy"—*i.e.,* they should learn about selecting, preparing, and cooking foods with both nutrition and taste in mind. One suggestion was that young people be encouraged to assist in shopping and meal preparation. Simple activities like tearing up lettuce for salads and pouring ingredients into a blender can stimulate creative interest in food preparation and taste experimentation. Many noted chefs and gastronomists, including Child, have offered to work with registered dietitians and school food-service professionals toward the goal of making food both enjoyable and nutritious for youngsters.

Another priority cited nearly as often by the participants at the meetings was the need to get people back to the family table, the place where the appreciation of food begins and social and cultural rituals are shared and passed on from one generation to another. Taste and health professionals unanimously agree that eating and the enjoyment of good food are rooted in the home. It is at the family table that "food memories" are born, which children carry with them for life. Participants joined Child in her concern that eating together has become a hit-or-miss proposition for many families and that this signifies the loss of an important and positive form of social interaction.

Above all, a collaborative effort

One of the most important outcomes of the new taste and health alliance was the sensitization of the two communities to the dangers of dilettantism. Although they may have the best of intentions, experts in one arena should not attempt to be experts in another. Most chefs and other taste professionals are not authorities on nutrition and physical activity. Nor are

Robert E. Daemmrich—Tony Stone Worldwide

Taste and health professionals believe that children need to develop "culinary literacy." Youngsters are most likely to develop lasting and healthy eating habits if they are introduced to a wide variety of foods at an early age. They can also gain an appreciation of the nutritional values of foods if they help with the shopping and are involved in meal preparation.

As part of the "Resetting the American Table" project, six leaders from the culinary world collaborated with six nutrition experts to create exciting new recipes for dishes that are undeniably delectable but also meet dietary guidelines. Taste testers were unanimous in awarding top marks to Robert Del Grande and Carolyn O'Neil's hearty vegetable and legume stew.

The American Institute of Wine & Food

health professionals in the best position to create exciting new menus or to be the originators of innovative methods of cooking.

Taste and health leaders must rely on each other's expertise. Who but local chefs know best how to cook the foods of a given region and to incorporate the taste preferences of the many diverse ethnic groups into healthful, appealing menus? Conversely, culinary professionals and those in the food industries must rely on the expertise and training of health and nutrition professionals to conduct and evaluate credible research, assess nutritional propriety, and evaluate and take action against nutritional claims that may mislead or harm the public.

Far from turning a deaf ear to the health community's call for less fat,

Gastronomists and nutrition experts need to work together to create exciting and tasty dishes that also meet recommended dietary guidelines. Students at New York's Culinary Institute of America, the country's leading school for professional chefs, spend 21 months in a rigorous training program that includes courses in nutrition and cost control—both vital to the contemporary diet of Americans. Their instruction emphasizes the preparation of a wide variety of regional and ethnic dishes that use natural ingredients and are at once simple, nutritious, uniquely flavorful, and visually appealing.

culinary professionals are exploring innovative cooking techniques and developing recipes to reduce fat but enhance taste. Meanwhile, health professionals are realizing that restrictive diet regimens do not work for the general public. Rather than a list of restrictions and foods to be avoided, taste and health leaders agree that an approach that emphasizes the enjoyment of eating and offers a range of choices within food groups *is* conducive to a healthful diet.

An example of this collaborative effort was the creation of six new recipes that celebrate the abundance of fine foods in America while meeting accepted dietary guidelines. Each of the recipes was developed by a gastronomist-nutritionist team; together they are solid proof that foods can be both delicious and nutritious. And, yes, one of the six recipes is for a "sinful" dessert. A scrumptious Raspberry-Cranberry Trifle is the creation of syndicated food writer and cookbook author Abby Mandel and registered dietitian Mary Abbott Hess.

Bon appetit!

The professionals who are responsible for creating the "new alliance of taste and health" agree that health recommendations alone are not enough to change the way that people eat. In preparing the *Standards for Food and Diet Quality,* it was their hope that the document would "encourage a shift from unduly restrictive dietary recommendations to a broader outlook and more integrated understanding of the varied and exciting ways to achieve a healthful diet." Above all, they desire that the *joy* of eating return to the American table. As Julia Child said in the introduction to her book *The Way to Cook,* food is "a delightful part of a civilized life."

Chef Abby Mandel and dietitian Mary Abbott Hess's Raspberry-Cranberry Trifle with custard sauce and fresh raspberries may look too divine to eat. Even when topped with a dollop of freshly whipped cream, however, one serving has but 250 calories (9 grams of fat and 170 milligrams of sodium) and is the kind of indulgence that everyone can enjoy now and then.

71

IN THE TIME OF

CHOLERA

by Mariam Claeson, M.D., M.P.H.,
and Ronald J. Waldman, M.D.

In late January 1991 cholera struck the Pacific coast of Peru. It was the first appearance in South America of this dread disease in more than a century. Within weeks, cholera had spread throughout Peru, where in the early stages of the epidemic it caused more than 1,500 cases of illness each day. In all, there were almost 300,000 cases (and 3,000 deaths) in that country alone during the year. It was not long after reaching Peru, undoubtedly carried there along shipping routes from the western Pacific, that the disease infected Ecuador, Colombia, Brazil, and Chile. Then, leaping northward to Mexico, the epidemic continued to spread, reaching throughout Central America. Cholera, which had erupted in Asia in 1961 and reached Africa 10 years later with an intensity which that continent had not known before, had finally encircled the globe—as it had done at least six times previously in history.

Cholera is a disease that incites populations to panic. Its reputation as a fierce and unrelenting killer is a deserved one; it has been responsible for the death of millions, for economic losses of immense magnitude, and for the disruption of the very fabric of societies in all parts of the world. In Peru in 1991, for example, the imposition of trade barriers by potential importers was responsible for the loss of up to $700 million in revenues, about one-fifth of the country's total exports in a normal year. In addition, cholera caused the loss of an estimated $70 million in tourist revenues; in Cuzco, a major tourist center, 40 of the 114 hotels were closed. Hospitals were overcrowded with cholera patients. In Iquitos, a coastal city that was among the earliest affected by the epidemic and where an average of 200 people out of a population of 350,000 fell ill each week, health care workers blocked the entrance to the hospital to protest low wages and poor working conditions.

Ironically, in spite of the chaos it continues to generate, cholera is perhaps the best understood of the modern plagues. The organism that causes it has been studied extensively for well over a century; its modes of transmission have been identified; and safe, effective, and inexpensive interventions for both preventing infection and treating clinical illness have been developed. Nonetheless, in 1991 cholera proved that it still cannot

Mariam Claeson, M.D., M.P.H., *is Medical Officer, Control of Diarrhoeal Diseases Programme, World Health Organization, Geneva.*
Ronald J. Waldman, M.D., *is a medical epidemiologist with the International Health Program Office, Centers for Disease Control, Atlanta, Georgia. He is currently on assignment to the World Health Organization.*

(Opposite page) Cholera victims, Lima, Peru, March 1991; photograph, Gustavo Gilabert—JB Pictures

Cholera is a disease with a reputation as a fierce and unrelenting killer that has always incited populations to panic. A cartoon depicting the tightening of quarantine and sanitation laws after an outbreak of cholera in the United States in 1883 was captioned "The kind of 'Assisted Emigrant' we cannot afford to admit." Quarantine of infected persons is an intervention for controlling cholera's spread that has been tried repeatedly but has rarely been effective.

be stopped, at least not in those large parts of the world in which poverty forces people to live without clean water or adequate sanitation.

The recorded history of cholera is relatively short and remarkable. Although Hippocrates (in the 5th and 4th centuries BC) and Galen (in the 2nd century AD) referred to an illness that may well have been cholera, and there are numerous hints that a cholera-like malady has been well known in the fertile delta plains of the Ganges River since antiquity, most of what is known about the disease comes from the modern era. Gaspar Correa, a Portuguese historian and the author of *Legendary India,* gave one of the first detailed accounts of the clinical aspects of an epidemic of "moryxy" in India in 1843: "The very worst of poison seemed there to take effect, as proved by vomiting, with drought of water accompanying it, as if the stomach were parched up, and cramps that fixed in the sinews of the joints." Many similar accounts of a devastating disease that was obviously cholera have come from India—evidence that outbreaks of the disease have occurred there sporadically throughout history. Cholera's appearance in Europe and the Americas dates only to the early 1800s, but more importantly, it was during the first half of the 19th century that researchers first began to make progress toward a better understanding of its causes and its appropriate treatment.

First six pandemics

In 1817 cholera became a disease of global importance. It was in that year that a particularly lethal outbreak occurred in Jessore, India, midway between Calcutta and Dhaka, then spread throughout most of India to Burma (now Myanmar) and Ceylon (now Sri Lanka). By 1820 epidemics had been reported from Siam (Thailand), Indonesia (where more than 100,000 people succumbed on the island of Java alone), and as far away as the Philippines. To the north and west, the Arabian Peninsula became involved in this first pandemic (as global epidemics are called) in 1821 when, in Basra, Iraq, an important port of the Persian Gulf, as many as 18,000 people died during a three-week period. In fact, wars between Persia (Iran), Iraq, and Turkey were disrupted when thousands of deaths were caused by this microbial enemy. The subsequent dispersion of these armies carried cholera to the threshold of Europe. Simultaneously, the disease spread along trade routes from Arabia to the eastern African and Mediterranean coasts.

Over the next few years, cholera disappeared from most of the world, returning to its "home base" in Bengal. Then in 1829 the second pandemic, which was the first to reach into Europe and the Americas, began. The disease arrived in Moscow and St. Petersburg in 1830, continuing on into Finland and Poland. Moving with tradesmen along shipping routes, cholera rapidly spread to the port of Hamburg in northern Germany and made its first appearance in northern England, in Sunderland, in 1831. In 1832 it arrived in the Americas, where in June more than 1,000 deaths were documented in Quebec. From Canada the disease moved quickly southward

Historical Pictures/Stock Montage, Inc.

Expiring cholera victims in Cairo during a late 19th-century epidemic showed all the typical signs of massive and rapid fluid loss. The dehydration that results from profuse diarrhea, often accompanied by vomiting, leaves the patient in an extreme state of lethargy, with weak muscles, slow pulse, and tremendous thirst. The skin is cold, clammy, and shriveled; the breathing rapid; and the eyes sunken and hollow.

An illustration from a French newspaper pictures residents of a working-class neighborhood of Hamburg, Germany, ill with cholera, being bundled into an ambulance during the devastating epidemic of 1892 that claimed the lives of nearly 10,000 in a period of just six weeks. In his book Death in Hamburg, *Richard J. Evans chronicles how as that city grew, "the problems of keeping its inhabitants alive and well, of supplying them with clean water, fresh air, pure food, and all the other basic requirements of human existence became steadily more acute, and led in the end to catastrophe."*

to the United States, disrupting life in most of the large cities along the Eastern Seaboard but striking hardest in New Orleans, Louisiana, where 5,000 residents died.

It is known that Mexico and Cuba were infected in 1833, and there are disputed reports of cholera's having reached as far as Peru and Chile at that time; it would undoubtedly have come from trade contacts with Spain, which, despite concerted efforts to quarantine infected individuals, suffered a severe epidemic in 1833.

Having spread, then, throughout most of the world, cholera receded from some areas but recurred in others, continuing to inflict a heavy toll. The extent of the epidemic in England was graphically and emotionally described by the statistician William Farr in 1852:

If a foreign army had landed on the coast of England, seized all the seaports, sent detachments over the surrounding districts, ravaged the population through the summer, after having destroyed more than a thousand lives a day, for several days in succession, and in the year it held possession of the country, slain 53,293 men, women and children, the task of registering the dead would be inexpressibly painful; and the pain is not greatly diminished by the circumstance, that in the calamity to be described, the minister of destruction was a pestilence that spread over the face of the island.

The third pandemic is generally considered to have been the most costly in terms of human lives. This pandemic is thought to have begun in 1852, with cholera once again erupting in India and spreading rapidly through Persia to Europe, the United States, and then the rest of the world. Perhaps the worst cholera year ever recorded in history was 1854; 23,000 died in Great Britain alone. Africa (at least those parts from which records exist) was also severely affected during this pandemic, with the disease spreading inland from the east coast to Ethiopia and Uganda.

The fourth and fifth cholera pandemics (beginning in 1863 and 1881, respectively) are considered to have been less severe than previous ones, at least in most of Europe and the Americas. However, in some areas extraordinarily lethal outbreaks were documented. These included the death of more than 5,000 inhabitants of Naples in 1884, 60,000 in the provinces of Valencia and Murcia in Spain in 1885, and perhaps as many as 200,000 in Russia in 1893–94. In Hamburg, which had consistently been one of the most severely affected cities in Europe, nearly 1.5% of the population perished during the cholera outbreak of 1892; cholera killed more people in that year than had died of the disease in that city in all previous epidemics combined.

The last quarter of the 19th century saw widespread infection in China and particularly in Japan, where more than 150,000 cases and 90,000 deaths were recorded between 1877 and 1879. The disease spread throughout South America in the early 1890s but did not become endemic there and was not to return for a century.

The sixth pandemic lasted from 1899 to 1923 and was especially lethal in India, in Arabia, and along the northern African coast. More than 34,000 people perished in Egypt in a three-month period, and some 4,000 Muslim pilgrims were estimated to have died in Mecca in 1902. (Mecca has been called a "relay station" for cholera in its progress from East to West: 27 epidemics were recorded during pilgrimages from the 19th century to 1930, and more than 20,000 pilgrims died of cholera during the 1907–08 hajj.)

Russia was also struck severely by the sixth pandemic, with well over 500,000 people dying of cholera during the first quarter of the 20th century. The extent of this pandemic was not as great as its predecessors, however, as it failed to reach the Americas and caused only small outbreaks in some ports of western Europe. Even so, extensive areas of Italy, Greece, Turkey, and the Balkans were severely affected.

In 1923 cholera receded from most of the world, apparently returning once again to its endemic home on the Indian subcontinent. The disease was not to spread widely again until 1961—when the seventh pandemic, different from all before it in a variety of important ways, began—not in Bengal but on the island of Celebes in Indonesia.

Cholera patients were isolated on a floating hospital at Nijni-Novgorod, on the Volga, in 1892 during the fifth pandemic, which claimed as many as 200,000 Russian lives. During the subsequent sixth pandemic, which lasted from 1899 through the first quarter of the 20th century, Russia recorded over 500,000 cholera deaths.

The current pandemic

The seventh pandemic began in 1961 and spread throughout Asia during the 1960s. During the next decade cholera spread westward to the Middle East and reached Africa, where it had not appeared for 70 years. The African continent is assumed to have been struck harder at this time than ever before, and by 1990 it was the origin of more than 90% of all cholera cases reported to the World Health Organization (WHO). In 1991, 19 African nations reported nearly 140,000 cases.

Then, early in 1991, cholera appeared unexpectedly and without explanation on the western coast of South America, in the country of Peru. As it entered its fourth decade, the seventh pandemic showed no signs of receding; on the contrary, more than 500,000 cases and well over 15,000 deaths were reported to WHO in 1991—more than in the previous five years combined. (Official reporting of cholera cases and deaths is known to represent only a small fraction of actual cases. Inadequate surveillance systems, lack of appropriate diagnostic equipment, and fear of significant economic losses from reduced trade and tourism inhibit many countries from reporting accurate figures.)

In the United States a total of 26 cases were reported through the end of 1991, all in people who either had traveled to infected areas or had consumed food products that had come from those areas. (A small endemic focus of cholera exists in the Mississippi Delta region, causing occasional cases, most of them from eating uncooked oysters, crab, or shrimp from the Gulf of Mexico, but only minimal pandemic-related transmission has occurred in the United States.)

On Feb. 19, 1992, an outbreak of cholera was detected in Los Angeles.

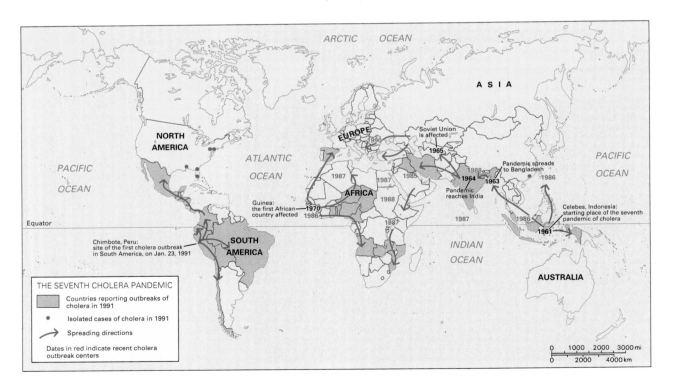

THE SEVENTH CHOLERA PANDEMIC

Countries reporting outbreaks of cholera in 1991

Isolated cases of cholera in 1991

Spreading directions

Dates in red indicate recent cholera outbreak centers

Chimbote, Peru: site of the first cholera outbreak in South America, on Jan. 23, 1991

Guinea: the first African country affected

Celebes, Indonesia: starting place of the seventh pandemic of cholera

Pandemic spreads to Bangladesh

Pandemic reaches India

Soviet Union is affected

Cholera in the Americas, 1991*			
country	reported cases	hospitalizations	deaths
Peru	285,438	108,271	2,720
Ecuador	40,465	32,326	623
Colombia	9,774	4,656	132
Mexico	2,107	767	27
Guatemala	2,536†	1,164	40
El Salvador	709	325	25
Panama	696†	156	20
Brazil	326	218	3
Bolivia	128†	62	10
Chile	41	not reported	2
United States	24 (8‡)	13	0
Honduras	5	5	0
Nicaragua	1	1	0
Canada	1‡	not reported	0
total	342,251	147,964	3,602

*reported to the Pan American Health Organization as of November 27
†includes probable and confirmed cases
‡not related to Latin-American epidemic

Source: *Morbidity & Mortality Weekly Report*, CDC, Dec. 13, 1991

All of the people affected had been passengers on a commercial flight originating in Buenos Aires, Argentina, which had stopped in Lima, Peru. By March 4, 76 cases of cholera had occurred among the 356 passengers and crew, and one elderly passenger had died. In spite of the growing potential for diseases to be transmitted rapidly from one continent to another as barriers to commerce and to personal travel disappear, to date, the more industrialized countries of the world have largely been spared during the seventh and current pandemic. As the disparity between industrialized and less developed nations grows, cholera, which previously was a global disease, now seems to have become yet another burden to be borne by impoverished nations of the Third World. Moreover, experts predict that this time cholera will not go away; instead, it will become endemic to many parts of the world, much as it has been for centuries in the Ganges Delta.

The seventh pandemic differs from its predecessors in two important ways. First, the world has essentially become a smaller place. As noted above, international travel is now commonplace; more people travel more quickly and more easily to more places. Thus, cholera is likely to be introduced many times into the same areas. Second, and most important, the bacterium responsible for this pandemic is the so-called El Tor biotype of *Vibrio cholerae* 01, not the classical biotype that is suspected of having caused all previous pandemics. Because there is no obvious way to prevent the introduction of cholera into new areas or to eliminate it once it has appeared, it is urgent that countries take active measures to improve their state of preparedness and that individuals be informed about what they can do to protect themselves.

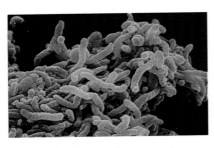

In 1883 the German physician and pioneer bacteriologist Robert Koch identified the comma-shaped bacterium whose presence in the intestines of cholera patients leads to the symptoms of the disease. The Vibrio cholerae 01 *organism (above), which Koch had called "Kommabacillus," is believed to have been responsible for the first six cholera pandemics.*

The microbial enemy

Credit for the discovery of the bacterium that causes cholera is usually accorded to Robert Koch, the renowned German bacteriologist who first enunciated the principles of modern germ theory. In June 1883, during the fifth pandemic, an outbreak of cholera occurred in Egypt. First France and then Germany sent teams of their top scientists to Alexandria to study the disease, hoping to head it off before it reached Europe. The French team tried to isolate the causative organism by infecting animals but failed to do so and returned home after one of its members, Louis Thuillier, became ill with cholera and died at the age of 27.

Koch and his team remained in Egypt and studied the disease both in patients and in cadavers. They were successful in visualizing a suspicious microbe in both stool specimens and intestinal contents but not in patients ill with other diseases or in organs other than the intestines. Before they were able to complete their investigations, however, the outbreak subsided. Koch requested and received permission to continue from Alexandria to Calcutta, where an epidemic was then under way. There, by employing a new technique—one that Koch had invented—of inoculating sterilized gelatin-coated glass plates with fecal material from patients, he was able to grow and describe the organism that he called "Kommabacillus" (because of its slightly bent, commalike shape) and to show that its presence in human intestines indeed led to the development of cholera in patients. While in Calcutta, Koch also made valuable observations on the role played by water in the transmission of the disease.

Koch's findings, however, were not original. Rather, they were rediscoveries of work that had been previously done by others. The Italian microbiologist Filippo Pacini had already seen the bacterium and named it "cholerigenic vibrios" in 1854 (a fact that Koch is assumed not to have been aware of). The principal mode of cholera transmission, contaminated water, had also been described previously—by John Snow during the course of the 1854 outbreak in London.

80

Vibrio cholerae is a member of the family Vibrionaceae, which includes three medically important genera of water-dwelling bacteria. It is a short, gram-negative, rod-shaped bacterium that appears curved when isolated. (By convention, bacteria are divided into two categories, according to whether they look blue under the microscope after being stained by a technique discovered by the Danish microbiologist Hans Christian Joachim Gram, hence the terms *gram positive* and *gram negative*.) *V. cholerae* are easy to grow, surviving best at temperatures of 18°–37° C (64°–99° F) and at a pH of 7 (neither acidic nor alkaline). While the organism can tolerate a very alkaline environment (up to a pH of 9), it is extremely sensitive to acidity; even a mildly acidic milieu (pH of 5–6) will effectively destroy it.

More than 60 of the most important kinds of *V. cholerae* are classified on the basis of a protein contained in their cell wall, the 0 antigen. Cholera-causing *V. cholerae* contain the 01 protein. The single-most-important characteristic of many *V. cholerae* 01 organisms is the ability to produce a potent toxin called an enterotoxin in the intestines. These toxigenic *V. cholerae* 01 bacteria are the only ones that cause the illness cholera, and neither *V. cholerae* 01 that do not contain enterotoxin nor *V. cholerae* that do not have the 01 protein are responsible for the disease.

Toxigenic *V. cholerae* can be further subdivided into two biotypes, called classical and El Tor, according to the way they react in laboratory tests. This distinction has enormous epidemiological importance at the present time because the seventh pandemic, which has been spreading through-out the world for the past three decades, is, as previously noted, in all likelihood the first caused by the El Tor biotype.

V. cholerae biotype El Tor was first described by the German physician E. Gotschlich in 1905 during the sixth pandemic at a quarantine station at El Tor in the Sinai Desert, which had been established to study the disease in victims returning from pilgrimages to Mecca. From the time of its discovery, scientists were in disagreement about whether the El Tor vibrio should be considered a separate biotype and whether the organisms could cause

Ann Ronan Picture Library

Sick pilgrims returning from Mecca in 1884 are quarantined in wooden sheds at El Tor in the Sinai Desert in Egypt. It was at an El Tor quarantine station in 1905 that Vibrio cholerae *biotype El Tor, the organism responsible for the seventh pandemic, was identified.*

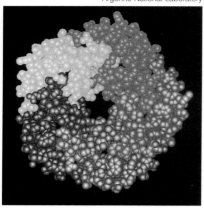

In 1991 scientists were able to crystallize and analyze the individual proteins of the cholera toxin—a task that had proved exceptionally difficult. Because producing a truly effective vaccine depends on knowing the precise structure of an infectious organism's key bacterial proteins—those that cause symptoms—this achievement may enable the development of a new and better cholera vaccine than any that now exists. It is the three-dimensional doughnut-shaped B subunit of the toxin (above) that anchors itself to the intestinal cell walls—the first step in a process that ultimately causes the body to excrete voluminous quantities of water and to lose essential salts, resulting in the profound dehydration of the patient.

disease. The latter issue was resolved in 1937 when El Tor was shown to be the cause of an outbreak of cholera on Celebes, but the organism was still largely ignored because of its apparent geographic localization. Interest in El Tor was vigorously renewed, however, when in 1961 it was shown to be the cause of the current pandemic.

The El Tor biotype possesses two characteristics that are of great epidemiological significance. First, it is a much hardier organism than the classical biotype. Although human beings had long been considered to be the only reservoir of *V. cholerae,* the El Tor biotype can survive for long periods of time in aquatic environments. Second, whereas a very high proportion of people infected with the classical biotype become ill, the El Tor strain can infect large numbers of people without causing clinical disease—*i.e.,* the organism causes only mild diarrhea or no symptoms at all. These people constitute an invisible pool of potential transmitters; they are, in effect, carriers of a potentially lethal disease. Although more seriously ill patients are more effective transmitters of cholera, carriers are more likely to travel and therefore play a crucial role in its spread.

The most significant disease-causing factor of both biotypes of toxigenic *V. cholerae* 01, the enterotoxin, was independently described by both S.N. De and N.K. Dutta in Calcutta in 1959. Its discovery came more than a century after Snow had theorized, with great prescience:

The morbid material producing cholera must be introduced into the alimentary canal . . . and the increase of the morbid material, or cholera poison, must take place in the interior of the stomach and bowels. It would seem that the cholera poison, when reproduced in sufficient quantity, acts as an irritant on the surface of the stomach and intestine . . . it withdraws fluid from the blood.

On the other hand, some 75 years before the discovery of the enterotoxin in *V. cholerae,* Koch had announced (wrongly, as it turned out):

Comma-bacilli produce a special poison [which] shows itself partly in an immediate manner [on] the epithelium . . . [and] in the worst cases . . . is partly reabsorbed and acts on the organism as a whole, but especially on the organs of circulation, which are as it were paralysed.

In fact, cholera enterotoxin neither destroys the intestinal epithelium (lining), as Koch implied, nor acts throughout the body. Koch's uncharacteristic mistake may have been partially due to the influence on his thinking of the recently discovered systemically acting toxins that cause diphtheria, tetanus, and botulism. Nonetheless, Koch's refusal to recognize what Snow had postulated 30 years previously and his failure to accept that most cholera patients either died or recovered rapidly without developing generalized illness, together with his enormous influence on the scientific thinking of the time, contributed to more than 60 years of unfruitful research into the mechanism by which *V. cholerae* exerts its effects. (In all fairness, probably more influential than Koch in retarding medical progress during this period was the fact that cholera simply disappeared from Europe and the Americas, thereby dimming the urgency of the problem in the West.)

It is now well understood that the *V. cholerae* 01 enterotoxin, upon its release from the external coating of the bacterium, acts by binding, irreversibly, to a receptor on the cells of the lining of the small intestine. Part of the toxin then separates from the rest and enters the intestinal cells. There it acts to increase the activity of an enzyme that is responsible for regulating the movement of water and electrolytes between the intestine and the circulatory system. (Electrolytes are essential to the body's tissues.) This action of locking this process in the "on" position results in the loss of enormous quantities of fluid, up to one liter (about one quart) per hour, into the intestinal tract. All of the clinical manifestations of cholera can be attributed to this extreme loss of water and salts. In 1991 researchers at Argonne (Illinois) National Laboratory and their colleagues at Yale University and Boston University identified the molecular structure of the cholera toxin, bringing to completion a search that had lasted for over 30 years. This discovery may lead to the development of improved cholera vaccines.

John Snow: cholera sleuth

Cholera is an intestinal disease that spreads through the fecal-oral route and is the archetype of waterborne illnesses. The London anesthesiologist John Snow is mainly credited with establishing it as such. In 1849 he published his pamphlet *On the Mode of Communication of Cholera,* in which he proposed that infection occurred as a result of the ingestion of contaminated water. Snow then confirmed his theories and earned a reputation as the father of "shoe-leather" epidemiology as a result of his elegant studies during the great London epidemic of 1854, which he vividly described:

The most terrible outbreak of cholera which ever occurred in this kingdom, is probably that which took place in Broad Street, Golden Square. . . . Within two hundred and fifty yards . . . there were upwards of five hundred fatal attacks of cholera in ten days. The mortality in this limited area probably equals any that was ever caused in this country, even by the plague; and it was much more sudden, as the greater number of cases terminated in a few hours. The mortality would undoubtedly have

A cartoon that appeared in Punch *in 1848 pictured "Dirty Father Thames," but the filthy water from the river had yet to be definitively linked to London's epidemic outbreaks of cholera.*

In the summer of 1849 the prominent London anesthesiologist John Snow published his pamphlet On the Mode of Communication of Cholera, *in which he argued that cholera was a contagious disease caused by a poison that reproduced itself in the bodies of its victims and that the most frequent source of infection was a contaminated water supply. His ideas, however, went largely unheeded for at least another half decade. The cartoon at right commented on the still-polluted state of the Thames in the 1850s.*

been much greater had it not been for the flight of the population. . . . In less than six days from the commencement of the outbreak, the most afflicted streets were deserted by more than three-quarters of their inhabitants.

Immediately suspecting that the Broad Street pump was dispensing contaminated water, Snow found that most of the deaths had occurred in its vicinity. The survivors he interviewed confirmed that cholera victims with whom they had been acquainted drew their water from it. Furthermore, although both a jailhouse and a brewery were near the pump, neither the inmates nor the brewery employees ever used water from it, and mortality in both groups was very low.

Even more elegant was Snow's analysis of the epidemic in South London. Here two water-supply companies, the Southwark and Vauxhall and the Lambeth, supplied houses in the vicinity by an arrangement Snow described as follows:

The pipes of each Company go down all the streets, and into nearly all the courts and alleys. . . . In many cases a single house has a supply different from that on either side. Each company supplies both rich and poor, both large houses and small; there is no difference either in the condition or occupation of the persons receiving the water of the different Companies. . . . As there is no difference whatever, either in the houses or the people receiving the supply of the two Water Companies . . . it is obvious that no experiment could have been devised which would more thoroughly test the effect of water supply on the progress of cholera than this.

Snow took advantage of the "natural experiment" after he learned that following the epidemic of 1849, the source of the Lambeth company's water but not that of its competitor had been moved to a part of the Thames River that was not contaminated by sewage from the city. Snow's diligence and sleuthing revealed that the Southwark and Vauxhall company served 40,046 houses, in which there were 1,263 deaths from cholera; the Lambeth company served 26,107 houses, in which only 9 died from cholera;

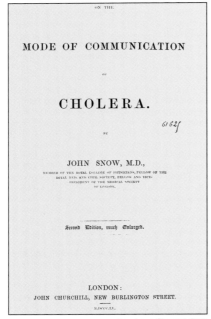

Jean-Loup Charmet, Paris

84

and in all of the rest of London, there were 1,422 cholera deaths in 256,423 houses that were served by other water-supply companies (*see* Table).

The water supplied by the Southwark and Vauxhall company, therefore, was responsible for an almost ninefold increase in mortality over that supplied by Lambeth. Snow brilliantly concluded that "if the effect of contaminated water be admitted, it must lead to the conclusion that it acts by containing the true and specific cause of the malady."

Unfortunately, Snow's work was not totally accepted at the time. Other theories of disease causation were prevalent, most notably that of "miasmatism," which claimed that cholera was contracted by breathing air contaminated by disease-containing "clouds." The notion of contagiousness had not yet become firmly established. It remained for Koch to provide the undeniable proof of the role of water in the transmission of cholera during his Calcutta studies in 1884.

Contaminated food

Other forms of transmission have also been identified. Food that has been either irrigated, washed, or cooked with contaminated water has been repeatedly implicated as a cause of cholera. Foods that have the greatest potential to transmit the disease include shellfish and seafoods, especially if eaten raw; fruits and vegetables grown in soil that has been either fertilized with human excrement (night soil) or irrigated with raw sewage; and foods packed in ice. Even foods that are fully frozen before shipping from areas known to be infected with *V. cholerae* can cause illness in those who consume them. *V. cholerae* has also been found to survive on cooked grains such as rice and millet.

As previously noted, most cases in the United States in recent years have been food-related. On March 30, 1991, for example, crabmeat that had been purchased in a fish market in Ecuador and then boiled, shelled, wrapped in foil, and stored unrefrigerated in a plastic bag was transported to the U.S. It was delivered to a home in New Jersey, refrigerated overnight,

Contaminated water and cholera London, 1849			
water supplier	number of houses	cholera deaths	deaths per 10,000 houses
Southwark and Vauxhall	40,046	1,263	315
Lambeth	26,107	9	37
all other London suppliers	256,423	1,422	59

The Bettmann Archive

The threat of food-borne cholera was the subject of a late 19th-century illustration depicting "the great battle between the Board of Health and the marketmen." Among the foods known to transmit the infection are shellfish and seafood— the most common source; fruits and vegetables that have been grown in night soil or irrigated with raw sewage; and foods packed on ice or frozen that are imported from an area where there has been a recent outbreak of cholera.

then served in a salad to eight people over the next two days. All eight developed cholera symptoms but recovered. In August 1991 three cases of cholera in Maryland were traced to a brand of frozen coconut milk exported from Bangkok, Thailand.

A particularly insidious mode of transmission occurs in areas where the funerals of cholera victims are followed by the consumption of communal meals; frequently the same people who prepare the corpse for burial prepare the subsequent feast. Although infrequent, such outbreaks have been reported in recent years in parts of Africa.

A treatable illness

The French physiologist François Magendie observed cholera patients in Moscow in 1831 and described the dread disease as one "which begins where others end, with death." The description by a U.S. Army surgeon in 1832 was also uncannily accurate:

The face was sunken, as if wasted by lingering consumption; . . . the hands and feet were bluish white, wrinkled as when long macerated in cold water; the eyes had fallen to the bottom of their orbs, and evinced a glaring vitality, but without mobility; and the surface of the body was cold and bedewed with an early exudation.

Cholera is marked by the sudden onset of profuse, watery diarrhea often containing flecks of mucus ("rice water" stools) and frequently accompanied by vomiting. The patient is very thirsty and has a dry tongue; cold, clammy skin; a weak pulse; rapid breathing; hollow, sunken eyes; and shriveled, wrinkled skin, especially of the hands ("washerwoman's hands"). The rapid loss of fluid from the bowel can, if *untreated,* lead to death, sometimes within hours, in more than 50% of those stricken.

However, with proper modern treatment, which essentially consists of replacing the fluid and salts lost through the intestines, mortality can essentially be prevented (rates kept to less than 1% of those requiring therapy). The history of the development of appropriate treatment is one

An elderly cholera victim lies dying in a refugee camp in West Bengal in the summer of 1971. Cholera struck savagely among the massive refugee populations created by the civil war between East and West Pakistan. In a single camp of 350,000 refugees, before the arrival of a medical relief team, mortality rates were as high as 30%.

Mark Godfrey

marked by isolated discoveries that often went unheeded, followed by subsequent rediscoveries.

Little is known about the treatment of cholera prior to its arrival in Europe. One of the early recorded advances was made by the chemist R. Hermann, a German working at the Institute of Artificial Mineral Waters in Moscow during the 1831 outbreak. Hermann was the first to analyze the chemical content of the blood and stools of cholera victims and, although most of his analyses were subsequently proved wrong, he believed that water should be injected into the victims' veins to replace fluids.

Early attempts at rehydration. A few years later, after the first cases occurred in Sunderland during the second cholera pandemic, William Brooke O'Shaughnessy, a young British physician, reported in *The Lancet* (1831) that, on the basis of his studies, he "would not hesitate to inject some ounces of warm water into the veins. I would also, without apprehension, dissolve in that water the mild innocuous salts which nature herself is accustomed to combine with the human blood, and which in Cholera are deficient." Although O'Shaughnessy never carried out his recommendations for treating cholera sufferers (and became better known for developing a telegraph system in India), his ideas were put into practice by Thomas Latta, a Scot, as early as 1832, with surprisingly good results. Latta's success in saving his patients was probably due to the fact that he persisted in infusing them with intravenous solution until they were better.

Nevertheless, intravenous rehydration rapidly fell into disuse because, *if* patients were kept alive, the voluminous diarrhea continued, often for days, necessitating still more replacement fluid. Many, including members of the medical community, incorrectly believed that the treatment itself was responsible for "reviving" the diarrhea. Consequently, few physicians followed Latta's example, and it would be more than a century before fluid replacement became universally accepted as the mainstay of cholera therapy.

In the meantime, mortality due to cholera remained high throughout the 19th century. Conventional treatment consisted of enemas, castor oil, calomel (mercurous chloride, a purgative), gastric washing, venesection (blood-letting), opium, brandy, and plugging of the anus to prevent fluid from escaping. In Hamburg in 1892, during its most devastating epidemic, the most widely used treatment was purging with a 2% solution of tannic acid, precisely the opposite of what should be done. In that year 3,994 of the 8,296 cholera patients hospitalized in that city died.

The search for an adequate treatment was renewed at the beginning of the 20th century. Among the leading investigators were Sir Leonard Rogers, an Englishman at Calcutta Medical College, and Andrew Sellards, an American in Manila. Rogers developed a replacement fluid that was better than all others that existed at the time. His intravenous solutions, which contained a much higher salt content than had previously been used, resulted in a halving of cholera deaths—from 60 to 30%. Sellards suggested that sodium bicarbonate be added to intravenous solutions in addition to sodium chloride—an idea that Rogers then adopted and that resulted in further reductions in mortality—to 20%.

The next round of major advances in cholera treatment did not occur until 1958, when Capt. Robert A. Phillips, a U.S. Navy physician, identified a solution that proved to be even more effective. Totally committed to rehydration therapy, Phillips had gone to Cairo in 1947, when the first epidemic there since 1919 resulted in 33,000 cases and 20,000 deaths. "Cholera cures itself, like a common cold," he wrote. "The problem is to keep the patient alive by giving him enough fluids fast enough. If he has no other complex diseases, any patient who can get treatment will survive." After a few months, during which a variety of rehydration methods were tried, mortality in Cairo fell to less than 10%.

Further refinements of Phillips' solution and the methods of administering treatment occurred in Bangkok, Taiwan, Manila, and Dhaka. By the mid-1960s Phillips' prophesy had essentially been fulfilled—mortality rates in those areas were under 1%.

Oral solutions. In spite of the incredible success of intravenous rehydration, which was finally accepted as effective more than 130 years after it had first been conceived by Hermann, the treatment still had many disadvantages. Cholera had the habit of appearing most frequently and most severely in some of the poorest countries in the world and in some of the most inaccessible places. The historian Charles E. Rosenberg called it the "poor man's plague."

Treating large numbers of patients during an epidemic required enormous amounts of fluids made up with distilled water. The delivery and storage of such quantities of rehydration solution could be logistically impossible. Furthermore, the need for sterile needles and tubes for injecting the solution surpassed the capacity of most local hospitals in an epidemic situation.

The next step in the conquest of cholera was to develop a rehydration fluid that could be administered orally. This would obviate the need for distilled water, needles, and intravenous tubing and theoretically would make simple and effective treatment available to all cholera victims. The

In June 1971 a medical supply firm in Geneva was producing 15 tons of intravenous rehydration solution daily for shipment to India. Although intravenous rehydration therapy had been established as a highly successful means of saving the lives of cholera victims, it required huge quantities of fluid prepared with distilled water and could be administered only by trained personnel using sterile needles and tubing. In large epidemics, such as the one that struck refugee populations in West Bengal in the summer of '71, such intravenous therapy on a mass scale became impossible; the need for a simple-to-administer, inexpensive oral rehydration solution was evident.

World Health Organization; photograph, E. Mandelmann

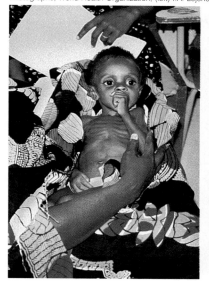

Cholera broke out with an intensity never before seen on the African continent during the second decade of the seventh pandemic, well before the pandemic reached South America. By 1990 more than 90% of cholera cases reported to the World Health Organization were from Africa, and in 1991 alone 19 African nations reported nearly 140,000 cases. The life of a young, severely dehydrated cholera victim in Nigeria was saved by oral rehydration therapy, a cheap and simple-to-administer treatment that can prevent fatal outcomes even in large populations and under the most adverse conditions. Premeasured packets of oral rehydration salts provide all the necessary components for effective fluid replacement, in the treatment not only of cholera but of other acute diarrheal diseases as well.

breakthrough that brought oral rehydration therapy from wishful thinking to reality was the discovery that the absorption of sodium, the principal ion lost during an acute cholera attack, is linked to that of glucose in the small intestine. Prior to this discovery, it was known that sodium is transported actively and independently from the intestinal lumen, through the epithelial cells, and into the blood. The cholera enterotoxin inhibits this means of sodium absorption, resulting in excess sodium loss, but the glucose-sodium transport system remains intact in these victims. In fact, glucose enhances the absorption of both sodium and water. Thus, it was clear that the presence of a solution of sodium, glucose, and water in the intestine would overcome the losses caused by the toxin, bringing about a net absorption that would maintain the hydration of the patient.

Oral rehydration solutions had been used by Ruth R. Darrow in the United States for dehydrated infants and by N.H. Chatterjee in Calcutta for successfully treating patients with mild cholera. Clinical studies carried out simultaneously by physicians Norbert Hirschhorn in Dhaka and Nathaniel F. Pierce in Calcutta helped define the optimal composition of an oral solution. Finally, in 1968 researchers David R. Nalin and Richard A. Cash, working in East Pakistan, developed an oral glucose electrolyte solution that was suitable for cholera patients of all ages with all severities of illness. In mild cases the solution was effective as the sole treatment.

A remarkable test. The big test for oral rehydration therapy came in the summer of 1971, during the civil war between East Pakistan and West Pakistan that resulted in the creation of Bangladesh. The war caused the exodus of six million refugees from East Pakistan into the neighboring Indian state of West Bengal and, not unexpectedly, cholera broke out with a vengeance in this exhausted and starving population, causing mortality rates of about 30%.

In late June, led by the Indian physician Dilip Mahalanabis, a medical relief team arrived in a camp of 350,000 refugees in West Bengal and by

89

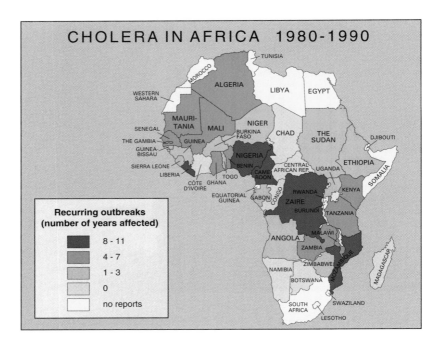

CHOLERA IN AFRICA 1980-1990

**Recurring outbreaks
(number of years affected)**

- 8 - 11
- 4 - 7
- 1 - 3
- 0
- no reports

the end of August had treated 3,700 cholera victims. Intravenous therapy was out of the question on a mass scale and therefore was reserved for patients in shock, but even those patients who were most severely ill were switched to oral therapy as soon as they were alert enough and physically able to drink. Oral rehydration was the only practical treatment, and the team managed to prepare 50,000 liters of oral solution (using table salt, baking soda, and glucose) at a total cost of $750. The relief team working with Mahalanabis often treated more than 200 cholera patients a day, in wards with makeshift beds on floors or with canvas cots that were occupied by two adults or four children. Despite these desperate conditions, the mortality rate was kept to 3.6%; in the demonstration ward, where 1,200 patients were treated, only 1% died.

This stunning achievement established oral rehydration salts (ORS) as the foundation of treatment not only for cholera but also for other forms of diarrhea. Moreover, the success of Mahalanabis and his team in treating refugees suggested that the ingredients needed for ORS could be prepackaged so that errors in mixing solutions in the field could be avoided, lay members of the community could easily recognize and begin treatment for cholera, and, most importantly, even under the most adverse conditions, ORS could be used successfully to treat all but the most severely dehydrated cholera patients.

Other medications and nourishment. In severe cases of cholera, antibiotics are a useful adjunct to rehydration therapy. Tetracycline, an inexpensive, widely available medication, can reduce the volume of severe diarrhea as well as its duration. It is also important for patients to resume eating as soon as they are able to. There is no truth to the adage that the bowel should "rest" during bouts of diarrhea; rather, getting adequate nourishment is vital to recovery.

Combating cholera: what works, what does not

The ability of the El Tor organism to infect without causing apparent illness, along with today's population mobility, increases the likelihood that cholera transmission will continue to occur on a global scale. Nonetheless, the current level of understanding of cholera infection and the wide availability of simple, low-cost treatment are sufficient to mitigate substantially the potentially devastating effects of an epidemic.

Successful strategies. Peru, the first country in South America struck by cholera during the current pandemic, is an example of a country that managed, for the most part, to limit the toll that the disease took when it arrived unexpectedly in 1991. Despite sudden and significant outbreaks, mortality rates in many parts of the country were kept to under 1%.

The principles of cholera prevention and control are basically the same as those for other forms of infectious diarrhea, the second most common killer of children in less developed countries (after pneumonia). Although the fear of cholera and the attention it is accorded are appropriate in light of the heavy toll it has taken over the years, with adequate oral rehydration supplies, properly administered, cholera deaths should be relatively few. Notably, epidemic cholera has less impact on children than on adults; even during the largest cholera outbreaks, more children succumb to diarrhea caused by other microbial agents. For example, in the first three weeks of the 1991 outbreak of cholera in Peru, an estimated 120 persons died from cholera, but in the same time period 10 to 20 times more Peruvian children died from diarrhea due to other causes.

Because of the high prevalence of diarrhea throughout the Third World, programs aimed at controlling diarrheal diseases have been established in most less developed countries. These programs are responsible for educating health professionals and the public about ORS. In addition, health officials need to promote effective means of preventing infection and controlling the spread of cholera while discouraging reliance on methods that have been proved to be relatively useless.

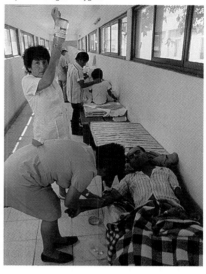

The first cholera case in Latin America in the current pandemic was reported in Peru on Jan. 23, 1991. By mid-February hundreds were falling ill each day and, nationwide, hospitals and clinics were hard-pressed to cope with the growing epidemic.

A vast field of garbage near Lima, Peru's capital, is a veritable breeding ground for cholera. The disease inevitably takes its greatest toll where sanitation standards are poorest.

In a Lima slum, water for home use is stored in poorly sealed containers that easily become contaminated. Drinking unboiled water from sewage-containing municipal water-supply systems has been a major source of cholera's spread. Peru, the country in Latin America that was hardest hit by cholera, is one of many that mounted public health campaigns to fight the disease. A billboard emphasizes that hygiene and cooperative efforts are the best means of preventing cholera infection. Although cholera's arrival in Peru was sudden and the spread of infection rapid, mortality rates in many parts of the country were kept to under 1%.

A safe and clean supply of water is the key to cholera prevention. Adequate chlorination of public water supplies and, in some cases, the distribution of chlorine tablets to households with instructions for their proper use are often effective measures. If chemical disinfection is not possible, people can be instructed to boil water before drinking it, but this may be difficult to accomplish, especially in poor countries where fuel may be either too expensive or unavailable.

Sometimes even simpler methods can be effective. In Calcutta, for example, where it is common for people to store water at home, changing from open containers, which allowed water to become easily contaminated, to narrow-necked jugs resulted in substantially reduced cholera transmission. Another important intervention is the improved, hygienic disposal of human waste. In areas lacking modern sewerage systems, the use of latrines can substantially lower the risk of infection.

Ensuring the safety of food is yet another important control measure. During an epidemic of cholera, it is important that people be instructed to cook all food thoroughly (to a core temperature of 70° C [158° F]) and eat it before it cools, to cover foods to avoid contamination during storage, and always to wash their hands after defecation and prior to food preparation. Foods sold by street vendors have been repeatedly implicated as sources of infection, and these should be avoided, especially by travelers to endemic areas. Foods that have a high acid content, if sterilized by irradiation or pasteurized, are considered to be safe.

Ineffective measures. In their attempts to control the spread of cholera, public health officials have learned that certain interventions, although tried repeatedly, are of little benefit. These include:

1. *Vaccination.* Only one year after Koch convincingly demonstrated that the "Kommabacillus" was the cause of cholera, the first attempt to develop a cholera vaccine was made by the Spanish scientist Juan Ferran. His results were dismal—no protection against infection was demonstrated, and

severe and sometimes fatal reactions occurred. Nevertheless, intensive efforts to develop an effective vaccine against cholera have continued. Even with the present level of sophisticated knowledge of the organism, these efforts have been disappointing.

At present, two vaccines are considered to be somewhat promising candidates for the future. However, although these vaccines appear to confer protection about two-thirds of the time, this effect tends to be short-lived, especially in children, and protection against the more prevalent El Tor biotype is substantially less than that for the classical biotype. WHO presently concludes that "there is no vaccine with established value for public health use in the control of cholera."

In fact, vaccination may even be dangerous in that its widespread use may divert scant resources away from the promotion of more important and more effective control measures and may give a false sense of security to populations that are most at risk. For these reasons, no country currently requires proof of cholera vaccination from travelers.

2. *Chemoprophylaxis.* As mentioned above, a short course of antibiotic treatment can reduce the duration of severe cholera. Accordingly, it has been suggested that treating the potential contacts of patients with antibiotics before they become ill might be an effective way to prevent the disease from spreading. However, so-called mass chemoprophylaxis has never been effective in controlling cholera outbreaks. In fact, as is the case with vaccination, the administration of oral antibiotics to large numbers of people, who would have to take several doses according to schedule, is logistically difficult and can detract attention from more important control activities. In addition, widespread use of antibiotics can hasten the emergence of organisms resistant to cheap, readily available antibiotics and thereby render the management of the ill who need the drugs more difficult. The use of antibiotics as a preventive measure at present is recommended only for the closest of contacts (mothers of ill children and sometimes

Gustavo Gilabert—JB Pictures

With their city in the grip of cholera, Lima citizens launch a vigorous cleanup effort at a local street market. Experts attribute the explosive outbreak of cholera in Peru to years of neglect of basic public health needs. Those who live in the country's crowded coastal cities have been and will continue to be the most vulnerable.

other family members) and even then only when it can be shown that the rate of transmission to close contacts is very high (15–25%).

3. *Travel restrictions.* Over the years, quarantine of infected persons has been tried on many occasions, and its role in stopping cholera's spread has been widely debated. Indeed, one factor that led to the persistence of the "miasmatic" theory of disease causation was the universal failure of quarantine to contain cholera. The recognition that most infected persons are free of symptoms and the inability to detect these healthy carriers have rendered this debate pointless. Restricting local or international travel will not limit the spread of cholera, and the enormous effort and expenditure required for mounting border checks and other quarantine measures will, as is true with vaccination and chemoprophylaxis, divert human and financial resources from more effective lifesaving activities.

4. *Restrictions on food imports.* The risk of cholera infection from foods that are imported from infected areas is real but relatively small. Because authorities of every country have the duty to protect their citizens from exposure to potentially infected foods, many countries have chosen to restrict the importation of certain foods from cholera-infected areas. WHO, recognizing that these restrictions can place a heavy burden on the economies of some less developed countries that rely largely on food exports for generating revenue, has urged that restrictions be applied conservatively and only when deemed absolutely necessary to protect the health of the public.

"Poor man's plague"

The issues surrounding quarantine and embargo are very real and help to demonstrate the impact that cholera has had on societies. When cholera was reported to have struck Hamburg in 1892, the response by that city's trade partners was immediate. Clothes, food, and other products coming from Hamburg were banned by many countries. Even mail was refused by some. Few ships docked in Hamburg's port, the heart of its once-thriving economy. Before cholera struck, the city's weekly trade revenues were

Within weeks of the widely reported cholera outbreak in Peru, fishing boats stand idle in Lima's port. The country's fishing industry was virtually paralyzed during the epidemic, and in 1991 its loss of revenues from exports and tourism amounted to hundreds of millions of dollars. Recognizing the extent to which the imposition of trade barriers can devastate a nation's economy, the World Health Organization has urged that such restrictions be applied only when absolutely necessary. In fact, no large cholera outbreak has ever been traced to commercial exports.

Mourners attend the funeral of a cholera victim in Peru in March 1991. Although cholera is a disease that is both well understood and highly treatable, its impact on that country in 1991 demonstrated that it still has the capacity not only to take lives but to disrupt the fabric of a society.

over 50 million Marks. Within a month of the cholera outbreak, they were reduced to only a few thousand. More recently, damage to the fragile economy of Peru in 1991 was placed at between $270 million and $700 million.

Cholera is a disease that science has mastered; although it was once a mysterious and fearsome illness, its causes are now well understood and effective interventions exist. Yet cholera continues to spread, causing panic, social disruption, and unnecessary mortality. The *Vibrio cholerae* organism can no longer be blamed; ignorance, poverty, and social injustice have become the principal perpetuators of this disease—as they have for so many others. Until adequate resources are made available for improving education and communications systems in less developed countries, for building new, safe water supplies, for improving standards of living, and for developing competent and effective public health programs, cholera will continue to exact a heavy toll.

FOR ADDITIONAL READING:

Evans, Richard J. *Death in Hamburg: Society and Politics in the Cholera Years, 1830–1910.* Oxford: Oxford University Press, 1987.

Longmate, Norman. *King Cholera: The Biography of a Disease.* London: H. Hamilton, 1966.

Pollitzer, Robert. *Cholera.* Geneva: World Health Organization, 1959.

Rosenberg, Charles E. *The Cholera Years: The United States in 1832, 1849, and 1866.* Chicago: University of Chicago Press, 1987.

van Heynigen, William E., and Seal, John R. *Cholera: The American Scientific Experience, 1947–1980.* Boulder, Colo.: Westview Press, 1983.

Pursuing Health
THE BRITISH WAY

by John Lister, M.D.

John Lister, M.D., *is a retired consultant physician and former Linacre Fellow of the Royal College of Physicians of London. Between 1952 and 1980 he wrote a monthly column for the* New England Journal of Medicine, *subsequently collected in the book* By the London Post: Essays on Medicine in Britain and America.

(Opposite page) Hiking in the Yorkshire Dales; photograph, Robert Harding Picture Library

At the time of this author's first visit to the United States in 1952, there was as yet no commercial television in Britain; post-World War II food rationing was still in force, and the National Health Service (NHS) was just four years old. His first impression of America was of a land of plenty, with forests of television aerials on the rooftops, vast numbers of large motorcars, and an abundance of household appliances and gadgets.

Television presented perhaps the greatest cultural shock. Especially fascinating were the advertisements for all kinds of products. One such ad assured viewers that their obesity was not due to heredity or their glands but was all "a matter of mind over platter," and if only they took "Fastabs," their hunger would be controlled. For a dime a day, they could lose all their ugly unwanted fat!

Americans, this author had been told, were more health conscious than Britons, and he soon found ample evidence of this when he heard people avidly discussing the dangers of dietary salt and fat and confiding the details of their annual physical exams (the annual checkup being almost unheard of in Britain). Forty years later Americans are probably still more health conscious than Britons, but now in the U.K. there is increasing emphasis on the importance of adopting a healthy life-style. The British are not as "set in their ways" as many believe. Thus, what is popularly considered the "full English breakfast"—porridge, followed by fried eggs and bacon, sausages, kippers, kidneys, and lots of buttered toast and marmalade—though featured in the enticements of the travel brochures, is largely a thing of the past. A much more typical English breakfast today is fruit juice with a slice of toast or a bowl of cereal and coffee. As in the U.S., cigarette smoking is now well recognized as *the* major health hazard and is indeed becoming a socially unacceptable habit; the virtues of exercise are widely promoted.

Interestingly, whereas Americans may be slightly ahead of Britons in making life-style changes—and much more money is spent on health care delivery in the United States (12% of gross national product) than in Britain (6%)—life expectancy in the two countries is virtually the same: 72.8 years for British men and 78.3 years for women, compared with 71.6 years for

Per capita spending on health care*		
U.S.		2,354
Canada		1,683
Sweden		1,361
France		1,274
Germany		1,232
Netherlands		1,135
Japan		1,035
Denmark		912
U.K.		**836**
Ireland		658
Portugal		464
Greece		371

Source: Health Affairs newsletter   *1989 (in U.S. dollars)

U.S. males and 78.6 years for females (1988 statistics). The infant mortality rates in 1988 were roughly comparable—9.1 per 1,000 live births in England and 10.1 per 1,000 in the U.S.

A revered system of health care

In Britain 90% of the population rely on the NHS for their health care. Every citizen has access to the health care system, without payment, at

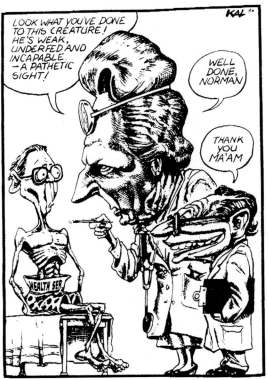

During her 11-year tenure (1979–90), Conservative Prime Minister Margaret Thatcher ordered sharp reductions in spending on all British social programs, including stringent cuts in expenditures on the National Health Service. A cartoon that appeared in the English newspaper Today *in October 1986 shows Thatcher praising Norman Fowler, then secretary of state for social services, for his "success" in carrying out her government's directives.*

Kevin Kallagher

the time of need. Every citizen has the right to register with a family practitioner (general practitioner, or GP) for primary care and the right to consult and be treated by a specialist upon referral by the GP. Since the time of its inception in 1948, the NHS has been immensely popular, and in spite of well-publicized deficiencies, it is now a jealously guarded national institution. Politicians tamper with it at their peril, and opinion polls show that expenditure on the health service is considered by the public to be a top priority, ranking above education, other social services, and defense.

Ironically, the sense of security that the NHS provides may have encouraged the average citizen to take a somewhat passive attitude toward health matters. People tend to rely on their family doctors for primary care and accept their advice about how to stay well. At the same time, Britons can be confident that hospital treatment will be available when they need it—though there may be lengthy delays for some elective surgical procedures. Compared with the populations of other developed nations, people in the U.K. have been slow to recognize just how much personal control they have over their own well-being.

Perhaps the major deficiency of the NHS has been that it is biased toward the provision of hospital care and places maximum emphasis on curative medicine. In the British health care system, preventive medicine and health promotion have typically received a low priority in the allocation of the nation's constrained resources.

That this is not the case in the U.S. was strikingly obvious to British health care professionals who visited that country in 1985. They found, rather, that health promotion enjoys a high profile in the U.S., with considerable commitment at the national, local, and individual levels. The British practitioners were particularly impressed with the multitude of activities being carried on outside of traditional medical settings—in the workplace, community centers, and churches and under the auspices of voluntary organizations. For example, the adolescent health specialists in the group traveled to several cities to observe health-promotion activities aimed at teens. Of the three

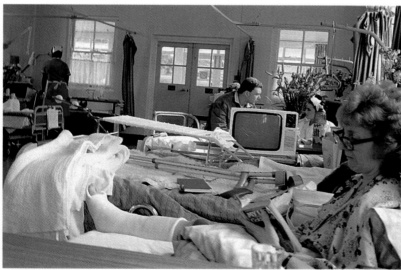

Robert Harding Picture Library

Patients in the orthopedic ward of a British hospital—like their fellow citizens—enjoy free medical care. However, hospitals often have waiting lists, and there may be lengthy delays for certain elective procedures. Some experts believe that, secure in the knowledge that their health needs will be met, the British public may have developed a somewhat passive attitude toward exhortations that they adopt a healthier life-style.

kinds of settings they visited—public schools, adolescent health centers in publicly and privately funded hospitals, and community-based youth projects—they concluded that only in the area of school health education did the U.K. have programs comparable to those in the U.S. It is worth noting, though, that they felt the British education system had a superior health curriculum.

A new health consciousness

While the U.K. may have got off to a later start, there is growing evidence of a new health consciousness among the British. Undoubtedly, this movement has been stimulated by the mass media, but there have also been three major governmental initiatives designed to encourage healthier lifestyles and foster the practice of preventive medicine.

The first of these initiatives was the introduction of a new contract for GPs, which took effect on April 1, 1990. This contract requires them to practice preventive as well as curative medicine; to ensure that goals are met, a certain portion of their earnings is linked to reaching specific targets—achieving a 90% immunization rate for children on their practice lists (*i.e.,* those registered as their patients) and carrying out cervical smear (Pap) tests on at least 90% of their female patients between the ages of 20 and 64. They are also required to see all patients aged 75 and older once a year for a review of their health.

Most GPs now work in group practices based in well-equipped health centers, and about 70% of their registered patients consult them at least once a year. This provides the opportunity for monitoring weight and blood pressure, encouraging life-style changes, and distributing consumer-oriented literature that has been prepared by various health education groups on such subjects as diet, smoking, exercise, the prevention of heart attacks, and the importance of screening tests for colon cancer and other diseases.

The second government initiative was the introduction on April 1, 1991, of radical reforms in the administrative structure of the NHS. These were in response to widespread criticism of the system, in particular the long waiting times for elective surgery—in the 1980s a patient might have waited 18 months for hip-replacement or cataract surgery, for example. The reforms that were enacted in 1991 placed new responsibilities on the administrative bodies known as district health authorities—190 local agencies that, in turn, report to 14 regional health authorities. Previously, the district health authorities had allocated funds out of their budgets to hospitals in their districts to pay for patient services; under the new system they must purchase these same services by negotiating contracts with the hospitals. Freed from the direct responsibility of providing hospital care, the district health authorities now have the task of assessing the state of health of the populations they serve and obtaining services to maintain good health and prevent illness.

"The Government has decided that the time is now right to launch a health strategy for England." With this pronouncement the U.K. embarked upon its third major initiative, a new strategy for public health, the goal of

---

Toward a healthier Britain: targets for improvement

causes of substantial mortality
    coronary heart disease
    stroke
    cancers
    accidents

causes of substantial ill health
    mental health problems
    diabetes
    asthma

contributing factors to mortality and ill health and potentially to healthy living
    smoking
    diet and alcohol
    physical exercise

areas with room for improvement
    health of pregnant women, infants, and children
    rehabilitation services for people with a physical disability

areas with great potential for harm
    HIV and AIDS
    other communicable diseases
    food-borne diseases

British youngsters improve their fitness level in a Health Education Authority-sponsored sports program. Promoting physical activity among the country's youth is one of the agency's top priorities.

which is to increase the British population's span of healthy life. The plan was unveiled in June 1991 with the publication of *The Health of the Nation*. In his introduction to this document, William Waldegrave, the secretary of state for health, pointed out that a government cannot by itself secure the health of its people; rather, this is a goal that can be achieved only through persuading ordinary citizens to change their behavior in such matters as smoking, alcohol consumption, exercise, diet, injury prevention, and sexual practices. What is required, Waldegrave noted, is a balance between government action and individual responsibility, with the government making certain that individuals have correct information on which to base their decisions.

While acknowledging that it is not possible to coerce people into adopting healthy habits, the U.K. is nonetheless fully committed to developing a nationwide health strategy. The main objective is to identify important areas responsible for premature deaths or avoidable illness and then to set targets for improvement by initiating effective intervention programs. A number of key areas were initially proposed (*see* Table, opposite page), but the government hopes to narrow this to about half a dozen. In many of the suggested areas, both statutory and voluntary agencies are already actively engaged in campaigns to induce people to give up unhealthy habits and forge new, healthful ones.

Getting the word out

If the U.K.'s new public health strategy succeeds, much of the credit will be owed to the Health Education Authority (HEA), now established as a special health authority (similar to the district health authorities but reporting directly to the Department of Health, a Cabinet-level bureau comparable to the U.S. Department of Health and Human Services). Its functions are to provide information and advice about health directly to the public and to support the educational efforts of other organizations and health professionals.

The HEA is engaged in an enormous range of activities. Its youth programs target those between the ages of 5 and 19 in schools, colleges, and youth clubs, sponsoring a variety of projects to encourage a healthy life-style. Efforts are made to help young people acquire social skills and thus the confidence to refuse cigarettes, for example, or to discuss with potential sexual partners the use of condoms. One HEA youth effort, the Happy Heart program, was designed to promote physical activity in the primary schools; another, the Health and Physical Education project, provides information on health-related exercise for youngsters in secondary schools and physical education training for teachers.

HEA programs have also been developed to reach people where they work. Health at Work encourages employers to make health-promotion activities a part of their overall management style—for example, by subsidizing healthy meals in company cafeterias or providing locker rooms and showers so that employees can exercise during work breaks. The Look After Your Heart Workplace project—a branch of the comprehensive program to prevent coronary heart disease in England—now involves 600 companies and 3.5 million employees. The project encourages employers to provide smoke-free areas in offices and factories, increase workers' opportunities for on-the-job physical activity (*e.g.,* encouraging the use of stairs rather than elevators), offer fitness testing and blood pressure screening for employees at the workplace, and publish health-promotion material in company magazines and newsletters.

The HEA is also developing support programs for GPs to help them carry out their new responsibilities in the area of health promotion. Millions of leaflets with advice on life-style—many produced by the HEA's own publications department—are distributed through general practitioners' offices, pharmacies, and various other NHS facilities. These provide advice on subjects ranging from low-fat diets to safer sex.

Discouraging smoking: top priority

The Queen does not smoke, and has just stripped Alfred Dunhill of its royal warrant as her suppliers of smokers' accessories.

This event, as reported in *The Times* (London) on Jan. 10, 1992, probably surprised no one. It represents the culmination of many years of work by British antismoking forces. As much as a hundred years ago, a National Antitobacco Society tried—unsuccessfully—to mobilize British sentiment against the habit. At that time even the medical establishment refused to lend its support. Commenting on the organizers' goals in an 1892 issue of the *British Medical Journal,* one editorialist wrote:

So far as [the society's] objects are connected with the desire to prevent the abuse and excess of tobacco smoking among the young, it will have general sympathy, but beyond this few will care to go. . . . Tobacco smoking is a habit in which

Close to one-third of British adults are smokers. Nowadays, however, there are increasingly fewer opportunities to light up in public places. For example, smoking is strictly forbidden throughout the London subway system. Bans on smoking are also in force on all British Airways domestic flights, in many factories and offices, and in a growing number of restaurants.

Stuart Goldstein

The princess of Wales, whose dislike for smoking is well known, makes a public appearance in support of the 1991 national No Smoking Day, which adopted as its slogan "Let's packet in." No-smoking days have been held annually since 1984 and are credited with having helped about 300,000 British smokers to quit.

divines, philosophers, and doctors have found solace and comfort for more than three centuries; it is practised so widely and so universally that it is idle to quote a few isolated opinions against it or fanatically to denounce it as pernicious. . . . [The society] should address [itself] to those excesses of smoking which are manifestly injurious, and should avoid the attempt to do the impossible by aiming at suppressing smoking altogether.

Today, of course, smoking is acknowledged as the greatest single cause of preventable premature death in the U.K., killing about 115,000 people each year. It is the cause of 30% of all deaths from cancer and 90% of all noncancer deaths from lung disease and contributes to 20% of all deaths from coronary heart disease. Passive smoking—the involuntary inhalation of "second-hand" smoke—is now believed to cause 1,000 deaths each year in nonsmokers. In 1992, 33% of British men and 32% of women smoked; even more worrying, 7% of 11–15-year-olds smoked.

British antismoking campaigns have received impetus from a series of recent reports from the Royal College of Physicians on the dangers of smoking and from the activities of the pressure group Action on Smoking and Health (ASH). Television campaigns have been directed particularly at young people; in some of these public service messages, celebrity

103

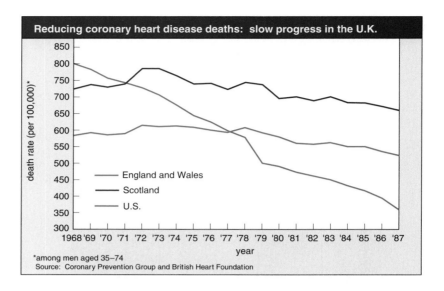

Reducing coronary heart disease deaths: slow progress in the U.K.

— England and Wales
— Scotland
— U.S.

death rate (per 100,000)*

year

*among men aged 35–74
Source: Coronary Prevention Group and British Heart Foundation

spokespersons deliver the message that smoking is an unattractive habit or that it is "not smart" to smoke. The government is also strengthening measures to deal with shopkeepers who sell cigarettes to children under the legal age of 16. In February 1992 the maximum fine for selling tobacco to underage youngsters was increased from £400 (about $700) to £1,000.

An estimated 300,000 Britons have stopped smoking for good since the first national No Smoking Day in 1984. In recent years Diana, princess of Wales—who reportedly threw away the ashtrays at Kensington Palace, her London home—has been an enthusiastic supporter of this annual event. The theme for the 1991 No Smoking Day was "Let's packet in!" This slogan, along with a picture of a crumpled cigarette pack dropping into a garbage can, appeared on posters, stickers, T-shirts, and other items that were distributed throughout Britain on that day.

Unfortunately, the young remain susceptible—especially when there is peer pressure to smoke and when parents smoke. Moreover, the tobacco industry continues to portray smoking in a glamorous light. Women are

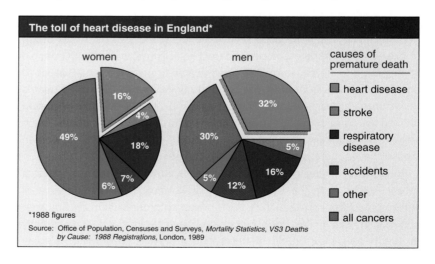

The toll of heart disease in England*

women

men

causes of premature death
■ heart disease
■ stroke
■ respiratory disease
■ accidents
■ other
■ all cancers

*1988 figures
Source: Office of Population, Censuses and Surveys, *Mortality Statistics, VS3 Deaths by Cause: 1988 Registrations*, London, 1989

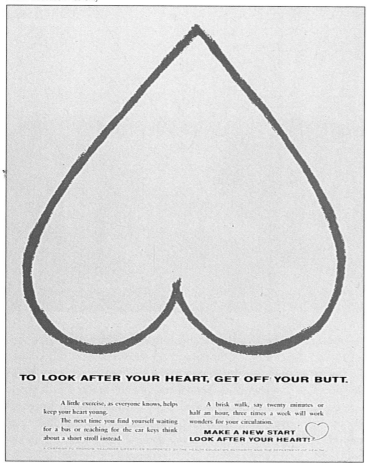

TO LOOK AFTER YOUR HEART, GET OFF YOUR BUTT.

A little exercise, as everyone knows, helps keep your heart young.

The next time you find yourself waiting for a bus or reaching for the car keys think about a short stroll instead.

A brisk walk, say twenty minutes or half an hour, three times a week will work wonders for your circulation.

MAKE A NEW START
LOOK AFTER YOUR HEART!

A poster urging people to give up their sedentary ways is one weapon in a massive government offensive against heart disease in England. The Look After Your Heart program, which was launched in 1987, is funded jointly by the Department of Health and the Health Education Authority. Several other initiatives against heart disease are under way in other parts of the U.K., including Heartbeat Wales and, in Northern Ireland, Change of Heart.

particularly influenced by advertising in women's magazines, many of which carry more ads promoting smoking than articles explaining its harmful effects. A recent study published in the *British Medical Journal* noted that more than 50% of women in Britain, including a majority of young women aged 15–24, are regular readers of these magazines. The authors of the study pointed out that the death rate from lung cancer in women is on the increase in the U.K.—in Scotland it has surpassed than the rate of breast cancer deaths.

The secretary of state for health has been urged by the HEA to press for regular increases in the price of tobacco, the prohibition of all tobacco advertising (none is permitted on television), the elimination of smoking in enclosed spaces and in the workplace, and the support of major antismoking education programs. An attitude survey published early in 1992 indicated that two-thirds of British voters would support a ban on tobacco advertising.

Already smoking is prohibited on the London Underground (subway system), on all British Airways domestic flights, and in many public places. A recent survey of 500 companies revealed that 79% had no-smoking areas and 22% had a complete ban on smoking. In a Sept. 8, 1991, article

105

Like their U.S. counterparts, British shoppers face an enormous array of choices at the supermarket and often feel confused by dietary advice they receive from the "experts." The British public is still trying to decide what to make of the ongoing controversy over cholesterol, and in 1990 a survey found that only 50% of Britons questioned knew whether certain foods contained predominantly saturated or unsaturated fat.

in the *New York Times*, London correspondent William Schmidt observed, however, that the British lag far behind Americans in banning smoking in public places: "Ask most Englishmen about the choking atmosphere inside a pub, and they dismiss it as part of the natural ambience. If you don't like it, they politely suggest, you don't have to come inside." Nonetheless, restaurants are now instituting no-smoking sections, and the idea is catching on. Indeed, in another British survey most of those responding favored restricting smoking in restaurants and public places, and 60% supported legislation to ban smoking on all public transport.

Clearly, smoking is becoming a socially unacceptable habit in Britain, and it constitutes one area of health promotion in which the example of the medical profession may have been helpful. British physicians in general no longer smoke; this has been true for many years. The steady decline in the number of smokers that is now occurring in the general population is indeed encouraging.

The huge toll of heart disease

In many ways your heart is a muscle just like any other. If you don't exercise it regularly it gets weak. Those of you who've seen what a limb looks like after it's been in plaster for weeks will know how bad a "wasted" muscle looks. In some ways, life in modern Britain is like encasing your whole body in plaster!

The above excerpt from the Coronary Prevention Group's leaflet entitled *Exercise and Your Heart* is an example of the earnest health-promotion effort under way in the U.K. to alert people to the risks of heart disease, now the most common cause of death, accounting for 30% of premature deaths in men. Death rates due to heart disease in England and Wales are among the highest in the world, and although they are falling, the decline is much slower than in the United States. The reason for this is not clear, but it may be that Britons have been less responsive than Americans to exhortations to eat wisely and get more exercise.

In cooperation with the British Heart Foundation and the Coronary Prevention Group (a nonprofit organization devoted to preventing heart disease), the HEA is conducting an intensive national heart disease education program. As part of this campaign, British television has produced special programs focusing on specific changes in life-style—"Quit and Win" (aimed at smokers) and "It Doesn't Have to Hurt" (promoting the virtues of physical activity). Through the Food for the Heart project, leaflets on dietary changes have been distributed to millions of customers in major supermarket chains, encouraging them to eat less fat and more fiber and to "Take Fish to Heart." As a result of this massive health-promotion effort, heart disease is now perceived by the public as the biggest killer in Britain, and there is an increased awareness that people can reduce their risk of a heart attack by developing better eating habits, quitting smoking, and being more active.

Who's afraid of cholesterol?

Facing an enormous choice, persuasive advertising, conflicting nutritional information about what is "good" for us, but, restricted by a limited budget—shopping for food can be a bit of a nightmare.

This quotation from a British Heart Foundation pamphlet could just as easily have appeared in any piece of U.S. health education literature. Like their U.S. counterparts, the British are confused by the plethora of advice they receive about diet and nutrition. A British survey conducted in April 1990, for example, showed that only 50% of respondents knew whether certain

Paul Massey—Sunday Times, London

On the pier in the seaside town of Brighton, a couple of sightseers enjoy an English specialty: crispy deep-fat-fried fish and chips (the latter better known in the U.S. as French fries). While most Britons still exceed the recommended limits for dietary fat, they have reduced their consumption of butter and are switching from full-fat (i.e., whole) milk to skim in increasing numbers. Programs promoting better eating habits have succeeded in alerting people to the need to cut down on such staples of the English diet as bacon and sausages and desserts topped with heavy cream.

foods contained mainly saturated or unsaturated fat, and most could not rank items in order of fat content. More than 80% of Britons eat more than the recommended level of fat (35% of total caloric intake according to British guidelines, which is 5% more than U.S. authorities suggest), and salt intake is needlessly high. Not surprisingly, 37% of men and 24% of women were found to be above their recommended weight in 1987, and 12% of women and 8% of men were frankly obese. Two-thirds of those studied had elevated blood cholesterol levels.

Nevertheless, there is evidence that the British are forsaking such traditional menu items as creamery butter and full-fat milk in favor of low-fat spreads and skim milk, and people are constantly being exhorted to eat more complex carbohydrates and foods high in fiber. Since 1980 there has been a 50% reduction in butter consumption; whole wheat and brown bread now make up 28% of all bread eaten in the U.K. There are many other positive trends. In interviews conducted at the conclusion of the Food for the Heart promotion, 70% of shoppers said that this and similar campaigns had increased their awareness of healthful foods.

Dietary advice is, of course, the area of health education that offers the greatest opportunity for commercial exploitation, and there has been some concern about the practice of literature and "teaching packs" on health issues being produced by organizations with a vested interest—*e.g.,* the Sugar Bureau, the Butter Council, and the Meat and Livestock Commission. Following in the footsteps of the pharmaceuticals industry, food manufacturers are now sponsoring health information for doctors. Such information may well be biased—cereal manufacturers could be tempted to overemphasize the value of dietary fiber or margarine producers the importance of polyunsaturates—but it is hoped that an independent body will be set up to assess such materials before they are distributed to the public.

Perhaps more important in terms of its effect on people's habits is the continuing controversy among the experts over the role of cholesterol in the causation of heart attacks. In a 1959 cartoon in the *The New Yorker* magazine, one cocktail-party guest asks another, "Are you a no-cholesterol doctor—or are you one of those no-cholesterol-is-all-bosh doctors?" Thirty-two years later the debate over restricting dietary cholesterol is still going strong. A headline in *The Sunday Times* on Dec. 22, 1991, went so far as to proclaim: "Cutting cholesterol can increase risk of heart attacks." Neville Hodgkinson, *Times* science correspondent, went on to advise readers, "Eat, drink, and be merry: Christmas pudding may be good for you after all." These provocative statements were prompted by the publication of the results of a Finnish study of two groups of business executives who were at risk of heart attack. Over a five-year period, those counseled to cut down on calories, saturated fats, cholesterol, alcohol, and sugar were twice as likely to have died as those in a control group allowed to continue their "unhealthy" life-styles. (It should be noted that noncardiac deaths from suicide, accidents, and violence figured largely in this increased death rate.)

Despite these findings, the HEA and the British Heart Foundation stood fast on their dietary recommendations, which, they emphasized, were based on a consensus of scientific evidence. However, *The Times* columnist

Bernard Levin was quick to seize upon the Finnish report as an occasion to celebrate the collapse of a medical myth and to call for the immediate abolition of the HEA. Levin wrote:

It has long been obvious to me that if we were to seek a single safe and inexpensive panacea for the improvement of the entire population's well-being, it would be the immediate closing down of the Health Education Authority.

This body, which is in danger of terminal indigestion from the quantity of our money it has swallowed, must by now have frightened to death so many people that it is no wonder that the population is falling. Well, would you want to live, much less bring children into the world, if you were daily assured by the HEA that your only chance of survival, and that a slight one, was to change immediately to an exclusive diet of pasteurised muesli washed down with turnip-juice?

However intemperate Levin's remarks may have been, the cholesterol controversy is confusing for all concerned. With a little effort, some bon viveurs may still be able to find a "no-cholesterol-is-all-bosh" doctor, but their numbers have dwindled.

A reasonable pursuit of fitness

There is a self-righteousness to many people who practise physical fitness and it can be very tiresome.

So wrote *The Times* columnist Barbara Amiel in January 1992, commenting on the U.S. fitness craze and, in particular, the intemperate exercise habits of Pres. George Bush, an ardent fitness enthusiast. Bush, suffering from jet lag and too much tennis, had recently become ill at a state dinner in Japan. Amiel was not the only European commentator to speculate that Bush's

Robert Harding Picture Library

"Ramblers" look out over a scenic vista in the Cumbrian countryside. While jogging has not caught on in the U.K. to the extent that it has in the U.S., the British public has long been aware of the pleasures— and, increasingly, of the health benefits— of physical exercise. Walking is the most popular outdoor activity of both men and women.

very public bout of "stomach flu" had been brought on by his relentless drive to project an image of robust health. Earlier, when the president had experienced an episode of heart trouble and collapsed while jogging, some overseas observers could not resist noting that a man of Bush's advanced years—he is officially a "senior citizen"—should have known better. Amiel put it all down to the well-known American obsession with fitness, the irresistible urge to "pound that quivering flesh into muscle" and to achieve the "new American dream—to die in perfect physical condition."

All this might seem to imply that Britons are impervious to the notion that exercise is beneficial to health, but such a view would be misguided. True, jogging is nowhere near as popular in the U.K. as it is in the U.S. Nonetheless, Britons are participating in sports in increasing numbers, and they are being urged to do so by their physicians, the HEA, and numerous voluntary organizations. Currently, more than 40% participate in some form of regular sports activity. Many more men than women take part in sports, but the gender gap began to close in the decade between the mid-1970s and mid-'80s and will probably continue to do so.

As in the U.S., participation is influenced by socioeconomic factors. Britons of the professional classes are two to three times more likely to engage in sports activities than are unskilled workers. Age and geography also play a part in determining how often people exercise and what kinds of activities they prefer. Among all of the outdoor sports, the category "walking/rambling/hiking" leads the list in popularity among British men and women. Swimming and gymnastics are favorite indoor activities—but so is darts, which, as it is usually accompanied by a pint or two, is probably not an exercise recommended by most GPs!

The Sports Council, a government-sponsored body incorporated by Royal Charter in 1972, encourages people to participate in sports and promotes the development of more and better facilities, particularly for the young. A recent increase in the popularity of swimming in the U.K. reflects at least in part an effort by the council and local authorities to build more indoor public pools. Recognizing the need for in-depth information about the fitness of Britons, the HEA has commissioned a two-year survey that will involve thousands of personal interviews, a program of cardiorespiratory fitness testing, and an examination of the relationship between sports participation and life-style factors such as drinking and smoking. Another area to be investigated is the degree to which people are prevented from exercising by physical disability, competing demands on their time, and financial constraints. The survey is being sponsored by Allied Dunbar, one of the country's largest life insurance companies.

Alcohol: how much is too much?

It's just social to go to the pub and have a drink. Our parents do it. If you were the only one having a coke you would feel a prat.

Except for colloquialisms such as *prat* (meaning "fool" or "jerk") and *pub,* these justifications for drinking—an excerpt from an interview with a 15-year-old English girl—could easily be taken for the reasoning of a U.S.

Genial Londoners exchange the day's news over a pint of ale in that quintessentially English institution, the local pub. Many drink more than a pint, however. Some six million people in Britain exceed the limits of "sensible" alcohol consumption set by the Royal College of Physicians and promoted by the voluntary organization Alcohol Concern, whose goal is to foster a responsible attitude toward drinking.

teenager. Certainly the factors cited—peer pressure, parental example—are familiar to Americans.

Alcohol abuse is a major problem in Britain. The Royal College of Physicians, which has established guidelines for "sensible" drinking, advises that men should limit their drinking to 21 units of alcohol each week and women to 14 units. (A unit is equivalent to eight grams.) One half-pint of beer, one glass of wine, or one small measure of spirits contains approximately one unit of alcohol. It is estimated, however, that 6 million people in Britain exceed these limits, and 1.5 million drink much more heavily.

While alcoholism is far less common among young people (those aged 15 to 24) than among their elders, recent surveys suggest that British children are becoming familiar with drink at earlier ages than ever before and that it is a regular part of life for many teens. In a survey of 15- and 16-year-olds in Scotland, for example, only 2% said they had never tasted an alcoholic beverage. Consequently, much of the literature produced by Alcohol Concern, a voluntary organization that attempts to promote a responsible attitude toward drinking, is aimed at British youth. The legal age for drinking alcoholic beverages in Britain is 18, and youngsters under 14 are not allowed in the bar area of restaurants or other premises licensed to sell alcohol. Underage drinking is nevertheless a pervasive problem. In a study of 17-year-olds, 91% of boys and 28% of girls admitted that they had drunk illegally in public houses. Alcohol Concern sponsors public service announcements and publishes books, pamphlets, and posters that attempt to educate people—particularly young people—about how alcohol affects the body, why people drink, and how much is too much. In addition to informing and educating the public, the organization supports services for people who have a drinking problem. As a result of Alcohol Concern's campaign to promote sensible drinking, 51% of people in the general population and 75% of young people are now aware of the sensible drinking limits.

The death from AIDS of rock singer Freddie Mercury in 1991 apparently had a greater impact on the British public than health information campaigns about the disease have had. Previously, in a survey of 16–34-year-olds, 80% said they did not feel that they were very much at risk of getting AIDS.

AIDS awareness

Condoms have come out from behind the counter. They're now such a part of everyday life that you can buy them from pharmacists, garages, record shops, supermarkets, barbers, some clothes shops, pubs, slot machines and by mail order. Many shops have self-service so you don't have to ask, and many are making condoms as easy to buy as records, toothpaste or petrol.

The above information, which appears in the leaflet *Your Guide to Safer Sex and the Condom,* published by the British Family Planning Association and the HEA, is typical of that being disseminated in Britain today. In March 1991 the cumulative total of diagnosed and reported cases of infection with HIV (the virus that causes AIDS) in England was in excess of 15,000. As is the case in the U.S., currently the most rapid increase in those testing positive for HIV is among heterosexuals.

Major AIDS education programs have been promoted by the government, and a television campaign featuring the personal testimonials of HIV-positive individuals won a recent award as the TV Campaign of the Year. This effort was launched in response to research showing that although 30% of British youngsters have had sexual intercourse by age 16, more than 80% of 16–34-year-olds claimed that they "did not feel very much at risk" of contracting AIDS. A report by the National AIDS Trust indicated that most young people get a majority of their information on AIDS and HIV from television. Since September 1992, however, AIDS education has been included in the national science curriculum for all 11–14-year-old British schoolchildren.

To encourage safer sex practices, cinema advertising campaigns have used humor to break down resistance to the use of condoms, and condom-information packs are distributed to all students entering college. In a study of the effectiveness of public health messages about AIDS, a psychologist at the London School of Economics found that posters showing sex in a positive light have a greater impact on sexual behavior than those featuring messages of fear and despair. One of the most effective posters in a recent British AIDS-awareness program pictured an attractive heterosexual couple in a romantic embrace. The woman is handing her partner a discreet foil-wrapped package. The caption reads: "It's that condom moment."

In the U.K. as in the U.S., a disease like AIDS has possibly the greatest impact on the public following the death of a well-known figure, particularly in the field of sports or show business, or the announcement by such a person that he or she is HIV positive. Thus, the November 1991 death of Freddie Mercury, lead singer of the popular rock group Queen, provided stimulus to the AIDS-prevention campaign. Surveys suggest that the number of young Britons who understand that HIV infection leads to AIDS has risen from 24 to 48%, and the number who understand the symptomless nature of the infection ("You cannot tell who has HIV by looking at them") increased from 74 to 81% in 1990. In fact, no one should now be ignorant of the basic facts about AIDS. Nonetheless, while there is strong evidence that homosexuals are practicing safer sex, the increase in the numbers of HIV-positive heterosexuals indicates that this population has not taken the AIDS message to heart.

112

Promoting responsibility, not fear

Although media coverage has greatly increased public awareness of health issues in Britain, the messages are sometimes confusing, and there are always those like Hodgkinson, Levin, Amiel, and others ready to exploit any disagreement among the experts—or, at least, to have some fun at their expense. Others will go even further to denigrate the concept of health promotion. An example is a recent publication entitled *Health, Lifestyle, and Environment: Countering the Panic,* which claims that Britain and other developed nations are in the grip of a "health panic" that is unsustained by fact and fueled by the misuse of science by well-meaning health activists. Certainly, making people fearful of myriad possible and potential hazards does nothing to improve their quality of life or health. One of the authors of the report pointed out that it is important to distinguish between health educators, who provide information and leave individuals to make their own decisions, and health propagandists, who decide what should be eaten and drunk and attempt to impose changes by bans and restrictions. Of course, however health messages are presented, there will always be those who will dismiss them and those who will go to the opposite extreme.

While most health professionals in Britain support the idea of a government-sponsored strategy to help people live longer, healthier lives, some authorities have been critical of the present schemes for achieving this aim. One faction feels than many of the current proposals overemphasize individual responsibility without considering the socioeconomic factors that make it difficult for some people to change their lives and life-styles. They may have a point. Nevertheless, all agree that it is important for people to recognize the impact of personal choice on health and to receive reliable information on which to base their decisions. The British government and the country's health care professionals now seem united in their determination to accomplish these objectives.

The Hutchinson Library

An Edinburgh city bus is the vehicle for spreading the word about AIDS to the Scottish public.

Sexually Transmitted Disease

KEEPING THE PUBLIC POSTED

by William H. Helfand

Although the devastating effects of sexually transmitted diseases (STDs), formerly known as venereal disease (VD), have been recognized for at least the last 500 years, programs to educate the public about them were virtually nonexistent until early in the 20th century. For one thing, these diseases were not a subject for polite discourse—even for doctors. As late as 1874 a Philadelphia physician apologized to his audience at an American Medical Association meeting for discussing a subject with such unpleasant aspects and expressed the hope that he would not give offense to his listeners. In 1908 the U.S. secretary of the treasury refused to allow a bulletin on venereal disease to be issued by his department, commenting, "The matter contained in this bulletin is not in keeping with the dignity of the fiscal department of the government." The press at the turn of the century also suppressed open discussion of sexually transmitted diseases and either did not cover the subject at all or did not directly refer to the diseases themselves (euphemisms, such as "rare blood disease," were used instead). What little was said about the generally taboo topic stressed moral behavior and continence.

There were rare exceptions to this rule of reticence. In 1906 the *Ladies' Home Journal* ran a series on the subject of VD; as a result, it lost up to 75,000 regular subscribers. That same year Robert N. Willson, a physician from Philadelphia, castigated his fellow professionals for their "studied propriety" and blamed them for what he described as "a world more full of venereal infection than of any other pestilence." Silence on the subject, however, continued to hold sway.

Fitness of the troops

At the start of World War I, concern over the fitness of the armed forces—particularly their fighting efficiency—made communicating the dangers of venereal infection essential; military leaders were forced to consider the potential ravages of VD as they planned battle strategies. As the conflict in Europe escalated, campaigns were mounted to instill a concern for health in the minds of fighting men. Warnings were presented in a continual barrage of propaganda materials—pamphlets, handbills, articles in news-

William H. Helfand is the author and coauthor of several books on art, medicine, and pharmacy, including Pharmacy: An Illustrated History *(New York: Harry N. Abrams, Inc., 1990). He is a consultant to the National Library of Medicine, Bethesda, Maryland, and to the Philadelphia Museum of Art, where in 1991 a major exhibit of prints, posters, caricatures, and ephemera from his personal collection, entitled "The Picture of Health: Images of Medicine and Pharmacy," was shown.*

(Overleaf) Photograph, Centers for Disease Control, Atlanta, Georgia

papers and magazines, exhibitions, lectures, tracts, and posters. The latter were particularly important pieces of artillery in these campaigns.

World War I posters, which were issued by the Social Hygiene Division of the U.S. Army Educational Commission, were among the first public health posters. They told the troops that shame and remorse were what they should feel for any sexual transgressions—for not living up to the high moral standards expected of them and for failing to properly support their comrades in the war effort. "Go back to them physically fit and morally clean" was the message of one that pictured a smiling mother and younger children decorating a cake for the returning soldier. Another, showing a pointing Uncle Sam, admonished: "He still needs your *best*." Yet another depicted a forlorn soldier in a hospital ward: "Not in line of duty." No two ways about it, the posters instructed, the moral path of righteousness was the only path to follow.

Posters also portrayed men in the U.S. armed forces as innocent victims away from home, who could all too easily succumb to the wiles of women.

Posters were important artillery in the American armed forces' anti-venereal-disease campaign throughout World War I and following the war. There was nothing ambiguous about their messages; during the war servicemen were expected to fully support their comrades in arms; afterward they were expected to continue to live up to the highest of moral standards and to avoid infection at all costs.

The Granger Collection

They gave persistent reminders to the soldiers, sailors, and marines that prostitutes presented the gravest of dangers. They also played on the conscience of the serviceman with reminders of the virtuous women (wives, mothers, "sweethearts") chastely waiting for them at home: "100%—she deserves the same."

In Europe many well-known artists of the day contributed to the wartime anti-venereal-disease campaigns. An elaborate poster by the French illustrator Théophile-Alexandre Steinlen had as its centerpiece a tombstone with this inscription: "Soldier, the country counts on you; keep healthy. Resist the temptations of the street where a sickness as dangerous as the war awaits you. It carries its victims to decay and to death without honor, without happiness." World War I posters were full of gravestones, cemeteries, skulls, corpses, specters, and similarly frightful images that very powerfully conveyed the dreadful consequences awaiting the soldier who contracted a venereal disease. European posters were more explicit in naming the threat. (Those issued by the American armed forces did not

Belgian artist Louis Raemakers' striking poster "L'Hécatombe" ("The Massacre"), c. 1916, ominously links sex, syphilis, and death.

117

mention the words *syphilis* or *gonorrhea*.) A particularly haunting poster created by the Belgian artist Louis Raemakers shows a woman in black standing amid rows of graves and holding a skull in a position that seems to equate sex with death.

Although truly effective chemotherapy against venereal disease was not yet available at the time of World War I, chemical prophylaxis to be taken after exposure was. In the book *No Magic Bullet: A Social History of Venereal Disease in the United States Since 1880,* the medical historian Allan M. Brandt described chemical prophylaxis as "a relatively simple procedure, but not a particularly pleasant one."

A soldier reporting for the treatment would first urinate. Then, on a specially constructed stool, he would wash his genitals with soap and water followed by bichloride of mercury, while the attendant inspected. The attendant would then inject a solution of protargol into the penis, which the soldier would hold in the urethra for five minutes, then expel. After the injection, calomel ointment would be rubbed on the penis, which would then be wrapped in waxed paper. For the prevention to be effective the soldier could not urinate for four or five hours following the treatment.

With the threat posed to the troops by the availability of French prostitutes, Gen. John J. Pershing, commander in chief of the American Expeditionary

After World War I, efforts to combat VD were redirected toward the public at large. In 1935 Connecticut was the first state to pass a law requiring couples to undergo premarital blood tests for the detection of venereal infection. Over the next several years, more than half the states in the nation passed similar laws. At the same time, many states also began requiring pregnant women to undergo prenatal blood testing to prevent the congenital transmission of syphilis. These two measures were hailed by public health officials as a great step forward in the battle against VD.

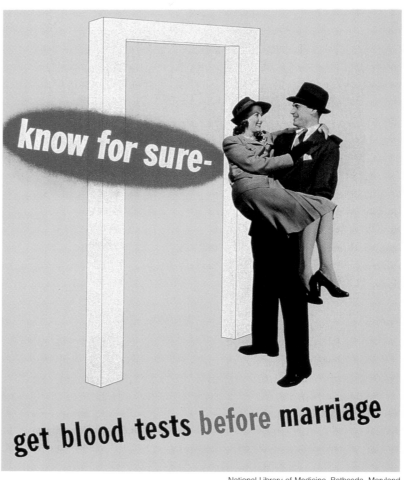

know for sure-

get blood tests before marriage

Forces (AEF), a firm believer in the merits of prophylaxis, ordered the medical department of each AEF division to make the treatments easily accessible, sanitary, and private. Despite the military's enthusiasm for preventing venereal disease with prophylaxis, it proved to be a not wholly reliable method; up to 60% of soldiers who developed syphilis or gonorrhea had taken the treatment.

Between the wars: "shadow on the land"

With the war's end, VD was rampant in Europe and the U.S., and propaganda was redirected to the public at large. Postwar posters still focused on the evils of sexual promiscuity but now also emphasized early detection and treatment. Beginning in 1935, many U.S. states began requiring couples to undergo blood tests and physical exams for venereal disease before marriage; by 1938, 26 states had laws prohibiting marriage between infected individuals. A poster addressing brides and grooms instructed: "Happiness ahead—for the Healthy but not for the Diseased—get full medical examination for VD before marriage."

Forthright as some public health messages had become, the time of frank and open discussion of infections that were acquired through sexual intercourse still had not arrived. In 1934 the New York state health commissioner, Thomas Parran, was forced to cancel a nationwide radio broadcast because he had planned to specifically mention syphilis and gonorrhea in his text. Parran, who was appointed surgeon general of the United States by Pres. Franklin D. Roosevelt in 1936, persevered nonetheless and proved to be a forceful leader in the campaign to battle venereal disease in the years before adequate chemotherapy became available. The year he became surgeon general, he wrote an article entitled "The Next Great Plague to Go," which called for massive, well-publicized information on the causes of and treatment for syphilis. The article was published first in the *Survey Graphic,* a women's magazine with a circulation of three million, and shortly thereafter in the even more popular *Reader's Digest,* thereby reaching a vast international audience. Even the highbrow *New Yorker* took note; its "Talk of the Town" section commented that publication of Parran's syphilis article would "go far towards making the 'hush-hushers' end their mental sit-down strike." Although Parran broke with tradition—he emphasized that he "deliberately minimized the morality issues"—he also noted, "So far as has been possible in dealing with a subject held intrinsically lurid by most people, I have avoided the lurid description and overstatement." As part of his continuing campaign to wipe out syphilis, Parran wrote the book *Shadow on the Land* (1937), which in a short time became a best-seller.

VD and the Axis

Parran's campaign, along with improved medical care, had some success in bringing down the incidence of VD. During World War I over 10% of whites in the U.S. armed forces had been diagnosed with VD (the rate among blacks was higher); by the beginning of World War II the incidence of drafted men with VD had dropped to about half that level. With the start of the war, however, many of the same issues that had troubled military

During World War I the troops were repeatedly warned of the evils of prostitutes. While the professional harlot was still presented as "a bag full of trouble" in World War II, there was a new and even more ubiquitous threat: the so-called amateur, or, as the British poster below, c. 1943, called her, the " 'easy' girl-friend"—a woman of loose morals, eager for a fling with a man in uniform.

119

leaders 25 years earlier were rekindled, and many of the same themes and messages were revived in the all-out anti-venereal-disease campaign that was launched by the military. Posters again stressed the danger of prostitutes—one even stating that "a German bullet is cleaner than a whore"—consideration of the folks back home, and the importance of being an active participant in the war.

Some new themes emerged as well. One was that professional prostitutes were not the only danger; in fact, the "girl next door" could be a source of infection more insidious than prostitutes themselves. "She may look clean—but . . ." was the message of a poster issued by the Army Medical Corps. By that time about 90% of VD cases in the U.S. Army could be traced to so-called amateurs—promiscuous young women (sometimes called "khaki-wackies," "victory girls," or "good-time Charlottes") who were quite eager and willing to have flings with soldiers. A British poster minced no words in blaming loose women for bringing down fighting men: the " 'easy' girl-friend spreads syphilis and gonorrhea, which unless properly treated may result in blindness, paralysis, premature death."

By World War II, however, it had become clear that no matter how strong, fear-inspiring, or often-repeated the messages were, men could *not* be persuaded to exercise continence. Thus, the armed forces took steps to provide them with adequate preventive measures—both before and after

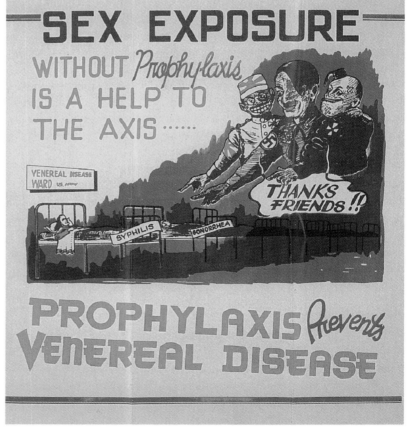

By the time of World War II, it was clear that men serving in the armed forces could not be prevented from having sexual encounters, no matter how grave the warnings. Prophylaxis was widely available, and the men were thus urged to visit the nearest "pro station"—for condoms (before an encounter) or chemical treatment (within three hours after sex without protection). A series of posters issued by the U.S. Army Medical Corps, including the one at right, c. 1942, presented prophylaxis as a matter of patriotism; the lack of it would help the Axis.

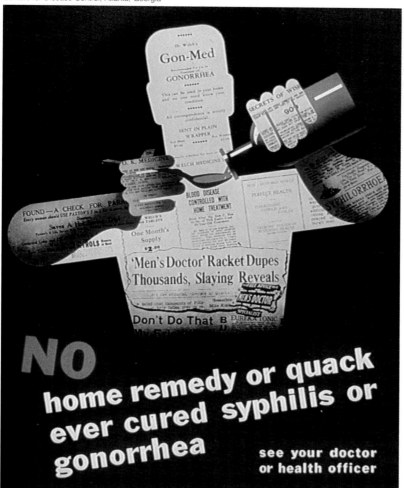

Although there were effective antibiotics to treat VD in the 1930s, the true "magic bullet" against both syphilis and gonorrhea—penicillin—first became available in 1943. After that, posters began to stress the importance of getting proper treatment. They also cautioned against "home remedies" and widely advertised quack treatments.

sexual encounters. Hundreds of "pro stations" were established, conveniently located at military bases and in downtown areas of large cities. The stations gave out (or charged 10 cents for) "pro-kits," containing condoms and lubricating jelly. Or the stations, with their beckoning green lights, were to be visited for chemical treatment within three hours after promiscuous intercourse. A poster distributed by the U.S. Navy showed a sailor in a dunce cap writing over and over on a blackboard: "I should have gone to the pro station."

The Army Medical Corps sought to make prophylaxis not only a matter of health but one of patriotism: "Sex exposure without prophylaxis is a help to the Axis." On one such poster Hitler, Mussolini, and Tojo, representing the three Axis powers, loomed above the VD ward of a military hospital, saying, "Thanks friends!!" Another portrayed the "prostitute," "streetwalker," and "pickup" as "Axis agents."

Although types of chemotherapy had been available even before the start of the war—Paul Ehrlich's "magic bullet" salvarsan, or "606," an arsenic compound used against syphilis, from 1910, and the sulfonamides,

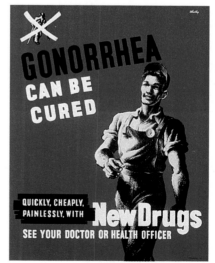

121

effective against gonorrhea, from the mid-1930s—the availability of penicillin toward the end of the war and its remarkable ability to cure both early syphilis and gonorrhea changed the face of the VD threat and provided clear incentives for servicemen to seek medical care. Posters thus could proclaim, "Penicillin cures gonorrhea in 4 hours; see your doctor *today*. He now has penicillin for your treatment." Posters also cautioned the servicemen to seek care from the medical staff only and advised that quack remedies offered by local drugstores were to be scrupulously avoided.

At the end of the war, the availability of effective antibiotics created the expectation that STDs soon would be completely eradicated. As the number of cases dwindled (syphilis rates in the United States declined from 76 cases per 100,000 in 1945 to only 4 per 100,000 in the late 1950s), public funds to combat them were steadily reduced, in some areas being eliminated completely. Hopes for eradication were premature, however. STD rates began to rise again in the 1960s as new bacterial strains of gonorrhea and syphilis that were resistant to available antibiotics began to appear—syphilis cases reaching 12 per 100,000 by 1965 and by 1990, 20 per 100,000 (with rates among blacks as high as 120 cases per 100,000).

Enter AIDS

The arrival of AIDS (acquired immune deficiency syndrome) in 1981 stimulated STD public education activities to new levels—far surpassing those of the war years. Because the disease is incurable, cessation of unsafe sexual practices has been the most important preventive strategy. Consequently, the demand for posters and other means of communicating the facts has been—and continues to be—enormous. Moreover, as the epidemic has grown, and the patterns of infection have changed, so, too, has the need to reach a broader and broader audience. The posters are now ubiquitous; a collection of them at the National Library of Medicine, Bethesda, Maryland,

With the advent of AIDS in the early 1980s, efforts to spread the word about the risks of sexually transmitted disease reached new heights. AIDS posters make it clear that no one is immune. As they strive to deliver lifesaving information to specific at-risk population groups, their messages can be quite compelling. A woman infected with the AIDS virus risks perinatal transmission of the infection to her child (below). The poster (below right) is one of a series of culturally sensitive educational materials that seek to enlighten Native Americans about the AIDS risk.

(Left) "Happy Birthday" designed by Ann Williams for the Shoshin Society; photograph, ibid inc.; (right) National Library of Medicine, Bethesda, Maryland

Don't Share Needles. Don't Get Stuck With AIDS.
Confidential help and information
1-800-872-AIDS
Michigan Department of Public Health AIDS Prevention Program

AIDS, of course, is not only a sexually transmitted disease. It is also transmitted through infected blood. Intravenous-drug users who share needles are another high-risk group, as the poster at left makes eminently clear. AIDS posters are quite frank about the consequences of taking risks, but most important, they emphasize that it is crucial to be well informed. Both posters on this page give toll-free telephone numbers—AIDS hot lines that can be called for the facts.

numbers over 2,000 examples, with new ones being added continually (*see* Sidebar, pages 124–125).

AIDS posters differ from those of previous STD campaigns in that they are bolder, broader in their appeal, and free of euphemisms as they strive to deliver lifesaving information to specific at-risk population groups. In the U.S. posters are aimed at homosexuals, bisexuals, heterosexuals, Caucasians, blacks, Hispanics, Native Americans, mothers-to-be, intravenous-drug users, and adolescents. One notable series of posters produced by the organization People of Color Against AIDS is called "Famous Last Words"—*e.g.,* "AIDS is a white man's disease"; "I don't need to wear one of those" (referring to a condom).

AIDS posters urge and describe "safer sex" practices, stress that condoms are crucial, highlight the dangers of promiscuity, and emphasize that those at risk should be tested. Because the AIDS epidemic has inspired many fears, posters have attempted to correct misinformation—emphasizing that donating blood is safe, that those infected with the AIDS virus deserve compassion, and that children with AIDS are not contagious. The

Center for Attitudinal Healing issued a poster in the mid-1980s in which a child says, "I have AIDS. Please hug me. I can't make you sick." Others inform that there is no risk of infection from doorknobs, handshakes, toilet seats, the sharing of plates and glasses, or kissing. One from Alaska, picturing a mosquito, says: "Go ahead! Spread the word! You can't get AIDS from Alaska's state bird!" (The state has a lot of mosquitoes!)

AIDS posters are an international phenomenon. In the Philippines posters tell prostitutes that they should supply their clients with condoms. Posters in many Third World countries are directed toward reducing the number of sexual partners. One from Trinidad and Tobago says, "You're safer with one partner." One from the island of Mauritius warns men to avoid *les partenaires faciles* ("easy women"). Early in the AIDS epidemic, the Ministry of Health in Uganda, where AIDS is chiefly spread among heterosexuals, issued posters that warned people to "Love carefully!" and urged them to learn the facts about " 'slim' AIDS disease" (so-called because of its emaciating effects).

AIDS Posters in the National Library of Medicine

The ever growing number of AIDS posters is a new and welcome component of the prints and photographs collection in the National Library of Medicine's History of Medicine division. The library, on the campus of the U.S. National Institutes of Health in Bethesda, Maryland, is the world's largest medical research resource. Its prints and photographs collection began as an indulgence of John Shaw Billings, the library's visionary leader during the Victorian era. In 1879 Billings had the opportunity to purchase engraved portraits of famous figures in medical history; he was keen enough on the idea to borrow funds in order to add this nonprint material to the holdings of the young library, then known as the Army Medical Library. Although pictorial material was subsequently added, the collection remained dormant and somewhat inaccessible until the 1950s, when a massive cataloging effort was undertaken.

Now numbering about 60,000 items, the library's prints and photographs serve a public interested in both the historic and aesthetic content of a remarkably diverse group of images. It is anticipated that there will be a substantial increase in use of these materials as the innovative image technology analog videodisc, combined with computerized captions, is adapted to provide total visual and bibliographic access to the collection. This system is particularly appropriate for the library's valuable poster holdings, which are too large, fragile, and cumbersome to be routinely retrieved.

The library now has some 6,000 public health-related posters. Certainly the AIDS posters—at latest count numbering over 2,000—are among the most compelling and dramatic and are a testament to the profound impact this disease has had on the world in its short life. By their very nature, however, posters are ephemeral; they are here today, gone tomorrow. If mounted outdoors, they can be quickly destroyed by the elements. Moreover, they are soon superseded by new public health materials.

Because AIDS posters provide a valuable record of the international response to a frightening and as-yet-incurable disease—in particular, the effort to sensitize the public to the growing health threat—the library sought to find the best way not only to collect them but to organize and preserve them. Bringing these documents into the collection was a task facilitated by one of the library's newer data bases, "Dirline," an on-line file of medically related organizations. In 1988 hundreds of letters seeking AIDS materials were sent to selected groups discovered through this directory; these inquiries soon yielded poster offerings from dozens of different organizations and from countries all over the world.

The key to storing these large, flimsy documents, often printed on cheap paper, is first to place them in durable Mylar; the plastic encasements prevent the posters from slipping during handling and protect them from chemical contamination, which might affect their

But posters are widespread in wealthy nations as well. A Swiss poster features the accoutrements of a well-dressed man—from necktie to watchband to condom. Japan has only recently joined the AIDS-awareness movement. The approach it has taken is to reflect the public's fears of the disease. Japanese subways are lined with posters featuring monsters, witches, mummies, and Dracula, proclaiming: "I am afraid of AIDS." The specific messages of AIDS posters are as varied as the countries they come from. Their aim, however, is the same: to motivate people to alter risky behavior.

Some AIDS posters have been quite provocative and indeed controversial. They have, for example, shown explicit photographs of gay men engaging in sexual activities—the rationale being that the images are justified by the urgency of their message. Nonetheless, even in the current era forthright messages in public health campaigns have not been entirely unrestricted. In 1986 a federal rule was imposed on U.S. government financing of AIDS educational materials that were deemed "offensive" to

Adam and Eve stand duly warned that marital fidelity offers the best protection against AIDS. The messages are in dozens of languages—in this case Russian—in the ever growing international collection of AIDS posters at the National Library of Medicine, Bethesda, Maryland.

color or condition. The well-protected posters are then safely stored in dust-free steel mapcases in a temperature- and humidity-controlled room, thus guaranteeing that the ephemeral material will last for many years. Not all the AIDS posters are mass productions printed on cheap paper; some are rare and quite valuable—for example, posters created by well-known artists to raise funds for AIDS research. Accordingly, these are specially mounted and stored to ensure their lasting value.

So that the AIDS posters are accessible to researchers, each one is catalogued. The catalog entry includes the poster's country of origin, the publishing and sponsoring organization, the date of issue, a brief description of the visual, the size (which is particularly helpful when the poster is to be lent for an exhibit), and other relevant information. Library users can view the catalogued AIDS posters in color on a computer screen, or they can specially request to see the actual documents.

The National Library of Medicine's unique collection of AIDS posters will only gain in significance as it continues to grow. The library is gratified to have these documents of what may be the most important public health crisis of the 20th century as part of its information resources.

—Lucinda H. Keister, Head
Prints and Photographs Collection
History of Medicine Division
National Library of Medicine

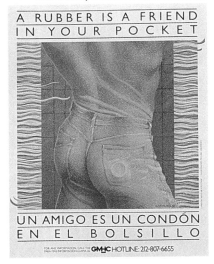

A RUBBER IS A FRIEND
IN YOUR POCKET

UN AMIGO ES UN CONDÓN
EN EL BOLSILLO

FOR ANY INFORMATION CALL THE **GMHC** HOTLINE: 212-807-6655
PARA MAS INFORMACIÓN LLAMA AL

Gay men—one of the groups hit hardest and earliest by the AIDS epidemic—have been the target of some of the most sexually explicit AIDS posters. The gay community is also one in which the most striking changes in sexual behavior have occurred and, consequently, the incidence of new AIDS cases among homosexual men has steadily declined. Presumably, the increased use of condoms by this group—along with reduced numbers of sexual partners—is a reflection of effective educational efforts.

"a majority of adults." In May 1992, however, a federal district court judge in New York City ruled that the restriction was both vague and unconstitutional. "Can educational material be offensive simply because it mentions homosexuality?" the judge asked. "Can a proposed education project be offensive because it traps a captive audience, such as subway riders, and forces them to look at a condom?" AIDS advocacy groups applauded the decision, which is expected to have an impact on the content of future posters and other materials in the campaign to conquer AIDS.

Nowadays social scientists study the effects of persuasion strategies that are used in public health campaigns in order to determine what approaches work best. Some psychologists have suggested that poster images must be personal and relevant to a target audience's life-style; otherwise, the intended viewers are likely to be oblivious to the message that the poster is meant to convey. Janet Stockdale, a psychologist at the London School of Economics, has studied and measured the effects of AIDS posters in the U.K. and found that if the message is delivered in a positive way, people are more ready to accept the information and alter behavior accordingly. In contrast, posters that provoke despair—saying that "AIDS is killing the human race," for example—are so frightening that there can be no practical response. Thus, a recent series of British AIDS posters has sought to convey the message that safer sex is "trendy" and that it is practiced by "attractive people."

Others contend that instilling fear is the best way to capture an intended audience. Certainly wartime anti-VD campaigns sought to frighten people about the unmentionable diseases. Even as late as World War II, nightmarish images dominated—to the point of fostering a climate of "syphilophobia." The scary approach is one the Japanese authorities have adopted to educate the public about AIDS, using Dracula as a spokesperson. While alarming words and images may be quite effective in gaining attention, in comparison with those at the low end of the "fear scale," studies show that they do not necessarily lead to positive changes in behavior. In fact, scare tactics can lead to denial; people assume that such horrors could never happen to them. A recent study found that adolescents "may be compelled to deny fear messages or to respond with dysfunctionally high levels of fear, thus developing a paranoia about disease."

Assessing the impact

Posters have been key contributors to public health campaigns for nearly a century. While their approaches and designs have changed, reflecting the times, they continue to be widely used to promote good health practices. Because of their large size, posters can have a strong impact; with their colorful graphics they can arrest the attention of the passerby and deliver vital health information in a matter of a few precious seconds. Moreover, because their information is provided in a visual format, even the nonliterate public can grasp the messages. Furthermore, posters are inexpensive to produce and are easily mounted in public places such as commuter railway stations, factories, offices, and public restrooms. During the world wars they were strategically placed in latrines.

It is now well recognized that the heterosexual spread of AIDS is a global—and growing—problem. A poster from Mauritius is reminiscent of World War II posters—warning that "easy partners" may be easy transmitters of sexually transmitted diseases. A poster from Thailand, where prostitution is widespread and as many as 50% of prostitutes are believed to carry the AIDS virus, delivers the message that condom use is a must. By recent projections AIDS cases in sub-Saharan Africa will number over three million by 1995. In the 1980s, well before this grim picture of the epidemic had emerged, the Ugandan Ministry of Health urged couples to play it safe.

Because they are inexpensive to produce, are readily mounted in public places, and can deliver lifesaving information in a matter of seconds, posters will undoubtedly continue to play a vital role in AIDS education campaigns around the globe.

How effective have the STD posters been? Their aim—to bring about changes in attitude and behavior in what is the most intimate and personal of contexts—is by no means an easy one to accomplish, and it is something they could not possibly do alone. Moreover, because they are rarely the sole artillery in the educational armamentarium, it is difficult to isolate their influence. During the major wars of this century, military leaders, faced with the seriousness of the problem of STD, could not run the risk of conducting controlled experiments to find out which materials in the massive propaganda campaigns reduced or did not reduce disease rates.

In the U.S. educational efforts have *not* been able to significantly curtail the level of teenage pregnancies or intravenous drug use. On the other hand, condom use and safer sex practices have increased. Among gay men the number of new cases of AIDS has been steadily declining since the early alarms were sounded.

In the U.K. two reports in 1991 found that despite the sale of over 140 million condoms in that country in 1990, the message about safer sex was still failing to get through to young sexually active people. The Health Education Authority found that among 4,000 16–19-year-olds, 72% understood that having sex without a condom was unsafe, but 20% would still have unprotected sex with a new partner. Another report based on a study by the London Rubber Co. found that 27% of those in an 18–20-year-old group would have sex with a new partner without using a condom. Social psychologists concluded that follow-up health education efforts were not sufficient; some 32% of young people reported that they did not have *enough* information. Moreover, it was found that many had

128

rejected "safer sex" in favor of the far less reliable practice of "safer choice" of a partner. Studies have found similar behavior among U.S. adolescents; young people know they should use condoms, but many take the risk of unprotected sex anyway.

The impact of posters thus appears equivocal. Nonetheless, because the AIDS problem is so deadly serious, public health education must continue. No single effort or medium can conquer a societal problem of the magnitude of AIDS; the war on AIDS will continue to require a massive effort on many fronts. The challenge remains to find the most effective ways to present vital information so that people will be less likely to take risks that will endanger their lives. Because they have the potential to reach a vast audience and to deliver potent messages, posters are certain to play an important part in the continuing campaigns.

The battle against AIDS requires not only a well-informed public but dollars to support research and benefit disease victims. The poster at left was created by the artist Paul Davis for an AIDS fund-raiser sponsored by the East End Gay Organization of New York.

DRUGS

SOME DO GROW ON TREES

by Jerry Mason

Recently the U.S. National Cancer Institute (NCI) hailed the drug taxol as the most important new drug for cancer patients in 15 years. Taxol was discovered about 30 years ago during a plant-screening program that involved 35,000 species. Researchers at Albert Einstein College of Medicine, New York City, have found that taxol works in a unique way: it causes the microtubules of cancerous cells to "gum up," thereby inhibiting their reproduction. While taxol is toxic to all cells, it appears to have some specificity for tumor cells.

The first successful clinical trials of taxol were reported in 1989 by William McGuire and colleagues at the Johns Hopkins School of Medicine, Baltimore, Maryland. In patients with advanced ovarian cancer for whom traditional therapies had failed, 30% responded to the drug; their tumors regressed in size following treatment. Encouraging results were also obtained in patients with lung cancer. Researchers at M.D. Anderson Cancer Center, Houston, Texas, found that taxol helped stem advanced breast cancer in several patients. The NCI believes that taxol holds promise in the treatment of malignant melanoma and colon cancer as well and has called for stepped-up production of the drug.

The only known source of taxol is the Pacific yew (*Taxus brevifolia*), a conifer of the family Taxaceae. The slow-growing evergreen, which reaches its mature height of about 9 meters (30 feet) after 100 years, is found scattered in the northwestern U.S. and Canada. It is the tree's thin, reddish bark that yields the drug. Until recently the tree was not considered to be of any commercial value. It was treated as a weed and regularly bulldozed during forest clear-cutting; its valuable product was burned along with the undergrowth.

It has been estimated that in the forests of Oregon and Washington there are anywhere from 20 million to 130 million yews. It takes bark from as many as 5,000 Pacific yews and costs about $200,000 to make one kilogram (2.2 pounds) of taxol; treatment for a single patient requires the

Jerry Mason is a London-based photojournalist.

(Opposite page) A lush Costa Rican rain forest is home to plants that may one day offer hitherto undreamed-of medicines. Photograph, Gary Retherford—Bruce Coleman Limited

Steven C. Wilson

*Taxol, which has been called the most promising new drug for cancer of the last 15 years, is extracted from the bark of the Pacific yew (*Taxus brevifolia*), a slow-growing conifer found primarily in the Pacific Northwest. The pharmaceutical company Bristol-Myers Squibb has invested $100 million in the commercial development of taxol; over a five-year period it will harvest up to 38,000 yews a year in order to produce the drug. However, because the demand for taxol is so great—and it takes bark from three to eight trees to make enough of the drug to treat a single patient—alternative sources are desperately needed.*

Raw taxol from Pacific yews is processed and purified in a chemical laboratory. Because the present method of producing the drug yields only very limited quantities, chemists around the world are vying to come up with more efficient means of boosting the taxol supply.

bark of three to eight trees. Extracting and purifying taxol is an extremely complex process, and its concentration in the bark can vary widely from tree to tree.

In June 1991 the U.S. Department of Agriculture and the Department of the Interior entered into an agreement with Bristol-Myers Squibb, allowing the drug company to harvest up to 38,000 trees a year for five years on federal land. Many environmentalists, fearing extinction of the tree, were dismayed by that action; they believe that because it shares a habitat with the threatened northern spotted owl, the Pacific yew should be declared an endangered species. Advocates of the drug, however, question whether yews should be preserved as a home for owls when they could be providing a lifesaving drug for cancer patients. Bristol-Myers Squibb speculates that in five years it will have harvested an adequate supply of bark to meet the needs of patients, and after that it will be possible to manufacture taxol synthetically or by genetic engineering techniques.

Spurred on by the present difficulty in obtaining adequate supplies of the active drug from the trees themselves, chemists around the world have been racing to come up with a synthetic version. Early attempts to synthesize taxol failed owing to its highly complex chemical structure. Consequently, researchers turned to tissue cultures. By manipulating plant cells in growth mediums, chemists can create laboratory "gardens" of plant parts that yield important chemicals. Chemical "elicitors" are added to the growth medium to prompt the culture to produce more than the usual amounts of the desired compound.

In 1991 a team of French scientists reported in the *Journal of the American Chemical Society* that they had produced a semisynthetic drug called Taxotère, the precursor of which was extracted from the needles of the English yew (*Taxus baccata*). The drug is in phase-one clinical trials in Paris and other cities, where so far it has caused fewer adverse reactions than taxol. (Taxol's side effects can include nausea, muscle pain, numbness

Jay Dickman

Interest in botanical products as pharmaceuticals is not new. In the Middle Ages medicinal plants, or "simples," were cultivated on the grounds of monasteries, and during the Renaissance "physic" gardens flourished throughout much of Europe. The woodcut at left depicts the gathering, drying, chopping, and distilling of plants for medicines in a 16th-century herbarium in Germany.

in the extremities, and hair loss; the most severe effect is neutropenia, a reduction in white blood cells.) Chemist Robert A. Holton at Florida State University has also produced a semisynthetic form of taxol from the English yew and has been granted a U.S. patent for his product. In San Carlos, California, the biotechnology firm ESCAgenetics Corp. has developed a genetic engineering process for making taxol. These developments suggest that a synthetic or semisynthetic form of the drug will eventually be available for cancer patients—but probably not for many years.

Drugs from plants: old idea, new interest

The taxol story illustrates some of the conflicting issues affecting the development of drugs from plants, and it highlights the need for more careful husbandry of the environment. Plants manufacture a vast and varied range of chemical products of ingenious design—products that are often beyond the imaginings of chemists. Taxol is just one of many therapeutic drugs derived from plants that may offer hitherto undreamed-of treatments for cancer and other illnesses. After a long period of neglect, interest in the pharmacologically active principles in plants—the science of pharmacognosy—is undergoing a major revival.

It has been estimated that man-made pollution and the process of development could lead to the extinction of some 60,000 plant species by the middle of the next century. As ethnobotanists (those who study the ways that traditional cultures use plants) have mounted efforts to collect disappearing species, particularly in the rain forests, the potential of natural products in drug manufacture has been reappraised. Pharmacognosy has received a further boost from technology; it is now possible for scientists to scour the plant world for novel compounds in ways that they never could before. Whereas once research on plants was slow and highly labor

133

A scientist working in a pharmaceutical company laboratory analyzes plant samples with the use of a fluorescent cell sorter. The contemporary search for new drugs from natural sources has received an important boost from technology.

intensive, today the pharmacognosist has highly efficient and automated methods for screening virtually unlimited numbers of plants.

There are four ways that medicines are derived from plants: (1) The medicine itself is contained in the plant—*e.g.,* alkaloids and glycosides, small molecules that effect changes in the biochemistry of organisms—and is used without modification after it has been extracted. An example is digoxin, a glycoside, from the foxglove (*Digitalis lanata*), which works as a heart stimulant. (2) A plant compound provides the basic material for a semisynthetic chemical process. Topical steroidal skin salves, for example, rely on natural precursors from the sisal plant (*Agave sisalana*). (3) An active principle in the plant acts as the stimulus to produce a new medicine by total synthesis. Observation of the active principle khellin of the khella plant (*Ammi visnaga*), which had been used in Egypt for skin, lung, and kidney complaints, led to the synthesis of three important drugs in the contemporary therapeutic armamentarium: nifedipine (for angina and hypertension), amiodarone (for abnormal heart rhythms), and sodium cromoglycate (for asthma). (4) The mode of action of a plant medicine is copied to provide a better synthetic drug. Widely used muscle relaxants today are based on the chemical structure and mode of action of the alkaloid tubocurarine from *Chondodendron tomentosum,* an Amazonian jungle vine from which South American Indians had long extracted curare for use as a paralyzing agent on arrowheads.

Saving the rain forests

Of the approximately 275,000 to 300,000 species of plants worldwide, only about 5,000 have been screened by modern scientists. Hidden among the disappearing plants may be drugs with the potential to combat cancer, diabetes, heart disease, and even unpredictable epidemics like that of AIDS. Estimates suggest that about 50% of the world's plant species are in the tropics—a large proportion being in the rain forests. Moreover, 50%

of all rain forest plants are thought to be indigenous and not a renewable resource. Many of the plants that are now being appraised as potential sources for pharmaceuticals come from those parts of the tropics involved in environmental and social upheaval.

By their very nature, tropical plants are well endowed with chemical defenses, which the plants presumably manufacture in order to repel predators (*e.g.,* insects or fungal diseases) or to protect themselves against a sudden temperature change. It is these potent defenses, known as secondary metabolites, that lend themselves to drug manufacture.

Numerous modern drugs have been derived from plants of the jungle. Just one notable example is quinine, which for many years was the standard treatment for malaria. Quinine comes from the bark of the cinchona tree, as does another alkaloid, quinidine, which is used in treating heart rhythm abnormalities. Peruvians traditionally used the bark of various species of cinchona trees to treat fevers. According to legend, Countess Chinchón, the wife of the viceroy of Peru, fell ill with malaria in 1663. The governor of a nearby province sent a remedy obtained from tree bark. The countess experienced a seemingly miraculous recovery, and word of the bark's remarkable powers spread quickly. The tree was named cinchona by the Swedish botanist Carolus Linnaeus, introducing a small spelling error. Subsequently, the powdered bark was taken to Europe by Jesuits, where it was widely touted for its healing powers (and often referred to as Jesuits' bark).

Wisdom of the shaman. Not only is plant life destroyed to make way for development, centuries of wisdom are lost as tribal communities disperse and die. The medicine men, or shamans, are repositories of vast botanical knowledge. Michael Balick, director of the Institute of Economic Botany at the New York Botanical Garden, has called the people living in the disappearing forests "encyclopedias of local flora." The disappearance of

The trunk of the cinchona tree, native to the Amazonian jungle, is the source of quinine (an antimalarial and fever-reducing drug) and quinidine (used to treat abnormal heart rhythms). The tree was named after the Countess Chinchón of Peru, who, according to legend, was miraculously cured of malaria by a remedy obtained from tree bark.

Medicine men, or shamans, in the Amazon River basin have vast knowledge of the local flora. For centuries they have relied on the plants of the rain forests to treat virtually every kind of human ailment, and many of their treatments are known to be highly effective.

the shamans' unwritten pharmacopoeias has been appropriately compared to the burning of the library at Alexandria, Egypt.

In Belém of Pará province in northeastern Brazil, a local shaman of the Kayopo tribe, Beptopoop, acts as adviser to a recently established medicinal garden project. In his own garden Beptopoop grows a variety of plants that he uses to treat epilepsy, toothaches, boils, and tumors on the skin. For other medicines he goes into the forest—for example, to seek *Epistephium lucidum,* a kind of orchid that is used as a contraceptive, or rhizomes (subterranean plant stems) known locally as piri-piri, which are said to induce sterility in women who no longer wish to conceive.

The medical practice of the Kayopo people is extremely sophisticated and includes a wealth of plant-derived remedies. For example, the Kayopo have long used the sap of the wee-dee plant, a member of the nutmeg family, to treat a variety of fungal infections. Western medicine, which is short on effective antifungal treatments, is particularly interested in the wee-dee. As far back as 1940, Harvard University researchers attempted to identify the plant's active components but failed to do so. More recent studies by scientists in Brazil demonstrated antifungal activity in at least two of the wee-dee's components.

Promising partnerships. Richard Evans Schultes, director of the Botanical Museum at Harvard University, who spent well over a decade collecting and studying Amazonian plants, has said that "the drugs of the future grow in the primeval jungle." Belatedly, the pharmaceutical industry has discovered that the tropical forests, especially those of Latin America, are a largely untapped resource for new medicines. Several major drug manufacturers are now investing in conservation of the valuable forests and are compensating indigenous people for sharing their botanical knowledge. In 1991 Merck & Co., the world's largest drug company, began a partnership with the tiny country of Costa Rica to develop its biological resources. The Costa Rican government has set aside 25% of its land as forest preserves. Merck will provide $1 million over two years in return for exclusive rights to screen rain forest plants (as well as microorganisms and insects). The collection of plants is being overseen by the National Institute of Biodiversity (INBio), a government-sponsored research center in Heredia. INBio is training so-called parataxonomists—natives who have no previous scientific training and often no formal education but know the forests well; these "bioliterate" workers are paid as "chemical prospectors," who help to both collect and identify specimens.

Scientists at Cornell University, Ithaca, New York, and the Strathclyde Institute for Drug Research at the University of Strathclyde, Glasgow, Scotland, have formal agreements with Merck to test biological extracts of special interest and are working with INBio scientists to find chemically promising plants. Among the compounds that are being most actively sought are those that may be effective against cancer, AIDS, and fungal infections. The collaborating scientists are also seeking new antibiotics because of the growing resistance of many pathogens to existing drugs.

In addition to the Merck venture and those of several other corporate giants, a number of smaller companies have been set up expressly to

Tirio tribesmen on the Brazil-Suriname border point out to ethnobotanist Mark Plotkin the many varieties of medicinal plants that are used by their people. As tropical forests are rapidly being destroyed and indigenous people forced to disperse, many healing plants are now in danger of being lost. Plotkin and other ethnobotanists emphasize the importance not only of preserving the intimate understanding that local shamans have of the rain forest flora but of classifying the plants and appreciating their natural relationships to each other.

explore the pharmaceutical potential of the rain forests—before it is too late. One of them is Shaman Pharmaceuticals of San Carlos, California, established in 1989. In its search for new drugs in the tropics, the company relies on the knowledge and experience of shamans and other local healers. Already Shaman has several promising products in development, each isolated from a plant used by natives. The company has also set up a foundation called the Healing Forest Conservancy to channel profits from rain forest-derived drugs back to the local communities.

Biotics Ltd., a British company based in Sussex, acts as a broker for less developed countries, finding them buyers for their medicinal plants and ensuring that the suppliers receive royalties for any profits that are made. The Biotics program has supplied large international pharmaceuticals companies such as Glaxo and SmithKline Beecham with medicinal plants from Malaysia, Thailand, Ghana, Costa Rica, and China.

A sampling of plant-derived drugs

Of course, medicines have been made from plants found in virtually every part of the world for centuries. In fact, about 120 drugs that are commonly prescribed today are plant derived.

Coca (*Erythroxylum coca*), native to Peru and Bolivia, yields the anesthetic cocaine. The Calabar bean (*Physostigma venenosum*) from western Africa, also known as the ordeal bean, is a source of physostigmine, used in treating myasthenia gravis and glaucoma, diseases that are also treated with the alkaloid pilocarpine obtained from the leaflets of the South American tropical plant jaborandi (*Pilocarpus microphyllus*). Opium, the milky resin from the seed pod of the opium poppy (*Papaver somniferum*), until recently was widely available over the counter as an analgesic. Morphine, derived from opium, was the first of the poppy's alkaloids to be isolated (early in the last century) and is the main source of the potent painkiller codeine.

137

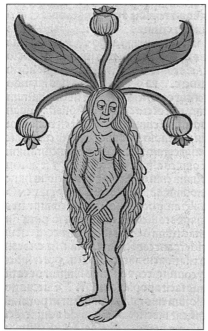

In 1776 William Withering, an English country doctor, learned of a complex herbal mixture used by a Shropshire woman to treat "the dropsy" (edema); he then determined that the principal active ingredient of this folk remedy was the foxglove plant (*Digitalis purpurea*). In 1785 Withering published *An Account of the Foxglove,* an exhaustive study now considered a medical literature classic. Digitalis and digoxin, two of the active principles in the foxglove, are potent cardiac glycosides that are still widely used agents for stimulating the heart. Important cardiac glycosides are also obtained from other plants, including the oleander (*Nerium oleander*) and lily of the valley (*Convallaria majalis*).

The willow tree (*Salix alba*) is a source of salicin, a bitter glycoside whose derivative acetylsalicylic acid (aspirin) is now the world's most commonly used painkiller. In the U.S. alone some 80 million tablets are consumed annually. In 1763 the Rev. Edmund Stone of Chipping Norton, Oxfordshire, England, wrote to the president of the Royal Society recommending the bark of the willow as "efficacious in curing aquish and intermitting disorders" (referring to the chills, fever, and sweating that occur with the flu and other febrile disorders). "I have no other motives for publishing this valuable specific," wrote Stone, "than that it may have a fair and full trial in all its variety of circumstances and situations, and that the world may reap the benefits accruing from it." Salicin is found in many other plants, including the meadowsweet (*Filipendula ulmaria*) and the myrtle tree (*Myrtus communis*). The mechanisms by which aspirin achieves its wide-ranging beneficial effects are only now being fully elucidated.

The isolation of the natural steroid diosgenin from various species of the Mexican yam (*Dioscorea composita, D. floribunda,* and others), from which the steroidal sex hormone progesterone is derived, enabled the large-scale production of the first oral contraceptives in the 1940s. Before the discovery of a plant source of the hormone, only tiny amounts could be obtained by synthesis or from animal sources (such as sows' ovaries).

Mandrake (*Mandragora officinarum*), recognized by its human-shaped roots, is a member of the family Solanaceae; the plant contains a powerful concoction of alkaloids with sedative and anesthetic properties. The mandrake was thought to have been a constituent of death sponges used to relieve the suffering of those crucified by the Romans. Its properties were known to Plato, and the plant was used in surgical operations and cauterization by Pedanius Dioscorides, the Greek army surgeon who served Nero from AD 54 to 68. Dioscorides also prescribed mandragora wine (*orinos mandragorites*) as a draft for insomnia and pain. The mandrake yields hyoscine, a potent alkaloid that, under the name scopolamine, remains a standard preoperative sedative. It is also used to prevent motion sickness and as truth serum in lie-detector tests. In a bizarre series of incidents, reported in the *New Scientist* in August 1991, robbers in Bogota, Colombia, gave their victims a concoction containing scopolomine before robbing them; the victims' memories were erased for several hours after the event.

A relative of mandrake, the thorn apple (*Datura stramonium*), which was formerly used to treat Parkinson's disease and asthma, yields hyoscine and another alkaloid, hyoscyamine. In America *D. stramonium* is com-

138

monly called jimsonweed, or Jamestown weed, commemorating an event in Jamestown in 1676 when soldiers who were sent to put down a rebellion encountered the plant and were waylaid by its toxic effects for several days.

Two other members of the family Solanaceae, henbane (*Hyoscyamus niger*)—the witch's plant—and *Atropa belladonna,* the deadly nightshade, produce a third potent alkaloid, atropine. Atropine-based drugs derived from these plants have been valuable remedies for spasmodic muscular contractions, nervous disorders, and hysteria. However, the drugs can be extremely toxic; for this reason they have largely been replaced by synthetic analogs.

Owing to their toxicity, quite a few plant medicines that were once in official pharmacopoeias have been discarded or supplanted by synthetic products. Ipecacuanha (*Cephaelis ipecacuanha*) was known in 17th-century Brazil as a remedy for the "bloody flux"—a form of diarrhea; its alkaloid emetine was the standard treatment for amebiasis (amebic dysentery) until the early 1960s, when it was replaced by less toxic synthetic drugs such as metronidazole and iodoquinol.

Snakeroot (*Rauwolfia serpentina*) was an old Indian remedy for snakebite and insanity. It yields the alkaloid reserpine, which was originally used as a tranquilizer and was later found to be effective in treating hypertension (high blood pressure). The drug works by depleting the nerve-impulse transmitter norepinephrine from nerve terminals, thereby reducing the ability of the sympathetic nervous system to maintain the degree of blood vessel constriction that is responsible for high blood pressure. However, reserpine is rarely a drug of choice in the treatment of hypertension today because it often has major side effects—most notably, severe and prolonged mental depression.

Some plants that have been used for decades, or even for centuries, to treat one ailment are now being studied as remedies with other therapeutic indications. Colchicine is an anti-inflammatory agent extracted

(Opposite page) The mandrake plant (Mandragora officinarum) *has long been identified by its human-shaped roots. Its medicinal properties were known to Plato (428/427 BC–348/347 BC), and Greek physicians of the 1st century AD prescribed mandragora wine for pain and insomnia. Mandrake yields the potent alkaloid hyoscine, or scopolamine, which is used today as a sedative in surgery and obstetrics, as a motion-sickness preventative, and as truth serum in lie-detector tests.*

*The world's most commonly used painkiller was advertised on trucks in Europe in the 1920s and '30s. Acetylsalicylic acid, or aspirin, is derived from the bitter compound salicin, found in the bark of the willow tree (*Salix alba*). Best known as a pain reliever, aspirin also reduces fever, redness, and swelling; inhibits blood clotting; and may prevent heart attacks and strokes. In fact, aspirin's full therapeutic potential probably has yet to be realized.*

G.G. Hunter—Bruce Coleman Limited

Flowering plants from virtually every corner of the globe are the source of novel therapeutic products used to treat countless human ills. (Above) The opium poppy, native to Asia Minor, is the source of the powerful narcotics morphine, heroin, codeine, and papaverine. A drug derived from the roots of the Chinese milk vetch (above center) enhances the immune system and is used in combination with other drugs in cancer treatments. The foxglove (above right) yields the potent cardiac glycosides digitalis and digoxin. Vinblastine and vincristine, drugs derived from the Madagascar periwinkle (right), are important anticancer agents used to treat Hodgkin's disease and leukemia.

(Top left and right) Jerry Mason;
(top center) Dick J.C. Klees—Bruce Coleman Limited;
(bottom) Isaac Geib—Grant Heilman

from the autumn crocus (*Colchicum autumnale*). The crocus, also called meadow saffron, was first recommended by the much-traveled practitioner Alexander of Tralles (AD *c.* 525–*c.* 605) for gouty joints. More recently, medical researchers at Rockefeller University, New York City, have found that colchicine may help slow the progression of the degenerative nervous system disorder multiple sclerosis. Clinical trials were begun in 1986.

The seeds of the castor-oil plant (*Ricinus communis*) of Brazil and India yield the oil that is commonly given to children and has been widely extolled for centuries as a purgative, but the seeds also contains the deadly poison ricin. In an infamous incident in September 1978, a Bulgarian diplomat was

The autumn crocus, or meadow saffron (above), is the source of colchicine, which has been used since the 6th century AD to treat gout. The European deadly nightshade, or belladonna plant (left), with its reddish bell-shaped flowers and shining black berries, yields the potent alkaloid atropine. Used alone, atropine works as an antispasmodic in the treatment of stomach and intestinal disorders. Atropine is most effective when used in combination with a mild sedative to manage functional disorders associated with anxiety and nervous tension, such as irritable bowel syndrome.

murdered in London by an agent whose weapon was an umbrella tipped with a lethal dose of ricin. Currently, cancer researchers are seeking ways to target specific tumor cells with this powerful poison.

China's pharmacopoeia: ancient but buoyant

The World Health Organization (WHO) estimates that 80% of the people in China depend on traditional medicine and herbal remedies whose effectiveness has been well documented through the dynasties. The legendary emperor Shen Nung, who may have lived as long ago as the 3rd millennium BC, is said to have been familiar with several hundred medicinal plants.

141

The legendary Chinese emperor Shen Nung, who may have lived as long ago as the 3rd millennium BC, is said to have documented several hundred plant-derived drugs. Many of those reputed remedies have been passed down through the dynasties and are still in use today. A traditional pharmacy in contemporary China (opposite page, top) dispenses many of the same herbal medicines as were contained in ancient pharmacopoeias. One ancient Chinese remedy that has long been regarded as a panacea is ginseng root (Panax schinseng)—often called the "herb of eternal life" or the "root of heaven." Ginseng is also native to and cultivated in Korea; the highly prized herb is sold in an apothecary shop in Seoul (opposite page, bottom).

In 1979 the Chinese Medical Material Research Center (CMMRC) was set up at the Chinese University of Hong Kong to survey the long tradition of Chinese medicine. CMMRC scientists are analyzing many ancient remedies for their true bioactivity (as opposed to placebo effects).

The root of the ginseng plant (*Panax schinseng)*, the Chinese "herb of eternal life," contains a number of active compounds that have been found to stimulate the nervous system, enhance circulation, and increase the secretion of hormones. CMMRC is comparing the saponin content of various types of ginseng. Saponins, which are potent glucosides, seem to act on the nervous system as either a depressant or a stimulant, depending on the dosage.

The 16th-century herbalist Li Shih-chen compiled a comprehensive catalog of Chinese materia medica known as the "Great Pharmacopeia." CMMRC is bringing this work up to date and with the help of IBM has created a reference data base of more than 700 commonly used Chinese herbs. One folklore remedy described in the catalog that has attracted considerable attention is the moon citrus (*Murraya paniculata)*, whose roots contain yuehuchukene, an unusual indole alkaloid, which has been found to prevent implantation of a fertilized egg; the plant is therefore a potential candidate as a morning-after contraceptive.

Despite the Chinese government's recent attempts to stamp out traditional healers, the market in herbal remedies continues to flourish, particularly because these natural drugs tend to have a less drastic impact on the body than synthetic ones. In modern hospitals throughout China, herbal and Western treatments are routinely combined. A mixture of the root of the milk vetch (*Astragalus glycyphyllus)*, a member of the pea family that is known in China as huang qi, and the Chinese privet (*Ligustrum japonicum)* is used to boost the immune systems of cancer patients so that they can better withstand chemotherapy and radiotherapy. Research at the M.D. Anderson Cancer Center has confirmed these effects and has also found that an extract of milk vetch appears to enhance the activity of interleukin-2, a natural protein secreted by the body that increases both the number and activity of cancer-fighting cells.

Many other plants in the Chinese pharmacopoeia appear in Western medicine. The joint fir (*Ephedra sinica)* was an ancient Chinese treatment for asthma, hay fever, and colds. In 1887 Japanese researchers isolated from *Ephedra sinica* the alkaloid ephedrine, which acts in a fashion similar to that of the hormone epinephrine (adrenaline). Most over-the-counter decongestant tablets contain a synthetic form of ephedrine, pseudoephedrine.

Simply stated, the philosophy behind Chinese medicine is to help the body cure itself. Artemisia or wormwood (*Artemisia annua)* was used to treat fevers as many as 2,000 years ago. Until recently, artemisia was being actively investigated as a treatment for hepatitis because of its ability to increase the secretion of bile and thereby act as an aid in detoxifying the liver. However, since the development of an effective vaccine against hepatitis B, financial support for this research has been discontinued. Since 1972 studies have been carried out on artemisinin, or qinghaosu, an active compound of artemisia, which has been found to sharply reduce the

number of malaria parasites in the blood. Chinese experience has shown the substance to be highly effective and well tolerated. Although it has not been widely adopted in the West because of questions concerning its purity and variability, a recent trial in Bangkok, Thailand (reported in the April 4, 1992, issue of *Lancet*), found that another qinghaosu derivative, known as artesunate, in combination with the drug mefloquine was "highly effective and well tolerated" in patients with acute, uncomplicated malaria.

GLQ223, or compound Q, continues to generate considerable excitement among Western researchers as a potential treatment for AIDS. Compound Q is derived from an extract of the Chinese cucumber root, traditionally used to procure abortions. Research in Hong Kong has demonstrated that compound Q blocks the action of HIV (human immunodeficiency virus, which causes AIDS) in the body's T cells (the white blood cells that are the targets of HIV). In San Francisco a phase I clinical trial showed the substance to be safe in a small group of HIV-infected patients. A phase II trial to test for effectiveness got under way in early 1992, involving 120 patients at centers in the U.S.

Discovering the secrets of Africa's tribal healers

A large proportion of the African population, perhaps 75%, still accepts traditional medicine, which is deeply bound up with African spiritual culture. In 1977 WHO recognized the need to evaluate traditional systems of medicine and their therapeutic claims; today medical scientists from many countries are cooperating with traditional healers. In an attempt to focus all the new knowledge, a computer data base called Napralert (an acronym for "natural

143

products alert") was established by ethnobotanist Norman Farnsworth at the Center for Traditional Medicine at the University of Illinois at Chicago. Napralert is collating the research findings of more than 20 collaborating research centers established under WHO's Traditional Medicine Program.

Some of the medicines used by African tribal healers have been evaluated at Obafemi Awolowo University, Ile-Ife, Nigeria. The juice of the fruit of the sandpaper tree (*Lagenaria breviflora*), for example, is used by tribespeople as an abortifacient, inserted into the vagina with a parrot feather. In the laboratory, extracts of *L. breviflora* have demonstrated significant anti-implantation activity.

The bark of *Balanites aegyptiaca* is used as a soap substitute in The Sudan and Chad; the tree's roots, fruit, bark, and seeds have been found to be lethal to the freshwater snails that act as intermediate hosts for the parasitic infection schistosomiasis. The WHO estimates that schistosomiasis, or bilharziasis, affects some 200 million people in tropical regions of the world. Slender, elongated trematode flatworms (blood flukes) multiply in snail hosts and are disseminated into fresh water; when humans and other mammals come into contact with the infested water, the blood flukes bore into their bodies, where they live in the blood vessels, releasing eggs that produce significant tissue damage; eventually schistosome eggs are evacuated in the feces of mammals and humans and hatch on contact with fresh water, releasing ciliated larvae that swim about until they find an appropriate snail host, thereby starting a new cycle of infection. Although the ultimate approach to controlling this scourge of the Third World is through ensuring a safe water supply and raising standards of living, *Balanites aegyptiaca* may offer a way of interrupting the human–snail host cycle.

When the eminent British anthropologist Nigel Barley was in East Cameroun in 1980 and developed hepatitis, he received information from the mission in Ngaoundéré that a decoction of guava leaves in hot water was a local cure for the condition. He credits the local remedy with bringing about his slow but steady improvement. A German pharmaceutical company subsequently began testing a similar compound for treating liver inflammation.

Recently a survey of plants, sponsored by the World Wildlife Fund in collaboration with the Camaroons Center for the Study of Medicinal Plants, was carried out in the Korup rain forest in western Africa. Among the plants that are now being studied for their therapeutic properties are species of Flacourtiaceae and several kinds of cola nut. Until modern antimicrobial drugs came along, chaulmoogra oil obtained from the fruit of a Burmese tree (*Taraktogenos kurzii*) of the family Flacourtiaceae was a standard treatment for leprosy. Cola nuts, of course, were one of the original ingredients of Coca Cola.

The unique flora of South Africa's Cape Province, which is one of the world's six biomes (ecological communities), is extremely rich in species. Local botanists and *sangomas* (medicine men) were alarmed by recent depredations of medicinal plants and so have joined forces with the government to set up nurseries to protect the precious species from extinction, thus ensuring that established medicines can continue to be harvested from plants and potential new ones discovered.

Learning from the chimpanzees

While traditional African and ancient Chinese civilizations have been documenting the effects of herbs on health for hundreds and thousands of years, respectively, recent studies carried out by Richard Wrangham, professor of anthropology at Harvard University, Toshisada Nishida, a zoologist at Kyoto (Japan) University, and others have shown that the closest relative of humans, the chimpanzee, is adept at self-medication. The scientists have documented that chimpanzees in Tanzania's Gombe Stream National Park and Mahale Mountains National Park consume several species of plants that are not normally a part of their diet, apparently for medicinal purposes. Those same plants are used by the local human population to treat a variety of complaints. For example, the chimpanzees were observed to dose themselves on the bitter leaves of several species of *Aspilia,* members of the sunflower family; the same leaves are brewed in a tea by the local Tongwe people to treat stomach disorders. Eloy Rodriguez, a pharmacognosist at the University of California at Irvine, analyzed *Aspilia* and discovered high concentrations of a potent antibiotic, thiarubrine-A. Low doses of this substance are effective against a variety of parasitic worms, and the compound has also been shown in the laboratory to have antibacterial, antifungal, antiviral, and even selective anticancer properties.

The scientists also observed a lethargic and obviously sick female chimpanzee carefully select and chew leaves of the *Vernonia amygdalina* bush—a plant that Tanzanians use to treat parasitic infections and gastrointestinal disorders. Shortly after eating *Vernonia* leaves, the ailing chimp showed signs of renewed health and by the next day had perked up quite visibly. The researchers believe that chimps eat more *Aspilia* and *Vernonia* during the rainy season, when they are more susceptible to illness.

Other researchers have observed similar self-medication behavior in Brazilian monkeys and in the howling monkey of Costa Rica. The study of

Richard Wrangham—Anthro-Photo

A chimpanzee in Gombe Stream National Park in Tanzania consumes the bitter leaves of Aspilia*, of the sunflower family; researchers believe that the plant is sought out by the animals for medicinal purposes. The same plant is used by the native people of the region to treat a number of common ailments. The study of medicinal plant use by animals in the wild (zoopharmacognosy) may offer new ways for humans to identify valuable medicines in nature.*

Photographs, Jerry Mason

Plants that have been cultivated in London's Chelsea Physic Garden for their potential medicinal value (above) await shipment to the British pharmaceutical company Glaxo, where they will be screened for unusual natural substances. Because plants contain complex mixtures of different molecules, their extracts must be separated, or resolved, into pure compounds for individual identification and testing. A scientist at Glaxo carries out such a task (above right) by means of high-performance liquid chromatography, a powerful chemical-separation technique capable of resolving samples as small as millionths or billionths of a gram.

medicinal plant use by animals in the wild (zoopharmacognosy) may offer a way for humans to identify new drugs for their own pharmacopoeias.

Treatments for cancer and AIDS: top priority

A few early successes in finding drugs effective against cancer fueled a major search of the plant world for other cancer-fighting agents. One of the first such finds came in the 1950s: alkaloids of the Madagascar periwinkle (*Catharanthus roseus*, formerly *Vinca rosea*) were found to be effective against Hodgkin's disease and childhood lymphocytic leukemia. The alkaloids, used in the drugs vinblastine and vincristine, are mitotic inhibitors; *i.e.,* they interfere with cell division. In the West Indies the periwinkle had developed a reputation as a cure for diabetes. The discovery of its anticancer properties was made by Canadian researchers during random screening of plants with folkloric associations.

Under a $4 million grant from the NCI, the pharmaceutical company Glaxo in the United Kingdom, in a consortium with the University of Illinois at Chicago and the Research Triangle Institute in North Carolina, is presently investigating plants that may have anticancer and other therapeutic properties. Since 1989, as part of its plant-screening program, Glaxo has been receiving some 250 to 500 dried plant samples a year for analysis from the Chelsea Physic Garden in London. (The Chelsea garden is one of Europe's oldest botanical gardens for the cultivation of medicinal plants.) Glaxo is interested in finding unusual molecules that occur in the natural chemistry of plants themselves. These may eventually lend themselves to the development of novel compounds that offer specific treatments for cancer and other diseases.

In the search for drugs against cancer, even that age-old Christmas decoration mistletoe has come under scrutiny. In the 1st century AD Pliny the Elder of Rome suggested mistletoe as a treatment for epilepsy; he also

146

said it must not touch the ground. Mistletoe ("all-heal") was the panacea of Druidical medicine in Britain in the Middle Ages. For the past three decades George Salzer at the Ludwig Boltzmann Institute in Vienna has treated several thousand cancer patients with injections of mistletoe extract in conjunction with other drugs or radiation. He has found that when mistletoe is included, the treatment regimen is more effective. The extract appears to boost the immune system, perhaps by inducing the production of natural interferons.

Those attending the 1992 annual convention of the American Association for the Advancement of Science in Chicago learned of a host of new bioactive compounds that have been isolated from plants. The Indiana banana, also called false banana or the papaw (*Asima triloba*), a member of the family Annonaceae, is a tree that grows wild, predominantly in the eastern U.S. Using new bioassay techniques, researchers at Purdue University, West Lafayette, Indiana, found that the active ingredient of this plant, asimicin, is many times more toxic to tumors in laboratory animals than are many conventional anticancer drugs.

Perhaps the most exciting development to date in the search for drugs against cancer is the sophisticated antitumor screen developed by the NCI as part of its Developmental Therapeutic Program. The screen enables research scientists to test the specific cytotoxic activity (*i.e.,* toxicity to cells) of drugs against 60 different human cancer cell lines. The cell lines, which were developed from tumors of cancer patients, are kept frozen in liquid nitrogen, where they remain alive but dormant. Plant samples found active against a particular type of cancer in the *in vitro* screen (*i.e.,* in a laboratory dish) are then tested *in vivo* (against tumors of the same kind that are implanted in laboratory mice). This screening process is extremely sensitive, allowing the discovery of substances that are present in a plant extract in only very minute concentrations.

The dawn of the AIDS epidemic in the early 1980s intensified the drive to find agents to help boost the body's immune system. At the same time it was developing its anticancer screen, the NCI also developed an anti-HIV screen, which, because the genetic makeup of the AIDS virus is much simpler than that of the myriad types of cancer cells, is proving highly useful. One of the first extracts to show potential anti-HIV activity comes from the bark of a small Samoan tree, *Homalanthus acuminatus*. The native population of Samoa has long used the leaves of the tree to treat back pains and abdominal swellings, the roots to treat diarrhea, and the bark against yellow fever.

Not just palate pleasing

Some familiar plants best known as foods are proving to have value beyond the gastronomic. Juice of the pineapple is an aid to digestion; its enzymes ananain and comsain are also applied externally to help the healing process of burn wounds. Bromelain, an enzyme that is present in large quantity in pineapples, can prevent blood clots by breaking down the protein fibrin. Cashew-nut oil controls infestation of the skin by barfly larvae and is effective against *Streptococcus mutans,* the cause of tooth decay.

At the National Cancer Institute's research facility in Frederick, Maryland, the crude materials from plants that have been collected from rain forests in South America and Africa are extracted and prepared for chemical analysis. Promising specimens are then subjected to an antitumor screen that tests their activity against 60 different human cancer cell lines. The NCI has also developed a screening process to test plant-derived drugs that may be effective against HIV, the virus that causes AIDS.

National Cancer Institute, NIH

147

*Garlic (*Allium sativum*), native to Asia, is prepared for market on a wharf in Thailand. As long ago as 1550 BC, garlic—a member of the lily family— was reputed to have health-giving properties. Over the centuries it has been advocated for everything from coughs to cancer. Recently researchers in India found that garlic supplements lowered cardiovascular risk factors in patients who had had heart attacks, and research in the U.S., China, and Italy has shown certain active compounds in garlic to be highly anticarcinogenic. These and other purported benefits still need to be confirmed by further studies.*

It can also destroy bacteria that cause acne and kill freshwater snails that harbor the parasites that cause schistosomiasis.

For centuries garlic (*Allium sativum*), often called the "stinking rose" and associated with bad breath and vampires, has been advocated as a treatment for cough, intestinal spasms, circulatory disorders, headaches, insect bites, wounds, worms, and tumors. Today researchers are finding that many of these traditional uses, in fact, have some virtue. A bulbous member of the lily family, garlic contains dozens of chemical compounds. One of these is the antibiotic allium, whose principal active agent is allicin, the sulfur-containing compound that, with its breakdown products, produces the pungent odor of garlic.

In a study conducted by Arun Bordia, a cardiologist at Tagore Medical College, Udaipur, India, over 400 patients who had had previous heart attacks were randomly assigned to one of two groups. One group took a garlic supplement; the other did not. The garlic-taking group had lower blood pressure and serum cholesterol levels, and after three years nearly twice as many patients in the control group (those not taking the supplement) had died of heart complications.

Researchers at the Illinois Institute of Technology have shown that another of garlic's compounds, diallyl disulfide, is a strong anticancer agent— findings confirmed by investigators at the University of Texas Health Service Center in Houston. Studies in China and Italy suggest that garlic eating is associated with low rates of stomach cancer. William J. Blot, a statistician at the NCI, agrees that these are impressive findings. He cautions, however, that it is too early to draw any definite conclusions.

Max Gibbs—Oxford Scientific Films

Piper Indicum maxi mum longum. Piper Indicum minus recurvis filiquis.

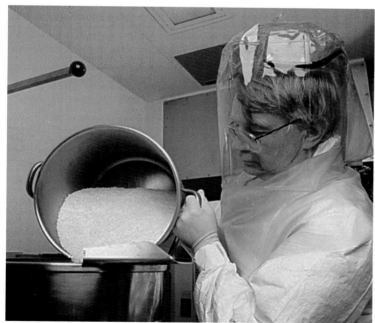

Chilies, the hot peppers that timid eaters dare not touch, contain the powerful alkaloid capsaicin, which is capable not only of setting the mouth on fire but of relieving excruciating pain. The substance is a main component of topical analgesic skin salves such as Zostrix and Axsain, used to treat the pain of postherpetic neuralgia, rheumatoid arthritis, and diabetic neuropathy. Shown in the process of crystallizing (above left), capsaicin works by interrupting pain signals from the sensory nerves of the skin to the brain. At left, Lloyd Matheson, the University of Iowa chemist who developed the capsaicin-based skin salves, pours a pure, powdered form of the material into a large vat for processing.

(Top left) Herb Charles Ohlmeyer—Fran Heyl Associates;
(top right) the Granger Collection;
(left) Harry Przekop—Discover Magazine

The chili pepper, the fleshy fruit of a plant of the genus *Capsicum*, which Mexicans use to spice tamales and other dishes and Texans put in "five-alarm chili," contains a fiery agent called capsaicin that, if modified, could be a powerful new analgesic. In laboratory tests capsaicin has been shown to interfere with pain signals that are relayed to the brain from sensory nerves in the skin. Capsaicin is already used in several chemically purified skin salves to relieve the severe burning of postherpetic neuralgia, caused by the herpes zoster virus, and the pain associated with nerve damage due to diabetes. The capsaicin in these remedies appears to work as a counter-irritant. Oral forms of the potent substance are presently being given in

149

In Africa up to 75% of the population relies on native healers for primary health care. Under the World Health Organization's Traditional Medicine Program, Western scientists are working closely with native African practitioners to better understand their treatments, including herbal medicines that have been used successfully for centuries.

clinical trials for the severe itching experienced by burn victims and kidney dialysis patients and for pain caused by crushing wounds and gunshots. Italian researchers tested capsaicin in sufferers of cluster headache, a one-sided headache that is considered the most severe of all headache types. Preliminary findings showed that 70% of the patients using a nasal spray containing the potent agent experienced dramatic relief.

Wonder drugs of the future—but some caveats

Every day the new plant-screening programs turn up compounds with properties that may be useful in treating illness, and reports of new drugs from plants abound. While many of the plants that are currently being screened have been used for centuries in folk medicine, their efficacy has yet to be proved. Today it is no longer adequate to prescribe a remedy simply because there is anecdotal evidence of its effectiveness. The only certain way of knowing whether a drug is effective is to conduct a controlled clinical trial involving the random allocation of patients to either a treatment or a control group (which receives a placebo), with neither the doctor nor the subjects knowing what substance is being given.

No matter how sophisticated their tools, pharmacognosists are not always able to substantiate therapeutic claims for plant-derived medicines. Ghanaians, for example, treat bacterial infections with an extract of the *Cryptolepis sanguinolenta,* but despite its apparent efficacy, laboratory tests have failed to reveal any biological activity of individual components of the plant. Other remedies from natural substances need to be significantly modified—an often laborious and difficult process—to make them safe and effective.

Even the excitement generated by taxol must be tempered. Susan Arbuck of the NCI, who is directing studies of taxol in women with ovarian cancer, points out: "Taxol does not provide a cure, nor does it promise to extend life at this point, because it is used in the more advanced diseases." Nonetheless, the hope is that curative therapies combining taxol with other anticancer drugs can be developed and that sufficient quantities will be available so that it can be used earlier in the course of the disease. Those possibilities are some time away, however.

A very important point that is stressed by those involved in the "back-to-nature" search for exciting new medicines is that the taxonomic study of plants—the orderly scientific classification of plants and understanding of their relationships to each other—is essential. Mark Plotkin, an ethnobotanist who has worked with native healers in the Costa Rican rain forests, has said, "As long as people think that the genetic engineers can cure everything, the world will think it does not need taxonomists anymore. But there is no biological diversity without the taxonomist to tell the stuff apart."

Peter Hylands of Kings College, London, has worked for many years on the taxonomy of feverfew (*Tanacetum parthenium*), a plant that is used in the prophylaxis of migraine and shows promise as a treatment for rheumatoid arthritis, elevated blood fats, and numerous other conditions. Hylands points out that there are many varieties of the plant and that these can be quite variable in terms of morphology and chemistry. His

150

work has shown that the amount of the active agent present in feverfew varies with the season and the plant part; moreover, cultivated varieties of feverfew often differ markedly from most of the wild types that have been studied and reported on in the medical literature. Nevertheless, a number of products are sold to the public under the name feverfew, often without having undergone chemical investigation.

"Natural" medicines are not benign. And, of course, the dangers inherent in self-medication apply equally to herbal remedies and synthetically manufactured pharmaceuticals. For example, the acute need for effective drugs to combat AIDS has created a brisk new black market business in plant-derived drugs; unfortunately, many desperate persons with AIDS seem willing to purchase virtually any product alleged to affect the course of the lethal infection—whether tested or not.

Pharmacognosy was at an all-time low in the 1960s and '70s, when virtually all pharmaceutical research was being carried out on synthetic agents. Now scientists and society are beginning to realize how much pharmacological potential there is in plants and especially in the plants and cultures of the less developed parts of the world. The offerings in nature's medicine chest have only begun to be discovered. How many of the plants of myth and legend can be collected before the world's invaluable forests and flora are destroyed is anybody's guess. Humankind stands to gain many previously unimagined remedies—but only if there are concerted and immediate efforts to save this rich resource.

A market stand in Seoul, South Korea, displays traditional medicines, including many varieties of herbs and other botanical products. The immense potential of plants as pharmaceuticals has only begun to be realized. The untapped secrets of nature's medicine chest can be discovered only if the many thousands of plant species now facing extinction are saved.

151

Advertising
ALCOHOL

THIS BREW'S FOR YOU

by Michael Jacobson, Ph.D., Patricia Taylor,
and Deborah Baldwin

A group of male "thirtysomethings" sits around a campfire somewhere far away from home, contemplating the twin glories of male companionship and cold beer. Sighs one contented camper: "Guys, it doesn't get any better than this."

Two attractive women jog down the beach together. "He loves my mind," confides one to the other as they lope along in their body-conscious bathing suits. "And," she adds, "he drinks Johnnie Walker."

A young black rap singer touts the high he gets from 40-ounce bottles of high-strength malt liquor, aiming his message directly at his age group: "I usually drink it when I'm out just clowning, me and the home boys, you know, be like downing it. Cause it's stronger but the taste is more smooth. I grab me a 40 when I want to act a fool."

Welcome to the world of alcoholic beverage advertising. In 1991 beer, wine, and liquor producers in the United States spent more than $1 billion to market their wares in the print and broadcast media. As the ads excerpted above suggest, the business of selling "booze" is indeed a curious one—and an increasingly controversial one as well.

The market is the message

About 66% of all U.S. adults drink alcohol, constituting a vast audience for the industry's inventive appeals. Nonetheless, drinking in general is declining, forcing alcoholic beverage companies to battle over a shrinking stein. The result—reflected in imagery that ricochets from yuppie beaches to blue-collar barrooms to gritty urban streets—is an all-out campaign to capture segments of the market where consumption is either dispropor-tionately large (young white males) or has plenty of room to grow (young black males). Other segments that are increasingly being "targeted," as the practice is known on Madison Avenue, include women, Latinos, and heavy drinkers.

The advertising industry defends targeting as a cost-effective way to reach select audiences. By slicing up a product's market into demographic

Young white males are the heaviest consumers of beer in the United States. Not coincidentally, they are also the prime target of ads that associate beer drinking—and having more than one—with good times.

chunks, the industry says, it can tailor messages to meet the varying needs and wishes of today's highly diverse society. In 1991, after the federal government took action to block the use of the brand name PowerMaster for a high-strength malt liquor targeted at inner-city males, marketing consultant John E. Calfee expressed obvious exasperation when he wrote in the trade paper *Advertising Age:* "Have we forgotten that to target a consumer segment is to work up a sweat giving that group what it wants?" Calfee, who worked for the Federal Trade Commission during the administration of Pres. Ronald Reagan, added that targeting "brings efficiency in marketing, including more closely tailored products, better information, and more convenient distribution."

Public health advocates, however, see things a bit differently. At a time of mounting awareness of the social costs of addictive substances, they point out that marketing campaigns that exploit ethnic, racial, and sexual stereotypes reflect not only poor taste but also glaring insensitivity to the high rates of alcohol problems among such vulnerable target audiences as young people and low-income minorities.

The high costs of imbibing

Some 18 million U.S. adults and 4.5 million young people (aged 15–24) are heavy drinkers. Among "recreational" drugs, alcohol is by far the most destructive, cutting across ethnic, age, and economic lines. It is linked to violent crime, suicide, accidental deaths, spousal and child abuse, and fetal alcohol syndrome (now the leading preventable cause of mental retardation). Alcohol destroys families, causes disease and injuries, and is responsible for inestimable emotional and physical pain. More than 7,000 Americans die annually from alcohol-related cirrhosis of the liver alone.

In 1990 excessive drinking cost the U.S. about $100 billion—and more than 100,000 lives. About a fourth of those alcohol-related fatalities occurred on the nation's highways, where the combination of alcohol and automobiles consumed the lives of more than 7,000 15–24-year-olds. Among

Michael Jacobson, Ph.D., *is Executive Director, Center for Science in the Public Interest, Washington, D.C.*
Patricia Taylor *is Director, Alcohol Policies Project, Center for Science in the Public Interest.*
Deborah Baldwin *is a writer based in Washington, D.C.*

(Overleaf) Advertisement for Miller Light ("Open the Gold") in Pilsen, a Latino neighborhood of Chicago; photo, Ralf-Finn Hestoft—Saba

teens, alcohol is by far the most widely used drug; at least eight million American junior-high- and high-school-aged teens use alcohol every week, and almost half a million go on a weekly drinking binge (five or more drinks in a row).

While its impact on the white population is indisputable, alcohol causes a disproportionately greater problem among minorities. There is little question that alcohol compounds health problems caused by poverty. Latinos, for example, are three times as likely as whites to die from cirrhosis and other liver disease. While blacks have a lower drinking rate than whites, they have a greater incidence of alcoholism and other alcohol-related illness starting after the age of 30. A 1985 government study found that the cirrhosis mortality rate for blacks is nearly twice that of whites.

Outspoken public health advocates, among them former U.S. surgeon general C. Everett Koop, have called for a number of restrictions on the marketing of alcohol, including a ban on all television advertising. Through such efforts as campaigns to remove the ubiquitous ads for alcoholic beverages from inner-city billboards, others are striving to stop the targeting of minority communities.

Alcohol is directly responsible for more accidents, acts of violence, injuries, and deaths than any other substance of abuse. Despite the tremendous toll it takes on society, the use of alcohol, unlike any other toxic drug, is widely condoned—indeed promoted.

(Left) Medford Taylor—Woodfin Camp, Inc; (top right) Matt Meadows—Peter Arnold, Inc.; (bottom right) Dan Miller—Woodfin Camp, Inc.

First identified in 1973, the congenital abnormalities known collectively as fetal alcohol syndrome (FAS) affect about 40% of offspring born to alcoholic women and as many as 11% of infants of women who ingest only "moderate" amounts of alcohol during pregnancy. The 10-year-old above has several of the striking facial features that are characteristic of the syndrome, including wide-set eyes with skin folds over the inside eye corners, upturned nose, thin upper lip, and receding chin.

FAS children may also be born with malformed joints and limbs, abnormalities of the upper airways, cardiac defects, and mental retardation and may subsequently suffer from delayed development, behavior problems, and learning disorders. While the actual thresholds of alcohol that result in FAS are not known, binge drinking, especially in the first 12 weeks' gestation, can be perilous. Moreover, many doctors now believe that any amount of alcohol consumed by the pregnant woman has the potential to damage her fetus.

Fulfilling every fantasy

The most important message of most alcoholic beverage advertising is that drinking alcohol is a safe, healthy means of achieving happiness—one, moreover, that makes people sexier, more sophisticated, more successful, and more lovable—or just about anything else they yearn to be. As the typically romanticized Madison Avenue imagery has it, drinking is *not* risky, does *not* cause violent behavior or deadly accidents, does *not* make people fat, and does *not* even give them hangovers. Not only is drinking fun, it is all-American.

Alcohol has long been woven into America's social fabric, and contemporary culture reinforces alcohol's appeal in countless ways—in the print media, movies, books, songs, and plays, on television and radio, and at major sporting events. One reason the ads are so effective is that by playing on deeply entrenched cultural beliefs about alcohol, they manage to blend into the background. Chief among those beliefs is that "everyone drinks" when, in fact, about a third of adults abstain.

The "normalization" of drinking starts early—before children are even conscious of why adults drink or what alcohol is. And advertising and promotion campaigns play a major role in that process. According to some estimates, long before they are old enough to drink legally, children see thousands of beer commercials on television—not to mention the countless scenes of inebriated people enjoying themselves in TV programs.

The savvy people who market alcohol did not invent the notion that good times go with drinking; rather, they use the culture's congenial associations with alcohol as a subtext. Like other products that are hard to promote on their objective merits, alcoholic beverages are largely sold by way of the emotions. Different audiences get different themes, playing on their particular culture and sentiments.

The most important target audience is actually relatively small. With a mere 10% of the adult population imbibing about 60% of the alcohol sold in the U.S., alcoholics and other problem drinkers basically keep the industry afloat. For this audience certain ads suggest that it is perfectly normal to view alcohol as a solace, that it is acceptable to consume large quantities of alcohol—"the joy of six," as one ad picturing a six-pack puts it—and that heavy drinking is something most people do on a regular basis; *i.e.,* every day.

While heavy drinkers come in all ages and colors, young white males are the heaviest consumers of beer and the prime target for beer ads that glorify "having more than one." Fantasy and wish fulfillment are leading themes for this group, which helps explain such TV ads as the one for the "King of Beers," Budweiser, in which two male companions trudge through the desert; they stop to rest, only to have one of them magically produce out of his backpack an inflatable swimming pool—complete with scantily clad girl and, of course, cold beer.

While such advertising appears harmless on the surface, there is nothing arbitrary or capricious about the strategies that lie behind it. According to Neil M. Postman, professor of media ecology and communications at New York University and well-known media and social critic, commercials

What is moderate drinking?

women

men

no more than
one drink a day

no more than
two drinks a day

one drink =

1.5 oz distilled
spirits (80 proof)

5 oz wine

12 oz beer

Source: *Dietary Guidelines for Americans*, U.S. Department of Agriculture and U.S. Department of Health and Human Services

further the myth that beer drinking is a suitable reward for hard work and repeatedly suggest that beer provides a true bond for masculine cama-raderie. In a study done for the American Automobile Association (AAA) Foundation for Traffic Safety, Postman and his three coauthors found that TV ads are "especially potent sources of sex-role learning for young boys" and that certain cultural myths in beer ads "may be implicated in the often fatal mixture of young men, automobiles, and beer."

Brought to you by . . .

Another study done for the AAA foundation was prompted by the alarm-ingly high incidence of traffic fatalities among teens. The study, "Beer and Fast Cars: How Brewers Target Blue-Collar Youth Through Motor Sport Sponsorships," criticized the beer industry for spending approximately $50

What could be more all-American than beer and baseball? Accordingly, Anheuser-Busch Cos., Inc., has purchased prominence on the scoreboards of major league ballparks across the nation, including that at Shea Stadium, home of the New York Mets. The idea that drinking is glamorous and sexy has long been ingrained in American culture. When silver-screen idol William Powell, playing Nick Charles in the film classic The Shadow of the Thin Man, *the 1941 sequel to* The Thin Man *(1934), pondered whether to drink milk or a martini, it was clear that the booze would win. As one reviewer noted, "Nick—none other—still drinks cocktails with an obvious zest that must be worth millions in advertising to the liquor industry."*

(Left) Evan Agostini—Gamma Liaison; (right) Kobal Collection/Superstock

million a year to sponsor motor sports events—sponsorships that, in targeting young blue-collar males, strengthen associations of beer with cars and speeding. The impact of those sponsorships is enormous; auto racing is the second largest spectator sport in the U.S. (football is the first). In 1988 a single beer manufacturer—the Adolph Coors Co.—handled 18 major national motor sports sponsorships and more than 4,300 smaller local sponsorships. Moreover, surveys have shown that motor sports fans drink more beer than do fans of any other sport.

As TV ads for beer and wine come under increasing fire and network audiences diminish, alcoholic beverage makers are spending a higher percentage of their marketing money on sponsorships, reasoning that these "brought-to-you-by" events can deliver "more bang for the buck." Sports events, including everything from women's volleyball to sled-dog racing, are the biggest draw because they attract heavy-drinking young males.

Beer and sports have had a long association—since the 1870s, when a local saloon keeper bought a stake in the St. Louis Brown Stockings in order to sell his beer inside the ball park. In 1992 Anheuser-Busch Cos., Inc., spent $1.8 million just to produce one 30-second spot on the TV broadcast of Super Bowl XXVI. In 1987 the brewing industry spent more than $180 million to promote its products at sporting events nationwide, making it second only to the tobacco industry in this endeavor. As the "Beer and Fast Cars" study noted, "Sponsorships enable the companies to reach prospective customers at their lifestyle level, in an environment they identify with, at a time when they are unguarded, open, and more receptive."

Breweries also look for—and find—receptive young audiences at youth-oriented music festivals and rock concerts. The *Los Angeles Times* reported in July 1989 that roughly 75% of the nation's key concert facilities had beer company sponsors, each paying $100,000 a year and up for the privilege of wallpapering their brand names over all available surfaces, including the tickets. The newspaper also noted that the beer industry alone spends $50 million annually to subsidize concert venues and performers'

Auto racing fans—largely blue-collar males—consume more beer than do spectators of any other sport, and beer manufacturers have discovered just how lucrative it can be to promote their brews to this target group. Through sole sponsorship agreements with individual racers, beer makers are able to plaster their brand names and logos over the driver's entire rig.

tours. It traced the involvement of the nation's number one event sponsor, Anheuser-Busch, to 1977, when the beer giant signed onto its first concert series. In 1982 Schlitz paid $1 million to sponsor a tour by the Who. By 1987 the Beastie Boys were using a giant replica of a Budweiser six-pack as a stage prop.

Sponsoring music events is one of the methods alcohol producers use to reach minority markets. The makers of Bacardi Breezer spent more than $1 million to sponsor Gloria Estefan's 1991 "Into the Light" tour, which capitalized on the pop siren's Cuban heritage. "We already have a franchise within the Hispanic market," a Bacardi spokesperson told the trade publication *Special Events Report,* referring to the company's Caribbean roots, "but going with Gloria certainly won't hurt our sales."

Alcoholic beverage makers also fund the traditional Mexican-American Cinco de Mayo celebration, an event commemorating Mexico's defeat of French invaders (May 5, 1862). The holiday is widely celebrated in Mexican-American communities across the United States and has been likened to a "Mexican St. Patrick's Day." In 1988 alcohol producers spent $25 million promoting and selling their products at Cinco de Mayo festivities in southern California alone. In 1989 ads for Cinco de Mayo in Los Angeles encouraged attendance and drinking, but the merrymaking had to be cut short when drunkenness and violence broke out. Vast sums are also spent by alcoholic beverage manufacturers on other popular annual Hispanic festivals, such as the Cuban-American Carnaval Miami and Puerto Rican Day parades in cities such as Boston, New York, and Chicago. Indeed, it was an advertising campaign by Coors that dubbed the 1980s "the decade of the Hispanic." In the 1990s the industry's efforts to forge ties in the Latino community are ever growing.

Power brews

To reach minority groups the $500 million malt liquor industry capitalizes on its products' supposed "power." Packaged in oversized bottles and often

The alcoholic beverage industry's efforts to forge ties in Hispanic communities is ever growing. Bacardi Breezer, a low-alcohol rum-and-fruit drink, which debuted in April 1990 and targets 21-to-29-year-olds, spent a reported low-seven-figure sum to sponsor the Cuban-American pop singer Gloria Estefan's five-month, 34-city "Into the Light" tour in 1991. (Below) Coors was the most prominent sponsor of the 1992 Cinco de Mayo festivities in the Mexican-American community of Douglas Park in Chicago. Owing to the amount of drinking—and drunkenness—that often occurs at 5th of May celebrations across the U.S., the holiday has been dubbed "Mexican St. Patrick's Day."

*The malt liquor industry has invested
hundreds of millions of dollars to promote
its "power brews" to inner-city youths—
apparently, quite successfully. According to
the* Wall Street Journal, *"Kids as young
as 13 now wield 40-ounce bottles of malt,
which corner grocery stores sell for $1.50."
Among the chief promoters of the potent
products, which contain 4.5–6% alcohol
(compared with 3.5–4% in most beers), are
highly paid rap stars, who tout malt liquor
products as a quick way to, among other
things, achieve virility, get a "buzz on," or
just "act a fool." Although one malt liquor,
PowerMaster, was forced off the market
in July 1991 for violating federal rules
that prohibit the marketing an alcoholic
beverage on the basis of its strength, other
"upstrength" malt liquors, despite highly
controversial promotional tactics, remain
on the market—with sales growing at
reported annual rates of 25–30%.*

sold at rock-bottom prices, malt liquor has reportedly become a symbol of
tough young manhood in the inner city, thanks in no small part to carefully
targeted advertising campaigns.

In the 1980s ads for the Anheuser-Busch malt liquor product King Cobra
used the slogan "Don't let the smooth taste fool you" and dubbed the
brew "The bite that's right." Advertisements for G. Heileman Brewing Co.
Inc.'s Colt 45 have, among other things, featured bulls smashing through
concrete walls—an image that apparently gets the desired message about
the brew's power across.

Ads touting malt liquor have frequently featured provocative sexual
messages. One such ad pictured a seductive model cradling a bottle of
Midnight Dragon, declaring, "I could suck on this all night." In one version
of an ad for Olde English "800," a bikini-clad black model posed atop a
tiger; the slogan was "It's the power!" A Spanish-language version of the
same ad (proclaiming "Es la fuerza") featured a buxom Latino model in
string bikini crouching next to a tiger on a beach.

In 1991 a particularly controversial television advertisement triggered
a rare case of government intervention when the McKenzie River Corp.,
which markets the high-strength malt liquor St. Ides (made by Heileman),
hired rap star Ice Cube as its singer-spokesman. With a 40-ounce bottle of
St. Ides in hand, Ice Cube made overt references to street gangs and sexual conquest and, over the airwaves, used language like this: "Why don't
ya grab a six-pack and get your girl in the mood quicker, and get your
jimmy thicker with St. Ides malt liquor." The U.S. Treasury Department's
Bureau of Alcohol, Tobacco and Firearms (BATF) persuaded McKenzie
River to take that commercial—and several others—off the air and ordered
the company to pay a $10,000 fine. The attorney general of the state of
New York also took action against McKenzie River, eventually reaching a
$50,000 settlement and securing an agreement from the company to stop
falsely advertising its product as a way for young men to achieve virility.

Selling sophistication

Drinking rates are lower among blacks than whites—a fact that may not be very obvious from the stereotypes that are furthered by advertising. A product that is marketed heavily to African-Americans is cognac—a traditional symbol of "the good life." In a typical effort to reach a young, mostly black audience, Hennessy Cognac sponsored a five-city Jazz Search talent contest.

Liquor and wine producers in particular aim to reach consumers yearning for status, so, of course, yuppies have not been left out of this part of the marketing game. According to *Special Events Report,* Absolut Vodka is marketed to "upscale, sophisticated consumers," and the manufacturer spends about $1 million a year sponsoring such tony events as opening-night "gala" performances of the Joffrey Ballet.

Historically, women have represented a relatively small segment of the alcohol-consuming market and mainly have been exploited as sex objects to sell booze to men. This, however, is changing. In keeping with the trend set by the tobacco industry, famous for its "You've come a long way, baby" campaign, alcohol ads aimed at women are now suggesting that drinking, too, is a means to freedom and independence. To reach this heretofore untapped market, the Seagram Beverage Co. has launched malt beverages in fruit flavors, marketing them not as beer but as "spritzers," according to the *Wall Street Journal* (April 6, 1992), which noted as well that Coors has similar products in the works. "New age" ads feature women who surf, teach aerobics, and ride rodeo. An ad campaign for Michelob beer appearing in *Cosmopolitan* and *Vogue* magazines presents women in "real-life situations," according to *Food & Beverage Marketing* (March 1992). A Coors ad showed women at a bike race knocking back a beer. Ignored in all this are the federal government's *Dietary Guidelines for Americans,* which states that "alcoholic beverages supply calories but little or no nutrients" and defines moderate drinking as no more than one drink a day for women who decide to drink.

With sales totaling 2.7 million cases a year, Absolut Vodka is the top-selling imported vodka in the U.S. In 1985 the late Andy Warhol, who apparently loved the brand and boasted that he wore it as perfume, conceived the idea of contemporary artists' doing paintings for Absolut ads; he did the first—"Absolut Warhol"—for which he was paid $65,000. The distributor of the Swedish import, Carillon Importers, has commissioned several hundred artists to create original Absolut ads, which run in glossy spreads in upscale magazines. Ads by Ivan Jenson and Romero Britto were featured in the May 1992 issue of Art in America *(below left).* Forbes *magazine has called the $9 million-a-year advertising campaign for the vodka "Absolut-ly ingenious."*

Brent Jones

Though the advertisers say they are not targeting children, it is obvious that certain characters featured in ads promoting both cigarettes and beer have enormous appeal to grade-school-aged youngsters. In February 1992, after a study published in the Journal of the American Medical Association *found that R.J. Reynolds' ubiquitous cartoon character Joe Camel had developed a vast following among children, U.S. Surgeon General Antonia Novello called on the cigarette manufacturer to stop using Joe in its ads: "It's time that we invite Old Joe Camel himself to take a hike," she said at a Washington, D.C., news conference. Novello's plea, however, was not heeded; Joe Camel still looms over Times Square in New York and on scores of prominent billboards nationwide. Similarly, a study found that Bud Light's endearing bullterrier mascot Spuds MacKenzie was both well known to and adored by children aged 10–13. In one ad (above right) Spuds was dressed up for St. Patrick's Day; his button says: "KISS ME. I'm an Irish Party Animal."*

Hey, kids, don't listen!

Only two industries in the world deny that they are trying to increase sales to current customers or bring in new—especially younger—ones: the makers of cigarettes and alcohol. The companies that peddle these addictive, health-endangering substances maintain that they are only trying to persuade existing users to try new brands and that they would be "shocked" to hear that in the process of glorifying their products, they attract new or underage users.

Yet just as Camel cigarettes' ubiquitous cartoon character, Joe Camel, has developed a vast following among youngsters—indeed as young as the first grade—Coors, Budweiser, St. Ides, and other alcoholic beverages enjoy fame in the same age group. According to a study headed by Lawrence Wallack, professor of public health at the University of California at Berkeley, an incredible 88% of children aged 10 to 13 knew that the irresistible English bullterrier Spuds MacKenzie sells Bud Light. (In contrast, only 10% were able to link "It's the real thing" to Coca-Cola.) "The more brands the children identify in commercials," Wallack told a congressional committee in 1990, "the more likely they are to have a positive set of beliefs about the social aspects of using beer" and the more likely they are to expect to drink as adults. Boys were significantly more likely than girls to recognize beer commercials—no doubt because they watch more sports.

In a survey of 8–12-year-old children in the Washington, D.C., area, the advocacy group Center for Science in the Public Interest found that the youngsters could name more brands of alcohol than they could presidents of the United States. One 10-year-old girl could name only four presidents, but when it came to booze, she was able to rattle off 14 brand-name products.

In U.S. high schools today, many students are drinking heavily. According to the inspector general of the Department of Health and Human Services, twice as many of those students skip school than do nondrinking

162

students; nearly five times as many damage school property; and twice as many receive grades of C or lower. The average age at which Americans begin drinking today is 13. Shortly before stepping down as surgeon general in 1989, Koop, a pediatrician, attacked the industry for using celebrities, rock concerts, and sporting events to sell their products, saying, "These practices tell youth that alcohol consumption leads to athletic, social, and sexual success. They send the message that drinking is a normal and glamorous activity without negative consequences. And our young people are believing these messages."

Koop's successor, Antonia C. Novello, also a pediatrician, has reinforced that message and turned up the heat on the advertising industry, especially when it comes to teen smoking and drinking. In testimony before Congress in November 1991, Novello called on the industry to voluntarily eliminate advertising that attracts young people on the basis of certain lifestyle, sexual, or sports appeal, as well as advertising that makes use of cartoon characters and youth slang:

The ads have youth believing that instead of getting up early, exercising, going to school, playing a sport, or learning to be a team player, all they have to do to fit in is learn to drink the right alcoholic beverage. The ads tell our youth that vacationing on an exotic island, playing at the beach, participating in major-league sports . . . or skiing, surfing, or mountain climbing go hand in hand with alcohol.

The myth of self-regulation

Historically, the relationship between the media and the alcoholic beverage industry has been an ambiguous one. While the makers of distilled spirits have voluntarily refrained from advertising their products on television and radio, beer and broadcasting have enjoyed an enormously lucrative symbiosis, with the former ponying up hundreds of millions of advertising dollars every year and the latter providing programming that appeals to drinkers. Voluntary advertising codes are popular with the alcoholic beverage industry because they keep the heavy hand of government out of the marketplace. But self-regulation has built-in limitations. When Bacardi wanted to introduce liquor-based coolers, the distilled spirits industry's code was simply rewritten to allow ads on radio and television. Similarly, voluntary codes that prohibit marketing to children winked at Budweiser's endearing mascot, Spuds MacKenzie, whose enormous appeal among young people has already been noted. And although brewing industry standards supposedly reject advertising references to alcohol products as "extra strength," it is hard to see how that rule has done anything to restrict the ads for malt liquor.

Industry guidelines have also proved less than effective when it comes to one of the most visible vehicles for minority-targeted advertising: the inner-city billboard. One study in Detroit, Michigan, found 118 billboards and signs advertising alcohol and tobacco within 10 blocks of a public school in an inner-city neighborhood. In 1990 outdoor advertising guidelines were revised in the wake of bitter criticism from citizens' groups about the peddling of addictive substances in African-American and Hispanic neighborhoods. The voluntary guidelines now prohibit alcohol and tobacco

163

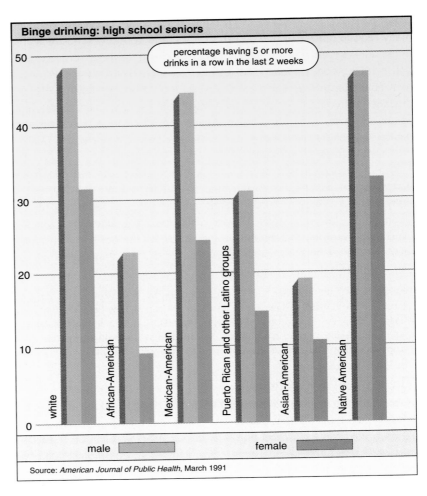

Binge drinking: high school seniors

percentage having 5 or more drinks in a row in the last 2 weeks

male female

Source: *American Journal of Public Health*, March 1991

billboards within 150 meters (500 feet, or about one block) of a school, church, or hospital. Meanwhile, billboards anywhere else advertising these products are fine.

Calling Uncle Sam

The federal government does regulate the alcoholic beverage industry to some extent, though its jurisdiction is fragmented (health experts at the Department of Health and Human Services notably have *no* regulatory authority). Moreover, the government does not take a consistently hard line against questionable advertising. For example, Bureau of Alcohol, Tobacco and Firearms rules discourage ads that associate athletic ability with drinking and advertising claims that are misleading or obscene. Nonetheless, Coors ads manage to suggest that "lite" beer is the beverage of choice among America's fitness buffs, while ads targeting men frequently use seminaked models to suggest that liquor is an aphrodisiac that magically improves a man's prowess—and a woman's willingness.

On the other hand, the BATF took steps in 1991 to stop the use of the brand name PowerMaster on the grounds that the alcoholic beverage industry had not followed its own standard of prohibiting manufacturers

164

from boasting about the strength of their brews in advertisements or on containers. The other federal agency with regulatory authority over alcohol advertising, the Federal Trade Commission, also responded to recent public pressure, ordering a halt to misleading ads for the drink Cisco and insisting that the product be repackaged. Cisco, which was sold as a wine cooler, has such a high alcohol content (four times as high as that of other products sold as wine coolers) that some young people were hospitalized after drinking it.

Despite these actions (and the fact that it is illegal for anyone under the age of 21 to purchase alcohol in the U.S.), neither agency has used its authority to challenge ads targeted at young drinkers or ads that encourage heavy drinking. Nor has either expressed concern about the exclusively favorable images of alcohol's effects that appear in ads.

Let's be friends

One response of the alcoholic beverage industry to the mounting criticism of its marketing techniques has been ads that are disguised as health information. So-called moderation messages with slogans like "Know when to say when" or "Think when you drink" do not provide information about when it is safe to drink and when it is not, but they give the distinct impression of showing concern for people's health and safety.

In another instance, an Anheuser-Busch public service magazine ad noted that from 1982 to 1990 the number of teenage drunk drivers involved in fatal accidents declined 40%; it claimed to have had a major role in the decline. That, however, seems unlikely, given that the company is the number one sponsor among alcoholic beverage manufacturers of events appealing to young people. The lobbying efforts of political action groups such as Mothers Against Drunk Driving (MADD) and Students Against Driving Drunk (SADD), on the other hand, have had a definite impact on the enactment of tough laws and on the increased social opprobrium toward driving under the influence.

Former U.S. surgeon general C. Everett Koop has been an outspoken opponent of ads promoting alcohol to young audiences and has called for a total ban on the ads in the broadcast media. In making that recommendation, he cited research conducted by the National Commission on Drunk Driving, which found that American children see approximately 100,000 beer commercials by the time they turn 18. Those ads persuade young people to drink by associating alcohol with sex, patriotism, active life-styles, and health. Koop believes that a ban is necessary because, in his words, "advertising works."

With its 6-meter (20-foot)-high inflatable "Bud Man," Budweiser beer's latest crowd-pleasing mascot, and even taller cans and bottles of Bud, there is no mistaking who is sponsoring the event. Red, white, and blue air-filled dirigibles are just one of the inventive ways used by Anheuser-Busch to tell Americans which beer is for them.

Another tactic of the industry is to try to build goodwill, especially in minority communities, by distributing money to charities, community groups, and arts, cultural, educational, environmental, and even medical organizations. For example, alcoholic beverage makers have contributed large sums to such black organizations as the National Association for the Advancement of Colored People and the United Negro College Fund. They have also supported research efforts to combat sickle-cell disease. In the Latino community alcoholic beverage companies have financed health fairs sponsored by the League of United Latin American Citizens, made large donations to the National Hispanic Scholarship Fund, and supported many other community causes.

Such efforts, of course, can have the effect of raising product awareness among target audiences and indirectly influencing sales. Coors signed a pact with the Hispanic community in 1984 to increase the hiring of Hispanics, purchase from Hispanic suppliers, and donate $500,000 annually to not-for-profit Hispanic causes. In this effort to win the hearts of the Spanish-speaking community, Coors also won its way into Hispanics' pocketbooks. Many critics of the industry believe Coors and other companies are directly contributing to high rates of alcoholism and other alcohol-related problems in minority communities. In 1991 the Remy Martin Foundation announced that it had raised $10,000 to benefit the Harlem Visitors and Convention Association by using a novel financing approach; the company donated to the cause 33 cents to $1.33 for each bottle of Remy Martin VSOP Cognac sold in upper Manhattan (*i.e.,* Harlem).

There is some evidence that such generosity can buy silence on the issue of alcohol and health, most notably when the recipient group seeks to play an advocacy role. For example, despite a ground swell of grass-roots opposition to alcohol and tobacco billboard advertisements flooding the inner city, the Detroit Urban League backed away from the controversy in 1988. It was reported that Urban League-supporter and Detroit-based Stroh Brewery Co. played a role.

Speaking out

Citizens' groups are becoming increasingly active in efforts to tone down the targeting of minorities, lower the alcohol content of malt liquor, remove alcoholic beverage ads from billboards, and quash specific advertising campaigns. In more and more cities across the country, African-American, Latino, consumer, parent, and health organizations have joined forces to protest alcoholic beverage advertisements that explicitly target minority groups.

The organized opposition has focused its energies locally on removing billboards and reducing the number of alcohol sales outlets in inner-city neighborhoods, at the state level on raising taxes and restricting alcohol advertising and promotions, and nationally on controlling advertising and pressing for stronger warning messages on product labels. There have also been numerous calls for the elimination of alcoholic beverage sponsorships at college and high school events. Critics have also lobbied to end the tax deduction that enables alcoholic beverage makers to write off the costs of

Hennessy Cognac, according to the company's senior public relations manager, targets consumers aged 25 to 44 who earn $25,000-plus, and about 40% of Hennessy ads are aimed at African-Americans. Although blacks drink less per capita than whites, they suffer disproportionately from alcohol-related problems. Nevertheless, the alcoholic beverage industry saturates black communities with billboards that use seductive imagery to suggest that "the good life" is readily attainable—all one has to do is consume the right brand of liquor.

Stephen Ferry—Gamma Liaison

A billboard featuring movie star Billy Dee Williams promoting Colt 45 as the malt liquor that "works every time" was one of the targets of a Saturday afternoon whitewashing campaign in Harlem, led by the Rev. Calvin Butts. Butts is a principal proponent of a nationwide ban on billboards promoting "drugs that kill"—namely, alcohol and tobacco—to minorities. Inspired by his example, activists in other areas around the country have taken similar actions to eradicate billboards that promote harmful products and are a blight on inner-city neighborhoods.

their advertising campaigns. On Capitol Hill a coalition of nonprofit groups is lobbying for changes in tax policy that would equalize federal taxation rates on beer, wine, and liquor—the present rates favor beer and wine—and adjust taxes for past and annual inflation. The coalition estimates that such changes would generate some $20 billion in revenues, which could finance alcohol-related education and treatment programs and almost certainly would reduce drinking—and drinking problems—by up to 15%.

Another coalition supports mandatory health warnings in both print and broadcast advertisements and improved warnings on alcoholic beverage containers. As of November 1989 all alcoholic beverages sold in the United States must carry a warning on the container that states: "GOVERNMENT WARNING: (1) According to the Surgeon General, women should not drink alcoholic beverages during pregnancy because of the risk of birth defects. (2) Consumption of alcoholic beverages impairs your ability to drive a car or operate machinery, and may cause health problems."

The United States is far behind some European and Scandinavian countries, where tight governmental restrictions on alcoholic beverage advertising are commonplace. In Norway, for example, there has been a complete ban on advertising of all alcoholic products since 1975. As of Jan. 1, 1993, producers of beer, wine, and distilled spirits will no longer be allowed to advertise on television in France. Billboard advertising will also be curtailed, and the sponsorship of sporting events and athletic teams will be outlawed.

Ultimately, one of the most important goals of those seeking changes in alcoholic beverage advertising is also one of the most challenging: to eliminate the glamour and romance of imbibing. Those qualities are easy enough to identify in ads but very hard indeed to excise with rules and regulations—and harder still to banish from the cultural landscape. Meanwhile, the prevailing atmosphere is one of tolerance—and few protections for young people.

167

Alcohol Warning Labels:

Are They Working?

by Kenneth R. Laughery, Ph.D., and Stephen L. Young, M.A.

In the U.S. today a seemingly endless variety of consumer products—from cigarettes to saccharin to liquid drain openers—are required by law to carry warnings of their potential dangers. These warnings take various forms, such as messages on product labels and detailed package inserts. Evaluating the impact of such warnings on the public has been difficult because people learn about a given product's hazards from a variety of sources: television news, magazine articles, posters, etc. Nevertheless, social scientists have attempted to assess the ways that warnings influence behavior, and from their studies certain conclusions can be drawn. The study of warnings on alcoholic beverage containers is a case in point.

Scientists scrutinize labels

In 1988, as a result of growing concern about the safety and health problems associated with alcohol consumption, Congress mandated that as of November 1989 the following message should appear on all alcoholic beverage containers marketed in the United States:

GOVERNMENT WARNING: (1) According to the Surgeon General, women should not drink alcoholic beverages during pregnancy because of the risk of birth defects. (2) Consumption of alcoholic beverages impairs your ability to drive a car or operate machinery, and may cause health problems.

The effectiveness of any product warning is ultimately evaluated in terms of whether it reduces rates of illness, injury, and death associated with the use of the product. For those engaged in the scientific study of such warnings, however, the process is a good deal more complicated. Researchers have therefore identified a number of important criteria that can be used to measure a warning's effectiveness. These criteria are based on the assumption that people process information in a specific step-by-step manner. According to this model, in order for a warning to have a decided impact—and ultimately to reduce mortality and morbidity—it must first be attended (noticed), next provide appropriate information and be understood, then affect beliefs and attitudes that in turn affect the person's intentions, and finally result in "proper"

Kenneth R. Laughery, Ph.D., is Henry Luce Professor of Engineering Psychology, Rice University, Houston, Texas. *Stephen L. Young, M.A.*, is a Graduate Student at Rice.

behavior. Failure of the warning to do any one of the above compromises the possibility that it will ultimately influence behavior. Thus, if the warning goes unnoticed, it cannot be effective; if it is noticed but not understood, it cannot be effective; and so forth.

Most studies evaluating the impact of warning messages on alcoholic beverage containers have attempted to determine the extent to which the warnings have been noticed by consumers and how they have affected people's knowledge and understanding of the consequences of alcohol consumption. The logic, again, is that if the warnings are not effective at these stages, they are not likely to have an impact on behavior. Another reason for focusing on these stages is that as a rule, the procedures for measuring effectiveness become increasingly complex and time-consuming as the investigation moves from the attention stage to the behavior stage.

Getting the consumer's attention

An alcohol warning label cannot be expected to have any effect on drinking behavior if those buying alcoholic beverages do not notice and read it. Thus, the Alcoholic Beverage Labeling Act of 1988 specified that the warnings were to be printed on a "contrasting background" in a "conspicuous and prominent place" in the overall label scheme. Some studies have evaluated the noticeability of warnings; others have attempted to improve upon it.

In one survey of noticeability, researchers questioned more than 2,000 people before and after the warning appeared. Interestingly, prior to its introduction, some 8% of the respondents incorrectly reported having noticed a warning. In July 1990, about six months after the labels had begun to appear, roughly 27% of those surveyed reported having seen such a warning label; however, about 6% of these responses were considered erroneous reports because subjects could not correctly recall the warning's content. The rate of notice of the warning was strongly affected by gender, age, and drinking pattern: males were more aware of the warning than females; younger people (aged 18–29) were more aware than older ones (aged 40 and over); and heavy drinkers showed greater awareness than other drinkers. These findings are perhaps to be expected—younger people, males, and heavy drinkers buy and consume more alcoholic beverages than the general population. However, the survey results may also have been influenced by the fact that only about 86% of beer, 34% of wine, and 30% of liquor products on the market actually had warning labels as of June 1990 because those containers that were bottled prior to November 1989 and remained in stock and on store shelves were not required to have the new label. More recently, two surveys have suggested that while more people are beginning to notice the warning, overall awareness rates are still low (between 21 and 51%).

Several studies have suggested reasons why the warning—in its current form—is not likely to attract the attention of consumers. There are many different ways to display the mandated warning and still remain in compliance with Bureau of Alcohol, Tobacco and Firearms (BATF) regulations. It was initially proposed that the warning be placed anywhere on the container except the bottom, top, or inside and that the lettering be no less than two millimeters (0.08 inch) in height (for containers larger than 237 milliliters [8 fluid ounces]). The regulations did not explicitly specify factors such as how dense the type must be, how large an area the warning should occupy, its location and orientation on the container, the degree to which the print must contrast with the background, or how readable it must be. In fact, there is currently a great deal of variation in the way that these warnings are displayed on labels. While the regulations are meant to give beverage manufacturers some degree of flexibility, several studies have demonstrated that the current standards probably allow too much license and that this has reduced the effectiveness of the warning.

To determine how noticeability might be improved, these authors and colleagues at Rice University conducted a study of warnings on actual alcoholic beverage containers. Roughly 250 different containers (of beer, wine, and liquor) were collected before and after the mandated warning appeared. Of these, 100 containers (50 with the warning and 50 without), which varied in size, type of container, label dimensions, and other design features, were shown to volunteers. It was found that larger warnings with less dense type and greater contrast were more prominent than smaller warnings with dense type and less contrast.

In addition, warnings that were printed horizontally were easier to locate than ones printed vertically, and warnings printed on the front label of the container were found more rapidly than those on any other label. While the quality of the warning presentations varied widely among the different containers evaluated, the researchers concluded that, overall, effective contrast and color, legible print, optimal location, and the inclusion of certain other attention-getting design features were the exception rather than the rule for alcoholic beverage products then on the market.

One of the more important findings of this study was that when the labels were "busy" or "cluttered"

A simulated alcohol warning label incorporates features that research has shown are likely to attract attention: a pictorial (bottom left), a signal icon (above warning message), and the message itself printed in a color that contrasts with the background.

with nonwarning information, the warning was less noticeable than when the labels were simple and sparse in design. Thus, it was the design of the entire label, and not just that of the warning, that seemed to determine whether the warning was seen.

In order to explore this finding further, these authors examined several alternative ways of increasing the prominence of warning information on beverage containers. Simulated labels were created with the following design features: a pictorial (*e.g.,* an automobile and three alcoholic beverage containers—a bottle, wine glass, and beer stein—depicted within a circle with a diagonal slash through the center); a signal icon (in this case, an exclamation point enclosed within a triangle, next to the word WARNING); contrasting colors—for example, red type on a white background; and a border around the warning.

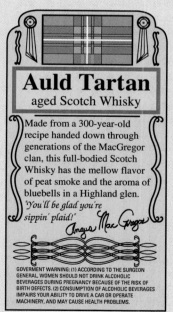

Label design can be used to minimize the noticeability of warning information as well as to maximize it; the busier and more cluttered the label, the less likely it is that the warning will be seen and read.

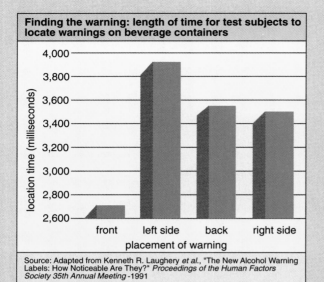

Finding the warning: length of time for test subjects to locate warnings on beverage containers

[Bar chart showing location time (milliseconds) on the y-axis ranging from 2,600 to 4,000, versus placement of warning on the x-axis. Bars: front ≈ 2,700; left side ≈ 3,920; back ≈ 3,550; right side ≈ 3,490]

y-axis label: location time (milliseconds)
x-axis label: placement of warning

Source: Adapted from Kenneth R. Laughery *et al.*, "The New Alcohol Warning Labels: How Noticeable Are They?" *Proceedings of the Human Factors Society 35th Annual Meeting* -1991

Subjects viewed the labels on a computer screen and indicated whether a warning was present. Of the above four features, all but the border increased the conspicuousness of warnings. This was confirmed by means of a technique that tracked the eye movements of subjects while they looked at different label designs. It was found that people's eyes were almost automatically drawn to the most salient combination of features, one that included the pictorial, the signal icon, and the use of contrasting colors. These studies suggest that warnings *can* be improved by maximum use of salient design features.

What do people really know about alcohol?

The purpose of employing an attention-getting format for the design of the warning is, of course, to increase the chance that consumers will actually read the message. Thus, an important aspect of assessing effectiveness is measuring the extent to which the warning, once noticed, is read and understood. A survey that evaluated the currently mandated warning demonstrated that awareness of alcohol-related health hazards was already very high prior to the introduction of the printed warning labels. In fact, 95% of those questioned knew that alcohol is associated with birth defects, may cause health problems, or interferes with driving. The researchers found modest but statistically significant increases (1–2%) in knowledge of these hazards once the printed warning came into use, but the fact that rates of awareness were already high suggests that the current message offers little in the way of new information. At the same time, other studies show that more than 50% of the population is *not* knowledgeable about or aware of alcohol-related hazards that are *not* addressed in the current warning—for example, the risks of cancer, liver disease, and

addiction; effects on blood pressure; and potential for alcohol-drug interactions.

Several other studies have assessed the impact of warning information on people's knowledge of health and safety risks associated with alcohol. In one investigation, prominent warning placards were posted on the walls of fraternity houses where beer was served. The placards addressed various specific hazards associated with drinking and included statistics on such things as the rates of alcohol-related death and injury and the effects of alcohol on reflexes and coordination. When questioned later about the content of the warning, students who had been exposed to the placards had high levels of recall. This finding suggests that awareness of a hazard can be increased if unknown information is presented rather than well-known facts.

Investigations to date indicate that because the current warning does not provide much in the way of new information, it would be unrealistic to expect it to produce substantial increases in people's knowledge of the hazards associated with drinking. However, although 95% of people may know that alcohol is associated with health hazards, this does not mean they have a *complete* understanding or appreciation of *all* the hazards listed in the current warning. Rather, most people have only a very general awareness of these hazards. Another reason that has been suggested for the current label's lack of effect is its vagueness with regard to the four different hazard categories that it does address; namely, birth defects, driving, operating machinery, and health problems. The warning is not likely to produce any appreciable increase in awareness—as general awareness rates are already high—nor is it likely to produce a greater understanding or appreciation of the hazards (because it is so vague). All this suggests that if labels included warnings that addressed the *lesser known* hazards of alcohol—such

Skip Williamson

Whereas billboard campaigns by advocacy groups such as Mothers Against Drunk Driving (MADD) have definitely reduced the incidence of alcohol-related injuries and deaths, research on alcoholic beverage warning labels indicates that since 1989, when the warnings were first mandated, they have not had any clear effect on people's beliefs about alcohol or their drinking behavior.

as those on the fraternity house placards—they might have a greater impact.

Seeing is believing—or is it?

Beliefs and attitudes affect not only the way people behave when using a product but also the way they process information about that product. For example, surveys have shown that warnings that address the less-well-known hazards—alcohol-related cancers and liver disease, addiction, and the like—are somewhat less believable than the currently mandated warning. This phenomenon, known to psychologists as "discounting," was pronounced in some groups, including frequent drinkers. Apparently, preexisting beliefs about a product affect the degree to which a warning about it is considered credible.

Because of the relatively short time that the current warning has actually been present on alcohol containers, there is little reliable evidence about its effect on beliefs and attitudes. However, several recent surveys have examined how people perceive alcohol-related health hazards. In 1989 and 1990 one researcher observed a small (and statistically nonsignificant) increase in the number of people reporting that alcohol consumption was "very harmful," but this trend reversed itself in 1991. Another survey suggested that there had been no change in the perceived dangers of drinking during pregnancy since the warning labels were introduced. Still another demonstrated that most people believe that "regular drinkers" are at no greater risk of being involved in automobile accidents or having babies with birth defects than are "nondrinkers."

Overall, these results suggest that the mandated warning has had no reliable impact on people's beliefs and attitudes. There are at least two reasons why this might be so. First, it could be that the warning has not had sufficient time to affect beliefs and attitudes. Second, and more likely, the information contained in the warning is both too vague to have a marked impact and already too familiar to most people.

Seeking warnings that work

The surveys conducted to date generally show that the current warning on alcoholic beverage containers has little or no effect on people's drinking behavior. One study concluded, for example, that the warning did not affect people's intentions with regard to driving after drinking, nor did it influence them to curb their drinking for health reasons. Inexplicably, the reported use of power tools or machinery after drinking apparently *increased* in the time period after the introduction of the warning. Again, since the warning has not been in the marketplace very long, these findings need to be validated by further research. Even so, the apparent failure of the warning to influence beliefs and attitudes suggests that it will have little effect on drinking behavior.

What is the future direction for alcohol warnings on beverage containers? There are several ways to increase the chances that the warning will be noticed—for example, reducing label clutter, adding visual devices such as pictorials and signal icons, and printing warnings in colors that stand out. The studies also show that alcohol warnings need to be more explicit and detailed and that there are important alcohol-related health hazards of which people are generally unaware.

Future warning messages, by addressing these hazards in a believable and persuasive manner, could effectively increase the understanding of health and safety issues associated with alcohol consumption. A number of consumer groups have called for "pithier" messages as well as rotating ones that would increase the chances that drinkers will be exposed to information about many potential hazards of alcohol. One that has been suggested is: "Warning: Alcohol Is a Drug and May Be Addictive." In 1991 the U.S. surgeon general convened a task force to assess the need for labeling revisions. It is hoped that these efforts will lead to new requirements that ultimately could bring about more responsible drinking behavior.

PRO FOOTBALL
The Team That Treats the Team

by John A. Bergfeld, M.D., and Andrew M. Tucker, M.D.

In 1905—15 years before the founding of the National Football League (NFL)—organized football was on the verge of being banned in the United States. An increasingly popular collegiate sport, football had been transformed from a merely violent and brutal game to a deadly one. Student players, who wore only the most rudimentary body pads and leather helmets, were using such "mass plays" as the flying wedge, in which the ball carrier would run closely behind a V-shaped "mass" of teammates. To help keep the wedge together, players sometimes held onto suitcase handles that were sewn onto their teammates' uniforms. Mass plays were effective but also painful and hazardous, causing broken bones and occasionally even death. After the 1905 college season, in which there were 18 deaths and more than 150 serious injuries, Pres. Theodore Roosevelt responded to public outrage and forced football officials to revise the rules. Mass plays were banned, but another offensive play, the forward pass, was legalized.

Football has seen dramatic changes since its early days, and improved equipment and further changes in the rules have afforded greater protection for players. Still, because of the demands made on the players, the game presents serious health risks. The use of artificial turf, for example, has led to a slight increase in the number of injuries, especially those of the knee, ankle, and foot.

Furthermore, the players have become stronger, heavier, and faster—increasing the injury odds. In 1921 the average weight on the starting lineup of the Chicago Staleys (later the Chicago Bears) was 88 kilograms (194 pounds). At 104 kilograms (229 pounds) the heaviest was the team's center, George Trafton, but the lightest, Pete Stinchcomb, who played quarterback and halfback, weighed only 69 kilograms (152 pounds). The legendary George Halas, at right end, played at just 83 kilograms (182 pounds). Today the average professional football player weighs 104 kilograms. Immensely strong 136-kilogram (300-pound) linemen are routinely showcased, and even the Bears' William ("Refrigerator") Perry, who weighs well over 136 kilograms, is remarkably mobile.

Today's professional football players, however, have an advantage that players of the past did not have. The highly sophisticated specialty of

John A. Bergfeld, M.D., is Head of the Section of Sports Medicine, Department of Orthopaedic Surgery, Cleveland Clinic Foundation, and Team Physician to the Cleveland Browns football team, Cleveland, Ohio.
Andrew M. Tucker, M.D., is Staff Physician, Cleveland Clinic Foundation, and Associate Team Physician to the Cleveland Browns.

(Opposite page) Greg Koch, an offensive lineman for the Minnesota Vikings, is taken off the field with a minor injury during a game with the San Francisco 49ers. Photograph, Otto Greule—Allsport

172

Players line up in the flying wedge, a "mass play" in which the ball carrier runs closely behind a V-shaped mass of teammates. After the 1905 college football season, during which there were 18 deaths and more than 150 serious injuries, U.S. Pres. Theodore Roosevelt forced football officials to ban such plays.

sports medicine has brought expert care to all NFL team members—on the field as well as before and after play. Each team employs a variety of medical professionals who use the latest knowledge and skills, along with state-of-the-art technology not only to treat injuries but to prevent them—and ultimately to enhance performance.

Sports medicine's evolution

Although the historical roots of sports medicine are buried in antiquity, it is known that the discipline existed in Greece at least as early as the 5th century BC, when practitioners were called "gymnastes." The first gymnaste recorded in ancient Greek sources was Herodicus, who was apparently a teacher of the "father of medicine," Hippocrates (c. 460–377 BC). Herodicus and other ancient sports physicians prescribed remedies such as herbal medicine, dietary regimes, and rudimentary surgery, but it is now thought that the effectiveness of many of their treatments was mainly coincidental. Although sports medicine today barely resembles what it was over 2,000 years ago, the Herodicus Society, a group of prominent international sports orthopedic surgeons, continues to honor the acknowledged founder of the discipline.

The first known counterpart of today's "team physician" was Galen (c. AD 130–200), who was charged with the medical care of the Roman gladiators. Generally criminals or former slaves, the gladiators were required to fight to the death, often with a sword but sometimes with unusual equipment

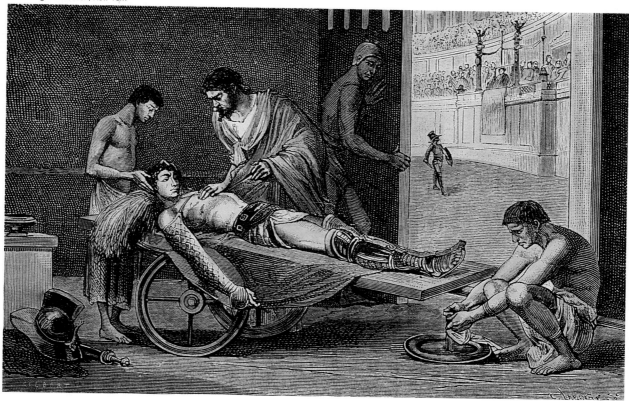

or by unusual means—for example, with a lasso, with a net and a trident, or while blindfolded. Galen took meticulous notes on the injuries suffered by the "athletes," and these notes enabled him to make important contributions to the sciences of anatomy, physiology, physical therapy, and biomechanics.

Sports medicine as a modern specialty really began in the 19th century with the rapid growth and development of organized sports and, in the United States, with the beginnings of interscholastic and intercollegiate athletics. The first U.S. team physician is generally acknowledged to have been Edward Hitchcock, Jr. In 1861 he was appointed professor of physical education and hygiene at Amherst (Massachusetts) College and was responsible for the care of its athletic teams.

Numerous organizations have since been formed for the advancement of sports medicine. One of the oldest, the International Federation of Sports Medicine (Fédération Internationale de Médecine Sportive), founded in France in 1928, has members from more than 60 countries. In the U.S. the American College of Sports Medicine, a diverse multispecialty organization that includes nonphysicians, was founded in 1954. The American Orthopaedic Society for Sports Medicine, founded in 1972, is an organization of orthopedic surgeons who devote much of their time to the practice of sports medicine; other "sister" organizations have emerged in many other countries. The American Medical Society for Sports Medicine, composed of nonorthopedic physicians, was formed in 1992.

The first known counterpart to the team physicians of modern sports was Galen (c. AD 130–200), a Greek physician who provided medical care for the Roman gladiators.

175

Edward Hitchcock, Jr., is generally considered to have been the first U.S. team physician. In 1861 he was appointed professor of physical education and hygiene at Amherst (Massachusetts) College and was responsible for the school's athletic teams.

Treating the team—from head to toe

Perhaps the least discussed influence on the care of professional football players has been their skyrocketing salaries, some now surpassing $1 million per year. With the high value placed on players, teams are spending increasingly larger sums of money on maintaining their health and prolonging their careers. Players, of course, also have a financial incentive to extend their careers, even in the face of a serious injury, as their incomes are likely to drop considerably when they retire.

The diverse group that cares for the players in the NFL generally includes a head physician (an orthopedic surgeon), a medical specialist (usually an internist or family practice doctor), athletic trainers, and a strength and conditioning coach. In addition, professional football teams often enlist the services of other specialists, such as neurosurgeons, cardiologists, general surgeons, psychiatrists, psychologists, and dentists. Increasingly, teams in the NFL today also use the services of nutritionists and substance-abuse specialists.

Head team physician. The orthopedic surgeon who heads the medical team must have extensive training and expertise in sports-related orthopedic problems. Teams may employ two or even three orthopedic surgeons, as the time and travel demands of the job make it difficult for one person to carry out the extensive responsibilities. When a medical problem arises outside the realm of the orthopedist's expertise, the head physician may call upon an appropriate specialist.

The bulk of time and energy of the team's orthopedic surgeons is spent evaluating and treating the large volume of musculoskeletal injuries that occur during the season. A major off-the-field responsibility of the head physician is reporting on the health of players to the team's owner or owners. Because the financial value of a team is partially dependent on the health of its current roster of players, the owner has a considerable business interest in the team's injuries and the medical care provided by the staff. Of course, the head physician also communicates frequently with the head coach.

One of the least appealing jobs of the head physician is working with the team's attorneys in settling worker's compensation cases. These cases are filed by retired players for injuries sustained during their professional football careers. When a player signs a contract with a team, that team becomes responsible for all of the player's medical and orthopedic problems, irrespective of when they occurred. Therefore, a team may be required to provide a monetary settlement for injuries sustained years earlier with another team. To help the attorneys determine an appropriate compensation package, the head physician is periodically required to pore over medical charts and past X-rays of an injured player. This task emphasizes the importance of teams' keeping detailed medical records of their players.

Medical specialist. Complementing the role of the orthopedist is the physician who takes care of the general health needs of the players—the management of both ongoing medical problems (*e.g.,* hypertension or peptic ulcer disease) and the common acute illnesses likely to affect the players during the season (*e.g.,* influenza, bronchitis, or gastroenteritis).

176

Other duties include providing preventive care, such as the giving of appropriate immunizations; informing players of the risks of alcohol, drugs, and anabolic steroids; and performing routine physical exams and screening tests (*e.g.,* chest X-rays, electrocardiograms, blood pressure evaluation, and cholesterol screening).

Both the head physician and the team's medical doctor play a role in the evaluation of prospective players. The former assesses the candidate's past injuries and possible susceptibility to further musculoskeletal problems, while the latter compiles a careful medical history and performs a general physical examination. Their joint assessment is sometimes an important factor in whether a team chooses to hire a particular player.

Athletic trainers. The scope of responsibilities and amount of individual contact with players that the head athletic trainer and his assistants have probably surpass those of all other members of the treatment team. During the season the trainers work exceedingly long hours. One of their responsibilities is to help recognize, evaluate, and keep detailed records of injuries, which occur not only in games but also in daily practice. Trainers are also required to be innovative craftsmen, capable of altering or designing new equipment, such as braces to protect existing injuries or to prevent new ones.

Perhaps the most important job of the trainers is to design individualized rehabilitation programs for injured players, working in conjunction with the team's orthopedist. Such rehabilitation commonly involves specific stretching exercises and progressive-resistance training utilizing various kinds of equipment, including free weights and state-of-the-art variable-resistance machines. These treatments must take into account each player's unique response to injury. For injuries that require surgery, the technical proficiency of the orthopedic surgeon is crucial, but most surgeons admit that the real key to operative success is proper rehabilitation. For a player recovering from a lower extremity injury, exercising in water provides an

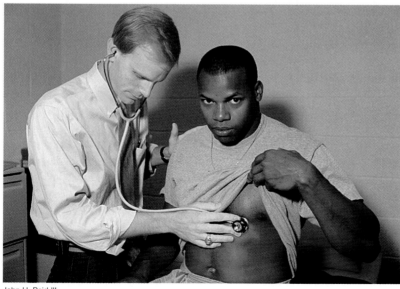

John H. Reid III

Andrew Tucker, a family practice physician who serves as the medical doctor to the Cleveland Browns, examines running back Kevin Mack. An NFL team's medical specialist takes care of the general health needs of the players.

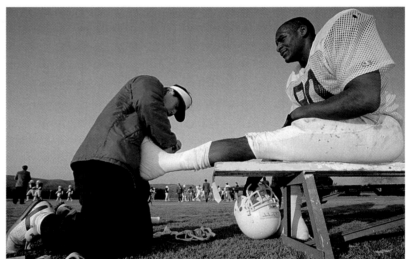

Athletic trainers are responsible for evaluating and attending to injuries. In conjunction with the team's orthopedist, they also design rehabilitation programs for injured players. Above, a defensive lineman works out in a miniature swimming pool that has an adjustable current to vary the intensity of the therapy; exercising in water is particularly helpful to players recovering from knee, leg, and foot injuries. Top right, trainers for the Phoenix Cardinals attend to cornerback Aeneas Williams after a minor injury. Trainers spend much of their time taping ankles, knees, wrists, elbows, and shoulders (right).

aerobic workout that places only minimal weight on the affected body part. The training facilities of some NFL teams now include a miniature swimming pool that has an adjustable current to vary the intensity of a player's exercise regimen. Other treatment modalities used by athletic trainers include ultrasound, electrical stimulation, phonophoresis, and iontophoresis. Ultrasound utilizes sound waves of various lengths that penetrate superficial tissue and can enhance the healing process. Electrical stimulation uses weak currents to stimulate muscle after injury or surgery in order to maintain muscle tone and prevent muscle atrophy. It can also be used to control pain because such stimulation interferes with the body's ability to perceive localized pain. Phonophoresis is the process whereby sound waves are used to help drive medication into the superficial body tissues in order to treat an inflammatory response associated with injury, while iontophoresis uses electric current as the driving force for transporting the medicine into such tissue.

The task that undoubtedly takes up most of the trainer's time is the daily ritual of taping countless ankles, knees, wrists, elbows, and shoulders for each day's practice and for every game. The trainers for the Cleveland Browns estimate that in a single season they use $40,000 worth of athletic tape!

Strength and conditioning coach. All professional teams employ a full-time strength and conditioning coach with a background in exercise physiology. Working closely with the athletic trainers, the coach not only instructs players in weight training and aerobic conditioning but also provides important advice to physicians and the coaching staff on the progress of team members returning to play after an injury.

Nutritionist. In order to maintain the health and maximize the performance of their players, NFL teams are increasingly turning to dietitians and nutritionists. These professionals can make important recommendations on general nutrition, as well as on appropriate foods and fluids for pregame meals, postgame recovery, and supplementation during practice and games. In addition, a nutritionist can help design strategies for individual players who must gain or lose weight.

Because of their size and the amount of energy expended during practices and games, professional football players must consume an extraordinary number of calories each day. A 136-kilogram lineman, for example, may need as many as 5,000–6,000 calories to maintain his weight. Of the nutrients critical for these players, carbohydrates are the most important, as they replenish glycogen in exercise-fatigued muscles. Carbohydrates taken into the body are broken down to glucose and then stored in the liver and muscles in the form of glycogen, which serves as the energy source for the body during exercise. Nutritionists working with NFL teams generally recommend that complex carbohydrates make up at least 65% of a football player's diet, while fat and protein should provide about 10–15% and 15–20%, respectively. Pregame meals, once dominated by steak and potatoes, now more commonly consist of such carbohydrate-rich foods as pastas and breads. After the game, players are provided with high-carbohydrate snacks.

During a two-to-three-hour practice or game in hot, humid conditions, players can lose as many as 4.5–6.8 kilograms (10–15 pounds). They are encouraged to drink as much as possible to minimize dehydration and the risk of heat illness. Each player's weight is monitored closely to evaluate daily hydration status.

Along with these recommendations for improving performance, nutritional specialists also try to help players meet long-term dietary needs—for example, designing an eating plan for a retiring player whose activity level and caloric and nutrient requirements often change radically when he is no longer playing football professionally. This role of nutritionists is especially important in light of the brief period—an average of just 4.5 years—during which a football player competes in the NFL.

Substance-abuse specialist. Some NFL teams employ the services of a chemical-abuse specialist, who may be a clinical psychologist or a psychiatrist. Instances of alcohol or drug abuse by professional athletes have

Jerry Simmons, strength and conditioning coach for the Cleveland Browns, works with a player. All NFL teams employ a full-time strength and conditioning coach, who instructs players in weight training and aerobic conditioning and advises physicians and the coaching staff on the progress of players recovering from injuries.

179

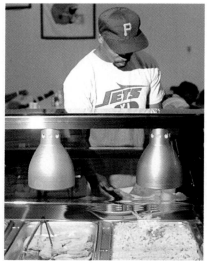

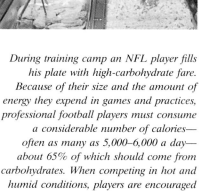

During training camp an NFL player fills his plate with high-carbohydrate fare. Because of their size and the amount of energy they expend in games and practices, professional football players must consume a considerable number of calories— often as many as 5,000–6,000 a day— about 65% of which should come from carbohydrates. When competing in hot and humid conditions, players are encouraged to drink as much as possible to minimize dehydration and the risk of heat illness.

been well documented over the past several years. Many clubs employ a specialist to help design programs to treat past offenders of the league's drug and alcohol policies and to provide education for all the players in hopes of minimizing future occurrences.

Injuries: part of the game

My first major injury came when I was a sophomore in high school. A couple of gorillas fell on me and my arm locked. I snapped it back in place, locating the dislocation, but I crushed all the tendons, so I couldn't lift the sucker for weeks. I came back sooner than I should have, and started throwing sidearm. Since then, it's been one thing or another.

I always used to tear up my ankles for some reason. Had casts on them both at various times. I've broken my left wrist, my right hand. . . . I've had three operations on my left knee and one on my right. I've split my chin wide open. I had cracked vertebrae, and a cracked tailbone. That was fun. I had to drive around while sitting on one of those plastic donuts, like a pregnant woman. There aren't many parts of me that haven't been wrapped in plaster at one time or another.

This list of injuries—described by former Chicago Bears quarterback Jim McMahon in his 1986 autobiography, *McMahon!*—is, unfortunately, not unusual. An unavoidable consequence of large men colliding at high speeds is that professional football players continually face the prospect of serious or even catastrophic injury.

Careful records of injuries are kept by the medical staffs of all NFL teams, and this information is compiled by the NFL Injury Surveillance System. According to the surveillance system, there are three types of injuries: a major injury, defined as one that puts a player out of action for at least 22 days; a moderate injury, 8–21 days; and a minor injury, less than 8 days. An example of a major injury is a sprain or tear of a knee ligament; a moderate injury is a moderate-to-severe ankle sprain; and a minor injury is a mild ankle sprain. Examination of the injury rates over a several-year period enables significant trends to be identified, although drawing conclusions from these results must be done cautiously. For example, from 1980 to

1989 NFL players experienced a slight decrease in moderate injuries but a slight increase in major injuries; however, because injuries are defined by the number of days a player is kept from participation, the data are unclear as to whether the increase in major injuries represents a true increase or a more conservative treatment approach.

Case study: the 1989 season. For the 1989 regular season and post-season, the number of injuries—whether major, moderate, or minor—occurred at an average rate of 35 injuries per 100 athletes. There were, however, a number of important variances. During in-season practice, teams try to minimize heavy contact between players by reducing scrimmages and other full-contact situations, which in a game are routine and unavoidable. Thus, on average, only 7.6 injuries per 100 athletes occurred during practice, but there were 68.1 per 100 athletes in games. Clearly, games represented the far greater risk for players. During game play the injury rates were 38.2, 14.5, and 15.4 per 100 for minor, moderate, and major injuries, respectively.

The injury rates also differed considerably by body part and playing position. The most frequently injured body parts were the knees, ankles, shoulders, upper legs, feet, forearms, wrists, and hands. Running backs and quarterbacks were the most often injured players, while offensive linemen were among the least frequently injured. The high rates among running backs and quarterbacks, who receive heavy pounding by defensive players, support the view that it is safer to hit than to be hit.

Catastrophic injuries. Darryl Stingley, who was knocked out of football on a single play, is happy just to be alive. Stingley was a star wide receiver for Purdue University, West Lafayette, Indiana, and in 1973 was selected in the first round of the NFL draft by the New England Patriots. He became one of the Patriots' top receivers.

In August 1978 his team was host to a preseason game against the Oakland Raiders, who were known to be exceptionally aggressive. Jack Tatum, a defensive free safety for the Raiders, was especially feared for his powerful—and some say unnecessarily rough—hits. As the game clock approached halftime, the Patriots were nearing the end of a successful drive. Only two plays earlier, Stingley had gained more than 20 yards on a pass from quarterback Steve Grogan, and the Patriots, with third down and 8 yards to go on the Raiders' 24-yard line, were in position to score.

The play brought in from the coaches was a "94 slant." One of three pass receivers on the play, Stingley lined up on the right side of the quarterback and ran a slant pattern across the middle of the field. Grogan saw Stingley but threw the ball too high, and even though Stingley had leaped into the air, the ball passed over his outstretched hands. It was then—as Stingley was falling back to the ground—that Tatum came in for the hit. Tatum's forearm smashed into Stingley's head and neck and instantly fractured two of his neck vertebrae, injuring his spinal cord beyond repair. From that point on, Stingley was a quadriplegic, with no movement at all below the neck.

The surveillance system has a category for such severe cases—those that cause "societally serious disability," such as amputation, permanent

The brace on his left leg and the extensive taping bear witness to the many injuries suffered by Jim McMahon during his career as a Chicago Bear quarterback.

181

paralysis, or death. These tragic outcomes are fortunately so rare that no such cases were reported in the NFL during the 1980s. In the 1991 season, however, Mike Utley, an offensive tackle for the Detroit Lions, suffered a cervical spine fracture-dislocation resulting in permanent paralysis below the upper chest.

Prevention of injuries. Although severe injuries are rare in the NFL, even a much less serious injury can be career threatening. Ironically, one player who has spoken out against the violence in football is Tatum. In his 1979 autobiography, *They Call Me Assassin,* Tatum blended an apparent concern for player safety with an obvious relish for causing pain and injury. He attributes violence on the football field to several sources, including the owners, the coaches, and the existing rules:

August 12, 1978, I was involved in a terrible accident with Darryl Stingley. . . . On a typical passing play, Darryl ran a rather dangerous pattern across the middle of our zone defense. It was one of those pass plays where I could have attempted to intercept, but because of what the owners expect of me when they give me my paycheck, I automatically reacted to the situation by going for an intimidating hit. . . . I want to be tough and I work at playing the game hard, but within the structure of the rules. . . . At the same time, I admit to using the rules to my advantage. Sure, I could just make tackles without really trying to blast through the man [a player], but I'm expected to, and the rules are designed in my favor because people [fans] want the excitement of violent play.

Severe injuries can occasionally end a player's career and, in rare cases, leave him permanently disabled. During an exhibition game in 1978, New England Patriot wide receiver Darryl Stingley (left) leaped into the air for a pass; as he was falling back to the ground, the forearm of Oakland Raider defensive free safety Jack Tatum (number 32) smashed into his head and neck. This fractured two of Stingley's neck vertebrae, injuring his spinal cord beyond repair and leaving him a quadriplegic, paralyzed from the neck down.

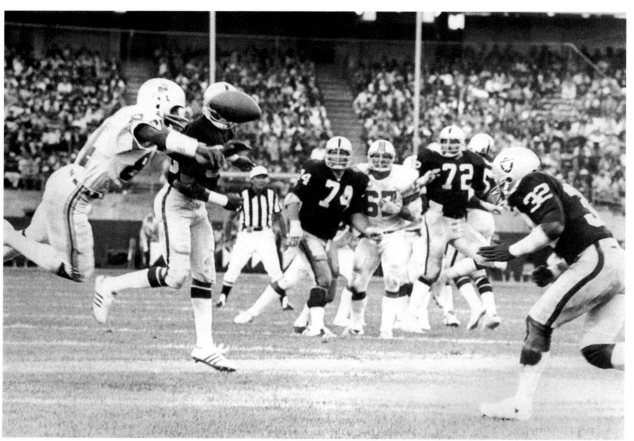

UPI/Bettmann

Where does the responsibility lie for the violence in football? On the owners and coaches, who, as Tatum charges, reward aggressive hits with greater playing time and money? On the rules, which allow extreme force to be used in tackles and which sanction certain plays and formations known to be dangerous? On the athletes, who sometimes try to hurt or injure their opponents, often by means not sanctioned in the rules? Or on the fans, who cheer when players make exceptionally aggressive hits?

The question of responsibility may not have an easy answer. Because the goal of the offense is to force the ball through a wall of human defenders, and the aim of the defense is to tackle the ball carrier—which often requires hitting the opponent at full strength—some amount of injury appears inevitable. Even so, with the help of statistics on the prevalence, type, and cause of football injuries, there have been a number of attempts at prevention. Two areas in which such efforts have been directed are rule changes and equipment improvement, both of which have dramatically reduced the number and severity of head injuries, one of football's greatest hazards.

In 1968, of the 36 deaths that occurred in football at all levels (high school, college, and professional), 20 were blamed on head injury. Why? According to the National Operating Committee on Standards for Athletic Equipment (NOCSAE), which is composed of representatives from consumer groups, manufacturers of sporting goods, and other organizations, head and neck position during a tackle was the most important factor in a fatal or catastrophic head/neck injury. Consequently, the NFL adopted a rule in 1976 that penalized football players who use the crown, or top, of their helmets as a battering ram—a practice known as spearing. The high forces that can be transmitted as a result of spearing are transmitted through the spine and can, in the worst cases, result in paralysis. Proper tackling utilizes the face and front part of the upper trunk as the areas of initial contact. NOCSAE has also campaigned for the use of improved helmets and has conducted research on other football equipment, such as face guards, shoulder pads, and knee braces.

In 1990, for the first time since record keeping began (in 1931), there were no deaths directly attributable to football in the United States. Subdural hematoma (a blood clot between the skull and the brain tissue), responsible for most head-injury deaths and the most debilitating injuries, averaged 35 per year from 1959 to 1963 at all levels of football, but in 1990 only three such injuries occurred. In addition, paralyzing neck injuries, which averaged 20 per year from 1971 to 1975, decreased to an average of 10 per year from 1977 to 1989.

The day of the game

From Monday until the team's next game—usually the following Sunday—NFL players prepare for their upcoming opponents by attending meetings and practices, viewing game films, and continuing a program of strength training and conditioning. The physical and mental demands of an NFL season, however, also require that players be given an adequate amount of time off for the healing of their bodies and the reduction of stress.

Scott Mersereau (number 94), a defensive tackle for the New York Jets, spears Jim Kelly, a quarterback for the Buffalo Bills. In 1976 the NFL ruled that spearing—using the crown, or top, of one's helmet as a battering ram—would be penalized because the high forces that can be transmitted as a result of spearing can, in the worst cases, result in paralysis.

183

During the week the head coach and the medical staff meet to determine each player's injury status for the upcoming game. The medical evaluation of the players' various injuries, of course, often affects the strategy for the upcoming game.

For both players and the medical staff, the most demanding time is the day of the game. Athletic trainers generally arrive at the stadium about four or five hours before kickoff. As the players arrive, trainers become immersed in the task of taping and bracing each player, a process that can take three trainers working continuously up to two hours. Other members of the medical staff may also have pregame work to do. The head physician may be involved in last-minute decisions on the readiness of a previously injured player, and the medical specialist may need to treat last-minute ailments—the most common being "nervous stomach."

Many players prefer to go on the field initially for a light, individual warm-up, especially if the team is not playing at home. A group warm-up generally begins about one hour before game time. Just minutes prior to kickoff, trainers are busy readjusting tape and braces that do not feel quite right to the players. Such readjustments are also made throughout the game and especially during halftime.

Once the game begins, so too does the risk of injuries, and the medical staff must be ready to handle anything from a minor sprain to a serious fracture or worse. If a player's injury is not severe enough to warrant removal from the game, the trainers work quickly to pad, tape, or brace the new injury, thus reducing the possibility of aggravation or more serious complications.

Although football players vary in their reactions to pain, many have a high level of tolerance and often want to continue playing despite injury. The decision to withhold a player from the game, however, ultimately rests with the head team physician, whose ability to make an accurate diagnosis requires careful examination and sometimes the performing of

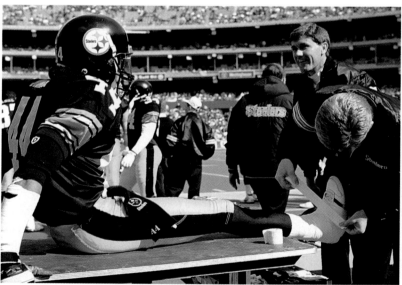

Defensive back David Johnson of the Pittsburgh Steelers is taped up before a game. On the day of a game, trainers tape and brace each player on a team, a task that can take as long as two hours for three trainers working continuously.

Greg Crisp—Sportslight

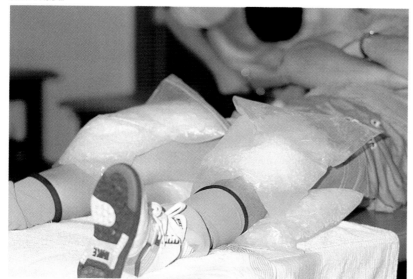

Ice packs are an effective means of limiting the extent of an injury. When applied to an injured body part, they reduce the flow of blood at the site and thereby reduce both swelling and pain.

certain diagnostic procedures, such as having X-rays taken. (All NFL stadiums nowadays have X-ray equipment on site.) In some circumstances—for example, a serious head or neck injury—a player may need to be sent to a local hospital for more definitive evaluation and treatment. During every game ambulance crews are at the stadium to respond to any emergency that arises.

After the game the medical staff evaluates each injured player in the training area and must decide whether X-rays, medication, or other treatment is necessary. Common pain-relief and anti-inflammatory agents, such as ibuprofen, are widely used medications for both acute and chronic musculoskeletal injuries. It is not unusual for players to take such medications for several weeks in a row, as the extreme exertion and physical abuse sustained during play cause persistent soreness, strained muscles, and sprains. With severe injuries more potent drugs are required. Ice packs also play a significant part in the treatment of players. Ice is a remarkably effective method of limiting the extent of an injury. Strapped to the injured body part, an ice pack reduces the flow of blood at the site, thereby diminishing both swelling and pain. Quarterbacks routinely ice their throwing shoulder and elbow after each game to help prevent inflammation in those critical joints.

The off-season

Although the regular season lasts from September to December (with the Super Bowl in January or early February), professional football and the care of its players is a year-round business. At the conclusion of the season, the medical staff performs comprehensive physical examinations and updates the status of the players' various injuries. A rehabilitation program is then planned for each player.

Team members with injuries that do not require surgery may need to complete a rehabilitation program, with periodic checkups at the team's training facility. A formal off-season program of weight training and conditioning, usually beginning in March, is designed for each returning player. Many players choose to live year round in their team's city so they can participate in this program at the team's training facility.

A major event for the medical staff each February is the NFL "combine," held in Indianapolis, Indiana. This four-day event—attended by some 400 college players eligible for the professional football draft—includes not only strength, speed, and agility tests supervised by the coaching staffs from every NFL team but also evaluations by each team's medical staff. For those athletes who are drafted by the teams, a minicamp is held at the end of April. Once again the medical staff is busy performing medical and orthopedic evaluations to assure the readiness of each team member to play. Another minicamp is held in early June for both rookies and returning players.

Formal preseason camp begins in mid-July. Grueling twice-a-day practice sessions place enormous demands on players, coaches, and medical staff alike. The team physicians make frequent trips to the campsite for injury evaluations. For trainers the preseason is the most rigorous of all, as the taping and treatment demands are practically doubled.

For players with chronic injuries that are given temporary treatment during the season, the off-season is the time when more definitive care, such as surgery, is undertaken. Operations for such problems as torn knee cartilage are usually performed as soon as possible at the season's end to allow the maximum recovery and rehabilitation time.

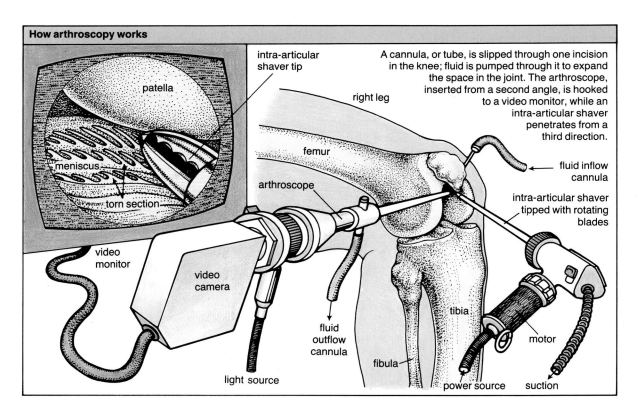

How arthroscopy works

patella

meniscus

torn section

video monitor

video camera

light source

intra-articular shaver tip

right leg

femur

arthroscope

fluid outflow cannula

fibula

tibia

A cannula, or tube, is slipped through one incision in the knee; fluid is pumped through it to expand the space in the joint. The arthroscope, inserted from a second angle, is hooked to a video monitor, while an intra-articular shaver penetrates from a third direction.

fluid inflow cannula

intra-articular shaver tipped with rotating blades

motor

power source

suction

Professional football players, as well as other big league athletes, have benefited from many treatments that have emerged as a result of advances in technology. In the 1970s advanced fiber-optic technology allowed for the development of the arthroscope—a long, thin tube that is inserted into a joint via a small incision in the skin. The instrument's field of view is displayed on a video screen. With this simple but highly sophisticated procedure, diagnosis and repair of an injured knee or elbow can be accomplished without opening up the joint. With the aid of extremely small surgical tools (*e.g.,* shavers, hooks, or clippers), the orthopedic surgeon, using the video screen to guide the instruments, can perform such procedures as the cutting away of damaged tissues without disturbing surrounding tissues. A football player with a tear in the knee cartilage, for example, can have the torn tissue removed in outpatient surgery and be ready to play again in a matter of weeks.

Major reconstruction procedures often combine conventional "open" surgery with arthroscopy in order to minimize the injured football player's recovery time. This hybrid technique is used in the reconstruction of the anterior cruciate ligament, located in the center of the knee, an injury that can occur when a running back is tackled from the outside (lateral) aspect of his knee when that foot is firmly planted on the playing field. In this operation the patient's ruptured ligament is replaced with a portion of the patellar tendon from his own knee. The new piece is threaded through holes drilled in the tibia and femur, fitted into a position approximating that of the former ligament, and secured by bone screws. Repair of this ligament used to involve a long incision extending across the knee joint. Using the arthroscope to carry out much of the operation not only minimizes the healing time but improves the aesthetic outcome. The rehabilitation time for this once potentially career-threatening injury nowadays is usually at most a single football season.

Another boon to physicians caring for injured football players is magnetic resonance imaging (MRI). MRI is capable of providing amazing pictures of the body's tissues, which can aid enormously in diagnosis. By recording energy emissions of the charged particles in body tissues, MRI is able to construct cross-sectional or three-dimensional computerized images of a body part without using X-rays or other radiation. With MRI, precise diagnoses can often be made without surgical intervention. This diagnostic technique is especially valuable for evaluating joints and soft tissues. MRI of the knee, for example, provides superior images for evaluation of ligaments, the menisci, and articular cartilage, and it is used frequently in the evaluation of spinal problems, such as herniated disks. With further technical improvements, MRI is expected to lend itself to the accurate diagnosis of other injured joints as well.

Ominous clouds over the big leagues

Many prominent professional athletes have been involved in well-publicized drug- or alcohol-related incidents. Some—for example, Don Rogers of the Cleveland Browns'—have tragically lost their lives to drug abuse. The NFL in recent years has stepped up its commitment to identifying play-

Don Rogers, a free safety for the Cleveland Browns, died of a cocaine overdose in 1986. Drug and alcohol abuse has remained a serious problem in many professional sports.

187

DRUG NOTICE

Any player or other club employee who violates National Football League policy on drugs is subject to disciplinary action by the Commissioner, which may include suspension or banishment from the League. Rehabilitative treatment may also be required. The following actions are among those prohibited:

1. Use, possession, purchase, sale, and/or participation in the distribution of illegal drugs, regardless of amount.

2. Use of anabolic steroids or related substances, or masking agents designed to hide their presence.

3. Serious misuse of alcohol, including violations of the law while intoxicated.

4. Illegal acquisition, distribution, and/or misuse of legal prescription or over-the-counter drugs. Use of such drugs in an effort to enhance on-field performance is also prohibited.

5. Association with drug-related activity in a manner detrimental to the integrity of, or public confidence in, NFL football.

Consult your playbook for the full text of the NFL drug policy.

Chemical dependency treatment is available for all employees; voluntary request for and submission to such treatment will not by itself result in disciplinary action by the Commissioner.

PAUL TAGLIABUE
Commissioner

The policy of the NFL with regard to illegal drugs, anabolic steroids, and alcohol is announced in a drug notice by NFL Commissioner Paul Tagliabue.

ers with substance-abuse problems and providing them with appropriate treatment.

Each player is tested during the preseason for so-called drugs of abuse (*e.g.,* cocaine, marijuana, heroine, and amphetamines). Also, certain players are subject to "reasonable cause" drug testing during both the season and off-season. Reasonable cause, as defined by the NFL, includes "prior established drug use, prior substance-abuse treatment, drug-or-alcohol-related involvement with the criminal justice system, or other medical or psychological evidence of substance abuse." The first time a player tests positive for a drug of abuse, he is required to undergo a mandatory evaluation and treatment directed by his team physicians. If later that player again tests positive, the penalty is removal from the active roster for six games without pay. A third positive drug test results in expulsion from the NFL, as occurred in the case of Dexter Manley of the Washington Redskins, but the player may petition the league commissioner for reinstatement after one year. The penalties for being found guilty of an alcohol-related charge, such as driving while intoxicated, are similar to those for using a drug of abuse.

Other substances commonly abused by football players are anabolic steroids—synthetic derivatives of the male hormone testosterone. These agents are capable of increasing lean body mass (muscle) and may improve strength in their users; thus, players in the "strength" positions—lineman, linebacker, tight end—are most likely to use them. The NFL is increasingly concerned about steroids for several reasons: (1) the drugs have the potential to improve performance, thus giving users of steroids an unfair competitive advantage over those who train without such aids; (2) steroids have potentially dangerous side effects that can affect the cardiovascular, reproductive, gastrointestinal, and central nervous systems; (3) since professional athletes are often seen as role models, it is feared that steroid use by well-known professional football players may encourage young people to experiment with these potent and dangerous drugs; and (4) steroids became controlled substances in the United States in February 1991, so the illegal distribution or use of these drugs is now subject to stiff government penalties. In an attempt to eradicate the use of steroids by professional football players, the NFL conducts random urine testing throughout the year, including the preseason and off-season. Offenders are subject to penalties similar to those outlined above for drugs of abuse, including suspensions from play and mandatory weekly testing. It is thought that the stringent NFL policies have had a significant effect on sharply reducing steroid use among professional football players.

In 1991 awareness of AIDS reached a new level with the announcement that professional basketball star Earvin ("Magic") Johnson had tested positive for the human immunodeficiency virus (HIV). The news was shocking to many people, in part because the guard for the Los Angeles Lakers was a popular personality who had been at the top of his sport for many years. More generally, however, in the United States AIDS had disproportionately afflicted two groups—homosexuals and intravenous drug users—and the case of Johnson, who contracted the virus through heterosexual contact,

188

made it clear that even a great sports figure was not impervious to AIDS. In fact, professional athletes may be at higher risk than the general population for all sexually transmitted diseases (STDs). Many athletes have confessed to a large number of sexual contacts in the many cities to which they have traveled. Some sexual contacts have also been shared among players, thus increasing the chance that HIV might be transmitted to more than one player by a single infected person.

A fear of many athletes, especially those in sports with a lot of physical contact, is the possibility of transmission from blood exposure on the playing field. Infectious disease experts have emphasized that there have been no documented cases of HIV transmission in this manner and that transmission other than by sexual contact, the sharing of needles, or exposure to infected blood products is extraordinarily unlikely. Although the NFL and other organizations have maintained that there is no need for widespread mandatory AIDS testing, this policy could, of course, change if transmission is shown to occur on the playing field. The medical staffs of NFL teams, which provide confidential HIV testing, have attempted to use the case of Magic Johnson to enlighten players about serious risks of STDs, especially AIDS.

Health after the NFL

The long-term medical and orthopedic health of retired professional football players has not yet been adequately studied. There is no conclusive evidence, for example, that such chronic medical conditions as hypertension and cardiovascular disease are any more prevalent in retired football players than in the general population.

What many specialists in sports medicine do believe is that professional football players experience a higher-than-average incidence of degenerative arthritis in various joints. Not only do collisions place joints at risk but vigorous weight training puts tremendous stress on the shoulders, elbows, and knees. Some of the strongest players routinely bench press as much as 180–225 kilograms (400–500 pounds). It should be noted, however, that many nonathletes suffer from the same arthritic conditions, such as "football knee." Heredity may actually play a more important role in the arthritis of some football players than the game of football does.

A popular stereotype of football players is that they all become obese after retirement. This belief stems from a common misconception that muscles turn into fat with inactivity. Although muscles cannot, in fact, turn into fat, diminished activity will result in decreased muscle mass and can be accompanied by increased body fat if a player does not reduce his caloric intake. In fact, many former professional football players maintain excellent fitness throughout their lifetime, and their health risks tend not to be any greater than those of the general population.

Caring for players in the intensely competitive world of professional football is an ongoing challenge for the medical staff. Indeed, the team that treats the team plays a vital part not only in helping players maximize performance during their careers but also in promoting the long-term health of every team member.

Earvin ("Magic") Johnson, a star professional basketball player for the Los Angeles Lakers, announced in 1991 that he had tested positive for the human immunodeficiency virus (HIV), which causes AIDS. His announcement underlined the fact that even a great athlete can fall victim to the disease.

Housing and Health

by Stella Lowry, M.B. Ch.B.

The connection between health and the dwellings of the population is one of the most important that exists.

—Florence Nightingale

The close association between housing and health has been recognized for centuries; the Romans were aware of the problems of overcrowding, and medieval London had building codes aimed at reducing the risks of fire and collapse. It was not until the Victorian era, however, that social reformers and medical professionals came to realize the full importance of the relationship between people's homes and their physical and mental well-being.

Squalor in the cities

But what a Chaos and Confusion is there: meer fields of Grass give way to crooked Passages and quiet Lanes to smoking Factors, and these new Houses, commonly built by the London workmen, are often burning and frequently tumbling down. . . . Thus London grows more Monstrous, Straggling and out of all Shape.

London, *c.* 1700, as described above by the contemporary British writer Peter Ackroyd in his 1985 novel *Hawksmoor,* was a filthy, disordered, and thoroughly disagreeable place. By the beginning of the 19th century, with the Industrial Revolution in England in full swing and the city's population swelling, living conditions for ordinary Londoners were even more wretched than in Ackroyd's dismal depiction.

The population of England and Wales, estimated to be about 6 million in 1750, had risen to almost 18 million by 1851. This growth was almost entirely an urban phenomenon. Liverpool, for example, grew from just over 20,000 in 1750 to 138,000 by 1820. The urban population explosion created a severe shortage of houses that pushed the laboring classes into more and more crowded and unsanitary accommodations. The word *slum,* referring to "a thickly populated neighborhood . . . where the houses and the conditions of life are of a squalid and wretched character," was coined in the early 19th century.

Stella Lowry, M.B. Ch.B., is Assistant Editor of the British Medical Journal.

Although social reformers publicly deplored the dreadful living conditions of urban working families, it was not until the introduction of social statistics—beginning with a system for registering births and deaths—that the full implications of poor housing were realized. It soon became apparent that death rates were higher in districts where poverty and overcrowding prevailed, and the vast health inequities of rich and poor became a matter of public record. In Liverpool in 1840, for example, the average life expectancy of a doctor or lawyer was 35 years, compared with 22 years for a grocer or draper; a laborer might reasonably expect to reach the ripe age of 15.

Sharing rooms, beds, and sickness

"Hard times" characterized life for the poor in Victorian Britain, and the squalid state of their dwellings was only one factor. Nonetheless, it was a factor that was amenable to change, and there was no shortage of those dedicated to bringing the disgraceful state of affairs to public—and parliamentary—attention. Edwin Chadwick, Thomas Southwood Smith, Florence Nightingale, Anthony Ashley Cooper (the earl of Shaftesbury), Joseph

Wood engraving after Gustave Doré, 1872; photograph, The Granger Collection

Rowntree and his son Benjamin, and others painstakingly documented the wretched living conditions of urban laborers and agitated for change. In his study of the "wage-earning classes" in York in 1899, Benjamin Rowntree, for example, found that a tenth of them lived more than two to a room. The same level of overcrowding could be found in many other British cities.

The detrimental effects of inadequate and substandard housing were perhaps best illustrated by the situation in the so-called common lodging houses of 19th-century Britain. Intended primarily to provide basic accommodation for single working men for a few nights, these fetid, warrenlike buildings often housed vagrants, prostitutes, and thieves and were sometimes home to large families for weeks at a time. Describing the conditions he witnessed in the "lowest" (*i.e.*, cheapest) of these unsavory domiciles in his book *London Labour and the London Poor* (1851–62), the English journalist and social reformer Henry Mayhew observed, "All was delapidation, filth, and noisomeness." Of the daily life of one lodging-house denizen, Mayhew wrote:

In the morning he drew, for purposes of ablution, a basinfull of water from a pailfull kept in the room. In the water were floating alive, or apparently alive, bugs and lice, which my informant was convinced had fallen from the ceiling, shaken off by the tread of some one walking in the rickety apartments above!

Another lodger told Mayhew how he regularly collected handfuls of bugs from his bedclothes and crushed them under the base of a candlestick. He also said he had "slept in rooms so crammed with sleepers . . . that their breaths in the dead of night and in the unventilated chamber, rose . . . 'in one foul, choking steam of stench.'" Understandably, infectious diseases such as cholera, typhus, and tuberculosis were rampant in these establishments. An outbreak of typhus in Leeds in 1851 was traced to one such dwelling, and this incident paved the way for the passage of Shaftesbury's Common Lodging Houses Acts, under which these buildings were required to be registered and inspected and to meet minimum standards of cleanliness, ventilation, and space.

Other housing reforms were introduced on moral rather than health grounds. Chadwick and other advocates of the poor, making door-to-door surveys of English tenements, witnessed sights that deeply shocked their middle-class Victorian sensibilities: dark, airless rooms in which people of both sexes and all ages were obliged to share beds. Mayhew, writing again of what he had seen in the lodging houses, described these conditions as follows:

The indiscriminate admixture of the sexes among adults, in many of these places, is another evil. Even in some houses considered of the better sort, men and women, husbands and wives, old and young, strangers and acquaintances, sleep in the same apartment, and if they choose, in the same bed. . . . There is no provision for purposes of decency in some of the places I have been describing.

The problems of inadequate housing were not, of course, confined to British cities but were characteristic of urban enclaves in every country touched by industrialization, the United States and much of continental Europe included. In Hamburg, Germany, for example, the population doubled

Two views of London in the 1870s (above and opposite page) capture the squalid conditions of life in the grime-encrusted slums and airless back alleys of that industrial metropolis.

In the second half of the 19th century, social activists such as Anthony Ashley Cooper, the 7th earl of Shaftesbury (above), committed to improving the lives of working people in Britain, went to view first hand the squalid conditions that prevailed in the slums of the burgeoning industrial cities. Often these well-bred Victorians were shocked by what they saw. Some of the worst circumstances were found in the multiple-occupancy dwellings known as common lodging houses. In a typical lodging-house room (below), children and adults of both sexes were obliged to share beds. Not surprisingly, infectious diseases such as typhus and tuberculosis were rampant in these establishments.

in size between 1850 and 1880; so many people moved to the port city that by the late 1870s fewer than 60% of the city's inhabitants had been born there. The influx of residents during this period resulted in overcrowding, inadequate sanitation, and continuous outbreaks of infectious disease. As rents increased, laborers' families typically took in lodgers, usually single men seeking work at the docks. One such family consisting of a tannery worker, his wife, their five children, and a lodger—described by Richard J. Evans in his book *Death in Hamburg*—lived in a two-room apartment without a toilet. All five children slept in a single bed. As late as the 1890s sanitary facilities remained primitive. In one building in an old quarter of Hamburg, a lavatory under a staircase in the courtyard served all who lived in the surrounding apartments. It contained a bucket that was emptied once a week. According to Evans, the situation was no better in the newer, cheaply built housing blocks in outlying areas, where one water closet on every floor was shared by an even larger number of people.

In New York City the 1834 annual report issued by the health inspector stated that the city's high death rate was related to overcrowding and filthy conditions. A U.S. Senate report issued in 1859 cited New York housing for overcrowding, inadequate light and ventilation, and insufficient sewerage. Certainly the tenements of New York rivaled those of London, Liverpool, and Hamburg in terms of density, filth, and disease. Some of the most compelling accounts of living conditions in New York in the second half of the 19th century were written by Jacob Riis, a photojournalist who documented the appalling situation of the city's urban poor in his book *How the Other Half Lives* (1890):

It is said that nowhere in the world are so many people crowded together on a square mile as here. . . . The Sanitary policeman, whose beat this is, will tell you that [this building] contains thirty-six families, but the term [family] has a widely different meaning here. . . . In this house, where a case of smallpox was reported, there were fifty-eight babies and thirty-eight children that were over five years of age. In Essex Street, two small rooms in a six-story tenement were made to hold a "family" of father and mother, twelve children, and six boarders. . . . These are samples of the

packing of the population that has run up the record here to the rate of 330,000 per square mile. The densest crowding of Old London . . . never got beyond 175,000.

Riis's writings and his poignant photographs of New York slum dwellers were an important force in the crusade for housing reform.

Good housing is good medicine

It is perhaps not an exaggeration to say that the major advances in public health in the late 19th century—the decline of the infectious scourges of cholera, typhoid, and tuberculosis—owed more to the housing movement than to innovations in the diagnosis and treatment of disease. London physician John Snow's demonstration of the link between cholera and polluted drinking water and epidemiological studies by others that showed the association between overcrowding and tuberculosis dramatically emphasized the extent to which the domestic environment could affect health. Unfortunately, the interest of the medical community in housing and other public health issues, embraced with such great enthusiasm during the Victorian era, was superseded in the 20th century by a philosophy and practice that focused more on curing illness than preventing it. With the advent of antibiotics in the 1940s, doctors became obsessed with treating and curing disease. Thus, the appreciation of the close connection between housing and health was all but forgotten. In recent years, however, the emphasis has shifted once again, and health care professionals now have renewed concern for these issues. The focus is no longer solely on the dwellings of the poorest segments of society but on how housing affects everyone's health.

Health care today ideally involves a holistic approach to patients—that is, treating the whole person rather than a limb, an organ, or an ailment. This approach requires, among other things, that physicians have an awareness of their patients' domestic environments. Furthermore, recent changes in health care delivery—in particular, increased emphasis on outpatient

195

treatment, same-day surgery, and short hospital stays—mean that sick people are now spending more time at home. Practitioners must therefore understand what kinds of living conditions their patients are coming from and returning to and how these may affect their health. For example, a patient undergoing knee surgery might formerly have spent several days in the hospital recuperating. Today he or she will probably have outpatient arthroscopic surgery and leave the clinic on crutches shortly after the operation. How will the patient who lives alone in a house with a steep flight of stairs manage?

Some of the current health problems seen by primary-care practitioners are clearly the legacy of construction techniques that were popular in the 1950s and '60s. The concrete-slab high-rise housing projects of that era, built primarily to house low-income families, have had notably detrimental effects on both the physical and mental well-being of residents. Physicians—particularly those who treat the economically disadvantaged—need to have an appreciation of these interactions.

Finally, there are compelling economic reasons for the revival of medical interest in the link between housing and health. Health care that focuses on treatment at the expense of prevention is highly costly to society in the long term. Governments that pay some or all of the costs of medical care are now acknowledging that preventive care makes good economic sense, and they are giving it a high priority. Consequently, physicians are being urged to learn more about how their patients' life-styles, habits, and environments may predispose them to disease.

Problems of studying housing and health

Although common sense suggests that poor housing would have an adverse effect on health, it can be difficult to prove that this is so. Moreover, there is surprisingly little strong scientific evidence of a link. One of the first difficulties encountered by anyone trying to study the effects of housing on health is the problem of defining the terms.

Blocks of cheerless-looking modern flats loom on the horizon of a run-down older London neighborhood. When they were constructed in the 1950s and '60s, these high-rise developments were intended to provide clean, low-cost housing for urban working families. In fact, such buildings proved to have a variety of detrimental effects on the physical and mental health of their inhabitants—a living demonstration of the principle that housing is a great deal more than structures that provide certain basic necessities. When defining "housing," public health experts take into account, among other things, the suitability of the buildings for those who will live in them and the proximity of transportation, shopping facilities, and other amenities.

J. Allan Cash

What is housing? Exactly what does the concept of "housing" include? Does one consider simply the basic construction—*i.e.,* a dwelling with a roof and walls? What about amenities such as water supply, heat, ventilation, sewage disposal, and electricity? Do interior furnishings and decor play a part?

Certainly some houses are so badly constructed as to be hazardous to life and limb, and a very simple definition, based on the brick-and-mortar shell, is enough to encompass the health risks and implications. For most discussions of the impact of housing on health, however, a broader definition is needed. The public utilities that supply a house are important in maintaining the health of its occupants; even a well-designed and soundly built home can become unhealthy if it is so overcrowded that the electrical circuits, water supply, and sewer systems cannot cope with the demand. Building materials and interior furnishings may contain hazardous chemicals that can adversely affect the health of the occupants.

Sometimes it is important to use a very broad definition of "housing" that includes the surrounding neighborhood. It would be foolish to study the effects of high-rise living on the psychological health of single mothers, for example, without taking into consideration factors such as the proximity of shops and health care facilities, access to public transportation, and availability of community support programs.

What is health? "Health," too, can be difficult to define. The World Health Organization favors a definition that encompasses total physical and emotional well-being. For most practical purposes, however, this ideal is unrealistic because those things are difficult to measure. Some studies rely on numbers of physician consultations or hospital admissions as indications of relative good or ill health. This system assumes that such statistics accurately reflect the individual health status of all members of a society. All people do not have equal access to health care though, and many ill people never seek care. Another option is to use self-reported assessments of health based on questionnaires, but this technique raises the possibility of reporting bias—for example, persons living in very poor housing may remember being ill more accurately or may exaggerate their ill health, while someone whose home provides more comforts may minimize his or her health problems.

Cause or effect? Many other confounding variables and biases further complicate investigations into the effects of housing on health. For example, in communities where good housing is in short supply, people need to be strong and assertive (or be represented by strong public advocates) if they are to obtain a decent place to live. People who are already disadvantaged by failing health may be less able to compete in the housing market and therefore end up living in the least desirable dwellings. Outside observers might erroneously conclude that poor housing was the cause, rather than the effect, of the health problems.

Researchers must also be aware of the way in which various social, economic, and environmental influences may interact to produce observed health effects. For example, children who live in damp houses are at increased risk of developing asthma. They are also likely to come from lower

A youngster in the Bronx, New York, surveys a grim urban landscape. High-rise public housing projects often have a grave impact on the emotional well-being of residents.

197

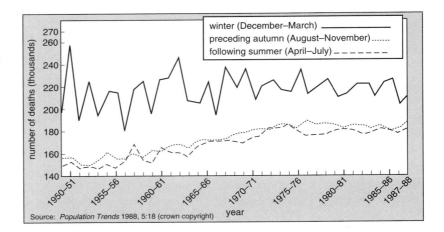

A graph showing seasonal mortality in the U.K. over a period of several decades demonstrates the markedly higher death rates that prevail during the damp, chill winter months.

Source: *Population Trends* 1988, 5:18 (crown copyright)

socioeconomic groups. Smoking is more common in lower income and education groups, and childhood asthma is known to be associated with exposure to cigarette smoke. Thus, the confounding variables of poverty and passive smoking must be separated from the effects of damp housing before any cause-and-effect relationship between housing and asthma can be proved.

A further difficulty is that the association between housing and health does not lend itself to traditional methods of scientific study. It is rarely possible to change a single aspect of people's housing and see an obvious, measurable health gain. For one thing, the effects of housing often accrue over a long term, and large numbers of people would need to be studied for many years before any effect would be evident. It is also difficult to establish a proper control group in such studies—people whose housing conditions would remain unchanged during the course of the experiment. Furthermore, it would be almost impossible for researchers to prevent their subjects from knowing the details of the experiment, as is the case, for example, in trials of new medications when patients take a drug or a placebo without knowing which they are receiving. There have been a few before-and-after studies of health in people who have been rehoused from slums, but because there is a tendency for those who want new housing to exaggerate their health problems, any improvement seen after relocation might be more apparent then real.

Despite these problems, physicians, social workers, economists, and a variety of other professionals are in a position to directly observe the effects of housing on health. Such specialists have identified several key elements of living conditions that have a major impact on physical and mental well-being.

Cold, mold, and wheezing

Some of the strongest scientific evidence of a link between housing and health concerns the effects of cold and damp indoor environments. Very cold weather is unequivocally known to cause health problems. In Britain, which is notorious for its chill, damp climate, about 40,000 more people die each year during the winter months than during the summer. Most of this increase in deaths occurs among elderly people, yet few of the deaths are from hypothermia (very low body temperature due to exposure to cold). Most are the result of exacerbation of existing conditions: respiratory problems, for example, become increasingly common at living temperatures below about 16° C (61° F), and at lower temperatures cardiovascular changes increase the risk of stroke and heart attack.

Many British studies have shown an association between damp housing and respiratory disease, especially in children, and damp conditions indoors encourage the proliferation of mold and house dust mites, both of which are known causes of asthma. The associations are not straightforward, however. Some researchers have found a relationship between damp homes and parents' reports of respiratory ailments in their children, but they saw no correlation with the families' number of doctor's visits or medical tests of the children's lung function. This discrepancy could be explained by reporting bias: parents living in damp, moldy homes may be more likely than those in dry homes to notice wheezing in their children or to report ill health. Some of the early studies did not control adequately for confounding variables such as income, social class, and parental smoking, all now recognized as important in determining a child's respiratory health. However, more recent investigations have taken into account the effects of these other factors, and their findings confirm a relationship between damp housing and poor health. The evidence is sufficiently strong that in the British courts several lawsuits have been settled in favor of tenants who claimed that their health or that of their children was being jeopardized by their wet, chilly homes.

Of course, any home can be made warm and dry if enough money is spent to heat it. In the U.K. the poor spend twice as much (as a percentage of their income) on heating as do the more affluent. The people who live in cold, damp houses are, however, the least likely to be able to pay large fuel bills or to have central heating (which has become common in Britain

Damp homes and children's health			
symptoms	housing conditions (%)		
	dry	damp only	damp and moldy
bodily aches and pains	12.5	21.6	15.7
diarrhea	18.5	21.6	18.2
wheezing	16.3	18.7	27.0
vomiting	12.0	18.0	19.0
sore throat	30.4	24.5	42.3
irritability	12.5	20.1	20.4
tiredness	13.6	20.1	17.5
persistent headaches	12.5	13.7	21.2
earache	14.7	10.8	17.2
fever	11.4	18.0	24.5
feeling depressed or unhappy	10.9	18.0	15.3
temper tantrums	20.1	26.6	27.0
bedwetting	22.3	20.9	23.4
poor appetite	16.8	26.6	24.8
persistent cough	31.0	37.4	42.7
runny nose	39.1	40.3	50.7
any symptom	79.9	85.6	90.5

Adapted from Stephen D. Platt et al., "Damp Housing, Mould Growth, and Symptomatic Health State," British Medical Journal, vol. 298, no. 6689 (June 24, 1989), pp. 1673–78

In 1989 Scottish researchers reported on their survey of families in public housing projects in London, Edinburgh, and Glasgow. Parents were asked detailed questions about their children's health (1,169 children living in 597 households) during the two weeks preceding the interview. The investigators also inspected the homes for signs of dampness and mold growth and measured spore concentration in the indoor air. They concluded that dampness and mold have adverse effects on children's health and are an important public health issue that deserves more attention.

only in fairly recent times). Many who live in drafty older houses try to economize by heating only certain rooms, but this practice merely sets up temperature differentials that encourage condensation and the growth of mold, contributing to the development of allergies and respiratory disorders. Laundry hung up to dry indoors further increases humidity, condensation, and mold. In newer apartment buildings, especially the high-rise projects designed for low-income families, cracks in concrete slabs and ill-fitting windows and doors are sources of drafts and water leakage.

Despite proof of the health hazards associated with dampness—and court actions upholding the connection—it remains difficult to persuade landlords to remedy the problem. Perhaps economic arguments would provide a greater incentive to them than the prospect of health gains for their tenants. Although it is costly to heat a damp house adequately, the structural elements of a damp building—wood, metal, concrete—decay faster then those of a dry one, and correcting underlying structural faults can be cost-effective. For example, a team of experts from Glasgow inspected one housing development that was plagued by dampness and suggested a series of structural modifications designed to correct the problem. It was estimated that the proposed changes could potentially increase the life of the buildings from 15 to 35 years at a cost of approximately £17,000 ($30,000) per individual unit, at the same time cutting the residents' heating bills in half.

Stairways, fires, and the high toll of home injuries

Every year about 5,500 people die in accidents in British homes, and more than three million require medical treatment. (U.S. statistics for 1990 show that 21,500 people were killed and 3.2 million injured in domestic accidents.) People in the U.K. spend about 80% of their time indoors, and three-quarters of this in their own homes, so it is hardly surprising that a large proportion of accidents occur at home. Young children, people with chronic diseases, and the elderly—society's most vulnerable groups—spend an even greater proportion of their time at home and are at particular risk from domestic accidents.

Common hazards around the home

- windows without locks or devices to limit how wide they open
- balconies with low, unsteady, or inadequate railings
- nonsafety glass in windows, doors, panels, and furnishings
- old or overloaded electrical wiring
- faulty electrical appliances
- faulty or incorrectly vented heating equipment
- inadequate lighting in stairwells
- medicines and household chemicals not kept in locked cabinets
- open fireplaces and stairs without protective gates in homes where young children live
- improperly fenced-in swimming pools and garden ponds
- storage cupboards that can be reached only with a stepladder
- shelves, cupboards, or drying racks above the burners or heating elements of the kitchen range
- loose mats or rugs on slippery floors
- absence of smoke detectors in main escape routes

Many people assume that accidents are unavoidable, but in fact most can be anticipated. That this is true is apparent from the study of children's accidents, in which the pattern of injuries almost always mirrors the developmental stage of the child. Thus, small babies are at greatest risk of being dropped, whereas older infants may roll off beds and other furniture; toddlers often fall after climbing onto high objects, stumble against the sharp edges of furniture and other household objects, or pull hot or heavy items down onto themselves. Older children spend more time playing outdoors and are at greater risk than younger ones of being injured on roads— *e.g.,* being hit by a car. A rudimentary understanding of child development and a bit of imagination allow many potential hazards in the home to be identified and eliminated.

Likewise, it is fairly easy to identify potential dangers to elderly people by recognizing how aging can limit people's abilities. Failing sight is a common cause of domestic injuries in the elderly. Many studies have shown that lighting levels in most homes fall far short of the standards required in industry. Elderly people (or any others with poor sight) are at increased risk of burns when they cook in dimly lit kitchens and are in greater danger of falling if they try to negotiate ill-lit flights of stairs. The remedy can be as simple as installing fluorescent lighting and painting the room a color that will reflect as much light as possible.

Simple, low-cost measures such as removing unnecessary furniture and other obstacles, installing nonslip pads under loose rugs or mats, and wearing comfortable, well-fitting shoes with nonslip soles are effective safety precautions for elderly people who are unsteady on their feet. Ideally any stairs in their homes should be arranged in short flights to minimize the distance that they could fall, and doors should not open onto stairwells. Certainly, furniture should not be placed at the bottom of a flight of stairs. Adaptations to the home in the form of grab rails, motorized chair lifts, and the like should be made only after consultation with a trained professional, such as an occupational or physical therapist, as too often people make expensive mistakes when choosing such modifications.

There are some home hazards that affect people regardless of age or frailty. One of the most common causes of death and injury at home is fire. Many house fires are caused by faulty wiring; ideally, domestic wiring should be checked every five years. Another major factor is the careless use of smoking materials. Installing smoke alarms will reduce the risk of serious injury should a fire occur. Homes occupied by more than one family pose a particular threat, as they are often poorly maintained and overcrowded, have overloaded electrical circuits, and may have inadequate escape routes.

If the causes of domestic accidents are so easy to identify, why do injuries continue to occur? One problem is that the people who live in the most rundown, poorly maintained, and hazardous homes are usually those who are least able to afford structural and other safety-related modifications. There is a strong correlation between the incidence of children's injuries and the socioeconomic status of families. Another major problem is that minimum safety standards cannot easily be enforced in private

Fires are one of the most common causes of injury and death at home. Older buildings—which often have obsolete wiring, overloaded electrical circuits, and inadequate escape routes—are among the most hazardous.

Homelessness was an established feature of urban life in Victorian England. A mid-19th-century engraving shows destitute men, women, and children huddled against the bitter cold as they wait for a night's shelter in one of London's several workhouses. Upon admittance, each was given six ounces of bread and one ounce of cheese; boards strewn with straw served as beds. In return for this "charity," vagrants were expected to perform three hours of labor.

homes. Even when builders are required by law to install certain safety features, proper functioning of those systems often depends on regular maintenance. People can be advised about safety hazards, but rarely can they be forced to do something about them. Research has shown that disseminating general information about injury prevention has little impact on people's behavior. They are much more likely to take action if they receive specific advice that is tailored to their individual circumstances, including practical information about how to implement change.

"Slab-block blues"

The health consequences of poor housing are not solely physical. Although the psychological effects may be hard to prove, again common sense and anecdotal observation play a part in documenting these influences.

Many aspects of housing could be expected to affect mental health. Overcrowding is an obvious one, but there is surprisingly little evidence that limited space per se has a harmful effect on psychological well-being (although the potential risks to physical health from inadequate sanitation are clear). Studies from Hong Kong of people who have a median allocation of only about 4 square meters (43 square feet)—a small amount by Western standards—have found that their mental health does not suffer. There is evidence that it is not the amount of space individuals have that matters as much as the degree of their personal control over it. This observation may help to explain some of the detrimental effects on mental health of living in modern housing developments or apartment buildings where there is a great deal of communal and very little personal space. In such dwellings there is often widespread littering and noise, as well as high rates of vandalism, burglary, and other crimes.

The type of housing most often blamed for psychological problems is the high-rise project that was the most popular form of public housing in the 1950s and '60s. In these structures lack of personal control over the immediate environment is often compounded by shoddy construction and the absence of community spirit. People become isolated in their own little "boxes," rarely meeting their neighbors but often subjected to the sounds of their radios, televisions, and family squabbles. In Britain the term *slab-block blues* was coined to describe the depression experienced by many project residents.

The depression associated with slab-block living is a good example of how difficult it can be to sort out the causes of observed health problems. Many studies of the mental health of high-rise inhabitants have failed to distinguish the contributions of social factors such as poverty, isolation from the extended family, and single parenthood. High-rise apartments are not intrinsically bad or unhealthy. In many U.S. cities, for example, they are among the most desirable and exclusive homes, but they must be well maintained. Then, too, high-rise living is not for everyone—it is, for example, rarely suitable for families with young children.

The tragedy of homelessness

It would be impossible to discuss the effects of housing and health today without considering the crisis of homelessness. Like other housing problems, it has a history rooted in the origins of urban industrial life. It had emerged as a major social issue in Britain by the mid-19th century—Friedrich Engels, the German political theorist, reported that in 1844 the homeless in London numbered about 50,000.

Mayhew interviewed many of the London homeless and inspected the city's Asylum for the Houseless Poor, which provided nighttime shelter for about 200 persons. A ragged, barefooted horde would gather outside the doors of this institution every evening waiting for admittance. Even Mayhew, who had observed much poverty and hardship, was deeply affected:

Laurie Sparham—Network/Matrix

A man camped in London's Charing Cross rail station advertises his plight—he is homeless, jobless, and not eligible for welfare ("no dole"). With no permanent address, most homeless persons find it difficult to obtain social services, receive welfare payments, or get medical care for chronic illnesses such as tuberculosis that require prolonged treatment. For such individuals even a minor ailment can turn into a major health problem.

The children of two homeless families play in the New York City hotel room that serves as a temporary residence for one family. A true picture of the extent of homelessness today must include not only those sleeping on park benches and under viaducts but also the countless individuals and families living in shelters and welfare hotels. These settings have their own health hazards; accidents are common, and the incidence of gastrointestinal and respiratory infections and depression is high. Moreover, the women often receive no prenatal care, which frequently contributes to adverse pregnancy outcomes (graph, below), and the children may fail to receive regular immunization against childhood diseases.

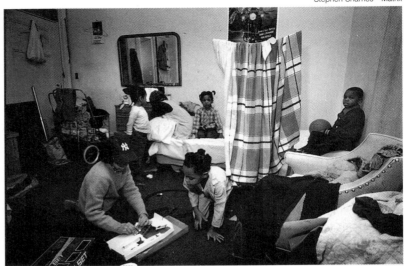

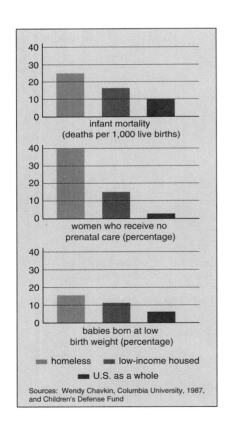

infant mortality
(deaths per 1,000 live births)

women who receive no
prenatal care (percentage)

babies born at low
birth weight (percentage)

■ homeless ■ low-income housed
■ U.S. as a whole

Sources: Wendy Chavkin, Columbia University, 1987, and Children's Defense Fund

It is a terrible thing, indeed, to look down upon the squalid crowd from one of the upper windows of the institution. There they stand shivering in the snow, with their thin, cobwebby garments hanging in tatters about them. Many are without shirts; with their bare skin showing through the rents and gaps of their clothes, like the hide of a dog with the mange. Some have their greasy coats and trousers tied round their wrists and ankles with string, to prevent the piercing wind from blowing up them. A few are without shoes; and these keep one foot only to the ground, while the bare flesh that has had to tramp through the snow is blue and livid-looking as half cooked meat. . . . To hear the cries of the hungry, shivering children, and the wrangling of the greedy men, scrambling for a bed and a pound of dry bread, is a thing to haunt one for life. . . . the shirtless, shoeless, breadless, homeless; in a word, the very poorest of this the very richest city in the world.

Few countries today are immune to the problem of homelessness, and even the world's wealthiest nations with well-established social services—including the U.K., the U.S., and most European countries—have substantial numbers of homeless people. Although the word *homeless* typically conjures up a picture of people sleeping on park benches and under viaducts, people whose circumstances force them to live in temporary shelters or unfit accommodations must also be considered homeless. In Britain there are probably over two million homeless people, yet fewer than 400,000 appear in the official statistics, and only about 3,000 sleep on the streets on any given night. The traditional image of the homeless person is of a down-and-out alcoholic or a crazed eccentric who has rejected society. Certainly there will always be some homeless individuals who have chosen to live that way; for most, however, homelessness is an unwanted condition and a tragedy.

The causes of homelessness are legion—mental illness, unemployment, breakdown of the family structure, bereavement, domestic violence, recent discharge from the armed forces, and so on. Whatever the initial cause, once a person becomes homeless, it can be very difficult to break out of what becomes a vicious cycle. It is hard to find a place to live when one has no money for a rent deposit, but it can be almost impossible to find a job to earn the money if one is sleeping on the streets and living hand-to-mouth. Welfare payments are, in effect, limited to people who can cite a permanent address. Thus, homeless people truly become disenfranchised.

The health effects of homelessness are too numerous to list. Tuberculosis, AIDS, pneumonia, severe skin infections, and malnutrition are all common. Ailments that would be a minor nuisance to most people can create major health problems for the homeless. Even fairly simple cuts and scratches can become secondarily infected and, without proper care, are unlikely to heal. Chronic medical conditions are almost impossible to manage. A homeless person with diabetes has no access to a refrigerator for storing insulin, cannot eat properly and at regular intervals, and finds it difficult to avoid such complications as foot sores when prevention requires that the feet be kept warm, clean, and dry. How does a homeless person with asthma, epilepsy, or schizophrenia obtain regular care and monitoring of long-term drug treatment?

It is not just the street homeless who have medical problems. People living in unfit or overcrowded shelters and welfare hotels are at increased risk of gastrointestinal and respiratory infections. Many pregnant women in these circumstances do not have adequate prenatal care or proper nutrition; a survey by New York City health officials in 1987 found that 40% of homeless women had no prenatal care during their pregnancies. These women are more likely than others to need hospital admission during their pregnancies. Their babies are likely to be of low birth weight and at higher-than-average risk of dying in infancy. Their children are less likely to be fully immunized against common childhood diseases and often suffer from malnutrition. A study of families in New York City welfare hotels found that 92% had no refrigerators in their hotel rooms and none had their own stoves. The risk of accidents is increased in these temporary accommodations; privacy is virtually nonexistent; and depression is common. Abuse and neglect are also pervasive problems.

It is obviously critical for any society to provide health care for its

John Lei—Stock, Boston

The only way to truly solve the serious and pervasive health problems of the homeless is to eliminate the problem of homelessness.

homeless, but the best ways of doing so are the subject of debate. Some authorities favor providing special outreach medical services for the homeless, such as mobile clinics that travel to places frequented by homeless people to provide them with primary health care. In New York City, for example, the New York Hospital-Cornell Medical Center operates a mobile clinic that provides free care to homeless children. In London's Soho district a walk-in clinic provides primary care; no appointments are necessary, so medical care is more accessible to this hard-to-reach population.

These kinds of services have certain advantages; they deliver immediate health care efficiently and effectively, but follow-up in these circumstances is difficult. Some also argue that providing separate services to the homeless in separate facilities only isolates them more from the rest of society—and thus runs the risk of marginalizing them still further. On the other hand, it can be difficult to provide care for homeless people within mainstream facilities—not least because other patients are often offended by the presence of a ragged, smelly "street person" in the waiting room. Also to be taken into consideration are such practical difficulties as maintaining continuity in the medical records of vagrants and arranging for follow-up appointments with someone who has no address. Even if primary care can be provided for this group, there remains the challenge of ensuring proper hospital care for people who do not come into any particular "catchment area" and have nowhere to go on discharge.

There is no single, simple solution to these problems, and for the foreseeable future some combination of services will probably be needed. In the long run, however, the only real solution to the health needs of homeless people is to solve the problem of homelessness.

Everybody's concern

The relationship between housing and health is too intricate to consider in depth in a single article, but the foregoing may at least provide some insight into this vital area of investigation. Although many of the examples cited are from the U.K., the lessons learned are applicable everywhere that people live in conditions adversely affecting their well-being. There are, of course, many potentially harmful aspects of contemporary housing that have not been mentioned here—lead-containing paint; asbestos in building materials; poor ventilation and indoor air pollution due to sources as varied as radon, household cleaning products, and improperly vented cooking and heating equipment; disease-carrying vermin; and unsafe drinking water. The list could go on.

Despite the problems inherent in studying these complex problems, it is possible to gather strong evidence of the effect of housing on health, and community leaders, residents, and concerned professionals should not be daunted by the difficulties. Recent changes in health care—increased home care, the growing emphasis on preventive medicine—have made it increasingly important that everyone understands the link between housing and health. Now that housing has become firmly reestablished on the public health agenda, professionals and nonprofessionals alike must ensure that it stays there.

EDITORS' CHOICE

An address to young people on World AIDS Day

by U.S. Surgeon General
Antonia C. Novello

Excerpts from Antonia Novello's speech on Dec. 2, 1991

It is especially important for me, as surgeon general and as a pediatrician, to focus the energies of my office as well as my personal energies on the health of our nation's young people. Today, on World AIDS Day, we focus those energies on the humbling fact that the AIDS pandemic, despite our best hopes and fervent prayers, has not slowed down. It has touched all of our lives—whether directly or indirectly—in all corners of this globe. Its urgency to me as your surgeon general increases every day.

The AIDS epidemic has clearly entered the population of some 17 million U.S. young people age 13 to 19. Many of you here today are young, curious, and inquisitive. I dare to say that many of you might know more about AIDS than most. Even though that might be the case, AIDS is something we just *cannot know enough about*.

One of the biggest goals of those in the health care professions is to emphasize the *risk* of HIV. If you participate in high-risk behavior, you must be prepared to deal with the fact that you might be exposing yourself to the AIDS virus, and as such, you must learn how to protect yourself.

Let me start out by highlighting the matter with some statistics to help bring this issue closer to home.

- As of Sept. 1, 1991, there were in the U.S. 737 cases of AIDS in young people age 13 to 19—less than half of 1% of the total 191,601 reported cases.

Not too much to be worried about, you might say? Well, maybe not. But let me give you a few other numbers.

- As of September 1, fully 7,704 cases of AIDS reported in the U.S. were in young people age 21 to 24—4% of the total number of cases and 10 times the number among those age 13 to 19.

Still not too worried? Now let me give you two other statistics.

- In June 1991 the number of AIDS cases in persons age 25 to 29 constituted 16% of all U.S. AIDS cases, meaning that *over 20% of AIDS cases are in persons under 29.*

Finally, another fact to add to this.

- Two-thirds of the 12 million cases of sexually transmitted diseases in the U.S. occur in persons under the age of 25.

Now you ask: So what does this mean? What it means is that the combination of HIV/AIDS and young people is like an accident waiting to happen—it is like putting a match next to a can of gasoline. Let me put these figures in perspective.

- The median latency period—or the period between being infected with HIV and the onset of AIDS—is estimated to be about 10 years. In other words, *most persons under age 29 with AIDS could have been infected with HIV before they were 21.*

- The prevalence of sexually transmitted diseases, or STDs, among young people is particularly alarming. In the U.S. *an adolescent gets an STD every*

30 seconds, and eight million STD cases are found in persons under age 25—the highest rates of gonorrhea and the highest rates of chlamydia of any age group!

I am particularly concerned about this because it is known that the presence of STDs may make a person more susceptible to HIV infection. It is absolutely essential that this message be heeded in the adolescent population. Let me give you another fact.

• In testimony before the National AIDS Commission in March 1991, Dr. Robert Johnson, a specialist in adolescent medicine at the University of Medicine and Dentistry of New Jersey, stated that the last four cases of heterosexually transmitted AIDS in New Jersey were in adolescents—and that they were adolescents who, interestingly enough, had been drinking the highly potent alcoholic beverage Cisco and *forgot* to use any protection.

There you have it. Sexual and risk-taking behavior in young people today might be a clear path to the probability of HIV infection, of AIDS, and consequently of premature death!

Let me talk about the two known avenues of HIV infection in young people—drug use and unprotected sex. In young people today, heterosexual transmission is the usual route of infection. In adolescents, it is not usually intravenous drug use that is itself a risk for AIDS. Nor is it the use of unsterilized needles or the sharing of drug paraphernalia. Instead, it is drug use that *leads to* risk taking, to frequent sexual activity, and ultimately to unprotected sex.

Let us look at the epidemiology of drug use in high school and college students as an indication of the general pattern of use in young people. Let me remind you that when we talk of drug abuse we are talking here of not only illicit drugs but also the abuse of alcohol and other substances.

• It is estimated that 3% of high school students use intravenous drugs, including cocaine or heroin—a direct avenue to HIV infection, especially through infected needles. I must add that steroid use—popular among athletes—is intravenous drug use as well!

• Nearly half (48%) of high school seniors have used an illicit drug. Two percent of students have used crack in the past year. And trading sex for drugs is frequently the way adolescents get into crack.

• Over half (57%) of senior high school students drink alcohol, and one-third (33%) of seniors drink five or more drinks in a row. Nearly one-half million college students, or 4%, drink every day. And college students get drunk more often than their counterparts not in college.

With regard to sex, let me share with you what we do know about adolescent sexual activity and how that might relate to HIV and AIDS:

• By their senior year, the majority of adolescents have already engaged in sexual intercourse. Among adolescents age 15 to 19 surveyed in 1988, 52% of women and 60% of men reported that they had engaged in sexual intercourse. The proportion of women who are sexually active increased between 1970 and 1988.

• Among adolescents in the U.S., the average age of the first sexual experience is 16 years. However, in some urban areas it may be as early as 12 years of age.

- Approximately 21% of high school students in 1989 said they had engaged in sex with four or more partners.

- Many adolescents know how HIV is transmitted; however, 63% of those who are sexually active do not consistently use condoms. For example, 99% of adolescents surveyed in Massachusetts in 1990 knew that HIV can be contracted through heterosexual and homosexual sexual activity. However, in a recent survey, 40% of sexually active adolescents reported "sometimes" using a condom, and 23% reported "never" using one.

- A substantial proportion of adolescents engage in anal intercourse, a principle risk factor for HIV. One survey indicated that between 10 and 26% of adolescents practice anal intercourse. Moreover, a recent study conducted among University of Puerto Rico students found that 31% of women and 40% of men practiced anal sex.

- Sexual contact is responsible for a greater proportion of adolescent AIDS cases than is intravenous drug use; however, the use of alcohol and drugs, including crack, increases the likelihood of engaging in unsafe sexual behavior.

- Some 40% of adolescents are exposed to AIDS through sexual contact, compared with 9% who are exposed through intravenous drug use.

- Since 1990, heterosexual contact has surpassed homosexual contact as the major mode of sexual transmission for adolescent AIDS. Among AIDS cases in adolescents age 13 to 19 reported in 1990, 51% of females and 4% of males contracted HIV through heterosexual contact; 29% of adolescent males were exposed to AIDS through homosexual/bisexual contact.

The need to address the issue of HIV infection among young people is absolutely essential *now.* The legal, ethical, social, and medical challenges that young people present to the current legal and health care system will make this a difficult process. For example, how should public health specialists handle the issues of HIV testing and partner notification among people your age? This is a particularly complex ethical dilemma for health care providers and local governments; they must balance parental rights against the autonomy of the young person, including the young person's right to confidentiality.

The legal status of young people in general presents a quandary to physicians, and a quandary that varies from state to state. For the purposes of treatment of an STD, for example, some states consider minors to be "emancipated" and thus not in need of parental consent for testing, counseling, and treatment. However, only 11 states legally classify HIV infection and AIDS as an STD.

In addition, the stage of their cognitive and emotional development influences the way in which young people understand and process standardized consent procedures and medical information. Is a young person capable—and, I might add here, is *anyone* capable—of consenting to HIV testing, counseling, and treatment, given the devastating impact on their lives of a positive HIV test result?

AIDS in young people also presents a plethora of *social* issues. As all of you can attest, adolescence is a period of profound physiological, psychological, and social change. Many young people often feel alienated from

the rest of society, and society, in turn, often finds it difficult to understand their emotions and behaviors. This alienation is significantly heightened in the presence of HIV. As Dr. Karen Hein, the head of an adolescent AIDS program in New York City, emphasizes, the behaviors that lead to HIV infection in adolescents are often deemed socially unacceptable, and there is a temptation to characterize most of the adolescent population as "high risk" or "hard to reach."

It is crucial for adults to understand that *most* young people find them-selves at times in situations that are risky for acquiring HIV, even if these situations are encountered only infrequently. It is certainly true that not all young people are at equal risk of acquiring HIV. Those who are at highest risk—the homeless, runaways, and prostitutes, particularly those in high-HIV-incidence areas—should be regarded as "youth in high-risk situations" not "high-risk youth." The emphasis should be on helping young people escape these situations rather than on assigning blame.

Those of us in the health professions must begin to address the many unanswered *medical* questions about HIV infection in adolescents. We need to understand how exactly the disease progresses in young people from infection to symptomatic AIDS; we need to discover the best treat-ment approach—what specific dosages of therapeutic drugs are needed for adolescents; and we need to recognize that adolescents clearly need to be actively recruited into AIDS research and that services provided to them during such research must be sensitive to adolescent physiological and psychosocial needs. This situation demands immediate action—action that needs to be built on existing systems of health care services. Given that 40% of recent adolescent AIDS cases were linked to sexual contact and that there are behavioral and physiological relationships between HIV and other sexually transmitted diseases, we must provide HIV-prevention education at the same time we give care for other STDs.

Irrespective of their age, adolescents must be treated with respect, and an atmosphere of trust must be fostered between them and the health care provider. And although HIV prevention is one of society's most important

211

obligations, we should not ignore the issue of care for HIV-positive adolescents. Young people must receive HIV-prevention education immediately—and not in isolation but as an integral element of a comprehensive health curriculum that, in addition to education, also provides sensitive training to help adolescents deal with their sexuality and drug use. A dialogue between adolescents and their parents will be critical to such education, and the views of both should be acknowledged and accommodated.

As I stand here before you, my heart is heavy with worry about the challenges that you, our young people, face while growing up in this second decade of AIDS. Let me share with you some of the questions that our society must find answers to, which reflect *my* deepest concerns about AIDS.

● How can our society move to end discrimination against those with HIV? How can you, as young people, with fresh faces and new perspectives, help the older generation to overcome old fears, old ways of doing things that prevent the creation of an environment in which those who need our help most may seek it freely and without fear?

● How can health professionals communicate the very real benefits of testing and early intervention to young people at high risk for HIV?

● How can communities, schools, and colleges be enlisted to treat those with HIV with compassion—as human beings first?

● How can health professionals reach young people to *personalize* the risks of HIV? How can we enlist youth to help us develop HIV-prevention programs that work?

● How can the administrative and logistic barriers to care for women, for young people, and for children be removed and the care they need be provided in one place—in their communities and under one roof?

● How can young people, who may have little control within sexual relationships, be empowered to negotiate a change in the rules? And where will they find support when they make such crucial decisions?

● And, finally, given the ways in which young people become infected with HIV, how can health professionals make sure that those young people know how to protect themselves? And how can we make sure that young men share equal responsibility with young women for safer sexual practices?

It is up to all of us, but especially to you—informed and concerned young people—to alert your peers about the risks and realities of AIDS. I urge you to share with them the information you have heard here today. The biggest hurdle we face in the health care professions today is the inability to get to you and, in turn, be credible in your eyes. We must pass not judgment but *information*. I urge you all to tell your friends, your classmates, your teammates to learn *all* that they can, to become aware of the dangers if they are not knowledgeable already. As surgeon general, I am asking for your help—I cannot do it alone.

From the 1992

ENCYCLOPÆDIA BRITANNICA

From the 1992 Printing of Encyclopædia Britannica

The purpose of this section is to offer the *Medical and Health Annual*'s readers articles from the *Encyclopædia Britannica* that have recently been completely revised or rewritten. In keeping with the goal of providing the broadest possible picture of "health," this year the *Annual*'s editors have chosen to reprint the article HUMAN MOTIVATION—a selection that offers a comprehensive treatment of a complex and fascinating topic in human psychology; like all *Britannica* articles, it is the work of distinguished scholars.

Human Motivation

Motivation in human psychology is the term used to describe forces acting either on or within a person to initiate behaviour. The word motivation is derived from the Latin term *motivus* ("a moving cause"), which suggests the activating properties of the processes involved in psychological motivation. Psychologists study motivational forces to help explain observed changes in behaviour that occur in an individual. Thus, for example, the observation that a person is increasingly likely to open the refrigerator door to look for food as the number of hours since the last meal increases can be understood by invoking the concept of motivation. As the above example suggests, motivation is not typically measured directly but rather inferred as the result of behavioral changes in reaction to internal or external stimuli. It is also important to understand that motivation is primarily a performance variable. That is, the effects of changes in motivation are often temporary. An individual, highly motivated to perform a particular task because of a motivational change, may later show little interest for that task as a result of further change in motivation.

Unlearned and learned motives

Motives are often categorized into primary, or basic, motives, which are unlearned and common to both animals and humans; and secondary, or learned, motives, which can differ from animal to animal and person to person. Primary motives are thought to include hunger, thirst, sex, avoidance of pain, and perhaps aggression and fear. Secondary motives typically studied in humans include achievement, power motivation, and numerous other specialized motives.

Motives have also sometimes been classified into "pushes" and "pulls." Push motives concern internal changes that have the effect of triggering specific motive states. Pull motives represent external goals that influence one's behaviour toward them. Most motivational situations are in reality a combination of push and pull conditions. For example, hunger, in part, may be signaled by internal changes in blood glucose or fat stores, but motivation to eat is also heavily influenced by what foods are available. Some foods are more desirable than others and exert an influence on our behaviour toward them. Behaviour is, thus, often a complex blend of internal pushes and external pulls.

The study of motivation

PHYSIOLOGICAL, PSYCHOLOGICAL, AND PHILOSOPHICAL APPROACHES

Motivation has been studied in a variety of ways. For instance, it has been analyzed at the physiological level using electrical and chemical stimulation of the brain, the recording of electrical brain-wave activity with the electroencephalograph, and lesion techniques, where a portion of the brain (usually of a laboratory animal) is destroyed and subsequent changes in motivation are noted. Physiological studies performed primarily on animals other than humans have demonstrated the importance of certain brain structures in the control of basic motives such as hunger, thirst, sex, aggression, and fear.

Motivation may also be analyzed at the individual psychological level. Such analyses attempt to understand why people act in particular ways and seek to draw general conclusions from individual cases. Through studies of individuals, for example, it has been found that both men and women proceed through a series of identifiable stages of arousal during behaviours leading to and culminating in sexual intercourse. The finding may be applied to people in general.

Motivation of an individual is also influenced by the presence of other people. Social psychologists have been active in discovering how the presence of others in a given situation influences motivation. For example, students and teachers behave in predictable ways in the classroom. Those behaviours are often quite different, however, from the way students and teachers behave outside the classroom. Studies of conformity, obedience, and helping behaviours (which benefit others without reward) are three areas in this field that have received considerable attention.

Aversive and positive views

Finally, motivation is sometimes also approached from a more philosophical direction. That is, analyses of motivation are understood, at least in part, by examining the particular philosophical point of view espoused by the theorist. For example, some motivational theorists conceive motivation to be an aversive state: one to be avoided. Sigmund Freud's view of motivational processes could be applied within this framework; his contention that blocked sexual energy could be displaced into acceptable behaviours implies that accumulation of sexual energy (motivation) is aversive. Other theorists see motivation as a much more positive experience. That is, motivation can produce behaviours that lead to increases in future motivation. The American psychologist Abraham H. Maslow's concept of self-actualization could be applied within this framework (see below).

DEBATES IN MOTIVATIONAL STUDY

The nomothetic versus ideographic approach. However motivation is studied, certain fundamental debates have typified the positions taken by researchers. One such debate concerns the question of whether it is better to study groups of individuals and attempt to draw general conclusions (termed the nomothetic approach) or to study the behaviours that make individuals unique (termed the idiographic approach). Although both approaches have added to the understanding of motivational processes, the nomothetic approach has dominated motivational research.

Innate versus acquired processes. A second debate among theorists concerns the degree to which motivational processes are innate (genetically programmed) versus acquired (learned). Since the 1890s this debate has swung from one extreme to the other and then back toward the middle. Early approaches viewed motivation as largely or entirely instinctive. When the instinctive approach fell into disfavour during the 1920s, the idea that all behaviours were learned largely replaced the instinctive approach. By the 1960s, and continuing to the present, research indicated that the answer to the debate is that both positions are correct. Some motives, in some species, do appear to be largely innate, as, for example, in the courting behaviour of the three-spined stickleback, a small fish of the Northern Hemisphere (see below). Other motives, such as achievement motivation, seem more closely associated with learning. Some motive states, such as extreme shyness, seem to result from an innate predisposition coupled with a particular environment where learning interacts with the predisposition.

Internal needs versus external goals. Another dimension along which debates concerning motivational processes have flourished is the question of whether motivation is primarily the result of internal needs or external goals. As noted earlier, this dimension describes differences between push and pull motives. Research suggests that some motive states are best classified as internal (push motives) while other motive states develop from goals external to the individual (pull motives). Many real-life situations are undoubtedly a combination of both internal and external motives.

Mechanistic versus cognitive processes. Finally, researchers have tended to view motivational processes as either mechanistic or cognitive. The first of these assumes that motivational processes are automatic; that is, the organism, human or otherwise, need not understand what it is doing in order for the processes to work. This point of view has achieved considerable popularity. Neither conscious awareness nor intent is assumed to be operative in the mechanistic approach. Researchers taking the mechanistic point of view are often interested in studying internal need states and genetically programmed behaviours. The second and newer approach, promoted by researchers more often interested in external and acquired motives, has emphasized the importance of cognition in motivational processes. The cognitive approach assumes that the way in which one interprets information influences motives. Cognitive motivational approaches assume that the active processing of information has important influences on future motivation. Given the complexity of motivational processes, most theorists feel safe in assuming that some motive states are relatively mechanistic while others are more cognitive.

The mechanistic approach

Historical overview

PHILOSOPHERS' CONTRIBUTIONS

The history of motivational thought reflects the considerable influence of philosophers and physiologists. For example, the concept of free will as proposed by Aristotle and others was a widely accepted philosophical position until it was generally rejected in favour of determinism. Determinism, as the term is used by psychologists, holds that every behaviour has some antecedent cause. One antecedent to which particular behaviours are often attributed is motivation. Thus, if one sees a woman hurriedly eating a sandwich while continually glancing at her watch, one might infer that she is late for an appointment rather than that she is ravenously hungry. Regardless of the eventual explanation that would allow us to understand her behaviour, we do not assume that she is behaving randomly. Rather, we assume some motive is causing her to behave as she does.

Aristotle's belief that the mind is at birth a blank slate upon which experience writes was the basis for studying the effects of learning on behaviour. The 17th-century philosopher René Descartes proposed the concept of mind-body dualism, which implied that human behaviour could be understood as resulting from both a free, rational soul

Descartes's mind-body dualism

and from automatic, nonrational processes of the body. His proposition that nonrational, mechanistic processes of the body could motivate behaviour under some circumstances led to the development of the concept of instinct and provided a counterpoint to Aristotle's emphasis on learning as the most important concept in the control of behaviour. Today, the mechanistic component of Descartes's dualism can be seen as the distant forerunner of the study of genetic components of motivation, while his other view of rational choices can be regarded as a precursor of modern cognitive approaches to motivation.

British empiricist philosophers, as exemplified by John Locke, also contributed to the development of modern motivational theory. Locke's emphasis on the importance of sensory experience can be understood as underlying the modern focus on external stimulation as motivating. Many psychologists believe that goals become valuable to us because of the sensory experience associated with these goals. Thus, for example, the motivating properties that cause a person to drive across the city to eat a particular food are thought to result from the desirable taste, smell, and perhaps texture of the food itself. If the food tasted and smelled like cardboard, it would not motivate future trips across the city to obtain it. Locke also provided the important concept of association. As proposed by Locke, one idea can become associated, or linked, to another to produce a new, more complex idea. The concept of association provides an explanation for how nonmotivating experiences can become motivating. If one pairs a nonmotivating stimulus with a highly motivating object several times, the formerly neutral stimulus begins to motivate behaviour in a fashion similar to the original object. Research has shown that, under some circumstances, phobias and other motives may be acquired through such association. The associative mechanism can serve as an example of Pavlovian classical conditioning. (Ivan P. Pavlov was a Russian scientist who taught dogs to associate food with the sound of a bell; the dogs learned to salivate at the sound of a bell, demonstrating what has been termed a conditioned response.) Perhaps the most commonly associated stimulus in Western society that is recognized for its strong motivational properties is money. Because money is paired with many strong motivators, it often becomes strongly motivating itself.

PHYSIOLOGISTS' CONTRIBUTIONS

Motivational research has also progressed through discoveries made in the field of physiology. The discovery of separate nerve fibers for sensory and motor information first suspected by the Greek physician Galen and separately confirmed by the English anatomist Sir Charles Bell in 1811 and the French physiologist François Magendie in 1822 led naturally to the development of the stimulus-response approach to motivation, which has become fundamental to the field.

The discovery of the electrical nature of the nerve impulse, first suggested by the Italian physician and physicist Luigi Galvani's experiments in the 1770s and '80s with frogs and later directly measured by the German physiologist Emil Du Bois-Reymond in 1848–49 using a galvanometer, showed that nerves are not canals by which animal spirits flow through the body, as had been commonly thought, but are rather the conveyors of signals sent from one area of the body to another. The German psychologist Georg E. Müller added the concept of specific nerve energies, which proposed that the electrical signals passing along the nerves were specific, coded messages, while the German scientist Hermann von Helmholtz measured the speed of the nerve impulse and found it to be about 100 miles (160 kilometres) per hour. These discoveries made it clear that the nervous system could be studied and paved the way for examination of its role in the motivation of behaviour.

Galvani's and Du Bois-Reymond's experiments

Studies of the localization of function within the nervous system, especially the brain, derived at least in part from the phrenology of the German physician Franz Josef Gall during the early 1800s. Although phrenology has been thoroughly discredited, it indirectly contributed to the localization of motivational systems within such brain areas as the hypothalamus.

BEHAVIOURISM

The contributions from philosophical and physiological sources have generated several stages of evolution in motivational theory since the late 19th century. In the 1800s Descartes' dualism was often used to distinguish between animal and human motivation. By the end of the 19th century, behavioral theorists such as the American psychologists William James and William McDougall had begun to emphasize the instinctive component of human behaviour and to de-emphasize, and in some cases eliminate from discussion, the more mentalistic concept of will. Other behaviourists, as exemplified by the American psychologist John B. Watson, rejected theories of both instinct and will and emphasized the importance of learning in behaviour. This group conceived behaviour to be a reaction or response (R) to changes in environmental stimulation (S); their S-R psychology subsequently gained popularity, becoming the basis for the school of behaviourism. By the 1920s, the concept of instinct as proposed by theorists such as James and McDougall had been roundly criticized and fell into disrepute. Behaviourism dominated the thinking of motivational theorists and a new motivational concept, drive, congenial to behaviourism's S-R approach, was born. Drive, initially proposed by the American psychologist Robert S. Woodworth, was developed most fully by Clark Hull, an American psychologist who conceived motivation to result from changed internal bodily needs, which were in turn satisfied by obtaining specific items from the environment. Thus, hunger motivation was thought to occur as a result of a changed internal need for energy that motivated food-seeking behaviour in the environment.

Behaviourism dominated motivational research until the 1960s, but even in the 1920s and '30s dissenting voices were heard. Researchers such as the American psychologist Edward C. Tolman and the German psychologist Wolfgang Köhler argued for the existence of a more active processing of information in both humans and animals and rejected the mechanistic S-R psychology. These early cognitive psychologists opened the way for other researchers to examine motivation resulting from the expectation of future events, choices among alternatives, and attributions concerning outcomes. In other words, with the advent of cognitive explanations of motivated behaviour, it became possible to argue that behaviours were sometimes purposive. The cognitive approach has proved useful in the analysis of several types of motivation, among them achievement behaviour, dissonance motivation, and self-actualization (see below).

Changing perspectives and research on motivation have led away from large, all-encompassing theories of motivation to smaller, discrete theories that explain specific motives or specific aspects of motivation under particular conditions. These microtheories of motivation are conveniently categorized as falling within three major areas: biological, behaviouristic, and cognitive explanations.

Biological approaches to motivation

The biological microtheories of motivation can be divided into three categories: genetic contributions to motivated behaviour, arousal mechanisms, and biological monitoring systems.

GENETIC CONTRIBUTIONS

As indicated above, the idea that some motivated behaviours are the result of innate programs manifested in the nervous system had been proposed by James and McDougall in the late 1800s and early 1900s. These early instinct approaches fell into disfavour during the 1920s because of their proponents' inability to discriminate between instinctive and learned behaviours and because of the realization that labeling an observed behaviour as instinctive did not explain why the behaviour occurred. In Europe, however, a group of biologists interested in the evolutionary significance of animal behaviours kept the concept alive and continued to study the genetic basis of behaviour. Three of these researchers (the Austrians Karl von Frisch and Konrad Lorenz and the Netherlander

Nikolaas Tinbergen) were awarded a Nobel Prize in 1973 for their work on the subject. They were early entrants in the field of study known as ethology, which studies the behaviour patterns of animals in their natural habitat. Ethologists argue that the evolutionary significance of a particular behaviour can best be understood after a taxonomy of behaviours for that species has been developed as a result of observation in nature. They propose further that the significance of a behaviour is often clearer when observed in the context of other behaviours of that animal. Ethologists use naturalistic observation and field studies as their most common techniques.

The research conducted by the ethologists showed that some behaviours of some animal species were released in an automatic and mechanical fashion when conditions were appropriate. These behaviours, known as fixed-action patterns, have several salient characteristics: they are specific to the species under study, occur in a highly similar fashion from one occurrence to the next, and do not appear to be appreciably altered by experience. Furthermore, the stimulus that releases these genetically programmed behaviours is usually highly specific, such as a particular colour, shape, or sound. Such stimuli are termed key stimuli or sign stimuli and when provided by a conspecific organism (a member of the same species) are known as social releasers.

One thoroughly researched example of this type of genetically programmed behaviour is the courtship behaviour of the three-spined stickleback, a small fish. During the reproductive season, male sticklebacks become territorial and defend a portion of the streambed against other intruding stickleback males. Ethological analysis of this aggressive behaviour reveals that it is a series of fixed-action patterns released by the reddish coloration of the ventral (under) surface of the intruding males. A female stickleback entering the territory is not attacked because she does not possess the red coloration. Instead she is courted through a complex series of movements termed the zigzag dance. This behaviour pattern performed by the male stickleback is released by the shape of the ventral surface of the female, which is distended as a result of the eggs she carries.

Although the largest number of studies conducted by ethologists has been on nonhuman animals, some ethological researchers have applied the same kinds of analyses to human behaviour. Prominent among these is the Austrian ethologist Irenäus Eibl-Eibesfeldt. In a book entitled *Love and Hate: The Natural History of Behavior Patterns,* he summarized many years of cross-cultural research on human genetic behaviour patterns. Interestingly, research on the facial expressions associated with emotion has provided some support for the existence of innate motivations in humans.

MOTIVATION AS AROUSAL

The James-Lange theory. A second biological approach to the study of human motivation has been the study of mechanisms that change the arousal level of the organism. Early research on this topic emphasized the essential equivalency of changes in arousal, changes in emotion, and changes in motivation. It was proposed that emotional expressions and the motivation of behaviour are the observable manifestations of changes in arousal level. One of the earliest arousal theories suggested that one's perception of emotion depends upon the bodily responses the individual makes to a specific, arousing situation. This theory became known as the James-Lange theory of emotion after the two researchers, William James and the Danish physician Carl Lange, who independently proposed it in 1884 and 1885 respectively. The theory argued, for example, that experiencing a dangerous event such as an automobile accident leads to bodily changes such as increased breathing and heart rate, increased adrenaline output, and so forth. These changes are detected by the brain and the emotion appropriate to the situation is experienced. In the example of the automobile accident, fear might be experienced as a result of these bodily changes.

The Cannon-Bard theory. Walter B. Cannon, a Harvard physiologist, questioned the James-Lange theory on

Decline of the instinct concept

Ethology

Study of the arousal level

the basis of a number of observations; he noted that the feedback from bodily changes can be eliminated without eliminating emotion; that the bodily changes associated with many quite different emotional states are similar, making it unlikely that these changes serve to produce particular emotions; that the organs supposedly providing the feedback to the brain concerning these bodily changes are not very sensitive; and that these bodily changes occur too slowly to account for experienced emotions.

Cannon and a colleague, Philip Bard, proposed an alternative arousal theory, subsequently known as the Cannon-Bard theory. According to this approach, the experience of an event, such as the automobile accident mentioned earlier, leads to the simultaneous determination of emotion and changes to the body. The brain, upon receiving information from the senses, interprets an event as emotional while at the same time preparing the body to deal with the new situation. Thus, emotional responses and changes in the body are proposed to be preparations for dealing with a potentially dangerous emergency situation.

The Schachter-Singer model. In 1962 the American psychologists Stanley Schachter and Jerome Singer performed an experiment that suggested to them that elements of both the James-Lange and Cannon-Bard theories are factors in the experience of emotion. Their cognitive-physiological theory of emotion proposed that both bodily changes and a cognitive label are needed to experience emotion completely. The bodily changes are assumed to occur as a result of situations that are experienced, while the cognitive label is considered to be the interpretation the brain makes about those experiences. According to this view, one experiences anger as a result of perceiving the bodily changes (increased heart rate and breathing, adrenaline production, and so forth) and interpreting the situation as one in which anger is appropriate or would be expected. The Schachter-Singer model of emotional arousal has proved to be popular although the evidence for it remains modest. Other researchers have suggested that bodily changes are unnecessary for the experience of emotional arousal and that the cognitive label alone is sufficient.

The inverted-U function. The relationship between changes in arousal and motivation is often expressed as an inverted-U function (also known as the Yerkes-Dodson law). The basic concept is that, as arousal level increases, performance improves, but only to a point, beyond which increases in arousal lead to a deterioration in performance. Thus some arousal is thought to be necessary for efficient performance, but too much arousal leads to anxiety or stress, which degrades performance.

The search for a biological mechanism capable of altering the arousal level of an individual led to the discovery of a group of neurons (nerve cells) in the brain stem named the reticular activating system, or reticular formation. These cells, which are found along the center of the brain stem, run from the medulla to the thalamus and are responsible for changes in arousal that move a person from sleeping to waking. They are also believed to function in relation to an individual's attention factor.

Sleep processes and stress reactions. Research on arousal mechanisms of motivation has furthered understanding of both sleep processes and stress reactions. In the case of sleep, arousal levels generally seem lower than during waking; however, during one stage of sleep arousal levels appear highly similar to those in the waking state. Sleep itself may be considered a motivational state. The biological motivation to sleep can become so overpowering that individuals can fall asleep while driving an automobile or while engaged in dangerous tasks.

Five stages of sleep have been defined using the electroencephalograph (EEG). The EEG records the electrical activity of neurons in the outermost portion of the brain known as the cerebral cortex.

According to EEG-based findings, everyone cycles through five stages during sleep. A complete cycle averages approximately 90 minutes. The two most interesting stages of sleep from a motivational point of view are stages 4 and 5. Stage 4 represents the deepest sleep in that the brain-wave activity as measured by the EEG is farthest from the activity seen when a person is awake. The brain-wave pattern is characterized by delta waves, which are large, irregular, and slow; breathing, heart rate, and blood pressure are also reduced. Because the overall activity of the individual in stage 4 is greatly reduced, it has been suggested by some researchers that stage 4 (and perhaps also stage 3) sleep serves a restorative function. However, a potential problem with such an explanation is that stage 4 sleep drops dramatically after age 30 and may be entirely absent in some people aged 50 or over who nevertheless appear to be perfectly healthy. Additionally, studies have shown that in the typical individual physical exhaustion does not lead to increases in stage 4 sleep as might be expected if it were serving a restorative function. The purpose of stage 4 sleep remains unknown.

Stage 5 sleep is also known as rapid eye movement (REM) sleep because during this stage the eyes begin to move rapidly under the eyelids. Interest in stage 5 sleep has been considerable since it was discovered that most, if not all, dreaming occurs during this stage. During stage 5 sleep the EEG pattern of brain-wave activity appears very similar to the brain-wave activity of an awake, alert person. Breathing, heart rate, and blood pressure rise from the low levels observed during stage 4 and can fluctuate rapidly. In addition to eye movements, fast, small, and irregular brain waves, and autonomic changes indicative of an aroused state, individuals in stage 5 sleep display a large loss in skeletal muscle tone that amounts to a temporary paralysis. Researchers have suggested that the muscle paralysis prevents the "acting out" of our dreams.

Another aspect of arousal processes concerns the high levels of arousal leading to a triggering of the stress reaction. The stress reaction can be triggered by a challenge to the physical integrity of the body, or it can occur as a result of some psychological challenge. Furthermore, the body appears to react in a similar fashion regardless of whether the demands made upon it are physical or psychological. Hans Selye, a Viennese-born Canadian medical researcher, showed that stressors trigger a chain of processes that begins with what is called the alarm reaction, may proceed to a second stage called the stage of resistance, and, if the stressor has still not been removed, may lead to a final stage called exhaustion.

The alarm reaction occurs when a stressor is first detected and activates a brain structure called the hypothalamus. The hypothalamus, in turn, stimulates the sympathetic nervous system and also produces a substance called corticotropin-releasing hormone that activates the pituitary to produce adrenocorticotropic hormone (ACTH). Both ACTH and activation of the sympathetic nervous system stimulate the adrenal glands. ACTH stimulates the adrenals to produce hydrocortisone, or cortisol, an anti-inflammatory substance, while the sympathetic nervous system stimulates the centre portion of the adrenals to produce epinephrine and norepinephrine (adrenaline and noradrenaline). All these hormones are secreted into the bloodstream and have the effect of mobilizing the body to deal with the stressor. This initial mobilization is a whole-body response and leads to increases in heart rate, blood pressure, and respiration and other responses associated with high arousal. The person so aroused is, in effect, in a high state of readiness. The alarm reaction often succeeds in changing the situation so that the stressor is no longer present, as would be the case, for example, if one were to run away from a physical threat.

In the second stage, the stage of resistance, localized responses within appropriate areas of the body replace the whole-body response of the alarm reaction, and blood levels of hydrocortisone, epinephrine, and norepinephrine return to just slightly above normal levels. During this stage the ability to fight off the stressor is high and may remain so for considerable periods of time.

If these localized responses to a stressor prove to be inadequate, eventually the third stage of stress, that of exhaustion, will be triggered, during which hormonal levels rise once more and the whole body becomes mobilized again. Selye proposed that if the stressor is not quickly defeated during this last stage, the individual can become withdrawn, maladjusted, and even die.

The cognitive-physiological theory

The five stages of sleep

The three stages of stress reaction

This three-part mechanism for coping with a stressor is called the general adaptation syndrome and appears to have evolved primarily to deal with systemic stressors. As noted earlier, however, this same set of processes is also triggered by psychological stressors and is often inappropriate to the situation. For example, the stress of an important upcoming test can trigger the alarm reaction, yet it is not apparent how increased levels of hydrocortisone, epinephrine, and norepinephrine would facilitate removing the stress-provoking test. It has been suggested that overstimulation of the stress response, in which psychological stressors produce physical changes in the body, can lead to psychosomatic illness. When the stress response, especially the alarm reaction, is triggered too often, it can lead to physical deterioration.

The Meyer scale of life-change stress

The relationship between stress and illness has been investigated most thoroughly in regard to the effect life changes have on the likelihood of subsequent illness. The pioneer in the field was Adolph Meyer, a Swiss-born American psychiatrist. Several life-change scales have been developed that measure the number and severity of various life changes, such as the death of a spouse, divorce, retirement, change in living conditions, and so forth. High scores on these scales have been found to be consistently associated with an increased probability of future illness, although the relationship is not especially strong. Presumably the life changes lead to increased stress, which in turn promotes an increased likelihood of illness.

Some research has also been conducted on the ways in which the negative effects of stressors can be reduced. A personality characteristic called hardiness has been associated with the ability to better withstand the effects of stress. People who score high in hardiness appear to have high levels of commitment toward the things they do, a strong need to control the events around them, and a willingness to accept challenges. These characteristics may serve to protect individuals from the effects of stress related to major life changes. Exercise, especially in conjunction with hardiness, was reported to relieve stress stemming from physiological and psychological causes. Other factors unrelated to hardiness, such as social support from others, optimism, and humour in the face of difficulty, also have been reported to reduce the stressful effects of life changes.

BIOLOGICAL MONITORING SYSTEMS

For some basic motives such as hunger, thirst, and sex, a biological approach emphasizing regulatory mechanisms has dominated the thinking of researchers. The fundamental premise has been that such basic motives are homeostatically regulated—that is, the nervous system monitors levels of energy, fluid balance, and hormone production (in the case of sex) and alters motivation when these levels deviate too far from some optimum level.

Hunger. The question of why we eat when we do appears to involve two separate mechanisms. The first mechanism, typically called short-term regulation, attempts to take in sufficient energy to balance what is being expended. It is usually assumed that time between meals and meal size are determined by this short-term mechanism. A second mechanism, called long-term regulation, is directed toward storing away sufficient energy for possible later use should the short-term mechanism fail to adequately replenish energy expended. Energy for long-term use is stored in the form of fat within the fat cells of the body. Short-term regulation processes have generally been assumed to monitor the blood glucose (blood sugar) level and to initiate eating when this level falls below some predetermined optimum. Long-term regulation processes appear to monitor fat levels and to initiate eating when fat stores fall below some optimal level.

The local theory of hunger

Explanations of short-term regulation of hunger motivation have revolved around two basic ideas. The earlier of these two, known as the local theory of hunger, suggested that the hunger signals that initiate eating originate in the gastrointestinal tract, specifically the stomach. Hunger pangs were thought to be the result of stomach contractions. Considerable research has shown that such an analysis is inadequate to explain hunger motivation. For example, it is known that much of the stomach can be removed without the loss of hunger motivation. Similarly, it is known that severing the vagus nerve, which causes stomach contractions to cease, does not eliminate the experience of hunger.

When it became apparent that the local theory of hunger was incomplete, researchers began to look for the hunger-initiating mechanism in the brain. It was quickly discovered that the hypothalamus, a small structure lying below the thalamus of the brain, is involved in the regulation of eating. Damage to the ventromedial (lower, middle) area of the hypothalamus produces a condition known as hyperphagia, in which animals overeat and gain enormous amounts of weight. Damage to a different area known as the lateral hypothalamus (located on the sides of the hypothalamus) produces a total lack of eating known as aphagia, as well as a lack of drinking, or adipsia. It was assumed that these two areas share in the control of hunger motivation by activating and deactivating hunger as glucose levels within the blood change. It was further assumed that the specialized cells (glucoreceptors) monitoring the levels of blood glucose reside in these two hypothalamic areas. This belief was weakened, however, when these glucoreceptors could not definitely be located in the brain. Additional research suggests that such glucoreceptors may reside in the liver, where new arrivals of glucose are first received and whence signals about glucose content are sent to these hypothalamic areas.

Theory of long-term hunger regulation

Less is known about the long-term regulation of hunger motivation, but one suggestion has been that there exists in each individual a genetically programmed body-weight set point that determines how much energy is stored away as fat within the fat cells. According to this theory, hunger motivation would serve to keep individuals close to this set point, even though the fat level maintained may not be what the individual desires nor what society dictates as beautiful or healthy. Such a system would help to explain why weight loss is so hard to maintain in many persons.

Thirst. Processes similar to the physiological control mechanisms of hunger are thought to regulate thirst motivation and sexual behaviour. In the case of thirst, the desire to drink appears to be initiated by fluid loss from within specialized brain cells known as osmoreceptors and also from fluid loss from the area outside of cells, such as from bleeding. Thirst, therefore, would seem to be triggered by mechanisms controlling the fluid integrity both within and around the cells of the body. Cells within the hypothalamus also seem to be involved in the control of thirst motivation.

Sexual motivation. In most animals sexual motivation is under stricter hormonal control than is the case in humans. The female of most species is not interested in sexual behaviour until cyclic hormonal changes produce estrus. The male, however, is usually sexually ready but is prevented from engaging in sexual behaviour by the female until estrus occurs. Research indicates that the anterior (front) portion of the hypothalamus is involved with the estrous cycle of female mammals; it has been demonstrated that destruction of these hypothalamus cells eliminates estrus. Similarly, destruction of the anterior region of the hypothalamus reduces or eliminates sexual behaviour in male rats. Since hormone replacement therapy in both males and females is ineffective in reestablishing sexual behaviours reduced by anterior hypothalamic damage, it has been suggested that this region contains receptors sensitive to changes in the levels of circulating sex hormones. Damage to the ventromedial hypothalamus (VMH) also arrests estrus in females and sexual behaviour in males, but hormone replacement therapy successfully restores these functions, suggesting that VMH is involved with the expression of sexual behaviour when hormonal conditions are appropriate.

Behavioristic approaches to motivation

The behavioristic approach examines how motives are learned and how internal drives and external goals interact with learning to produce behaviour. Learning theorists have taken a somewhat more global perspective when studying motivation than researchers using the biological approach. These researchers have regarded motivation as one component out of several that combine to cause behaviour. Thus, for example, one major theory regards learning and motivation as combining multiplicatively to determine behaviour. Among the behaviouristic approaches, three concepts are especially prominent: drive, learned motives, and incentives.

DRIVE

Wood-
worth's
early
concept
of drive
theory

Although in many respects Freud's psychoanalytic theory of behaviour was a drive theory, the term drive was first used by Robert S. Woodworth, an American psychologist, in 1918. The concept of drive is closely tied to the concept of homeostasis. It was assumed that drive would be triggered when internal conditions changed enough to be detected and to initiate the motivational changes that amounted to drive. Thus it was assumed that some tissue need within the body would instigate drive, which would, in turn, instigate behaviours aimed at reducing the drive. According to this sort of analysis, energy depletion would lead to a hunger drive, which would in turn lead to food-seeking behaviours. Drive, then, would serve to energize appropriate behaviours, either innate or learned, which would effect a lowering of the need state of the individual.

The most extensive theoretical model of drive was developed by Clark Hull in the 1940s. Hull argued that drive is general in nature and that various motives such as hunger, thirst, or sex add to the overall drive level of an individual. Since drive was regarded as the instigator of behaviour, increases in drive level were expected to lead to increases in activity. According to Hull's model, drive is directed by what he termed drive stimuli. These internal stimuli were thought to be different for different motives and to direct the activity of an individual in ways appropriate for the particular motive state present. Thus, for example, a hungry person might go to the refrigerator seeking food because drive stimuli linked with hunger had been associated with responses of obtaining food from the refrigerator in the past.

Finally, Hull suggested that learning itself depends upon adequate drive. Responses were thought to be strengthened when followed by drive or drive-stimulus reduction. If drive or drive stimuli were not reduced, then learning would not occur.

Assessment
of Hull's
drive
theory

Hull's drive theory generated a tremendous body of research, but the model of motivation that he evolved was not more effective than others were in explaining behaviour. For example, studies showed that increases in activity that occur when subjects are deprived depend largely on the species of the subject and on the manner in which the activity is tested. Some species do not become more active when they are deprived, and changes in activity that are apparent when one type of apparatus is used (*e.g.,* a running wheel) are not seen when other types of apparatus (*e.g.,* a stabilimeter cage—for measuring caged animal activity) are used. Furthermore, drive stimuli, the proposed directional mechanism in Hull's model, have proved to be very elusive, and it is not clear that under normal circumstances their presence, if they exist, is crucial to the direction of behaviour. Finally, a number of studies have shown that learning can occur under circumstances that would seem to preclude any reduction in drive or drive stimuli. Since Hull's model tied learning to a reduction in drive, these studies pose a problem. Although explicit theoretical models of drive have not proved to be any better at explaining motivation than have other approaches, the drive concept, in general, would seem to have some validity if only because people often express their subjective feelings of motivation in terms that suggest that they are driven. In particular, the drive concept would often seem to apply to feelings that are associated with human sexual motivation. The drive theory no longer has wide acceptance in the motivational field, however.

LEARNED MOTIVES

One of the most significant contributions that the learning approach has made to the study of motivation is its emphasis on the ability of individuals to learn new motives. It has been demonstrated that new motives may be acquired as a result of three learning techniques: classical, instrumental, and observational learning.

Classical conditioning. In classical conditioning, also called Pavlovian conditioning, a neutral stimulus gains the ability to elicit a response as a result of being paired with another stimulus that already causes that response. Such learning situations can then lead to changes in motivated behaviour. Pavlov, for example, showed that dogs would develop what appeared to be neurotic behaviour if they were required to make finer and finer discriminations between stimuli in a classical conditioning discrimination experiment. The dogs became motivated to avoid the experiment room, were restless during the experimental session, and sometimes bit the apparatus. The neurosis developed when the dogs were no longer able to discriminate between the two stimuli presented to them. Later researchers have noted that this motivational change may have resulted from a lack of predictability or control on the part of the animal rather than from the classical conditioning process per se.

Induce-
ment of
a fear
response
through
condi-
tioning

In 1920 the American psychologists John B. Watson and Rosalie Rayner demonstrated the development of an emotional response in a young boy using classical conditioning techniques. The presentation of a white rat was paired with the striking of a steel bar, which induced fear in the little boy. After only a few pairings, the white rat became capable of inducing fear responses similar to those produced by striking the bar. This early demonstration of learned emotional responses has suggested to psychologists that many human motives may result from the accidental pairing of events. It has been proposed that some fears, phobias, taste aversions, and even eating problems can result from classical conditioning.

Instrumental learning. The second type of learning technique is instrumental learning, or conditioning, also called operant conditioning. In this type of conditioning a response is followed by some consequence which then changes the future probability of that response. For example, instrumental conditioning appears to be one way in which aggressive motivation can be changed. If an aggressive response by one child toward another child is followed by some positive event such as the aggressor getting to play with a desired toy, then the motivation to behave aggressively can be expected to increase in the future. Furthermore, through a process called conditioned reinforcement, neutral stimuli associated with a reinforcer can become reinforcers in their own right. These stimuli can then be used to motivate behaviour. Perhaps the most common example of a conditioned reinforcer is money. A piece of paper with numbers and intricate drawings on it can motivate all sorts of behaviour if that paper has previously been associated with important reinforcers such as food, clothing, sex, and so forth. Money is in effect a token of the things it can buy. Psychologists have used different types of tokens as rewards to implement reinforcement, and token economies, involving the principles of conditioned reinforcement, have been successfully used to alter behaviour in schools, institutions, and hospitals (see below).

Observational learning. In the third type of learning technique, observational learning, or modeling, a new behaviour is learned simply by watching someone else behave. In a very real sense, such learning is the ability to profit from another's successes or mistakes. This type of learning is important because the learning can occur without an individual ever having to perform the behaviour. Thus, watching another child put a finger in an electrical outlet and get shocked is often enough to keep the observing child from behaving the same way. Similarly, noticing that friends do well in school because they study hard may be a sufficient stimulus to motivate students. Albert Bandura, a Canadian psychologist, has proposed, and provided a wealth of support for, the observational learning of aggression in humans. He has shown that young children will mimic the aggressive responses they see performed by adults. Such aggressive responses can potentially be learned by observation of violent acts on television or in movies or by reading or hearing about violent behaviour. If the observed violent acts are further perceived to lead

Learned
aggressive
responses
in children

to desired goals, then the observed aggressive behaviours may be utilized at some future date by the observer.

Research indicates that persons also learn their society's rules of sexual conduct through observation. These sexual values are taught in part by parents, clergy, political leaders, books, movies, and television. Although the learning is often indirect, people nevertheless learn how to express their sexuality. The rules for sexual behaviour in a given culture appear to be learned during adolescence. In monkeys, social isolation impairs sexual functioning. Although isolated monkeys seem to have adequate sexual motivation, the lack of appropriate social skills results in inappropriate behaviours. Thus, learning would appear to be a significant factor in normal sexual behaviour. It is generally thought that certain sexual preferences are also learned, by one technique or another. In one experiment a boot fetish was established in three males by pairing pictures of boots with pictures of nude women (at the conclusion of the experiment the fetish was extinguished). Such a demonstration would seem to indicate that some sexual preferences are learned.

INCENTIVE MOTIVATION

One area within the study of human motivation that has proved fruitful is research on incentives. Incentive motivation is concerned with the way goals influence behaviour. For example, a person might be willing to travel across the city to dine at a special restaurant that served a favourite dish. On the other hand, that same person might not be willing to travel the same distance to eat an ordinary frankfurter. The two meals have different incentive values and motivate behaviour to differing degrees.

It is often assumed that the stimulus characteristics of the goal are what produce the goal's motivating properties. Thus, the taste, smell, and texture of one food would motivate behaviour better than these qualities in another food. Unlike drives, which were thought to be innate, incentives are usually considered to be learned. An individual is not born preferring one goal over another, but rather these preferences develop as new goals are experienced. Incentive motivation is not restricted to goals associated with the primary motives of hunger, thirst, sex, or avoidance of pain. Indeed, one of the most important aspects of this type of motivation is that any goal one seeks can motivate behaviour. For example, the goal of obtaining a high-paying job could serve as a strong motivator for studying hard in school. Goals serving as incentive motivators do not even need to physically exist at the time they activate behaviour, such as might be the case for someone who is motivated to get high grades now in order to eventually get into medical school.

Theoretical explanations of incentive motivation have ranged from mechanical stimulus-response approaches based on classical conditioning to cognitive approaches emphasizing the learning of expectancies, as discussed in the section below. Several theories have emphasized the role of predictive cues in the development of incentive motivation. Researchers concerned primarily with human motivation have suggested that much of human behaviour can be understood as being directed toward specific goals.

Cognitive motivation

Cognitive theories of motivation assume that behaviour is directed as a result of the active processing and interpretation of information. Motivation is not seen as a mechanical or innate set of processes but as a purposive and persistent set of behaviours based on the information available. Expectations, based on past experiences, serve to direct behaviour toward particular goals.

Important concepts of cognitive motivation theory include expectancy-value theory, attribution theory, cognitive dissonance, self-perception, and self-actualization.

EXPECTANCY-VALUE THEORY

According to expectancy-value theory, behaviour is a function of the expectancies one has and the value of the goal toward which one is working [expressed as $B = f(E \times V)$]. Such an approach predicts that, when more than one

behaviour is possible, the behaviour chosen will be the one with the largest combination of expected success and value. Expectancy-value theory has proved useful in the explanation of social behaviours, achievement motivation, and work motivation. Examination of its use in achievement motivation can serve to represent the various types of expectancy-value motivations.

Achievement was initially recognized as an important source of human motivation by the American psychologist Henry Murray in the late 1930s. Although Murray identified achievement motivation as important to the behaviour of many people, it was the American psychologists David McClelland and John Atkinson who devised a way of measuring differences in achievement motivation. These researchers used Murray's Thematic Apperception Test (TAT), a series of ambiguous pictures about which people were asked to write stories (as a determination of personality traits), to measure differences in achievement motivation. Using a technique known as content analysis, the stories were scored for achievement imagery. Based on a substantial body of research, a theoretical model was developed that rested upon the fundamental concepts of expectancy and goal value.

The expectancy-value model of achievement motivation proposes that the overall tendency to achieve in a particular situation depends upon two stable motives—a motive for success and a motive to avoid failure—and the subjective evaluation of the probability of success in the situation. The motive for success is regarded as a relatively stable personality characteristic by the time adulthood is reached. One's motive for success is believed to result from learning in prior achievement situations where the individual has performed successfully. Thus, someone who has, for the most part, had successful experiences in the past is thought to be highly achievement-oriented. The motive to avoid failure is also assumed to be relatively stable by adulthood and represents the compilation of those prior instances where achievement behaviours were unsuccessful. It is argued that someone who has made many unsuccessful attempts in achievement situations will develop a strong motive to avoid failure.

Since almost everyone has experienced both successes and failures during development, the theory assumes that each person has differing degrees of both motivation for success and motivation to avoid failure. These two motivations are opposing tendencies, and as a result the difference in strength between the two will determine whether a given individual is an "achiever" or not. People with high motivation for success and low motivation to avoid failure will be achievement-oriented, while people with strong motivation to avoid failure and weak motivation for success will try to avoid most achievement situations if possible.

The expected probability of success in a particular achievement situation is also important in this achievement theory. The theory predicts that persons highly motivated for success will tend to choose to participate in achievement situations that they judge to be moderately difficult, while the theory also predicts that people highly motivated to avoid failure will tend to choose tasks that they judge to be either very easy or extremely difficult. The choices made by people either highly motivated to achieve success or to avoid failure differ because of the differing value of easy, moderate, and difficult goals for these two types of people. The model mathematically predicts that goals that require moderate effort to achieve will have the greatest value for persons highly motivated for success. Stated another way, high achievers want to obtain goals that are difficult enough to have some value but not so difficult as to be impossible or so easy as to be worthless. Persons with strong motivation to avoid failure believe they are likely to be unsuccessful. For this reason, the theory predicts that they would prefer easy tasks where success is likely or tasks so difficult that little embarrassment would ensue if they fail.

Attempts to test these predictions have met with mixed results. Some studies have found that people scoring high in motivation for success do often choose tasks that they consider moderately difficult, while other studies have failed to find such results. Also, persons scoring high in

Effect of goal-seeking on behaviour

The motive for success

motivation to avoid failure do sometimes choose very easy tasks, as the theory predicts, but often do not choose very difficult tasks as also predicted. Clearly much research remains to be done before the model's accuracy in predicting achievement behaviour can be judged.

ATTRIBUTION THEORY

Rejection of the expectancy-value concept

A second major approach to achievement motivation rejects the expectancy-value formulation and analyzes instead the attributions that people make about achievement situations. In general, attribution theory concerns how people make judgments about someone's (or their own) behaviour—that is, the causes to which they attribute behaviour. Considerable research has found that people typically attribute behaviour either to stable personality characteristics, termed dispositions, or to the situations that were present at the time the behaviour occurred.

In regard to achievement behaviour, it is argued that the attributions of ability, effort, task difficulty, and luck are especially important in determining motivation for future achievement. For example, when a person is successful at a certain task and attributes that success to ability, that person is likely to approach new achievement situations in the future. Similarly, if the success was attributed to an intense effort, future achievement behaviour would depend upon the person's willingness to expend such an effort in the future.

Task difficulty appears to be judged from social norms. If most people are unsuccessful at a task, it is judged to be difficult, and, if most people are successful, the task is judged to be easy. The attribution of success to task difficulty therefore, would be expected to modify future achievement behaviour. If success was judged to be due to the fact that the task was very easy, future achievement behaviour would not be expected to change much; however, success in a task judged to be very difficult might prompt a person to expand the range of tasks he or she is willing to attempt. Ascriptions of luck in an achievement task would also influence future achievement behaviour. Basically, luck is assumed when a person expects to have no control over the outcome in the task. Success attributed to luck is not expected to increase future achievement behaviour much, nor would failure attributed to bad luck be expected to decrease it much.

Locus, stability, and controllability

Research on the attributions that people make in achievement-related situations suggests that the four causal ascriptions mentioned above and perhaps other ascriptions as well can best be understood as falling along three dimensions: locus, stability, and controllability. Locus refers to the location, internal or external, of the perceived cause of a success or failure. Ability and effort, for example, are seen as internal dispositions of a person, while task difficulty and luck are situational factors that are external to the person. Stability refers to how much a given reason for success or failure could be expected to change in the future. Ability and task difficulty are stable and therefore not expected to change much, while effort and luck are unstable and could therefore change dramatically over time. Controllability refers to how much control the individual has over the events of the situation. Causes such as effort are considered to be controllable, whereas luck is uncontrollable.

COGNITIVE DISSONANCE

One of the most popular cognitive approaches to the study of motivation has been the theory of cognitive dissonance, first systematically studied by the American psychologist Leon Festinger. This theory proposed that people attempt to maintain consistency among their beliefs, attitudes, and behaviours. According to this theory, a motivational state termed cognitive dissonance is produced whenever beliefs, attitudes, and behaviours are inconsistent. Cognitive dissonance is considered to be an aversive state that triggers mechanisms to bring cognitions back into a consistent relationship with one another. Much of the research on cognitive dissonance has centred around what happens when attitudes and behaviours are inconsistent. This research suggests that behavior inconsistent with one's beliefs—if there is insufficient justification for the behaviour—will often bring about modification of those beliefs. Suppose, for example, that a person is required to undergo a stressful initiation in order to join a select group. After undergoing this initiation the person discovers that becoming a member of the group does not provide the satisfaction originally expected. Such an outcome should produce cognitive dissonance because the behaviours required and the current belief about the group are inconsistent. As a result, the theory suggests that motivation will be triggered to bring the dissonant elements back into a consistent relationship. The behaviour cannot be changed because it has already occurred; the belief, on the other hand can be changed. Under these conditions dissonance theory predicts that the person's attitude will change and that he will actually come to believe that he likes the group more. Several studies have supported this prediction.

SELF-PERCEPTION THEORY

Cognitive dissonance approaches have not gone unchallenged. An alternative approach, known as self-perception theory, suggests that all individuals analyze their own behaviour much as an outside observer might and, as a result of these observations, make judgments about why they are motivated to do what they do. Thus, in the example above, self-perception theory would argue that the person, in observing his own behaviour, assesses the effort involved and decides that the initiation was endured because he really wanted to be a member of this group. Dissonance theory and self-perception theory are not necessarily mutually exclusive; several studies suggest that both processes can and do occur but under different conditions.

SELF-ACTUALIZATION

Cognitive motivational approaches have also explored the idea that human motivation is heavily influenced by a need for competence or control. Although there are several varieties of these theories, most have in common the idea that human behaviour is at least partially motivated by a need to become as much as one can possibly become. One example of this approach is the self-actualization theory of Abraham Maslow previously mentioned.

Maslow's hierarchy of needs

Maslow has proposed that human motivation can be understood as resulting from a hierarchy of needs. These needs, starting with the most basic physiological demands, progress upward through safety needs, belonging needs, and esteem needs and culminate in self-actualization. Each level directs behaviour toward the need level that is not being adequately met. As lower-level needs are met, the motivation to meet the higher-level needs becomes active. Furthermore, as an individual progresses upward, it becomes progressively more difficult to successfully fulfill the needs of each higher level. For this reason Maslow believed that very few people actually reach the level of self-actualization, and it is a lifelong process for the few who do.

On the basis of his observations of individuals he believed to be self-actualized, including historical figures such as the U.S. presidents Abraham Lincoln and Thomas Jefferson, Maslow outlined a cluster of 14 characteristics that distinguish self-actualized individuals. Summarized, these characteristics define individuals who are accepting of themselves and others, are relatively independent of the culture or society in which they live, are somewhat detached but with very close personal ties to a few other people, and are deeply committed to solving problems that they deem important. Additionally, self-actualized individuals intensely appreciate simple or natural events, such as a sunrise, and they sometimes experience profound changes that Maslow termed peak experiences. Although difficult to describe, peak experiences often involve a momentary loss of self and feelings of transcendence. Reports of peak experiences also include the feeling of limitless horizons opening up and of being simultaneously very powerful, yet weak. Peak experiences are extremely positive in nature and often cause an individual to change the direction of his or her future behaviour. Maslow believed that everyone is capable of having peak experiences, but he believed that self-actualized persons have these experiences more often than most people do.

Applications in society

Behavioral control through motivational reinforcement

Attempts have been made in society to use motivational methods to achieve certain goals. In the control of animal behaviour, for example, it is clear that depriving an organism of food is a powerful means for accomplishing reinforcement. Appropriate use of food under these circumstances is an effective procedure for shaping an animal's behaviour, maintaining it, and controlling the rate of its occurrence. Likewise, it is clear that animals have preferences (within, for example, the range of foodstuffs) and that their behaviour can be controlled with relatively greater effectiveness by the proper selection of preferred substances for use in training.

In many cultures, deprivation cannot be used so readily with human beings as it can be with other animals, although there are many human examples. Thus, some success has been reported in effecting desired behaviour in the classroom by depriving children of some of their recess time when they behave in ways deemed undesirable by the school authorities. Economies based on the use of tokens (*e.g.,* poker chips) have been set up in schools, psychiatric hospitals, and institutions for retarded people. The result typically has been an improvement in the subjects' behaviour and personal care and in the ease with which they may be managed. In such economies, tokens can be exchanged for privileges and commodities (*e.g.,* candy and toys). The individual's ability to obtain tokens is made contingent on socially desirable acts, such as making beds, being personally clean, being cooperative, and being generally acceptable to others. There have been reports of marked improvement in scholastic achievement among institutionalized juvenile delinquents who have been placed in such token economies.

The effectiveness of these and similar procedures has been most easily demonstrated in institutions, in which the situation permits a great deal of control over the subjects' conditions of life and over their activities. In society at large, of course, this degree of control is effectively not feasible. There also are widely endorsed moral or ethical concerns about the desirability of instituting such control even if it were possible. The use of particular kinds of motivational devices in the control of human behaviour seems to many to be incompatible with the ethical idea of personal freedom and fraught with potential for immoral misuse in the hands of those who seek to manipulate others for ends that are politically or socially conformist.

On the other hand, it often is observed that many of society's problems are motivational. This observation usually means that the goals and values of economically affluent groups in the Americas, Europe, and Asia are not shared by members of deprived urban populations or by millions of poor people in industrially less-developed countries. Or, it may mean that the goals of those who own or control profit-seeking enterprises (to make a product or deliver a service for the investors' profit) are not shared by workers below the level of middle management.

Motivational techniques in business and industry

Many techniques have been tried in business and industry to effect so-called motivational involvement with production on the part of ordinary employees. Some of them have had success. Incentive systems, employee participation in company planning and decisions, and human-relations training exemplify the procedures used. A substantial corps of specialists throughout the world provides programs to industry designed to improve the motivation, morale, and satisfaction of workers at all levels. Although these programs have wide acceptance, most of them have received very little objective evaluation.

Summary

Motivation is a complex topic that spans virtually all areas of psychology. No one theory is capable of explaining all that we know about motivational processes. Some motives such as hunger, thirst, and sexual activity seem best understood from a biological viewpoint. Other motives appear to be learned, and such motives help to account for the diversity and complexity of human activities. Still other motives are influenced by the cognitive processes in which we engage. Our interpretation of the events around us influences our future motivation.

A complicating factor in human motivation is the fact that even basic motives are influenced by a variety of elements. For example, we may eat because of energy needs, but some people also eat when stressed or anxious, when depressed or alone, or because of social influences such as other people eating. The taste qualities of certain foods may also cause us to eat when not hungry. This interaction of many factors in determining the motivation of behaviour seriously hinders our ability to understand even basic motivational processes; the contribution of various motivational components must be carefully separated and analyzed. When the study of more subtle motives is attempted, these complicating factors hinder understanding even more. In spite of the large amount of information we have on motivation, much yet remains to be understood.

BIBLIOGRAPHY. The following works are broad studies in psychology, and they, if not cover, then at least touch upon many aspects of the subject of motivation. CHARLES N. COFER, *Motivation & Emotion* (1972), is a concise discussion of the basic relevant psychological concepts. Good overviews of the major approaches to motivation are presented in HERBERT L. PETRI, *Motivation: Theory, Research, and Applications,* 3rd ed. (1991); and DAVID C. MCCLELLAND, *Human Motivation* (1985). NIKO TINBERGEN, *The Study of Instinct* (1951, reissued with a new preface by the author, 1989), offers an excellent survey of early research using the ethological approach. Development of the ethological school in the behavioral sciences is exemplified in KONRAD LORENZ and PAUL LEYHAUSEN, *Motivation of Human and Animal Behavior* (1973; originally published in German, 1968). IRENÄUS EIBL-EIBESFELDT, *Love and Hate; On the Natural History of Basic Behaviour Patterns* (1971; originally published in German, 1970), examines the role of instinctive behaviour in human motivation. CHARLES N. COFER and M.H. APPLEY, *Motivation: Theory and Research* (1964), is a monumental survey, which for years was considered a standard in the field. Another broad survey of developments in the period until the mid-1960s, though not as extensive, is M.D. VERNON, *Human Motivation* (1969). CLARK L. HULL, *Principles of Behavior: An Introduction to Behavior Theory* (1943, reissued 1966), includes a discussion of the learning approach, excluded from Vernon's book. ROBERT C. BOLLES, *Theory of Motivation,* 2nd ed. (1975), provides a review of the drive concept and its failure to explain all aspects of motivated behaviour. JOHN JUNG, *Understanding Human Motivation: A Cognitive Approach* (1978), covers also all traditional motivational approaches. HANS SELYE, *The Physiology and Pathology of Exposure to Stress: A Treatise Based on the Concepts of the General-Adaptation-Syndrome and the Diseases of Adaptation* (1950), and *The Stress of Life,* rev. ed. (1976, reissued 1984), provide a good introduction to the understanding of the concept of stress and the body's reaction to it. JOHN W. ATKINSON and DAVID BIRCH, *An Introduction to Motivation,* 2nd ed. (1978), examines the expectancy-value model of achievement motivation and the relevant research. ABRAHAM H. MASLOW (ed.), *New Knowledge in Human Values* (1959, reissued 1970), and the two books authored by Maslow, *Eupsychian Management: A Journal* (1965), and *The Farther Reaches of Human Nature* (1971), outline his ideas concerning self-actualization. NATHAN BRODY, *Human Motivation: Commentary on Goal-Directed Action* (1983), provides an overview of all mainstream scientific theories of motivation beginning with Hull. EDWARD L. DECI and RICHARD M. RYAN, *Intrinsic Motivation and Self-Determination in Human Behavior* (1985), offers a comprehensive look at the literature of motivation from Freud to the latest working theories.

CHARLES N. COFER. Research Professor of Psychology, University of North Carolina at Chapel Hill; Lecturer in Psychology, Duke University, Durham, N.C.
HERBERT L. PETRIE. Professor of Psychology, Towson (Md.) State University.

WORLD OF MEDICINE

A review of
recent developments

Aerospace Medicine

Among the goals of aerospace medicine are ensuring the health, safety, and productivity of humans in space; developing an understanding of the role of gravity in the normal function of living systems; and promoting the application of life sciences research to improve the quality of life on Earth. To fulfill these goals, the National Aeronautics and Space Administration (NASA) established its life sciences program. The program includes a planned series of missions dedicated to conducting biomedical experiments in space approximately every two years.

For these missions NASA has designed the Spacelab Life Sciences (SLS), a 9,500-kg (21,000-lb) pressurized module, about the size of a small bus, to be carried inside the payload bay of the space shuttle orbiter. It provides a shirtsleeve environment for astronauts and scientists to perform investigations much as they could on Earth. The modular design of the experiment hardware allows each Spacelab mission to be outfitted with equipment specific to its objectives. Many of the SLS studies are designed to solve physiological problems associated with extending shuttle flight durations from the current 10 days to 16—and eventually to 28—days. The studies also have relevance for projected long-duration operations aboard the space station *Freedom,* NASA's future gateway to planetary exploration and permanent platform for research.

The first spaceflight dedicated entirely to biomedical research was the highly successful SLS-1 mission in June 1991. This mission, together with biomedical studies conducted during the year's five other shuttle missions and the ongoing ground-based studies conducted in NASA laboratories, provided scientists with a better understanding of human physiological responses, both in space and on Earth.

Studying physiology in space

Spaceflight is associated with numerous environmental changes that influence biological systems—the most significant being the absence of gravitational forces. Throughout evolution all biological systems have been shaped by the constant presence of gravity and have adapted to function in its presence. Upon entering weightlessness, astronauts have been observed to experience almost immediate effects, such as increases in height, changes in posture, and a redistribution of bodily fluids. Other factors play a role in adaptation to spaceflight. During launch, astronauts are exposed to increased acceleration force, vibration, and noise, as well as some emotional stress. Once they are in space, there may be the psychological stress of living in a confined artificial environment and relying on the spacecraft's life-support system for survival. This factor, along with increased radiation

The space shuttle Columbia *carries the Spacelab Life Sciences module on its highly successful first mission, launched June 5, 1991. The SLS-1 mission was devoted entirely to biomedical research.*

and altered geomagnetic and electrical fields, may have more importance during long-duration flights. Prolonged stays in weightlessness have effects on the cardiovascular system, muscles, and bones. Finally, the return to Earth imposes acceleration forces during reentry into the atmosphere, followed by the return of gravitational forces after landing. The physiological adaptations observed during and after spaceflight are responses of various organs, tissues, and systems to all these factors.

The study of physiology in space is hampered by several factors. First, although space travel may now seem almost commonplace, it is still a relatively special event, and very few individuals have the opportunity to participate in it. This small sample population size (to date, only about 300 people have flown in space) makes it very difficult to draw general conclusions regarding human physiological changes. Second, spaceflight durations have been limited—thus restricting the time available for observing some of these changes. Current flights on the shuttle, although each may include up to seven crew members, are less than two weeks in length. The Russians, on the other hand, routinely fly crew members for six months at a time and have flown one crew for one year; but again that was a very small sample population. Third, the opportunities to conduct thorough biomedical investigations on most spaceflights are limited since crew time must be devoted to many other specific mission objectives—deploying or repairing satellites and planetary explorations among them. Fourth, because a primary objective of medical investigators who design the physiological experiments conducted in space is to ensure the health and well-being of astronauts—individuals who are as a rule exceptionally healthy and fit—certain measures are taken to minimize or prevent some of the adverse effects of spaceflight, such as space motion sickness. These countermeasures may mask the true effects of weightlessness. The SLS series of missions is designed to overcome some of these obstacles and carry out in-depth studies of physiological adaptation to spaceflight.

First Spacelab mission

The space shuttle *Columbia*, carrying the SLS-1 mission, was launched from the Kennedy Space Center in Florida on June 5, 1991, with 7 astronauts, 29 rats, and 2,478 jellyfish. During the nine-day mission, all scientific objectives were met. Moreover, some additional data that may provide valuable new understanding of physiological processes were collected. After a flight lasting 218 hours 15 minutes, *Columbia* made a successful landing at Edwards Air Force Base in California.

The seven-member SLS-1 crew was led by Commander Bryan D. O'Connor of the Marine Corps, with Sidney M. Gutierrez of the Air Force serving as pilot. Astrophysicist Tamara E. Jernigan was a mission specialist with a primary role as a flight engineer. The science crew consisted of two NASA career astronauts—mission specialists James P. Bagian and M. Rhea Seddon, both physicians—and two payload specialists chosen from the scientific community— F. Drew Gaffney, a physician, and Millie Hughes-Fulford, a chemist. This crew was unique in several respects. First, with three M.D.'s and two Ph.D. scientists, the crew had more members with life sciences backgrounds than any previous NASA crew. Second,

this was the first crew to include three women, allowing physiological responses to be measured in both sexes and distinct gender differences observed. And third, the crew members were probably the best-trained group of astronauts that NASA had sent into space thus far, having spent approximately seven years preparing for the mission.

The SLS-1 experiments

The principal objective of the SLS-1 mission was to characterize the magnitudes, time courses, and mechanisms of certain physiological changes that occur during spaceflight. The consequences of adaptation to weightlessness and readaptation to gravity after spaceflight were also to be investigated. A third objective was to test the validity of using animals as models for human responses in spaceflight studies. In all, SLS-1 included 18 human and animal investigations—studies of the cardiovascular/cardiopulmonary, musculoskeletal, and neurovestibular systems; kidney function and fluid regulation; red blood cell regulation; protein metabolism; and immune cell function. Previous experience had indicated that all of these systems and processes are affected to a certain degree during spaceflight, but SLS-1 was the first attempt to investigate all of these changes in a truly comprehensive manner. Some of the investigations, although designed to study physiology in the unique environment of spaceflight, also have the potential to help scientists understand important earthbound medical conditions such as osteoporosis, hypertension, and heart failure.

Cardiovascular/cardiopulmonary studies. When a person is standing on Earth, the force of gravity causes blood and bodily fluids to pool in the legs. Upon entry into weightlessness, the lack of gravity causes a redistribution of these fluids from the legs to the upper body. This fluid redistribution is thought to have consequences on the function and structure of the heart and lungs as well as on blood pressure in the arteries

NASA

The SLS-1 crew spent some seven years preparing for the biomedical experiments they would carry out on their nine-day flight. Pictured on board (clockwise from upper left), the seven members of the crew are: Commander Bryan D. O'Connor, Tamara E. Jernigan, Millie Hughes-Fulford, Sidney M. Gutierrez, M. Rhea Seddon, James P. Bagian, and F. Drew Gaffney.

and veins. On Earth the heart is forced to work hard every time a person stands up, walks, runs, climbs stairs, or performs any activity that opposes gravity. But the lack of gravity in weightlessness means the heart is no longer being stressed, and like any muscle that is not properly exercised, it will lose some of its strength. This phenomenon, called cardiovascular deconditioning, is also observed in patients who are bedridden for long periods of time. On Earth, gravity causes a relatively greater amount of blood flow, or perfusion, to the lower portion of the lungs and a relatively greater volume of air, or ventilation, in the upper lungs. The absence of gravity was believed to bring about changes in the normal distribution of perfusion and ventilation in the pulmonary system.

Four experiments to study the cardiovascular/cardiopulmonary system were performed on SLS-1. One experiment, led by cardiologist C. Gunnar Blomqvist of the University of Texas Southwestern Medical Center in Dallas, was designed not only to measure the body's fluid redistribution but also to document changes in the pressure of blood as it returns to the heart (central venous pressure), the size of the heart chambers, the electrical activity of the heart, and blood flow in the legs. The subject of the experiment was crew member Gaffney, who is also a cardiologist. Central venous pressure was measured by a thin flexible catheter, connected to a pressure recording system, inserted into Gaffney's arm vein and advanced to a point in the vena cava, the large vein that returns blood to the heart. Although this procedure is fairly common in hospitals and laboratories on Earth, its performance on SLS-1 marked the first time that it had been attempted during spaceflight. The catheter was inserted before launch and measured central venous pressure before and during liftoff as well as for the first several hours of weightlessness. Changes in the sizes of the heart chambers were measured by echocardiography, a technique that uses ultrasound

waves to produce images of the heart. An electrocardiogram simultaneously recorded the heart's rhythm and electrical activity. Cardiovascular function was measured at rest and also during exercise on a bicycle ergometer.

A closely related experiment led by Leon E. Farhi of the State University of New York at Buffalo focused on cardiovascular and cardiopulmonary deconditioning. Noninvasive techniques measured changes in the function of the heart and blood vessels, oxygen used and carbon dioxide produced, and function and volume of the lungs. The astronauts were tested at rest and while performing various levels of exercise on a bicycle ergometer. Through comparisons of results of the test performed before, during, and after flight, the crew members' cardiovascular status could be determined.

Blood pressure control was the subject of a study by Dwain L. Eckberg of the Hunter Holmes McGuire Veterans Administration Medical Center and the Medical College of Virginia in Richmond. Natural sensors called baroreceptors—located in the carotid arteries, the principal arteries on each side of the neck, and in the aorta, the main artery arising out of the left ventricle of the heart—sense changes in blood pressure, such as those that occur when a person moves from a sitting or supine to a standing position on Earth. In weightlessness, however, these pressure changes are eliminated, and the ability of the baroreceptors to control blood pressure may therefore decline during spaceflight, contributing to orthostatic intolerance, or a tendency to faint upon standing, which had previously been observed in some crew members after flight. Orthostatic intolerance would be a safety concern if an emergency required the crew to rapidly evacuate the spacecraft shortly after landing. In the SLS-1 experiment, an inflatable neck cuff applied positive and negative pressures to stimulate the carotid baroreceptors, and heart rate and blood pressure responses

Mission specialist Bagian removes a thin, flexible catheter from the vein of payload specialist Gaffney, who was the subject of an experiment looking at cardiovascular adaptation in the absence of gravity. The catheter was inserted before launch and measured central venous pressure during liftoff and in the first hours of exposure to weightlessness.

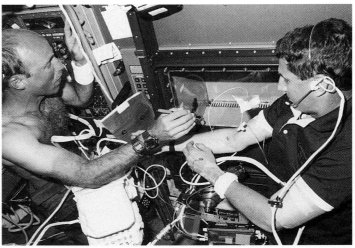

NASA

were monitored to determine the effectiveness of the baroreceptors. This type of study had not been performed previously during spaceflight.

Comprehensive testing of pulmonary function in space was also done for the first time during SLS-1. An experiment designed by John B. West of the University of California at San Diego examined the ability of gases to diffuse through the lungs and the distribution of blood flow and ventilation in the lungs. The crew members breathed different gas mixtures, and the exhaled air was then analyzed by a mass spectrometer to determine lung function. Results from the spaceflight tests were then compared with the results from ground-based tests to determine the effects of weightlessness.

Studies of bodily fluids and kidney function. The body's volume and pressure receptors may perceive the headward redistribution of bodily fluids as a fluid overload. To reduce the blood volume, hormones that control kidney function promote the excretion of excess fluid as urine, but the exact mechanism responsible for this was not known. A comprehensive study of these responses had never been done during spaceflight, particularly in the very early phases of flight, when rapid changes may be occurring. Therefore, immediate and adaptive changes in kidney function, in blood, water, salt, and mineral content, in the amount of fluid in cells and tissues, and in blood and urine levels of hormones that affect the kidneys and circulation were monitored in an experiment led by Carolyn S. Leach of the NASA Johnson Space Center in Houston, Texas. During the flight, crew members' intake of food, fluids, and medications was monitored, as was their body mass.

One of the results of the shift and loss of bodily fluids (*e.g.,* blood plasma) that occur during weightlessness is hemoconcentration, a relative increase in the cellular component of blood. The body responds to this perceived excess by reducing the number of red blood cells—a phenomenon that had been observed during experiments on previous spaceflights. Again, however, the precise mechanism by which this occurs was not known. Three experiments sought to characterize the magnitude and time course of blood volume and red blood cell changes as well as to define the mechanisms responsible for the changes. Clarence P. Alfrey of Baylor College of Medicine in Houston conducted two related experiments, one using the astronauts as subjects and the other using rats; by measuring plasma volume, red blood cell mass, and red blood cell production and removal in both humans and rats, scientists are able to validate the use of animals as models for human studies. A related study by Robert D. Lange of the University of Tennessee Medical Center in Knoxville examined in great detail the regulation of erythropoiesis, or red blood cell production, in rats.

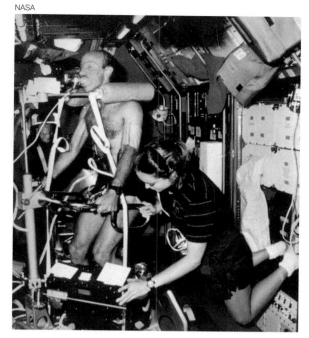

As part of a study measuring the deconditioning effects of spaceflight on cardiovascular/cardiopulmonary function, astronaut Bagian, assisted by flight engineer Jernigan, takes his turn exercising on a bicycle ergometer.

Assessing immune function. Space shuttle crew members have shown a decrease in the number of circulating lymphocytes, a type of white blood cell important in fighting infections. However, the astronauts have not shown increased susceptibility to infections, and their lymphocyte levels have returned to normal soon after landing. An experiment designed by Augusto Cogoli of the Institute for Biotechnology in Zürich, Switz., examined the effects of weightlessness on lymphocyte activation. Lymphocytes isolated from donors and from the astronauts at various times before, during, and after the mission were placed in a culture medium in an incubator. The reaction of the isolated lymphocytes to a substance that causes their activation was studied to determine the effects of spaceflight on their functioning.

Musculoskeletal system studies. In the absence of gravity during spaceflight, muscles and bones are no longer required to support the body's weight; astronauts tend to float instead of walk. The leg muscles of astronauts become weakened, losing mass as well as protein, the major component of muscle. This phenomenon is also observed in patients who are chronically bedridden. The changes may occur as a result of a decrease in protein synthesis, an increase in protein breakdown, or both, and the specific biochemical mechanisms regulating them are unknown. Minerals such as calcium and phosphorus have been shown to be lost from bones during spaceflight, most of the

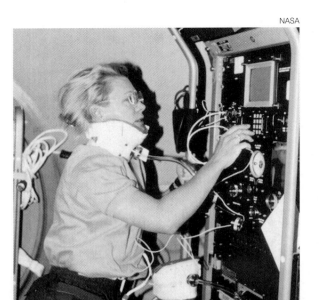

Wearing an inflatable neck cuff, mission specialist Seddon applies positive and negative pressure to the baroreceptors in the carotid arteries of the neck to test their ability to control blood pressure in the absence of gravity.

loss occurring in the legs and spine. The loss of calcium through the urine is of particular concern since it may predispose astronauts to kidney stone formation. Exercise during spaceflight has been shown to minimize the changes in muscles and bones but not to eliminate them completely.

Four experiments, one using astronauts and three using rats, examined changes in muscles. A study designed by T. Peter Stein of the University of Medicine and Dentistry of New Jersey in Camden examined muscle protein synthesis and breakdown rates: crew members ingested a labeled amino acid that is incorporated into protein, which was then measured in urine. Nitrogen balance was investigated through measurements of levels of nitrogen-containing products of muscle protein breakdown in urine samples. Kenneth M. Baldwin of the University of California at Irvine examined the biochemical and metabolic properties of rat skeletal muscles by analyzing the concentration of certain key enzymes in the muscles of animals that flew in space and in control animals on the ground. In a study led by Dan A. Riley of the Medical College of Wisconsin in Milwaukee, light and electron microscopy were used to study morphological changes in the muscles of rats flown in space; the muscles were analyzed for enzymes that cause muscle breakdown. An experiment by Joseph Foon Yoong Hoh of the University of Sydney, Australia, examined the effects of weightlessness on the speed of muscle contraction by analyzing different forms of myosin, an enzyme responsible for muscle contraction.

Two experiments examined changes in bone and calcium metabolism. Claude D. Arnaud of the University of California at San Francisco measured the levels of parathyroid hormone, calcitonin, and vitamin D metabolites in the blood and urine of crew members. These substances are involved in bone and calcium metabolism. A closely related experiment led by Emily M. Holton of the NASA Ames Research Center at Moffett Field, California, examined bone growth and strength in rats by using markers that are incorporated into growing bone.

Studies of neurosensory changes. The lack of gravity during spaceflight affects the neurosensory and neuromuscular systems. Space motion sickness was recognized from the earliest days of spaceflight, and most neurological research in space has focused on understanding, treating, and preventing it. Subtle changes in balance, orientation, and proprioception (a sense of the position of the body) have also been reported by astronauts but had not been studied in great detail. Experiments using humans, rats, and jellyfish (*Aurelia aurita*), which have gravity receptors to maintain balance and direction, were designed to investigate these phenomena.

Laurence R. Young of the Massachusetts Institute of Technology led a comprehensive experiment to investigate neurovestibular function in humans during spaceflight. One part examined the influence of weightlessness on the interaction of the otolith organs and the semicircular canals, vestibular organs within the labyrinth—the tortuous cavities of the inner ear—that sense linear and rotational acceleration, respectively, and their combined effect on eye movements. Another part of the experiment examined the specific manifestations of space motion sickness and the relation between head movements and symptom severity. Susceptibility to motion sickness was also examined before and after flight. The relative importance of visual, tactile, and vestibular information on the perception of body orientation was the subject of another part of the study. The interaction of the otolith organs and leg muscles, the so-called vestibulospinal reflex, was also studied, as was the ability of crew members to sense the correct position of their limbs or of an external target with their eyes closed.

Muriel D. Ross of the Ames Research Center investigated the structural changes that may occur in the otolith organs of rats during spaceflight. The otolith organs contain microscopic calcium crystals whose displacement by gravity or linear acceleration stimulates nerve endings, with the resulting signals interpreted by the brain. Prolonged weightlessness may cause morphological changes in the crystals. In a related study, Dorothy B. Spangenberg of the Eastern Virginia Medical School in Norfolk examined the development and function of jellyfish statoliths, which are analogous to the human otolith organs. The swimming patterns of jellyfish that developed in weightlessness were assessed for any differences from those of earthbound jellyfish.

Analyzing the data: preliminary findings

Complete analysis of the wealth of data gathered during the SLS-1 mission may take years, but some preliminary results are available. The expected fluid shift from the legs to the upper body was observed. An unexpected result was a decrease in central venous pressure following entry into weightlessness; the excess blood near the heart caused by the fluid redistribution was expected to cause an increase in pressure. Although these data are available from an experiment on only one crew member, current concepts about acute cardiovascular adaptation to weightlessness may require revision. Exercise capacity was reduced after flight, possibly as a result of altered fluid status, but it had returned to normal within one week. The expected postflight orthostatic intolerance was observed, and there is good evidence that baroreceptor function was altered during flight. The relative contributions of fluid status changes and altered baroreceptor function to orthostatic intolerance are not yet known. Small changes were seen in pulmonary function, but expected alterations in the distribution of ventilation and perfusion in the lungs caused by the absence of gravity were not observed.

Preliminary analysis indicates that plasma volume is significantly reduced early in flight, contributing to a decrease in total body water. As the mission progressed, the fluid volumes tended to increase toward preflight levels. The rate of blood filtration through the kidneys was elevated during flight. The responses of regulatory hormones were consistent with the observed bodily fluid changes. In both humans and rats, red blood cell mass was reduced after flight, apparently because of decreased red blood cell production. The proliferation of lymphocytes was decreased in the cells cultured in weightlessness, but a direct link to reduced immune function cannot be made.

Spaceflight caused an increase in muscle protein synthesis, probably as a result of increased stress. In rats a significant decrease in muscle mass was observed, and the efficiency of muscles that are normally used for weight bearing was reduced. There was also increased vulnerability to muscle fiber damage caused by muscle atrophy. The ability of muscles to use fatty acids as an energy source was reduced in flight but recovered immediately after the mission. An increase in serum calcium levels was observed, probably caused by resorption of bone and not by hormonal factors.

As expected, spaceflight offers at least temporary immunity against motion sickness upon return to Earth. During spaceflight the central nervous system tends to rely primarily on nonvestibular cues such as vision and touch to maintain orientation, but crew members' responses were found to be very individual. The ability to point to remembered targets with eyes closed was poorer in weightlessness but returned to normal within one week after landing. A temporary postural instability, caused by a combination of altered muscular and vestibular functions, was observed in the astronauts. The rats' otolith organs, however, showed no adverse effects from the nine-day spaceflight. While the jellyfish developed normally in weightlessness, their swimming behavior in space was different from that on Earth.

Ongoing life sciences research

The five other space shuttle missions in 1991 were in early April (*Atlantis*), April–May (*Discovery*), August (*Atlantis*), September (*Discovery*), and late November (*Atlantis*). As noted previously, biomedical studies have been flown on every space shuttle mission. The initial focus was on characterizing the immediate adaptation to weightlessness and specifically on the causes of space motion sickness. More recently, these have expanded to include investigations of cardiovascular deconditioning, muscle loss, changes in coordination and balance, effects of radiation exposure, and changes in the body's biochemistry and in pharmacokinetics (the absorption, distribution, metabolism, and excretion of drugs). The development of appropriate countermeasures to minimize or prevent some of the adverse effects of spaceflight has been the goal of many of these studies. Most experiments are considered to be investigations-in-progress and are flown on several missions to increase the statistical reliability of the results.

Various aspects of cardiovascular adaptation to weightlessness and particularly the consequences of this adaptation for normal function after spaceflight are the focus of several of these ongoing investigations. In space the effects of weightlessness on heart rate and rhythm are studied by 24-hour ambulatory electrocardiographic monitoring. Blood pressure and its control are monitored through the responses of the baroreceptors (as described above). During the critical final phases of the mission and the immediate postflight period, heart rate and blood pressure are monitored for signs of orthostatic intolerance; hormonal responses during orthostasis are also monitored. Tests of possible countermeasures to postflight orthostatic intolerance include having crew members ingest a salt solution prior to landing and applying negative pressure to the lower half of the body to simulate the pull of gravity.

The effects of spaceflight on neuromuscular function are also continually being studied: crew members' aerobic exercise capacity; aerobic and anaerobic metabolism; and muscle size, strength, and composition are measured on virtually all shuttle flights. Postflight postural equilibrium, a combination of muscular and vestibular effects, is studied, as are the interactions among visual, vestibular, and proprioceptive systems for head and gaze stability.

Future plans

Work is already well under way in preparation for SLS-2, the next mission in the Spacelab Life Sciences series, scheduled for 1993. Many of the experiments performed on SLS-1 will be continued in order to increase the number of subjects involved in the various studies and to enhance some of the methodologies. Future missions in the series will investigate the muscular and neurological systems in greater detail. Biomedical experiments will also be flown as part of the other NASA shuttle missions, including on flights sponsored by Japan, Germany, and the European Space Agency. Life sciences studies will continue to be a significant focus of the scientific investigations carried out in space, which will ultimately ensure crew health and safety during long-duration space station *Freedom* operations and beyond.

—*Arnauld E. Nicogossian, M.D.,
and Howard Schneider, Ph.D.*

AIDS

When a new and puzzling illness was first reported in 1981, very few people had any idea of the incredible changes—personal, social, economic, legal, and political, as well as medical—that would occur as a result. After much confusion and controversy, it was finally determined that the baffling constellation of symptoms was indeed a distinct clinical entity; because the hallmark of the disorder was a gradual failure of the immune system, it was given the name acquired immune deficiency syndrome, or AIDS. There were many theories about its cause, but in 1984 scientists isolated the virus that is responsible for AIDS, subsequently named the human immunodeficiency virus (HIV). Today this disease, unknown a little over a decade ago, has been found in virtually every country in the world and in all types of populations. It has emerged as the major public health problem of the last two decades of the 20th century and is likely to remain so well into the 21st.

Reported cases: alarming increase

There are many ways of viewing the numerous changes wrought by this devastating disease. However, no assessment of the impact of AIDS would be complete without a look at the sheer numbers involved. In the United States alone, from mid-1981 through the end of 1987, 50,000 cases were reported to the Centers for Disease Control (CDC). The total number of U.S. cases reached the 100,000 mark in August 1989. Then, between September 1989 and November 1991, another 100,000 cases were reported. Probably the most alarming aspect of these statistics is that while the first 100,000 cases were reported over an eight-year time period, the second 100,000 occurred in only two years. By June 30, 1992, a cumulative total of more than 230,000 cases had been reported to the CDC; AIDS deaths in the U.S. numbered more than 150,000. Of the one million individuals in the U.S. believed to be infected with HIV, slightly more than 20% have now developed AIDS, and that number will increase. Experts currently do not know how many of those who are infected will die of AIDS, but estimates range from 50 to 90%. In May 1992, when the CDC published its statistics on the leading causes of death for 1990, AIDS was tied with birth defects as the sixth most important cause of premature death and was the second fastest growing (just behind homicide).

Worldwide a similar rapid increase in the number of persons affected has been observed and documented in studies by the World Health Organization (WHO). In July 1991 WHO estimated that about 10 million people were infected with HIV. Six months later, however, WHO's Global Program on AIDS published a report

An AIDS patient is looked after in a hospital in Thailand, one of the first Asian countries to report a significant number of cases of the disease. Epidemiologists monitoring the global spread of AIDS predict an increasingly serious situation throughout Asia in the coming decade.

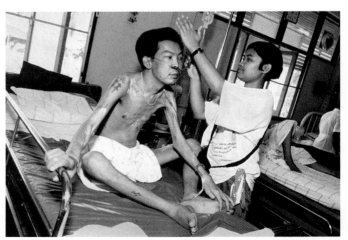

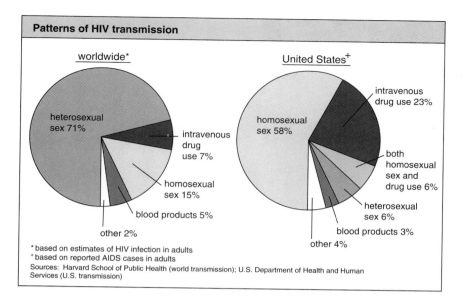

Patterns of HIV transmission

worldwide*

heterosexual sex 71%

intravenous drug use 7%

homosexual sex 15%

blood products 5%

other 2%

United States⁺

homosexual sex 58%

intravenous drug use 23%

both homosexual sex and drug use 6%

heterosexual sex 6%

blood products 3%

other 4%

* based on estimates of HIV infection in adults
⁺ based on reported AIDS cases in adults
Sources: Harvard School of Public Health (world transmission); U.S. Department of Health and Human Services (U.S. transmission)

assessing the dimensions of the AIDS pandemic, in which the agency estimated that as many as 12 million individuals around the world had already contracted HIV. The WHO report also indicated that AIDS would very soon be the major cause of premature death in many U.S. and western European cities. In less developed countries—which accounted for 90% of all new infections—the situation was even more disturbing. According to the WHO estimates, by the end of the decade 10 million African children will have been orphaned by AIDS. Moreover, WHO statistics show that the rate of AIDS in Asia is rising rapidly; by the end of the decade, Asians could surpass Africans—currently the largest reservoir for the virus—in the numbers becoming infected each year.

How accurate are the WHO predictions? A group of experts at the Harvard School of Public Health believe the international agency has seriously underestimated the true extent of the epidemic, which, according to their projections, could affect as many as 110 million people by the end of the decade. Whereas the WHO statistics are based on official government reports, the Harvard researchers based their figures on interviews with authorities around the world and analysis of hundreds of AIDS programs. The Harvard group suggested that the WHO estimates might have been influenced by political pressures exerted by member nations.

Shifting demographics

When the U.S. data on the first and second 100,000 cases are compared, it becomes clear that there have been significant changes in the population groups affected by AIDS. Among the first 100,000 cases, the major groups of patients were homosexual or bisexual men with no history of being intravenous (IV)

drug users (61%) and female and heterosexual male IV drug users (total, 20%). In contrast, in the second 100,000, 55% of reported cases occurred in homosexual or bisexual men with no history of drug abuse; female and heterosexual male drug users constituted 24%. (Smaller percentages of cases were reported in other groups, including a small proportion for whom no specific risk factors could be identified.)

Although the transmission of HIV in less developed countries in Africa and elsewhere has been predominately (90%) heterosexual in nature, this has not been true in the United States. There are signs, however, that this pattern is also beginning to change. Of the first 100,000 U.S. cases, 5% were attributed to heterosexual transmission; 7% of the second 100,000 cases were transmitted heterosexually—a 44% increase.

The number of AIDS cases reported among women went up as well, from 9% of the total in the first 100,000 to 12% in the second 100,000. Thirty-four percent of these were attributed to heterosexual transmission; further, of the reported cases of HIV infection attributed to heterosexual transmission, women account for 61%. The most recent CDC data show that while most causes of death among U.S. women are not changing in incidence, AIDS deaths are climbing at an alarming rate. In 1987 AIDS was the number one cause of death among black women aged 25–34 in New York and New Jersey. The number of U.S. children with AIDS is also increasing. In the first 100,000 cases there were 1,683 children, 81% of whom acquired the disease from their mothers. The second 100,000 cases included 1,702 children, of whom 87% acquired the infection perinatally.

Major variations continue to be noted in infection rates among different racial and ethnic populations in the U.S. In the first group of 100,000 cases, 27%

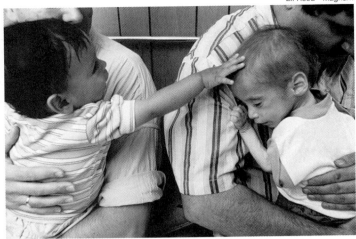

Two youngsters who were infected with the AIDS virus at birth are among the fortunate few who, though abandoned by their mothers, have found loving adoptive parents. As the number of female AIDS patients grows, so too will the number of infants born with the disease.

occurred among blacks and 15% among Hispanics. In the second 100,000 cases, these percentages changed to 31 and 17%, respectively. What has not changed is that these numbers show minorities to be at disproportionate risk of acquiring HIV infection.

While blood transfusions were a significant cause of infection in the earlier years of the epidemic, the advent of a blood-screening test and better regulation of the blood supply have resulted in a steady decrease in such cases. The number of transfusion-related cases of AIDS declined from 2.5 to 1.9% in the case of adults and from 11 to 5.6% in children.

As already noted, the most significant change in the U.S. pattern of infection is the increasing number and percentage of cases due to heterosexual transmission. Originally AIDS was considered to be a condition chiefly of homosexual men; belatedly and somewhat reluctantly, it has been recognized that this is clearly not the case. In fact, according to recent estimates, by 1995 the number of cases due to heterosexual contact may double. There are two main reasons for this trend. The first is the tendency of sexually active people to have multiple sexual partners. The second is the rapid escalation in the number of cases of other sexually transmitted diseases (STDs) among heterosexuals. The presence of certain STDs (herpes and other diseases associated with open ulcers or sores) has been shown to significantly increase the risk of HIV transmission.

Another recently noted demographic shift is that the largest number of new AIDS cases is occurring in the southern U.S., the region that had the largest increases in cases in both 1990 and 1991. Thus, AIDS is no longer primarily a concern of the urban northeast and California.

Debate over the definition of AIDS

Early in the AIDS epidemic, problems were encountered in trying to formulate an official case definition (a list of criteria that, when present, confirm that an individual has the disease in question). Putting together such a definition for AIDS proved to be very difficult inasmuch as AIDS per se has no clear clinical picture. Multiple definitions were considered, most of them originating from the CDC, which is responsible for collecting and publishing data on infectious diseases in the U.S.

AIDS has been diagnosed in terms of the presence of certain characteristic opportunistic infections—those occurring in people whose immune systems have been damaged by HIV—the primary ones being *Pneumocystis carinii* pneumonia (PCP), toxoplasmosis of the brain, Kaposi's sarcoma (a form of skin cancer), genital herpes simplex with chronic ulcers, dementia, encephalopathy, and wasting syndrome (progressive weight loss and emaciation). These conditions are rarely seen in people with intact immune systems.

In recent years, however, this definition has come under criticism because it does not include many of the conditions typically seen in women and IV drug users with AIDS. As a result, those people are often refused benefits by insurance companies and government agencies, which have used the official case definition to decide who is eligible. Consequently, many health care workers and patient advocates are in favor of the adoption of a broader definition, and in 1991 an addition to the original definition was proposed. This states that any HIV-infected person with a blood count of 200 or fewer CD4 lymphocytes (the white blood cells that are a major target of the virus) per cubic millimeter of blood should be considered to have AIDS even in the absence of clinical symptoms. (A normal, healthy individual has about 1,000 CD4 cells per cubic millimeter.)

Adoption of this proposed expansion of the case definition of AIDS could have far-reaching implications. For one thing, it would allow more accurate tracking of the numbers of people affected by the AIDS epidemic. Even more significant, the new definition would greatly expand the number of people classified as having AIDS; although it would have no impact on the total incidence of HIV infection itself, the expanded definition might well double the number of people officially classified as having AIDS—potentially adding from 150,000 to 200,000 cases to the existing totals. Further, the expanded definition would, in particular, increase the number of recognized cases in women and IV drug users—two groups that already represent a rapidly growing proportion of AIDS patients. In addition, with the use of drugs such as AZT that delay the onset of opportunistic diseases in those who test positive for HIV, retaining the narrower definition could well mask the true number of people who actually have AIDS, leading to health care planning and allocation of resources based on unrealistically low estimates.

There has also been considerable concern that the new definition could have untoward consequences for health care costs and provision of services. In New York City, for example, which has the largest number of AIDS cases in the U.S., the already overburdened health care system might well be swamped as a result of this proposed change. Adoption of the broader criteria would undoubtedly add to the number of laboratory tests being requested and would probably substantially increase the numbers entitled to medical care.

It has also been pointed out that the new definition would not solve the problem of the large numbers of HIV-positive indigent people and IV drug users who are undiagnosed; they would remain so even under the changed definition simply because they do not avail themselves of or have access to testing or medical care. Moreover, many diagnoses of AIDS would continue to be missed because people with HIV are susceptible to a host of other diseases and conditions that are not mentioned in either the present definition or the proposed new one. These include tuberculosis, now occurring in rapidly growing numbers of HIV-infected individuals; some viral STDs; major bacterial infections such as pelvic inflammatory disease; chronic vaginal candidiasis; endocarditis (inflammation of the lining of the heart and its valves); lymphoma; and cervical cancer. A particularly important disease in this group is syphilis, which is being seen in increasing numbers in both adults and children (congenital syphilis). Public health authorities are particularly disturbed by the apparent resurgence of this disease, which for many years was believed to have been virtually eliminated. It remains to be seen what, if any, changes will be made to the official case definition of AIDS.

Doctors, patients, and HIV

In July 1991 the CDC asked the major U.S. professional health care organizations to develop lists of

Sarah Krulwich—The New York Times

Actor and playwright Jim Hansen is one of many HIV-infected individuals who do not meet the case definition of AIDS; overlooked in the official statistics, this group is also denied disability benefits accorded to AIDS patients.

procedures that should be classified as "invasive" to indicate the potential risk of HIV transmission from an infected health care worker to a patient. Probably the major impetus for this action was the tragic case of Kimberly Bergalis, a Florida woman who died of AIDS in December 1991; Bergalis and four other persons were allegedly infected by their dentist, who had continued to practice after discovering that he was HIV positive.

After much debate, almost all professional medical and dental organizations concluded that drawing up such a list would be scientifically unjustified and medically irrelevant. Further, by creating the false impression that some procedures are more risky than others, such a step would actually be counterproductive. Subsequently, the CDC abandoned its plan to develop a list of "exposure-prone" procedures and instead suggested new guidelines that would allow case-by-case decisions regarding whether individual HIV-infected health workers should be allowed to carry out specific procedures. A decision would be based on the procedure in question, the worker's adherence to standard infection-control practices, and his or her medical condition. The various specialty groups pointed out that the best strategy for avoiding transmission of HIV from health care workers to patients is increased emphasis on infection control—so-called universal precautions—that had already been developed. The American Medical Association—having abandoned its support for the plan to list exposure-prone procedures—was nevertheless supportive of voluntary testing for doctors who perform surgical and other high-risk procedures. Specifically, it recommended that HIV-positive physicians be carefully

233

Testifying before a congressional committee in September 1991, less than three months before she died, Kimberly Bergalis—one of five people believed to have acquired AIDS from an infected dentist—urged lawmakers to pass a bill requiring health care workers who perform invasive procedures to undergo testing for the AIDS virus. Accompanied by her parents, Bergalis told the committee, "My life has been taken away. Please enact legislation so other patients and health care providers don't have to go through the hell that I have."

supervised by panels of experts appointed by local health departments to ensure that they conform to strict infection-control practices.

In order to grapple with the practical problems of overseeing practice by HIV-infected health care workers, several states decided on their own procedures. After some deliberation, a New York state commission announced that it was opposed to and would not require mandatory HIV testing of health care professionals. The commission believed, rather, that the most effective way to prevent transmission to patients was rigorous adherence to the universal precautions previously outlined by the CDC. It further stated that HIV-infected health care workers in New York would be able to perform invasive procedures without being required to disclose their HIV status to patients. The Michigan Department of Public Health also took the position that infected health care workers should

continue to practice unless review of the particular situation by a local committee indicated that there was a significant risk. Finally, in June 1992 the CDC decided to authorize state and local health departments throughout the U.S. to decide, on a case-by-case basis, the kind of care that may be provided by HIV-positive professionals, thus apparently ending the attempts to establish an official list of high-risk procedures that infected health care workers would be forbidden to perform.

While health care professionals debated the merits of specifying high-risk procedures, Congress considered the passage of laws that would restrict the activities of HIV-infected health care workers. There was strong feeling—on the part of physicians and other scientists, AIDS advocates, and others—that such proposals derived more from the desires of some individuals for political aggrandizement than from con-

Removing a sterile instrument from its sealed package, a Manhattan dentist reassures a patient of the precautions his office is taking to reduce the risk of AIDS transmission. After much deliberation about restricting the activities of infected health care workers, almost all organizations representing U.S. health professionals agreed in 1992 that rigorous infection-control procedures would be more effective in protecting the public than legal sanctions against individuals.

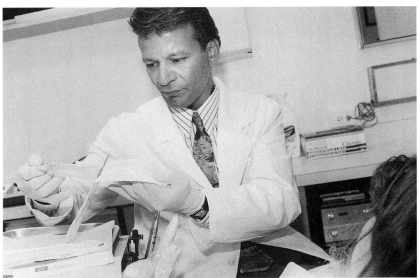

cern with scientifically documented risks. Sen. Jesse Helms (Rep., N.C.) attracted publicity—and, perhaps, some votes—when he suggested that the failure of a physician to disclose HIV-positive status should be classified as a criminal offense punishable with a prison sentence.

Not surprisingly, Congress rejected this extreme position and instead approved a bill that suggested—but did not require—that health care workers be tested for HIV and left it to the states to adopt specific rules regarding disclosure and continued medical practice. In commending this decision, Rep. Henry Waxman (Dem., Calif.), chairman of the House Subcommittee on Health and the Environment, declared, "Mandatory testing is not an answer. Gloves and sterile instruments will protect more patients and workers than any testing program possibly could." Waxman said he felt that the legislators had acted responsibly in resisting political pressures to come up with a "quick fix."

In the meantime, studies of more than 15,000 patients of health care workers known to be HIV positive failed to find a single one—other than those in Florida—who had acquired the disease from an infected practitioner. Further, while sophisticated molecular genetic techniques strongly suggested that Bergalis and four others had indeed been infected by the dentist, an extensive investigation had been unable to determine exactly how the transmission had occurred.

The future

At the present time, the AIDS epidemic continues to grow and spread. The concept that it can be controlled by vigorous public health efforts is no longer tenable. What is needed is more biomedical research, leading eventually to the development of an effective vaccine. Of great interest is a recent study in chimpanzees in which a new vaccine was shown to protect against infection both before and after exposure to HIV. This experiment might indicate the ultimate feasibility of using vaccines to protect individuals in the aftermath of exposure—for example, following needlestick injuries. In the U.S., vaccine testing and other promising research efforts by the National Institutes of Health have been hampered by budgetary cuts, but even so, the agency still hopes to have an effective vaccine by the end of the decade. In the U.S. alone about 18 universities and a dozen different drug manufacturers are actively involved in attempts to develop a vaccine, as are a number of European researchers. The major obstacle all must overcome is the remarkable ability of HIV to mutate when exposed to a particular vaccine. Moreover, because of differences in HIV strains around the world, promising vaccines will have to be tested on small populations in the countries where they will be used before mass vaccination can be undertaken.

—Elizabeth B. Connell, M.D.

Asthma

The rates of illness and death from asthma are increasing. From 1979 to 1989 the prevalence of asthma in the U.S. climbed 60% (from 3% of the population in 1979 to 4.8% in 1989); death rates for asthma as the first-listed diagnosis rose 31%. Paradoxically, these changes, which remain to be explained, are occurring at a time when scientific advances are providing a better understanding of asthma and offering new therapies. Appreciation of the nature of the disease and implementation of effective treatment strategies may help reverse this disturbing trend. In 1991 the U.S. National Heart, Lung, and Blood Institute's National Asthma Education Program (NAEP) expert panel issued the report *Guidelines for the Diagnosis and Management of Asthma*. The discussion that follows emphasizes new approaches to controlling asthma, which are based on those guidelines.

Key features of asthma

Asthma is a chronic disease of the air passages of the lungs. Key abnormalities include obstruction, or narrowing, of the airway that is usually reversible either spontaneously or with treatment; inflammation of the airway; and hyperresponsiveness of the airway to a variety of stimuli.

Airway obstruction is responsible for the symptoms of wheezing, difficulty in breathing, and coughing experienced in asthma episodes (attacks). Airway narrowing may worsen gradually and persist, but it can also develop abruptly and produce acute breathing problems. It was long considered that asthma episodes resulted only from bronchospasm caused by muscular constriction of the bronchi (the larger airway passages in the lungs), progressing to airway obstruction. For several decades asthma therapy was based on this concept and relied primarily on such bronchodilator agents as beta$_2$-adrenergic agonists (beta$_2$ agonists) and theophylline, which relax bronchial smooth muscle and thus open the airway.

Recently it has become recognized that asthma is more than bronchospasm. Airway obstruction is also influenced by other factors, including swelling of the bronchial wall, excessive production of mucus, and hypertrophy, or thickening, of the airway's smooth muscle. Airway obstruction is now thought to be initiated by inflammatory events in the airway—a view that has led to the current emphasis on anti-inflammatory agents in long-term control of asthma.

The tissues of the airways of people with asthma are populated with a number of different inflammatory cells, which interact in a complex way through the release of a variety of chemicals that mediate the inflammatory response. The process produces injury to the cellular lining, or epithelium, of the airway passages; it increases airway smooth-muscle responsiveness to stimuli; and it contributes to airflow obstruction. Epithelial injury in turn can lead to increased sensitivity to inhaled substances and inflammatory mediators; in addition, it can allow fluid leakage into airway tissues and reduce the ability of the airway to clear inflammatory substances and respiratory secretions. The inflammatory process may chronically irritate the airway. Lung-tissue studies of people with asthma indicate that inflammatory changes are present in the airways of individuals with mild or inactive disease as well as in the airways of those with severe asthma. This finding suggests the importance of the inflammatory process in virtually all cases of asthma.

Airway hyperresponsiveness, or hyperreactivity, is an exaggerated bronchoconstrictor response to a number of physical and chemical agents; e.g., allergens (substances that provoke allergic reactions) like pollen or animal dander, environmental irritants like automobile emissions or cigarette smoke, viral respiratory infections, cold air, or exercise. Whether airway hyperresponsiveness, a fundamental characteristic of asthma, is present at birth in genetically predisposed individuals or is acquired later in life is a subject of current debate, although it is well known that individuals can develop asthma occupationally as a direct result of exposure to various substances found in the work environment.

Airway inflammation appears to be a key factor in hyperresponsiveness, given the evidence suggesting the presence of airway inflammation in all cases of asthma and the observation that treatments that reduce bronchial inflammation in asthma patients appear to decrease airway hyperresponsiveness. Abnormalities in neural mechanisms of the airway may also contribute to hyperresponsiveness.

Essence of asthma treatment

With proper medical management, people with asthma should not have to miss work, school, or a night's sleep because of their disease. The specific goals for therapy are to (1) control chronic symptoms, including nighttime symptoms, (2) maintain normal activity levels, including exercise, (3) maintain normal or near-normal lung function, (4) prevent acute asthma episodes, and (5) avoid adverse effects from asthma medications.

Asthma treatment is based on an appreciation of the key features and course of the disease and has four critical components: the use of objective measures of lung function to assess the severity of asthma and to monitor the effect of therapy, comprehensive drug therapy in which the primary goal for all but mild occasional asthma is to suppress and prevent airway inflammation, environmental measures to reduce or control exposure to allergens and irritants, and patient education.

A page from a peak flow meter diary records a week of lung-function measurements made each morning and evening by a patient with asthma. The drop into the "yellow" zone on day 2 alerted the patient to the need for additional medication, while the more serious decline into the "red" zone later in the week called for both additional drugs and medical attention.

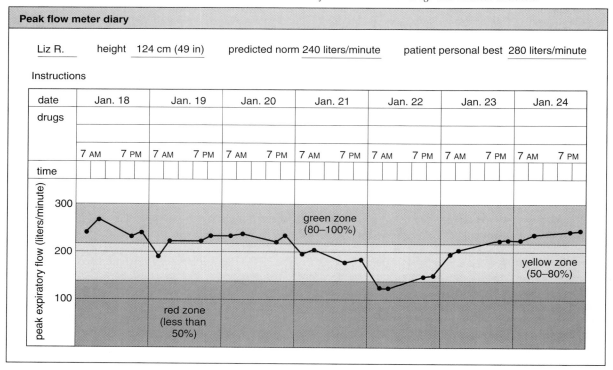

Measuring lung function

Lung-function studies are essential for diagnosing asthma and for assessing its severity in order to plan and monitor therapy. They also appear to reflect the degree of airway hyperresponsiveness, which may correlate with airway inflammation. Objective assessments of lung function, made with measuring devices, are particularly important because subjective measures, such as patients' symptom reports and physicians' physical examination findings, often do not correlate with the variability and severity of airflow obstruction. By the time wheezing can be heard through a stethoscope, a person's peak expiratory flow (PEF; the highest rate of exhalation achievable, measured in liters per minute [l/min]) may have already decreased 25% or more. Poor perception of severity by the patient and the physician is a major cause of delay in treatment.

Objective measurements of lung function should be performed in the physician's office during each visit. Furthermore, patients over five years of age who have moderate to severe asthma, and therefore are receiving daily drug treatment, should have daily (preferably morning and evening) home PEF measurements, which can be taken with a simple hand-held device called a peak flow meter. Home PEF measurements become an especially useful monitor of the course of asthma for the patient and physician and a guide to adjustments in therapy when they are charted in a daily diary that has been developed in accordance with the patient's personal asthma-management plan. Such a diary, for example, may be divided into zones analogous to the colors of a traffic signal light. When the patient's readings are in the "green" zone, remaining above a certain minimum level, the message is "all clear"; the patient should follow the regular management plan. When the readings dip into the "yellow" zone, the message is "caution"; PEF has declined and may well fall further—additional medication is required. Readings that drop still more, into the "red" zone, signal a medical alert; PEF has declined significantly—additional medication and medical attention are necessary.

For example, a female patient who usually has a peak flow rate greater than 225 l/min measures a decrease in PEF to below 200 l/min, without significant symptoms, following a brief encounter with a sensitizing agent (a friend's cat). After she uses a $beta_2$ agonist, her PEF returns to normal. A few days later, in the course of a respiratory tract infection, her PEF falls steadily through the yellow zone, but she cannot distinguish her asthmatic symptoms from those of the infection. She ignores the declining PEF, her symptoms become marked, and her PEF enters the red zone. She now requires more intensive and prolonged therapy than if she had acted upon the first signs of declining PEF.

A nurse shows a patient with asthma how to use a peak flow meter to measure lung function. Employed regularly at home, the device is a particularly valuable tool for monitoring the course of an individual's disease and response to therapy.

Drug therapy: "preventers" or "relievers"

The two main groups of medications for asthma therapy are anti-inflammatory agents and bronchodilators. Anti-inflammatory agents interrupt the development of airway inflammation and have a preventive and suppressive action; they have no direct bronchodilating action and thus do not reverse the immediate bronchospasm experienced in an asthma episode. Bronchodilators act principally to dilate the airways by relaxing bronchial smooth muscle; although they reverse or inhibit bronchoconstriction and related symptoms of asthma episodes, they do not reverse airway inflammation and hyperresponsiveness. Thus, anti-inflammatory agents are considered "preventer" agents in asthma therapy, whereas bronchodilator agents are "relievers."

The development of inhaled forms of asthma medications has led to greatly improved therapy. Asthma treatment via inhalation is preferable to treatment with oral (swallowed) or injected drugs because a higher concentration of the drug can be delivered directly and more effectively to the airways with relatively little systemic absorption and associated side effects.

Anti-inflammatory agents include corticosteroids, cromolyn sodium (sodium cromoglycate), and nedocromil sodium. Because of the importance of airway inflammation in asthma, anti-inflammatory agents are used as primary therapy for moderate and severe asthma.

Corticosteroids are the most effective anti-inflammatory agents for asthma. Inhaled forms appear to be safe for treating chronic asthma when administered at currently recommended doses. (Although the clinical importance of the side effects of long-term high doses has not been established, some studies suggest the association of systemic side effects with doses above 800–1,000 micrograms a day—and possibly with

237

doses below 800 micrograms a day in some patients.) Regular therapy with oral corticosteroids is employed for severe chronic asthma, but because their long-term use is associated with serious side effects, they are reserved for patients who have not responded well to high doses of inhaled corticosteroids. Short-term use of oral corticosteroids for severe asthma episodes is important because they prevent the episode from worsening, speed recovery, and prevent relapse.

Cromolyn sodium, a nonsteroidal, inhaled anti-inflammatory drug, is virtually devoid of side effects and thus is preferred as the initial anti-inflammatory asthma preventive for children. Nedocromil sodium has a mechanism of action similar to that of cromolyn sodium, but studies indicate that it is more potent and may have more extensive anti-inflammatory action. As with cromolyn sodium, this drug may be used for preventive therapy early in the disease. Employed in Europe and pending approval in the U.S., nedocromil sodium is not associated with significant side effects. It is a newer medication, and clinical trials are needed to establish its role in treating childhood asthma.

Bronchodilators include beta$_2$ agonists, theophylline, and anticholinergics. Short-acting, inhaled beta$_2$ agonists, which have a duration of action of 4–6 hours, are the drugs of choice for treating acute asthma episodes and for pretreating exercise-induced asthma. Although inhaled beta$_2$ agonists also have been commonly used on a scheduled daily basis for managing chronic asthma, recent reports suggested that such use was associated with diminished control of asthma. The nature of this connection is unclear and requires further study, but it is possible that beta$_2$ agonists may increase airway hyperresponsiveness when used regularly. Thus, the NAEP guidelines recommend that regularly scheduled inhaled beta$_2$ agonists be kept to a minimum. Furthermore, because well-controlled asthma requires only occasional use of inhaled beta$_2$ agonists, increased use is an indication of deteriorating control. If a patient relies on a beta$_2$ agonist inhaler every day to relieve symptoms, or more than three to four times on the day of an asthma episode, the experience usually means that anti-inflammatory therapy should be either initiated or intensified.

Two newer long-acting, inhaled beta$_2$ agonists, formoterol and salmeterol, have a duration of action of more than 12 hours. Preliminary work suggests that it is not appropriate to use long-acting beta$_2$ agonists for asthma episodes. They may be considered for maintenance therapy when standard doses of inhaled corticosteroids fail to control asthma, especially at night, and before the dose of inhaled corticosteroids is raised. Some specialists prefer to use them only after trying higher doses of inhaled corticosteroids.

The bronchodilator theophylline is available in either oral or injectable form but not as an inhaled medication. When given as a sustained-release preparation, it is useful in controlling nighttime symptoms. Although theophylline has the potential for significant side effects, they generally can be avoided by blood-sample monitoring and dosage adjustment. Theophylline once was used extensively, but inhaled beta$_2$ agonists have gained preference owing to their higher potency, fewer potential side effects, and simpler monitoring needs.

Inhaled anticholinergic agents (*e.g.,* ipratropium bromide) are less potent bronchodilators than inhaled beta$_2$ agonists and in general have a slower onset of action. Ipratropium bromide's benefits in asthma management have not been established, although it may be considered an alternative bronchodilator for patients who experience such adverse effects as tachycardia (abnormally rapid heartbeat) and tremor from beta$_2$ agonists.

A number of drugs currently under investigation show promise in asthma therapy. Immunosuppressive agents like methotrexate, gold compounds, and cyclosporine have significant anti-inflammatory activity, but their potential side effects may limit their use in patients with severe asthma who are either dependent on oral corticosteroids or steroid-resistant. Yet other drugs that inhibit key biochemical steps in the inflammatory process or in smooth muscle contraction are being assessed for asthma therapy.

There is only anecdotal evidence that some people benefit from the use of room-air ionizers, acupuncture, homeopathy, or other nonstandard treatment, and their effects in controlled clinical trials so far have been disappointing. Therefore, it is strongly recommended that conventional drug therapy be continued if these treatments are tried.

Stepwise management

Asthma is a disease that varies among patients. Furthermore, the degree of severity for any individual may change from one season or year to the next. Therefore, therapy must always be tailored and adjusted to individual needs and circumstances. The NAEP guidelines call for a stepwise approach to drug therapy in which the selection of treatment is based on asthma severity—mild, moderate, or severe—and the patient's current treatment. With increasing severity, the variety and frequency of medications are increased. Upward progression from one step to the next is indicated when control cannot be achieved at the current step and there is assurance that the patient is using medication correctly. The aim is to achieve the best possible control with the least possible medication. Once control has been sustained for several weeks or months, reduction in therapy—a step down—can be considered. In all cases treatment requires regular, continuous medical care and monitoring.

Patients with *mild* asthma are those with wheezing, coughing, and difficulty in breathing less often than twice a week; night cough or wheeze less than twice a month; and no symptoms between episodes. Short-acting, inhaled beta₂ agonists taken as needed are usually sufficient. If symptoms disappear and lung function becomes and remains normal, this treatment can be used indefinitely on an as-needed basis. However, the use of beta₂ agonists more than three or four times a day, or even daily use, indicates moderate disease and the need for additional therapy.

Patients with *moderate* asthma, if not treated adequately, experience symptoms more than twice a week and show diminished lung function. They need daily doses of anti-inflammatory agents—either inhaled corticosteroids, cromolyn sodium, or nedocromil sodium—as their primary therapy, plus short-acting, inhaled beta₂ agonists as needed to relieve symptoms. If the latter drugs are required daily or more than three or four times in one day, asthma control is poor, and anti-inflammatory therapy should be increased accordingly. Theophylline, an oral beta₂ agonist, or a long-acting, inhaled beta₂ agonist may be added, especially for the control of night symptoms.

Patients with *severe* asthma have continuous symptoms; frequent nighttime symptoms; frequent, often severe worsening of symptoms; impaired lung function; and limited activity levels. They should be evaluated by an asthma specialist. They require several different medications on a daily basis, including high doses of inhaled corticosteroids, oral bronchodilators, inhaled beta₂ agonists once a day and as needed, and frequent courses of oral corticosteroids.

Long-term management of asthma also includes attention to associated conditions and special problems. For example, bacterial ear and sinus infections require antibiotics for 10 days to 3 weeks. Swollen nasal passages may need decongestants, while allergic and nonallergic rhinitis (inflammation of the nasal mucous membranes) should be treated with antihistamines, cromolyn sodium nasal spray, or topical nasal corticosteroids. Upper respiratory viral infections can worsen asthma, especially in young children; parents need to ensure adherence to the regular medication schedule and to be alert for early signs of acute worsening so that asthma medication may be started or increased immediately. Treatment with beta₂ agonists, cromolyn sodium, or both prior to exposure to a known trigger such as cold air or specific antigens can prevent or diminish an asthmatic response.

Exercise-induced asthma—airway narrowing that occurs minutes after one begins vigorous activity—should be anticipated in all asthma patients. Exercise-induced asthma is one expression of airway hyperresponsiveness, not a special form of asthma. For some patients exercise is the only stimulus that provokes asthma symptoms. A history of cough, shortness of breath, chest pain or tightness, wheezing, or endurance problems during exercise suggests exercise-induced asthma. Traditionally, people with asthma have either avoided physical activities or limited their exercise to those activities or sports that are less likely to provoke asthma symptoms for them. It is now emphasized, however, that physical activity should not be avoided and that the goal of asthma management is to enable people to participate in any activity they choose without experiencing symptoms. The presence of exercise-induced asthma often indicates that the person's disease is not properly controlled; appropriate anti-inflammatory therapy generally abolishes exercise-related symptoms. For those who still experience exercise-induced asthma despite appropriate therapy and for those who have symptoms only upon exercise, an inhaled beta₂ agonist (or cromolyn sodium) used 5–60 minutes before exercise will prevent symptoms for as long as several hours.

Asthma episodes

Asthma episodes are occurrences of progressively worsening shortness of breath, coughing, wheezing, chest tightness, or some combination of these symp-

A simple environmental precaution like wearing a face mask can help individuals whose asthma is provoked by cold air enjoy regular outdoor exercise. For modern asthma management the goal is to enable people to participate in any physical activity they choose without experiencing symptoms. Good control of asthma can usually be achieved with appropriate medication and avoidance of triggering irritants and allergens.

The importance of controlling irritants in asthma prevention was highlighted by a 1992 U.S. Environmental Protection Agency draft report on passive smoking. In the document environmental tobacco smoke was held responsible for aggravating from 400,000 to one million existing cases of childhood asthma in the U.S. each year as well as causing 8,000 to 26,000 new cases.

toms. They are characterized by decreases in expiratory airflow that can be measured by PEF or other techniques. Prevention and early on-the-spot treatment to reverse symptoms are the best strategies for managing episodes. Written action plans help the patient recognize early indications of an episode, begin appropriate treatment, assess the response to therapy, and decide to seek medical help if symptoms and lung function do not improve.

Airflow obstruction in an asthma episode is best relieved by repeated use of a beta$_2$ agonist inhaler and removal of the allergen or irritant that may have brought on the episode. For patients who respond insufficiently to inhaler treatment, early addition of a short course of oral corticosteroids will speed improvement. Patients must understand the limits of bronchodilator therapy in acute episodes. If there is no immediate relief, no improvement within two hours, or no sustained improvement (for example, if improvement does not last more than four hours), the episode is severe enough to require urgent medical attention.

Controlling allergens and irritants

The association of asthma and allergy has long been recognized. An allergic reaction in the airway can cause both immediate bronchial narrowing and a later increase in airway hyperresponsiveness to a variety of stimuli that can persist for several weeks. The patient's history is essential in determining whether the asthma is tied significantly with allergy; skin tests can determine the presence of allergy to specific agents.

Controlling allergens and irritants is an important prevention strategy; avoiding these triggers may reduce symptoms, the need for medication, and the level of airway hyperresponsiveness. Emphasis is on avoiding airborne allergens (outdoor allergens like plant pollen and mold spores and indoor allergens like animal dander and protein substances from cockroaches and house-dust mites) and irritants (for example, tobacco smoke, strong odors and sprays, and air pollutants). For people who are allergic to pets, it is recommended that furred and feathered animals be removed from the home—or at least kept out of the person's bedroom at all times and heating and cooling vents in the room covered with filters to trap out airborne particles carrying the allergen from the pet hair, dander, dried saliva, or urine.

Environmental control and medication together usually provide good control of allergy-related asthma. Immunotherapy (desensitization shots) may be considered when avoiding allergens is not possible, when appropriate medication fails to control symptoms, and when specific immunotherapy is available. Immunotherapy prevents the development of allergic inflammation and perhaps the resulting bronchial hyperresponsiveness; it has been shown to reduce asthma symptoms for such allergens as house-dust mites, animal dander, grass pollen, and spores of *Alternaria* fungus. Allergy immunotherapy should be administered only in a physician's office, where facilities and trained personnel are available to treat potential, though rare, life-threatening reactions.

Importance of patient education

Asthma management is more effective when a partnership exists among the patient, the patient's family, and the physician. Such a partnership involves open communication about expectations for therapy and the patient's concerns about asthma and its treatment, joint development of a treatment plan by the physician and patient, and encouragement of the family's efforts to improve asthma management. The focus of education is on helping persons with asthma learn and practice specific management skills, which include identifying and avoiding asthma triggers, recognizing early signs of deterioration, peak flow monitoring, taking medicine correctly, following a treatment plan, and seeking help appropriately.

—*Albert L. Sheffer, M.D., and Virginia S. Taggart, M.P.H.*

240

TB: The Captain of All These Men of Death Returns

by Artin Mahmoudi, M.D., and Michael D. Iseman, M.D.

> The captain of all these men of death that came against him to take him away, was the Consumption, for it was that that brought him down to the grave.
> —John Bunyan, *The Life and Death of Mr. Badman* (1680)

Pulmonary tuberculosis, or TB, a disease that since the 1950s has lost its age-old reputation as the grim conqueror described by Bunyan, is making a comeback. Worldwide, more new cases were reported in 1991 than at any previous time in history. The 8 million people who developed active TB and the 2.9 million who died from it that year made the disease the leading infectious cause of sickness and death. In Africa, in some western European countries like Italy, and in large urban areas of the U.S., the dramatic increases seen in the number of active TB cases have been due to the fulminant spread of the human immunodeficiency virus (HIV), the cause of AIDS. Similar epidemics of coexisting TB and HIV infection are appearing in South America and Asia. Worse, the new TB threat has come at a time when proportionally fewer resources are being allocated to public health programs—particularly to the prevention of TB, which is widely held to be a problem of the past. The emergence of TB strains that are resistant to today's widely employed, effective, cheap, and well-tolerated medications threatens to make TB again the untreatable scourge it was in the preantibiotic era.

An ancient, opportunistic enemy

Tuberculosis, historically known as white plague or consumption, is a chronic infectious disease caused by the bacterium *Mycobacterium tuberculosis*, often called the tubercle bacillus. Evidence of human infection with *M. tuberculosis* has been noted in fossils dating from the prehistoric era, and accounts of the disease can be found in ancient Egyptian and Greek writings. It was not until 1882, however, that the causative agent of TB was discovered by the renowned German scientist Robert Koch. Although forms of the disease caused by other varieties of the bacillus are found in cattle, swine, fowl, and other animals, humans are the only natural reservoir of *M. tuberculosis*. For practical purposes pulmonary tuberculosis is spread only directly from person to person, thus accounting for the fact that TB rates have always been higher in crowded urban areas than in rural communities.

Although it can involve virtually any organ in the body, TB affects the lungs in most cases. Owing to the chronic, slow-developing nature of the disease, its early stages often go unnoticed or are blamed on another illness. As the disease evolves, the victim experiences progressive coughing, which generates an airborne discharge of sputum loaded with tubercle bacilli. Those in close contact with the victim may inhale the bacilli. Although short casual contact with a highly contagious person can result in infection, TB is passed much more often by intense and repeated contact, as occurs among family members or those living in crowded quarters. In persons who become infected after exposure, there is initially an uninhibited growth of bacilli and dissemination via the bloodstream, during which small numbers of the microorganisms may be deposited in the kidneys, bones, liver, spleen, brain, lymph nodes, or other sites. Within 4 to 20 weeks, however, the body's immune system develops effective defenses against the infection, mediated primarily through lymphocytes (a variety of white blood cell) and macrophages (a variety of scavenging cell, or phagocyte). This response results in the accumulation of defensive cells in a palisade around the organisms, thereby controlling the infection. These microscopic foci of walled-in bacteria and inflammatory cells are called granulomas and are highly characteristic of TB in laboratory analyses of tissue samples.

In about 90% of immunologically normal individuals, the disease is checked at this stage, and the only effects are a positive tuberculin skin test and, in a minority of people, small spots on their chest X-rays. Such people then possess some immunologic resistance to future exposures to the bacillus. Nevertheless, viable bacilli exist within the granulomas, and if the immune system is weakened by such factors as infection with HIV, advanced age, alcoholism, malnutrition, or diabetes, bacilli may escape the body's defensive forces, resume growth, and cause overt TB. In this sense *M. tuberculosis* is an opportunistic infectious agent, stepping in like Bunyan's "captain" after the other "men of death" have taken their toll.

Paradoxically, it is the body's effort to fight off the proliferating hordes of tubercle bacilli that produces most of the manifestations associated with the consumption, or wasting, seen in TB: fever, sweats, blood in the sputum, chest pain, weight loss, and profound weakness. The microorganisms themselves do not elaborate toxic products as do the bacteria that cause typhoid fever or tetanus. Rather, the lymphocytes involved in the immune response secrete substances that bring on fever, wasting, and tissue damage. An infection centered in the lungs may damage the tissues so extensively that holes, or cavities, appear. Inside a typical cavity bacilli can number in the millions or billions. Each cough from a person with such lesions discharges into the air a large number of bacilli having the potential to infect others. When tubercle bacilli proliferate outside the lungs, they can result in damage to various organs and structures including kidneys, spinal vertebrae, lymph nodes, and hip bones.

Tuberculosis is usually diagnosed by the detection of tubercle bacilli in the microscopic examination and culture of sputum, although tissue or secretions from other organs may be examined when appropriate. Given the very slow replication of the organism (once every 20–24 hours, compared with once every 15 minutes for staphylococci), the culture may not show growth for as long as eight weeks. If needed, characteristic results of chest X-rays and skin tests are used as supportive evidence of active infection.

Decline and resurgence

Until the mid-20th century, no effective therapy for TB existed. Indeed, from the 18th to the early 20th century, the disease was the leading cause of death for all age groups in the Western world. During the late 1940s and early '50s, researchers identified three effective antituberculosis agents: isoniazid, streptomycin, and *para*-aminosalicylic acid (PAS). Treatment with a combination of these drugs for 24 months resulted in 90–95% cure rates (then considered miraculous) and revolutionized TB therapy. Later a few more drugs, including rifampin and ethambutol, were added to the antituberculosis arsenal.

Hitherto, most TB patients had been cared for in special sanatoriums, where treatment included strict and prolonged bed rest, heliotherapy (exposure to sunlight), and occasionally lung-collapse therapy (pneumothorax). As the new antibiotics became available, treatment of TB shifted to outpatient clinics, and eventually the sanatoriums were phased out. Current treatment of patients infected with drug-susceptible strains of bacilli entails a combination of three or four drugs for only six months, which includes an initial two-week isolation period, after which the patient is no longer infectious to others. Over the years, however, some strains have acquired drug resistance, which has made treatment much more difficult, toxic, and expensive and the period of contagiousness much longer. Treatment of patients infected with strains that are resistant to two or more of the standard drugs involves the administration of combinations of less potent, more toxic drugs for a prolonged period (up to two years) and, in some cases, the surgical removal of diseased lung tissue. In a recent study it was calculated that the cost of treatment for such multidrug-resistant cases may exceed $180,000; by contrast, uncomplicated cases of drug-susceptible TB can be cured for $500 to $1,000.

Whereas the annual incidence of tuberculosis in the U.S. dropped markedly after the introduction of effective drug therapy, evidence exists for a steady decline in incidence even prior to the modern antibiotic era. Large-scale isolation of infectious patients in TB sanatoriums and improvements in the nutritional and housing status of the general population must have contributed to this trend. In the late 1980s, however, the number of new cases of TB began gradually increasing. In 1990, 25,701 cases were reported in the U.S., a jump of 9.4% over 1989 and the single largest increase since the inception of national reporting on tuberculosis in 1953. In 1991 reported cases

Death, eyeglass in hand, watches the neck and neck race between tuberculosis and syphilis for the leading cause of death in France in a 1926 public health poster. Tuberculosis reached nearly epidemic proportions in the urbanizing societies of Europe and North America in the 18th and 19th centuries. It was the number one killer among all age groups in the Western world until the early 20th century, when improved health and hygiene began effecting a gradual decline in TB death rates.

Children afflicted with TB bask outdoors in the sunshine as part of their treatment at a Cleveland, Ohio, sanatorium in 1918. Prior to the discovery of effective antituberculosis drugs in the mid-20th century, strict bed rest, sun treatment, and lung-collapse therapy in special isolated facilities offered the best chance for a cure.

in the U.S. climbed again—to 26,283, an increase of 2.3% over 1990.

Furthermore, the epidemiology, or pattern of cases, of TB in the U.S. has changed from that seen in the first half of the 20th century. Two-thirds of cases now occur among people of racial and ethnic minorities, a number of whom have recently immigrated to the U.S. Also, increasing numbers of patients infected with both HIV (*i.e.,* who test positive for HIV) and *M. tuberculosis* are being reported, among whom the manifestations of TB can vary widely and make recognition of the disease difficult. For many of these individuals, access to health care is delayed and limited. In addition, owing to the receding case rates of TB since the 1950s and diminishing professional education on the topic, the medical community has become progressively unfamiliar with the subtleties of diagnosis and treatment of the disease. These and other factors have now set the stage for a substantial reemergence of tuberculosis in the U.S.

The HIV connection

As mentioned above, reactivation of latent tuberculous foci often follows a decline in the immune defenses of a previously infected individual. In the modern era the most dramatic example of a faltering immune system is seen in people infected with HIV. The combination of HIV infection and TB has severely challenged public health programs in many countries, including the U.S., where it is estimated that 10 million persons harbor a latent TB infection. The connection between the two infections was noticed very early in the AIDS epidemic, particularly among Haitians in Florida and intravenous drug abusers in New York City. The effect on TB of immunosuppression by HIV infection is profound; whereas an individual free of HIV but with latent TB has a 10% likelihood of developing active TB over his or her lifetime, for the HIV-infected individual the risk approaches 10% per year. Even more dramatic is the risk for a person whose HIV infection has advanced to AIDS; among such individuals, whose

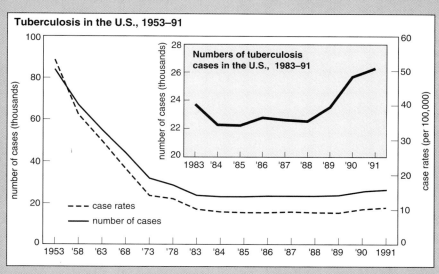

Tuberculosis in the U.S., 1953–91

Numbers of tuberculosis cases in the U.S., 1983–91

immunity is sorely disrupted, exposure to persons with active TB is associated with a likelihood of 30% or more of contracting TB, a rate never before observed. Furthermore, the time from infection to appearance of overt, often life-threatening TB is orders of magnitude less for AIDS patients than for AIDS-free persons: 30 to 100 days versus 6 months to 60 years.

Most authorities agree that the resurgence of tuberculosis in the U.S. is largely due to the spread of HIV. A unique aspect of this coepidemic is that TB is the only opportunistic infection in the HIV-infected individual that can be transmitted to his or her contacts with only casual exposure, thus increasing the risk of TB for HIV-free persons as well. Additionally, tuberculosis in the presence of HIV infection can manifest itself quite differently from the "classic" picture described above. Sputum samples and skin tests more often test negative, leading to delays in diagnosis, which result in more severe disease and increased likelihood of death for the patient and increased exposure of health care professionals and the patient's contacts. The propensity for such people to develop severe TB was highlighted in 1991 and early 1992 in reports from Florida and New York, where scores of dually infected individuals (many of them carrying drug-resistant bacilli) died before effective therapy could be started.

Although the medical regimen and the response to treatment for the HIV-infected person are very similar to those for other individuals, most medical authorities favor extending the drug regimen by three to six months. Once appropriate therapy has been started, the patient whose disease is caused by drug-susceptible bacilli usually finds that symptoms improve in 14 to 21 days.

Erratic therapy and drug resistance

Unfortunately, such rapid improvement with treatment can have drawbacks. As the debilitating symptoms of TB subside, the cost of continued treatment or other factors may discourage an individual from continuing therapy for the full requisite time. In fact, noncompliance is the largest problem with TB control in the U.S. and globally; as a result of high rates of nonadherence to prescribed therapy, very expensive programs of institutional or supervised outpatient treatment are required. In a recent study at a New York City hospital, only 11% of those diagnosed with TB completed the prescribed therapy; homelessness and substance abuse contributed significantly to their lack of compliance.

Alarmingly, erratic administration of antituberculosis drugs can encourage the selection of drug-resistant strains. Brief or sporadic treatment kills only the more drug-susceptible bacilli, leaving the resistant fraction to proliferate and take over the infection. Carried to extremes, tubercle bacilli resistant to all of the first-line drugs have been found in explosive TB epidemics in U.S. hospitals and prisons. Compounding the problem of erratic therapy are poverty, alcoholism, crowded living quarters, drug abuse, poor nutritional status, and poor access to health care, all of which further assure the propagation of the infection among the inner-city poor. The drastic reduction of federal and state financial assistance for urban TB-control programs has been particularly telling. Combined, these factors have brought the U.S. to the brink of a potentially extensive TB epidemic unprecedented in the modern era—one that is certain to be marked by great difficulty and expense in treatment, no proven means of prevention, and high rates of illness and death.

Homelessness and poverty are major factors contributing to the recent resurgence of TB in the U.S. Crowded living conditions, malnutrition and lowered disease resistance (including immune systems compromised by HIV infection), and poor access to health care encourage transmission of the tubercle bacillus, particularly in inner-city populations. Among the TB-infected poor who have access to treatment, those who start drug therapy often do not comply with the full course of treatment, thus encouraging the multiplication and spread of drug-resistant strains.

UPI/Bettmann Newsphotos

Testing those at risk

The federal Centers for Disease Control (CDC), Atlanta, Ga., has published extensive recommendations for skin testing of individuals at risk of developing TB. Such people include but are not limited to those infected with HIV, intravenous drug abusers, residents of chronic care facilities, individuals from countries where the incidence of TB is still high (for example, Africa and Southeast Asia), contacts of active cases, and health care workers. For all individuals identified as having latent tuberculous infection, 6 to 12 months of preventive therapy with a single drug, isoniazid, can reduce their chances of developing active tuberculosis over their lifetime by 65 to 90% if the infecting strain is susceptible to isoniazid. If it is not isoniazid susceptible, there is no proven preventive therapy.

Preventing a possible epidemic

After three years of planning, the CDC in 1989 initiated a plan to eliminate tuberculosis from the U.S. by the year 2010. The plan calls for the allocation of more resources and the application of newer technologies to combat TB. Given the sharp rise in the incidence of TB in the U.S., however, and the overall decline in financial support for public health institutions, the likelihood of achieving the CDC's goal on schedule appears remote. To offset these unfavorable trends, several actions are needed.

First, public health programs must be adequately funded to ensure compliance with prescribed therapy. Such an approach would have workers directly supervise the administration of medication for most of the required period. Only in this way can the high rates of treatment failure and the rise of drug-resistant bacilli be arrested. The first model of this kind of program in North America has operated in Denver, Colo., for the past 25 years with excellent results.

Second, centralized diagnostic centers must be established where high-quality culture and drug-susceptibility testing can be performed and the results communicated in a matter of weeks to physicians. Currently the process can take three to six months.

Third, new tools of molecular biology need to be applied to the diagnosis and drug-susceptibility testing of TB. The polymerase chain reaction (PCR), for example, is a recently developed laboratory technique that can vastly increase the quantity of genetic material extracted from sources as small as a single cell. By means of PCR, genetic material from any specimen can be amplified and tested for the presence of DNA from *M. tuberculosis*. If the result of the PCR assay is positive, a tentative diagnosis of TB can be made. A second PCR assay would then determine the drug-susceptibility pattern of the isolated bacillus, thus assisting in correct drug selection. In contrast to conventional culture and drug testing, which even under ideal circumstances can take three to six weeks, a

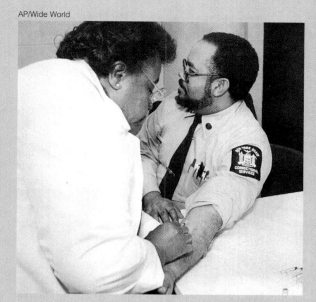

Annual TB skin tests are now the norm for officers and other employees at New York state prisons, where 13 inmates and a guard contracted fatal infections of drug-resistant tuberculosis in 1991.

PCR-based system could give identification and susceptibility results in as little as two days.

Fourth, commitment must come from the pharmaceutical industry to develop new antituberculosis medications. The last major TB drug, rifampin, was introduced in the early 1970s. Fifth, in concert with new drugs, newer modes of drug delivery such as prolonged-release, subcutaneous-implant, and transdermal-patch systems need to be investigated.

Finally, research must be conducted to develop an effective preventive vaccine. Although a vaccine (bacille Calmette-Guérin, or BCG) currently exists, it has proved useful primarily in reducing severe forms of childhood tuberculosis. BCG has had little effect on reducing the risk for adult pulmonary tuberculosis, the form in which TB is most contagious, and thus little effect on the transmission and epidemiology of TB. A better vaccine is particularly vital to the less developed nations in which case rates are high and preventive drug therapy (the U.S. model) is financially and administratively impractical.

The implementation of all of these plans will require substantial fiscal support. Without such, TB case rates in the U.S. will accelerate. Unfortunately, the situation in the Third World countries is even more grim; high levels of initial drug resistance, increasing numbers of people infected with HIV, and lack of financial resources may result in the largest epidemic of the white plague in history. Only with the combined global assistance of more affluent nations and leadership of international health agencies is there hope of warding off such a threat.

Bone Marrow Transplantation

Over the past four decades, bone marrow transplantation has evolved into a treatment of choice for several forms of cancer and blood disease. In the U.S. about 4,000 patients a year undergo the procedure. While "bone marrow transplantation" appears to describe a type of complex surgery, in reality the procedure is quite simple.

Bone marrow, a jellylike substance found inside virtually all bones, is removed by being sucked out with needles inserted through the skin into the interior of the bone. Although in theory any bone could be used, the pelvic bones are the safest source because they are relatively large, close to the body surface, and far from vital organs. To remove sufficient marrow (usually about one liter [or quart]), up to 200 needle punctures may be needed. For this reason, the donor is given either general anesthesia (put to sleep) or regional anesthesia (numbed from the hips down). The procedure is carried out in an operating room, both to allow safe delivery of the anesthesia and to ensure that the marrow obtained is free from germs; there are few risks involved for donors, whose bodies replenish the donated marrow in about two weeks. The procedure takes two to three hours from start to finish.

After the marrow is removed, it is filtered through stainless steel mesh to remove any small bone or fat particles. Further processing is needed only if the patient and donor have different blood types. In any case, the marrow is usually infused into the patient's veins within a few hours of the harvest. The critical "seed" cells in the marrow have the ability, through unknown mechanisms, to "home" to the marrow and begin growing. During the several days before receiving the marrow, the patient has been receiving intense chemotherapy and sometimes radiation treatment in order to both destroy the underlying cancer and decrease the chance that his or her body will reject the new marrow graft.

Four decades of progress

The impetus for bone marrow transplantation came in the early 1950s, when it was realized that cancer of the blood (leukemia) and cancer of the lymph glands (lymphoma) could respond dramatically to treatment with chemotherapy (potent drugs that seek out and attack cancer cells in the body). Unfortunately, these diseases could be cured only rarely because the doses of the drugs that were necessary for cure also could cause dangerous side effects. One such effect is temporary or even permanent damage of bone marrow function. Because bone marrow is responsible for producing white blood cells that fight infection, platelets that prevent bleeding, and red blood cells that carry oxygen, this particular side effect can in some cases lead to death of the patient.

When former Massachusetts senator Paul Tsongas made his bid for the 1992 Democratic presidential nomination, he had been cancer-free for over five years, having undergone a bone marrow transplant in 1986 for non-Hodgkin's lymphoma.

Crucial discoveries. In the 1950s experiments in rodents and dogs proved that treatment-related toxicities could be minimized by infusion of marrow after the animals received high doses of chemotherapy or radiotherapy. On the basis of these observations, several human patients with incurable acute leukemia were treated with high doses of radiation followed by infusion of bone marrow donated by a relative. All of those early efforts were unsuccessful owing to incomplete destruction of the leukemia or failure of the infused bone marrow to grow properly. Despite the discouraging results, a small group of medical scientists, including the 1990 Nobel laureate E. Donnall Thomas, began to study the problems that led to the initial failures, in hopes that these problems could eventually be overcome.

It became obvious that the evolving field of tissue typing would be vitally important to the success of marrow transplantation. It was discovered, first in animals and then in humans, that the body has the ability to recognize tissues from another individual as different and then attempt to destroy those foreign tissues. Molecules called antigens, which are proteins present on the surface of every cell of every tissue in the body, were found to be responsible for determining the foreign nature of tissues transplanted from another individual. Most important, it was discovered that the specific antigens critical to this foreign tissue reaction are genetically determined and thus inherited from one's parents. Furthermore, the genes for these human leukocyte antigens (HLA) are located on one small portion of one chromosome—chromosome 6. Therefore, if a patient and his or her sibling have inherited the same relevant chromosomes from their parents (a 25% chance), they will be matched for HLA and hence would be far more likely to have a successful transplant. With the realization of the importance of HLA and the refinement of technology to determine HLA types, it became possible to identify family member donors who would be acceptable. As a result, the advent of HLA typing led to the rapid development of marrow transplantation in the early 1970s. Thomas and others soon published the first reports of long-term cures in otherwise incurable patients with acute leukemia.

Overcoming complications. Despite this success, with longer patient survival other serious problems became evident. In marrow transplantation, as in solid organ transplants such as heart, kidney, and liver, there is always the possibility that the patient could reject the incoming tissue or organ. Bone marrow transplantation, however, is unique in that it is also possible that the new marrow graft can attempt to reject the patient's own body, a process called graft-versus-host disease (GVHD). GVHD can attack the skin, liver, stomach, and intestines, with severe and sometimes fatal consequences. Borrowing from experience in animal models and in human solid organ grafting, physicians quickly discovered that by giving the patient medications to suppress this effect of the new graft, it was possible to decrease the incidence and severity of GVHD. With the advent of the wide use of the drug cyclosporine in the 1980s, the incidence of GVHD diminished still further. (Cyclosporine is a rejection-preventing drug, derived from a soil fungus, that significantly improved the outcome of all types of organ transplants when it was introduced in the 1970s.) Ironically, however, decreasing the incidence of GVHD is not entirely beneficial; in many instances GVHD can attack the original cancer in addition to the patient's normal organs. Thus, among patients with advanced acute leukemia, those with a moderate degree of GVHD may ultimately have a higher survival rate, as the chance of recurrence of their leukemia is much lower than that in similar patients who did not develop GVHD. Research efforts are now under way to discover how to separate these good and bad effects of GVHD.

Another major complication of bone marrow transplantation occurs in the months between destruction of the patient's diseased bone marrow and the full development of the new marrow graft. During this critical time, the patient is extremely vulnerable to infections. By remaining in a special germ-free room and eating a diet low in bacterial pathogens—*i.e.,* one that has no uncooked vegetables or unprocessed milk—patients can usually be prevented from acquiring overwhelm-ing infections caused by bacterial organisms in the surrounding environment.

Other infections, such as those caused by fungi or viruses, are more difficult to prevent or treat, particularly as many arise within the body when the patient's ability to fight infections is suppressed or destroyed. Successful treatment therefore requires careful monitoring for the earliest signs of fungal and viral infections, such as a fever, dry cough, or shortness of breath. Many transplant centers are exploring the use of recently developed antifungal medications that both prevent and treat fungal infections. A particularly difficult viral infection is that of cytomegalovirus (CMV), a member of the herpesvirus family. As with other members of the herpes family, it often resides within a host without causing any ill effects but can suddenly activate or reactivate. In marrow-transplant patients CMV can cause major problems, including fatal pneumonia, during the critical first three months following the transplant. A patient who does not carry the virus and who receives marrow from a donor who likewise does not carry the virus usually can be prevented from acquiring CMV by the careful screening of all blood products to ensure that they are CMV negative. In the majority of cases, when either the patient or the donor is CMV positive, infection can often be prevented or treated with the antiviral drug ganciclovir. In addition, the biotechnology industry is now producing new drugs from growth factors, which

Before their new marrow has fully developed, bone marrow transplant recipients are protected against overwhelming infections, to which they are extremely vulnerable, in special germ-free isolation units.

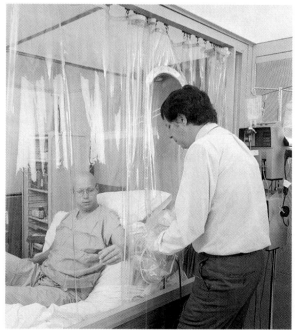

R.J. McDougall—Fred Hutchinson Cancer Center

treatment of choice

chronic myelogenous leukemia (both
    in the chronic phase and in the accelerated
    phase, or "blast crisis")
acute myelogenous leukemia after first relapse
acute lymphocytic leukemia after first relapse
multiple myeloma
severe aplastic anemia
myelodysplastic syndromes ("preleukemia")
genetic immune diseases, such as severe
    combined immunodeficiency disease (SCID),
    DiGeorge syndrome, and Wiscott-Aldrich disease
lymphomas after first relapse
thalassemia major

treatment of choice in some circumstances

acute myelogenous leukemia in first remission
acute lymphocytic leukemia in first remission
lymphoma in first remission
breast cancer
ovarian cancer
sickle-cell disease

someday may play a role

AIDS
small-cell lung cancer

are effective in speeding up the growth of the marrow graft and in decreasing the probability of severe infections. Granulocyte-macrophage colony-stimulating factor (GM-CSF) and granulocyte colony-stimulating factor (G-CSF) are particularly promising. A number of other growth factors, such as hematopoietic stem cell factor and interleukin-3, may further accelerate marrow engraftment.

Expanding applications

These improvements in the safety of marrow transplantation have allowed the treatment to be utilized in an increasing number of diseases (*see* Table). Nowadays patients with almost any disease that is highly responsive to chemotherapy may be considered candidates for treatment with marrow transplantation. Examples include acute lymphocytic leukemia and acute myelogenous leukemia; chronic myelogenous leukemia (a more indolent form of leukemia); several forms of lymphoma, including Hodgkin's disease that has relapsed after initial therapy; multiple myeloma (another type of cancer of the blood); and several nonmalignant blood disorders such as thalassemia and sickle-cell anemia (both inherited blood disorders) and severe aplastic anemia (a condition in which the bone marrow ceases to function). In addition, there are re-

cent encouraging data suggesting that solid tumors sensitive to chemotherapy, such as breast cancer and ovarian cancer, may be particularly responsive to the higher doses of chemotherapeutic drugs that are possible with bone marrow transplantation.

For all of these disease categories, it is clear that transplantation sooner rather than later in the course of a patient's disease is critical. Patients at the end stage of their disease generally have been through several cycles of chemotherapy, which in effect trains the cancer cells to be resistant to further treatment. Furthermore, the patients' organs may have been damaged by previous treatment and by the disease itself, plus the patients may have acquired infections that would be difficult to treat. Therefore, efforts must be made to identify candidates for marrow transplantation whose disease is still in the early stages but who nevertheless have diagnoses known to be ultimately fatal. As an example, patients with acute myelocytic leukemia who have relapsed after previous therapy might have a cure rate of only 10–15% with a marrow transplant. However, this cure rate climbs to 50–60% if these patients receive a transplant of bone marrow during their first remission, while the disease is inactive and still responsive to chemotherapy and radiation.

The Chernobyl experience

With the increasing efficacy and safety of marrow transplantation, it was only natural that this form of treatment might be applied in new arenas. Following the 1986 accident at the Chernobyl nuclear power station in the Soviet Union (now Ukraine), when many were exposed to doses of radiation high enough to destroy their bone marrow, marrow transplantation was attempted as a rescue. Unfortunately, transplantation was not successful in any of these cases. Indeed, it now appears that marrow transplantation per se has little if any value in cases of acute radiation exposure because any dose of radiation that can destroy the victim's bone marrow would almost certainly destroy other vital organs, particularly the lungs. However, Chernobyl and other radiation victims benefited from several treatment advances gained during the 40 years of marrow transplantation experience. These developments included use of specialized blood products such as platelets, isolation of the patient in order to reduce infections, and use of the new growth factors to facilitate regrowth of the patient's own bone marrow.

A more likely application of marrow transplantation to radiation victims will be in those who develop cancer years or even decades after their initial exposure. Expected cancers would include cancers of the blood such as acute myelogenous leukemia and multiple myeloma, both of which can be treated by marrow transplantation. The number of such victims is impossible to predict accurately but may run into the hundreds or even thousands.

Success with unrelated donors

With a growing consensus that marrow transplantation is indeed the treatment of choice for many diseases, the lack of an HLA-matched brother, sister, or other immediate family member has become a significant issue for many if not most patients. Given the genetics of inheritance of the HLA antigens, the chance of a patient's being HLA matched with a given brother or sister, as previously noted, is 25%. In the U.S. the average number of siblings in a family is 2.7; if one is a patient needing a transplant, only 1.7 possible donors are left. Thus, the chance of having an HLA-matched brother or sister within the family is only about 40%. Consequently, several transplant centers have begun exploring the possibility of using donors other than HLA-matched brothers and sisters. Attempts to use family members who are not HLA identical are routinely successful only if the amount of HLA difference between the patient and donor is minimal, but the use of HLA-matched donors who are not related to the patient has the potential for greater applicability.

With the continuing evolution of HLA typing, it is now possible to determine very precisely the level of compatibility between unrelated individuals. In the 1980s several early successes using HLA-matched unrelated donors led to the development of the National Marrow Donor Program in 1987. Established by three blood bank systems—the American Red Cross, the American Association of Blood Banks, and the Council of Community Blood Centers—and a $3 million federal grant, the donor program is a large registry of HLA-typed individuals willing to donate marrow. Given the extremely large number of possible HLA types, it was calculated that up to a million donors might be needed. As of June 1992, over 630,000 potential donors had been recruited, and over 1,200 patients had had transplants from donors from this registry. As with transplantation from HLA-matched brothers and sisters, the success of the transplants depends most heavily on the stage of the patient's disease. Although there has been a higher incidence of GVHD and other complications than is seen when related donors are used, a substantial number of patients with marrow from an unrelated donor have survived 5 to 10 years, with no signs of disease.

As the registry has grown, it has become apparent that patients of different racial groups have very different probabilities of finding donors. This is due to the small number of donors who belong to racial minorities and who have joined the registry to date as well as to substantially different mixes of HLA types among racial groups. At present, Caucasians have a better than 50% chance of finding a donor among those in the national donor registry, while the chance that blacks and Asians will find a suitable donor is 5% or less. This has led to a strong movement to recruit donors who represent all racial and ethnic backgrounds, which will require cooperation among registries in many countries to provide a broader representation of donors of various racial and ethnic backgrounds. Countries with active registries include most in western Europe, Japan, Hong Kong, Australia, Israel, Argentina, and, recently, several in eastern Europe.

A new treatment tool: the patient's own marrow

Over the last 5 to 10 years, rapid developments have made marrow transplantation sometimes possible by use of the patient's own bone marrow rather than that of another individual. Of course, this is possible only if

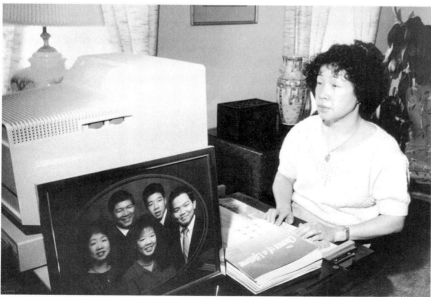

Elaine Chin of Naperville, Illinois, works at a computer in her home organizing a drive to locate a bone marrow donor for her 19-year-old leukemia-stricken son, Raymond (on the right in the family photo). Whereas Caucasians have better than a 50% chance of finding a donor whose marrow is suitably matched through the National Marrow Donor Program, Asians have less than a 5% chance. Sadly, time ran out before either his mother or the national program was able to find a donor for Raymond.

James C. Svehla—Naperville Sun Newspaper

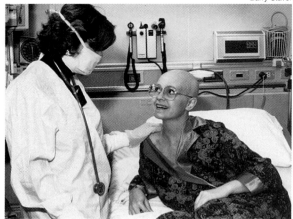

A patient recuperates after an autologous bone marrow transplant for metastatic breast cancer. In this promising new form of therapy, some of the patient's bone marrow is removed; she then receives high-dose chemotherapy, after which her own cancer-free marrow is reinfused.

the patient's bone marrow either has no cancer or has been cleansed of cancer. This approach, known as autologous bone marrow transplant, or autotransplant, has been successfully used in patients with leukemia or lymphoma who lack an HLA-matched donor. For patients with breast cancer, autotransplant is showing great promise. Breast cancer is highly responsive to chemotherapy, but once the tumor has progressed outside the involved breast and adjacent armpit, the chance of cure is extremely low. As with other forms of cancer treatment, the dose of chemotherapy that can be administered has heretofore been limited by the risk of damage to the bone marrow. Therefore, marrow is removed from the patient, frozen, stored in liquid nitrogen, and reinfused after the patient has had very high doses of chemotherapy. It is clear that this approach is superior to other forms of treatment in metastatic breast cancer and may indeed be curative for some patients.

The potential of autologous marrow transplants for breast as well as several other types of cancer has led to considerable debate about the optimal use of scarce health care dollars. Owing to the intense doses of chemotherapy required and the need for at least a month of meticulous in-hospital care, the treatment is extremely costly. Given the high cost (usually over $75,000) and the fact that breast cancer is a very common disease, many insurance companies are unwilling to pay for the procedure, labeling it as "experimental." In some cases the issue has become highly politicized, with women asserting that they are being denied a potentially curative procedure, whereas a similar procedure in males, were it appropriate, would likely be paid without question. As a result, many women have resorted to lawsuits in order to force

their insurance companies to pay for the procedure. In most cases the patients have been successful, with the result that autologous bone marrow transplantation is likely to become increasingly standard in years to come.

—*Patrick G. Beatty, M.D., Ph.D.*

Burns

Today among children and young adults in the United States, burns and trauma are the leading cause of accidental death and disability. Of all major injuries, only those that are motor vehicle related cause more accidental deaths than burns. Conservative estimates indicate that in the U.S. over 2.5 million people seek medical care for burn injuries each year, more than 100,000 thermally injured patients are hospitalized, and approximately 12,000 individuals die of their injuries.

There are few areas of modern medicine that have advanced as rapidly as burn care. These advances are largely due to the commitment of physicians, surgeons, clinician-scientists, and many other health care specialists from the fields of nursing, physical and occupational therapy, nutrition, and social services. Together this diverse group constitutes the burn care team. In terms of its capacity to respond to the enormous challenges presented by burn injuries, the whole has clearly become greater than the sum of its parts.

Social interaction is encouraged in the burn unit as part of the rehabilitation process. Thanks to the highly sophisticated care that is available in specialized burn centers today, adult and child burn victims can make excellent recoveries.

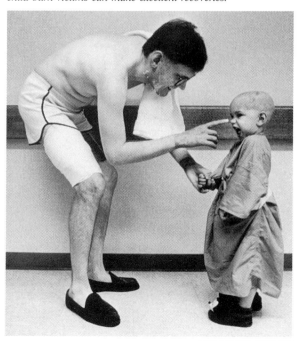

Prior to World War II the average burn size associated with a 50% mortality rate in healthy young adults was one that covered less than 30% of the total body surface area. Today in specialized burn centers the mean burn size associated with a 50% chance of dying has more than doubled and ranges from 65 to 75% of the body surface area. This major advance in burn survival can be attributed to (1) better understanding of the pathophysiology of the burn injury, which has led to improvements in all aspects of critical care, (2) improved methods of administering fluid therapy ("volume resuscitation"), which prevents the development of burn-induced shock and acute kidney failure, (3) the development of topical (locally applied) antimicrobial agents such as silver sulfadiazine and mafenide, which reduce the incidence of infections originating in the burn wound, (4) the development and implementation of improved methods of nutritional support that optimize the patient's ability to fight infection, enabling burns to heal, and (5) the discovery that early surgical removal of the burn wound and immediate skin grafting shorten the period of physiological stress and promote recovery.

Before 1958 there were fewer than 10 hospitals specializing in burn care in the U.S. Today the country has 1,809 beds dedicated to specialized burn care in 148 hospitals. In patients with burns involving more than 20% of their body surface area, the mean hospitalization period has been reduced by almost half in the past two decades. Currently, initial acute hospital stays average slightly less than one day per percentage of the body burned. Thus, for patients with burns covering 20% of their body surface area, hospitalization would be about 20 days; for patients with burns over 40% of their body, 40 days; and so forth.

Because of the sophisticated nature of the technology required for providing optimal care for these severely injured patients and the labor-intensive demands of the care (three to five full-time medical professionals providing round-the-clock care for a single patient), such hospitalization is costly. In the U.S. daily inpatient charges of $2,500–$4,000 for patients with major burns are common.

Classifying thermal injuries

In classifying a burn injury, it is important to consider the depth and extent of the injury as well as the presence or absence of smoke poisoning (inhalation injury). These three factors plus the patient's age are vital for determining both the prognosis of the patient and the appropriate medical care. Most burns are classified as first-, second-, or third-degree.

First-degree burns involve only the epidermis; the skin is red and painful, but blisters are not present. These burns heal in less than a week and rarely result in permanent scars. Second-degree burns can be superficial or deep. In superficial second-degree

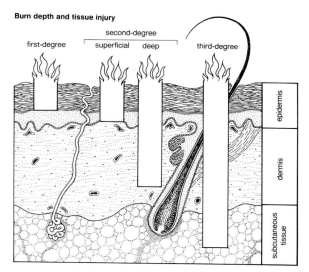

Burn depth and tissue injury

Burn depth is one of the factors used to determine prognosis. First-degree and superficial second-degree burns usually heal spontaneously, often without scarring. Deep second-degree burns are slower to heal and may require skin grafting, while third-degree burns rarely heal without grafting.

burns, damage is limited to the epidermis and the upper portion of the dermis. These burns are painful and characterized by the formation of blisters. Underneath the blisters, the skin is moist, pink, and tender. Healing generally occurs spontaneously over a two-week period. In contrast, deep second-degree burns spare only the deepest portion of the dermis. Although more severe, these burns are less painful than superficial ones because the sensory nerves of the skin have been destroyed along with the dermis and epidermis. Deep second-degree burns generally take three or more weeks to heal and frequently require skin-grafting operations for optimal wound closure. Third-degree burns are full-thickness skin injuries. The entire dermis and epidermis are destroyed. They are less painful than first- or second-degree burns, have a milky white or tanned leathery appearance, and are dry rather than moist. Third-degree burns will not heal spontaneously unless they are very small; in most cases, skin grafting is required.

A common way of estimating the extent of the burned body surface area is to follow the "rule of nines." In this system each portion of the body is divided into a multiple of nine. For example, each upper extremity is considered 9% of the body surface area, while each lower extremity is 18%. Although other factors are involved, such a quick approximation is extremely valuable for predicting survival.

Burns can also be classified according to the mechanism of injury. The most common burns are scald or flame burns, followed by contact, chemical, or electrical burns. Scald burns due to household accidents are the most commonly occurring burns in infants,

251

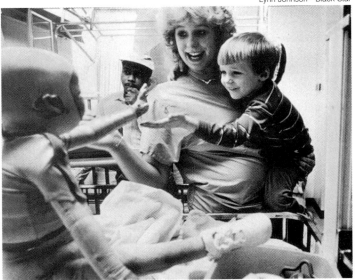

A young patient in the burn center of West Penn Hospital in Pittsburgh, Pennsylvania, greets her brother for the first time since the accident in which she suffered massive burns over her entire body when a propane gas tank exploded at their home. She is wearing a specially fitted pressure garment that will help minimize scarring as her wounds heal.

toddlers, and the elderly, while flame burns due to home fires or clothing's becoming ignited occur more frequently in older children and adults. Chemical and electrical burns are most often the result of industrial accidents.

Burn pathophysiology and management

A burn can amount to a quite trivial injury, or it can be the most devastating and severe of all human injuries. Once the burn wound exceeds 15–20% of the body surface area, it evokes a large number of systemic disturbances. These include major metabolic stress, impaired immunity, and massive fluid shifts. In addition, increased demands are placed on the cardiac, pulmonary, and renal systems. Moreover, the magnitude of these physiological changes tends to increase as the size and depth of the burn wound increase. Owing to the severe nature of these burn-induced insults, thermal injury victims are at increased risk of dying from shock, organ failure (heart, lung, or kidney), and infection.

One of the early, distinctive characteristics of a serious thermal injury is the rapid and massive development of edema (fluid retention and swelling) in burned and unburned tissue, which, in the absence of adequate fluid therapy, or volume resuscitation, may result in shock (hypotension), renal failure, and death. In fact, prior to the discovery that hypotension after thermal injury was due to the internal redistribution of fluid and not to the presence of burn-induced poisons, as had been previously thought, the leading cause of early death after thermal injury was burn shock with acute renal failure. Today, owing to the more sophisticated knowledge of the physiology of burn-induced fluid and electrolyte disturbances, burn shock is no longer a common cause of death.

Fluid therapy. In order to understand the importance of fluid therapy for major burn injuries, it is necessary to understand the normal distribution of fluids within the body. Sixty percent of the body is water, which is contained primarily in three separate but exchangeable fluid spaces, or compartments—the intravascular, interstitial, and extracellular spaces. The intravascular space is within the blood vessels and contains only a small fraction of the body's water (about 8.5%). The interstitial space is larger than the intravascular space and contains all the water that is outside the intravascular compartment but not within the cells; it can be viewed as the aggregate of all fluids that bathe the cells of the body and contains approximately 25% of the total body water. Fluid contained within the cells of the body is intracellular fluid. The intracellular fluid compartment is the largest fluid space, containing about two-thirds of the body's water.

After a thermal injury blood vessel permeability increases, resulting in leakage of intravascular fluid into the interstitial space. Accumulation of fluid in the interstitial space results in the rapid formation of edema within the wound and to a lesser extent in nonburned tissues. Additionally, because the cells at the site of the thermal injury are damaged, they swell, and more fluid leaves the intravascular space to enter these injured, swollen cells. What this means physiologically is that the fluid normally contained within the intravascular space is depleted. The body's initial response to a drop in intravascular volume is vasoconstriction (narrowing of blood vessels). This constriction of the vessels initially enables the patient to maintain a normal blood pressure. However, as more fluid is lost from the intravascular space, the body's ability to maintain normal blood pressure fails; the patient becomes hypotensive and develops burn shock.

Unless it is corrected, the uncompensated loss of fluid from the intravascular space after a thermal injury will result not only in shock but in inadequate blood flow to vital organs and, ultimately, death. Thus, the immediate goal of therapy is to restore the intravascular fluid volume to a normal level. This goal is accomplished by administration of salt-containing intravenous fluids. Since the blood vessels will continue to leak, tremendous amounts of fluid are frequently required, not only to refill the intravascular space but also to keep it filled. In fact, patients with burns involving over 50% of their body surface frequently require more than 14–20 liters (3.7–5.3 gal) of fluid during the first day of therapy.

Immediate volume resuscitation is now routine in the management of thermally injured patients and rarely fails. However, one of the chief side effects of large volume resuscitation is an accentuation of tissue edema. Since massive burn-wound edema impairs the availability of oxygen to reach the injured cells, it may lead to further cell injury and cell death. Thus, it seems likely that if the magnitude of burn-wound edema could be reduced, it might be possible to limit the ultimate depth of the burn and thereby improve outcome and survival of burned patients. Consequently, one active area of burn research is the investigation of the mediators and mechanisms responsible for burn-wound edema. As more information is generated from these studies, it may be possible to identify or develop specific drugs that would modulate burn-induced vascular permeability. Alternatively, more effective resuscitation formulas that limit the extent of edema yet are effective at maintaining the intravascular volume might be developed.

Respiratory system complications and their treatment. Upper airway and pulmonary problems are a major cause of morbidity and mortality in the burn victim. Pulmonary injuries range from a lack of oxygen (hypoxia) and carbon monoxide poisoning, both occurring at the scene of the accident, to the development of pneumonia days to weeks after the injury. Approximately 20% of all patients admitted to the hospital with a thermal injury will experience a pulmonary complication at some time during their hospital course. In fact, respiratory complications have become a major cause of death in patients who survive the fluid resuscitation phase of their injury. This is especially true in burn victims who have suffered a smoke-inhalation injury; the presence of an inhalation injury superimposed on a cutaneous burn significantly increases the mortality rate of these patients regardless of the size of the burn. This was quite clearly shown in a recent study that found that the presence of a smoke-inhalation injury increased the mortality rate from 13 to 56% in patients with equal-sized burn injuries. Moreover, the physiological effects of an inhalation injury are not limited to the lungs; patients with inhalation injuries frequently require up to 50% more fluid for adequate volume resuscitation.

Among the respiratory system complications that can develop either at the time of the injury or subsequent to it, carbon monoxide poisoning and hypoxia, occurring at the scene of the accident, are most common in patients who have been burned in house fires or fires occurring in a closed space. Similarly, patients who have been burned in a closed space where smoke can accumulate are at increased risk of having a smoke-inhalation injury. Most patients who have sustained severe inhalation injuries will be hoarse, and they may have difficulty breathing. The presence of a facial burn, singed nasal hairs, or soot in the airways is a sign of potential inhalation injury. Recent diagnostic advances have documented that the incidence of smoke-inhalation injury is several times higher than had been previously known or suspected. One technique that makes such definite diagnosis possible is the use of a small fiber-optic bronchoscope that can be passed through the mouth to directly visualize the bronchial tree and inspect for the presence of injury. If a smoke-inhalation injury is found to be present, these patients can be prophylactically placed on a ventilator before they develop respiratory complications.

Improvements in respiratory therapy over the last decade combined with a better understanding of inhalation injury and breathing mechanics have resulted in the improved care of these patients. Progress is also being made in elucidating the underlying pathophysiology of pulmonary injury at the cellular level. As more information is generated, treatment options should improve.

As was noted above, pneumonia is a major risk factor in the burn patient, and its occurrence is associated with a high mortality rate. There are several reasons why the burn victim, even in the absence of an inhalation injury, is predisposed to pneumonia: (1) burn patients are immunocompromised; (2) they have a poor cough reflex because of skeletal muscle wasting; and (3) they require frequent operations (skin grafts and burn wound removal) under general anesthesia. (The latter are described below.) Once pneumonia has developed, therapeutic options are limited to respiratory support, including mechanical ventilation when necessary, antibiotics, and nutrition. Consequently, the prevention of pneumonia by the use of good aseptic techniques and maneuvers to minimize bacterial contamination of the lower airways is of major importance.

Metabolic complications and nutritional therapy. The hypermetabolic response that occurs after thermal injury, which is characterized by fever, weight loss, and progressive skeletal muscle loss, is greater than that observed after any other form of trauma or during severe infections. The magnitude and duration of the hypermetabolic response parallels the severity of the burn injury and generally is at a maximum when the burn size is 60% or greater of the body surface area. Recent research has begun to clarify why the metabolic response of these patients is so deranged. It has been found that through a process of "autocannibalism" the body liberates protein stored in skeletal muscle to serve as building blocks for new proteins and substrates that are important in wound healing and marshaling defenses against infection. This complex metabolic response is orchestrated primarily by hormones (insulin, cortisol, catecholamines, and glucagon) plus factors released from inflammatory and immune cells (cytokines).

Because both massive weight and nitrogen losses result from accelerated muscle protein breakdown, the burn patient requires significant amounts of calories and protein. Failure to meet these metabolic needs will result in muscle wasting, decreased immunologic reserve, and impaired wound healing. Recognition of the unique nutritional needs of burn victims has been one of the crucial advances in burn care over the past decade. In particular, it is evident that the increased protein needs of these patients greatly exceed their increased caloric requirements. Furthermore, it is becoming clear that certain nutrients have major physiological effects that transcend their metabolic effects. For example, two amino acids, glutamine and arginine, have been found to improve immune function and foster wound healing by mechanisms that are independent of their traditional metabolic effects. Similarly, it is clear that certain types of fats are more immunosuppressive than others. Thus, a highly sophisticated "nutrient pharmacology" has evolved in which specific nutrients are given or withheld in order to directly augment specific physiological processes. Studies are presently under way to determine the optimal mix of dietary fats and other nutrients for burn victims.

Another advance in nutritional therapy is the use of specific hormones to directly increase the body's ability to synthesize protein and diminish the hypermetabolic response. The two hormones that appear to be most useful are human growth hormone and the insulin-like hormone growth factor I. The development of genetic engineering techniques now allows the mass production of these two hormones; previously, adequate quantities were unavailable for experimental investigation or therapeutic use.

A further important advance in the nutritional therapy of severely burned patients comes from the recognition that failure of the barrier function of the intestine can lead to systemic infections, potentiate organ injury, and contribute to the hypermetabolic response after thermal injury. This understanding has led to major conceptual changes in nutritional therapy. That is, it has been discovered that in these patients, bacteria or their products (endotoxins) that are normally contained within the gut escape and reach the systemic

circulation and internal organs, where they fuel the metabolic response and potentially lead to organ injury. Experimentally, orally administered nutrients that pass directly through the intestines have been shown to be physiologically superior to parenterally administered (intravenous) nutrients in maintaining intestinal barrier function and limiting the hypermetabolic response. This concept of providing immediate enteral feeding—nutrients that are administered by nasal tube directly to the gut—is now being tested clinically.

Infection and infection control. Once the patient has been successfully resuscitated, the major threats to survival are burn wound infections and, as previously noted, pneumonia. Although it is clear that thermal injury can lead to a widespread depression in immunity, controversy and confusion still exist over the mechanisms of burn-induced immunosuppression. Most infections are caused by bacteria that are colonizing in the patient, and these infections tend to originate at sites of tissue injury. Because the combination of impaired immunity and loss of the normal barrier function of the skin renders the burn patient uniquely susceptible to infection, much attention has focused on methods of reducing the bacterial counts in the burn wound.

Topical antimicrobial agents, local wound care, and strict infection-control practices are all parts of the strategy to prevent a fatal outcome. The topical agents that are available today allow high concentrations of antimicrobial medications to be used directly on the

An important advance in the treatment of thermal injuries came from the discovery that early surgical removal of the burned tissue and immediate skin grafting shorten the period of physiological stress, thereby promoting recovery.

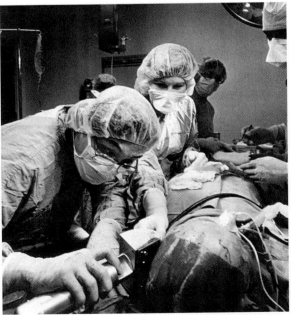

Lynn Johnson—Black Star

burn, thereby limiting or eliminating bacterial growth within the wound itself. Local wound care also involves meticulous cleaning of the burned skin area and frequent removal of tissue debris, which also minimizes bacterial growth by removing the nutrients on which these microorganisms depend. In addition, the wearing of caps, gowns, gloves, and face masks by hospital personnel coming in contact with the burn victim reduces the chances of transmitting bacteria to the burn wound or other body sites.

Although all of these measures will reduce the incidence of burn wound infections, they will not totally eliminate them. While systemic antibiotics play a major supportive role in the eradication of infections, in most cases the infected burn wound must be surgically removed. Early excision of burned tissue and immediate skin grafting before infection can develop have been shown experimentally to be beneficial. Consequently, over the last decade many burn centers have adopted a policy of excision and grafting of burn wounds beginning within a few days of admission in burn patients of all ages. Although the effectiveness of this approach has not been fully proved, it clearly shortens hospital stays of patients and appears to have resulted in improved survival.

The burn wound and its treatment. The vast majority of burn injury victims sustain burns that involve less than 15% of the body surface area and are non-life-threatening. The primary goal of treatment then is the promotion of optimal wound healing that both preserves function and produces the best possible cosmetic result. Since shallow second-degree burns will usually heal with minimal scarring if infection is prevented, care generally is limited to meticulous and frequent cleansing of the burn wound plus the application of topical antimicrobial agents. However, since deeper second-degree and third-degree burns frequently heal with extensive scarring, excision of the burned tissue and immediate skin grafting are currently recommended.

Unfortunately, the larger the size of the burn, the less nonburned skin is available for skin grafts to cover the area of the excised burn wound. This problem becomes particularly acute when burns involve more than 65–70% of the body surface area. In patients with such massive burns, it is often the lack of available donor skin rather than the size of the burn that compromises survival. Consequently, one of the most intense areas of research has involved the search for effective skin substitutes to permanently close the excised burn wound.

To date, no synthetic skin substitutes that can be used on a permanent basis have been developed. Although some synthetic skin substitutes have been used to achieve temporary burn wound closure until sites from which skin has already been taken for grafting have healed and are ready for reuse, these

Tissue-culture methods make it possible to grow sizable sheets of graftable skin from a dime-sized piece of a burned patient's skin; this approach holds promise for closing burn wounds that cover a large body surface area.

substitutes have met with inconsistent results. There are many reasons why the various types of skin substitutes have not been effective over the long term. For example, although cadaver skin functions as an effective skin substitute, its effectiveness is a short-term phenomenon since the skin graft is eventually rejected by the host.

However, recent advances in cell biology, molecular biology, and the biology of wound healing have led to the development of several different types of skin substitutes that show promise as permanent replacements; such advances have also led to the use of topically applied growth factors to hasten wound healing. One approach has been the use of tissue-culture methods to grow skin outside the body. With this technique a piece of skin about one square centimeter (0.155 sq in) in size is taken from the patient, processed into individual cells, and the skin cells placed into a tissue culture medium, where they multiply and form a shell of new skin. In the best of circumstances, the amount of new skin produced by this technique (over a 30-day culture period) is 10,000 times greater than the original piece. Although these approaches are exciting, it is too early to know what their ultimate clinical impact will be either in terms of achieving immediate closure of the burn wound or in the long-term quality of the skin cover.

The four R's

Optimum care of the burned patient can be summarized as the four R's: resuscitation, resurfacing, reconstruction, and rehabilitation. The "resuscitative" phase

A youngster rides on the shoulders of his doctor at a summer camp sponsored by the burn center of Pittsburgh's West Penn Hospital. The camp program encourages children recovering from burn injuries to participate in group activities in an atmosphere where they need not feel self-conscious about their physical disfigurement. The ultimate goal of the rehabilitation phase of therapy is to help the burn patient return to society.

consists of immediate volume resuscitation as well as the ongoing medical therapies directed at preventing infection and providing the individual organ systems and tissues with specific physiological support until the burn wound has either healed spontaneously or been surgically closed. This phase can last from a few days to up to three months, depending on the burn's severity. The "resurfacing" phase, during which burn wound closure occurs, is generally measured in weeks and overlaps the resuscitative phase.

The "rehabilitation" and "reconstructive" phases of therapy for a major burn frequently take months to years. The ultimate goal of rehabilitation therapy is to allow the patient to return to society. To accomplish this goal, reconstructive procedures to improve the cosmetic and functional outcomes are frequently required. For example, surgical procedures may be needed to improve the function and mobility of hands and joints so that the patient can accomplish daily living tasks (personal hygiene, preparing meals, etc.) or that will allow the patient to return to work and in some cases even to engage in physically demanding recreational activities.

Rehabilitation begins as soon as the patient is admitted to the burn center. It initially involves the construction and use of splints and various devices to prevent joint contractures (scar bands that cross joints and limit mobility) and the initiation of an exercise program to maintain muscle strength and joint mobility. Once the burn wounds have healed or been surgically closed, patients frequently benefit from wearing special pressure garments that prevent or limit hypertrophic scarring—*i.e.,* skin that becomes thickened, raised, red, and hard. These pressure garments are specially constructed for the individual patient and are usually worn for 23 hours a day for an average of 12 to 18 months.

Physical pain and emotional scars

Because of the complex nature of a burn injury, to accomplish one goal it may be necessary to sacrifice other goals. For example, since burns are extremely painful, an important therapeutic goal is pain control. Although movement or cleansing of the burned tissue is painful, failure to adequately exercise leads to weakness and joint contractures. And failure to adequately cleanse the burned tissues essentially guarantees infection. Thus, one major area of research is the development of improved methods of pain control. Currently, most burn centers use a combination of sedatives and narcotic or nonnarcotic agents. But research is now being conducted into the use of alternative methods, including meditation and hypnotherapy. Another method that is being explored is the use of devices that allow the patients to self-administer intravenous pain medications—so-called patient-controlled analgesia. The patient can infuse medication as needed, or "on demand"—thereby limiting unnecessary doses.

Since the emotional scars of a thermal injury may last long after the physical scars have faded, and psychological factors frequently play as important a role as physical factors in the patient's ultimate ability to return to society, psychological support is a major component of burn care. Thus, social workers and psychologists are essential members of the burn care team. Psychological counseling for patients as well as family members and other loved ones can help facilitate the many emotional adjustments that are required during and for months following the initial hospitalization period. In addition, many burn centers have inpatient and outpatient support groups to help the patients and their families cope with the stresses imposed by the burn injury and its treatment.

The future

Although spectacular progress has been made in all aspects of the care of the burn patient, death and disfigurement still occur. Further improvements in the care of the burn victim must await advances in several fields. Considerably more needs to be learned about wound healing, immunity, inflammation, cardiovascular physiology, and nutrition. For example, further study of host immune defenses is needed because in spite of the development of successive generations of increasingly powerful antibiotics, infection remains a major cause of death in the burn patient. However, no matter how powerful the antibiotic or which microorganism is causing the infection, the patient will not recover if his or her own antibacterial defenses cannot respond.

Consequently, a new area of research is the use of various natural products to stimulate or bolster specific aspects of the immune system that fail after a major thermal injury. As discussed above, these immunoadjuvant substances may include specific nutrients. In addition, experimental and some early clinical studies indicate that the administration of specific immune system growth factors helps restore immune function and prevent infection. These growth factors are of the cytokine family and include interleukin-1, interleukin-2, tumor necrosis factor, and the macrophage and neutrophil colony-stimulating factors. All of these cytokines are normally produced by the body; however, prior to the development of molecular biological technologies, it was not possible to obtain sufficient amounts of these agents in pure form for experimental or clinical testing.

Work also continues on techniques to aid in closure of the burn wound. When the wound is closed, evaporative water and heat loss are reduced, thus enabling the metabolic response to begin to return to normal and increasing the resistance to infection. Therefore, a large effort is being directed toward the development of temporary and permanent skin substitutes.

—Edwin A. Deitch, M.D.

Cancer

The United States declared war on cancer on Dec. 23, 1971. Pres. Richard M. Nixon, urged on by members of Congress and various lobbies, had proposed that the same kind of concerted effort that resulted in the splitting of the atom and put a man on the Moon go toward conquering the dread disease. Congress passed the National Cancer Act of 1971, seemingly unmindful of the difference between solving space problems by means of known engineering principles and vanquishing cancer, about which little was understood. On the 20th anniversary of that declaration, the war still raged. Although impressive battles had been won, the inescapable conclusion was that the war itself was being lost.

At an estimated cost of $22 billion over two decades, significant progress was made toward understanding cancer at the research level and providing better treatments and longer survival for patients. Victories were won against cancers of the stomach, cervix, uterus, rectum, testis, thyroid, mouth, and larynx and against rare childhood malignancies. But incidences of major killers such as lung, prostate, breast, colon, and skin cancers rose. Much, but not all, of that rise came from better methods of detection. Finding cancer early significantly increases the chances of successfully containing or curing it with the more effective treatments that have become available.

However, in the area that counts most—reducing deaths—the war continues to be lost. In 1971, 335,-000 people in the U.S. died from cancer; it was projected that in 1992 the number of deaths would reach 520,000, an increase of some 55%. The fact that the population is larger and older accounts for most but not all of the increase. A progress report on cancer deaths and incidence prepared by researchers at the University of Southern California School of Medicine in Los Angeles, published in the Nov. 22, 1991, issue of *Science* magazine, mainly covering the years 1973–87, indicated a frustrating increase in age-adjusted mortality. (Age adjustment is a statistical way to make comparisons by assuming that the same distribution of ages occurs in the different groups being studied. It allows valid comparisons, for example, between prostate cancer—most victims of which are older than 65—and childhood leukemias.) Deaths from lung cancer, melanoma (the most serious form of skin cancer), multiple myeloma (bone marrow cancer), and non-Hodgkin's lymphoma (a type of lymph cancer) rose more than 15% between 1973 and 1987. Mortality also increased for kidney (13%), esophageal (11%), brain (9%), prostate (7%), and breast (2%) cancers during the same period.

In contrast, mortality from heart disease declined markedly, although it remained the leading cause of death in the U.S. About 600,000 people died of coronary heart disease in 1971, compared with 498,000 in 1989, a drop of 34%, despite an increasing and aging population. Deaths from all types of cardiovascular disease totaled 945,000 in 1989, down 23.4% from 1971. If the increase in cancer deaths and the decrease in deaths from heart disease continue, cancer will be the leading cause of all deaths in the United States by the year 2000. It already is the leading cause of death among U.S. women, largely as a result of the sharp rise in lung cancer within that group.

Gains and losses

The *Science* magazine report further revealed that overall cancer mortality rose 6% between 1950 and 1987. This figure, however, includes a 60% decrease in deaths from testicular cancer and 50% from Hodgkin's disease between 1973 and 1987, as well as increases of 34% from lung cancer and 30% from melanoma.

Cervical cancer. Deaths from cervical cancer dropped 40% and incidence fell 36% during 1973–87. The decrease to 13,500 cases and 4,500 deaths in U.S. women annually is mainly due to early detection of the disease by Pap smears. This test costs about $15 and involves a cervical smear that is judged by technicians, who pass questionable ones on to experts for further evaluation. The process takes a week or two and is subject to errors of judgment. Consequently, a less expensive test that gives surer, quicker results is needed. In 1991 researchers developed a promising candidate, a new detector that relies on differences in the way that normal and precancerous cells absorb infrared light. The cells emit different infrared signatures at various stages in the transfor-

mation to malignancy. Initial testing on ideal samples from a limited number of women have shown promise. If the technique proves to be reliable in further studies with random samples of women with and without cancer, it might eventually be automated to screen large numbers of samples rapidly. Suspicious cells could then be examined more closely by specialists. Automated screening systems designed to increase handling speed without loss of diagnostic accuracy have been under development for a number of years.

Because an estimated one-third of U.S. women are not receiving Pap tests annually or even at three-year intervals, even in the absence of a better test, a group of experts from the Centers for Disease Control (CDC) and National Cancer Institute (NCI) recently recommended that Pap smears be offered whenever female patients see physicians for treatment of other conditions. The majority of cervical cancer patients are members of minority and low-income groups who do not receive adequate screening. The same group also recommended that research be done on "determinants of screening behavior and on characterizing the populations at risk for noncompliance."

In another recent development, a genital wart virus was found in up to 90% of women with cancer of the cervix. When the virus lands on a healthy cell, it remains harmless until the cell is damaged, typically during sexual intercourse. Once the virus has entered the cell, it takes over the cell's molecular machinery and begins making copies of itself, a process that can cause warts and ultimately cancer. This knowledge may make it possible to design a vaccine containing wart virus material that would cause the immune system to attack the invading virus.

Stomach cancer. Paralleling the fall in cervical cancer mortality, deaths from stomach cancer decreased 29% between 1973 and 1987. This is attributed in part to a reduction in the food-preservation methods of salting and pickling (which have a corrosive, carcinogenic effect) and in part to the increased consumption of fruits and vegetables (which are thought to have an anticancer effect). During the same period, there was also a 20% decline in the number of new cases of stomach cancer in the U.S. (to an estimated 23,200 cases in 1990). A parallel decline occurred worldwide, presumably for the same reasons. The change in dietary trends was stimulated by the aggressive public education campaigns of various cancer institutions. In fact, the significance of diet grew so sharply that in 1992 the American Cancer Society announced that it would make prevention through diet its main focus.

While high-salt diets have been identified as a major cause of stomach cancer, in 1991 researchers at Stanford University School of Medicine implicated another cause—*Helicobacter pylori,* a treatable bacterium associated with gastritis and peptic ulcers. If further research proves this organism to be a cause of stomach cancer, the potential will be enormous for fighting the disease in poorer nations where stomach cancer incidence and mortality have not decreased as they have in the U.S.

Uterine cancer. Deaths from cancer of the uterus (usually the endometrium, or lining) have also decreased after having shown an alarming upswing in the early years of the war on cancer. Investigators traced the rise in incidence of endometrial cancer to an increase in the use of estrogen replacement therapy by women to alleviate short-term symptoms of menopause—hot flushes, vaginal tract dryness, mood changes, insomnia, fatigue, and others—and to reduce the more serious, long-term risks of osteoporosis and heart disease. However, with the coadministration of a progestin (a steroid hormone that opposes estrogen), which in recent years has become the common practice in postmenopausal hormone replacement therapy, the incidence of endometrial cancer in the U.S. decreased 26% between 1973 and 1987, and deaths decreased by 20%.

Obesity is also associated with endometrial cancer. Recent studies have yielded evidence that hormonal and metabolic abnormalities are associated with certain types of obesity and that the distribution of fat may be more important than the amount. Researchers at the University of South Florida found that the risk of this cancer rose progressively with accumulation of fat in the upper body.

Testicular cancer. Steep declines have occurred in mortality from testicular cancer in the U.S.—60% between 1973 and 1987. The five-year survival rate rose from 63% in 1971 to 91% in 1991, when deaths fell to an estimated 375 men. However, incidence rose by 39% during the 1973–87 period and was projected to reach 6,300 in 1992. The lower death rate has resulted from better detection and drug treatments, while the increased incidence remains largely unexplained. Education programs that urge men to check their testes regularly for lumps may be one important factor in improved detection, however.

Cancer of the bladder. More effective treatment also reduced the toll from cancer of the bladder (by 23%) between 1973 and 1987, and noteworthy new ground has been gained in the battle against it. In 1991 oncologists announced a new method for detecting this malignancy as well as others that involve a mutated gene known as p53. Through a simple urine test, it may be possible to find evidence of bladder cancer before the mutation occurs. Since the same gene characterizes other malignancies, the same approach might be used to search for signs of colon cancer in stools, lung cancer in sputum, and ovarian cancer in vaginal secretions.

Once detected, bladder cancer might be successfully fought with a bacterium that causes tuberculosis in cows. When infused into a cancerous bladder, a weakened strain of the parasite known as bacille Calmette-Guérin, or BCG, bolsters the immune system in its fight against tumors. In May 1990 the Food and Drug Administration (FDA) approved BCG for fighting a shallow but aggressive form of the malignancy. In about 50% of patients, the tumors proceed to burrow farther into the organ and spread to other sites. BCG offers the promise of eliminating tumors before that happens, thus obviating the need to surgically remove the bladder.

The risk of getting tuberculosis from BCG is low but not zero, so the treatment cannot be used on patients with deficient immune systems. Studies of patients with healthy disease defense systems show that up to 82% receiving BCG stayed in remission from the shallow form of bladder cancer for an average of four years. Proponents of the treatment believe that it might also be used to treat other types of bladder cancer in the early stages. It was expected that all forms of bladder cancer would kill about 9,500 people in the U.S. in 1992, and an estimated 51,600 new cases, about 38,500 of them in men, would occur.

Childhood cancers: ups and downs. Other victories have been won in battles against leukemia and blood cell cancer, and some of them even predate the official declaration of the cancer war. For example, since the early 1960s the five-year survival rate for children with acute lymphocytic leukemia has jumped from 4 to as high as 73%. By 1991 childhood malignancies in the U.S. were thought to be rare (although they are still the chief cause of death from disease among children aged one to 14). However, a mysterious and disturbing rise in childhood leukemias and brain tumors came to light in 1991. For the period 1973 to 1988, the NCI reported an 11% rise in acute lymphocytic leukemia and a staggering 30.5% rise in brain and nervous system tumors. Non-Hodgkin's lymphoma, a lymph node cancer often associated with AIDS, increased among children more than 19% during the same period. Research could not confirm whether the rise in overall childhood cancers was real or the result of improved diagnoses and collection of information. Detection of brain tumors, for example, has surged with the use of new technologies, such as computed tomography (CT) and magnetic resonance imaging (MRI).

Meanwhile, cancer experts noted that even if childhood cancers are cured at an increased rate in the 1990s, the survivors remain at higher risk for other cancers than the general population. A notable additional finding comes from a British group, which determined that childhood leukemia is significantly more prevalent among the upper socioeconomic classes; the reason was not clear.

Other gains. The U.S. death toll from cancers of the mouth and pharynx, rectum, and thyroid was also reduced between 1973 and 1987, by 16, 40, and 21%, respectively. These reductions are largely attributed to

Come to where the Cancer is.

Smoking kills more Americans each year than alcohol, cocaine, crack, heroin, homicide, suicide, car accidents, fires, and AIDS combined.

An award-winning antismoking poster designed by a grade-school child is carried in subway cars in New York City. The Metropolitan Transit Authority has allotted 5% of its advertising space for messages that discourage smoking—the leading preventable cause of cancer deaths.

more effective treatments. However, despite research advances, new treatments, and earlier detection, the war continues to be lost on many fronts.

Smoking-related cancers. Increased smoking has made lung cancer the leading cause of U.S. cancer deaths. Mortality and incidence have increased more than 30% since 1973; an estimated 146,000 deaths and 168,000 new cases were projected for 1992. Cigarette smoking accounts for 85% of this toll.

Increasing evidence implicates tobacco as a killer of nonsmokers; an estimated 3,000 lung cancer deaths occur in the U.S. annually among nonsmoking people who breathe other people's smoke. A study by the NCI concluded that such passive smoking increases the risk of lung cancer by 30% even among those who never smoked. For the nonsmoking spouse of a smoker, the risk rises with the frequency and duration of exposure. Other research cites increased risks for brain cancer, lymphomas, and acute lymphocytic leukemia among children whose parents smoke.

Nevertheless, some heavy smokers escape the disease, and new evidence suggests the reason may be genetic. One NCI study concluded that those who possess two copies of a particular gene have a six times greater risk of developing lung cancer than people with one or no copy. Located on chromosome 22, the implicated gene makes an enzyme (P-450) that researchers believe may activate cancer-causing compounds in cigarette smoke.

Scientists are also probing the role of diet in lung cancer and other malignancies. In 1992 several groups were testing findings that vitamins C and E and beta carotene (an ingredient of carrots and leafy vegetables) may lower the risk of lung, esophageal, and colon cancers. (*See* below.)

Melanoma, myeloma, and lymphoma. Deaths from malignant melanoma jumped 30% in the U.S. from 1973 to 1987, while new cases soared a startling 83%. It was projected that annual deaths would reach 6,700 and new cases would reach 32,000 in 1992. The latter were increasing at an annual rate of 4%. One study concluded that severe sunburns in childhood result in an excessive risk of melanoma later in life.

The alarming loss of ozone over the Northern and Southern hemispheres has become the focus of research seeking to find a cause for the increase in melanoma. Unlike noxious ground-level ozone, which belches from vehicle exhausts, stratospheric ozone (above 600 m [20,000 ft]) forms a protective umbrella against ultraviolet (UV) radiation coming from the Sun. Ultraviolet B (UVB) apparently can cause genetic damage that leads to skin cancer. A suspected main cause of ozone depletion is the extensive use of certain chemicals, such as chlorofluorocarbons used in aerosol sprays and other products.

Scientists estimate that every 1% decrease in stratospheric ozone allows 2% more UV radiation to shine on the Earth's surface. This prompted the Environmental Protection Agency to warn that ozone losses could result in 12 million additional cases of skin cancer and 200,000 additional deaths worldwide between 1991 and 2040. During several weeks in winter, a huge ozone hole over Antarctica expands to the latitudes of Australia (which has the world's highest incidence of melanoma) and South America. At this time people in those regions are urged not to wear shorts or short-sleeved shirts and to use sunscreen on their hands and faces to block out harmful rays. Wearing a large-brimmed hat also is advised.

If UVB actually has caused the surge of melanoma cases, measurements should show a comparable increase in the amount of that radiation reaching the Earth's surface over the last few decades. No such increase has been found. However, this may be due to the lack of instruments sensitive enough to detect a UVB increase or to the radiation's being filtered out by pollutants in the air.

Sunbathers can take no solace in this, however, because all evidence points to ozone depletion's becoming much worse. Satellite and aircraft flights in 1991 and 1992 found indications that future ozone holes may extend from the Arctic to as far south as Texas and the Mediterranean countries. No matter how many treaties are signed to curtail use and production of ozone-depleting chemicals, enough of the chemicals already exist in the atmosphere to justify concern in the coming decades.

Despite the lack of convincing measurements, a growing number of experts believe that ozone loss combined with an increase in outdoor activities accounts for the rapidly rising melanoma incidence. In fact, sunscreens may add to the latter by giving people a false sense of security, according to the findings of a recent study conducted by a research team from the University of California at San Diego. Thinking that they are fully protected, sunbathers tend to increase their exposure time. This can result in massive doses of ultraviolet A (UVA), which is not absorbed by UVB sunscreens but can still cause skin damage that—it is suspected—could lead to a malignancy.

One solution to the rapidly increasing melanoma incidence would be a vaccine. Researchers have made varying degrees of progress toward this goal.

In the meantime, in April 1992 University of Michigan researchers received final FDA approval to begin a radical new gene therapy, which was begun in June. Rather than removing cells from the patient, modifying them with a therapeutic gene, and returning them to the body, the new therapy would transfer genetically engineered DNA directly into the tumor. The experiment was to involve patients suffering from metastatic melanoma and given no chance of survival. The DNA is designed to enter the cancer cell, where it would activate the immune system's killer T cells to seek out and destroy the cancer cells.

Studies completed in 1991 link squamous cell carcinoma, a less deadly skin cancer than melanoma, to the effects of the UVB component of sunlight on the p53 gene. The radiation apparently disables the gene, which normally prevents uncontrolled growth of cells characteristic of this and other cancers. Ozone in the upper atmosphere absorbs UVB, and dramatic decreases in this protective layer are suspected of accelerating skin cancer incidence.

Fewer clues exist to help explain increases in deaths from and new cases of multiple myeloma—24 and 11%, respectively, between 1973 and 1987—and of non-Hodgkin's lymphoma—22 and 51% in the same period. Improved means of detection may account for the increased incidence of myeloma and non-Hodgkin's lymphoma, as may the rise in AIDS cases and infections from the human immunodeficiency virus (HIV), both of which can lead to these malignancies.

Prostate cancer. In 1992 it was projected that 132,000 new cases of prostate cancer would be diagnosed in U.S. men and 34,000 would die from the disease. By the late 1980s carcinoma of the prostate was the second most common malignancy among U.S. men and the second biggest cancer killer after lung cancer. Over the period 1980–88, prostate cancer incidence increased 30% among white men and 8% among blacks. However, the incidence rate for blacks remained higher than for whites. The disease kills over two times as many blacks as whites. Overall death rates during the period 1980–88 increased 2.5% among white men and 5.7% among black men. The increasing incidence in white men—particularly since 1984—may be associated with the greater use of newer diagnostic methods. The extremely high death rates among black men may reflect the fact that they seek medical attention later and have less access to medical care in general.

Early detection of small tumors on the prostate gland during rectal examinations has increased the five-year survival rate from 50 to 74% in the past 30 years. However, the majority of men (85% by one estimate) do not submit to such exams. They regard the digital probe, in which the doctor inserts a rubber-gloved finger into the rectum, as uncomfortable and embarrassing, and they fear that surgery to remove a cancerous gland will leave them impotent.

Recent advances in surgery make impotence unlikely, while new testing methods have decreased

Melanoma: drastically rising rates*				
	1953–63		1978–82	
selected location	men	women	men	women
Denmark	1.6	2.2	5.9	8.4
New Zealand (non-Maori)	4.5	7.7	15.6	21.4
Sweden	2.4	2.8	7.2	8.2
U.S. (Connecticut)	3.0	3.6	8.4	7.7
Israel	2.4	3.3	8.5	7.4
Canada (Alberta)	2.2	2.7	4.3	5.7
Yugoslavia (Slovenia)	1.3	1.4	2.4	2.7
U.K. (Birmingham)	0.9	1.6	1.6	3.3

*number of cases per 100,000 population in primarily white population

Adapted from Howard K. Koh, M.D., "Cutaneous Melanoma," *New England Journal of Medicine*, vol. 325, no. 3 (July 18, 1991), pp. 171–182

discomfort and improved detection accuracy. Probing the prostate with ultrasound can reveal tumors too small to be felt in a digital exam, and a blood test now available detects abnormal levels of an antigen that increases when the gland becomes malignant. In one study of 2,425 men, 73% more cancers were found by a combination of all three techniques than with a digital examination alone. When tumors are detected before they spread beyond the prostate, the survival rate is as high as 85%. However, a study by a Swedish group published in April 1992 indicated that 10-year survival rates for men with early prostate cancer that went initially untreated (which has been standard practice in some centers in Europe) were about the same as for those who had more aggressive treatment (radical prostatectomy, local irradiation, and hormonal manipulation). The Swedish team therefore suggested that the option of surgery required further study. Reaction in the U.S., where aggressive treatment is standard practice, was generally that it would be unwise and could be harmful for men with diagnosed cancer of the prostate to forgo treatment. Meantime, doctors are struggling to gain better understanding of prostate cancer and its alarming surge in frequency.

Breast cancer. In many ways the battle against breast cancer reflects lack of progress in the war in general. More than $1 billion was spent on this part of the struggle from 1971 to 1991. While treatment has improved and survival has increased (the five-year rate having reached 77%), the death rate has not been reduced. In 1973, 26.9 of every 100,000 U.S. women died of the malignancy; by 1988 the number had grown to 27.5 per 100,000. Incidence has risen from 82 to 110 per 100,000 women since 1971, and it is projected that the number of new cases in 1992 will reach 181,000. Much of this increase resulted from the timely discovery of localized lumps by self-examination and X-ray mammography, but there remains an unexplained portion of the rise that has been linked to a variety of causes, including hormonal changes, diet, breast-feeding, breast implants, and radiation.

Long-term use of estrogen replacement therapy produces about a 10% increase for each five years of therapy. Risk of breast cancer is apparently lowered 10 to 20% for each year menarche (the onset of menstruation) is delayed. Women who stop menstruating before age 45 experience half the risk of those who continue to menstruate at age 55 and beyond. Progestin, taken to counteract estrogen's tendency to cause uterine cancer, has been shown in trials to increase the risk of breast cancer rather than reduce it, as had been originally assumed.

In trials completed in 1991, Swedish researchers found that the estrogen-blocking drug tamoxifen, a synthetic hormone, reduced by 40% the chance that women who have had cancer in one breast will develop it in the other. The NCI launched a large study

of this drug in April 1992. There is strong statistical evidence that adjuvant (postsurgical) therapies (such as tamoxifen) increase survival among breast cancer patients.

Attempts to link breast cancer with animal or vegetable fats have been inconsistent. A better case can be made for the claim that women who nurse their babies reduce their risk of this malignancy. Some women with silicone breast implants have tested positive for a substance suspected of causing cancer, but the risk is not clear enough to warrant removal of the devices. In 1991 researchers reported that women who carry a single copy of the gene responsible for the rare nervous system disorder ataxia-telangiectasia might be especially sensitive to damage from low-dose X-rays. Some physicians recommend that such women avoid mammography when possible in favor of periodic physical examinations by an expert who feels for lumps.

If a tumor is found, is there an ideal time to remove it? Several small statistical studies conclude that recurrence and death can be decreased if surgery is performed during the latter part of the menstrual cycle. In 1990 William Hrushesky of the Stratton Veteran Affairs Hospital in Albany, N.Y., examined patients' records and reported that premenopausal women who had their operations between days 7 and 20 of the cycle experienced 75% less recurrence and death than those who had surgery at other times. His study included 44 women who were followed for 10 years after surgery. A second study of 44 patients, published in 1991, concluded that those who had tumors excised between days 7 and 14 suffered a greater rate of recurrence than those who had mastectomies between days 20 and 30. The studies are small and the periods do not match, but some oncologists are heeding the results. At Guy's Hospital in London, surgeons have decided to perform all breast tumor operations in premenopausal women at least 12 days after the last period.

Proponents of this timed approach suggest that it works because estrogen secretion, which dominates the first two weeks of the cycle, might promote growth of any malignant cells that escape during surgery. Progesterone, more dominant during the second two weeks, may have the opposite effect.

Many cancer specialists do not embrace this idea. The connection between menstrual cycle and recurrence may, they say, be due to a statistical fluke. Some surgeons recommend against any delay in surgery once a tumor is detected.

Other skirmishes

X-rays as utilized in CT scans receive much of the credit for early detection of brain cancer and other tumors of the central nervous system. On the other hand, some increase in such malignancies may have

Marty Katz

Researchers Paul Talalay (left), Yeusheng Zhang (right), and colleagues at Johns Hopkins University, Baltimore, Maryland, recently isolated a potent anticarcinogen, sulforaphane, in the least favorite vegetable of U.S. Pres. George Bush. The potent chemical, which is abundant not only in broccoli but in other cruciferous vegetables such as kale and brussels sprouts, apparently activates enzymes that ward off tumors. Until sulforaphane's protective potential is more fully investigated, however, it is unlikely that doctors will begin prescribing a spear of broccoli a day—for either Republicans or Democrats.

resulted from older dental X-ray equipment, which exposes people to much higher radiation doses than newer machines. The incidence of these cancers rose 23% and mortality rose 9% between 1973 and 1987.

Cigarette smoking, besides being the primary cause of lung cancer, is at least partially responsible for increases in cancer of the kidney, mouth, larynx, bladder, and pancreas. Oncologists also implicate tobacco combined with alcohol as a factor in the rise in deaths from and incidence of esophageal cancer (11 and 12%) and in liver cancer incidence (14.5%).

During the same 1973–87 period, colon cancer deaths dropped 2%, but incidence rose 10%. Studies show that colon cancer risk can be reduced through early detection of lesions by sigmoidoscopy, in which a fiber-optic device is inserted into the rectum to search for lesions there and in the colon.

Epidemiological studies reveal a consistent association between colon cancer and consumption of animal fat and low fiber intake. A Harvard Medical School study found that men who ate a high-fat, low-fiber diet quadrupled their risk of developing precancerous polyps. This research, conducted by questionnaire, involved more than 49,000 male health professionals. A previous investigation of 121,700 nurses found a positive connection between animal fat consumption and risk of colon cancer among women.

Other medical reports published in 1991 concluded that taking aspirin or similar anti-inflammatory drugs regularly may cut the risk of death from colon cancer by as much as 50%. If further research proves this to be true, taking 16 or more aspirin a month might substantially reduce mortality from this disease, projected at 58,300 in 1992. Some scientists suggest that

aspirin's effect might come from its interference with the production of prostaglandins (hormonelike substances), which spur the growth of cells.

Other promising drugs are not as readily available as aspirin. Taxol, a drug used to fight ovarian cancer, is a case in point. Deaths from this malignancy dropped 6% and new cases almost 7% between 1973 and 1987, but in 1992 it was still expected to kill an estimated 13,000 women, and 1.4% of U.S. women are expected to develop it in their lifetime. The NCI plans to investigate whether the new drug, extracted from the Pacific yew tree, can cut this toll as well as that from breast cancer and as many as eight other malignancies.

Anticancer agents in food

The NCI is also investigating the potential of natural chemicals found in food to prevent malignancies. Much interest centers around beta carotene, a pigment that the body converts to vitamin A. It is found in and named after the carrot, but it is also plentiful in such vegetables as broccoli, brussels sprouts, cabbage, cauliflower, collard greens, kale, and spinach, as well as in fresh fruits. Studies in the U.S. and Europe have produced strong evidence of a decrease in lung cancer with increased consumption of beta carotene. Researchers consistently find that people who develop lung, mouth, throat, and other smoking-related malignancies have lower levels of this nutrient than do healthy men and women. For a study being conducted by researchers at Harvard Medical School, 22,000 doctors are taking daily doses of beta carotene in pill form to determine whether they will develop fewer cancers than a control group. Various investi-

263

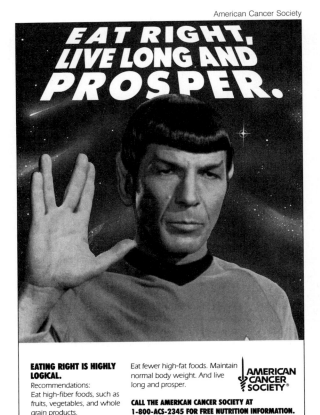

gations have also linked the pigment to decreased risk of cervical and skin cancers, but these are less convincing than the association with lung cancer.

Vitamin A, into which beta carotene is transformed, may protect against cancer by neutralizing unstable oxygen molecules known as free radicals that can kill or injure healthy cells. Besides this antioxidant effect, vitamin A inhibits the rapid proliferation of cells so characteristic of cancerous growth. This capability provides a rationale for testing both natural vitamin A and synthetic substances called retinoids. In 1990 researchers at the M.D. Anderson Cancer Center in Houston, Texas, found that treatment with a retinoid compound prevented patients with head and neck cancers from developing more primary tumors. However, the compound failed to stop the spread of the original tumor.

The NCI is testing retinoids in a large study appropriately called CARET. Seventeen thousand men at high risk of lung cancer from smoking or asbestos exposure take daily doses of beta carotene and the vitamin A derivative retinol to determine if this treatment can prevent or slow the development of malignancy. Other studies are under way to investigate the potential of retinoids for preventing breast, cervical, and skin cancers.

Vitamins C and E are also receiving attention in this

search because they, too, may protect against cancer-causing mutations resulting from oxygen-free radicals. A number of studies have shown such an effect, but the data remain far from conclusive. A 12-year investigation in Switzerland linked low blood levels of vitamins A and C and beta carotene with increased risk of death from cancer. The research associated low levels of vitamin C with increased deaths from stomach and gastrointestinal cancer, especially in men older than 60 years. Deficiencies of beta carotene and vitamin A were tied to an increased risk of lung cancer death and overall cancer mortality. Contrary to other studies, the Swiss found no link between low levels of vitamin E and increased incidence of malignancy. In 1992 a major U.S. study was planned to test whether a combination of vitamin E and beta carotene can prevent lung cancer in women smokers.

The discovery of another significant anticarcinogenic food chemical was announced in March 1992 by researchers at the Johns Hopkins School of Medicine, Baltimore, Md. The ingredient, called sulforaphane, was originally isolated from broccoli, but it is probably contained in other of the cruciferous vegetables, as is beta carotene. The research group found that the chemical activates "good" enzymes, which counteract the effect of other enzymes that cause cells to become carcinogenic.

The largest-ever investigation into diet and cancer was launched in Europe in December 1991, with more than 250,000 people in seven countries keeping detailed daily records of what they eat and providing blood samples for analysis by scientists. The project is slated to run for at least five years and will measure such factors as the relationship between cancer (and other diseases) and levels of vitamins in the blood.

Personal battles—cancer and life-style

Victories in the cancer campaigns have produced notable increases in survival times for patients under age 65 but have not decreased overall mortality. That sad fact has caused the NCI to drop its target of reducing cancer deaths by 50% before the end of the century. An increasing number of experts want to see greater emphasis on prevention. They insist that evidence strongly shows life-style to be more significant than environmental factors such as pollution. They point to the role of reduced smoking, low-fat diets, and exercise in lowering the number of deaths from heart disease significantly while cancer deaths rose.

Such a strategy would shift more responsibility for waging the cancer war to individual battles against smoking, alcohol use, consumption of animal fat, obesity, exposure to sunlight, and other factors. Personal victories in day-to-day encounters with food and other factors may do what $22 billion spent in laboratories and clinics over two decades has failed to do.

—*William J. Cromie*

Special Report

"Vaccines" for Cancer— Can They Succeed?

by Edward P. Cohen, M.D.

Almost 100 years ago, the German immunologist and Nobel laureate Paul Ehrlich theorized that throughout each person's lifetime cancer cells arise frequently but, like germs that cause infection, the cells are destroyed by the body's immune system. In this way people are protected from the development of malignant disease. Ehrlich's theory implies that the immune system distinguishes between malignant and nonmalignant (normal) cells of the body. Thus, tumor cells and normal cells of the same individual must differ from each other in some important way. According to the theory, cancer develops when the immune system fails to recognize and destroy the newly emerging malignant cells. Under these circumstances, the cells that have escaped destruction grow into tumors that spread throughout the person's body.

Scientists today have come to realize that much of Ehrlich's early hypothesis is correct and that this has exciting implications for cancer therapy. The hope of medical scientists is that the immune system can be mobilized to aid in the treatment of cancer patients. If it is true that malignant and nonmalignant cells are not the same and that these differences can be recognized by the body, then it might be possible to exploit those differences to develop a cancer "vaccine." Efforts in numerous medical centers throughout the world are being made to develop effective strategies to stimulate immunity to cancer, and the results, although still very preliminary, are encouraging.

Cellular differences

What evidence supports the notion that there are differences between cancer cells and normal cells of the same individual and that these differences can be recognized by the immune system? In the 1940s immunologists used the "transplantability" of cancer cells to investigate this question. Since the structure of all cells, both malignant and nonmalignant, is extraordinarily complex, and very small differences can be recognized by the immune system, tumor immunologists detected cellular differences by attempting to transfer cancer cells to normal recipients (laboratory animals without malignant cells). If the transferred cells differed from normal, they were recognized as "foreign" by the host and rejected.

The early investigators surgically removed tumors from individual mice, killed the cancerous cells, and then injected them into normal mice as a "tumor vaccine." Tumor vaccination, it was reasoned, would protect against cancer much as an immunization against polio or measles protects against those infectious diseases. After waiting several weeks—to allow the immunity to develop—the scientists then "challenged" the immunized animals with an injection of live cancer cells. This worked as predicted—in the same fashion as immunizations against infection. That is, the mice were protected. Because the immune system had been mobilized to reject the live tumor cells, the transplanted tumor did not grow.

Unfortunately, in these early studies the investigators failed to include an important control. They neglected to test the immune reaction against normal, nonmalignant cells. When this important control was included, they found that the normal cells, too, were rejected—just like the cancer cells. The mice had been immunized against all cells from the donor, both malignant and nonmalignant. In other words, the reaction against the normal cells was no different from the reaction against the cancer cells. The reason was that the animals were not inbred; genetic differences between donor and recipient, rather than differences between malignant and normal cells, were responsible for the rejection response.

Investigations into the structural differences between malignant and nonmalignant cells of the same individual could not be continued until inbred strains of mice became available in the 1950s. Inbred mice are just like identical twins; that is, they are genetically identical. Laboratory scientists breed these strains through repeated brother-sister matings over many generations. Eventually, all genetic differences between the animals are eliminated. The inbred mice look alike and share the same blood and tissue types. Like human identical twins, they will accept skin and organ grafts from each other without the need for drugs that suppress the immune system; across non-inbred strains of mice, grafts of normal tissues and injections of live tumor cells are rejected.

Once geneticists had developed strains of inbred mice, which are ideal for studying transplantation and tumor rejection, further investigations into cellular differences could proceed. When the previously described experiment was repeated and inbred mice were immunized with killed tumor cells, subsequent injections of viable cancer cells *were* rejected (as Ehrlich had postulated they would be), whereas under similar conditions normal, nonmalignant cells such as blood cells or a skin graft were accepted by the inbred recipient. Conversely, mice of the same inbred strain that had not previously been immunized accepted the tumor and eventually died from cancer. This experiment strongly implied that there must be differences between the structures of malignant and nonmalignant cells and that these differences formed the basis of rejection by the host's immune system. Still, critics of the theory argued that small but significant genetic differences between the animals remained and that it was those differences that were responsible for the rejection of the tumor by the immunized recipients.

The question was finally settled in 1960 when George Klein at the Karolinska Institute in Stockholm reported that an individual mouse whose cancer had been excised had evidence of immunity to its own tumor. The animal's immune system killed the malignant cells following reinjection of the viable cancer cells, and the animal survived. In this case, because the cancer was removed and then reinjected into the same animal, there could be no question of rejection's being due to genetic differences. Mice of the same inbred strain that had not had a tumor removed ("naive" mice) accepted the malignant cells and died of cancer. These animals that developed a malignancy also had evidence of antitumor immunity; it was apparent, however, that the immunity was insufficient to control the growth of the tumor. Although different from normal, the injected cancer cells must have been only weakly antigenic (*i.e.*, not potent enough to stimulate a reaction against them as foreign cells).

This experiment provided the first conclusive evidence of structural differences between malignant and nonmalignant cells of the same individual, and it revealed that those subtle differences could be recognized by the immune system of the host. Possibly, the weak immunity could be strengthened by the administration of a tumor vaccine or through the use of an immune stimulant.

Tumor cells: diverse and complex

The actual development of a tumor vaccine was complicated, however, when investigators found that an animal resistant to one tumor showed no resistance to another, independently arising tumor from a different mouse of the same inbred strain. Viable tumor cells from a second animal grew with no inhibition in a mouse immunized with cancer cells from the first animal. It turned out that although differences between malignant and nonmalignant cells could be detected, each tumor appeared to have its own unique structural property. The experiment indicated that the structural differences that tagged, or distinguished, the malignant cells were not all the same. Thus, the hope for

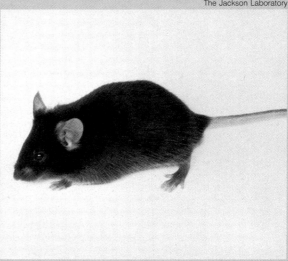

Inbred mice have made it possible for scientists to study the complex immune processes that cause the body to recognize and reject newly emerging cancer cells; potential "tumor vaccines" may result from this research.

a single, universal tumor vaccine that would be useful in all patients diminished.

In the case of a vaccine against an infection (*e.g.*, polio), the unique structures associated with the infectious microorganism are all the same, and one form of the vaccine is sufficient to protect all recipients. In cancer, each independently arising tumor is unique. Thus, the development of a single, universally effective cancer vaccine would be difficult—and perhaps impossible. A number of recent investigations have addressed this problem and attempted to answer the question: What is the nature of the tumor-associated structures that distinguish malignant and nonmalignant cells? The answer could lead the way toward the rational construction of an effective tumor vaccine.

Thierry Boon and his colleagues at the Ludwig Institute for Cancer Research in Brussels reported in 1990 that they had found that mouse mastocytoma (breast cancer) cells included some cells that formed tumors in inbred mice and others that were rejected. They reasoned that the difference between the cells that escaped the immune system and grew (called tum⁺, because they formed tumors) and those that were rejected (known as tum⁻) was the presence or absence on the cells per se of a distinguishing structure, or tumor antigen. Tum⁺ cells did not have such a distinguishing structure and escaped detection, whereas tum⁻ cells did have the antigen and were rejected. However, an analysis of many tum⁻ cells indicated that there was considerable diversity among them; that is, many of the tum⁻ cells expressed a slightly different tumor antigen.

Since there were a number of nonidentical tumor-associated antigens, Boon chose one tum⁻ cell type as a model. He grew large numbers of the cells in his laboratory, isolated the cells' DNA, and then transferred various genes from the tum⁻ cells into tum⁺ cells. His purpose was to isolate the gene responsible for forming at least one tumor-associated antigen and to characterize the molecular structure of an antigen that led to rejection of the cells by the host's immune system.

Boon searched among thousands of colonies of tum⁺ cells to find one clone that had been converted to tum⁻ following gene transfer. He was able to recover a gene specifying a tumor antigen. The gene that he found was a medium-sized protein that was similar to a protein found in normal cells. The gene had a very small but highly significant change—*i.e.,* a mutation—that converted the protein from a normal one to one that stimulated host immunity and led to rejection of the cancer. Tumors that grew (*i.e.,* the tum⁺ cells) failed to express the slightly altered structure; rather, they formed antigens that were present in normal cells. This meant that tumor cells expressing the normal protein were unrecognized by the immune system and grew, whereas tumor cells that were rejected expressed the altered structure. If Boon transferred a mixture of tum⁻ and tum⁺ cells to mice that had been immunized with tum⁻ cells, the animals developed a tumor, but the growing tumor cells were all tum⁺. Thus, the immune system recognized and killed the cells that expressed the aberrant, tumor-associated antigen.

Late in 1991 Boon and colleagues reported that they had subsequently discovered specific tumor antigens in cells of patients with melanoma, a highly metastatic and often fatal tumor that arises in the skin, and that these antigens might be mutant by-products of cancerous transformation, which suggested that they could be targets for a vaccine.

Analogous conclusions have been reached for a variety of cancers found in both animals and patients. The tumor-associated antigens are minor variants of structures associated with normal cells of the body. They are found inside the cell and are associated with portions of the cell's external membrane. There are many different types, consistent with the earlier observation that immunity to one tumor does not confer immunity to a second. Adding to the complexity of the problem is the fact that within a single population of tumor cells there is considerable diversity of tumor-antigen expression; different cells express different antigens.

Tumor immunization: early strategies

Since malignant cells express tumor-associated antigens that can be "targets" of an immune-mediated attack, why do tumors grow at all? Why does the immune system not reject such cells? There are two reasons. As already indicated, some tumor cells fail to express tumor-associated antigens and thus escape detection. In other instances the antigens, although present, fail to stimulate strong immune responses. Thus, a nonspecific stimulation of the immune system in cancer patients might lead to rejection of at least some tumor cells.

In some cancer patients the administration of novel adjuvants—substances (often of bacterial origin) that enhance the effectiveness of treatment by stimulating the immune system—has led to the rejection of established tumors. In selected patients with melanoma, adjuvants injected into the tumor itself led to a severe inflammation at the site and regression of the cancer; however, tumors at distant sites and internal tumors continued to grow. Moreover, for most other types of cancer, adjuvant treatment has not proved to be effective.

In other cases attempts have been made to "vaccinate" patients against their cancer. A cancer vaccine differs from other vaccines in that it is intended not to *prevent* the disease but to kill the tumor in cancer patients. In principle, however, the early attempts followed the strategy used to vaccinate against infectious disease except that instead of killed germs, killed cancer cells were used. In the case of an infectious disease such as smallpox, polio, or tetanus, the infectious organism is isolated and treated in such a way that it no longer poses the threat of infection but retains its antigenic properties (*i.e.,* it is attenuated); the immune system responds to the attenuated vaccine just as it would to an actual infection. In an analogous manner, physicians vaccinated against cancer by taking portions of the patient's tumor and treating the cancer cells with high doses of X-rays or with chemical substances to prevent the cells from dividing. The killed cells posed no threat to the patient and were used for immunization.

In most instances such vaccinations against cancer have not worked. Patients with breast cancer, for example, who were immunized with killed portions of their own tumors failed to live longer than patients who were not immunized. Moreover, there was no evidence that the patients' tumors regressed. However, for some tumors in some patients, immunization with extracts of cancer cells has led to objective evidence of tumor regression.

In the late 1980s Jean-Claude Bystryn and his colleagues at New York University found that immunization of patients who had malignant melanoma with killed melanoma cells stimulated immune responses to their tumors in 40% of cases, and those patients survived longer than patients who failed to develop immunity to the melanoma vaccine. Malcolm Mitchell at the University of Southern California and Donald Morton at the University of California at Los Angeles have used similar approaches to immunize patients with melanoma, with analogous results. Mitchell grew melanoma cell cultures from biopsies of patients with widespread disease, then mechanically disrupted the tumor cells and combined them with an adjuvant—an immunostimulant known as DETOX. In these various immunization attempts, each involving relatively small groups of patients, a significant proportion showed objective evidence of tumor regression in the absence of other forms of cancer therapy. In most instances the regression was temporary, and the tumor returned. These successes are particularly notable because melanoma is one of the most difficult forms of cancer to treat in its advanced stages.

In studies begun in the mid-1980s, Michael Hanna of the Biotechnology Research Institute in Rockville, Md., immunized colon cancer patients with killed tumor cells combined with an adjuvant following surgical removal of their tumors. Recurrence of the cancer was delayed, and the patients survived for longer periods than nonimmunized colon cancer patients. Here again, tumor regression following tumor vaccination provided objective evidence that patients' immune systems had the underlying capacity to recognize and destroy malignant cells. Whether this capacity will enable immunizations against all forms of cancer is uncertain. Attempts to vaccinate against other types of cancers—lung cancer, for example—thus far have not succeeded in slowing the growth of tumors.

The promise of interleukin-2

Steven Rosenberg and colleagues at the National Cancer Institute (NCI) chose another approach. Beginning in the early 1980s, they used interleukin-2 (IL-2) to stimulate the immune system of patients with advanced cancer. IL-2 is an immune mediator, a "hormone" of the immune system, that was isolated and characterized by NCI scientists in 1976. (Hormones are substances produced by and released from specific cell types that circulate in the bloodstream and affect the function of other cells. Insulin, for example, is produced in the beta cells of the islets of Langerhans in the pancreas and regulates the body's glucose metabolism.) IL-2 is a lymphokine—a product of a class of cells of the immune system (T lymphocytes) that affects the specialized function of other classes of cells. Cells stimulated by IL-2 undergo division to increase their numbers and engage in activities that protect the host from infection.

In one trial Rosenberg found that tumors of some patients with advanced cancer regressed following the administration of IL-2. Approximately 10% of his patients with widespread melanoma and about the same percentage of patients with metastatic renal cancer had a complete regression of their tumors following treatment. About 10 to 25% of other patients had partial tumor regressions. Unfortunately, as occurs with other forms of cancer immunotherapy, the tumors later returned. Although their survival was prolonged, the patients were not cured.

To increase the effectiveness of the treatment for larger numbers of patients, Rosenberg modified the approach. He took blood from the patients, recovered the white blood cells, and treated them outside the body with IL-2. Some of the cells so treated began dividing and over a two-week period increased dramatically in number. These cells, known as lymphokine-activated killer (LAK) cells, were then reinfused into the patients, with improved results. In one group studied by Rosenberg, approximately 30% of both melanoma and renal-cell cancer patients receiving LAK cells along with additional IL-2 showed objective signs of improvement. Tumor regression did not occur in all patients, however, and in most instances the improvement was only temporary. Nevertheless, the results clearly indicated that the immune system recognized and destroyed the cancer cells and, significantly, normal cells were unaffected. IL-2 and LAK cells were not effective in patients with most other types of cancer. (Responses of two early groups of patients studied by Rosenberg are shown in the table below.)

To improve the effectiveness of the treatment yet further, Rosenberg recovered lymphocytes from tumors themselves and stimulated those cells with IL-2. Known as tumor-infiltrating lymphocytes (TIL), these cells were 50 to 100 times more potent than LAK cells

Response to immunotherapy*

type of advanced cancer	IL-2				LAK cells plus IL-2			
	total number of patients	complete response	partial response	minor response	total number of patients	complete response	partial response	minor response
renal-cell cancer	21	1	0	0	36	4	8	7
melanoma	16	0	5	1	26	2	4	1
colorectal cancer	6	0	0	0	26	1	2	1
non-Hodgkin's lymphoma	0	—	—	—	2	1	1	0
sarcoma	0	—	—	—	6	0	0	0
adenocarcinoma of lung	1	0	0	0	5	0	0	1
other	2	0	0	0	5	0	0	0
	46	1	5	1	106	8	15	10

*Complete response = tumor disappeared; partial response = 50% decrease in tumor size; minor response = 25–49% decrease in tumor size

Adapted from Steven A. Rosenberg, M.D., *et al.*, "A Progress Report on . . . Lymphokine-Activated Killer Cells and Interleukin-2 . . .," *New England Journal of Medicine*, vol. 316, no. 15 (April 9, 1987), pp. 889–897

in mediating the regression of established tumors. Still, the success of this approach, as with other forms of immunotherapy, was short-lived. Although tumor regression occurred, the cancer returned, usually in less than two years. Moreover, the treatment itself was toxic. Most patients receiving IL-2 infusions experienced massive edema (fluid accumulation), which regressed when the treatment was discontinued. Some patients receiving the therapy experienced serious circulatory problems, including heart attacks, heart failure, and stroke. The importance of this experiment is that it provided still further objective evidence that the immune system has the underlying capacity to recognize and destroy at least some types of malignant cells.

To avoid toxicity associated with IL-2 administration, Mary K.L. Collins and her colleagues at the Institute of Cancer Research in London carried out studies in rats. They transferred the gene for IL-2 into a rat sarcoma cell line that would be used for treatment. (Sarcomas are cancers arising in bone, connective tissue, and muscle.) The idea was that the local formation of small quantities of IL-2 by the tumor itself would stimulate a strong antitumor immune response without the systemic toxicity that followed intravenous administration of the hormone. A retrovirus was used to carry the IL-2 gene into the cancer cells. (A retrovirus is a virus that is incorporated into the DNA of a cell and is duplicated when the cell divides.) By means of recombinant DNA technology, the gene for IL-2 was thus inserted into a defective virus (to prevent generalized viral infection from taking place), which was then used to infect the cancer cells. The IL-2 gene functioned inside the virally infected cell, and the cancer cells were thus able to produce large quantities of IL-2. Collins found that viable sarcoma cells modified by the insertion of the IL-2 gene were rejected, whereas unmodified cells grew and killed the inbred recipients. Significantly, the animals that had rejected the IL-2-secreting cancer cells had evidence of immunity to the unmodified tumor. Thus, infection of the tumor with a retrovirus carrying the gene for IL-2 stimulated an antitumor immune response.

In related experiments, Drew Pardoll and colleagues at Johns Hopkins School of Medicine, Baltimore, Md., in 1991 found that in mice with renal cell cancers the immunity that followed immunization with interleukin-secreting cells (in this case interleukin-4, a related lymphokine, was used) was powerful enough to cause the regression of established tumors. Together, these experiments pointed toward the promising use of lymphokine-modified tumor cells as an approach to cancer therapy that was new in principle.

These newest approaches are now being extended to human patients. Rosenberg recently received approval from the U.S. Food and Drug Administration to undertake a clinical study involving the infection of patients' tumor cells with an IL-2-specifying retrovirus. The IL-2-secreting cells will be reinjected into patients as a cancer vaccine. Since the earlier NCI trials, efforts to improve the potency of the therapy but lessen its toxicity have been made, as have attempts to find the optimal schedule of administration. Nevertheless, because the therapy is so new, and unforeseen harm might result, only patients who have exhausted other, more conservative forms of therapy are to be tested.

Many problems remain. First, modification of patients' tumors by retroviral infection for vaccination means that the patient receives an injection of his or her own viable cancer cells. Conceivably, the cells might grow in the patient. Working jointly, Collins in London and this author at the University of Illinois College of Medicine in Chicago have addressed this problem in experimental animals by inserting genes for tumor antigens *and* IL-2 into a foreign cell type. The foreign cells are rejected, just as a graft of tissue would be from an unrelated donor. Mice rejecting the modified cells subsequently develop tumor immunity.

A second remaining problem is that tumors are themselves highly heterogeneous, consisting of tumor-antigen-positive (tum⁻) and tumor-antigen-negative (tum⁺) cell types. Therefore, selection for tum⁺ cells would be expected to occur, and tumors that recur following immunotherapy are usually immunoresistant. Furthermore, the tumor antigens within the population of tumor cells are not all the same. Some tumor antigens strongly stimulate the immune system, while others do not. Thus, in unstimulated animals and patients, cells expressing weak antigens may escape immune destruction and grow.

The future: prospects for a cancer vaccine

Few believe that a cancer vaccine, even when fully developed, will be a cure for cancer. As yet, the immunotherapy approach has not proved to be effective for patients with the most common types of tumors— cancers of the large bowel, the breast, and the lung. The diversity of tumor antigens within the population of cancer cells within an individual patient may make a cure following the administration of a single form of therapy an insurmountable goal.

Many medical scientists view immunization against cancer as another means of therapy. When feasible, the patient's tumor is removed surgically. In many instances, however, the cancer has spread before symptoms have occurred and surgery can take place. In these cases chemotherapy and radiation are used in an attempt to kill remaining tumor cells. Immunotherapy is likely to find a place as yet another cancer treatment option. The hope is that immunotherapy used together with surgery, chemotherapy, and radiation will cause more and more cancer cells to be killed, enabling greater numbers of patients to survive this often lethal disease.

Chronic Fatigue Syndrome

Everyone gets tired—the pace of life in the late 20th century is fast. Not surprisingly, many people feel tired a great deal of the time. Sometimes, though, people feel that they are experiencing a degree of fatigue that cannot be explained by ordinary circumstances, and they seek medical attention. A majority of these individuals are found to be suffering from overwork or depression. On occasion, specific physical illnesses are found to be responsible. In some cases, however, neither psychological disorders nor known physical ailments can be identified as the cause of the debilitating fatigue, and these people may be suffering from chronic fatigue syndrome (CFS), an elusive ailment that has so far resisted scientists' attempts to understand or explain it.

CFS is not the "normal" persistent tiredness that occurs as a result of overwork or inadequate amounts of sleep, and it has features that distinguish it from fatigue that is clearly secondary to depression or to well-recognized physical diseases. CFS (known as postviral fatigue syndrome in the U.K.) is a devastating illness that can render its victims so exhausted that they are unable to perform the simple daily activities that most people take for granted. Many patients are unable to hold a job or maintain their family responsibilities. In some cases the illness has led to divorce and even suicide.

To help physicians determine which patients are indeed suffering from this poorly understood disorder, researchers have developed a detailed set of criteria known as a case definition (see Table, page 271). According to this definition, a true case of CFS is characterized by fatigue that starts suddenly and is usually accompanied by a flulike illness with symptoms of low-grade fever, sore throat, aching muscles, and related problems. These symptoms are severe, persist for at least six months, and cause the patient to curtail his or her level of activity by more than 50%. Along with fatigue, the most debilitating symptoms for most patients are difficulty with concentration and memory and an increased feeling of ill health that lasts for a day or two following even modest physical exertion. The case definition also requires that a variety of physical ailments—including cancer, autoimmune diseases, and infections—and psychiatric disorders be ruled out as possible causes of the symptoms.

Many people have the erroneous idea that CFS is a "new" disease. In fact, illnesses quite similar to it have been described in the medical and general literature for thousands of years. The condition called neurasthenia in the 19th and early 20th centuries could well have been CFS. And today the illnesses known variously as myalgic encephalomyelitis, epidemic neuromyasthenia, chronic Epstein-Barr virus infection, and fibromyalgia bear a close resemblance to CFS.

A "legitimate" disease?

CFS is currently a controversial illness. Some authorities claim that there simply is no such disorder and that those with CFS symptoms have other, undiagnosed ailments. One reason for the debate is that no single, definitive *objective* abnormality—*e.g.,* a physical anomaly, such as swollen lymph glands, found upon clinical examination or an unusual finding in the laboratory tests, such as elevated liver enzymes or white blood cell count—has yet been identified in all patients with CFS. This does not mean, of course, that no such abnormality or cause will be found. Many conditions that today are well established—for example, multiple sclerosis (MS), systemic lupus erythematosus (SLE, or lupus), and rheumatoid arthritis—were at one time also similarly controversial until definitive markers of the disease were identified.

Another reason that CFS is the subject of dispute is that many of its symptoms are not specific to a single illness; they can be found in patients with many different types of physical and psychological conditions. In particular, because some of the symptoms of CFS also are reported frequently by patients suffering from depression and anxiety, some doctors (understandably) think that CFS is more a psychological than a physical ailment. Others who have studied CFS, however, believe that it is not a purely psychological disorder. They also believe that the distinction between physical and psychological illness with regard to CFS—and many other diseases—is of little utility. (This issue is discussed in more detail below.)

A third reason that CFS is controversial is that many patients who do not have the illness believe—and insist to their doctors—that they do. Often these are individuals who are suffering from a psychiatric disorder but will not accept such a diagnosis because to them there is a stigma associated with psychiatric problems, a sense of a personal failing. Prompted by the enormous media attention given to CFS in recent years, some individuals have come to imagine that they actually suffer from the symptoms that they have read and heard so much about; others, well versed by media accounts, are adept at fabricating symptoms. These factors can make it very difficult for even the most astute physician to arrive at a correct diagnosis.

Who gets CFS?

Australian and U.S. studies indicate that between 10 and 40 of every 100,000 people have serious, unexplained fatigue that meets the case definition of CFS. It is not yet known if CFS is found worldwide. To date, most of the research has been conducted in Australia, the U.S., and the U.K., the countries that have the greatest number of well-documented cases. The U.S. Centers for Disease Control (CDC) currently estimates that there are at least 100,000 cases of CFS in the U.S. alone.

Although about 75% of those who seek care for CFS are female, this does not necessarily mean that women are disproportionately affected. In fact, in the U.S. 60% of patients seen in a doctor's office, with all kinds of illness, are female. Women seem to seek medical care more often than men do. Also, many illnesses that involve abnormalities of the immune system predominantly affect women; for example, 70–90% of all patients with MS, lupus, rheumatoid arthritis, and Graves' disease (an autoimmune thyroid disorder) are women. This observation is relevant because CFS may involve abnormalities in immune function, as will be discussed below.

In some epidemic-like outbreaks of CFS, such as a widely publicized one that occurred in the Lake Tahoe (Nevada) area in the 1980s, a majority of patients were well-educated persons aged 25–45. Because CFS often affects upper-middle-class young adults, some media reports have dubbed it the "yuppie flu." Implicit in the epithet is the idea that it is a contrivance of over-ambitious young adults, whose fast-paced life-styles became "too much" for them, causing them to seek some way to "get off the merry-go-round." This patient stereotype simply does not reflect the true case. In an ongoing study being conducted by the CDC at four surveillance sites (in Atlanta, Ga.; Reno, Nev.; Grand Rapids, Mich.; and Wichita, Kan.), it appears that CFS patients in each of the four communities have the same level of education and only a slightly higher income than the community at large; the typical patient is not a "yuppie." Virtually all studies of persons with CFS, however, have reported relatively few black, Hispanic, Native American, or Asian patients. It is unclear at this time whether the illness really is found less often in these racial and ethnic groups or whether they seek help less often for this problem—or simply have less access to health care.

Cases of CFS are usually sporadic—i.e., an individual becomes ill, but others in close contact with the patient remain well. However, sometimes a family member or a co-worker also suffers from a similar condition. Moreover, in the past 60 years there have been many apparent epidemics—such as the Lake Tahoe one—of CFS or an illness very much like CFS.

Different diseases, similar symptoms

An enormous number of physical and psychological maladies can cause a person to suffer from fatigue, among them depression, MS, and lupus. Along with overwork, depression is by far the most common cause of persistent tiredness. Furthermore, depression is often accompanied by some of the same physical symptoms (for example, headache and muscle aches) seen in CFS; moreover, some depressed patients complain mainly about their physical symptoms and do not readily admit to feeling chronically sad. Nonetheless, while depression shares several symp-

---

CFS case definition

a case of chronic fatigue syndrome must fulfill both of the major criteria and the following minor criteria: 6 or more of the symptom criteria and 2 or more of the physical examination criteria; or 8 or more of the symptom criteria

major criteria
- debilitating fatigue of sudden onset that persists for a period of at least six months
- appropriate tests must have ruled out cancer; viral, bacterial, and other infections; chronic psychiatric disorders; inflammatory diseases; drug abuse; other chronic conditions

minor criteria
symptom criteria (must have begun at or after onset of increased fatigability and must persist or recur over six months)
- chills or low-grade fever
- sore throat
- tender lymph nodes
- muscle weakness
- muscle pain
- prolonged fatigue after exertion
- headaches
- joint pain (without swelling)
- neurological problems (confusion, memory loss, visual disturbances)
- sleep disorders
- description of main symptoms as developing over a few hours to a few days

physical examination criteria (must be documented by a physician on at least two occasions at least one month apart)
- low-grade fever
- throat red but without discharge covering throat or tonsils
- palpable or tender lymph nodes in front or back of neck or in armpits

Source: Centers for Disease Control, Atlanta, Ga.

---

toms with CFS, it is also different in several important respects. Depression does not start suddenly with an infectious disease-like illness, and it is not associated with chronic low-grade fevers, joint pain, swollen lymph glands, and unusual sensitivity to bright light—all of which are often characteristic of CFS.

MS is a well-defined clinical entity in which the immune system, for unexplained reasons, attacks and damages the brain and spinal cord. Often the impairments caused by MS are clear and unambiguous; for example, patients lose the sight in one eye for a period of time or experience weakness in an arm. With MS, however, as with virtually all diseases, there can be a "gray zone"; in mild cases the diagnosis can be quite unclear. Moreover, fatigue, burning or tingling sensations of the skin, dizziness, and difficulty in concentrating can be common in patients with MS and in those with CFS. The situation is much the same for lupus—some patients receive an unambiguous diagnosis, whereas others fall into a gray zone. Also, as is

271

the case in MS, many patients with lupus experience fatigue, aching muscles, aching joints, and low-grade fevers as their most prominent symptoms.

A mind-body connection

There is considerable evidence to suggest that CFS is indeed a "physical" disorder. Laboratory tests of CFS sufferers have shown a variety of immune system changes, possible brain inflammation, and the reactivation of dormant viruses. In addition, some cases of CFS begin with an infection caused by a well-recognized infectious agent—for example, CFS may follow in the months after the onset of Lyme disease.

At the same time, it is clear that many patients with CFS develop psychological disturbances, particularly depression and anxiety, *after* the onset of CFS. In some individuals the psychological manifestations become a dominant part of the illness, and it is imperative that doctors recognize and treat them.

The question of whether CFS is a physical or psychological illness is not likely to be productive for those attempting to treat or understand the disease. First, the distinction tends to imply that psychological illness is not "real," that it does not produce real suffering; this, obviously, is not the case. Second, especially in a society where, unfortunately, emotional, or mental, illness still carries a stigma, there is an implication that such an illness is the patient's "fault." It is becoming increasingly clear, however, that ailments of a psychological nature, while sometimes triggered or exacerbated by life experiences, are frequently linked to physical phenomena such as changes in the chemistry of the brain.

Third, insisting on a distinction between bodily illness and mental disorder implies that diseases neatly fit into one of two mutually exclusive pigeonholes; instead, most diseases have both physical and psychological elements. Furthermore, individual reactions to physical illness can vary considerably. For example, two men of the same age who have had heart attacks and whose hearts are pumping with 80% of their former strength can have quite different levels of function. One may be severely limited by a psychological reaction to the heart attack, living the life of an invalid, whereas the other may be back at work full-time, involved in a program of rehabilitative exercise, and feeling he has a "new lease on life."

Finally, as research in the fascinating field of psychoneuroimmunology is demonstrating, actual physical connections exist between the mind and the body. In the case of CFS, chronic stress may lead to changes in both the endocrine and immune systems that could render the body more vulnerable to infection. Conversely, a long-lasting immunologic battle against a chronic infection could alter the chemistry of the brain in such a way as to induce psychological changes. Thus, although there are individuals who meet the case definition for CFS who appear to have only physical symptoms and others who appear to have only psychological manifestations, in CFS (as in most diseases) there appear to be both physical and psychological elements to the illness.

Many uncertainties about cause

There are a number of theories about the cause of CFS. While there is evidence to support many of the theories, there is as yet no scientific proof of any theory.

One cause or many? The first question is whether CFS has one or many causes. Some disorders have a single source, such as a virus or a discrete genetic defect. Most diseases, however—heart disease, cancer, and stroke, for example—clearly have multiple causes. Many infectious illnesses also have multiple causes. The common cold, pneumonia, hepatitis, and intestinal flu—each of these can be caused by any of a number of different viruses, bacteria, and other infectious agents. Most researchers studying CFS currently believe that this illness may have multiple causes; several different infectious agents may be involved, along with genetic predisposition, psychological makeup, and other influences.

Impairment of immune function. Many authorities believe that a disturbance of immunity plays a central role in CFS. The nature of this disturbance is subtle; unlike people with certain types of cancer or those with AIDS, CFS patients do not show evidence of seriously impaired immune function. Rather, their immune systems seem to be perpetually struggling, or chronically overactive, while at the same time showing signs of exhaustion from this continuous fight.

Why is the immune system in CFS patients chronically at war, and what is it battling against? One possibility is that it is attempting to subdue an infectious agent such as a virus. The battle is chronic because the immune system can never achieve complete victory—i.e., it can never completely eradicate the agent from the body. There are many infectious agents that operate in this manner, agents that can survive indefinitely inside the human body. In most people the immune system keeps these agents in a dormant state, without having to work very hard to do so. In persons with CFS, on the other hand, one theory holds that the immune system is constantly working overtime. Normally, the system has ways to regulate its own activity, turning its responses on and off. Some scientists think that in CFS the mechanisms for turning off the immune response may be impaired. Indeed, some features commonly seen in CFS—for example, a susceptibility to allergies and a diminished level of stress hormones—could lead to a chronically overactive immune system.

If this were the case, the symptoms of CFS could be caused primarily by the overstimulated immune

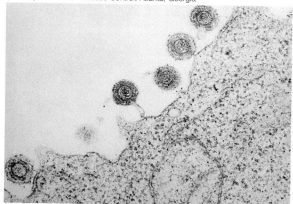

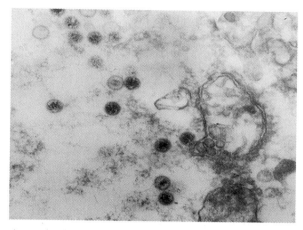

Agents that have come under scrutiny in studies of chronic fatigue syndrome include the human herpesvirus type 6 (top) and the Epstein-Barr virus (above). Researchers remain unsure if such viruses are a cause of the disorder—or an effect of it.

system itself rather than the pathogen it is mobilizing against. The immune system makes chemical substances that regulate the production of infection-fighting cells, and these substances, called cytokines, can themselves produce fatigue, fever, aching muscles, difficulty in concentrating, mood disorders, and other symptoms commonly seen in CFS.

Role of infectious agents. Disease-causing agents such as viruses, bacteria, and fungi could contribute to CFS in two ways. First, a newly acquired infection with an agent that directly affects the immune system could account for the changes in immune function seen in CFS. Alternatively, a change in the immune system could allow infectious agents lying dormant in the body to be reawakened. Indeed, both processes could be going on simultaneously, at least in some patients.

Although no infectious agent has been proved to cause CFS, several have been associated with the disorder in some preliminary studies. New infection with a variety of agents has been clearly shown to trigger

CFS in a few cases. For example, some patients with Lyme disease (which is caused by a bacterium) have developed CFS even though they have received standard antibiotic therapy, and in a few cases infection with parvovirus has been shown to trigger CFS.

As already noted, in some patients certain dormant viruses have been found to be reactivated. The unanswered question is whether these are the cause of CFS or whether they are an effect of the disease—that is, a reflection of some underlying disorder that prevents the immune system from keeping them dormant. Examples of such viruses include the Epstein-Barr virus (indeed, several years ago CFS was misnamed chronic Epstein-Barr virus infection), Coxsackie virus (related to the virus that causes polio and widely studied by British CFS researchers), and human herpesvirus type 6.

Some researchers have suggested that some cases of CFS may be caused by the family of viruses called retroviruses. The scientific community is divided about how to interpret this finding. Nonetheless, the possibility of involvement of retroviruses in CFS attracted a great deal of public attention because HIV (human immunodeficiency virus), the virus that causes AIDS, is a retrovirus. However, HIV itself is not related to CFS, nor does CFS lead to AIDS. In summary, there is no convincing evidence at the present time that any kind of retrovirus is a cause of CFS.

Brain and neurohormonal changes. Some of the symptoms of CFS—for example, sleep disturbances, irritability, memory impairment—suggest that the brain is somehow involved. While it could be that these symptoms reflect psychological conditions rather than actual physical problems in the brain, several recent preliminary studies indicate the possibility that some patients with CFS have a degree of inflammation in the brain. Either an overactivated immune system or infection by certain viruses could account for brain inflammation.

In 1991 investigators at the University of Michigan Medical School found that many of the CFS patients they were studying had a brain abnormality that resulted in unusually low levels of cortisol, an important stress hormone. Since cortisol serves to quiet, or suppress, immune function, low levels of cortisol could lead parts of the immune system to be overstimulated. Low levels of cortisol or of other hormones that lead to the production of cortisol could also directly produce fatigue.

Recently, by means of magnetic resonance imaging (MRI), it was shown that one large group of patients with CFS (or an illness very much like it) had brain changes that could explain the memory and concentration difficulties experienced by many CFS sufferers. The finding of abnormalities in the brain by means of MRI scans could provide objective confirmation of the problems in brain function that characterize CFS.

Stricken with chronic fatigue syndrome in 1979, Marc Iverson (left) heads a national patients' group that issues a quarterly publication for CFS sufferers. When necessary, Iverson manages to carry on his work in bed.

Since the technique has not been widely used, it is not yet known if other patients with CFS will also show such changes in MRI scans of their brains.

Psychological and other factors. As discussed above, psychological factors could affect how a person with CFS responds to being ill and could also affect the immune system directly. Several other influences not already mentioned could theoretically trigger the immune system disturbance that may lie at the heart of CFS. Stress, for example, can impair immune function and seems to play an important role in CFS. Theoretically, environmental toxins could affect the immune system, too, but there is not much evidence that they play a role in causing CFS.

Getting a correct diagnosis

Because so many different conditions can cause fatigue, a general physician—an internist, family physician, or general pediatrician in the case of children—is usually the first doctor consulted for a problem of unusual and long-lasting fatigue. The general physician then can refer the patient to a specialist if the features of the case so indicate.

The doctor will determine which tests are likely to yield the most useful diagnostic information. There is no mandatory set of tests that should be ordered for all patients seeking medical care for chronic fatigue. If the persistent fatigue is not accompanied by depression, some laboratory tests are likely to be ordered. A recent conference on CFS diagnosis sponsored by the U.S. National Institutes of Health identified the following tests as reasonable: a complete blood count (measurement of the number of red and white cells in the blood), a differential white blood cell count (measurement of the different types of white blood cells), an erythrocyte sedimentation rate (a simple blood test that indicates inflammation), a battery of blood chemistry tests to measure levels of various minerals, glucose, and cholesterol and to evaluate liver and kidney function, tests to assess how well the thyroid gland is functioning, and possibly tests for lupus and rheumatoid arthritis if the patient has significant symptoms of joint pain.

At this time there is no role for routine Epstein-Barr virus (EBV) antibody tests or for the sophisticated assays of immune function that have been used in some research protocols. These have not proved to be useful in the diagnosis of the individual patient, and they are expensive and are not yet done reliably by all laboratories. At this time there is also no role for routine use of MRI scans of the brains of patients with suspected CFS.

Treatment options

With the possible exception of a class of drugs called tricyclics, there are no proven treatments for CFS. In patients with fibromyalgia, a syndrome of muscle pain and tenderness that is very similar to CFS, several scientific studies have shown that very low doses of tricyclics improve the symptoms. Tricyclic drugs are also known to improve certain sleep disorders that have been found in CFS. Those most frequently used for this purpose are amitriptyline and doxepin. (Tricyclics also are prescribed to treat depression but in larger doses than are used in CFS.) Drugs of another class—the nonsteroidal anti-inflammatory agents, which include aspirin, acetaminophen, and ibuprofen—appear to be useful in relieving pain (headaches and joint and muscle aches) that many patients with CFS experience.

Several studies of the administration of intravenous gamma globulin (a blood product that boosts immunity) have come to different conclusions about the efficacy of such treatment in CFS. Many physicians feel that there is not yet enough evidence to justify the routine use of this expensive and potentially risky form of therapy.

Numerous other treatments have been used by some doctors, but none of them has been proved scientifically to be of any benefit; among them are vitamin B_{12} shots, medication and dietary changes directed at eradicating an alleged (but unproven) disseminated yeast infection caused by the fungus candida, and the drug naltrexone, which opposes the action of narcotics. Unfortunately, sufferers from CFS, like many people with chronic debilitating illnesses, are particularly vulnerable to unscrupulous practitioners. It would be wise for patients with CFS to be particularly skeptical of all those who offer sure cures.

Some physicians prescribe exercise as a remedy for CFS. This must be initiated very cautiously because patients commonly experience an exacerbation of their illness after exercise. While some CFS patients respond well to a carefully graded program of light aerobic exercises, others cannot tolerate even very moderate physical exertion.

Many people with CFS find that changes in diet are helpful—although no foods have been implicated as causes—but no particular dietary regime is beneficial to a majority of patients. Most patients agree, however, that they feel better if they reduce or eliminate alcohol and caffeine and reduce their intake of fat and sugar. But then these kinds of dietary modifications are reported by most people, even the healthiest, as increasing their energy level and improving their overall sense of well-being.

It is important for patients to learn to pace themselves, to try to minimize periods of intense physical, mental, or emotional activity, and to increase the number of hours of sleep they get. This is, of course, easier said than done. At the same time, most physicians advise CFS sufferers to "keep going" and to avoid becoming passive. It is easy for people with any chronic illness to fall into a psychological state of helplessness, and this creates even more stress in relationships with those who are most important in the patient's life: family, friends, and co-workers.

Future outlook

By definition, a patient diagnosed with CFS has been ill for at least six months. Most, in fact, have been ill for several years. The disorder has a cyclic nature; there are good days and bad days, good weeks and bad weeks. For most patients, unfortunately, the "good" days are only relatively good, and even then patients do not feel healthy. However, patients have only rarely been observed to get progressively worse over time, and most physicians have found that the majority of patients gradually improve their level of functioning, if for no other reason than that they become adept at pacing themselves and learn how to cope with having only a very limited store of energy.

There are now support groups for CFS in all U.S. states and in many foreign countries. Many patients find these groups useful because they provide information about the illness, along with the companionship of others who are going through a similar experience. On the other hand, others have complained of having been given erroneous information by some groups or feeling that they have not received the emotional support that they expected.

CFS is clearly a complex disease. Medical science does not yet have answers to the fundamental questions about causation, diagnosis, treatment, and prognosis. With more studies being supported by the CDC and the National Institutes of Health in the U.S., and a growing research effort around the world, solutions to these lingering problems will, it is hoped, be forthcoming in the not-too-distant future.

—Anthony L. Komaroff, M.D.,
and Walter J. Gunn, Ph.D.

Death and Dying

Much of the debate swirling around the issues of death and dying has focused on what physicians are required, permitted, or forbidden to do for their patients. In the recent past, old controversies such as the definition of brain death and the moral suitability of using anencephalic infants as organ donors were revived. The debate over what constitutes futile medical treatment and whether patients can insist on it over physicians' objections sharpened. In the United States the moral and public-policy dimensions of physician involvement in active euthanasia and assisted suicide became the subjects of a best-selling book and ballots. In The Netherlands, where doctors have been known to participate in the "merciful" killing of hopelessly ill patients for over a decade, the first official survey of the practice was conducted and captured the attention of countries throughout the world. Meanwhile, in December 1991 the first U.S. federal law intended to give people more say about their own dying quietly went into effect.

Baby Theresa and the definition of death

Theresa Ann Campo Pearson was born in Florida on March 21, 1992, with the condition known as anencephaly, in which the brain fails to develop and the skull does not close, leaving the top of the head open to a mass of disorganized tissue. Babies with anencephaly may live a few hours or days if they are born alive and with a functioning brain stem.

Baby Theresa's parents, accepting that their daughter's situation was hopeless, wished to see some good come out of her inevitable death and requested that her organs be removed for transplantation. There was a problem with their request, however; according to Florida law, Baby Theresa was not yet dead, and it is illegal to remove vital organs from living donors. A circuit court judge ruled that all of Baby Theresa's brain functions would have to cease before her organs could be taken. By that time, however, her organs would be too damaged to be useful.

The quandary faced by Baby Theresa's parents is a consequence of the current legal definition of brain death: the loss of function of the entire brain, including the brain stem. Though her death was imminent, Baby Theresa was not yet dead.

Under a whole-brain-death standard, there are two alternatives that would permit taking organs from babies such as Theresa. One would be to redefine brain death to include anencephaly. The other would be to permit an exception to the prohibition against taking organs from donors who are not yet dead. The first alternative, redefining brain death so that it includes infants who clearly do not meet the settled criteria for brain death, strikes some as a form of ethical gerrymandering, while the second, making a categor-

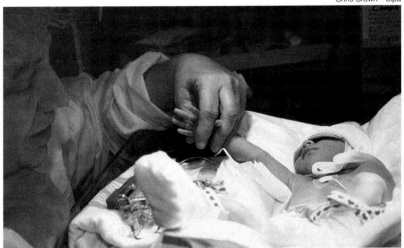

Theresa Ann Campo Pearson was born without a fully formed brain and had no chance of life. Theresa's parents, who knew of their baby's condition before her birth, wished to have her organs removed so that they could be used to benefit others, but a court ruled that the infant's total brain function would have to cease before the parents' desire could be fulfilled. By that time it would have been too late for the organs to be used for transplantation. The Pearsons' case focused attention on long-standing ethical questions concerning the present legal definition of brain death.

ical exception to the rule against taking vital organs from living persons, raises the question of who will be next. There are, for example, babies with related disorders such as hydranencephaly, in which the top of the head is covered by skin; however, the brain itself in these infants may be as devastated as it is in anencephaly. Would such children then be included as potential donors even though they might live much longer? The conclusion of many medical ethicists is that neither option is more attractive than the occasional loss of potential donated organs from anencephalic infants.

Helga Wanglie and medical futility

Helga Wanglie was admitted as a patient to the Hennepin County (Minn.) Medical Center on New Year's Day 1990 with difficulty breathing; she was placed on a respirator. By May of that year, all attempts to wean her from the respirator had failed, and the 85-year-old patient was transferred to a chronic care facility. On May 31 she was taken back to the Hennepin County Medical Center after her heart stopped and she was resuscitated. By mid-June her physicians had determined that she was in a persistent vegetative state and were convinced that her treatment, including the respirator, was doing her no good. Nonetheless, her husband and children insisted that full treatment be continued.

The hospital went to court, asking that an independent conservator be named to decide whether the respirator was beneficial to Wanglie; her husband, meanwhile, asked to remain as the primary decision maker. The hearing on Wanglie's case was held in May 1991, and the decision was announced on July 1: the husband was given continued authority to make medical decisions for his unconscious wife. Three days later, however, on July 4, 1991, Helga Wanglie died at the age of 86.

The Helga Wanglie case was the first widely publicized case in which health care professionals wished to discontinue life-prolonging treatment but the family insisted that such treatment continue. Previously the battle for control over the circumstances and timing of dying had centered on the concept of family decision making. People in the vanguard of the right-to-die movement stressed family decision making as a way of wresting control from doctors and hospitals, allowing a family member to die with a minimum of suffering, unencumbered by tubes and the paraphernalia of the intensive care unit. In the Wanglie case, family decision making resulted in just the opposite—a patient in a persistent vegetative state being kept on a respirator despite the protests of the physicians and nurses who cared for her.

The Wanglie case brought to the fore another issue that had been mired in ambiguity—the concept of medical futility. In the practice of medicine, the maxim that physicians are not morally obliged to do what will be futile is well accepted. Doctors have no moral duty, for example, to carry out a heart transplant on someone who is also dying of cancer. Though such an operation would replace the failing heart, it would not improve the prognosis for one whose life would soon be ended by an untreatable cancer. In the larger context of that person's life, the heart transplant would be futile.

Futility is a more complicated concept when applied to life-prolonging treatments for people in a persistent vegetative state. Wanglie's husband believed her respirator was not futile care because it postponed her death. Steven H. Miles, the physician who was the hospital's medical-ethics consultant for the case, believed her respirator may not have been futile in that narrow sense but neither was it providing any benefit. It was Miles's conclusion that "the husband's request seemed entirely inconsistent with what medical care could do for his wife, the standards of the community, and his fair share of resources that many people pooled for their collective medical care."

Humphry's best-seller

Since 1987 the Hemlock Society, named after the poison drunk by Socrates, has doubled its membership. The society's founder and executive director, Derek Humphry, has been an advocate of suicide and euthanasia since assisting in the suicide of his first wife, who had terminal cancer. After the March 1991 publication of Humphry's book *Final Exit*—a collection of do-it-yourself suicide "recipes"—it rose to the number one spot on the *New York Times* best-seller list in the hardcover advice-books category, where it remained for four months. Within a year it sold over 500,000 copies.

Humphry's book received a mixed response from medical ethicists. The central message of the book— that each individual can and should have control over his or her own death—is compatible with two important themes in medical ethics. First is the emphasis on individual autonomy—the moral right of individuals to make their own decisions about what shall be done to them by health care professionals. Second is the conviction that much of the standard treatment of people who are terminally ill is pointless. Such treatment not only strips dying persons of their pride but, paradoxically, it isolates them from meaningful human contact in their last days, weeks, or months, as they are surrounded by professionals who are often more intent on the technologies utilized in their care than on the very individuals those technologies are presumably meant to save.

Final Exit also provoked serious concerns. One obvious danger of the publication of explicit suicide instructions is that some unknown but possibly significant number of people who may be temporarily disillusioned with life and might have unsuccessfully attempted suicide (and lived to be grateful for their failure) would now be "successful" because they had the means at hand. Such an unfortunate outcome seems quite possible among adolescents who, in the callowness of youth, feel they have suffered a terrible blow. Similarly, persons with treatable psychiatric depressions might take their lives before getting professional help or before gaining a reasonable perspective on their situation.

The rush toward what Humphry calls "self-deliverance" also has the effect of diverting efforts away from attempts to change the inhumane circumstances of dying—such as by reforming hospitals and nursing homes, educating professionals, and encouraging both candor and depth in the public discussion of dying. Suicide thus offers a technological "fix" for what is to a significant extent a problem caused by technology. By assuring the most articulate and passionate defenders of the right to die in dignity that they need not face the horror of dying in an institution, promoters of suicide in fact distract precisely those people most capable of forcing institutions to become more humane.

Kevorkian: three more deaths

Final Exit was published at a time when the public's attention already had been fixed on physician-assisted suicide by the escapades of the Michigan physician Jack Kevorkian. Kevorkian, the inventor of a suicide machine, added three more deaths to that of his first subject, Janet Adkins, in 1990. On Oct. 23, 1991, both Sherry Miller, aged 43, who had multiple sclerosis, and Marjorie Wantz, aged 58 and said to have had an unspecified pelvic disease, died in a cabin in the Bald Mountain Recreation Area near Detroit. Both women had pleaded with him for over a year to help them commit suicide. It was Kevorkian's decision that the women should die on the same day in the same room. Then on May 15, 1992, Kevorkian was present in the home of Susan Williams, aged 52, who, like Miller, had multiple sclerosis. Williams' death apparently occurred after she breathed from a canister containing carbon monoxide and nitrogen that Kevorkian had taken to her home.

Though Kevorkian had previously been charged with the murder of Adkins, the charge was dismissed because her death had been ruled a suicide, and Michigan has no laws against assisting in a suicide. The coroner's ruling on the deaths of Miller, Wantz, and Williams, however, classified them as homicides, and in February he was indicted on two counts of murder for the October deaths—charges that were then dismissed in July. Thus, for the time being, Kevorkian remained free to espouse his beliefs about the control of death and the role he purports physicians should have in terminating lives.

The AMA's pronouncement on dying

In April 1992 the Council on Ethical and Judicial Affairs of the American Medical Association (AMA) updated its position on end-of-life decisions. Noting that in 1987 an estimated 75% of all deaths occurred in hospitals and long-term-care institutions, the AMA council took on the issues of physician-assisted suicide and euthanasia, reaffirming its commitment to respecting informed and competent patients' refusal of treatment. The ethically troublesome question the council faced was whether people can call on physicians to provide the expertise and the means either to end their own lives or to have a physician do it for them.

The report issued by the council members conceded that physician-assisted suicide is probably not a new phenomenon. It also recognized that there may be enormous variation in the thoughtfulness and care with which individual physicians engage in assisting suicides. The physician's association, however, did not—at least not yet—condone the practice. Instead it urged its members "to identify the concerns behind patients' requests for assisted suicide, and make concerted efforts at finding ways to address these concerns . . . including providing more aggressive comfort care."

In its conclusion the report seemed to be of two minds. On the one hand, it declared unequivocally: "Physicians must not perform euthanasia or participate in assisted suicide." On the other hand, it justified this, in part, by claiming that "the societal risks of involving physicians in medical interventions to cause patients' deaths is too great . . . to condone euthanasia or physician-assisted suicide *at this time*" [emphasis added]. Times change, however, and it may not be long before the AMA revisits this issue.

Euthanasia in The Netherlands

Since the 1980s Dutch physicians have been performing active euthanasia—the act of "merciful" killing of hopelessly sick or injured patients—with the wary tolerance of the legal system. Although euthanasia is technically murder in The Netherlands, physicians can expect to escape prosecution if they follow strict guidelines. Despite this assurance, it is assumed that Dutch physicians may have certified as deaths from "natural" causes an unknown number of cases of active euthanasia. Therefore, the first official survey of the practice of euthanasia in The Netherlands was conducted, and its findings were published in September 1991.

The study was commissioned by the Dutch government and included responses to questionnaires concerning over 9,000 deaths and extensive interviews with over 400 physicians. It examined three kinds of medical decisions at the end of life: decisions to forgo life-prolonging treatment, aggressive treatment of pain or other symptoms with drugs that might shorten the patient's life, and active euthanasia and assisted suicide.

About 30% of the 9,000 deaths considered were sudden and unexpected, offering no opportunity for medical decisions that might shorten life. Of the remaining 70%, an estimated 54% involved decisions in the three categories above.

Decisions to forgo life-prolonging treatment occurred in 17.5% of all deaths. Such decisions were more common for older patients and slightly more common for women than for men. Surprisingly, in only 30% of nontreatment decisions was the decision discussed with the patient, although in most (88%) of the cases where nontreatment was not discussed, the patient was not competent.

Of the physicians surveyed, 82% said that they had given painkillers or other drugs to relieve symptoms even at the risk of shortening the patient's life. Another 12% said they would be willing to do so; only 7% said they never would. Such decisions were involved in another 17.5% of all the deaths in the study. The patients for whom the drugs were prescribed were most likely to be young, female, and dying of cancer. It is notable that in 6% of cases where drugs were given to relieve symptoms when they might have shortened life, the physicians said that ending life was their primary goal. Why these were not counted among the cases of active euthanasia is unclear.

Over one-half (54%) of the Dutch physicians said they had participated in active euthanasia or assisted suicide; almost a quarter (24%) had done so in the previous year. Only 4% of those who had not participated in patients' deaths said that they would not

On Oct. 23, 1991, two women, previously unknown to each other, committed suicide in a remote cabin in the Bald Mountain Recreation Area near Detroit, Michigan, by using the "suicide machine" of Jack Kevorkian. One of the women had multiple sclerosis; the other had an unspecified pelvic disorder. The physician, who has been outspoken in his belief that doctors should be allowed to assist patients who choose to terminate their lives, first gained international attention in June 1990 when he assisted in the suicide of another woman, who was thought to be in the early stages of Alzheimer's disease. In May 1992 Kevorkian allegedly provided the gas that a fourth woman used to kill herself.

refer patients to other physicians with more permissive attitudes toward euthanasia. The most common means of killing cited by the respondents was giving a hopelessly ill patient a large dose of barbiturates to bring on coma, followed by the muscle relaxant curare to stop breathing and heart function.

Of the 187 cases of active euthanasia described in detailed interviews with physicians, 96% were the result of repeated and explicit patient requests. The typical patient in such cases was male, aged 63, and suffering from cancer. Few requests came from patients over age 75. Perhaps surprisingly, pain was not the principle reason given for euthanasia pleas; loss of dignity was most frequently cited, followed by "unworthy dying," pain, being dependent on others, and being tired of life.

The study estimated that active euthanasia by drug overdose without express and persistent requests from the patient accounted for slightly under 1% of all deaths. In most such cases the patients had indicated their interest in euthanasia earlier in their illness but could not later communicate their wishes. The physicians interviewed claimed that they typically discussed their decision to administer a lethal dose with the family, nurses, or other doctors and that their injection typically shortened the patient's life only by a matter of hours or days.

How common are requests for euthanasia in The Netherlands? The study estimated that over 25,000 patients each year ask their physicians if they will aid them if needed. An estimated 9,000 patients ask for active euthanasia or help in suicide. The number of requests that physicians agree to honor is probably under 3,000 per year—the bulk of those, an estimated 1,900, carried out by general practitioners or family doctors, probably because they tend to know their patients well and are likely to have formed the emotional bond that many physicians felt was essential to performing euthanasia or assisting in suicide. The study found that most such deaths took place in the patients' homes.

In January 1992 the *British Medical Journal* reported on the ferment surrounding euthanasia in a number of countries around the world. In Germany, for example, where killing of the disabled and others has taken place under the rubric of euthanasia, active euthanasia is expressly identified as a crime, punishable by up to five years in prison, but passive euthanasia—withholding nonbeneficial treatment from the dying—is regarded as a private matter between physicians and patients and their families. In 1992 in the United Kingdom, a senior physician was charged with having given a lethal injection to an elderly woman with severe arthritis; a battle over euthanasia loomed in Parliament between pro-life advocates and those sympathetic to euthanasia. The Canadian Medical Association endorses passive euthanasia. France's National Ethics Committee opposes legalizing active euthanasia. In Australia three states have approved some form of advance directives. Although there are surely national differences in the euthanasia debate, it is clear both that passive euthanasia is widely accepted and that active euthanasia is a highly charged and morally and politically problematic issue.

The Netherlands remains the pioneer of what has come to be called "physician aid in dying." If activists in the right-to-die movement in the U.S. are successful, one or more states may soon join The Netherlands in legally tolerating physicians' direct involvement in the deaths of their patients.

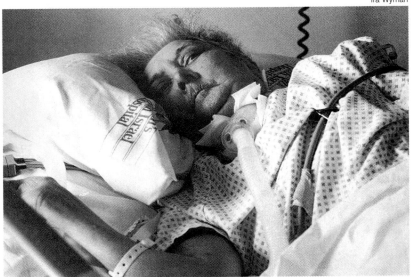

On Dec. 1, 1991, a U.S. federal law took effect that requires hospitals to inform patients of their right to have their wishes made known in advance about the use of life-prolonging treatments when they are facing death and no longer mentally competent. So-called advanced directives give patients the option of specifying what they would want done under such circumstances either through an explicit document—a living will—or by entrusting the decisions to someone else—durable power of attorney for health care.

Citizens say no to Initiative 119

This did not occur in the state of Washington, however, when on Nov. 5, 1991, 54% of citizens voted against and 46% voted for the amendment known as Initiative 119. The narrowly defeated initiative had been proposed as an amendment to the state's Natural Death Act of 1979. If adopted, it would have legalized so-called physician aid in dying, which was interpreted by both its supporters and opponents to authorize active euthanasia and assisted suicide.

The proposed law contained some procedural safeguards. The request by a patient for physician assistance in dying would have had to have been in writing and confirmed by two independent witnesses; two physicians would have been required to state in writing that the person would die in six months or less from a terminal illness. Nevertheless, the majority of Washington's voters agreed with the majority of physicians nationwide and worldwide in rejecting the legalization of physician involvement in euthanasia and suicide.

The debate in Washington illuminates a superficial inconsistency that is often mistaken for a deeper one. It is possible to believe both that active euthanasia and assisted suicide can be justified at times and that legalizing them, especially with physician participation, would be a mistake. This apparent inconsistency is explained by the conviction held by many physicians, ethicists, and members of the public that the good that would come with legalization (more euthanasia and suicide when they were morally justified and fewer prosecutions of physicians who participated in them) is outweighed by the harm legalization would cause (more cases of unjustified and unwise euthanasia and suicide and greater patient mistrust of doctors and hospitals). Those who are opposed to the legal-

ization of physician aid in dying often point out that only 11 doctors in the United States have ever been charged with murder for performing active euthanasia; of those, only two were convicted, and none has gone to prison—at least not yet.

Decisions about death: a new law

On Dec. 1, 1991, the Patient Self-Determination Act, the first U.S. federal law on so-called advance directives, went into effect. The new law requires all hospitals and other health care institutions in the country to inform patients of the laws of their particular state regarding advance directives for health care and of their right to have their wishes known. Advance directives are arrangements intended to give persons a say in the decisions that are made about potentially life-prolonging treatment when they are no longer mentally competent to make those decisions themselves. There are two distinct kinds of advance directives. One is a living will, in which the person makes a statement, which can be very general or excruciatingly specific, about his or her preferences for treatment or nontreatment. The other is durable power of attorney for health care, in which the person entrusts those decisions to someone else—one who understands his or her values and can make necessary decisions when the time comes.

Despite a few dire predictions that patients being admitted for minor procedures would be terrified by discussions about medical catastrophes and nontreatment decisions, the Patient Self-Determination Act seems to have been implemented with very little fuss. In its first year there was a paucity of evidence about whether the act was having its desired impact. In the near future that information should emerge.

—*Thomas H. Murray, Ph.D.*

Special Report
Once Stung, Twice Shy?
by Charles-Gene McDaniel, M.S.J.

On a hot June Sunday afternoon, C.W.M. was fishing with his son and grandson from a boat near the shore of a lake in Arkansas. Without much ado, the oldest of the party slapped his neck and muttered, "A dratted wasp just stung me." A few minutes later, the grandson worriedly said to his father, "I think you'd better see about Grandpa." His grandfather was sitting, fishing pole in hand, chin on his chest, comatose. Within 20 minutes he was dead.

Weeks after the funeral, a pathologist's autopsy report gave the cause of death: anaphylactic shock, an allergic hypersensitivity reaction of the body resulting from wasp sting. C.W.M. had been 62 years old and in excellent health. An ardent outdoorsman all his life, he was unaware of his sensitivity to insect stings.

In September 1990 a 60-year-old male golfer in suburban Chicago died after being stung inside his mouth by a bee trapped inside an open beer bottle he was carrying on the course. Like C.W.M., the golfer had been stung numerous times in the past and had never had an adverse reaction.

In the summer of 1991, U.S. Pres. George Bush was more fortunate. While golfing near his vacation home in Kennebunkport, Maine, he, too, was stung by a bee. In Bush's case the bee died, and the president had only minimal discomfort. Previously, in the early 1980s, Bush had had a severe reaction to a sting, after which he started taking shots to desensitize him to the venom.

More than a nuisance

As the above cases illustrate, insect stings can be far more than a nuisance. Anaphylactic reactions to insect stings have always amounted to a serious medical problem. In the United States the problem may be growing worse, as new and nastier varieties of stinging insects have been introduced.

The earliest recorded fatal allergic reaction to an insect sting was that of the ancient Egyptian king Menes, of Memphis. Hieroglyphics on his tomb describe his death in 2621 BC after being stung by a "great wasp." It was not until AD 1914, however, that sudden systemic symptoms of anaphylaxis were recognized as an allergic reaction rather than as the result of inherent toxicity of insect venoms.

Nowadays an estimated 50 persons in the U.S. die each year from the stings of insects of the order Hymenoptera—an order that includes more than 110,-000 species—the main troublemakers being bees, wasps, yellow jackets, hornets, and fire ants. About three to four times more people are killed by stings than die from snakebites, a fate that is considerably more feared. The actual number of insect sting deaths is probably much higher; because there may be no easily detectable external indication that a person who has died of anaphylaxis has been stung—e.g., a rash—many such deaths undoubtedly go unrecorded. Only an autopsy with laboratory tests can prove the cause of death. A person who is alone—gardening, mowing the lawn, or cleaning the attic or garage—may be found dead, and the presumed cause of death is a heart attack. Moreover, as the foregoing cases illustrate, anaphylaxis is most likely to occur and be fatal in individuals who have never previously had a systemic reaction.

Bees to beware of

The most familiar stinging bees in North America are European honeybees, small honey-colored pollinators—the source of commercially produced honey—that were imported into the North American continent in the 17th century, and bumblebees, which are large, noisy, fuzzy, and colored black and yellow. Both types of bees are relatively unaggressive, stinging humans only when provoked. A newer member of the bee family—and a growing menace—is the Africanized bee.

Of great concern to entomologists and public health officials in Central, and now North, America is the relentless progress of the aggressive "killer," or Africanized, bees from South America. The Africanized bee is a hybrid of the common honeybee and bees that were imported into Brazil from South Africa in 1956. The crossbreeding was carried out at an experimental station in Brazil in an attempt to produce bees that would increase honey production. Several queen bees escaped from the station, however, and Africanized bees have been out of control ever since, traveling not only on their own but in the cargoes of trucks, trains, and ships. By 1990 the bees had reached southern Texas, and they were expected to continue to migrate throughout the central and southeastern states. (Ironically, the Africanized bees have been found to produce not more but less honey than the European bees with which they were crossed.)

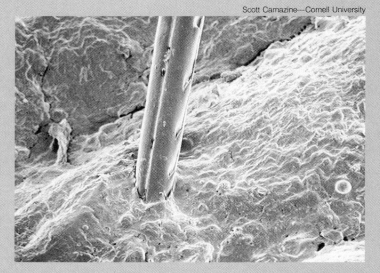

The barbed stinger of a European honeybee is shown embedded in the skin of its victim (magnified 140 times). When the bee attempts to fly away or is brushed away, the stinger and venom sacs to which it is attached are torn from its body, and shortly thereafter the bee dies. The majority of those who are stung experience pain, irritation, itching, redness, and swelling, which generally subside within a few hours. However, if the stinger is not removed from the skin fairly promptly, additional venom may be released, worsening the reaction.

The bees migrate about 300 to 500 km (200 to 300 mi) a year. The number of deaths from killer bees since they began migrating is estimated to be in the hundreds, with close to 40 fatal attacks having been reported from Mexico alone. In addition to humans, the bees also attack animals, including pets and livestock. The bee arrived in Panama in 1985 and caused the collapse of that country's honey industry. The government formed squads that destroyed 27,000 colonies of the killer bees. Terrified neighbors burned hives to force beekeepers to give up honey production.

Although the migrating Africanized bees did not reach the U.S. until 1990, a swarm of killer bees had arrived in the country five years earlier on a cargo ship from South America that docked in California. These, however, were quickly destroyed. The massive numbers of northern-migrating bees common today are more difficult to control. Potent pesticides cannot be used in an attempt to kill the killer bees because more docile European honeybees, which are necessary for the pollination of plants and which kill many harmful insects, would also be poisoned. When killer bee swarms are detected, professional exterminators garbed in protective clothing are summoned to spray them with a solution of water and dishwashing liquid, which smothers them.

The venom of killer bees is like that of ordinary honeybees. The problem is that the killer bees are much more aggressive and attack in frightening swarms. Ordinary bees typically nest in predictable places, such as the hollows of trees, logs, stumps, and the eaves of buildings. But Africanized bees, which are slightly smaller but virtually indistinguishable from the European bees, nest almost anywhere they find a protected cavity. Africanized bees are more easily riled than their domestic cousins. The noise of a lawn mower or farm equipment can rouse them to attack. In addition, they remain defensive longer than ordinary

bees, sometimes for more than 24 hours. Further, the Africanized bees defend their colonies in significantly greater numbers than do other bees, and they will pursue an antagonist for distances of nearly a kilometer (0.6 mi).

In September 1991 a farm worker in Abram, Texas, near the Mexican border, came into painful contact with killer bees when he disturbed a hidden nest while clearing brush. He was left unconscious but survived. Doctors counted 60 stings on each hand and 100 more on both his back and face before they stopped counting.

Bees are unique among stinging hymenopterans in that they have barbed stingers. The stinger becomes embedded in the victim's skin, so a single bee can sting only once. When it then attempts to fly away or is brushed away by the victim, both the stinger and the venom sacs to which the stinger is attached are torn from its body, and shortly afterward the bee dies. If the stinger is not removed promptly from the skin of the person who has been stung, additional venom is released, worsening the reaction.

Wasps and their kin: vicious picnic spoilers

In the late summer of 1991, the northeastern United States fought off a plague of nasty, stinging yellow jackets, which made themselves unwelcome guests at picnics and barbecues in areas along the Atlantic coast. Combined forces of nature—a mild winter followed by a hot, dry summer that ended with a hurricane—conspired to produce a "bumper crop" of the feisty insects. Some hospitals in metropolitan areas reported record numbers of patients arriving in emergency rooms with sting reactions. The Yale-New Haven Hospital had to abandon its policy of not giving treatment advice over the phone because the number of calls from those with local reactions to yellow jacket stings was so high.

Yellow jackets are members of the Vespidae family of Hymenoptera, which includes several species of wasps and hornets. The vespids are slender-bodied and hairless, have distinctly notched eyes, and are prone to sting their victims painfully and with little provocation. The stingers of wasps and their kin are unbarbed, so the insects can—and do—sting their victims multiple times and do not die as a result.

Invasion of the fire ants

Several types of ants are nonwinged hymenopterans, and in areas where they are indigenous, their stings are a major cause of allergic reactions. The fire ant is one of these. Fire ants were apparently imported into the U.S. accidentally in the early 20th century in sod and nursery stock arriving from South America at the port city of Mobile, Ala. The ants are now widespread in the southeastern United States. Entomologists are concerned because the red fire ant (*Solenopsis invicta*) and the black fire ant (*S. richteri*) have crossbred, making them more resistant to cold temperatures. The ants have recently moved north as far as New Jersey and west to California and eventually are expected to inhabit one-quarter of the country. An estimated 67,000 to 85,000 people in the U.S. annually seek medical attention for reactions to the stings of fire ants. In infested urban areas 30–60% of the inhabitants are stung per year, with up to half having large local reactions (with the formation of pustules that can become infected) and up to 1% having an anaphylactic reaction. Seizures and other neurological sequelae have also been reported after fire ant stings, and three people are known to have died between 1987 and 1990 from such stings.

The fire ants are omnivorous, attacking not only humans but farm animals, crops, and the electrical insulation of air conditioners and other appliances. When flooding occurs, the ants become waterborne, invading houses and attacking the inhabitants.

The social behavior of fire ants, like that of other ants, is remarkable. Their mounds now dot the landscape of the southeastern U.S., with as many as 80 mounds per hectare (200 per acre), not only in rural areas but in urban yards, playgrounds, and open fields. Above ground the mounds are usually 0.25 to 0.38 m (10 to 15 in) high but can stand as high as 0.9 m (3 ft). Below ground the mounds extend 0.9 to 1.5 m (3 to 5 ft) and radiate up to 39 m (130 ft), with systems of connecting tunnels that make it exceedingly difficult to destroy the ants. The fertile queen ant, whose lifespan is six years, lays eggs deep within the burrows of a mound; often fire ant colonies have as many as 500 queens, and within three years the mound of a single colony may be inhabited by 250,000 fire ants.

Fire ants are intractable. The pesticides heptachlor and mirex, which were used in early attempts to control them, were banned because they proved to be toxic to wildlife. Current attempts to control fire ants include treating individual mounds with pesticides such as diazinon or chlorpyricides, but this is not entirely effective because ants inhabiting a mound's perimeter survive. Another control measure is "broadcast treatment." Bait made of soybean oil, corn grits, and toxic chemical agents is scattered near the mounds. Worker ants pick up the bait and take it into the mound, where it eventually reaches the queens. This treatment can be effective for months at a time.

The sting of the fire ant is unique. The ants have powerful mandibles with which they attach themselves to the skin of a victim. They then arch their bodies and inject venom through their stinger, located in their abdomen. With mandibles still in place, the ants can then rotate their body in order to sting again and again.

Sting reactions

Most people who are stung by a bee or wasp experience pain, irritation, itching, redness, and swelling, all of which gradually disappear within hours after the

Scott Camazine—Cornell University

A sign at a Mexican apiary warns beekeepers to be cautious when working with easily disturbed Africanized honeybees. Since the highly aggressive "killer" bees began migrating north from Brazil, nearly 40 fatal attacks have been reported from Mexico alone.

sting. Others are quite sensitive to the venoms and develop more severe local reactions, often with symptoms including headache, nausea, malaise, fever, and fatigue. Toxic reactions can occur when a sting injects a large volume of venom or as a result of multiple stings. It is generally assumed that it would take 100 or more stings for most nonallergic adults to succumb to a lethal dose of venom, but cases of individuals who have survived more than 2,000 stings on a single occasion have been reported.

The type of treatment given depends upon the degree of reaction. Ice packs and rest sometimes are all that is required for a large local reaction, but oral corticosteroids may be required in extreme cases. Generalized skin reactions are treated with topical and/or oral antihistamines.

Severe allergic reactions to insect stings occur in about 3% of the U.S. population, but there is no way of knowing who the susceptible are because some who are allergic may lose the allergy and others may develop it years after having been stung uneventfully. There also is no correlation between allergy to insect venom and other allergies, such as those to pollen

An exterminator prepares insecticide to apply to an infested home in New York in the late summer of 1991, when the northeastern Atlantic states experienced a plague of stinging yellow-jacket wasps (Vespula germanica).

Stephen Castagneto—The New York Times

or particular foods. Allergic reactions can occur in people of all ages, with sensitivity tending to increase with age. Most victims of serious insect sting reactions are over age 30, and males are more commonly affected than females—possibly because they spend more time outdoors. It is unusual for children to have severe reactions, although some do.

Anaphylactic reaction is caused when a person's immune system produces too much of an antibody (a blood protein), specifically immunoglobulin E (IgE), which in combination with the insect venom triggers the allergic reaction. People who are venom-allergic have varying reactions to stings, which compounds the problems of identifying and treating them. They may develop potentially fatal anaphylaxis within minutes, or they may have local reactions, systemic symptoms, or no reaction at all to a particular sting. Some have local reactions on some occasions and systemic symptoms on others. In this regard they are similar to those who are allergic to penicillin, which also produces no consistent reactions.

It is known that people who have had multiple stings on a single occasion or repeated stings within a period of weeks are more likely to have an anaphylactic reaction, but most deaths occur in people who have had no previous allergic reaction to a sting. Although effective desensitization treatment (immunization) is available, most people who have minor reactions never seek medical advice. Immunization, therefore, is unlikely to have much effect on the incidence of fatal stings.

Fatalities occur most often in people over age 45. An anaphylactic reaction is, in effect, an internalized version of the skin reaction, with swelling of the tongue, epiglottis, larynx, and lungs. The swelling causes difficulty in swallowing and severe wheezing as it impedes breathing. Blood pressure may drop to the point of vascular collapse. The reaction may also include abdominal or pelvic cramps, mental confusion, nausea, vomiting, diarrhea, headache, palpitations, and chest pain.

Epinephrine (adrenaline), given by injection, is necessary as initial therapy if there are respiratory or circulatory symptoms. Some patients require cardiopulmonary resuscitation and other lifesaving measures.

Fire ant stings produce reactions that are similar to those caused by bee and wasp stings, ranging from mild skin itching and hives to anaphylactic shock. While only about 2% of those stung by fire ants have a life-threatening anaphylactic reaction, local reactions requiring antihistamine treatment are common.

Venom immunotherapy

Studies have shown that a person who has had a previous reaction to an insect sting has a 60% chance of having another reaction if stung again. Since the mid-1980s physicians have been able to desensitize those

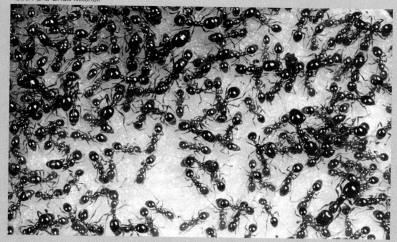

*Stinging red fire ants (*Solenopsis invicta*) feed on a cantaloupe in central Texas. In highly infested urban areas in the southeastern United States, an estimated 30–60% of the inhabitants are stung by fire ants each year. About half of those stung have large local reactions, requiring medical treatment.*

who are known to be allergic to stings of flying hymenopterans with injections of highly potent purified venoms taken from honeybees, yellow jackets, yellow hornets, bald-faced hornets, and *Polistes* wasps. The venoms are injected once or twice a week for several months, then every six to eight weeks, in increasingly stronger doses to stimulate the patient's immune system until it is resistant to the effects of a sting. The treatments generally last about five years.

Venom immunotherapy has been shown to be 97% effective in adults who have had a previous allergic systemic reaction to a sting. Moreover, studies have documented that the immunity achieved through desensitization treatment remains long after the shots are stopped. The need for venom immunotherapy for children has been more controversial. A recent study of 242 children by researchers at the Johns Hopkins University School of Medicine, Baltimore, Md., found that for most children desensitizing injections to prevent recurrence of mild allergic reactions to stings are unnecessary. However, children who have experienced severe systemic reactions should, like adults, be given the desensitization shots.

The composition of fire ant venom differs from that of the venoms of other hymenopterans. Previously, immunotherapy for allergy to bee-wasp-hornet stings relied on so-called whole-body extract—refined from the whole bodies of the insects—but these were found to contain too little pure venom to be reliable. Because it is not possible to obtain sufficient amounts of fire ant venom from the ants' venom sacs alone, whole-body extracts are used in immunotherapy. However, the amount of venom in the extracts is variable, and the efficacy of fire ant immunotherapy has not been established.

Avoiding stings

People who are known to have severe reactions to insect venom are advised, whenever they are at risk of being stung, to carry a self-treatment kit, prescribed by a physician, which contains antihistamines and a syringe with premeasured, preloaded epinephrine. The epinephrine works quickly to open up the airways to enable breathing. Even after using a kit, those who are allergic to stings should seek medical attention as soon as possible because additional treatment may be required.

To avoid the stings of hymenopterans, one should observe the following precautions:

● Have an exterminator remove the nests of stinging insects from porch roofs, eaves, and other places around the house.

● Wear long pants, tops with long sleeves, shoes, and socks when outdoors in gardens, fields, and woods.

● Wear subdued colors rather than bright, patterned, or pastel-colored clothing that bees may mistake for flowers.

● Do not wear perfume, cologne, after-shave lotion, or hair spray, which attract stinging insects.

● Picnic or play away from brightly colored and aromatic flowers where bees congregate in search of nectar.

● Do not drink from a beverage bottle or can that has been opened outdoors; stinging insects can easily get inside but often are not seen by a person, who then takes a drink.

● Avoid sweet, sticky foods on picnics (*e.g.,* jam, cola drinks, Popsicles).

● Keep tight lids on garbage cans.

● Inspect automobiles for insects before getting in, and drive with windows and sunroof closed.

● Do not swat a bee or wasp while driving; pull over and let it out of the car.

● Move away quietly if an insect is hovering; brisk movements may excite an insect to sting.

● Drop to the ground, with face down, if confronted by a mid-air swarm of hymenopterans.

Disability

As a result of major new federal legislation adopted on July 26, 1990, the final decade of the 20th century will be one in which America's melting pot expands to include as enhanced participants the 43 million U.S. citizens who have physical or mental impairments. The sweeping new law, the Americans with Disabilities Act (ADA), constitutes a remarkable leap forward, having created not only equal opportunities for persons long denied them but a fundamental new public awareness of these vital members of society.

The long road to ADA

ADA has been called the most important civil rights legislation since the Civil Rights Act of 1964, the law formally ending discrimination based on race, color, religion, or national origin. Although ADA is by far the most comprehensive legislation to date giving rights to persons with disabilities, federal laws concerning those with disabilities actually date back to the 19th century, when Pres. Abraham Lincoln signed bills giving aid to special schools for blind and deaf students.

In the 20th century several pieces of legislation have afforded important but limited rights and opportunities for persons with disabilities. Following World War I federal programs were initiated for the rehabilitation of the thousands of returning American soldiers injured in active service. In 1920 the Smith-Fess Veterans' Rehabilitation Act established the first broadly based federal program to assist those with disabilities with vocational training and job placement. In 1935 the Social Security Act included the allocation of federal funds to assist workers with disabilities and authorized vocational rehabilitation programs on a permanent basis. Although the Civil Rights Act did not include specific provisions related to persons with disabilities, it gave impetus for them to view their cause as one

of equal rights and opportunities. In 1968 the Architectural Barriers Act mandated that physical barriers be eliminated in all federal buildings, and in 1970 the Urban Mass Transportation Act required that all public transportation services be made accessible to persons with disabilities in order to qualify for federal funding.

The most crucial legislation for Americans with disabilities prior to ADA was the Rehabilitation Act of 1973, which, in addition to extending various federal training programs, prohibited recipients of federal financial assistance from discriminating against those with impairments and required federal contractors to take affirmative action to employ persons with "handicapping" conditions. Two years later the Education for All Handicapped Children Act of 1975 guaranteed children with physical and mental impairments free and appropriate special education within public schools (known as "mainstreaming"). The latter two pieces of legislation, along with the increasing availability of many important technological aids, enabled more and more persons with disabilities to receive high-level education, making them qualified for many more positions in the work force. Two years before ADA became law, in 1988, still further barriers came down: amendments to the Fair Housing Act added persons with disabilities to the minority groups entitled to protection from discrimination in housing, and the Technology-Related Assistance for Individuals with Disabilities Act sought to make high-technology aids and devices more readily available to persons who could benefit from them.

Equality of opportunity: the momentum gathers

ADA was originally conceived by the National Council on Disability (formerly the National Council on the Handicapped), an independent federal agency with 15 presidentially appointed members, which later was at the forefront of the congressional hearings. In the

A child works at a specially designed computer keyboard at a learning center in Berkeley, California. In the U.S. children with disabilities have the opportunity to receive high-level special education that meets their unique needs, thanks to the increasing availability of technological aids and the passage in 1975 of the Education for All Handicapped Children Act.

James D. Wilson—Woodfin Camp & Associates

Proclaiming that "every man, woman, and child with a disability can now pass through once-closed doors into a bright new era," Pres. George Bush signs into law the Americans with Disabilities Act on July 26, 1990.

1980s the council issued two reports, *Toward Independence* and *On the Threshold of Independence,* which were the "germs" that led to the first draft of ADA legislation, introduced in Congress in April 1988 by Sen. Lowell P. Weicker (Rep., Conn.) and Rep. Tony Coelho (Dem., Calif.). Other key congressional supporters of the legislation were Sen. Tom Harkin (Dem., Iowa), Edward M. Kennedy (Dem., Mass.), Paul Simon (Dem., Ill.), Orrin G. Hatch (Rep., Utah), and Robert Dole (Rep., Kan.) and Rep. Major R. Owens (Dem., N.Y.), Hamilton Fish, Jr. (Rep., N.Y.), Don Edwards (Dem., Calif.), and Steve Bartlett (Rep., Texas).

In 1986, at the request of the National Council, Louis Harris and Associates conducted the first major national survey to study the attitudes and experiences of people with disabilities. Respondents identified a variety of types of discrimination—including workplace discrimination, denial of educational opportunities, lack of access to public buildings and bathrooms, the absence of accessible transportation, and other forms of social ostracism. These findings were further supported in the council's 1986 report *Toward Independence,* which noted: "People with disabilities have been saying for years that their major obstacles are not inherent in their disabilities, but arise from barriers that have been imposed externally and unnecessarily."

In 1990, with overwhelming bipartisan support in Congress, the final version of ADA was passed in the House on a 377–28 vote and in the Senate by a vote of 76–8. Then, on July 26, with more than 2,000 persons gathered on the White House lawn for the largest bill-signing ceremony ever, Pres. George Bush signed into law the act guaranteeing equal opportunities for all individuals with disabilities.

ADA's scope

The scope of ADA, whose legislation will be phased in over several years, extends far beyond building ramps and providing parking spaces for wheelchair users. An estimated four million businesses and five million buildings will be affected by the new law, and four governmental agencies have been charged with overseeing its enforcement. The American with Disabilities Act consists of five critical "titles"—employment (Title I), public services (Title II), public accommodations (Title III), telecommunications (Title IV), and "miscellaneous" provisions (Title V).

"Americans with disabilities" include those who (1) have a physical or mental impairment that substantially limits a major life activity; (2) have a record, or past history, of such an impairment; or (3) are regarded by others as having such an impairment. A "major life activity" can be anything from caring for oneself to performing manual tasks, walking, standing, sitting, reaching, lifting, seeing, hearing, speaking, breathing, learning, and working. An example of a person with a "record" of an impairment is a former cancer patient who is now cured but who may encounter discrimination because of his or her past medical history. Another example is one who may have been misclassified or misdiagnosed as having a learning disability or as being "mentally retarded." An example of one who is "regarded" as having an impairment is a person with controlled high blood pressure who is disqualified from a job involving strenuous work because the employer fears that the individual might suffer a heart attack on the job. ADA also specifies that persons who have a business, social, or familial relationship with a person with a disability may not be discriminated against because of that relationship.

The National Council on Disability breaks down "major disabling conditions" as follows: 44% physical disabilities; 32% serious health impairments including cancer, heart disease, and respiratory diseases; 13% visual, hearing, and speech impairments; 6% mental retardation and mental illness; and 5% "other." ADA has been criticized for being confusing because of its sheer comprehensiveness, but its proponents point out that it was written to be *inclusive* rather than exclusive. Among those covered by the legislation are those having AIDS or infected with the human immunodeficiency virus (HIV). Persons with alcoholism who are in treatment are covered, as are former or recovering drug addicts. (In an employment situation such individuals may be expected to provide evidence of participation in a rehabilitation program or results of drug testing, and they must be able to do their work safely.) ADA does *not* give rights to *active* users of illegal substances.

Homosexuality, bisexuality, transvestism, transexualism, and other similar conditions are expressly *not* impairments or disabilities under ADA. Nor are compulsive gambling, pyromania, or kleptomania considered impairments. Physical characteristics and conditions that are within the "normal" range and are not the result of a physiological disorder are also not impairments. These would include eye color, hair color or length, left-handedness, height, weight, and personality traits such as a quick temper or poor judgment. Advanced age, in and of itself, is not an impairment under ADA (but age-related medical conditions such as arthritis or hearing loss *are*).

Employment provisions

According to the office of the U.S. attorney general, 58% of all working-age men with disabilities and 80% of women were not employed at the beginning of 1990. Americans with disabilities were thus the single largest unemployed demographic group aged 18 to 65. ADA will change that situation significantly. For employers with 25 or more employees, Title I became effective on July 26, 1992. Coverage expands to include employers with 15 or more employees on July 26, 1994.

Title I prohibits discrimination by employers in all aspects of the employee-employer relationship: hiring, promotion, benefits, training, transfers, terminations, etc. "Employers" include all businesses engaged in an industry affecting commerce. ADA covers not only the traditional private business employer but unions, employment agencies, and joint labor-management organizations. ADA applies to all state and local government employers but not the federal government, which is covered by the 1973 Rehabilitation Act. Title I of ADA provides that an American Indian tribe is not an employer. In addition, under the law, religious entities are permitted to exercise a preference in employment practices based on religious affiliation.

The regulations to implement Title I, which were issued by the Equal Employment Opportunity Commission in July 1991, require equal employment opportunity for qualified individuals—*i.e.,* those who satisfy the requisite skill, experience, education, and other job-related requirements and who, with or without reasonable accommodation, can perform the essential duties of the position they seek or hold.

The concept of "reasonable accommodation" is one that evolved under the Rehabilitation Act and is at the core of ADA. In using this term, ADA enables employers to draw on the almost 20 years of experience under the 1973 act. The concept attempts to balance the bona fide needs of the employee against the costs and administrative burden to the employer. The act's formulators emphasize that the law was designed to be both flexible and reasonable. "Reasonable accommodation" may include making existing work and nonwork facilities readily accessible to and usable by individuals with disabilities—*e.g.,* by widening aisles or lowering elevator buttons for a person who uses a wheelchair. Reasonable accommodation also may include job restructuring: allowing part-time or modified work schedules (*e.g.,* "flex-time," a popular system already in place in many workplaces); reassignment to a vacant position; acquisition or modification of equipment or devices (*e.g.,* installing an amplifier for a telephone or obtaining a telecommunications device for the deaf [TDD; a machine that employs graphic communication in the transmission of coded signals through a wire or radio communication system] to aid a hearing-impaired employee).

Reasonable accommodation may also include adjustment or modification of training materials, policies, or examinations, such as making such materials available in Braille or large type, giving an oral test in lieu of a written one, or allowing an individual with a learning disability extra time to complete a skills test (*e.g.,* a person with dyslexia may need more time to read the test questions). Such accommodation may also

At a training center in Oakland, California, a man with cerebral palsy, who is unable to use his hands, manipulates a computer keyboard by using a special mouth-stick device to produce elaborate architectural drawings. The Title I provisions of the Americans with Disabilities Act guarantee that as a skilled draftsman he will now have the same opportunity for employment as other qualified individuals who are able-bodied.

James D. Wilson—Woodfin Camp & Associates

A deaf guest at a Marriott Hotel uses a telecommunications device for the deaf (TDD) machine. Upon request, TDDs can be hooked up to the public phones in the hotel's lobby. The Americans with Disabilities Act requires that commercial facilities serving the public offer the same services to deaf customers that are provided for hearing customers. Necessary alterations to make public accommodations and commercial facilities accessible to persons with disabilities were to have been made by Jan. 26, 1992.

include providing qualified sign interpreters or readers for hearing-impaired and visually impaired persons, respectively.

In determining whether the accommodation is reasonable, the net cost to the employer, the resources of the employer, and any administrative burden are to be considered. An unreasonable accommodation—one that is not required to be provided—presents an "undue hardship" in terms of cost or disruption of the business. While there was initially much hue and cry from business about the costs of making accommodations, Congress weighed the costs and concluded that the investment required of businesses would *not* be excessive. A study conducted in 1987 by the Job Accommodation Network, a branch of the President's Committee on Employment of People with Disabilities, found that for a sample of 10,000 employees with disabilities, 69% required accommodations that cost under $500; for 50% the cost was under $50, and for 31% there was no additional cost to employers. A considerable expenditure (of over $5,000) on the part of the employer was necessary for only 1% of employees. Other studies have shown that most workers with disabilities can have their needs met with "quick fixes." Moreover, human resources experts point out that turnover rates among employees with disabilities tend to be extremely low, which helps justify any costs that are incurred when accommodations are made for their employment.

Not only will the Americans with Disabilities Act open employment doors, but, according to a recent poll conducted by Louis Harris and Associates, 82% of the public think that the greater employment of persons with disabilities will be a "boost to the nation." That survey found that 78% of the public viewed people with disabilities as having underused potential in the work force, whereas only 11% viewed them as creating a burden on taxpayers.

Nonetheless, some employers have been quite vocal in their criticism of the new law, claiming the provisions are too broad and the language of the act too vague. Many employers fear that ADA will spur a rash of lawsuits. Although fewer than 400 suits were engendered by the Rehabilitation Act over a period of nearly two decades, ADA offers legal remedy for a much larger group. Whether the predicted complaints against employers will indeed occur and result in litigation remains to be seen.

Public services

Title II, providing that no qualified individual with a disability shall be excluded from any state or local government services, activities, and programs, became effective Jan. 26, 1992. Under this title meaningful access to services, programs, and activities is required. New buildings and alterations of existing ones must be accessible and usable. Historic properties, to the maximum extent feasible, are to be made accessible (if need be by alternative, nonstructural means, such as a portable ramp). New and altered streets must have accessible curb ramps. Telephone emergency services, including 911 services, must provide direct access to individuals who use TDDs and other such aids. Likewise, where a state or local government in the normal course of its activity communicates by telephone with applicants and beneficiaries, it must use TDDs or other methods for communicating with individuals who are hearing- or speech-impaired. All such "public services" are under the regulation and enforcement of the U.S. Department of Justice.

Title II also contains statutory provisions relating to public transportation services; these provisions are administered by the Department of Transportation. Implementation regulations for public transportation services specify that all new buses ordered on or after Aug. 26, 1990, must be accessible. Government rail

The provisions of the Americans with Disabilities Act requiring public transit system buses to be accessible to all riders mean that the wheelchair-bound now have a greater chance than ever before to be a part of mainstream American society.

systems must have at least one accessible car per train by July 26, 1995. New transit facilities and alterations of older structures must be accessible to and usable by all persons. With regard to subways, rapid rail, commuter rail, and light rail systems, "key" stations (*i.e.,* stations at critical junctions such as transfer points or points of heavy usage) must be accessible by July 26, 1993, unless an extension (of up to 20 years, with possible extensions to 30 years) is granted.

Public accommodation

Title III, also regulated by the Department of Justice, provides that persons with disabilities must have access to existing private businesses that serve the general public. On Jan. 26, 1992, all public accommodations and commercial facilities should have been made accessible to people with disabilities. The sweep of this title is reflected in the definition of *public accommodation,* a term that includes hotels, motels, restaurants, bars, movie houses, concert halls, auditoriums, convention centers, bakeries, grocery stores, clothing stores, shopping centers, banks, barber shops, gas stations, self-service laundries, travel agencies, offices of accountants or lawyers, pharmacies, insurance offices, professional offices of health care providers, hospitals, public transportation facilities, museums, libraries, galleries, parks, zoos, amusement parks, private schools (at all levels from nursery through postgraduate), day-care centers, senior citizen centers, shelters for the homeless, social service centers, gymnasiums, health clubs, and bowling alleys.

Owners and operators of public accommodations may not discriminate against patrons with disabilities and must make facilities accessible to and usable by them. Reasonable modifications to existing practices and policies must be undertaken unless they would fundamentally alter the goods or services offered or create an undue burden. An example of a reasonable modification would be that a salesperson in a department store may orally inform a visually impaired person of the cost of an item (in lieu of the store's providing Braille price tags). Existing structural barriers are to be removed from these facilities if doing so is "readily achievable"—*i.e.,* if it is feasible both structurally and financially. If the site is not accessible, the service must still be provided.

Prior to the implementation of the Title III provisions of the Americans with Disabilities Act, a supermarket in Oklahoma City, Oklahoma, had widened its checkout aisles and provided electrically powered shopping carts for customers in wheelchairs. However, to be in full compliance with the law, the store would have to make still further accommodations, such as making the meat counter service bell reachable.

An exhibit of touchable monuments at the National Building Museum in Washington, D.C., enables the blind to discover the city's architectural treasures. The sign, lower left, is in Braille.

Places of public accommodation and commercial facilities such as factories and office buildings designed and constructed for first occupancy after Jan. 26, 1993, must be accessible to people with disabilities. Alterations to such accommodations and facilities after Jan. 26, 1992, must also be accessible. To be considered accessible, a new or altered facility must comply with ADA "accessibility guidelines," published as an appendix to the Department of Justice regulations, which contain both scoping (*i.e.,* which elements must be accessible, how many must be accessible) and technical requirements.

Title III also includes provisions concerning transportation services. As of Aug. 26, 1990, private transportation companies that are primarily in the business of transporting people in vehicles that carry 16 or more persons were required to purchase or lease accessible vehicles for all fixed-route service. Also, "demand-responsive" systems—those that do not have a fixed route—with vehicles seating 16 or more persons must be accessible, and services for persons with disabilities must be equivalent to those provided for persons who are not disabled. Over-the-road buses (those with baggage compartments below the seating area) must be accessible by July 26, 1996, or a year later for smaller companies. (A study, due to be completed in 1993, could be the basis for extending these deadlines by one year.) The enforcement of these Title III transportation provisions is by the Department of Justice.

Telecommunications

Title IV, under the enforcement jurisdiction of the Federal Communications Commission, issued regulations that require telephone companies serving the public to provide telecommunication relay services 24 hours a day by no later than July 26, 1993. Implementation of this title will enable hearing- and speech-impaired individuals to interact and communicate in important ways that have not previously been available to them. It will lead to greater linkages between any individual who utilizes a TDD and persons who do not use such a device. The enhanced availability of these telecommunication relay services will also allow more employers and more places of public accommodation to be more readily accessible and more easily serve persons with disabilities. The law states that the implementation of this title must encourage the use of existing technology but should not *discourage* the development of improved technology.

Title IV of ADA also requires that all federally funded television public service announcements have closed captioning of the oral content of the message.

Miscellaneous provisions

There are several critical provisions under Title V. Most importantly, ADA makes clear that it does not preempt or supersede state and local laws that afford persons with disabilities greater protection than ADA. Almost all of the states and many localities have certain existing laws prohibiting discrimination against persons with disabilities, many of which cover small businesses with fewer than 15 employees, which would not be subject to ADA.

Another Title V mandate is that health insurance and benefit plans be nondiscriminatory. This means that while preexisting conditions may be excluded from coverage under an insurance policy or company-wide plan, such preexisting conditions may not be used to deny overall coverage or coverage for nonpreexisting conditions. For example, a visually impaired person may be denied coverage for treatments, medications, and medical appointments for the vision-related condition but not for orthopedic, cardiovascular, or other conditions.

Title V also contains provisions applying ADA to the House of Representatives and the Senate. This was the first time that in passing a major civil rights bill, Congress expressly and simultaneously stipulated its application to itself. Both houses of Congress are prohibited from discriminating against persons with disabilities in all employment practices, and all services and premises of the legislative branch of the government must be accessible to persons with disabilities.

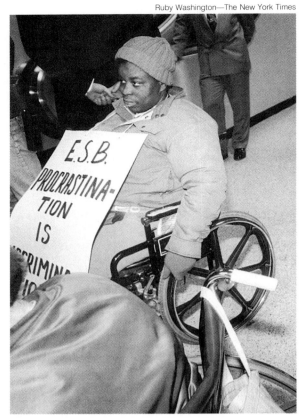

On Jan. 27, 1992, the day after most facilities serving the general public were to have been barrier-free, would-be patrons demonstrate outside New York City's Empire State Building, whose restrooms and observation deck were not wheelchair-accessible.

Related tax incentives

The same year that it adopted ADA, Congress also passed tax incentives to help businesses comply with the law. It extended the Targeted Jobs Tax Credit, which gives a tax credit for hiring "disadvantaged persons," a term that includes persons with disabilities. Also enacted was a tax credit of up to $5,000 per year for small businesses (*i.e.,* those with 30 or fewer employees and less than $1 million in gross sales) for providing auxiliary aids and services for employees with disabilities. And all businesses, regardless of size, are eligible for a tax deduction of up to $15,000 per year for removing architectural, transportation, and communication barriers.

Impact

Former White House press secretary Brady has pointed out that "most people don't like to think about disability at all. But disability can happen to anyone." The number of Americans with disabilities is growing rapidly with the aging of the baby boom generation. Most disabilities occur after the age of 40—fewer than 5% of those under 17 have disabilities, compared with almost 25% of people between ages 45 and 64. If current trends continue, it is expected that there will be a 42% rise in disability prevalence by the year 2010.

The term *handicapped* is clearly inappropriate when applied to persons who have disabilities. Americans with disabilities should now be thought of in terms of what they *can* rather than what they *cannot* do. Although attitude changes per se cannot be legislated, the Americans with Disabilities Act should go a long way toward raising the consciousness of people nationwide. The manager of one business put it quite succinctly when he observed, "The biggest change I had to make was in mind, to recognize the person's ability, not his disability."

Enactment of the Americans with Disabilities Act was accompanied by much fanfare. When President Bush signed ADA into law, he proclaimed that "every man, woman, and child with a disability can now pass through once-closed doors into a bright new era of equality, independence, and freedom." Indeed, persons with disabilities were imbued with a new sense of belonging and empowerment as equal members of society. Just as other civil rights legislation has changed American society in fundamental ways, so, too, will ADA. As various provisions of the law are phased in over a several-year period, those with disabilities will increasingly enter the marketplace as equal consumers, the work force as equal employees, and mainstream American society as full and equal citizens. New buildings will be accessible. Existing barriers will be removed where that is feasible. With the removal of those barriers will come the greater participation of persons with disabilities as vital members of the general public.

—*Sandra Swift Parrino*

Eye Diseases and Visual Disorders

To people the world over, eyesight is a very precious sense, yet eye diseases and visual disorders exact a huge toll. Worldwide there are some 27 million–35 million people who are blind. The impact of blindness in less developed countries is particularly tragic, as many of the most common eye diseases that threaten sight are preventable. It is estimated that in sub-Saharan Africa alone there are at least three million cases of untreated, yet surgically curable, cataract. Ocular disorders are also very common in the world's wealthiest countries. In the United States some 6.4 million new cases of eye disease occur each year; at least 11 million people have impaired vision that cannot be corrected by glasses, and 800,000 of them are considered legally blind (usually defined as having vision worse than 20/200).

Numerous advances in the understanding of the

eye and the conditions that affect it have been made in just the past few years. Continuing research offers the hope of even better methods of diagnosis, prevention, treatment—and perhaps cure—in years to come. Several areas in which there have been noteworthy recent developments are described below.

Correcting refractive errors

It has been estimated that about 140 million people in the U.S. have refractive errors. Most refractive errors fall into the categories of nearsightedness (myopia), farsightedness (hyperopia), and the need for reading glasses that generally begins during the fourth decade of life (presbyopia). For clear vision, light rays coming from an object must be perfectly focused on the back portion of the eye (the retina), specifically on a single point on the retina called the fovea. When this occurs, the eye is said to be emmetropic. Before reaching the retina, light rays must pass through the cornea, lens, and vitreous. Both the cornea and lens of the eye can bend light and therefore play an important role in how clearly people see.

About one-quarter of adults in the U.S. are myopic. Myopia occurs when the light rays from an object are focused not on the fovea but rather somewhere in front of it, in the vitreous. Under these circumstances, the eye is said to be "too long," and distant objects appear blurred. Conversely, in hyperopia the eye is "too short," and light rays are focused behind the retina, or, theoretically, beyond the back of the eye; the hyperopic individual sees close objects as blurred. Presbyopia is a virtually inescapable condition that occurs as the eye ages. When they are in their forties, most people become unable to see near objects clearly; however, their distance vision remains good. This is due to the decreased ability of the lens to change shape, which is a prerequisite for good near vision.

The most common way to correct any of these refractive errors is with glasses. The lenses placed into eyeglass frames focus light either backward or forward, depending on whether the eye is myopic or hyperopic. Contact lenses perform the same functions. Those with presbyopia require reading glasses or, if they are farsighted, bifocals or trifocals (so that they can see images clearly at various distances). Within the past few years bifocal contact lenses have become available as well.

In the past decade ophthalmologists have been studying other ways of correcting refractive errors. One technique that has received considerable attention is that of radial keratotomy, a surgical procedure performed under local anesthesia that attempts to correct myopia. Though several variations of the technique exist, the approach that has been most extensively studied involves making from four to eight surgical incisions in the cornea in a radial, or spokelike, configuration. Essentially the incisions have the effect of rendering the cornea less curved—*i.e.,* flattening it—and thus making it a less powerful lens. The desired effect of radial keratotomy is to move the focal point of light backward, just as glasses would.

A long-term study of the procedure, which was conducted at nine medical centers, began in 1981. It was sponsored by the National Eye Institute of the U.S. National Institutes of Health and was known as the Prospective Evaluation of Radial Keratotomy, or PERK, study. The study was designed to answer questions regarding the relative safety and predictability of radial keratotomy as well as the long-term effects of such a weakening procedure on the cornea. Attempts were made to standardize the operation as much as possible; eight incisions were made with a specially developed fine-angled diamond blade, the length of the cuts being dependent on the amount of myopia the patient had—the greater the myopia, the more

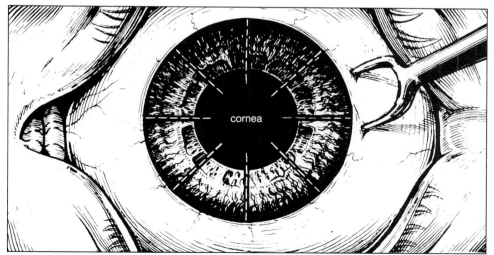

cornea

The radial keratotomy procedure to correct myopia is performed under local anesthesia. The eyeball is fixated with a double-pronged forceps, and four to eight spokelike incisions are made in the cornea, decreasing its curvature and thereby moving the focal point of light backward.

From *Highlights of Ophthalmology,* Triweekly Letter, vol. 10, no. 18 (1982); illustration, Stephen F. Gordon

the cornea needed to be flattened and, therefore, the longer the incisions.

At the end of 1991 the PERK study group published its analysis for three years of follow-up of radial keratotomy performed in 757 eyes. In all, 88% of all eyes operated on had a visual acuity of 20/40 or better without the need for glasses or contact lenses. However, the ability to fully correct the myopia was achieved more frequently in those with less severe nearsightedness, dropping the success rate to 56% in those eyes with moderate or greater myopia. Slight to moderate overcorrection had occurred in 17% of the eyes, meaning that they became hyperopic with the procedure, and those individuals then required reading glasses. In 3% of 752 eyes, radial keratotomy caused a decrease in visual acuity; on a standard Snellen eye chart, these patients could read fewer lines of letters after the surgery than they could before it. The multiyear review of ocular complications, including infections, excessive scarring of the cornea caused by the operation itself, and new vessel growth on the treated corneas, showed that these occurred very infrequently and therefore did not appear to be a major clinical concern.

Among the subjects in the study, the degree of satisfaction with the procedure was high; 90% were "moderately to very satisfied" with the result. More than 50 of the patients who elected not to have surgery on their second eye were interviewed in detail for their reasons. The reasons most often cited were a bad experience with the first eye, perception of a glare that was thought to result from the surgery, fluctuating vision, and pain after the first operation.

These results have left many unanswered questions. It would appear that radial keratotomy is a method by which myopia can be effectively treated. The relative safety of the procedure has been shown, although whether there will be continued change in the corneal curvature and what the long-term health of the eye will be remain to be determined. The major problems appear to be the relative unpredictability of the procedure, which is probably due to the fact that individual corneas have different biomechanical properties as well as different wound-healing potentials, and the instability of the result; notably, one-fifth of the subjects in the study had an increasingly hyperopic shift in their correction between six months and five years after the surgery.

It should be noted that the procedure of radial keratotomy continues to be improved, with some improvements being a result of the PERK study itself. One observation that has great clinical significance is that the effect of the same amount of surgery is greater in older patients than in younger ones. Also, patients with smaller amounts of myopia (ranging from 1.5 to 5 diopters) are the best candidates for the procedure. The number of incisions made in the cornea is now usually four, and improvements in the surgical instruments used, as well as in the way the incisions are made, have helped to standardize the procedure.

Recent interest has centered on the possible use of the excimer laser as an alternative way to reshape the cornea. A trial sponsored by the U.S. Food and Drug Administration (FDA) began in 1990 to test a surgical technique known as photorefractive keratectomy on 1,000 young adults with moderate myopia. The approach uses pulsed excimer laser beams to fragment, or vaporize, some of the corneal tissue; the amount of tissue removed is proportionate to the amount of energy (number of pulses) delivered to the corneal surface. Unlike radial keratotomy, the procedure does not weaken the cornea and thus may not affect the structural integrity of the eye. However, to date, certain technical problems have limited the effectiveness of this approach. One problem is that the laser pulses needed to penetrate the different thicknesses of the cornea—from its center to the periphery—can vary considerably. Also, the linear excisions made by the laser create a wide, V-shaped trough as opposed to the narrow trough made with a blade, posing problems of wound healing. Although these problems may eventually be worked out, at the present time neither excimer laser surgery nor radial keratotomy offers a better correction of myopia than do glasses or contact lenses.

Retinopathy of prematurity

The human eye begins to form fairly early in the embryonic period—at about six weeks. However, its maturation—particularly that of the retina—continues through the perinatal period (the time around birth). This ongoing development of the retina has great clinical import for children born prematurely. Because they do not have fully functioning pulmonary systems, they are often in need of high concentrations of oxygen to survive. When low-birth-weight newborns are given oxygen therapy, it stimulates blood vessels to grow in the eye, often causing a proliferation of abnormal peripheral retinal vessels, which can lead to retinal detachment and often total blindness. This constellation of problems is termed retinopathy of prematurity (ROP).

In the 1950s widespread use of oxygen in nurseries caused an epidemic of an estimated 10,000 cases of ROP worldwide. A study conducted over 30 years ago by the National Institutes of Health showed that careful screening of premature infants could identify those at high risk for retinal damage at an early stage and that with the prudent use of oxygen—giving it only as needed—the number of cases of ROP could be reduced dramatically. With this observation, centers that took care of such high-risk infants curtailed their use of oxygen. Over the past decade, however, as neonatal care has become increasingly sophisticated, permitting many more of these extremely low-birth-weight babies to survive, oxygen use has resurged. Today it is estimated that over 500 newborns a year in the U.S. develop sight-threatening ROP. Moreover, this problem occurs in spite of continuing very close monitoring of oxygen use.

Although ROP can regress in a relatively small number of cases, leaving these babies with the possibility of good vision, the vast majority of such low-birth-weight children are at high risk of becoming irreversibly blind. There had been some evidence that cryotherapy, a form of therapy that freezes the outer edge of the developing retina, from which new blood vessels grow, could double the possibility of a favorable visual outcome in those patients who require oxygen for survival. In the mid-1980s a randomized controlled trial involving 23 centers to evaluate the role of cryotherapy in the treatment of ROP was initiated. The infants included in this study were those weighing under 1,251 g (44 oz) who had developed ROP to a point that they were at high risk for blindness.

About 4,100 very-low-birth-weight infants born between Jan. 1, 1986, and Nov. 30, 1987, were eligible. Ultimately 291 children had retinopathy that progressed to the point where they were eligible for cryotherapy—over 80% having disease in both eyes. Infants who had treatable disease in both eyes were randomly chosen to receive either cryotherapy or no therapy. This was considered acceptable at that time because it was unknown whether cryotherapy would be any more beneficial than would simple observation. The cryotherapy involved treatment of the entire circumference of the developing retina. One year after treatment, important differences between the two groups were apparent; photographs of the backs of each infant's eyes revealed unfavorable changes in 47.7% of the untreated eyes, whereas the outcome was unfavorable in only 25.7% of the eyes in the cryotherapy group. The outcome was considered "unfavorable" if a fold was present in the retina running through the macular region or if there was a retinal detachment—changes that would have a negative effect on the eye's capacity to see well. Tests that measured the functional capacities of the infants' eyes also revealed differences in the two groups—poor functional capacity was noted in 56.3% of the eyes in the control group, compared with 35% poor functional capacity in the cryotherapy group.

While these findings indicate that cryotherapy is effective, the data did not indicate whether both eyes, if they have reached the stage where there is evidence of deleterious changes, should be treated concomitantly or whether eyes that have not progressed to this stage should be treated. Furthermore, long-term follow-up is needed to determine what eventually occurs to eyes that have been treated apparently successfully with cryotherapy.

Studies are under way to determine whether the common aging-related ocular disorders cataracts and macular degeneration can be prevented with specific nutrients. Cataracts, in which the eye's lens has become clouded, cause vision to be hazy (as in the top photograph); macular degeneration (as shown above) results in decreased central vision because of a deterioration of the retina.

Nutrients and eye disease: is there a connection?
In the United States more than $2 billion worth of vitamin and mineral supplements are sold each year. Recently it has been suggested that the taking of such supplements may be helpful in the prevention of ocular disorders, particularly those of cataract, a progressive clouding of the lens of the eye, which is the third leading cause of blindness in the United

States, and age-related macular degeneration, a sight-robbing deterioration of the retina. If it were true that supplements could indeed prevent these disorders, the economic and public health impact would be enormous. It has been estimated that the number of cataract operations performed annually in the U.S.—now over one million—could be halved if the development of cataract were postponed by 10 years. Further, the toll of age-related macular degeneration is huge; some 10 million elderly Americans experience visual impairments associated with this disorder. Moreover, there is presently no known treatment for age-related macular degeneration.

What evidence is there supporting the role of vitamins and minerals in staving off these common and devastating disorders of aging? Animal studies have evaluated the protective potential of a large number of nutrients in the development of cataracts. In general, the experimental approach has been to either remove from the diet or give in large doses the nutrient in question. Preliminary research has focused on certain minerals and vitamins that function as antioxidants. Oxidative processes in the lens of the eye are thought to play an important role in the development of cataracts. Activated forms of oxygen, which can be formed as a result of normal metabolism or certain outside stimuli such as ultraviolet light, are believed to be highly damaging to the lens of the eye in particular. A variety of chemical processes that can counteract oxygen's activation and subsequent harmful effect on the lens are present in the eye. In animal studies naturally occurring antioxidant enzymes such as superoxide dismutase, catalase, and selenium-dependent glutathione peroxidase have all been implicated in such protective mechanisms. Consequently, glutathione, vitamins C and E, carotenoids, selenium, calcium, zinc, riboflavin, and tryptophan have all been suggested as supplements that may have the potential to enhance the protection from cataracts.

Some human studies have also suggested an association between increased amounts of nutrients, such as vitamins C and E, and a decreased incidence of cataracts. One study, however, found no such protection in those taking multiple vitamin supplements. Still another study found no association at all between nutrient intake and development of cataracts. Studies carried out to date evaluating the roles of calcium and selenium offer little support for the notions that either deficiencies of or increases in either of these minerals play a role in cataract formation in humans. Unfortunately, virtually all the observational studies carried out thus far in humans noting associations of various nutrients and cataracts are fraught with confounding variables, making it very difficult to interpret the available data. Perhaps the most important confounding variable is that a higher socioeconomic status is strongly associated with a decreased risk of cataracts.

The available evidence from animal studies supporting the role of nutrients in the prevention of age-related macular degeneration is not overwhelming; studies in rats have shown that vitamin C appears to protect retinas from injury induced by excessive amounts of light, while studies in primates have shown that deprivation of vitamins A and E can lead to retinal damage. In human studies perhaps the most provocative finding is that a deficiency of zinc may be present in older individuals. This is of interest because zinc is present in high concentrations in the retina and pigment epithelium, a layer of cells that underlies the retina and whose health is imperative for the proper functioning of the retina. In a small preliminary study, subjects who were considered at high risk for the development of macular degeneration were treated with oral zinc and may have had less visual loss than a group taking a placebo. However, the interpretation of these results has been the subject of some debate; the investigators themselves emphasized the pilot nature of the study. Moreover, because of the possible toxic effects of oral zinc supplementation, it is not recommended that the treatment be given to patients with early evidence of macular degeneration.

Recently, a multicenter case-control study to determine risk factors for age-related macular degeneration was sponsored by the National Eye Institute. Those with the highest intake of carotenoids had a significantly (70%) reduced risk of the disorder, while higher serum levels of vitamins C and E were associated with a smaller risk reduction. However, this study did not support the notion that higher zinc levels in the blood reduced the risk of macular degeneration.

In order to arrive at more definitive answers about how age-related eye disorders develop and progress, the National Eye Institute is now conducting a 10-year investigation, the Age-Related Eye Disease Study, which will ultimately enroll close to 5,000 subjects aged 60 to 75. The provocative questions about whether vitamin and nutrient supplements have a preventive role in cataract development and age-related macular degeneration are among those that will be investigated.

The ocular complications of AIDS

The human immunodeficiency virus (HIV), which causes AIDS, affects many organs of the body. As the various characteristics of HIV-related disease became better defined, it was noted that the eye is often affected. More than half of AIDS patients, for example, develop so-called cotton-wool spots, changes in the retina that usually have no ocular significance.

A prominent feature of AIDS is the problem of recurring infections caused by opportunistic organisms. These are organisms that are often present in the body but are not pathogenic under normal circumstances; however, with the decreased ability of the immune sys-

Photographs, Don C. Bienfang, M.D., Brigham and Women's Hospital, Boston

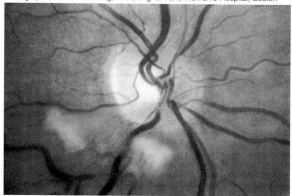

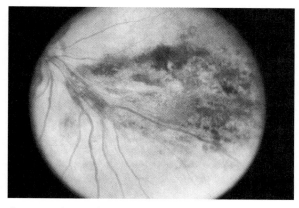

Cotton-wool spots, benign retinal changes, are present around a branch of blood vessels in the eye of a patient with AIDS (top). The most common and serious ocular complication of AIDS is cytomegalovirus retinitis, seen in the active phase in the eye above; in this opportunistic infection, retinal tissue death can lead to irreversible blindness.

tem to fight off infections, these organisms proliferate and cause disease. The most common opportunistic infection of the eye is cytomegalovirus (CMV) retinitis. Before the AIDS epidemic, ocular infections caused by CMV were relatively rare, usually seen only in patients who were severely immunosuppressed, either because of an underlying cancer or from medication taken for certain life-threatening diseases or to prevent rejection of a grafted organ after transplantation.

Approximately one-third of AIDS patients will ultimately develop sight-threatening CMV retinitis, which can lead to necrosis (*i.e.,* death) of the retina and irreversible blindness. Until recently there was no effective treatment for CMV retinitis. In the past several years, however, it has been shown that two medications, ganciclovir and foscarnet, can significantly impede the progression of the infection. Ganciclovir was approved for the treatment of CMV retinitis in 1989; foscarnet as a treatment for CMV retinitis was approved in September 1991.

In January 1990 the National Eye Institute initiated a randomized multicenter clinical trial comparing ganciclovir and foscarnet in the treatment of CMV retinitis. The study demonstrated that both drugs were essentially equally effective in impeding the spread of the infection. The study was suspended in October 1991, however, when it was found that patients receiving foscarnet survived an average of four months longer. Although there was a difference in the amount of antiviral therapy (*i.e.,* therapy against HIV itself) between the two groups—more patients in the foscarnet group were also taking zidovudine (AZT)—this could not totally explain the differences seen. It may be that foscarnet has an additional antiviral effect on HIV that accounts for the therapeutic benefit resulting in a prolongation of life. Further research is needed to explain why patients survived longer.

Unfortunately, a number of problems are associated with both drugs, thus limiting their effective use. Neither drug cures the patient of the infection; they can only hold it in check. Both therefore require long-term "maintenance" use, and stopping the medication will almost certainly result in a reactivation of the CMV infection. Both drugs need to be given intravenously several times a day; patients thus need to learn how to administer the medications themselves so that they can live at home. Some patients who cannot tolerate the drugs when they are given systemically are instead given injections of anti-CMV drugs directly into the vitreous of the eye. Furthermore, both drugs have major side effects, which can lead to the discontinuation of their use. Ganciclovir, like AZT, is known to decrease bone marrow function. Therefore, AZT and ganciclovir cannot be administered together at full therapeutic doses. Foscarnet in effective doses can be toxic to the kidneys; it may also cause low serum electrolyte levels that can lower the threshold for seizures.

Because serious side effects, the need for long-term maintenance therapy, and the frequency of recurrent infections all remain significant and unresolved problems, better ways to administer these antiviral medications are now being actively pursued. An oral form of ganciclovir is being developed, and new antiviral medications that do not affect the bone marrow are also being evaluated. Currently a sustained-release device that is implanted in the eye, allowing the slow continuous release of medication over a four-month period, is being tested, with initially promising results. However, the long-term safety and efficacy of this intraocular approach and its effect on survival still need to be determined.

Although CMV retinitis is the major cause of visual loss, there are other ophthalmologic complications of AIDS. As the epidemic continues, it will be important to identify new and unexpected ocular manifestations of HIV infection that could have disastrous consequences for sight.

—*Robert B. Nussenblatt, M.D.*

Caring for Patients with Alzheimer's Disease: An Innovative Approach

by Kevan H. Namazi, Ph.D.

Walter, a 75-year-old retired office manager in the moderate stage of Alzheimer's disease, lives in a traditional nursing home. About 6:30 each morning he is awakened so that he will be ready for breakfast before the nursing home staff starts its new shift. His breakfast is prepared in a remote main kitchen, where portions and choices have been preselected by a dietician, and then served to him in a dining area on a cafeteria-style tray. If Walter does not like the food or is not hungry, he may go without breakfast, eat a cold breakfast later, or proceed to eat the unappealing offering in front of him. The food is removed when most of Walter's coresidents in the home are finished eating or when trays are scheduled to go back to the kitchen.

Karen, a 78-year-old former dance instructor who also has moderate Alzheimer's disease, lives in a different kind of nursing home. She has long been a late riser and remains so now, getting up around 9. Aroused by the smells of cooking food, she puts on a robe and slippers and leaves her room for the adjacent central dining area, where she can see some of her earlier rising coresidents already at breakfast. The staff responsible for Karen's daily needs greets her and asks what she would like to eat. Although she is free to choose cereal, bacon and eggs, or some other food, Karen asks for her usual light breakfast of muffins and coffee, which the staff prepares in an open kitchen along one side of the dining area. Karen may decide to sit with a few of the other residents or to eat alone and look through the newspaper. As she has done throughout her life, she carries her dishes to the kitchen counter after breakfast. Then she may return to her room to dress for the day.

The examples of Walter and Karen reflect two different approaches to nursing home care. Walter's "home" follows the traditional "medical model": in design and operation it resembles a medical institution and as such offers residents little independence in their daily lives. Karen's "home," by contrast, is nontraditional and purposely supports decision making in a homelike setting. Its unique physical layout and operation have emerged from an effort to learn how Alzheimer's disease patients—whose progressive memory loss and disorientation over a period of years or decades mark their irreversible decline into demen-

tia—can be cared for in ways that will keep them safe, satisfied, and functioning on their own as much and as long as possible.

Such knowledge is sorely needed in light of expectations that by the end of the 1990s more than 35 million people in the U.S. alone will be 65 years of age or older. It is morally imperative that society find ways of assuring the frail and dependent segment of its elderly population, including those cognitively impaired with Alzheimer's disease, a reasonably autonomous and dignified life-style. Part of that search must involve a scrutiny of the differences in operations, general environment, and effectiveness of nursing homes and a reevaluation of the current philosophy of nursing home care.

Traditional nursing homes

The traditional nursing home has the physical characteristics of a hospital. Residents' rooms are small, often semiprivate, and typically outfitted with hospital beds and a few pieces of nondistinctive institutional furniture. Bathrooms may be hidden from view and thus offer no visual reminder to a person with a failing memory of the need to urinate; they may also be inaccessible to persons who use walkers or wheelchairs. The rooms open onto people- and equipment-crowded corridors, through which resonate frequent sounds of intercoms. Heavy fire doors keep occupants within different wings and hallways. A nurse's station, located strategically in the middle of intersecting hallways to oversee care of the residents, serves as a constant reminder of staff authority and patient dependency. Shiny linoleum floors, with geometric designs and frequently slippery surfaces, meet the sanitary and maintenance needs of hospitals with surgical and acutely ill patients but are unsafe for the elderly and limit their mobility.

The hospital-like concept for the building also extends to the way the institution is organized and operated. Meals and activities may be strictly scheduled and timed to accommodate staffing needs rather than residents' habits or preferences. Following breakfast, residents may wait in their rooms for a scheduled activity or may be taken to a dayroom, where there may be music, television, reading materials, and selected activities or where they can visit with family or friends.

Traditional nursing home residents have limited access to the outdoors and must be chaperoned when they do leave the building.

Traditional ideas about nursing homes and their residents are also based on a medical model. Such features as white uniforms and the organization of the facility into specific departments with specific jobs emphasize sickness and encourage dependency. The concept of home in the term *nursing home* can be forgotten in residents' lives. Administration and staff often think that if the institutionalized elderly's abilities to perform some daily routines are impaired, then the institution must assume total responsibility for all care. This belief runs counter to the person's need to maintain a sense of dignity, privacy, and independence. It is not coincidental that almost a quarter century ago Robert Butler, the first director of the U.S. National Institute on Aging, remarked after visiting many nursing homes that they were places with few nurses and hardly qualified as homes.

The continuity model

Because many elderly people lose the ability to deal effectively with their physical and social surroundings, special features and programs are necessary in the planning and operation of any long-term-care facility. An environment that does not impose excessive demands yet supports and nurtures remaining abilities may help reduce many of the problems encountered in living in a nursing home.

One recent trend in long-term care has been toward a "continuity model," in which residents' social, physical, and emotional needs, their past experiences, and the concerns of care-giving staff are included in the design and operation of the facility. *Continuity* suggests that nursing home life should be an extension of past life experiences. As such, the facility should provide care that combines the comfort, freedom, and privacy of one's home with a psychologically and physically supportive environment.

Surroundings play an especially crucial role for people with Alzheimer's disease, who appear to benefit highly from a network of sights, sounds, smells, and other sensory cues that remind them how to respond to particular situations. For example, adequate signs should be present to help residents locate washrooms in common areas. The signs must be simple to read and understand and must be placed where residents are likely to see them, since Alzheimer's patients may lose some of their ability to recognize familiar objects. Ideally the surroundings should limit stress but be rich in enjoyable experiences, provide a protective setting, and allow independent decision making when possible.

An example of a facility based on the continuity model is the Corinne Dolan Alzheimer Center (CDAC), part of the Heather Hill long-term care facility in Chardon, Ohio. The CDAC was designed around the concept that because Alzheimer's disease only gradually restricts one's ability to make decisions, people with the affliction have different needs at different times during the remainder of their lives. The CDAC works to provide an individualized program in an atmosphere that enriches the life of each resident through social interaction, exercise, and music therapy while promoting independence and productivity in its occupants and research into optimal nursing home care.

The idea of pertinent autonomy

The idea of individual independence is interwoven into the fabric of a "free" society. As children grow up, they gradually break the ties of dependence; they make friends, go to school on their own, choose their own clothes, develop food preferences, and acquire a variety of other likes and dislikes. Later the right to make decisions and do as one pleases, within social bound-

Marguerite B. Campbell

Rising unobtrusively behind its landscaped park, the Corinne Dolan Alzheimer Center (CDAC), Chardon, Ohio, represents the first application of Frank Lloyd Wright's concept of "organic architecture" to a care-giving facility. Inside and out, the design of the center works to support pertinent autonomy and self-sufficiency in its intellectually impaired residents by fostering harmony between the physical structure and its occupants.

aries, becomes a hallmark of adulthood. As people age, however, their ability to act independently and safely may diminish and ultimately disappear. Nevertheless, the need for autonomy does not diminish with age, even though the context in which autonomy is expressed may change. The philosophy of the CDAC is founded in the belief that all individuals, including nursing home residents with or without physical or mental impairments, are entitled to "pertinent autonomy" and rightful control over their lives.

At the CDAC pertinent autonomy is defined in terms of residents' choices; *e.g.*, when to rise, when and what to eat, what to wear, and the freedom to roam independently indoors and outdoors. To this end the physical design of the CDAC contains specific features that reduce the need for restrictions on residents and encourage successful navigation. The interaction between building design and the overall philosophy of care fosters self-sufficiency in a wide range of activities, be they as simple as getting a cup of coffee or as fundamental as finding and using the bathroom.

Architecture for care giving

The CDAC was established in 1989 on a 60-ha (150-ac) estate east of Cleveland to provide care exclusively to Alzheimer's patients. The center was designed by Stephen Nemtin of Taliesin Associated Architects, a subsidiary of the Frank Lloyd Wright Foundation, Scottsdale, Ariz. The CDAC design is the first instance in which Wright's concept of "organic architecture" has been applied to a care-providing facility. The goal of organic architecture is to foster harmony between the physical surroundings of the structure and the people who occupy it. Thus, the architectural features of the CDAC are intended to enhance the remaining abilities of residents in a supportive, flexible, and non-regimented milieu.

The triangular building consists of two mirror-image units with shared bathing facilities placed between them in the center of the structure. Each unit has 12 private rooms and a family room that can be used for small group activities and family visits. Both units share a craft room and a large central living room with comfortable chairs, a fireplace, and a serene view of the outdoors. The living room is integral to the living space of the facility; small groups and individuals use it to relax, listen to the radio or taped music, or interact with friends, as they would in a living room at home.

Residents' rooms encircle the dining area and nourishment center of each unit. Architectural features of the rooms help occupants function on their own despite their intellectual and perceptual limitations. For example, residents have a clear view of the toilet from anyplace in the room. Dutch doors at room entrances may be closed for privacy, opened at the top to bring natural light into the central areas and to prompt residents to recognize their own rooms, or left fully open. With family help each resident furnishes his or her own room with a bedroom set and linens, as well as a comfortable chair, lamps, decorations, and other items that reflect individual tastes and interests. Personal objects, especially ones brought from home, can provide a sense of familiarity in an unfamiliar place. Display cases just outside each resident's doorway make it easier for the occupant to locate his or her own room. Most residents include family photographs in the case, but others choose to show such significant objects as a doll collection or war- and work-related service awards and medals. One woman has a variety of miniature crystal shoes, along with dried flowers and crochet work. The sight of these prized possessions stirs deep memories still intact, evoking better recognition than do room numbers or nameplates.

The triangular building of the CDAC comprises two mirror-image units arranged around a central axis that contains shared bathing facilities and a common living room. In each unit 12 private rooms and a family room surround a kitchen and dining area. Looping through each unit is a walking path that connects with the opposite unit and the living room. The design of the walking paths eliminates long hallways and dead ends and encourages residents to be mobile. Side exits extend the walking paths to a protected outdoor terrace.

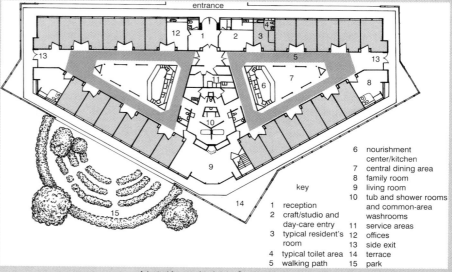

key

6 nourishment center/kitchen
7 central dining area
8 family room
9 living room
10 tub and shower rooms and common-area washrooms
11 service areas
12 offices
13 side exit
14 terrace
15 park

1 reception
2 craft/studio and day-care entry
3 typical resident's room
4 typical toilet area
5 walking path

Adapted from a drawing by Stephen M. Nemtin, the Robert Wood Johnson Foundation, *Advances*, vol. 3, no. 2 (Summer 1990)

Marguerite B. Campbell

Two residents of the CDAC meet at the doorway to a private room. With family assistance, residents furnish their own rooms with furniture and decorations that are familiar and that reflect personal taste. The Dutch doors at the entrances, when left open at the top, help residents find their own rooms without disturbing others. Another recognition cue is provided by the lighted showcase just outside the doorway, in which the room's occupant can display special possessions that evoke deep memories still intact.

The centrally located household-style kitchens help residents experience another homelike feature. The sight and smell of brewed coffee, baking bread, or homemade soup stimulate the appetite and continue everyday experiences established over a lifetime. A nonregimented policy about food gives residents a chance to practice pertinent autonomy. Meals are served family style in the dining areas rather than on institutional trays, and residents' guests are welcome to join them for meals. Residents may help set the tables, serve food, and clear or clean the tables. For safety, all kitchen appliances are specially adapted to prevent accidental harm. Hinged countertops at the entrances to the food-preparation areas can be locked down to restrict residents' access during meal preparation. Between meals residents have direct access to a specially designed transparent refrigerator in which they can see nutritious snacks like fruit, yogurt, and juices—and thus be reminded to eat.

Another purposeful feature of the CDAC is the open "walking paths" that separate the dining and central core areas from residents' bedrooms and also connect all areas of the center. This design eliminates confusing long hallways and dead-end corridors commonly found in traditional facilities. The pathways encourage residents to be mobile. For example, for two women who often wander together about the building, the pathways are conducive to their companionship and eventually direct them through the living room or past the kitchen or their own rooms. Staff can see where residents are without the need for a central station or unpleasant institutional messages over an intercom.

The walking paths on both units lead toward side exit doors that are equipped with an electronic locking system. During good weather the doors are unlocked and offer residents access to the outdoor terrace and park, another manifestation of pertinent autonomy. The terrace has protective walls and encircles the building so that residents can walk out from the end of one unit and reenter the building from the other unit. From the terrace an open walkway leads to a 0.8-ha (2-ac) secured park that is landscaped with a variety of plants and shrubs, all of which are nonpoisonous. Interconnecting paths in the park link the terrace, park, woods, and grassy areas where residents may enjoy the outdoors without constant supervision.

Personal programs

In nursing facilities that operate on the medical model, residents with Alzheimer's disease are separated from other residents and treated as a group with the same type of needs. Research shows, however, that needs and level of disability vary from one person to another in accordance with disease progression. Given the many differences among Alzheimer's disease patients, flexible program alternatives are an essential part of the continuity model.

To ease successful adjustment, a new arrival at the CDAC is often placed into a care group in which he or she receives personalized attention and assistance with specific needs. The care group also accommodates residents who are restless and unable to concentrate on tasks and who become stressed or overstimulated. Such activities as one-on-one crafts, music, and body movements and stretches are designed to increase or maintain attention span and encourage social interaction. Each newcomer is continuously evaluated and, when it is appropriate, is assigned to another group whose goals and activities are more in keeping with individual needs.

For example, a male resident eventually may join an all-male group, in which well-being and self-esteem draw support from the traditional male-oriented association of these qualities with productivity. The program for this group emphasizes masculine interests. Outdoor activities like sweeping the sidewalk or raking leaves are regularly scheduled, as are day trips to farm markets, fishing spots, and museums.

For those who still communicate verbally, daily discussion groups encourage interaction and self-expression. The topics discussed in these lively groups range from the weather to plans for trips to past experiences to sports and politics. Others enjoy listening to short stories, magazine articles, or romance novels read by staff. Some residents benefit most from activities that are rooted in their pre-Alzheimer's disease experiences; simple household tasks like making soup or folding laundry, which rely on long-term memory associations, enable them to maintain familiar routines that provide a sense of security.

Staff and residents

Staff members of traditional nursing homes are usually assigned to specific departments and particular positions. The responsibility for each of a resident's different activities—for example, recreation, music, or rehabilitation—may fall to a different specialist from the appropriate department. Consequently, a resident's contact time with a specialist may be intensive but limited. Between scheduled activities the resident may rest, read, write letters, or watch TV. For the frail elderly who are intellectually sound, this may be adequate. However, for residents with Alzheimer's disease whose ability to initiate self-directed activities is limited, other approaches are more suitable.

At the CDAC the continuity model places increased responsibility on both staff and residents. The same care giver who sees to the physical care of a small group of five or six residents also organizes activities based on those residents' abilities, needs, and interests. Activities are scheduled throughout the day and evening hours. Care givers adjust individual daily activity plans on the basis of the behavior of the group, the lucidity and physical abilities of each resident, and

other factors. For example, on a rainy day a care giver may postpone a walk to see the fall foliage and substitute an art project.

A guideline for recruiting employees at the CDAC is that they have no prior nursing-home work experience. This minimizes preconceived stereotypes about the elderly in general, and dementia in particular, that experienced employees might take to the center. To the CDAC the ability to relate to persons with Alzheimer's disease, to work effectively with them and family members, and to learn new approaches to nursing home care is more important than previous experience. Staff, who wear street clothes instead of uniforms, treat residents as individuals with specific needs rather than as a homogeneous group. All staff take part in an 80-hour orientation and training program.

Individuals in the early and intermediate stages of Alzheimer's disease—those who can still carry out some ordinary daily activities like eating, washing, or grooming—are most likely to benefit from residency at the CDAC. As of mid-1992 there were 23 full-time residents, 17 of whom were women. Ages ranged from 69 to 87, with an average of 80. The center can also accommodate a few day-care or overnight persons, depending on the needs of the full-time residents. All residents have an established diagnosis of probable Alzheimer's disease prior to admission and may receive further evaluation by staff from the Alzheimer's Center of the University Hospitals of Cleveland.

Research

Many institutions provide care to those afflicted with Alzheimer's disease, but few work systematically to learn more about the best methods of care. The CDAC combines both activities in a cooperative way. Its research center collaborates with the resident treatment team, sharing the latest information with staff while learning from them which care issues need more re-

Residents of a unit at the CDAC eat family style in the central dining area, sharing food prepared in the adjacent kitchen. The open architecture and closeness of the nourishment center to the private rooms help residents maintain continuity with their previous experience by providing them with some of the long-familiar sights, sounds, and smells of mealtimes at home. Encouraged to practice pertinent autonomy, residents may also help set tables, serve food, and clean up after meals.

Marguerite B. Campbell

Between mealtimes residents of the CDAC are reminded to eat with the aid of a specially designed transparent refrigerator, from which they may choose such nutritious snacks as fruit, juices, and yogurt.

search attention. Current research interests focus on those changes in the physical environment that may affect residents' activities of daily living like dressing, using the toilet, and wandering. Several recently completed projects illustrate how such research can be integrated with the continuity model.

Recognizing that incontinence is a common problem among Alzheimer's disease patients, the research center studied certain environmental features that could encourage independent toilet use. One project addressed two questions: is a visible toilet in the resident's bathroom more likely to be used than one usually hidden from view, and what types of identification signs help residents locate the public toilets?

To answer the first question, privacy curtains that screen the toilet area of each resident's room were left in either an open or a closed position for three weeks. The position then was reversed for the next three weeks. Observations were made hourly for six hours a day in each room to see if the toilet had been used. From nearly 2,600 observations the researchers learned that visible toilets were used seven times more often than concealed toilets.

To answer the second question, large signs with various colors, words, and picture cues were displayed to help residents find the public toilets in the central area of the building. Results indicated that a simple noun like *toilet* was more effective than either a compound word like *restroom* or a picture of a toilet. Signs on the floor that combined the world *toilet* with short directional arrows proved to be the most effective way of helping residents find the common toilets.

To test the importance of autonomy and independence to residents, a second project examined the ways in which locked and unlocked doors influenced residents' behavior. Initially, exit doors to the terrace were locked to prevent access to the outdoors. Later, unlocked doors gave residents the option of going outside during good weather or of remaining inside. Differences in residents' behavior were compared. When the doors were locked, residents walked, paced, wandered, and showed general agitation much more often than when the doors were unlocked. Although many residents decided not to go outside even when they could, the freedom to choose seemed to be significant in reducing stress and agitation.

Because ordinary activities of daily living are an important aspect of independent functioning, another project examined typical problems in dressing and the effectiveness of a specially modified closet design. It revealed that a closet that displayed clothing in the order in which it was to be put on increased the level of independence by 19%. The need for direct physical assistance was reduced by one-third to one-half, while the frequency with which residents dressed on their own in response to verbal prompts from staff increased—an indication that some residents became less dependent on physical assistance and were better able to dress themselves with simple verbal cues.

Yet another project tested the idea that establishing a daily pattern similar to a resident's former routine could help the person orient to the real world, help dispel periods of boredom, and enhance self-esteem by establishing links to the past. In this study residents were allowed to choose among familiar tasks like dusting, dishwashing, folding towels, and preparing simple food and among less familiar tasks like stuffing envelopes, putting paper in a binder, untangling coat hangers, and placing coins in a coin roll. Residents expressed clear preferences for the familiar. Moreover, they were able to concentrate better on familiar activities than on unfamiliar ones.

Until a cure is found

With a better understanding of the nature of cognitive disabilities has come an increased awareness of the needs of people with Alzheimer's disease. Until such time as the cause and cure for the affliction can be found, the physical, social, and psychological elements of a supportive environment must be integrated into the design and operation of nursing homes. The CDAC is demonstrating one way in which such institutions can respond to the current needs of their residents while looking to the future needs of the cognitively impaired and furthering essential research.

The booklet *Home Modifications: Responding to Dementia,* which describes changes in the home environment that families can make to ease the demands of care giving, may be obtained for $4.00 from The Research Center, Corinne Dolan Alzheimer Center, 12340 Bass Lake Road, Chardon, OH 04024-9364.

Genetics

In 1992 gene therapy passed from the realm of experimentation into the arena of clinical practice. By midyear there were several programs under way throughout the world in which the technique, which involves using DNA to treat disease, was incorporated into therapy for rare hereditary conditions, AIDS, and cancer. In other studies, gene therapy techniques were being used to assess the effectiveness of cancer treatment. Moreover, reports on the progress of the first gene therapy experiments, initiated at the U.S. National Institutes of Health (NIH) in 1990 and 1991, indicated that the therapy was proving both safe and effective.

Scientists continued to identify genes that are responsible for disease, including a genetic defect that causes one form of non-insulin-dependent diabetes and a gene that regulates lipoprotein production and is believed to play a part in atherosclerosis. Researchers studying three different conditions—the form of muscular dystrophy known as myotonic dystrophy, fragile X syndrome (the most common genetic cause of mental retardation), and the rare neurological disease called X-linked spinal and bulbar atrophy—discovered that the genes causing them have the ability to expand, adding numerous repetitions of the defective DNA sequence, when they are passed from one generation to another. Further, they found that the number of repetitions—and thus the length of the mutated DNA segment—correlates positively with the seriousness of the disorder, a discovery that could explain how it is possible that disease ranging from mild to severe can be seen in different members of an affected family.

Spanish hurdler María José Martínez Patiño was disqualified from world competition in 1985 when a chromosome test showed her to be genetically male. Most authorities opposed genetic screening of female competitors at the 1992 Olympics.

Peter Freed

Two recent studies added credence to the notion that homosexuality may have an organic, inheritable component. In the first, neuroscientist Simon LeVay of the Salk Institute in La Jolla, Calif., autopsied the brains of homosexual and heterosexual men and found an anatomic difference in a region believed to control sexual behavior. A short time later, researchers from Northwestern University, Evanston, Ill., and Boston University School of Medicine published the results of a two-year twin study that found that 52% of identical twin brothers of homosexual men were themselves homosexual, compared with 22% of nonidentical twins and 11% of genetically unrelated adoptive brothers.

Genetic tests became a focus of controversy as athletes assembled for the 1992 Olympic Games. Debate was touched off by the introduction of a new gender test for women athletes that screens for a gene for maleness. (It replaced a chromosomal analysis of the X and Y—or sex—chromosomes.) Although a few authorities still feel there is a need for some kind of sex-determination test for female competitors—to prevent men from impersonating women and competing unfairly against them—most felt that the use of genetic tests was unfair and stigmatizing for those who, although anatomically female, are chromosomally male. While the International Olympic Committee remained firmly in favor of the genetic screening, there was strong support for substitution of a standard that would determine sex simply on the basis of anatomic characteristics. The International Amateur Athletic Federation, the body that governs track and field sports, had already adopted such a criterion.

The following are some of the most newsworthy recent developments in the field of human genetics.

Gene therapy: new applications

In June 1992 researcher Gary J. Nabel and colleagues at the University of Michigan Medical Center initiated the first human experiment in which "naked" DNA was injected directly into a patient's body. All previous gene therapy experiments had involved removing cells from the body, treating them with viruses into which DNA had been inserted, and returning the altered cells to the patient.

The Michigan team is treating patients with advanced malignant melanoma—the most lethal form of skin cancer. Their protocol calls for inserting a gene for a transplantation antigen directly into the skin tumors. Transplantation antigens are molecules on the surface of the cells that act as each individual's molecular "identity card." The immune system is programmed to recognize cells bearing a certain combination of transplantation antigens as "self" and to identify cells with any other transplantation antigens as "nonself," or foreign. The immune system then mounts an attack on these foreign cells, the process that is responsible for the rejection of transplanted tissues.

The Michigan researchers believe that if they can cause tumor cells to produce the foreign antigen, the patient's immune system will be activated against the tumors and thus will destroy them. In earlier experiments in mice, the same researchers encased trillions of copies of an antigen-encoding gene in microscopic fat capsules called liposomes and injected the liposomes directly into cancerous skin tumors. Because they carry opposite electrical charges, the positively charged liposomes carry the genes directly to the negatively charged DNA in the cell, where the new genes are incorporated into the cell's genome. For treatment of human patients, the scientists chose the gene for HLA-B7, an antigen found in only 10% of the population and thus considered "foreign" in the remaining 90%.

The first studies in cancer patients, which involve injecting DNA into a single skin tumor, are not expected to arrest the disease. However, by removing and examining the tumors, the researchers will be able to tell how many cells have the HLA-B7 antigen—indicating a successful gene transfer—and whether they were attacked by the body's immune defenses.

In a second University of Michigan study, which also got under way in June 1992, a team headed by microbiologist James M. Wilson began using genetically altered liver cells to treat patients with the hereditary disease called familial hypercholesterolemia (FH), which predisposes to early coronary heart disease. Each of the patients chosen for the treatment must have the most severe form of the disease, in which blood cholesterol levels exceed 700 mg/dL and coronary artery disease develops in childhood. People with this form of FH have a pair of defective genes for the low-density lipoprotein (LDL) receptor. This is a molecule on the cell surface responsible for ferrying LDL cholesterol—the so-called bad cholesterol—out of the blood. As a result, their bodies are unable to remove cholesterol from the bloodstream, and it accumulates in fatty deposits inside the vessel walls, eventually blocking blood flow.

Because the liver is the body's principal cholesterol-removing organ, as well as the only organ with the capacity to regenerate itself, Wilson and colleagues decided to use liver cells in their experiment. Their procedure calls for removing a small portion of the patient's liver and treating it with an enzyme to release individual cells. The liver cells are then maintained in culture and infected with a retrovirus whose harmful genes have been replaced with the normal LDL-receptor gene. After a few days the cells are tested to see if they contain the receptor gene. Cells that bear the LDL receptor are infused back into the liver through a catheter inserted in the patient's hepatic vein, the major blood vessel leading to the liver. On the basis of earlier experiments in a strain of rabbit that also has defective LDL-receptor genes, the researchers expect that the genetically modified liver cells will remove approximately 10% of the cholesterol from the patients' blood.

Another gene therapy study scheduled to begin in 1992 is one at the University of Washington involving patients who are infected with HIV (human immunodeficiency virus), the virus that causes AIDS. The patients will first receive high doses of radiation to destroy HIV-infected lymphocytes. Because the radiation will destroy healthy blood cells as well, the patients will be given bone marrow transplants containing cells capable of reconstituting the blood system. As part of the transplant procedure, they will be treated with extra doses of CD8 cells (a specialized type of lymphocyte), which will carry a copy of a gene that will transform the cells into a biological equivalent of kamikaze pilots. The gene will trigger the release of herpes simplex thymidine kinase, a "suicide" enzyme that should destroy the treated cells if they attack cells other than those infected with HIV.

In December 1991 physicians in Shanghai began gene therapy treatments on two patients with hemophilia B, a bleeding disorder caused by a deficiency of a blood-clotting agent called factor IX. The treatment involved removing skin cells called fibroblasts from the patients and infecting the cells with a retrovirus containing the gene that controls production of factor IX. Once they had begun to secrete factor IX, the modified cells were injected back into the patients' skin.

Gene therapy: ongoing projects

Physicians at many centers are continuing to employ inserted genes as markers to gauge the effectiveness of treatments for cancer and other diseases. Clinical trials under way at St. Jude's Children's Research Hospital in Memphis, Tenn., M.D. Anderson Cancer Center in Houston, Texas, and the University of Indiana Medical Center in Indianapolis tested the ability of such markers to track the progress of the cancer treatment known as autologous bone marrow transplantation. In this procedure doctors take samples of a patient's bone marrow and treat the marrow to kill any cancer cells that might be present. They then give the patient chemotherapy and radiation at doses high enough to kill most of the remaining tumors in their bodies. Because extremely high-dose chemotherapy destroys bone marrow function, and thus the patient's immunity, the treated, presumably cancer-free bone marrow is reinfused to restore immune function.

Even with such aggressive treatment, however, patients often suffer recurrences. Yet it is impossible to tell whether the tumors that develop after the bone marrow transplant are generated by cancer cells not eradicated during radiation and chemotherapy or by cancer cells not purged from the reinfused bone marrow. To provide at least a partial answer to this ques-

"We finished the genome map, now we can't figure out how to fold it!"

tion, researchers will insert a gene that is resistant to the drug neomycin into the marrow cells before they are returned to the body. If the cancer recurs, they will remove some tumor cells and examine them for the gene. If the neomycin-resistant gene is found in tumor cells, the scientists will know that the tumor originated in the reinfused marrow and that more aggressive approaches to purging the marrow of cancer cells are needed. However, because it is impossible to get the marker gene into every marrow cell, the gene may not be present in every tumor cell; thus, the usefulness of this tracking method is limited.

In May 1992 W. French Anderson of the National Heart, Lung, and Blood Institute reported that the first two patients to receive gene therapy for severe combined immunodeficiency syndrome were doing well and had no significant side effects from treatment. Both patients—girls who were aged 6 and 10 when they began the therapy in 1990 and early 1991, respectively—lack functioning genes to make the enzyme adenosine deaminase (ADA), which is necessary for the activation of T-lymphocytes, the white blood cells that coordinate the body's immune response. The youngsters are being treated through a process in which their lymphocytes are withdrawn, injected with a virus carrying the ADA gene, and infused back into blood circulation. Since they have been receiving the ADA-bolstered lymphocytes, supplemented by injections of the ADA-containing drug pegademase, both girls have been able to attend public school and have not suffered an unusual number of infections.

However, laboratory tests have indicated that the girls' lymphocytes cannot respond to foreign substances they have not encountered before—something that the normal, healthy immune system can do. The researchers speculate that the reduced immune response is due to the fact that only mature T-cells, which cannot be provoked to respond to new substances, are receiving the ADA gene. To correct this problem, Anderson and colleagues plan to modify the treatment by identifying stem cells—precursor cells capable of diversifying into many types of blood cells—and supplying them with copies of the ADA gene. If this treatment is successful, it should not only increase the girls' immune function, because the gene will be present in a self-perpetuating blood cell, but also reduce the number of treatments that are necessary.

Prenatal diagnosis: innovative blood test

In October 1991, at the Eighth International Congress of Human Genetics, genetic researchers reported the development of a test by which a pregnant woman's blood can be screened to determine if her unborn child has certain genetic defects. The procedure, which involves isolating and analyzing the few fetal blood cells circulating in the mother's bloodstream, can detect chromosomal abnormalities in the first trimester of pregnancy. Because it requires only a routine blood test, it does not carry the 1–2% risk of fetal death associated with the two currently employed prenatal tests, amniocentesis and chorionic villus sampling (CVS).

The new procedure, developed by investigators at the University of Tennessee in Nashville and the University of California at San Francisco, relies on identifying fetal red blood cells. The test involves first treating the mother's blood sample to remove all the lymphocytes. Then fluorescently labeled antibodies are added to the remaining sample, which consists largely of red blood cells. The antibodies seek out two proteins, transferrin and glycophorin, that are more plentiful in fetal red cells than in maternal cells. The sample is then fed into a cell sorter, a device that separates the fluorescent cells from the other red cells. Technicians can double-check that the cells are of fetal rather than maternal origin because unlike mature red blood cells, in which no nuclei are present, fetal cells still have nuclei. The next step is to extract the DNA from these fetal cells, just as would be done with DNA from cells collected by amniocentesis or CVS, and analyze it for known genetic defects.

In early studies researchers at the two centers reported that they had used the technique to predict the sex of 41 fetuses of women who subsequently had amniocentesis or CVS. The results of the latter procedures confirmed that they made only one error. They also discovered one genetic abnormality, a fetus that had three copies of chromosome 18 (trisomy 18), in that sample. Another team, comprising researchers from Harvard Medical School and two Boston-area biotechnology companies, Genzyme and Integrated Genetics, reported that they had used the technique to identify Down syndrome, a diagnosis that was later confirmed by CVS. Although the technique is non-

Photographs from James H. Asher, Jr., and Thomas B. Friedman, "Mouse and Hamster Mutants as Models for Waardenburg Syndromes in Humans," *Journal of Medical Genetics,* vol. 27 (1990), pp. 618–626

A mother and daughter with Waardenburg syndrome exhibit several physical features that are typical of the syndrome. In 1992 geneticists identified the gene responsible for the condition, which is the most common heritable cause of deafness. In addition to hearing impairment, which affects about 20% of those who have the syndrome, other characteristics that can occur include a white forelock, widely spaced eyes, and unmatched eye colors.

invasive, less expensive, and less risky than either amniocentesis or CVS, for the present it is not expected to replace those procedures until large-scale studies have proved that it is a comparable diagnostic tool. The researchers predict that for the present it is more likely to be used to identify women who should undergo amniocentesis or CVS.

DNA fingerprinting: a reprieve

In April 1992 a panel convened by the U.S. National Academy of Sciences (NAS) advised that DNA fingerprinting, if properly performed, should be admissible as evidence in criminal cases. The technique, which has made it possible to match DNA samples from blood, hair, skin, and semen taken from the scene of a crime with DNA samples from suspects, has been in forensic use for several years. However, its admissibility as evidence has been determined on a case-by-case basis. The NAS panel's recommendation is expected to standardize DNA analysis sufficiently to make DNA "fingerprints" as universally acceptable as the conventional kind.

Creating a DNA fingerprint entails subjecting a sample of DNA to enzymes that function as chemical scissors, cutting the long strands of DNA into smaller segments. The enzymes are designed to snip at specific points that mark the boundaries of regions of DNA called variable numbers of tandem repeats (VNTRs). These are stretches that contain a sequence of DNA bases (the chemical subunits of DNA) repeated several times. VNTRs are found in regions of DNA between genes and thus do not code for proteins. The number of times they repeat—and thus their length—varies widely among individuals; while one person may have only two repetitions of a particular sequence, another may have scores. The wide variability in lengths of VNTRs makes it possible to distinguish among DNA samples from different people.

The debate over admitting DNA fingerprints in court centered on questions of mathematical odds and probabilities. The use of DNA fingerprints for identification purposes rests on the fact that the odds against any two randomly selected people sharing the same collection of VNTR fragments are in the millions. They

are significantly reduced, however, if the two people in question are selected from the same ethnic group. VNTRs, like eye color and a variety of other traits, are more likely to be shared by people who have common ancestors. Several population geneticists argued that in some segments of the population, the frequency of certain VNTRs is quite different from that in the population at large. For example while the chance of any two people in the population having exactly 27 repetitions of a particular DNA base sequence may be one in 10,000, the chance for two Americans of Irish descent may be as low as one in 200. Thus, the geneticists asserted, VNTRs should not be used as legal evidence until studies had been conducted to determine the exact frequency of the markers in all segments of the population, a process that would take 10 to 15 years. Others argued that the technique of DNA fingerprinting is still basically reliable and is too valuable to be shelved for a decade.

As a compromise, the NAS panel recommended sampling DNA taken from 100 members of 15 to 20 ethnic groups and calculating the frequencies for each group of the VNTRs most commonly used in DNA fingerprinting. Scientists would then reconstruct the odds in terms of the highest frequency—*i.e.,* the greatest likelihood of a chance match—in each of the groups. It was believed that this approach would reduce the likelihood of false matches without interfering with the rate of authentic matches. The panel also recommended the adoption of universal standards for laboratory tests and a system for certification of technicians who do DNA fingerprinting.

Disease-causing genes: new suspects identified

In October 1991 scientists at Baylor College of Medicine in Houston reported that they had located the gene responsible for Kallmann syndrome, a disorder that affects approximately one in every 10,000 persons. Affected individuals are usually male. The manifestations of Kallmann syndrome are varied and may include abnormal development of male genitalia, absence of the sense of smell, nervous system malfunction, and kidney malformations. The gene, located on the X (or female) chromosome, is active in a fetal cell that eventually differentiates into two types of cells. One releases hormones necessary for genital development; the other forms olfactory nerves that transmit signals from odors to the brain. The discovery will make it possible for scientists to develop a genetic test to diagnose the disorder and thus will enable physicians to begin hormone treatments in young patients, ensuring normal genital development.

In February 1992 geneticists at Boston University School of Medicine reported that they had identified the genetic defect responsible for Waardenburg syndrome, the most common cause of inherited deafness. Approximately 20% of those who have the syndrome are deaf. Other characteristics include unusually widely spaced eyes, a shock of white hair over the forehead, and unmatched eye colors. The researchers determined that Waardenburg syndrome originates with an alteration in a single DNA base in a gene on chromosome 2. This gene regulates the production of a DNA-binding protein that attaches to other genes to control their activity. This discovery should enable scientists to gain a better understanding of deafness and may lead to the development of a prenatal diagnostic test for the syndrome. Diagnosing the disease before birth or in early infancy would enable parents to begin special education programs to prevent the development of the learning disorders that often accompany unrecognized deafness.

Genes and cancer

Two recently reported studies shed light on how genes may be affected by environmental carcinogens. In November 1991 researchers at Yale University School of Medicine announced that they had found DNA mutations in tumor cells taken from patients with skin cancer apparently caused by overexposure to the sun. The mutations occurred in a gene called p53, which in its normal state is thought to repress tumor formation. When the researchers examined skin tumors from 24 U.S. and Swedish patients, they found that a majority contained a particular type of mutation in the p53 gene that was identical to a mutation produced by ultraviolet radiation in laboratory experiments. By counting the number of times a characteristic mutation has occurred in tumor cells, they hope to be able to determine the length of time from sun exposure to carcinogenesis.

In a highly publicized report published in December 1991, researchers at the University of North Carolina announced that women who are carriers of the gene responsible for ataxia-telangiectasia (A-T), a rare nervous system disorder, have a heightened risk of breast cancer when exposed to even low doses of radiation. A-T affects both sexes; it occurs in one in 100,000 people, but one in 5,000 is a carrier. People who have the disease inherit a pair of defective genes (the culprit gene has yet to be identified); they are also known to have a high rate of radiation-induced cancer. The researchers wanted to know whether radiation exposure increased the risk of cancer in A-T carriers, people who have one defective A-T gene and one normal one. They first compared the incidence of cancer among relatives of people with A-T, who supposedly carried only one gene for the disorder, and their spouses, who presumably had no A-T genes. They found that the A-T carriers were three to four times more likely to develop cancer than their spouses. They further determined that women A-T carriers who had been exposed to even relatively low doses of radiation from standard diagnostic X-rays were six times more likely

Mapping the human genome: progress report

chromosome	1	2	3	4	5	6	7	8	9	10	11	12
estimated number of genes	4,150	3,950	3,200	3,050	2,900	2,750	2,700	2,250	2,200	2,200	2,200	2,050
number mapped	234	133	78	100	89	136	109	61	72	69	143	119
number disease related	56	25	25	25	23	27	25	22	26	15	47	23

chromosome	13	14	15	16	17	18	19	20	21	22	X	Y
estimated number of genes	1,800	1,750	1,650	1,400	1,350	1,250	1,150	1,050	900	950	2,350	*
number mapped	31	73	62	80	128	29	111	39	32	51	244	16
number disease related	13	21	17	17	26	9	24	14	8	17	111	1

*unknown; has very few genes other than that for testis-determining factor

From Victor A. McKusick and Joanna S. Amberger, "The Human Gene Map: A Synopsis," Online *Mendelian Inheritance in Man,* Johns Hopkins University, Aug. 12, 1992

Randy Santos—Randolph Photography

J. Craig Venter, a U.S. researcher credited with having developed a rapid method of isolating and sequencing DNA fragments, found himself at the center of a scientific furor in 1992. The National Institutes of Health filed for patents on the newly identified DNA fragments, presumably so that the corresponding genes and their products could eventually be commercially licensed. This action was denounced by many in the field, who questioned both the legality and the practicality of such patent claims.

to develop breast cancer than were carriers who had not been exposed to X-rays. Because as many as one million American women are thought to be A-T carriers, the investigators estimate that the gene may account for 7 to 14% of all U.S. breast cancer cases.

Human Genome Project: year two

As the Human Genome Project—the international effort to determine the sequence of the three billion individual DNA bases that constitute human DNA and to arrange in order the 100,000 genes in the human genome—completed its second year, the scientific progress was often eclipsed by political squabbling. Since the program's earliest stages, researchers have debated whether the best approach was to first isolate genes and then determine the sequence of the bases they comprise or to sequence the entire genome and then try to identify the bases that make up the individual genes. Although the major advances in sequencing technology suggested the latter approach, the difficulty of separating the 5% of DNA bases that encode genes from the remainder—to winnow out the genetic chaff—seemed insurmountable. In October 1991 at the Human Genome III meeting in San Diego, Calif., researchers from the Oak Ridge (Tenn.) National Laboratory reported that they may have found a solution: a computer program called GRAIL, which employs artificial intelligence to identify the coding regions in a DNA sequence. The program employs a problem-solving system that "learns" by trial-and-error. By feeding the program hundreds of examples of both coding and noncoding DNA sequences, the researchers "trained" the program to distinguish coding regions. In early tests GRAIL was able to correctly locate 90% of the coding regions in 19 human genes; it misidentified only 20% of noncoding regions.

Although sequencing was proceeding at a faster-than-expected pace, many scientists involved in the project were outraged at the way the resultant data

were handled. In a highly controversial action in September 1991, the NIH applied for patents on hundreds of unidentified gene fragments that molecular biologist J. Craig Venter had isolated while doing research for the project. The NIH's action was criticized by several scientists, including James D. Watson, codiscoverer of the molecular structure of DNA and then director of the NIH Center for Human Genome Research, who argued that the information was in the international public domain. On the other hand, NIH director Bernadine Healy argued that patent protection was necessary if the discoveries were to be commercially developed into medically useful products. In the wake of this dispute and several other disagreements between himself and Healy, Watson resigned his post in April 1992. Michael M. Gottesman of the National Cancer Institute was named acting director until a permanent successor to Watson could be named. Meanwhile, researchers from the Medical Research Council of the U.K., who initially condemned the NIH's action, filed patent applications for more than 1,000 gene fragments that they had isolated.

—*Beverly Merz*

Health Policy

During 1992 election campaigns, candidates across the U.S. seized upon health care as an issue whose time had come. Many even seemed to consider it a new issue. However, the realization that the country's health care system is in serious trouble is not new.

Health care in crisis: a recent history

In the early 1970s then president Richard Nixon declared a "crisis" in the country's health care system. That particular declaration came after health costs had already been rising precipitously for years and lack of access to care for the poor had become a matter of national concern. Especially in the business community, cost increases had begun to cause widespread alarm as health benefits began to take larger and larger chunks out of profits.

Under the leadership of Paul M. Ellwood, Jr., a physician and health policy analyst, who founded the Minneapolis, Minn.-based think tank Interstudy, Nixon and his advisers came up with the health maintenance organization (HMO) model of prepaid health insurance. The HMO model is premised on the notion that the traditional model of retrospective reimbursement—a patient receives care, then sends the bill to his or her insurance company—is unnecessarily costly. If providers are reimbursed by their patients' insurance companies for virtually any medical care they give, neither providers nor patients have any incentive to think about cutting costs or being more efficient.

According to Ellwood's prepayment scheme, which now includes HMOs, preferred provider organizations (PPOs), and other variations on what has come to be known as the "managed care model" of health care delivery, the insured individual pays a fixed contract fee in advance, then receives care as needed from physicians, hospitals, or other providers. These providers are usually drawn from a list of participants in a particular managed care plan. The provider profits if services rendered cost less than the prepaid revenues; the incentive, therefore, is for the provider to keep costs down. The patient sacrifices a certain amount of freedom of choice for the ostensible cost savings down the road.

In 1983 the federal government fell into step behind the private sector by initiating the prospective payment system (PPS) under Medicare. (Medicare is the federally administered program of compulsory health insurance that covers acute care and hospital and physician services for most Americans 65 years of age and over.) Under PPS, patients are assigned to a so-called diagnosis-related group (DRG), reflecting their diagnosis and the prescribed treatment. There are several hundred established DRGs that are used to delineate the maximum allowable payment for each medical condition. A hospital bills the federal government for the Medicare cases it has seen over a particular time period and is paid according to the DRGs into which those patients have been assigned. Patients under PPS are not required to select from a predesignated group of providers. Again, the incentive behind this major cost-containment initiative of the 1980s was efficiency. Under PPS a hospital is motivated to minimize the length of patients' stays, to utilize the least expensive possible treatment procedures and technologies, and to attract a high volume of short-stay, minimum-intervention cases.

Continuing cost escalation

However, prepayment, whether through federally defined PPS or private sector managed care, has not alleviated escalating health costs. Hospitals and physicians have widely claimed that the DRG system under PPS is unfair; poorer patients, who tend to be sicker for longer periods of time than their more affluent counterparts, often exceed the limitations of DRGs in terms of the intensity of care they require. This is an especially serious issue for hospitals that treat large numbers of high-risk patients since it has proved difficult to factor severity of illness into the calculus used to compute DRG payment ceilings.

Since the 1970s, when the managed care strategy was first envisioned, health care expenditures have escalated to over 12% of the gross national product. National expenditures for health care increased by approximately $580 billion between 1960 (when they

Delegates to the July 1992 Democratic national convention in New York City show their support for affordable health care for families. A frequently reiterated theme of the four-day convention was that affordable quality health care should be available to all Americans—not as a privilege but as a right.

In New York City in the South Bronx, patients wait for care in the walk-in clinic of Lincoln Hospital, which serves what has been described as "one of the most medically desperate communities in the country." Like many local community hospitals in the United States, Lincoln has had to drastically curtail its services to the poor and uninsured. If economic pressures force the clinic to close, many community residents now receiving primary care will receive no treatment at all until they are seriously ill; the hospital's executive director has said that "the absolute bottom line is that more people in this community will die."

totaled $30 billion) and 1990 (when they totaled $610 billion). Furthermore, it is apparent that neither the public sector nor the private sector has had success in holding down costs; in the 1980s health care expenditures of private insurers, Medicare, and Medicaid (the federally administered, state-financed system that pays for care for economically disadvantaged people who meet state-determined eligibility criteria) all rose at approximately the same rates as the overall health expenditure.

The medically indigent: a growing population

Despite these high expenditures, health care is not readily accessible to vast numbers of Americans. Although estimates vary, it is generally accepted among health policy analysts that between 35 million and 40 million Americans either have no health insurance or are inadequately insured. *Medical indigence* is the term used for a lack of health insurance and the inability to afford health care; like *homelessness,* it describes a condition that less than 25 years ago would have been considered unimaginable for most Americans.

Surprisingly, the vast majority of medically indigent persons in the United States are employed. In 1988 it was reported that approximately 78.3% of all uninsured people under age 65 were employed or were family members of an employed individual. The majority (76%) were employed by firms or companies with fewer than 100 employees, and 60% worked for businesses with fewer than 25 employees. The majority of medically indigent persons were also low wage earners; 77% earned less than $10 an hour, and 38% earned less than $5 an hour. These data reflect a disturbing new pattern of employment in the U.S.—one that is leaving more and more people without any insurance; moreover, the data illustrate the growing inability of the country's economy to sustain the current health care system.

"Deindustrialization" of the U.S. economy has led to a large-scale shift in employment structure, especially in older "rust belt" cities, such as Detroit, Mich., and Youngstown, Ohio. As well-paying, unionized blue-collar jobs have disappeared, workers have increasingly been forced to take less lucrative employment in the service and information industries (*e.g.,* in fast-food businesses and data processing). Most of these jobs are nonunion and do not include health insurance as a benefit. Other workers have become self-employed, often in hazardous occupations such as construction. They may earn moderately good incomes, but the risky nature of their work makes health insurance unattainable or prohibitively costly.

The human cost

In the U.S. access to health care depends on financial resources more than it does in any other industrialized nation. The U.S. and South Africa are the only developed countries without some form of national health insurance or national health care system. The poor are at risk for a wide range of health problems: some are associated with the condition of poverty; others are a direct result of the difficulty poor people experience in obtaining treatment.

Of the world's major industrialized countries, more than half have higher rates of longevity (defined as life expectancy at birth) and lower rates of infant mortality (deaths during the first year of life) than the United States. Among the nation's poor and nonwhite populations, life expectancy rates are even lower and infant mortality rates higher than among the general population. Notably, black infant mortality rates are nearly double those of white infants. This discrepancy is, in large measure, due to the fact that blacks and other minorities in the United States receive less prenatal care—which has been shown conclusively to be vital to the health and well-being of infants—than their white counterparts.

311

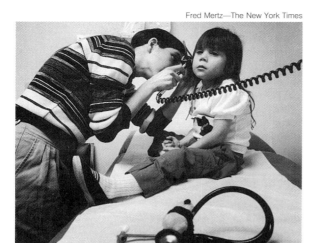

A young patient with an ear infection is examined at the Maxicare clinic in Oakland, California. In early 1992 the clinic closed its doors, leaving thousands of patients on public assistance without ready access to health care.

In 1990 Thomas A. LaVeist of the Johns Hopkins University School of Hygiene and Public Health, Baltimore, Md., reported in the *Journal of Public Health Policy* that the postneonatal mortality rate (percentage of all infant deaths occurring between the first and 12th months of life) for all infants in the U.S. declined throughout most of the 20th century but had increased steadily since 1970. During this time, however, the mortality rate for white infants has been maintained at a level approximating the average for all industrialized societies, while African-American rates have been drastically higher, approximating those in some less developed nations. LaVeist went on to show a statistical correlation between poverty rates and infant mortality, indicating that poverty is directly responsible for the vast majority of this black-white discrepancy. It is also of consequence that minorities and women are overrepresented in low-paying, nonunionized service jobs in deindustrialized urban areas, putting them at high risk for medical indigence.

Other studies have shown that these discrepancies between rich and poor occur for a wide variety of health conditions. It was recently reported in the *Journal of the American Medical Association* that survival rates after surgery for cardiovascular disease are largely dependent on income level; individuals in households with annual incomes of $40,000 or greater have an average five-year survival rate of 0.91, compared with a rate of 0.76 for those in households with incomes below $10,000.

Hospitals in crisis, lives at stake

Hospitals in the U.S. have also been hard hit by economic stress. Not only is the future financial viability of the hospital industry threatened, but this situation

has serious implications for public health. The urban poor are those who are most affected.

The 1980s saw drastic changes in the institutional structure of the U.S. health care industry, many directly related to the spiraling costs and growing insurance crisis outlined above. Economic pressure on local community hospitals has forced many to drastically curtail their services to the poor and uninsured; some have closed altogether. As early as 1983, many inner-city communities had lost all or most of their hospitals.

Hospital closures follow racial and economic patterns similar to those that affect individuals' access to care. Recent research has shown that urban communities at highest risk for losing their hospitals are those with greater numbers of African-American residents. In these same urban communities, the hospitals most at risk of closure are freestanding, for-profit institutions with limited capital for purchasing costly technology and diversifying services. (For both urban and rural hospitals, membership in a multi-institutional health care system appears to protect against such closures.)

The present cost crisis faced by hospitals, insurers, and other health care providers is, on one hand, a "sign of the times." Thus, health care can be considered one more U.S. industry—not unlike the automobile and construction industries—reeling from economic hard times and cutting back production or services in order to maximize profits and try to stay afloat. On the other hand, such cutbacks in health care may have life-or-death consequences.

Hospitals in financial straits sometimes resort to the practice known as "patient dumping"—refusing to provide services to poor and uninsured patients and sending them to the nearest available public hospital, which is usually legally mandated to take them. Although some would argue that, in fact, public hospitals are meant to function as a "safety net" for the urban poor—to be the health care provider of last resort for patients unable to afford insurance—studies have shown that some patients are transferred at much higher rates than others; "dumping" affects black patients more often than white patients. Even more telling was a study conducted in Chicago that showed that poor pregnant women were at risk of being transferred to a public hospital while in active labor, a clear violation of the Consolidated Omnibus Budget Reconciliation Act (COBRA) of 1985.

Another consequence of patient dumping and hospital closures is that public hospitals, particularly public hospital emergency departments, are so overcrowded that indigent patients have to wait for an excessively long time to be seen. In fact, many patients, even seriously ill or injured ones, leave the hospital without ever being seen. In addition, many public hospitals have too few available in-patient beds to accommodate those who need to be admitted.

Responses to cost crisis

There have been a wide range of responses to the present crisis in health care. Health insurance providers have responded with a number of new strategies, some of them quite controversial. Most of the schemes are designed to increase participation in insurance plans while minimizing the risk to those plans.

Increasingly, insurance plans sold to employee groups have begun to depart from the traditional approach of charging universal rates. Instead, a number of companies are now charging different workers different rates according to their age, family status, length of employment, and health risk status. Workers with families often have to pay more for insurance than empty nesters; elderly workers may have to pay more than younger workers; and workers with perceived health risks (*e.g.,* smokers) may also be charged higher premiums. The ethic that formerly underlay group insurance was that all who are covered by a company's policy subsidized the risks of others—the young subsidized the old, the healthy subsidized the sick, and so forth. That ethic is now being replaced by an approach that focuses on individual rather than group risks.

Another insurance industry response to escalating costs of health care coverage has been to offer basic coverage ("bare-bones") policies, making insurance of some sort affordable to small businesses, many of which cannot afford more comprehensive plans. These bare-bones plans offer limited benefits and generally require greater out-of-pocket expenses on the part of the insured (higher monthly premiums and greater deductibles), and the plans often do not cover services such as mental health care or prescription drugs. For the most part, however, small businesses have not been eager to incur even these minimal expenses to insure their employees, and the future of bare-bones policies seems uncertain.

In this atmosphere of uncertainty and retrenchment on the part of health care providers, calls for increased public sector involvement in health care financing came initially from an unlikely source—the corporate world. Business leaders in the private sector have long contended that the federal government will eventually have to take an increased role in funding health care for the poor and uninsured. The role of the public sector, according to this argument, is to provide for those who cannot provide for themselves, thus reducing the financial stress on private providers and purchasers of care. This approach would ease the burden of providing free care on hospitals and reduce the rates employers have to pay to insure their workers. Meanwhile, private insurance would remain the dominant source of health care payment for those who could afford it.

National health care debate

Recently, however, there have been calls for an even more comprehensive federal role, and the extent to which the federal government should complement or replace the current role of the private insurance industry has become a major focus in the national health care debate. In fact, despite the confusing plethora of national health care proposals currently being debated—in early 1992 there were more than 30 health insurance bills before Congress—most can be seen as falling into one of two major categories: a "single-

Baker Hughes: multirate health insurance plan*	
worker	annual rate
not covered by company's insurance plan	$240 bonus
single nonsmoker who passes wellness checkup and selects the lowest benefit plan	$84 ($100 rebate)
married smoker with uninsured spouse and children who fails wellness checkup and selects the highest benefit plan	$1,080
early retiree with 20 years' service and no dependents who passes wellness checkup and selects the lowest benefit plan	$156 ($100 rebate)
early retiree with 10 years' service and an uninsured spouse who fails wellness checkup and selects the highest benefit plan	$2,292

*sample employee rates

Source: Baker Hughes Inc.

Company health insurance policies traditionally spread costs equally among all employees. Now, however, many companies are beginning to charge different rates for different workers. An example of such a policy is that of Baker Hughes Inc., an oilfield services company in Houston, Texas, with 12,000 U.S. employees. A variety of benefit plans, with varying deductibles, are offered. The company gives nonsmokers and those who pass a "wellness checkup" a rebate; smokers, on the other hand, pay a surcharge. Rates for early retirees depend on how long they have been with the company. Those covered by a spouse's plan receive a bonus.

payer" system of nationalized health insurance or a "multipayer" system under which the federal government would take a more active role in guaranteeing coverage for the poor and uninsured but with current private sector mechanisms of financing health care remaining largely in place.

Advocates of a single-payer system—a system under which the federal government would be the sole source of health insurance, replacing or significantly reducing the role of the private sector—argue that only if the profit motive is eliminated from health care, or at least drastically reduced, will the poor and indigent be guaranteed coverage. According to this view, the for-profit insurance industry stands as an obstacle to a viable system of coverage and, therefore, the financial structure of U.S. health care must undergo significant change. Most single-payer plans mandate that the entire population be covered. They strive to eliminate financial barriers (deductibles, copayments, and extra charges by providers). Financing would be provided by the federal government and states, usually on a prospective payment basis. Most of these proposals place a strong emphasis on disease prevention and health promotion.

The proposed single-payer systems share a common goal of making government the primary insurer for health care and of expanding access to include as many people as possible, regardless of income or employment status. Alternatively, proposed multipayer plans would maintain the current structure of health care finance but provide incentives or mandates that would guarantee coverage for most working Americans. Advocates of multipayer plans suggest that single-payer plans do not provide necessary mechanisms for cost control. They feel that the business, or private, sector must be included in any national health care policy because it is in business' self-interest to lower the cost of insuring workers. They fear that the establishment of a new federal bureau-

cracy to administer health insurance would be cumbersome, inflationary, and inefficient. They also fear the political and economic repercussions of gutting the multibillion-dollar insurance industry, especially in times of nationwide economic slowdown.

An example of such a multipayer plan is the "prescription for reform" proposed in the Oct. 7, 1991, issue of *Business Week*. A variation on the system of "managed competition" originally conceived by Stanford University economist Alain C. Enthoven, *Business Week*'s proposal was structured around the idea that small businesses need help insuring their workers, whereas larger firms generally can afford commercial health insurance. Under this system, all employers with more than 100 workers would be required to purchase health insurance for their employees. Smaller firms, those with 100 or fewer employees, would pay a payroll tax to a health care purchasing corporation. These purchasing corporations would be regional not-for-profit agencies set up by the states to buy coverage from existing commercial insurance companies for small firms. The unemployed poor would continue to be covered by the federally administered Medicaid system; the elderly would be covered by Medicare; and workers not covered by public or private insurance, such as the self-employed, could purchase insurance directly from the purchasing corporation.

Commercial insurers would compete to sell insurance to the purchasing corporations, thereby keeping the market-oriented nature of the U.S. health care sector intact. In theory, this would keep costs down. A minimum acceptable benefits package would be mandated by the federal government; the employee would pay 20% of the cost of this basic package, and those who wanted higher benefits could pay higher premiums.

Variations on this theme include so-called pay-or-play models in which businesses would be required to either provide a basic insurance plan to full-time

Highly politicized issues in the current U.S. health care debate include the extent to which the federal government should complement or replace the private insurance industry and the role that the public sector (taxpayers) should play in providing for those who cannot afford to pay for themselves.

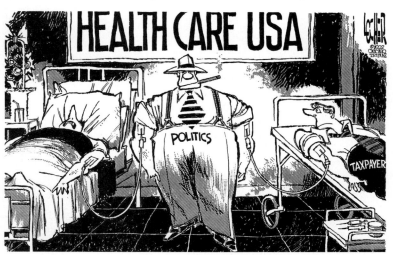

workers or pay into a state-wide pool that would finance health insurance for uncovered workers. Small businesses, fearing prohibitive costs, tend to be leery of such proposals. Conversely, advocates of single-payer plans feel that pay-or-play schemes are insufficient to address the health care needs of the poor, elderly, and unemployed. Moreover, they distrust the dominance of commercial insurers whose profit motive may be incompatible with the provision of what they see as a "social good."

Future of the debate

Some analysts feel that the current debate about universal health care, while long overdue, has obscured a vital element: many health problems have less to do with the adequacy or availability of medical care than with living conditions and personal habits that affect people's health.

Research has shown that a significant proportion of health problems can be addressed outside the medical care system. Smoking is the cause of one in every six deaths in the U.S.; in 1987, 87% of all deaths due to lung cancer, 82% of all deaths from chronic obstructive pulmonary disease, 21% of all deaths from heart disease, and 18% of all deaths caused by stroke were at least partly attributable to smoking.

Injuries and violence also take a huge toll, especially among nonwhites. In Maryland between 1980 and 1986, fully 30% of all deaths of nonwhite males between the ages of 15 and 34 were handgun related. Another 12% were due to other forms of "intentional injury" (*i.e.,* violence); 19% were due to unintentional injury (*i.e.,* accidents). Although few political aspirants have addressed such issues as smoking, handgun control, on-the-job safety, air pollution, and alcohol abuse as components of their health care reform proposals, these issues are increasingly becoming crucial to a meaningful debate on national health policy.

Within a relatively short time, health care policy has evolved from a topic that was once the province of academicians and policy analysts to one that is a matter of general public debate. The complexity of the alternative proposals, the dauntingly esoteric nature of the jargon of health care economics and financing, and public uncertainty about possible unintended consequences of even the most well-meaning proposals have led to a significant amount of frustration and confusion on the part of the general public and health policymakers alike. In a notable effort to gauge the public response to health care reform issues, Democrats in the House of Representatives held 285 "town meetings" with their constituents around the country on Jan. 14, 1992. Rep. Benjamin L. Cardin, speaking to residents in Towson, Md., near Baltimore, underscored the sentiment of politicians and highlighted what had emerged as a major 1992 campaign issue: "We know we have a national problem, we

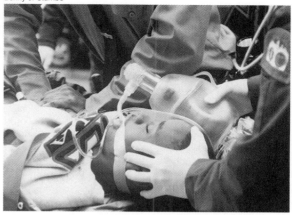

Paramedics attempt to save the life of a student, shot in the hallway of his New York City high school by another student in March 1992. Violence—particularly the toll it takes on nonwhites—is a public health issue that can no longer be ignored in the U.S.

know we have to do something about it, . . . three-quarters of the people in this country believe it's time for a radical change in our health care system."

Although much remains in doubt about the future direction of health care in the U.S., a few things are quite certain. It is clear that government will play a greater role in determining the structure and extent of health care financing. Escalating costs will increasingly affect both the quality and the quantity of health care. As the population ages and as social problems such as unemployment and poverty become more entrenched, access to care will become a matter of vital importance to greater numbers of Americans and will play a growing role in the national debate.

Eventually a balance will have to be struck between health care as a necessary social good and the health care industry as a financially viable private sector entity. Among the trade-offs that policymakers attempting to devise a workable solution to the current health care crisis will be forced to consider are: equity versus economic efficiency; consumer freedom of choice versus equal access to primary care; and cradle-to-grave high-technology medicine versus primary care, prevention, and palliative care for the terminally ill. Solutions to these and other difficult questions will have to be found before any long-range public health policies can be implemented.

With health care, as with many other present-day social realities, the American dream of limitless growth and wealth is slowly being replaced by a modified optimism that involves compromise, limitations, and sacrifice. As the *Business Week* "prescription for reform" concluded, "Those who yearn for the days of unlimited care at no cost and with no questions asked should stick to watching reruns of *Marcus Welby, M.D.*"

—David Whiteis, Ph.D.

315

The Gag Rule: Who Shall Be Silenced?

by George J. Annas, J.D., M.P.H.

For the past two decades some of the most important debates in U.S. health law have been waged over the bodies of American women. The abortion and "right-to-life" issues are only the most discussed examples. The two most widely publicized "right-to-die" cases, those of Karen Ann Quinlan (1976) and Nancy Cruzan (1990), also focused on women. Moreover, in the years between birth and death, women are the patients in almost 70% of all physician-patient encounters, and their experiences with intrauterine devices, breast implants, and a number of medications have helped shape an agenda for a review of the way drugs and medical devices are approved and monitored in the U.S. Women have also been leaders in the movement to change the way medical research priorities are set, demanding, among other things, more research on breast cancer and other diseases unique to women.

The outcomes on these issues affect all Americans, as either health care providers or patients, not just women. On its surface the U.S. Supreme Court's 1991 decision in *Rust* v. *Sullivan,* upholding the so-called gag rule, applied only to women, and to many observers it appeared to be simply another in a series of opinions designed primarily to limit abortion rights. But the decision in the Rust case has profound implications for the way the government views its obligations to the poor; it also has the potential to affect the nature of the doctor-patient relationship. Further, it raises the issue of federal funding that is conditional on the relinquishment of constitutional rights by those receiving the funds.

Evolution of the gag rule

In 1988 the U.S. Department of Health and Human Services (HHS) announced radically revised regulations governing the more than 4,000 family-planning clinics that had been receiving federal financing since 1970 under Title X of the Public Health Service Act. These clinics serve approximately four million poor women and girls, a large majority of them teenagers. The announced purpose of the regulations was to redefine what Congress meant by section 1008 of the act, which read: "None of the funds appropriated under this title shall be used in programs where abortion is a method of family planning." While Title X clinics had never been in the business of performing abortions, the administration of Pres. Ronald Reagan

wanted to prohibit them from making referrals for—or even discussing—abortion.

The 1988 revisions therefore directed that "a Title X project may not provide counseling concerning the use of abortion as a method of family planning." It is this provision that is usually called simply the "gag rule"; the regulations state that if a pregnant woman herself requests information on abortion, it is permissible to tell her that the clinic "does not consider abortion an appropriate method of family planning and therefore does not counsel or refer for abortion." The regulations were almost immediately declared unconstitutional by two U.S. circuit courts of appeal. Another circuit court, however, found them constitutionally acceptable, and in May 1991 the U.S. Supreme Court, in a five-to-four decision, agreed.

The Supreme Court was faced with two questions in *Rust* v. *Sullivan,* in which Irving Rust, medical director of a Title X Planned Parenthood-run clinic in the South Bronx, N.Y., alleged that HHS regulations (the agency was represented in the case by Secretary Louis W. Sullivan) violated free-speech rights of doctors and patients: (1) Did the revised 1988 regulations reflect the original congressional intent? (2) Were they constitutional? If the regulations were struck down as an implausible interpretation of the earlier statute set forth by Congress, thus amounting to an abuse of discretion on the part of HHS, the question of constitutionality would not arise.

What the majority said—and what that implies

In stating the opinion of the five-justice majority, Chief Justice William Rehnquist made the case appear quite straightforward. As to the first issue, he noted that the language of section 1008 is very broad and thus provided HHS with almost unlimited freedom to interpret its meaning. Furthermore, he found (as other courts had) that the legislative history of the 1970 statute was "ambiguous" and that it was therefore difficult to determine what Congress had intended when passing the law. In such a circumstance, the court found it reasonable to defer to the expertise of HHS, giving the agency license to determine what the law meant.

The constitutional issues were treated by the majority as being equally uncomplicated. The court had previously held that the government may not erect a "barrier" to prevent citizens from exercising their con-

In July 1991 demonstrators in Washington, D.C., graphically express their displeasure over the Supreme Court's decision to ban abortion counseling in federally funded clinics. Those who oppose the so-called gag rule emphasize the distinction between prohibiting an action—in this case, the performing of abortions—and limiting people's right to discuss it.

stitutional rights. On the other hand, the government may pay for one constitutionally protected activity, such as childbirth, yet refuse to fund another protected activity, such as abortion. As an analogy, Justice Rehnquist noted that Congress could constitutionally establish a National Endowment for Democracy to encourage other countries to adopt democratic principles without financing organizations to promote Communism and fascism. But can the government prohibit physicians from *saying* certain things to patients—as opposed to engaging in certain activities—in a federally funded clinic? The court concluded that it may.

A further question was whether the government can constitutionally promote childbirth over abortion by restricting the content of conversations in the context of a doctor-patient relationship that is funded partially by the government. The court conceded that it is possible that the doctor-patient relationship in general might be a "traditional relationship" and, as such, should be protected from government regulation under the First Amendment, "even when subsidized by the government." However, the court decided that it need not determine the constitutional status of the doctor-patient relationship in this case because the doctor-patient relationship in a Title X clinic (which offers only family-planning and related services) is not "sufficiently all-encompassing so as to justify an expectation on the part of the patient of comprehensive medical advice." In the court's view, if poor women are in fact unable to get abortion information elsewhere, it is because of their poverty and not because of any obstacle raised by the Title X regulations. According to this reasoning, poor women remain in the same position after *Rust* as they would have been in had the government not funded Title X clinics at all—*i.e.*, the government has done nothing to make their plight worse.

Dissenting view: regulate action, not speech

Four justices dissented; all agreed that there was no need to rule on the constitutional issues because the Title X statute could reasonably be interpreted simply as prohibiting the use of federal funds to perform abortions—not as prohibiting federally financed personnel from talking about them. However, Justice Harry Blackmun, in an opinion joined by Justices Thurgood Marshall and John Paul Stevens, also argued that the majority was wrong on the constitutional issues. In his view the regulations are the kind of "intrusive, ideologically based regulation of speech" that cannot be justified simply because the government is paying part of the cost.

In addition, Blackmun reasoned that by both forbidding conversation about abortion and simultaneously requiring referral for prenatal care, the regulations violate the pregnant woman's Fifth Amendment rights to make decisions about her pregnancy free from government interference. Thereby, wrote Blackmun, the government "places formidable obstacles in the path of Title X clients' freedom of choice." Justice Blackmun would also constitutionally protect the doctor-patient relationship on the basis that it "embodies a unique relationship of trust," in which physicians provide patients with "guidance, professional judgment, and vital emotional support," involving not only their health but "often their very lives."

Beyond *Rust*

It might be thought that the decision in the Rust case applies only when doctors talk to female patients about abortion in clinics that are funded by the federal government. Legal rulings cannot be so easily confined, however, and the opinion provides precedent giving Congress and the executive branch the constitutional authority to limit what doctors can say to their patients whenever the encounter between the two is being paid for wholly or partly by the government.

Even more central to an understanding of the Rust decision is what it revealed about the government's attitude toward the poor and the doctor-patient relationship. Poverty (unlike race, religion, and national

317

origin) does not fit the legal definition of a "suspect classification." When a law will predominantly affect people of a certain race, religion, or ethnic background, courts must generally consider the classification "suspect" and will therefore closely scrutinize the law's purpose. In the absence of a compelling justification, such a law denies the group equal protection under the law, as guaranteed them by the Constitution. This is not the case, however, when a law will apply primarily to people of lower socioeconomic status. Thus, legislation that affects the poor as a group has not been subjected to a high degree of scrutiny by the courts. On the other hand, as Justice Thurgood Marshall had argued passionately in the past, the court should not use poverty's lesser legal standing to completely ignore what is happening in the real world. In Marshall's words, "It is perfectly proper for judges to disagree about what the Constitution requires. But it is disgraceful for an interpretation of the Constitution to be premised upon unfounded assumptions about how people live."

The Rust opinion, based as it is largely on the false assumption that poor women will have access to responsive, understanding physicians outside the setting of the family-planning clinic, is untenable in its application to the real world of these women. In this sense the decision supported the perpetuation of a two-tiered health care system in which poor people and minorities are disproportionately represented in the lower tier. The fact that such a system is not unconstitutional does not justify the court's implying that its decision will not directly affect the constitutionally protected choices of poor women.

On the other important issue, the nature of the doctor-patient relationship, the majority opinion raises many more questions than it resolves. The court's description of the doctor-patient relationship, like its view of poor women's health resources, seems highly unrealistic. If physicians are told that in a given setting they have a restricted (not "sufficiently all-encompassing") relationship with their patients, does this mean that they cannot convey certain medical information to them? And whose "expectation" does the majority opinion refer to? The 1988 regulations themselves were adopted by the Reagan administration because pregnant patients were going to Title X clinics to inquire about abortion. Certainly these patients expected that they would be given appropriate answers to their questions. Perhaps most important, physicians can mislead patients as much by silence as by direct advice. In the doctor-patient context, a half-truth may be the same as a lie and may violate both medical ethics and the doctrine of informed consent.

Real-life implications

How much control over doctor-patient conversations can the federal government now claim for medical care that takes place in the federally funded Medicare and Medicaid contexts? Could the government limit the amount of information physicians can give such patients about alternative treatments (for example, experimental interventions such as the bone marrow transplant that saved the life of former senator Paul Tsongas) that are not paid for by Medicare or Medicaid? Could federal regulations limit the information that physicians practicing in government-financed prospective payment systems are allowed to provide their patients? Under a system of national health insurance, could all the types of doctor-patient dialogues that take place in public health care facilities be prescribed by federal regulation, at least as long as some "private" physicians were available for

Dan Wasserman; © 1991 Boston Globe. Distributed by Los Angeles Times Syndicate; reprinted with permission

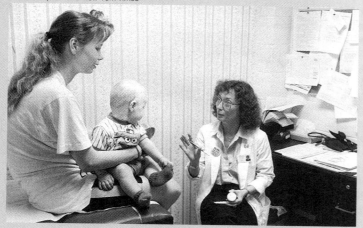

A nurse in a federally funded Kentucky clinic discusses prenatal care with a patient—an expectant mother with a seven-month-old child. Under the ruling in Rust v. Sullivan, *health care workers in clinics covered by Title X regulations are forbidden to counsel women about abortion or even to answer their questions about it. Following the court's decision, some clinics were considering forfeiting government funds so that they could continue to fully serve the four million women, most of them poor, who depend on such facilities for comprehensive health care.*

those who could pay for them? If so, how could such regulations be enforced? Would, say, videotaping of all doctor-patient contacts be required for monitoring of compliance? To take this example further, could videotaping also be required in the examining room or in the operating room? Could the government use "agents" posing as "patients" to check on what physicians actually say to patients?

Although their opinion in the Rust case would certainly permit affirmative answers to the above, even the five justices in the majority would probably want to answer all of these questions in the negative. Because the Rust decision ultimately seems to rest on the proposition that the challenged regulations apply only to poor women, this could be taken to mean that the poor should be grateful that the government is willing to spend any money on them at all. In this sense the court seems to view Title X funding as being almost a charitable act—recipients are free to take it or leave it but cannot expect to have any right to determine what is given or withheld. If these regulations were applied to middle-class Americans, they would almost certainly be seen as intolerable not only by the Congress and the court but by the executive branch of government as well.

Trying to undo the gag rule

Efforts to reverse the Rust decision got under way almost immediately. During the summer of 1991 the governing bodies of both the American Bar Association and the American Medical Association voted unanimously to condemn the decision—and any similar restrictions on doctor-patient conversations. In October 1991 Congress passed a statute rescinding the gag rule and restoring free-speech rights of physicians in federally funded family-planning clinics. Pres. George Bush, however, vetoed the measure, and the vote in the House of Representatives was 12 short of the two-thirds majority needed to override his veto. Thus, the Title X regulations remain in force even though over-whelming majorities of both the U.S. House and Senate believe that Congress never did intend and does not presently intend to grant the executive branch the authority to issue these regulations.

Perhaps even more chilling was the president's Nov. 19, 1991, veto message to Congress. It simultaneously reiterated his support of the regulations and insisted that there was no gag rule. Bush wrote, "I have directed that in implementing these regulations, nothing prevent a woman from receiving complete medical information about her condition from a physician." This statement seems to purposely miss the point. Under the Rust decision, there is nothing to prevent a pregnant woman from being told about pregnancy; the question is whether she can be told that abortion is one alternative to continuation of the pregnancy.

In March 1992 HHS sent to all Title X clinics a memorandum on the gag rule that essentially restated Bush's earlier message to Congress. The memorandum received considerable publicity, and some newspapers reported it as saying that the gag rule no longer applied to doctors but applied only to nurses, social workers, and other nonphysician clinic personnel. In fact, the memorandum—which did not have the legal force of a regulation—did nothing to change the federal regulations on this subject and in no way affected the Supreme Court's ruling in *Rust* v. *Sullivan*.

Tomorrow's victims

During his last day on the bench before his retirement in 1991, Justice Marshall warned that "power, not reason" has been the driving force behind recent Supreme Court decisions and that tomorrow's victims of the court's new conservative majority are likely to be "minorities, women, [and] the indigent." The Rust decision seems to bear out his prediction. It also underlines once again how health care law for everyone in the U.S. is so often made by decisions in cases that primarily involve women.

319

Heart and Blood Vessels

Cardiovascular diseases are the single most important cause of death in Western countries. However, research efforts have considerably reduced death and complication rates, particularly from coronary artery disease (CAD), and continued research advances promise to further reduce their impact on the lives of millions of people worldwide.

New weapons against atherosclerosis

A major step forward in the prevention of cardiovascular disease is the development of new weapons to prevent or reduce the progression of atherosclerosis. CAD is characterized by the deposition of lipids—primarily fats—and the accumulation of various cell types in the walls of the coronary arteries that feed the heart muscle. This process, called atherosclerosis, starts very early in life; the first microscopic manifestations of atherosclerosis have actually been found at autopsy in arteries of infants. These initially tiny lesions may progress to form a plaque large enough to narrow the opening of the coronary artery, thereby reducing its capacity to deliver blood to the heart muscle. Plaques are also susceptible to rupture—a process that can completely occlude the coronary artery, with catastrophic consequences for the individual.

The rate of progression of atherosclerotic disease is more rapid in persons with known risk factors, such as elevated plasma cholesterol levels (the condition known as hypercholesterolemia). Numerous studies have demonstrated that elevated cholesterol levels are associated with both increased prevalence of CAD and an increased rate of complications and that treatment of hypercholesterolemia reduces the risk of cardiac death. Such benefit has been found whether cholesterol levels are lowered by diet, by drug treatment, or even by a surgical procedure in which the terminal part of the small bowel is excluded from the digestive tract to prevent reabsorption of bile acids, thus producing a decrease in the concentration of cholesterol in the liver.

One common problem with traditional cholesterol-lowering drugs is that because of their many side effects, they are not well tolerated during long-term treatment. For this reason, the development of the cholesterol-lowering agent lovastatin (Mevacor) in the late 1980s holds promise for the successful medical treatment of hypercholesterolemia. Recently published results from the Expanded Clinical Evaluation of Lovastatin study, involving over 8,000 patients with moderate hypercholesterolemia, demonstrated that lovastatin decreases blood cholesterol, including low-density lipoprotein cholesterol (the type most closely associated with the development of atherosclerotic heart disease). In contrast to other cholesterol-lowering drugs, lovastatin is very well tolerated by patients,

and its most frequent side effect (liver dysfunction) can be avoided by periodic monitoring of liver enzymes. Thus, lovastatin offers a new and powerful weapon against the development and progression of CAD. It remains to be determined, however, whether lowering cholesterol levels with lovastatin decreases the frequency of heart attacks (as has been shown for other cholesterol-lowering drugs) and whether it reduces total death rate, not just deaths due to CAD (a result that has *not* yet been demonstrated with any cholesterol-lowering medication).

It must be emphasized that in studies designed to test the effects of agents to reduce cholesterol levels, drugs are always utilized in conjunction with a diet that is low in cholesterol and saturated fats. Thus, a prudent diet continues to be the primary approach to treating hypercholesterolemia.

Stress echocardiography: a new tool

Unfortunately, accurate screening of large populations of completely asymptomatic men and women for CAD has several problems, which to many physicians seem to outweigh the potential benefits to be derived. First, it is not uncommon for a screening test, such as an exercise electrocardiogram (ECG), or exercise stress test, to appear abnormal in a perfectly normal subject (a false-positive result). Since most asymptomatic individuals do not have CAD, the majority of the "abnormal" screening tests will be false positive—making it difficult to decide whether to proceed with invasive testing. Moreover, when asymptomatic individuals are screened for CAD by exercise ECG tests, most of the subjects who subsequently have a heart attack or die

Fatty deposits in the wall of a coronary artery (left) have regressed with drug therapy (right), thereby improving blood flow to the heart. A recent study has shown the well-tolerated drug lovastatin to be singularly effective in lowering blood cholesterol and halting atherosclerotic progression.

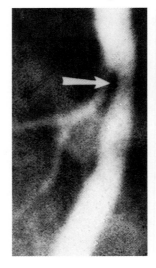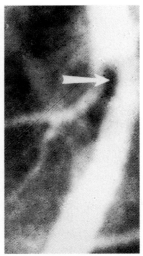

Photographs, B. Greg Brown, M.D.

320

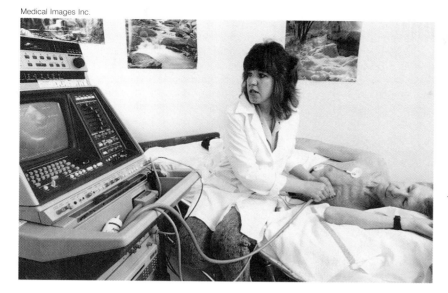

The technique of stress echocardiography enables the assessment of coronary artery disease in patients for whom the traditional exercise treadmill test is not suitable. The patient remains at rest while a medication is administered intravenously, causing the heart to work harder (pharmacological stress). At the same time, high-frequency sound waves are used to produce clear images of cardiac structures and functioning.

during the follow-up period actually had normal exercise test results.

Screening studies are more useful for those who have symptoms of CAD—*e.g.,* chest pain, or angina—or who have several risk factors. The tests are also important in determining which patients among those known to have CAD are at higher risk of dying and which might benefit from coronary revascularization with either coronary artery bypass surgery or coronary angioplasty.

The most traditional test for noninvasive assessment of CAD is exercise electrocardiography; the patient exercises, usually on a treadmill, with simultaneous recording of the ECG. When specific changes in the ECG appear during exercise, myocardial ischemia, the condition in which the heart muscle does not receive an adequate supply of blood and, therefore, of oxygen, is strongly suggested. Although exercise stress testing is reasonably sensitive for detecting CAD and can provide predictive information that helps the physician to decide on appropriate therapeutic strategies, it is of no use in the many patients who cannot exercise because they have arthritis, leg injuries, or physical debilities. Nor is it of use in those who have sedentary life-styles and are simply reluctant to exert themselves.

A recently developed technique to deal with this limitation of exercise testing employs echocardiography (a technique that utilizes ultrasound energy to create an image of the heart) at the same time as the heart is stressed by the intravenous administration of a medication that causes the heart to work harder even though the patient remains physically at rest (pharmacological stress). Not only does this technique help assess CAD in patients who would have difficulty exercising, but the pharmacological stress also avoids the excessive chest wall movement associated with

vigorous exercise, which can impair the quality of the echocardiographic image obtained.

A heart supplied by normal coronary arteries is able to respond to pharmacologically induced or exercise-induced stress by increasing the vigor of its contraction, with all portions of the heart muscle responding uniformly. However, when the coronary arteries are narrowed, the increased oxygen demands of the stressed heart muscle cannot be matched by a parallel increase in blood flow because the arteries are obstructed. This situation results in myocardial ischemia, which causes the affected portion of the heart to contract abnormally, a change that echocardiography will detect.

Stress echocardiography not only detects ischemia but can also determine the number of segments of heart muscle that are contracting abnormally and thereby can assess the extent of CAD. Because extent of disease is a major determinant of risk of death, and echocardiography provides this information, it has a further advantage over conventional exercise electrocardiography.

Although this noninvasive technique for the assessment of the presence and extent of CAD is an attractive one, certain features of its application place constraints on its routine and widespread use in clinical practice. Its major shortcoming is that echocardiographic imaging of the heart is not possible in some patients even during resting conditions—a problem most commonly seen in elderly patients, obese individuals, and those with chronic lung disease, in whom ultrasound waves suffer significant attenuation in their travel through the chest, resulting in suboptimal images of the heart. These characteristics are not uncommon in CAD patients. Another important factor limiting its widespread or routine use is that it requires special expertise to properly perform and interpret the study.

Medical therapy versus revascularization

Once the process of CAD is established and produces narrowing of one or more coronary arteries, therapy is directed toward relief of symptoms and prevention of more serious complications. There are basically two therapeutic options: medical treatment using various drugs and revascularization procedures—coronary artery bypass surgery or balloon angioplasty.

Coronary artery bypass surgery involves bypassing the obstructed segment of coronary artery either with a segment of vein taken from a leg (saphenous vein) or with one of the two arteries that supply the breast tissue (internal mammary arteries). The bypass vessel essentially functions as a bridge linking the aorta (the body's main artery) and the coronary artery beyond the area of narrowing. Coronary artery balloon angioplasty involves positioning a catheter (a long flexible tube) with a deflated balloon placed at its tip into the coronary artery at the point of maximum narrowing; the balloon is then inflated at high pressure in an attempt to compress and fracture the atherosclerotic plaque, thereby opening the narrowed coronary artery.

There are two major factors that are considered in determining whether a patient with CAD should be treated medically or by revascularization. The first is the severity of symptoms; the second is the existence of abnormalities in the coronary arteries and in the function of the left ventricle (the major pumping chamber of the heart), which would indicate that the patient is at increased risk of experiencing a heart attack or of dying suddenly. Thus, in the absence of life-threatening disease, medical treatment is generally the treatment of choice to alleviate symptoms; a revascularization procedure is appropriate only when anginal chest pain continues to restrict daily activities in a significant way, despite medical management. On the other hand, revascularization is indicated in those patients considered to be at high risk of suffering a serious event (heart attack or sudden death) even though there are no symptoms or only mild ones.

Several studies have helped define the high-risk patient. The heart is fed by three major coronary arteries; it has been shown that the patient is at high risk of experiencing a heart attack or sudden cardiac death when all three are narrowed by the atherosclerotic process and when myocardial ischemia occurs during a stress test. Revascularization is indicated in such patients, even in the absence of severely limiting symptoms. Survival may also be enhanced in those patients who have narrowing of two major coronary arteries and have evidence of impaired function of the left ventricle (usually as a consequence of a previous heart attack).

One particular group of patients for whom the best therapeutic approach is still controversial includes those with narrowing of only one major coronary artery and with no symptoms or only mild ones. Studies of these patients have demonstrated that coronary artery bypass surgery neither reduces heart attack risk nor prolongs survival. It is then reasonable to ask which of the two nonsurgical approaches to the treatment of symptoms in patients with single-vessel disease is better—medicines or balloon angioplasty?

A recent randomized trial compared the short-term (six-month) results of balloon angioplasty and medical therapy in patients with one-vessel CAD. Balloon angioplasty was superior to medical therapy for relieving symptoms and increasing exercise tolerance. However, some patients undergoing balloon angioplasty had acute myocardial infarctions (heart attacks), and others then required emergency bypass surgery. Although these rates were low, patients treated with angioplasty had a higher overall complication rate. Thus, although balloon angioplasty appears better than medical treatment for alleviating symptoms, the incidence of serious complications is increased. This technique also entails a greater initial cost and longer hospitalization period. It appears, therefore, that angioplasty should be considered only when patients find that their quality of life is compromised by their symptomatic state, even with medication.

A special group of patients consists of those who have ischemia on stress testing and critical narrowing (i.e., more than 90% reduction of the vessel lumen) of the left anterior descending coronary artery (the most important of the three major coronary arteries) at a point close to its origin. Although no definitive studies exist, some evidence suggests that such patients may benefit from balloon angioplasty.

Thus, of the different therapeutic approaches available for CAD patients, there is no single best form of management. Treatment must be individualized according to the type and extent of the patient's coronary obstructions and severity of symptoms.

"Bridges" to cardiac transplantation

The patients who fall at the most serious end of the spectrum of heart disease are those who have severe deterioration in the pumping function of the left ventricle, for whom corrective surgery is no longer possible and medical therapy no longer effective in treating their symptoms. For these patients cardiac transplantation is the only option available that can improve symptoms and prolong life.

Unfortunately, these patients now face a new dilemma. As the surgery has become more common and more in demand, the patients in need of it have had to wait longer for a donor heart. While in 1986 the average waiting time for cardiac transplantation was three months, that interval has lengthened to between six months and one year. For each patient who undergoes cardiac transplantation, there are two on waiting lists. Such a delay is of critical importance because, of those patients in whom cardiac transplantation is

A 33-year-old patient was among the first recipients of a new battery-powered portable heart-assist device that serves as a temporary "bridge" to cardiac transplantation. The device is implanted just below the diaphragm and is designed to take over the work of a failing heart until a donor heart is available.

indicated but not carried out, one-third will die (usually suddenly) during the first year. Therefore, survival is most likely if the transplant is performed within the first few months after the recommendation is made. In fact, because most of the deaths of patients awaiting cardiac transplantation occur soon after the initial evaluation (*i.e.,* the sickest patients die early), the survival rate of those patients still alive without transplantation six months after the recommendation for surgery is made is no worse than that of those patients who do receive donor hearts; at one year survival of both groups is 85–90%.

A paradoxical situation thus has developed: those patients most in need of a new heart may die while awaiting transplantation, while those patients who receive a new heart may be those in whom the benefit of cardiac transplant is not as great (*i.e.,* the surgery may not be critical). It therefore appears that the need for cardiac transplantation should be reconsidered in those patients who have survived more than six months on a waiting list. It also appears that once the initial recommendation for cardiac transplantation has been made, transplantation should be performed with the shortest possible delay. However, since the availability of donor hearts is not increasing, other forms of cardiac stabilization, or "bridges," to keep these patients alive until cardiac transplantation can be performed have been developed.

These mechanical devices serve to take blood as it enters the heart and then pump it back into the general circulation, thereby decreasing the actual work the heart must perform and, at the same time, improving the perfusion of blood to other vital organs, such as the kidneys and liver. Several different types of mechanical bridges have been used for the

past decade—in some cases with spectacular results. Probably the most significant recent advance in the design of these devices is a so-called portable heart-assist device that was first used at the Texas Heart Institute in Houston in May 1991.

Cardiologists are now trying to determine which patients are appropriate candidates for this form of therapy, which, although transient, can still sustain those awaiting a donor heart for several months. Although it is widely accepted that patients with severe bleeding or generalized infection should not be considered as potential candidates for the portable heart-assist, more controversy exists with regard to patients who, in addition to a failing heart, have other organs that are failing. In particular, severe liver and kidney dysfunction had been considered contraindications to the use of a temporary mechanical bridge. Recent studies, however, have raised questions about this conclusion because such organ failure is often reversed after successful cardiac transplantation.

Another potential temporary "bridge" to cardiac transplant is an implantable defibrillator. An implantable defibrillator is similar to a cardiac pacemaker; however, instead of sending electrical stimuli to the heart to make it beat, the device constantly senses the electrical activity of the heart so that if a life-threatening rhythm disturbance develops, it delivers an immediate shock to the heart, thereby restoring normal rhythm and preventing sudden death. Because the most frequent form of death in CAD patients awaiting transplantation is one that often can be prevented by a defibrillator, these devices could serve as important bridges for some patients. Multicenter trials are currently being conducted to determine the actual utility of the devices.

Circadian variation: new clues to CAD

The study of circadian rhythms in cardiovascular disease may prove important in expanding present knowledge of the mechanisms that trigger the occurrence of such events as heart attack, transient myocardial ischemia, and even sudden cardiac death. Circadian rhythms are fluctuations in physiological systems over 24 hours that are controlled by a biological clock. One of the great puzzles of CAD is what precipitates sudden adverse events, particularly in patients whose conditions had previously followed a stable or uncomplicated course.

A circadian pattern is evident if the occurrence of a disease-related event is unevenly distributed throughout the day so that the majority of such events are clustered at one, or sometimes two, times of day. Such an increase in the frequency of an event at one particular time of day, rather than randomly throughout the day, implies that internal or external influences with a similar circadian pattern may be acting as triggers of the event.

In fact, it has been established that the frequency of cardiovascular events is not evenly distributed during the day. Large multicenter trials have revealed that heart attacks are most likely to occur in the morning hours. Similarly, sudden deaths also occur with a higher frequency in the morning. It is now known that the most common precipitating cause of a heart attack is the sudden development of a blood clot that forms on the atherosclerotic plaque and worsens the coronary artery obstruction. The similar circadian distribution of heart attacks and of sudden death suggests that both events are caused by occlusion of a coronary artery by a blood clot (thrombus) and that the factors responsible for thrombus formation, if identified, must also exhibit a circadian pattern.

This, in fact, has proved to be the case, as studies have demonstrated that the tendency for clots to form is increased in the morning. It has been shown, for example, that the ability of circulating platelets to aggregate (the initial step in the process of clot formation) is augmented during the early morning hours. Also, the ability of the fibrinolytic system (the system normally present in the blood that dissolves clots) to dissolve a thrombus is reduced during the morning. This suggests that if clot formation is initiated, it is less likely to be curtailed in the morning than at other times of the day.

A morning increase in frequency has been demonstrated even more objectively for episodes of transient myocardial ischemia, which occur frequently during daily life in patients with stable CAD. The distribution of these episodes can be assessed with an ambulatory electrocardiographic monitor (Holter monitor), a device that is worn by the patient to record the electrical activity of the heart during a period of 24 or 48 hours. This monitoring permits the detection of specific electrocardiographic changes that are indicative of myocardial ischemia. Analyses of these tracings in large populations of patients with stable CAD have demonstrated not only that episodes of myocardial ischemia occur with an increased frequency during the morning hours but that the timing of ischemic episodes is closely related to the time of awakening—the highest frequency of episodes occurring during the first two hours after awakening.

A similar circadian pattern has been found in certain other physiological mechanisms of the cardiovascular system. These mechanisms include heart rate (number of beats per minute), blood pressure, and the vigor of the heart's contractions, all of which are increased during the morning hours.

A morning heart attack victim is rushed to the hospital by paramedics. Recent studies have shown that more patients suffer heart attacks, chest pain (angina), and sudden cardiac death in the morning hours than at other times of day. Ultimately, medical scientists hope that a better understanding of the role of circadian patterns in the occurrence of sudden adverse cardiovascular events will lead to more effective therapies.

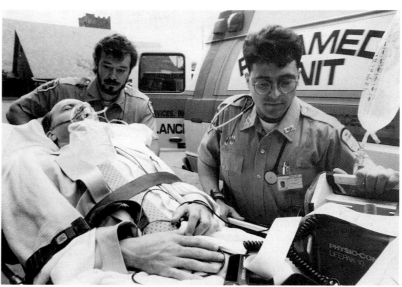

Still further circadian changes have been observed that may add to the likelihood of a heart attack or sudden cardiac death occurring in the morning. Blood vessels constrict and dilate in response to various stimuli acting through the blood or through the nervous system. Factors favoring constriction are known to be increased during the morning, and such increase in vascular tone may have significant implications. For example, a constriction of a coronary artery that is already narrowed by an atherosclerotic plaque could lead to further narrowing. This, in turn, could lead to a cascade of events that produce more stress on the plaque, resulting in its rupture and the formation of an occluding thrombus. The consequence of this process would be severe worsening of angina (chest pain resulting from myocardial ischemia), a heart attack, or even sudden cardiac death. These diurnal changes in vascular tone also help explain why blood pressure increases in the morning and why episodes of myocardial ischemia in patients with stable CAD are more prevalent at this time of day.

A role for such vasoconstrictor influences (changes in vascular tone) in myocardial ischemia was demonstrated in a recent study. The ischemic threshold—i.e., the ease with which ischemia can be induced during exercise—is reduced in the morning hours; thus, myocardial ischemia occurs in the morning, when the heart is working less hard than at other times of day. This reduction in ischemic threshold is associated with a concurrent increase in the constrictor tone of the blood vessels, resulting in their becoming narrowed, suggesting that the constrictor influences that act on both the coronary vascular beds—an intricate network of minute blood vessels with branches throughout coronary structures—and on the vessels supplying the rest of the body are increased during the morning hours and that this increase in vascular tone influences the function of the heart.

The complex mechanisms underlying this morning increase in vasoconstrictor tone are still not clearly understood. However, it has been demonstrated that vasoconstrictor activity exerted by the sympathetic nervous system is increased in the morning—a finding that is compatible with the hypothesis that sympathetic vasoconstrictor activity plays an important role in a number of cardiovascular conditions, including hypertension and effort-induced myocardial ischemia.

Several studies have investigated the effect of different therapies on the circadian patterns of cardiovascular events. In particular, a greater beneficial effect during the morning hours than during other times of the day has been demonstrated for beta-adrenergic blockers (drugs that block the stimulatory effects of adrenaline on the heart—e.g., propranolol, atenolol, metroprolol) in reducing the frequency of transient myocardial ischemia, heart attacks, and even sudden cardiac death. Aspirin, which reduces the incidence of heart attacks and deaths due to infarction, also appears to exert its greatest effect on these events during the morning hours. Because different medications affect different mechanisms involved in the process of cardiovascular disease, continued investigation of the effect of drugs on circadian rhythms may provide valuable information about the mechanisms that lead to the occurrence of adverse events in coronary artery disease. Indeed, further investigation and appreciation of the role of the intriguing circadian patterns in the complex pathophysiology of cardiovascular disease may eventually lead to the development of more effective therapies.

—Julio A. Panza, M.D.,
and Stephen E. Epstein, M.D.

Influenza

La grippe has been almost universally prevalent, striking down the young, middle-aged and old; and always leaving its victims in a prostrate condition, from which recovery is slow and often imperfect, the patient being peculiarly susceptible to inter-current affections.
—*Journal of the American Medical Association,* 1892

The influenza is once more in the air, wafted hither and thither throughout the habitable globe, a formidable, disabling and fatal pandemic.
—*British Medical Journal,* 1892

Each winter influenza viruses circulate, causing the acute respiratory illness referred to in the past as the grippe and today commonly called the flu. Compared with most other respiratory viruses that affect humans, influenza viruses typically cause a more severe illness and are more often associated with serious medical complications. They also have a distinctive epidemiology.

While influenza viruses have a characteristic seasonal pattern, circulating virtually every winter in most parts of the world, they are highly variable in other respects. The viruses themselves change over time by continually mutating; thus, people can be infected many times during their life. The viruses also change unpredictably, which contributes to the year-to-year variations in timing, intensity, and overall impact of flu outbreaks during a given season.

Facts about flu

Influenza is an infection of the respiratory tract. Typical manifestations include fever and respiratory symptoms (e.g., cough, sore throat, runny or stuffy nose), as well as headache, muscle aches, and often extreme fatigue. Although nausea, vomiting, and diarrhea sometimes accompany influenza, gastrointestinal symptoms are rarely prominent. The term stomach flu is often used to describe an illness that is more correctly referred to as gastroenteritis and that can be caused by a variety of viruses, bacteria, and other agents.

In an attempt to protect themselves against the deadly "Spanish flu," office workers wear surgical masks on the job. The most severe flu outbreak in history, the influenza pandemic of 1918–19 caused more than 20 million deaths worldwide, including about 500,000 in the United States.

While most people who get the flu recover completely in one to two weeks, some develop serious and potentially life-threatening complications, such as pneumonia. In an average year influenza is associated with about 20,000 deaths in the U.S. alone and many more hospitalizations. Although flu-related complications can occur at any age, the elderly and people with chronic health problems such as diabetes and heart, lung, or kidney disease are much more likely to develop serious conditions after a bout of flu than are younger, healthier people.

The influenza virus: ever changing

Influenza viruses are divided into three types, designated A, B, and C. Influenza type C differs from types A and B in some important ways. Type C infection usually causes either a very mild respiratory illness or no symptoms at all; it does not produce epidemics and does not have the severe public health impact that A and B do. For these reasons, efforts to control the spread of flu are aimed at type A and B viruses.

Flu viruses continually change over time, usually by mutation. This enables the virus to evade the immune defenses, so people are susceptible to infection throughout their lives. A person infected with influenza develops antibodies against the specific virus that caused the infection. However, as the virus mutates, the existing antibody no longer recognizes the new version, or strain, of the virus, and another infection can occur. However, the older antibody can sometimes provide partial protection against the new strain, thus reducing the severity of the illness.

Currently there are two distinct influenza type A viruses and one type B virus in worldwide circulation. Type A viruses are divided into subtypes on the basis of differences in two viral proteins called hemagglu-

tinin (H) and neuraminidase (N). The current subtypes of influenza A are designated A(H1N1) and A(H3N2), the numbers designating specific variations of hemagglutinin and neuraminidase molecules.

Influenza type A viruses undergo two kinds of changes. One is a series of mutations that occur over time and cause a gradual evolution of the virus. This is called antigenic drift (it also occurs in influenza type B viruses). When a virus mutates (*i.e.,* drifts) enough to be distinguishable in laboratory tests from its predecessors, then a new strain is designated. Within a given influenza A subtype, for example, many different strains may evolve over time. The other kind of change that influenza A viruses undergo is an abrupt change in either the hemagglutinin, the neuraminidase, or both. This is called antigenic shift, and it results in the sudden emergence of a new subtype.

Influenza A and B viruses often undergo antigenic drift. This process accounts for the changes that occur in viral subtypes from one season to another and the consequent need to update influenza vaccine strains frequently. Antigenic shift, on the other hand, takes place only occasionally. When it does occur, large numbers of people, and often the entire population, have no antibody protection. This results in a worldwide epidemic, called a pandemic. In recent history, antigenic shift occurred in 1918, 1957, and 1968.

Influenza A past and present	
virus subtype	period of circulation
A(H1N1)	1918–57, 1977–present
A(H2N2)	1957–68
A(H3N2)	1968–present

In 1977 the influenza type A strain A(H1N1), which had vanished in 1957, reappeared. Before 1977 the previously circulating influenza A subtype had always disappeared when a new subtype emerged (that is, when antigenic shift occurred).

Flu season, 1991–92

The 1991–92 U.S. flu season began—and reached its peak—earlier than usual. Substantial virus circulation was documented, and cases of associated illness were reported in some parts of the country as early as October 1991; widespread outbreaks of flu began to occur as early as November. Nationwide, peak influenza activity occurred from early December 1991 through mid-January 1992 and began to decline thereafter. By comparison, in recent decades influenza usually has not begun to circulate at high levels until mid- to late December, reaching a peak during January or February. In most countries in 1991–92, influenza activity did not appear as early as it did in the U.S. And although, as in the U.S., most flu viruses isolated worldwide were type A(H3N2), some countries isolated a larger proportion of type B and A(H1N1) viruses, and in a few countries one or the other of the latter was the predominant strain.

The early appearance of influenza in the U.S., combined with widely publicized predictions of a severe season and, consequently, a higher-than-usual demand for flu vaccine, contributed to localized shortages of vaccine during the fall of 1991. These short supplies occurred despite the fact that the amount of vaccine produced has increased greatly in recent years; approximately 32 million doses of vaccine were manufactured in 1991, compared with about 28 million doses the previous year and only 23 million in 1985. Although the U.S. Centers for Disease Control (CDC) estimated that somewhat fewer than the available 32 million doses were actually used for the 1991–92 flu season, more than the usual number of doctors' offices and clinics ran out of vaccine, while others had more than they needed. By redistributing the supply, health officials were able to make more vaccine available in areas where there were shortfalls, and the experience prompted a variety of public and private organizations to develop plans for improved vaccine distribution in future years.

Four pharmaceutical companies provide all of the flu vaccine used in the U.S. As profit-making enterprises, the different manufacturers make only as much vaccine as they think they will be able to sell. State and federal governments have no control over the amount of vaccine manufactured, nor do they regulate distribution, except of the vaccine they purchase for use in public programs and clinics, which has accounted for less than 15% of all flu vaccine sold in the U.S. in recent years. The pharmaceutical companies cooperate with governmental agencies to some ex-

tent, but certain types of information, such as patterns of vaccine distribution, are kept secret by the dictates of free-market competition. In the winter of 1991–92, when it became clear that demand for vaccine was high and supplies relatively low, one company was able to make an extra 650,000 doses in the month of December. All of these were sold. This type of late production is unusual because the growing of vaccine antigens is a complex, multistep process that must be begun well in advance of the time the vaccine will be needed.

International surveillance

While the earlier-than-usual occurrence of influenza in 1991–92 was not anticipated, researchers were able to accurately forecast which virus strain would predominate. In spite of the fact that the behavior of influenza viruses is notoriously unpredictable, decades of systematic observation have led to the ability to make at least educated guesses about what may occur in the near future. One important method of observation is the continuous global surveillance of influenza viruses. Since 1947 the World Health Organization (WHO) has coordinated this surveillance system, which includes approximately 100 laboratories in more than 70 countries throughout the world, in addition to about 60 WHO-collaborating laboratories in the U.S.

The process begins with the isolation of viruses from people who have caught the flu. Doctors and nurses in a variety of health care settings obtain specimens by swabbing the noses and throats of patients with flu symptoms and sending these specimens to the nearest WHO laboratory. Flu viruses that are grown in these laboratories are then tested with diagnostic agents that are regularly updated as the different strains evolve, enabling the labs to identify organisms that are different from the predominant flu virus strains. Such viruses, called variants, offer important clues about the direction in which the strains are changing and help researchers decide which ones should be included in each year's influenza vaccine. A sample of viruses is forwarded from the worldwide network of collaborating WHO laboratories to one of the three WHO influenza reference centers located at CDC headquarters in Atlanta, Ga., in London, and in Melbourne, Australia. At these centers more extensive studies are conducted, and viruses from all over the world are compared.

The making of flu shots

Because it takes six to eight months to manufacture, package, and distribute the influenza vaccine, and because the vaccine must be administered in the fall before influenza activity begins, the choice of strains to be included in a given year's formulation must be based to a large extent on information obtained during the previous flu season. The vaccine components cho-

A laboratory worker inoculates culture plates with samples of viruses obtained from throat cultures of flu patients. The laboratory-grown viruses will be used for vaccine production.

sen for the 1991–92 season were based on changes detected from late 1989 through early 1991 in two of the currently circulating influenza strains. A new variant of the type A(H3N2) strain, designated A/Beijing/353/89, was first detected in China in 1989. (Viruses are identified according to type, place of isolation, and number of isolates of that type of virus from that place and year.) Similar viruses were later found in the Southern Hemisphere from May through September 1990, the influenza season (*i.e.,* winter) in that part of the world. Although in the U.S. influenza type B viruses predominated during the winter of 1990–91, viruses similar to the A/Beijing/353/89 strain were also isolated, particularly during the latter part of the season. This information led researchers to believe that viruses resembling the A/Beijing strain were likely to circulate at higher levels in the Northern Hemisphere during the winter of 1991–92, and this strain was chosen in early 1991 to be included in the vaccine for the 1991–92 season. Changes were also detected in the prevailing type B strain, and this vaccine component was changed, too. However, many experts speculated that the predominant flu virus during the 1991–92 season would be very much like A/Beijing/353/89.

The prediction that the 1991–92 season would be more severe than usual was based primarily on the fact that of the currently circulating strains, type A(H3N2) is associated with the largest number of "excess" deaths (*i.e.,* the number over and above what would be expected without the effect of influenza on the death rate). This strain may be inherently more virulent, although this is not at all clear. The most obvious reason for the higher death rate associated with outbreaks of type A(H3N2) is that at this time in history elderly people are most susceptible to this strain, and it is in this age group that deaths as a result of flu are most likely.

Identifying the strains that should be included in the

next influenza season's vaccine can be compared to investing in the stock market. In both cases a great deal of information is available on which to base the choices, and decisions are made through analysis of past performance and current data and trends. A well-researched choice may be more likely than a guess to yield a future benefit, but in both influenza epidemiology and the stock market, unforeseen events can upset even the most educated prediction. In the case of the 1991–92 flu season, the choice of vaccine strains turned out to be correct; virtually all influenza type A(H3N2) strains isolated in the U.S. resembled the A/Beijing/353/89 virus.

Because the A/Beijing/353/89 virus did not appear to have changed during the winter of 1991–92, it was chosen again as the representative A(H3N2) strain for the 1992–93 influenza vaccine. The 1991–92 influenza type B component also was not changed for the 1992–93 vaccine. Of the three distinct influenza viruses, influenza type B viruses were isolated least frequently in most parts of the world during the 1991–92 season, and the viruses that were isolated did not appear to be significantly different from type B viruses isolated the previous season.

The one component of the 1992–93 flu vaccine that was changed is the type A(H1N1) virus. This subtype has shown little antigenic drift since it was discovered in the spring of 1986. The virus that was found at that time, called A/Taiwan/1/86, was sufficiently different from the previously circulating A(H1N1) strain that a supplemental A(H1N1) vaccine was produced for the 1986–87 season. This was necessary because the standard influenza vaccine was already in production by the time the new variant A/Taiwan/1/86 strain was detected. The difference between the A/Taiwan/1/86 strain and the A(H1N1) variants found during the 1991–92 season is not as great as the difference between the pre-1986 A(H1N1) viruses and the A/Taiwan/1/

328

86 strain. However, the differences were enough to warrant changing the A(H1N1) component for the first time in six years.

As in other influenza seasons, the 1992–93 vaccine became available in September. Public health authorities recommend that flu vaccine be given from September through mid-November. It can be given later, but because flu viruses start to circulate in November and early December in the Northern Hemisphere, and it takes two weeks or more to develop antibodies from the vaccine, late vaccination increases the risk that infection will occur before vaccine-induced immunity has developed. On the other hand, receiving vaccine far in advance of the time flu viruses start to circulate increases the chance that the highest levels of vaccine-induced antibody response will occur before they are needed and will have begun to decline before the flu season is over. Although it is impossible to predict precisely when the flu season will begin in a given year, most authorities believe that the optimal time to receive the vaccine is from mid-October to mid-November.

Prospects for new vaccines

The degree to which the virus strains chosen for the vaccine match the influenza strains that actually circulate during a given season is an important determinant of the vaccine's effectiveness. Because the strains to be used in the vaccine must be chosen 9 to 10 months before the influenza season and because influenza viruses mutate over time, sometimes mutations occur in the circulating strains between the time vaccine strains are chosen and the beginning of the next influenza season. These mutations sometimes

A nursing home resident receives a flu shot in preparation for the winter influenza season. Vaccination does not provide complete protection in the elderly, but it does reduce flu-related complications and deaths in this vulnerable population.

Arthur Grace—Stock, Boston

reduce the ability of the vaccine-induced antibody to inhibit the newly mutated virus, thereby reducing the efficacy of the vaccine.

Even with the best match between the vaccine and epidemic virus strains, the currently available killed-virus vaccine is not 100% effective because individual responses to the vaccine vary. Studies of healthy young adults have shown influenza vaccine to be as high as 70–90% effective in preventing any degree of illness caused by influenza. However, in the elderly and in people with certain chronic medical conditions, the vaccine is often less successful in completely preventing illness than in reducing its severity and the risk of serious complications and death. In some of the groups of people at highest risk for influenza-related complications, research has shown the vaccine to reduce flu-related hospitalization by as much as 70% and to lower the risk of death by up to 85%. Among elderly nursing home residents, vaccine can reduce hospitalizations by about 50%, the risk of developing pneumonia by about 60%, and the risk of death by 75–80%. When the circulating virus has drifted away from the vaccine strain, the overall efficacy of the vaccine may be lessened, but it is still likely to decrease the severity of the illness and reduce the incidence of complications and deaths.

One approach to improving the effectiveness of influenza vaccine has been the development of live-virus vaccines. Studies of immunity that develops naturally following infection provide strong evidence that infection produces longer-lasting immunity than that induced by the currently available killed-virus vaccines, as well as conferring broader protection against related flu virus variants. Development of the live-virus influenza vaccine has been based on the same principles used to produce other live-virus vaccines—that is, a virus strain is developed that retains the ability to induce protective antibodies against the naturally occurring virus but also has properties that prevent it from causing illness. The process by which such viruses are developed is termed *attenuation*.

One method for attenuating influenza viruses has been the development of a virus strain that grows at 25° (77° F), a temperature considerably lower than the usual optimal range of 38°–39° C (100.4°–102.2° F). A very important characteristic of these viruses that makes them good candidates for a live attenuated virus vaccine is that they have been shown to be genetically stable; that is, in spite of the ability of naturally occurring influenza viruses to adapt by mutation, these viruses have not been shown to revert to a form that causes illness. Vaccines using viruses attenuated in this manner have been used for many years in Russia. These viruses and the experimental vaccines produced with them have also been studied for more than 20 years in the U.S. In 1990 an American pharmaceutical company was granted permission by the Food and Drug Administration (FDA) to begin the process of developing a live attenuated vaccine against influenza type A viruses for potential marketing. Although further studies are needed, including studies to develop a better live influenza type B component, the progress that has been made is an encouraging step toward development of a new type of flu vaccine that may improve vaccine effectiveness in some groups.

Antiviral drugs and resistance

At present there is only one anti-influenza drug, amantadine (Symmetrel), licensed in the United States. This drug, which is effective against influenza type A viruses but not against type B, was first licensed in 1966 for use in preventing influenza type A(H2N2), the only type A virus circulating in the world at that time. In 1968 type A(H3N2) viruses emerged, and studies had to be conducted to show that amantadine was also effective against these new viruses. A decade passed before the drug was approved for treatment and prevention of all type A influenza viruses.

During the 1960s, when amantadine was first developed, another chemically related drug, rimantadine, was found to have similar activity against influenza type A. The reappearance of type A(H1N1) viruses in 1977, after an absence of 20 years, contributed to a renewed interest in rimantadine in the United States. When these viruses first appeared, widespread outbreaks occurred among children and young adults since most people who were younger than 25 years of age had never been exposed to this subtype. Because initially there was not time to develop and distribute vaccine against this subtype and, further, it would not have been feasible to vaccinate large numbers of healthy children and young adults, short-term use of antiviral agents for prevention and treatment of influenza A infection seemed appropriate. Thus, several clinical studies of amantadine and rimantadine were conducted, including some in which the two were compared. These studies showed both drugs to be 70 to 90% effective in preventing illness caused by influenza A infections. The drugs were also shown in many cases to be beneficial in the treatment of influenza A infections when administered within 48 hours of the onset of symptoms.

While amantadine and rimantadine were shown to be equally effective in prevention and treatment of influenza A, most studies in which side effects were evaluated found that rimantadine was associated with fewer and less troublesome side effects when given at equivalent doses, especially in older people. Studies of rimantadine use among the elderly, combined with knowledge of its pharmacological properties compared with those of amantadine, led many researchers and clinicians to view rimantadine as the drug of choice for this age group. The anticipated licensure

of rimantadine was viewed as a positive development in reducing the impact of influenza among the elderly, the group that is at highest risk for severe illness or death from flu.

FDA approval of rimantadine had been expected in time for the drug to be available during the 1989–90 influenza season, when, in retrospect, one of the most severe epidemics in recent years appears to have occurred. However, in 1989, before the drug was approved, a report was published indicating that simultaneous administration of rimantadine to individuals with flu symptoms and to their household contacts resulted in rimantadine-resistant flu viruses developing in the contacts. Because of fears that rimantadine use might promote the development of drug-resistant organisms, approval was delayed indefinitely.

In fact, the potential for the emergence of both amantadine- and rimantadine-resistant influenza A viruses had been recognized since these drugs were first developed. Resistant viruses emerge readily in the laboratory when either of these drugs is added to an influenza A virus culture. While the evolution of resistant strains in living patients was not anticipated during the early development of these drugs—partly because the mechanism of drug action was not well understood—the emergence of drug-resistant viruses was no surprise to researchers knowledgeable about the relative ease with which flu viruses mutate.

These investigators also observed that resistant viruses quickly reverted to being amantadine- and rimantadine-sensitive when the drugs were withdrawn from an influenza A virus culture. This finding suggests that resistant viruses are genetically disadvantaged compared with drug-sensitive ones and that sensitive viruses will dominate resistant ones when the pressure to mutate (that is, the presence of drug) is removed. It might also suggest that unlike some types of antibiotic-induced resistance in bacteria, which can be perpetuated even when the antibiotic is no longer present (*i.e.,* when the drug is withdrawn from culture or discontinued by patients), influenza A virus resistance to amantadine and rimantadine will not persist over time to any appreciable degree.

The concerns about the implications of amantadine and rimantadine resistance of influenza A viruses have now subsided, and it appeared that the FDA was about to approve rimantadine for the prevention and treatment of influenza type A. However, for reasons that are believed to be related to business agreements and developments within the various pharmaceutical companies that have had an interest in rimantadine, the companies have not pursued the licensure of this drug. For now, rimantadine, a drug that is as effective as amantadine and has no greater potential for inducing the emergence of resistant viruses—and that is, moreover, a safer drug than amantadine—remains unavailable. While research is under way to develop newer antiviral agents that might protect against both influenza types A and B, it may be many years before such a drug is developed, tested, approved, and marketed.

Future outlook

The variability of influenza viruses presents a unique challenge to researchers who seek better ways to control the impact of the disease. Knowledge of the molecular biology of viruses has expanded rapidly in recent years, providing reasons to be optimistic that more effective vaccines and antiviral agents may be developed. It is hoped that when newer technologies are discovered, tested, and approved, they will be made available in a more timely fashion than has been the case with rimantadine and, to some extent, the attenuated live-virus flu vaccines.

—*Nancy H. Arden, M.N.*

Injury Prevention

Throughout the world, injuries are the leading cause of death for more than half of the average human lifespan and the greatest single source of lost productive years of life. In the United States, China, and many other countries, injuries are the leading cause of death among people aged 1–44. In some less developed countries, the importance of injuries is not recognized because infectious diseases claim the lives of many infants and young children, yet virtually everywhere injuries take a great toll of older children, adolescents, young parents, and workers of all ages. As a result, injuries are the greatest source of lost productive years of life.

Injuries are caused primarily by mechanical energy transferred to the body upon impact with another object, as in collisions, falls, shootings, and other events involving motion. Thermal energy (heat) is the causal agent in burns. Other causes include electricity, chemicals, and ionizing radiation. The science of injury prevention involves keeping these hazards from reaching people in amounts or at rates that will harm them.

For example, exposure to a bathtubful of water that is 65° C (149° F) can produce an extensive third-degree burn in as little as two seconds, whereas exposure to a few drops of equally hot water will do little harm. On the other hand, when the water temperature is as low as 50° C (122° F), exposure for even two minutes is not likely to cause permanent damage. In a fall, spreading out the forces of impact can reduce the effect of mechanical energy; thus, a child who falls onto an energy-absorbing pad under a playground swing is much less likely to be injured than one who lands on a hard surface, such as concrete or asphalt, where the energy is transferred to the body very suddenly and therefore is more apt to cause a fracture, concussion, or other serious injury.

Until fairly recently, the study of injury prevention focused on "accidents" that happened to "victims." However, that emphasis was based on the erroneous assumption that injuries result from chance events and are beyond human control. In fact, injuries do not occur at random but usually result from predictable circumstances that can be foreseen and often prevented. Most health professionals have therefore abandoned the use of the term *accident* with its fatalistic implications, adopting instead a more scientific approach that emphasizes the most effective means of preventing *injuries*.

Indeed, a large proportion of injuries are by no means unintentional or "accidental"; more than one-third of U.S. injury deaths are due to homicide or suicide. However, prevention of even these intentional deaths can often be achieved by measures aimed at reducing unintentional deaths. As an illustration, the change in fuels for household use in the U.S. from coal gas (with its potentially lethal carbon monoxide content) to the much safer natural gas virtually eliminated both suicides due to gas inhalation and unintentional deaths from gas leaks in homes. A study conducted in England also illustrates the point; it was found that with the elimination of coal gas, overall suicide rates declined. This finding suggests that suicidal persons who are unable to kill themselves by one method (*e.g.,* coal gas) do not inevitably seek an alternate means.

Fatal injury: how it happens	
cause	number*
motor vehicle, total	48,024
occupant	37,063
pedestrian	7,219
motorcyclist	2,837
bicyclist	859
other	46
firearm, total	35,303
unintentional	1,501
suicide	18,181
homicide	13,666
other/unknown	1,955
poisoning, total†	9,782
unintentional‡	5,353
suicide	3,133
other/unknown	1,296
nonfirearm suicide	12,226
nonfirearm homicide	8,118
falls	12,096
drowning	4,966
residential fires	4,088
other	18,672
total	153,275

*based on 1988 statistics from the National Center for Health Statistics
†excludes poisoning by gases and vapors (*e.g.,* suicides by motor vehicle exhaust)
‡99% are age 15 or older

Injury prevention

Toward safer roads and vehicles

Motor vehicles, the primary source of fatal injury in the U.S., cause about 31% of all injury deaths. The average American aged one to 34 is more apt to die of motor-vehicle-related trauma than of any disease.

About two of every five motor vehicle fatalities result from single-vehicle crashes, in which a car, truck, or motorcycle strikes a tree or other fixed object, overturns on a poorly graded curve, or tumbles down a steep embankment. The contribution of good road design to injury prevention is amply demonstrated by the mortality statistics for interstate highways, where the death rate per million vehicle miles of travel is less than half the rate on other roads. Much of this difference results from careful highway planning, employing features such as a wide median strip between lanes going in opposite directions, wide shoulders, and roadsides that are free of unyielding obstructions. These design features reduce the risk of a head-on collision and improve the chances of avoiding a crash when a driver loses control—whether because of a tire failure, ice on the road, excessive speed on a curve, sudden braking by another vehicle, or any other reason. The "breakaway" light poles that are sometimes seen lying at the side of a highway illustrate the benefits of a design principle called energy attenuation. Typically, occupants of a vehicle that strikes this kind of pole escape with little injury, whereas collision with a rigid pole is likely to have devastating effects.

Many of the safety features of interstate highways could be extended to other roads, where roadside ditches, uncontrolled intersections, and steep embankments without guardrails contribute to high fatality rates. It is also possible to identify stretches of road having a high potential for fatal crashes—e.g., where a downhill gradient is combined with a curve—and to make selective improvements that are almost certain to pay off in terms of lives saved.

Vehicle design also plays a significant part in the degree to which motorists are protected in a crash. Vehicle size is a major factor: death rates are highest in small cars. Some have suggested that this problem could be remedied if all cars were small, thus eliminating the situation of a large car hitting a small one. In fact, about half of the deaths of people in small cars result from collisions with trucks or from single vehicle crashes—a small car hitting a tree, etc. Small cars are generally more economical to run than large cars, and manufacturers often ignore safety considerations when building vehicles that they intend to promote primarily for their fuel economy.

Automobile safety features have been proved to be effective in reducing motor vehicle deaths and injuries. Seat belts, child restraints, and air bags help to spread out the forces of a crash so that they act over a longer period of time and are not concentrated on a vulnerable part of the body. Seat belts alone, how-

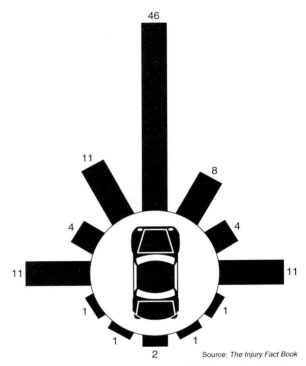

In the U.S. motor vehicles are responsible for nearly a third of all deaths due to injury. The diagram above compares the percentages of fatal injuries sustained in car crashes according to the direction of impact.

ever, may not keep a person from striking the steering wheel, instrument panel, or other unyielding interior structures, because the belts stretch when the body is thrown forcefully against them in a crash. In the event of side and rear impacts, seat belts and high-backed seats are the only effective restraint systems currently available. However, frontal and front-corner collisions are responsible for the majority of fatalities (*see* diagram); in these kinds of crashes, air bags greatly reduce injuries and deaths, adding substantially to the protection provided by seat belts. For those who may not be wearing seat belts when involved in a collision, air bags are even more essential.

As air bags have become more commonplace, the public's qualms about them have been laid to rest by the rarity of undesired deployments or failures and the many instances in which these devices have saved lives and prevented devastating injury. While injuries are occasionally caused by air bags, they are generally very minor in comparison with those that would have been likely to occur in their absence.

Speed and speed limits have been a major safety issue in recent years in the U.S. because of attempts in many states to raise the 55-mph speed limit on rural interstate highways. Such attempts, when successful, have resulted in increased numbers of fatalities. Higher speeds contribute to the likelihood of crashes by decreasing the time available to drivers to respond to emergencies. Moreover, at higher speeds the number and severity of injuries increase because crash forces increase exponentially with velocity—for example, the forces in an impact with a stationary barrier at 70 mph are almost twice those at 50 mph ($50^2 = 2,500$; $70^2 = 4,900$).

Head injuries to bicyclists have been the focus of much recent attention because of their frequency and potential for causing permanent disability and also because many are preventable through the use of bicycle helmets. However, recent figures show that fewer than 10% of all bicyclists—and only 2% of children riding bikes—wear helmets. Helmets have been shown to reduce head injuries in children by as much as 80% and are now required in a small but increasing number of jurisdictions and by most cycling groups. A 1991 study by researchers at the U.S. Centers for Disease Control (CDC) analyzed data on bicycle-related deaths and head injuries and concluded that between 1984 and 1988 helmet use could have prevented as many as 2,500 fatalities and more than 750,000 head injuries.

Firearms: likely to be lethal

Firearms are second only to motor vehicles among manufactured products associated with fatal injuries. In the state of Texas, firearms actually surpassed motor vehicle crashes as the leading cause of death in 1990.

The case-fatality rate (the number of deaths for every 100 injuries) from intentional shootings is extremely high. For this reason the availability of firearms alone is a major factor in the high U.S. death rates from firearm-associated suicide and homicide. An individual who does not have a gun and wants to commit suicide or kill another person is likely to seek some other means, and virtually any other means—poisons, knives, other weapons—is much less apt to prove fatal, regardless of intent.

The design of a gun—such factors as size and ease of firing—influences the likelihood that it will cause death. In contrast to rifles and shotguns, small handguns can be easily concealed, kept close at hand (such as in a pocket), and thus made readily available. Automatic weapons that fire repeatedly without reloading can kill many people in a single incident, as happens in drive-by shootings. Built-in safety features are another factor affecting the chances of a gun fatality. For example, guns can—and should—be designed so that they cannot be fired by small children. In addition, they can be manufactured in such a way that only the owner can fire them; for example, research is under way to develop handguns that "recognize" the owner's fingerprint.

Falls: hazard to old and young

Falls, the major cause of injury death in the elderly, are specified as the underlying cause in more than 12,000 deaths in the U.S. each year. That statistic does not tell the whole story; in probably another 10,000 or more cases, a fall initiates a chain of events that ends in death. For example, an 85-year-old man falls and breaks his hip; he is eventually discharged from the hospital to a nursing home, but during his convalescence there, he develops a blood clot from

Bob Mack—Florida Times-Union

An official at a Florida high school uses a metal detector to search students for concealed weapons before allowing them to enter the building. Guns are more likely than any other weapon to cause fatal injury; their wide availability is a major factor in the high rate of U.S. firearm-associated deaths.

lack of mobility. The clot eventually migrates to his lung and leads to his death.

High fracture rates in older people are most often related to osteoporosis, a weakening of the bones that begins in adulthood and accelerates with aging. A number of strategies are known to reduce fractures in the elderly: regular exercise, an adequate intake of calcium, and, in postmenopausal women, hormone replacement therapy.

Falls do not affect only the elderly, however. They are also the leading cause of nonfatal injury for people of all ages in the U.S. While falls occur under a variety of differing circumstances, the injuries they cause are generally preventable by the same basic measures—namely, by spreading out the forces of impact, as previously mentioned in the case of energy-absorbing playground surfaces, or by reducing the distance of the fall and, therefore, the velocity of the impact. For example, a tumble from a piece of playground equipment is less likely to cause serious injury when the equipment is installed close to the ground; in the case of a slide, this might mean building it into the side of a hill so that the distance traveled in a fall from the top would not be much greater than that from the bottom.

In addition to cushioning the surfaces that people are likely to strike in a fall, protection can also be provided for vulnerable parts of the body. Common examples include knee pads, shoulder pads, and helmets worn by ice hockey and football players. Similar specially padded garments are now being designed for the elderly to reduce the chance of hip fractures—an innovative and promising approach.

Preventing drowning

Drowning takes its highest toll among teenage males—a group known for their attraction to risk taking—and very young children. Many tragedies involving home swimming pools could be prevented if pool owners received training in resuscitation of drowning victims in a Red Cross program or other, similar program. Equally important is childproof fencing surrounding the pool to prevent direct access to the pool area from the house or the yard. Such fencing is now mandatory in some locales. The fact that the drowning rate is higher at age one to two than at any other age is testimony to the ease with which a toddler can momentarily escape a caretaker's watchful eye.

Cigarettes, matches, hot water: hazards at home

Residential fires are an especially important cause of death in young children and the elderly, in part because of their inability to escape without help and also, especially in the case of the elderly, because of their reduced capacity to survive any form of trauma. Common ignition sources include heating and cooking appliances and children playing with matches and cigarette lighters. The most important source, however,

Were it not for the heroic intervention of fire fighters, this three-month-old might have perished in an Oneida, New York, apartment house blaze. Unable to escape without help, infants are all too frequently the victims of residential fires.

is the cigarette itself. There are many health-related reasons why people should not smoke cigarettes; the fires they cause are yet another. Cigarettes that fall unnoticed onto upholstered furniture often smolder for hours, filling a home with deadly carbon monoxide fumes that kill people as they sleep. It is possible to reduce ignition potential by manufacturing cigarettes that smolder at lower temperatures or for shorter periods of time; because a "smoke-free" society is not yet within sight, federal statutes requiring such safety features are expected in the near future.

When fires erupt, smoke detectors and automatic sprinkler systems can play important roles in preventing injury and death. Smoke detectors are limited, however; they are effective only when in working order and when people are present who are capable of responding to them. These limitations magnify the importance of sprinkler systems, which are increasingly being required in new housing. Such systems have the ability to extinguish fires before substantial damage can be done to either the building or its occupants. The initial cost of sprinkler systems is often offset by long-term reductions in insurance premiums and by lower construction costs for other aspects of the dwelling related to fire containment. While it is true that water damage may result from sprinkler systems, it is minor compared with the much greater devastation caused by fire and smoke. In addition, damage from a sprinkler's discharge of 68 liters (18 gal) per minute is hardly comparable to that of a fire engine hose spewing 1,213 liters (320 gal) per minute.

Scalds, the most common nonfatal burns, can be very serious when they involve exposure to large amounts of very hot water. For this reason it is important that baths and showers have antiscald devices or other means of limiting the water-heater temperature to 50° C (122° F) or less.

Human factors: how they influence risk

A variety of demographic factors influence the risk of injury, including age, sex, and socioeconomic status. The kinds of injuries that are most common among specific age groups are as follows.

Injuries in the elderly. The highest death rates from injuries are seen in elderly people. Contributing factors are their lower injury thresholds (a blow or fall is more likely to cause injury to an elderly person than to a younger one) and greater susceptibility to infections and other complications of trauma. The latter accounts for the fact that relatively minor injuries such as fractures often prove fatal in older people. In some cases elderly people are injured because of age-related decreases in visual acuity (especially at night) and sense of balance and impaired ability to respond rapidly—for example, to move out of the path of an approaching vehicle. That some older drivers have difficulty in judging the speed of other vehicles is suggested by their especially high rates of collisions at intersections.

On the whole, however, statistics show that older drivers do not have higher rates of fatal collisions, although they are involved in more crashes when the figures are adjusted for the distances they drive. This finding indicates that many older drivers voluntarily compensate for age-associated decrements by reducing the amount of driving they do and restricting driving at night and under other challenging circumstances. As a result, older drivers as a group do not contribute disproportionately to the incidence of fatal crashes. Individual cases of elderly drivers who should not be operating vehicles are best managed by families, family physicians, and medical boards of state motor vehicle departments. Some U.S. states have introduced "graded licenses"; drivers over 55 are required to take road tests every four years, those 75 and over every two years. And some impaired drivers are given limited licenses allowing them to drive only on certain roads at certain times.

Childhood injuries. Unable to recognize or avoid many hazards, young children have a special need for protection. This need is reflected in the many safety measures designed specifically to reduce risks for infants and children—flame-retardant nightwear, automobile safety seats, childproof medicine containers, swimming pool enclosures, and the like. Death rates from injury are highest in the first year of life, especially from homicide (usually abuse by a caretaker) and motor vehicle crashes.

In the early 1980s the high death rates of infants in automobile crashes were a major incentive for state laws requiring that children be protected by well-designed child restraints. All U.S. states now have such laws, and federal statistics show that in the period from 1983 to 1990, the use of child safety seats increased dramatically, from 38 to 84% for children aged one to four and from 60 to 83% for infants under a year old. Fatalities have decreased most among infants, the very age group for whom safety seat usage is now most common; their death rate as motor

After some of his classmates were jolted out of their seats when their school bus came to a sudden stop, Aaron Gordon, a Miami, Florida, youngster, spearheaded a campaign to develop an effective—and affordable—seat belt for school buses.

vehicle occupants in 1984–86 was 37% lower than in 1977–79, when only one state (Tennessee) had such a law. Children riding in other types of vehicles—school buses, taxicabs, pickup trucks—often are not protected against injury, however. A recent study from Utah examined the special risks to youngsters riding in the back of pickup trucks; during the 40-month study period, 40 children required hospitalization for injuries suffered in such vehicles.

A special vehicle-safety problem in younger age groups is that many rear-seat lap belts "ride up" over a child's abdomen (rather than remaining in place over the upper thighs), with resulting injuries to the abdomen and spine. Combination lap-shoulder belts in rear seats are expected to reduce this problem, and booster seats that raise the child's body up higher on the seat may be helpful, but much still needs to be done to optimize child passenger protection in cars.

Children in the first few years of life are at particular risk of suffocation from choking on small objects—including foods—especially bite-sized, round, or pliable substances that can easily block an airway. Peanuts, grapes, chunks of hot dogs, round candies, and small balls and marbles share these characteristics and have often been involved in such tragedies. Federal law prohibits the marketing of toys with small parts to children under 3 years of age, and manufacturers have complied by labeling such toys "for age 3 and over." Nonetheless, some buyers choose them for younger children because they interpret the age labels as referring to the child's interest level rather than to safety concerns. The Consumer Product Safety Commission is considering changing its standard to require warnings that specify that small parts create a choking hazard.

Teenage and young adult injuries. Among the 15–24 age group, injuries cause 78% of deaths from *all* causes. Half of these injury deaths are related to motor vehicles. According to statistics from the Johns Hopkins University Injury Prevention Center, Baltimore, Md., traffic deaths peak sharply in both sexes at about age 18. For drowning and many other causes of injury, however, females in their teens and early adult years do not exhibit the dramatic increase in death rates seen in their male counterparts. Homicide rates increase sharply in the late teens and are highest in the twenties. Suicide, the third leading cause of death in this age group (after motor vehicles and homicide), is a major problem, and in recent years suicide rates have risen alarmingly in teenagers.

Injuries in other high-risk groups. Other people at especially high risk of injury include residents of rural areas, where greater exposure to certain kinds of hazards and reduced access to expert trauma care often have fatal consequences. Motor vehicles, farm machinery, firearms, and drowning take an especially heavy toll in remote areas.

High-risk occupational groups include loggers, pilots, fire fighters, truck drivers, farmers, and construction workers—as well as workers who are likely to be shot in connection with their jobs, such as police officers, taxi drivers, people who work in all-night convenience stores, motel clerks, and others whose work hours, isolated locations, and proximity to cash make them likely targets for armed robbers.

Prevention: strategies that work

The groups of people at greatest risk of being injured tend to comprise individuals whose behavior is extremely difficult to change. To appreciate this fact, one need only consider how difficult it is to keep a toddler from investigating the cleaning products under the sink, to ensure that an 18-year-old boy will choose a safe place to swim, or to persuade an intoxicated driver to call for a taxicab. The very people who are most likely to be in a car crash are also the ones who are least likely to wear their seat belts—for example, drivers who have been drinking or those who run red lights or follow other cars too closely. These considerations underscore the importance of designing people's working, living, and traveling environments in such a way that an individual's error or poor judgment does not lead to a serious injury. Such safety features are well established in electrical appliances and home electricity supply, where the lifesaving benefits of fuses and ground-fault interrupters are taken for granted by today's homeowners.

In many situations, however, where such protective features are lacking, easily made mistakes can have fatal consequences. For example, major pieces of farm machinery are not required to meet federal product safety standards; consequently, limbs lost as a result of entanglement in corn pickers and deaths from tractor rollovers have been tragically common on American farms. Between 1930 and 1980 the U.S. death rate from incidents involving farm machinery actually increased by 44%. During the same period, the death rate caused by other types of machinery dropped by 79%, largely because of governmental regulations that require shielding and other automatic protection for the operators.

Most research evaluating the effectiveness of preventive measures has shown that for injuries, as for disease, the best means of protecting people is with measures that do not require frequent actions on the part of the individual. Thus, air bags and well-designed roads have proved to be more successful in preventing injury than educational messages that attempt to motivate people to drive more carefully. Future developments in injury prevention are therefore likely to concentrate more on specific interventions that protect people from harm than on exhortations that they change their behavior.

—*Susan P. Baker, M.P.H.*

Special Report

Japan's "Golden Plan"

by Linda G. Martin, Ph.D.

The population of Japan is aging faster than that of any other industrialized country, and the government of Japan is responding with new policies and programs to address this challenge. Of particular interest in the health field is the proposed 10-year, $43 billion "Golden Plan"—an innovative and farsighted plan that is designed to reduce hospitalization and encourage rehabilitation and home care of the elderly.

The demography of aging

In 1950 the proportion of Japan's population that was aged 65 and over was only 4.9%, but by 1990 it was 11.7%, and it is projected to be 23.9% by 2025. The number of older persons is expected to increase from approximately 14.4 million in 1990 to 30.5 million in 2025. The populations of the other industrialized countries of the world, as well as those of many of the poorer ones, are also aging, but the speed of the process in Japan is unprecedented. The reasons for the phenomenally rapid aging of Japan's population are twofold: in the post-World War II period there were remarkable declines in both fertility and mortality.

The total fertility rate had already declined from 5.1 children per woman of childbearing age in 1925 to 4.1 in 1940. Although a postwar baby boom saw the fertility rate increase to 4.5 children in 1947, it lasted only three years, in contrast to the United States, where the postwar boom lasted 17 years. Moreover, fertility plummeted to two children per woman by 1960, and by 1990 the total fertility rate was 1.5. A fertility rate under 2.1 is known as "below-replacement fertility"; that is, allowing for some mortality, the couples in the population are no longer replacing themselves with children in the next generation. Sustained below-replacement fertility levels ultimately result in decline in the size of the population, a phenomenon that is likely to occur in Japan early in the next century. Another consequence of lower fertility is that with relatively fewer babies being born into the population, the population as a whole becomes older.

In the early stages of socioeconomic and demographic transitions, a decline in mortality typically benefits younger people more than older people—*i.e.,* it contributes to a rejuvenation of the population as more children survive. This mortality change, then, is not the primary reason for population aging in its early stages (though a decline in mortality is clearly

essential for individual extension of life). Nevertheless, once infectious and parasitic diseases are controlled (replaced by chronic degenerative diseases), and infant and child mortality are extremely low—as they are in Japan—further improvements in life expectancy are achieved through lower death rates in the adult and elderly populations. Such has been the case in Japan since about 1970 and, accordingly, the decline in mortality is playing a bigger role in the aging of the country's population.

In the early 1950s life expectancy for Japanese males was about 62 years and for Japanese females about 66 years. By the late 1980s it had increased to 75 and 81 years, respectively—the highest on Earth. In most industrialized countries heart disease is the number one killer, followed by cancer and cerebrovascular disease. Since 1958 these three causes of death have been the most prominent ones in Japan, too, but in a different order. Until 1981 cerebrovascular disease (primarily stroke) was first, followed by cancer and heart disease. In 1981 cancer became number one, and in 1985 heart disease became number two. Despite progress in reducing the death rate from cerebrovascular disease and its relegation to third place, it remains high relative to rates in other industrialized countries. For example, in 1988 the death rate from cerebrovascular disease among those aged 65 and over in the United States was 431 deaths per 100,000, compared with 779 per 100,000 in Japan. The high incidence of cerebrovascular disease is also thought to contribute to the relatively high proportion of older Japanese who are severely debilitated or bedridden. (Unfortunately, suitable data for international comparisons are not readily available.)

Aging's social context

In simple terms, there are three basic sources of support for elderly persons—their families, the public, and themselves. There has been increasing concern in Japan that families in the future will take less responsibility for caring for those elderly who need help, leaving the elder individuals themselves and the state to fill the gap.

Although financial and emotional support from family members can be given across household boundaries, the decline in multigenerational coresidence in recent decades may be cause for concern. Between

1970 and 1990 the proportion of Japanese people aged 65 and over living with their children declined from 77 to 59%, and the proportion living alone or with spouse only increased from 18 to 37%. Although the proportion living with their children remains high by Western standards, the decline represents a major departure from the traditional Japanese ideal of elderly parents living with the eldest son and his wife.

Of course, one should not assume that all or even the majority of the support in multigenerational households flows from younger to older generations. With increasing labor shortages as a result of population aging and an increasing demand for female workers, having an elderly parent in the household to assist with child care and household chores may be to the advantage of the younger generation. Also, it must be acknowledged that the increased independence of elderly Japanese in their living arrangements may reflect their increased ability to pay for privacy—something they may in fact desire—rather than abandonment by their children.

Although, as in other industrialized countries, participation of older Japanese in the labor force has declined in recent decades, a relatively large proportion of them continue to work. In 1988, 35.8% of Japanese men and 15.7% of women aged 65 and over were employed—about twice the percentages for those 65 and over in the U.S. Many of these older workers in Japan, however, may have officially retired from their so-called lifetime careers and then found new jobs, perhaps with an intervening period of unemployment. The average mandatory retirement age enforced by large Japanese companies has only recently increased from 55 to 60 years, so such transitions are not uncommon.

Besides earned income, older Japanese can also rely on their savings and public pensions for economic well-being. The Japanese public pension system has now reached maturity and is the most commonly cited source of support among older Japanese. Even so, if older persons become ill and unable to care for themselves, the family or the public will have to step in.

When asked who they want to look after them should they need help, the majority of older Japanese males mention their wives, while the majority of older females mention their daughters-in-law or daughters. Many of the men may have their wishes met, given the longer survival of women plus the fact that Japanese husbands tend to be several years older than their wives. The fulfillment of the wishes of older women, who now constitute about 60% of the 65-and-over population, is less likely, given the aforementioned change in living arrangements and the increased participation of their daughters and daughters-in-law in the labor force. Moreover, for both men and women, there may come a time when the younger family care givers simply can no longer cope with the situation.

Japan's population is aging faster than that of any other industrialized nation. By the year 2025, 30.5 million Japanese—nearly one-quarter of the population—will be 65 or older, creating many challenges for policymakers.

Although the number of nursing homes in Japan has tripled since 1970, there has been growing concern that hospital services are being misused in providing services to the elderly. The institutionalization rate for the older Japanese population increased from 1% in 1955 to over 6% in 1987, and in recent years as many as two-thirds of the institutionalized elderly were in hospitals and clinics as opposed to nursing homes. This high usage of hospitals is reflected in the average length of hospital stays of the elderly in Japan, which is roughly eight times greater than the average length of stay for the elderly in hospitals in the United States.

There are both financial and social incentives to families for such hospital utilization. Hospitalization is virtually free (less than $150 per month) under Japan's health care plan for the elderly. Moreover, hospitalization may help the family save face when it is no longer able or is not willing to care for an elderly member of the family. Instead of the family's having to take the step of moving the older person into a nursing home, a physician may be willing to prolong hospitalization—a practice that is known as "social hospitalization." Given these incentives to families, plus the rapidly increasing proportion of the population that is 65 years old or older, it is not surprising that the elderly account for a third of national health care expenditures in Japan.

338

Introduction of the Golden Plan

In 1989 the Japanese parliament approved a 10-year program, known as the Golden Plan, to span the final decade of the 20th century and prepare for the expansion of the older population by providing rehabilitation services and encouraging residence in the community for the country's elderly citizens. The seven main goals of the plan are: (1) to increase services for older people who live at home; (2) to reduce the number of bedridden elderly; (3) to improve the quality and appropriateness of home services; (4) to expand institutional facilities; (5) to promote productive aging and a high quality of life for the elderly; (6) to promote a national research agenda on aging; and (7) to develop comprehensive institutions for the health and welfare of the elderly. The specifics of each of these goals are discussed below.

Increasing services for the elderly who live at home. Provision of home helpers—housekeeping assistants or nurse's aides who visit the elderly several times a week—is viewed as an important component of promoting continued residence of the elderly in the community. In 1970 there was only one home helper for every 1,210 elderly persons, but the goal is to increase the ratio to one for every 204 by 2000. This change will require a tripling of the number of home helpers over the decade. Users of the services may bear some of the costs on the basis of their ability to pay (up to about $5 per hour); otherwise, the national government pays half the costs, with prefectures (states) and municipalities sharing the other half.

To provide respite care for elderly living with their families, the number of beds in temporary-stay facilities of nursing homes will be increased by a factor of more than six. These beds will also be available for night care of persons suffering from senile dementia. The charges for these services are approximately $15 per day, with the national government, prefectures, and municipalities subsidizing the rest of the costs.

Day-care services at special centers are designed to reduce burdens on families as well as enhance the mental and physical functioning of the elderly who continue to live at home. Services include bathing, the provision of meals, and training in activities of daily living—bathing, dressing, grooming, eating, shopping, etc. It is expected that the number of such centers will be more than quintupled over the decade (from 1990 to 2000).

Domiciliary-care support centers provide consultation and guidance on health and welfare services for families looking after elderly persons. These centers, which are being established for the first time under the Golden Plan, are expected to number 10,000 by the year 2000. Finally, model communities where the elderly are encouraged to lead active lives and the families to provide support will be established in over 20% of Japan's 3,000-plus municipalities by the end of the decade.

Reducing the number of bedridden elderly. Centers for outpatient rehabilitation will be established in all of Japan's municipalities. A more than 10% increase in the number of sites was expected in the first year of the plan—1990—alone.

Through newly established stroke information centers, a hospital will be able to communicate with municipalities about the needs of stroke patients upon their release from the hospital. Such centers were to be established in 10 of the 47 prefectures by 1990. The government also plans to improve its health education programs to prevent disease and disability among the elderly and thereby limit the number who are bedridden.

Improving the quality of services. A newly established Social Welfare Fund will seek to adapt environments to meet the special needs of the elderly as well as to support research on the improvement of social services for the elderly who live at home. Social services corporations will use volunteers and resources from

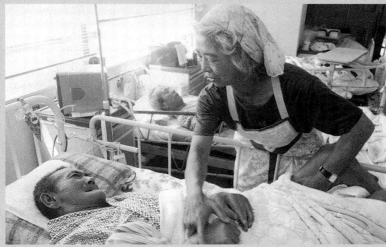

Torin Boyd

As many as two-thirds of Japan's institutionalized elderly who require long-term care are kept for extended periods in hospitals, where care is virtually free—a practice known as "social hospitalization." Among the aims of the comprehensive Golden Plan is the reduction of the number of elderly being cared for in hospitals. This will be accomplished largely through an increase in the number of beds in nursing homes and rehabilitation centers.

the public and private sectors on a regional basis to promote productive aging and a high quality of life for the aged.

One example of an innovative corporation can be found in Musashino City, a suburb of Tokyo, which provides care until death for elderly persons who use their property as collateral for services rendered. Many elderly own their own homes but lack sufficient cash to pay for services they may need, such as meal delivery, household help, and legal assistance. The corporation provides the services plus a monthly living allowance, if needed, and the accumulated debt plus interest is paid back after the death of the elderly person from the proceeds of the sale of the property.

Expanding institutional facilities. Under the Golden Plan, the number of beds in nursing homes for the elderly will be increased from about 162,000 in 1989 to 240,000 in 2000. These facilities care for those aged 65 and over who need constant nursing care because of debilitating physical or mental conditions. The goal is to eliminate waiting lists, which have been most prevalent in urban areas. Charges are based on ability to pay, and subsidization is equally divided between national and prefectural or city levels.

Japan also intends to expand by 10-fold the number of beds available in rehabilitation centers. These centers provide functional training and nursing care for rehabilitation purposes. Medical expenses (on average about $1,700 per month) are paid by the municipalities, and users pay the cost of meals and daily necessities (usually about $400 per month).

Alternative residence facilities known as care houses provide apartments for older people who can live independently but require the assistance of wheelchairs or home helpers, at least upon admission. If residents become frail but can be maintained with the provision of community-based services, they are allowed to stay. The goal is to provide such facilities for 100,000 elderly Japanese by 2000. There will also be a special effort to establish multipurpose senior centers to meet the needs of elderly people living in depopulated areas of the country.

Promoting productive aging. Model projects that encourage the elderly to remain productive and active— *e.g.,* through continuing education and participation in sports and various creative activities—will be expanded, as will regional administrative offices to oversee and coordinate these projects. Such activities are especially needed for older Japanese males, many of whom are at loose ends upon their retirements, given their typical unstinting devotion to their jobs. For example, a 1986 survey of people aged 60 and over in the U.S. and Japan found that 23% of retired American men participated often in social activities (*e.g.,* clubs and hobby groups), compared with 4% of retired Japanese men. The percentages of American versus Japanese male retirees often active in sports were 19 and 6, respectively.

Promoting aging-related research. Under the Golden Plan, a National Research Center for Aging and Health is being established. The tentative list of research fields includes biomedicine, social sciences, geriatrics, rehabilitation, nursing, basic care, technology development (of health care devices for aging-related impairments—*e.g.,* hearing aids, mobility aids, etc.), and various applications of traditional Oriental approaches to medicine. A private foundation to support aging research has also been established, and the national government has begun to give grants to researchers for aging-related studies, which in 1990 amounted to more than $7 million.

Developing comprehensive institutions. Finally, the Furusato 21 program ("my hometown in the 21st century") provides aid to municipalities and institutions to develop services appropriate for their regions that will help older Japanese live active and healthy lives. The goal of this program is to provide an atmosphere free from anxiety and with a sense of purpose for

Especially needed in Japan are programs that encourage the elderly—particularly elderly males—to remain active and productive beyond their working years. Japanese working men are known for their unstinting devotion to their professions. Because they tend to develop few interests or activities outside their jobs, they often find themselves at loose ends upon retirement.

World Health Organization; photograph, E. Schwab

Elderly women enjoy the fresh air on the grounds of a Tokyo nursing home. Like many urban institutions for the aged, this one cannot begin to accommodate the huge numbers in need of its services; typically, nursing homes in metropolitan areas have long waiting lists. In part because of the rapid expansion of the elderly population and in part because increasingly fewer older people are cared for by their children in multigenerational homes, Japan has an urgent need for alternative residential facilities for its older members of society.

the elderly through the integration of government and community services.

A major investment

Altogether, the 10-year Golden Plan is expected to cost over $43 billion, nearly four times the expenditure on services for the elderly in Japan in the 1980s. In general, costs are to be shared by the national, prefectural, and municipal governments, and designing programs and services appropriate to specific locales is being emphasized. As mentioned earlier, a central concern is the treatment of bedridden elderly Japanese. Of the approximately 730,000 bedridden in 1990 (about 5% of the 65-and-over population), 42% were in hospitals, 20% in nursing homes, and 36% at home. It is the objective of the Golden Plan to change these percentages by 2000—when it is expected that over one million elderly citizens will be bedridden—to 12, 24, and 36, respectively, with the remaining 28% receiving care in rehabilitation centers.

Of course, human capital as well as physical plant will be required if these goals are to be met. In 1988 approximately 2.2 million Japanese, or 3.6% of the labor force, were working in the health and welfare fields, a 1.6-fold increase from the 1975 figure of 1.3 million. With continued aging and this new initiative, it is expected that 3.5 million workers, or 5.1% of the labor force, will be working in these areas by the year 2000. Efforts are being made to improve salaries and fringe benefits, upgrade training, and attract people who are just entering the labor force to the health and welfare fields. Given the shortage of younger workers as the population grows older, the new workers will have to include more women, the middle-aged, and the elderly themselves.

Beyond the Golden Plan

The Golden Plan represents a significant commitment to addressing the long-term-care challenges of population aging. However, it is not the only major policy initiative in the area of aging, and the development of appropriate policies is an ongoing activity.

As mentioned earlier, the Japanese public pension system has now matured. A major reform in 1986 established the rights of women to pension benefits on their own, not just as employees or dependents of employees. The reform also reduced benefits that future retirees were expecting to receive in an effort to hold down required contribution rates.

Virtually all Japanese, including the elderly, are covered by a form of national health insurance. In 1973 copayments were eliminated for those over age 70, but usage and costs increased dramatically, and in 1983 nominal fees for service were reinstituted.

The government has also paid particular attention to employment programs for the elderly, spending $1.3 billion in 1987, up 60% in two years. There is presently no legislation on mandatory retirement age, but the Ministry of Labor uses its influence and financial incentives to encourage employers to raise the retirement age and reemploy retired workers.

Critical to all these policy and program developments have been political commitment at the highest level and public awareness of the dimensions of population aging. For example, the 1982 report of the top-level Long-Term Outlook Committee of the Economic Planning Agency cited population aging as one of the three major challenges facing Japan in the 21st century, along with internationalization and maturation of the economy. In recognition of the important consequences of aging for the society and the economy, Japanese prime ministers have regularly mentioned aging as they set the nation's policy agenda.

Continued attention to aging issues and refinement and redirection of initiatives will be required. Even so, the Golden Plan represents a bold step forward in meeting the needs of the Japanese elderly. Moreover, the plan is one that other countries may well study as they, too, attempt to cope with the challenge of their aging populations.

341

Medical Education

Medical education in the United States is a complex and constantly changing enterprise. In 1992 this enterprise involved 126 accredited medical schools, 1,250 hospitals providing educational settings for physicians-in-training, 65,602 medical students, more than 80,000 resident physicians and fellows, 74,621 full-time medical school faculty members, and more than 180,000 others who provided medical instruction on a part-time or voluntary basis. Foremost among the developments that have deeply affected academic medical centers in the last decade are changes in the pool of applicants and students seeking medical education and a variety of efforts to change and reform the very process of medical education. Today perhaps the greatest challenge facing medical education is the need to produce more primary care physicians who will meet the nation's present and future health care needs.

Applicants and students: changes and trends

The 1960s and '70s were a period of enormous growth in the medical education enterprise. Spurred by government programs to address a perceived shortage of physicians, the number of fully accredited medical schools increased from 81 in 1960 to 115 in 1980 and eventually rose to 127.

Numbers. Concomitantly, the number of medical students more than doubled from 30,228 in 1960 to 65,189 in 1980. However, this expansionary era was followed by a sharp decline of interest in medicine as a career, for which medical schools were unprepared. The erosion in medical school applicants began after

a peak was reached in 1974, when applicants for the entering class numbered 42,621—2.8 applicants per first-year medical school position. A nadir in the number of applicants to medical school was reached in 1988, when only 26,721 applied—a 37% total reduction in the applicant pool. There seems to be no single explanation for the decline, and the reduced number of applicants was not associated with changes in the overall size of the medical education enterprise. Except for one medical school that discontinued operation—Oral Roberts University in Tulsa, Okla.—neither the number of medical schools nor the size of medical school classes underwent major change, nor are they expected to do so in the immediate future.

It now appears that the decline in the number of applicants is over and a new trend is under way. There was a modest increase in the number of applicants for the class of 1989 over the previous year, followed by an 8.6% increase in 1990 and a robust 14% increase in 1991. An increment of similar size was projected for the 1992 entering class.

Quality. Although the major focus during the 1980s was on the declining number of applicants, another important concern was the quality of the potential students—particularly concern about whether the caliber of student had declined. However, an assessment of two measurable criteria—college grade-point averages and scores on the Medical College Admission Test (MCAT)—showed at most a very marginal decrease in academic qualifications.

Gender. During this period of considerable fluctuation in the number of applicants to medical school, a number of changes occurred in the composition of the applicant pool. Half as many women entered

At Massachusetts General Hospital in Boston, attending physician Edwin O. Wheeler leads medical students and residents on rounds. In the U.S., medical students typically spend their third and fourth years in clerkships in teaching hospitals in order to gain clinical experience in the major medical and surgical disciplines and various elected subspecialties. Residents then spend three to seven years in intensive hospital-based clinical training in their chosen specialty. While this traditional system has produced physicians who are among the best trained in the world, American medical education now finds itself at a crossroads, in need of alternative curricula and settings for clinical instruction.

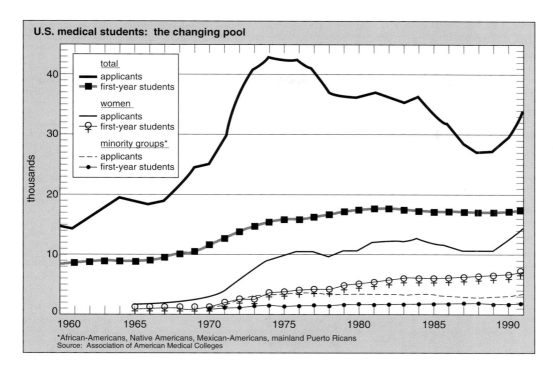

U.S. medical students: the changing pool

thousands

Legend:
total
— applicants
— first-year students
women
— applicants
— first-year students
minority groups*
- - - applicants
— first-year students

*African-Americans, Native Americans, Mexican-Americans, mainland Puerto Ricans
Source: Association of American Medical Colleges

medical school in 1991 as had entered during the entire five-year period from 1965 to 1969. After a fairly steady rise in female applicants for two decades beginning in 1965, the number of female applicants then declined between the years 1984 and 1988, but it has been rising again ever since 1988. In 1991–92 women constituted 39.9% of first-year students. During the late 1970s and early 1980s when the total number of applicants declined, the number of female applicants continued to increase. Even when the number of female applicants started to decline after 1984, the rate of decrease was less than that for males, and so the percentage of women in the applicant pool continued to grow. In 1991 there were 6,804 female first-year students—about 550 more than there had been three years previously.

Racial and ethnic mix. Although there has also been an increase in the number of minority students, their pattern of growth has been less consistent than that of women students. After an initial spurt some 20 years ago, the number of applicants from minority backgrounds (defined as those who are under-represented in medicine—African-Americans, Native Americans, Mexican-Americans, and mainland Puerto Ricans) stabilized at about 3,500 per year in the early 1980s, peaking, as did the number of female applicants, with the 1984 entering class. This was followed by a decline to fewer than 2,900 in 1988. A large rebound was then seen with the 1991 entering class, comprising 3,600 minority students. Minorities constituted 11% of the first-year enrollment in the 1991–92 academic year.

Age and educational background. Although a majority of students still enter medical school immediately after receiving a baccalaureate degree, recent years have seen more older candidates interested in beginning a career in medicine. For the 1991 entering class, 16.6% of the applicants and 12.3% of those accepted were aged 28 and over. This compares with 10.4 and 5.8%, respectively, in 1972. In general, it is believed that older students may have a stronger commitment to their pursuit of a career in medicine than do their younger counterparts.

Although there are now more "untraditional" students in medical school, certain characteristics of the medical student body have not changed much. Despite an expressed desire by medical schools to encourage application by students with undergraduate studies in the arts and humanities, three-quarters of all applicants and matriculants have earned bachelor's degrees in the sciences. The MCAT, sponsored by the Association of American Medical Colleges (AAMC) and used by nearly every medical school as one evaluation criterion for entrance, was substantially revised for the 1991 tests with the objective of encouraging students interested in medicine to pursue broad undergraduate study in the social sciences and humanities. The new test emphasizes critical thinking, logical reasoning, problem-solving, and communication skills. The most radical feature of the new MCAT is the inclusion of a graded essay component in which all examinees prepare an essay on a uniform subject. For example, they must reflect on a statement such as "Progress seldom comes from the deliberations of a group.

343

Rather, progress most often comes from the creative thinking of individuals working alone." The essays are graded according to examinees' ability to address and resolve conflicts inherent in the statement.

The medical curriculum: a time for change

At the beginning of the 20th century, the most rigorously academic medical schools had established a curriculum of two years of the basic sciences essential to the study of medicine followed by two years of clinical experience. This model was the basis against which Abraham Flexner (1866–1959), who played a major role in the assessment and improvement of medical education in North America, evaluated existing medical schools. The response by educational institutions and the public to his seminal 1910 report, *Medical Education in the United States and Canada: A Report to the Carnegie Foundation for the Advancement of Teaching,* established the "two-plus-two" pattern as the model for medical school education—a model that has endured throughout the century.

Accordingly, most U.S. medical students now spend their first two years in the study of anatomy and cell biology, biochemistry and molecular biology, physiology, pharmacology, microbiology, and pathology. This is followed by a year of required clerkships that generally include internal medicine, pediatrics, psychiatry, obstetrics and gynecology, surgery, and, in some schools, family medicine. The fourth year provides additional clinical experiences—generally a mixture of elective and required course work in disciplines such as radiology, anesthesiology, and the medical and surgical subspecialties. Following the award of the M.D. degree, young physicians begin an intensive period of hospital-based clinical training—the residency—which lasts from three to seven years and prepares them for the practice of a particular medical specialty.

Stimuli for change. This system has served U.S. medical education well by establishing the nation's physicians as among the world's best trained and most scientifically based. However, 80 years after the Flexner report, the academic medicine community is trying to define a post-Flexner model of medical education that will carry the profession into the next century. The stimuli for such a change are several:

• There has been an exponential growth in biomedical knowledge. In particular, advances in molecular and cell biology have refined the understanding of mechanisms controlling health and disease. While many of these scientific discoveries are currently of more interest and value to researchers than to practitioners, their eventual impact on medical education will be significant.

• Recent discoveries in biochemistry, immunology, and genetics that explain fundamental biological processes mandate more integral study of the basic sciences along with clinical medicine. Such integration

can be achieved only through a more interdisciplinary approach to medical education.

• A number of recent studies of medical education, including a report for the AAMC on the general professional education of the physician, emphasize the desirability of making education more "student-and-learning-oriented" rather than "faculty-and-teaching-oriented." This requires that medical faculties offer educational experiences in which students are active, independent learners and problem solvers rather than passive recipients of information.

• Greater attention is being given to the crucial dynamics of the patient-physician relationship and therefore to ensuring that students acquire the skills and attitudes to make this relationship more meaningful. Whereas previously U.S. medical practice had focused on treating and curing patients' illnesses, there is now an increased emphasis on the physician's responsibility to work with individual patients and communities to promote health and prevent disease.

• Heretofore, most clinical education has taken place in the teaching hospital. However, in recent years medical educators have come to recognize that the teaching hospital has significant deficiencies as an educational setting. The environment of the hospital has changed; as a consequence of recent cost-containment efforts, most hospitalized patients are sicker and are kept in the hospital for a briefer period. Thus, it is now more difficult to structure a coherent learning situation that enables students to follow the full progress of patients and their problems. Additionally, new technologies have enabled certain treatments and procedures to be performed in settings other than the hospital—settings that have not traditionally been used for medical education. Medical school faculty now realize that a broader and more representative patient population exists outside the hospital than in it.

Revisionary tactics. In response to these stimuli for change, the process of medical education, particularly in the undergraduate four years, is under active review at most U.S. medical schools, and alternative curricula and teaching approaches are being tested and evaluated. The objective of most of the revisions is to develop medical students as self-starters, problem solvers, and critical thinkers and to link the content of their course work more closely with the treatment of patients. Schools that have initiated significant curriculum changes include the University of New Mexico School of Medicine, Albuquerque; Rush Medical College, Chicago; Harvard Medical School and Tufts University School of Medicine, Boston; the University of Rochester (N.Y.) School of Medicine and Dentistry; Southern Illinois University School of Medicine, Springfield; the State University of New York Health Science Center at Syracuse; and the Bowman Gray School of Medicine of Wake Forest University, Winston-Salem, N.C. A few traditional medical schools

Students in the alternative curriculum at Rush Medical College in Chicago exchange ideas with the program's director, Harold Paul. Rush is one of a handful of U.S. medical schools that offer a nontraditional educational option—one based on a Socratic method of teaching that requires students to be active and independent learners and problem solvers rather than passive recipients of information. Paul believes that in the near future the Rush experiment—and others like it— will become "the Cadillac of medical education."

have established highly innovative curricula as separate tracks that a small subset of students within the school follow from matriculation to graduation.

First-year curricula in most U.S. medical schools now include fewer scheduled hours and fewer lecture hours. From 1983 to 1990 the average number of scheduled hours in required first-year courses decreased from 933.6 to 854.5 hours. The aim is to add learning experiences that are less didactic. In many schools more emphasis is now placed on tutorials, small group sessions, and independent study.

Several relatively new pedagogical approaches are receiving increased attention in medical schools. One of these is so-called problem-based learning, which allows students to accept responsibility for their own learning. An example of such an approach is a program that was begun at Rush Medical College in 1984. In addition to its standard curriculum, Rush offers an alternative curriculum in which the teaching of basic science is carried out by Socratic method. The students meet in small groups to work through sets of clinical problems. A facilitator who has been instructed in Socratic principles encourages students to test hypotheses and solve problems. Initial effects of this experience were seen in the oral examinations of the first such matriculating students in 1987; those in the alternative curriculum scored significantly higher than standard curriculum students in several areas. Instructors involved in the Rush program emphasize that as innovative programs in medical education increase in number, new evaluation methods will be needed to measure how well they are working.

Another educational innovation is the use of so-called standardized patients, sometimes real but of-ten simulated, who participate in the clinical learning experiences of students. Simulated patients are usually laypersons who are taught to make a uniform presentation of a "case" by acting out the signs and symptoms of a particular illness. In a typical evaluation based on such simulated patients, students rotate through different examination stations so that all students see the same "patients." These standardized patients evaluate the students' abilities in history taking and physical examination and assess their interpersonal skills. Much research is under way on this approach, which has been shown to have validity in strengthening medical students' clinical skill but which is, at present, administratively complex and costly.

The use of standardized patients is one of many innovations of interest to medical educators today as they strive to make medical learning more competency-based. Multiple-choice examinations, long a staple evaluative tool in medical education, are now recognized as being of quite limited use in predicting how well an individual will perform when engaged in the clinical practice of medicine. Knowledge alone is insufficient for the successful practice of medicine; it must be accompanied by the ability to use it effectively to treat individual patients. New ways of assessing clinical skills are being studied at many schools in order to link the process of education more closely with the desired outcome of clinical competence.

Medical informatics. Medical schools are also finding new ways to use computers in the evolving science of medical informatics—to improve the efficiency of information storage and retrieval, to assist in medical decision making, and to provide educational opportunities. Computers are now routinely used for electronic medical literature searches, for storage of medical information systems, and for computer-based medical education. In the latter application, computer simulations—in particular, interactive videos that simulate patient-physician encounters—provide a number of instructional advantages. These powerful educational tools enable a wider range of cases to be "seen" by students. They allow more control over the complex problems presented at different points in the students' learning and make it possible to follow diseases over longer periods. They also provide "standard" cases that can be used to measure and evaluate students' problem-solving skills.

More advanced computer-assisted medical decision-making systems have also been developed in selected disciplines, but at present their use in medical education is limited. The development of both expert systems and interactive computer instructional packages is costly and time consuming. Currently only a small number of physicians have training in this still-developing information science, but this situation is likely to change in coming years.

From medical school to residency. In recent years several experimental approaches have been proposed that would alter the current structure of medical education in such a way that the overall length of medical training would be reduced. Specifically, the aim would be to prepare greater numbers of physicians to be "general practitioners."

Writing in the journal *Health Affairs* in 1988, Robert H. Ebert, emeritus dean of Harvard Medical School, and Eli Ginzberg, professor emeritus of economics and director of the Conservation of Human Resources at Columbia University, New York City, proposed a scheme in which the fourth year of medical school would be merged into the period of postgraduate

medical education, thereby eliminating a year or two in the overall period of physician training. At the conclusion of a six-year educational continuum, the individual would be certified as a generalist physician. Although the principle is sound, the proposal has been met with skepticism by many in academic medicine. Currently residency training is the responsibility of independent certifying and accrediting bodies and hospital program directors; the role of the medical school in residency training is limited. A few programs have secured special permission from certifying authorities and have experimental programs under way in which a small number of trainees combine the clinical years of medical school with residency training in primary care disciplines.

The challenges ahead

There appears to be a consensus not only on the directions to be taken toward altering the content and process of medical education but on means of accomplishing the ultimate goal—*i.e.,* of preparing doctors who will function more effectively in the next century. However, such a system of medical education in which the nation's medical schools are producing the type of physician who is more likely to meet the needs of society is not yet close at hand.

As already indicated, there is a need for more generalist, or primary care, physicians. Specifically, U.S. medical schools must take stronger steps to interest young people in careers as generalist rather than as specialist physicians. Although the government has recognized this need for two decades, medical schools continue to produce an ever increasing supply of specialists. Among the 1987 graduates only one-quarter chose careers in one of the primary care disciplines—general internal medicine, general pedi-

Because hospital settings may not be relevant to the future practices of many of today's physicians-in-training, medical schools are increasingly offering clinical education experiences in other milieus. Students from Northwestern University Medical School in Chicago attend elderly patients in the Methodist Home, a residential nursing facility on the city's north side.

Steve Kagan

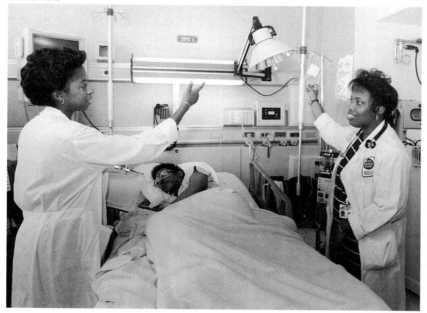

Recent graduates of the Sophie Davis School of Biomedical Education of the City University of New York attend a patient at New York University Medical Center. The Sophie Davis program, which began in 1973, is one of several in the country that seek out minority and economically disadvantaged students in inner-city high schools. The students are then given financial aid and the opportunity to take accelerated courses that prepare them to pursue a medical education. About 85% of college freshmen entering the Sophie Davis program have gone on to become physicians, and once they receive their medical degrees, most then return to the inner city to practice.

atrics, or family medicine. By contrast, in Great Britain 70% and in Canada 50% of doctors are primary care physicians, or general practitioners.

Another great need is to modify the clinical education of young physicians to make it more typical of the practice they will enter at the completion of their training. Nowadays the types of exposure that young physicians receive in hospitals may not be relevant to their future practice, particularly because hospitals have become progressively more specialized settings for complex services—*e.g.,* critical care medicine, transplantation surgery, neonatal intensive care, etc. Therefore, medical schools must identify new settings for clinical education, which may include physicians' offices in private solo or group practice, health maintenance organizations, skilled and nonskilled nursing facilities, hospices, day-care facilities for special populations, outpatient clinics, ambulatory surgery centers, and free-standing emergency facilities. While some of these may be considered surrogate inpatient settings, their modi operandi differ radically from the classical inpatient ward. It is hoped that the educational imperative to train medical students and residents in ambulatory settings will provide the means to attract more young physicians into primary care. However, such a shift to more teaching in the ambulatory care setting will require substantial curriculum changes.

Medical schools must also consider what needs to be done to improve educational opportunities for minority students and to increase minority participation in medicine. This will be necessary if medicine is to reflect national demographic patterns, in which the rate of increase among U.S. minority populations is greater than that in the Caucasian population.

Many medical schools are in the process of developing enhanced educational opportunities for minorities and for economically disadvantaged students. Academic medical centers, which are staffed by a large number of exceptionally qualified and scientifically trained professionals, are among the most respected, influential, and economically important institutions in their respective communities. In this milieu the stage is set for the development of potentially productive partnerships between local public schools and the academic medical center.

A model program was begun in 1971 by the Baylor College of Medicine, Houston, Texas. Baylor founded a magnet high school in the health sciences designed to serve a predominantly minority population. Over the years, nearly one out of every 20 graduates of Houston's High School for the Health Professions has become a physician or is now in medical school, and three-quarters of the graduates have pursued a science or health-related degree in college. Other medical schools, such as the University of California at San Francisco School of Medicine, the University of Kentucky College of Medicine in Lexington, and the University of Texas Medical School at San Antonio, are also working to improve the quality of premed science education in their respective communities for both minority and majority students.

Financial integrity of medical schools. Medical schools are expensive enterprises. In order to meet their multiple mission of education, research, and patient care (the latter in conjunction with their cooperating teaching hospitals) and to meet societal goals, they must maintain financial health. In the last three decades medical school revenues have grown from

347

$1,713,000,000 to $18,771,000,000. The ability of any sector of the economy to sustain such growth in the present era of resource constraint is questionable. Currently some schools are heavily dependent on revenue from research activities and clinical practice. The financial stability of academic medical centers and their ability to thrive in the future will be assured only if they maintain a balance in revenues from all three activities—education, research, and patient care.

At a crossroads. A survey of medical educators at all U.S. medical schools was conducted in 1989. A majority of educators expressed the belief that "fundamental changes" were needed, and nearly three-quarters of the deans and associate deans voiced the need for either "fundamental changes" or "thorough reform" of the U.S. medical education system. Many changes are now well under way; many more are inevitable in the decade to come.

—*Robert G. Petersdorf, M.D.,*
and Kathleen S. Turner, M.P.A.

Medical Imaging

Medical imaging first became a reality nearly 100 years ago when in 1895 Wilhelm Conrad Röntgen in Würzburg, Germany, discovered the X-ray. His announcement of a hitherto unidentified type of electrical-magnetic energy—which he designated X, for "unknown"—stimulated much research into its potential medical applications on both sides of the Atlantic. This remarkable discovery soon granted physicians the ability to look inside the human body without having to do surgery. By the beginning of the 20th century, many medical X-ray techniques had been established, and diagnostic radiology had achieved the status of a distinct medical specialty.

For many years X-rays were used in medicine much as they had been in Röntgen's time—*i.e.,* primarily to image the bones and the lungs. In the 1920s, however, a series of discoveries in the engineering and biological sciences rapidly expanded the specialty and increased its complexity. Many improvements were made to the equipment that provided the energy for the process (the X-ray generator) and produced the actual radiation (the X-ray tube). Advances in materials that could capture and record the X-ray (X-ray film) were also instrumental in broadening the application of the technology. Chemists and pharmacists became interested in this evolving medical specialty and developed hundreds of new compounds, called contrast agents (or contrast media), that enabled doctors to create images of virtually all internal human organs. Innovative research by radiologists (physicians with several years of specialty training in radiological techniques) and other physicians and scientists resulted in the development of methods that made X-ray imaging useful in many different kinds of diagnosis.

The success of the X-ray in medical diagnostics encouraged further research, and by the 1950s medical imaging began to use other forms of energy—for example, radioactive isotopes and sound waves. The development of new imaging techniques burgeoned with the linking of the computer to the X-ray; in the 1970s this partnership produced sophisticated imaging methods such as CT (computed tomography) and MRI (magnetic resonance imaging). The extraordinary advances that have occurred in just the past several years could not have taken place without the nearly 100 years of previous scientific discovery and development.

Röntgen's rays: today's applications

Diagnostic radiology is the most common form of medical imaging. The process uses conventional X-rays, created by an X-ray tube and transmitted through a portion of the human body. The resulting image is then developed on film. Approximately 85% of all medical imaging performed today uses X-rays. More than 100 different kinds of examinations can be ordered by a physician for diagnostic use, ranging from a single image of the chest to a coronary arteriogram requiring hundreds of individual images that are produced on a series of films in a movielike fashion and enable doctors to see blood flowing through the arteries that supply the heart muscle.

Advances in medical imaging can take many forms—methods to improve the accuracy of diagnosis, to make the imaging process safer for the patient, or to reduce the costs. One important recent development was the creation of a new type of contrast agent that is safer than previously available materials. Iodinated contrast agents are chemicals containing iodide that are given to a patient, usually by injection into a vein or artery, for use along with X-rays in order to identify structures such as the kidneys and blood vessels that are not clearly visible with X-rays alone. Iodinated agents have been in use for approximately 50 years; recently, however, a new kind of agent was developed, which is safer than older contrast media because it has approximately the same number of molecules per cubic centimeter of fluid—a property known as osmolality or osmolarity—as flowing blood. These so-called low-osmolality agents provide the same kind of diagnostic information as older agents but have a much lower rate of side effects such as discomfort and nausea. In addition, some patients have more serious physical reactions after injections of iodinated contrast media—for example, disturbance of heartbeat or impairment of kidney function—and some even die. Although severe reactions are unusual and death is rare (about one death per 75,000 injections), the new low-osmolality agents are two to three times safer than those employed previously. Consequently, they have become widely used in the past few years.

Unfortunately, this improvement in safety has come with a high price tag; low-osmolality contrast is approximately 10 times costlier than the older agents. This increase in cost adds up to as much as $1 billion annually in the U.S. alone, a factor that has made the widespread use of the newer agents controversial. Two recent studies, by Earl P. Steinberg and colleagues at Johns Hopkins University, Baltimore, Md., and Michael Bettman of Boston University, suggested that only patients at high risk for a contrast reaction—*i.e.,* those with the most severe illnesses—should get the newer and more expensive agents, while most patients, in whom adverse reactions are rare, can safely receive the traditional and considerably less expensive contrast media. However, the definition of "high risk" depends on a subjective judgment, which might not be agreed on by all clinicians.

Mammography, the use of X-rays to image the breast in order to identify cancer at an early stage, is currently the fastest growing diagnostic procedure in the U.S. Breast cancer is the most common cancer in American women, and its frequency of diagnosis is rising. Approximately one in every nine U.S. women will be diagnosed with breast cancer during her lifetime. Several clinical studies have shown that if a breast tumor is found when it is small (less than 2.5 cm [one inch] in diameter), the chance of a cure is high. Until recently, most breast cancers were found by the woman or by her doctor during a physical examination. The size of the cancer by the time it is palpable is almost always larger than 2.5 cm, and the possibility of a cure is then reduced to approximately 50% or less. Studies have shown that if a tumor is found by means of mammography during an annual screening exam, the cure rate rises dramatically to 90% or more. Because of this potential for saving

lives, the American Cancer Society and other groups are now emphasizing the need for mammograms to be performed every other year beginning at the age of 40 and annually after age 50.

In the U.S. initial efforts to screen large numbers of women were not successful; the primary reasons were the high cost of the exam and the inaccessibility of facilities (hospitals or medical offices) where mammography is performed. Efforts have therefore been made to reduce the cost of the procedure (to approximately $50 per examination) and to make the exam more readily available to women throughout the country. One method of increasing accessibility has been the use of mobile mammography vans, which travel to shopping centers, churches, residential neighborhoods, and workplaces, where women can conveniently schedule exams.

Mammography is also safer today than several years ago because the radiation dose required for producing a satisfactory image has been reduced considerably by improvements in X-ray tubes and film and in the way in which the procedure is performed (*i.e.,* positioning of the breasts, taking of different views). A remaining problem is the use of mammography in the hundreds of thousands of women who have had breast enlargement or reconstruction with silicone implants. Silicone can prevent the X-rays from reaching the film, making the detection of tumors difficult and sometimes impossible. This problem has been the focus of considerable public concern and deserves further research.

Another major advance in the field of radiology is the development of the specialty called interventional radiology. A variety of techniques now make it possible for doctors to place tiny flexible tubes, or catheters, as well as miniature devices (needles, wires, coils, etc.),

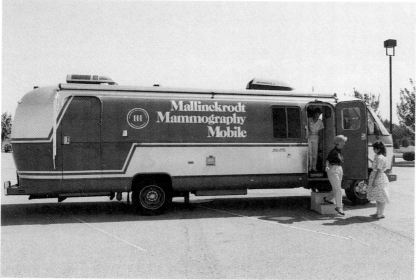

In St. Louis, Missouri, a mobile van enables large numbers of women who might not otherwise have mammograms to undergo regular breast cancer screening.

Mallinckrodt Institute of Radiology

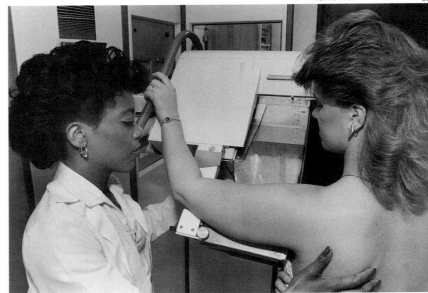

Improvements in the mammography process—for example, better methods of positioning the breasts and the taking of more than one view— have increased the procedure's effectiveness. Advances in X-ray technology have also made the process safer by reducing the amount of radiation needed to produce a satisfactory image.

into virtually any blood vessel in the human body in order to correct abnormalities that are beyond a surgeon's reach. The interventional radiologist guides the instruments by viewing X-ray images of the vessels on a television screen.

For the patient the procedures require only mild sedation and small amounts of local anesthesia. The most common interventional procedures are performed in arteries and veins, where the catheter is often used to insert a special balloon that can be guided to a location where the vessel is narrowed or blocked. The balloon is then inflated, clearing the obstructed area. Such vascular constrictions can occur throughout the body but are most common in the arteries of the heart and in peripheral arteries and veins of the legs. Interventional balloon angioplasty is now a frequently performed treatment for both problems. Vascular constrictions are also common in the carotid arteries (the vessels in the neck that supply blood to the brain), but balloon angioplasty treatment for this condition is only in an experimental stage. Procedures to correct problems such as aneurysms and arteriovenous malformations within the brain are newer and still considered investigational. Although they have been undertaken only at a few specialized centers, interventional techniques may one day become standard.

Isotopes in action

Nuclear medicine is a type of medical imaging that uses radiation-emitting atoms, called radioactive isotopes, and techniques of nuclear physics that were developed after World War II when the scientific efforts that produced the atomic bomb were focused on peaceful goals. Isotopes that are injected into the blood circulation concentrate within a specific organ, which can then be imaged with equipment that detects the radiation being given off by the isotopes. A variety of nuclear medicine procedures have been developed to study and diagnose diseases of the liver, lung, bones, and heart. For example, special isotopes and equipment are now available in most hospitals to examine patients with chest pain to determine if they are having a heart attack (myocardial infarction) and to predict whether various treatments will reduce the pain and keep the heart muscle alive. The treatment options for heart attack patients include surgery to bypass blocked arteries, balloon angioplasty to clear obstructions, and medications to reduce blood pressure and help the heart work more efficiently. Recent advances in nuclear medicine allow the doctor to predict which of these is likely to help a given patient. The procedure is called a thallium scan. The isotope thallium is injected intravenously and concentrates in heart muscle that is still living but not in heart muscle that is dead (infarcted). If the thallium scan reveals that the heart muscle beyond a blocked coronary artery is already dead, then neither surgery or angioplasty is likely to benefit the patient, and therapy with cardiac drugs is the appropriate treatment.

One fairly recently developed nuclear medicine technique, called PET (positron emission tomography), is increasingly being applied to the study of the human brain. Positrons are special kinds of isotopes, and tomography means a "slicing" technique that produces images that are a slice, or cross section, of human anatomy. PET has an advantage over other forms of medical imaging in that positron isotopes are capable of showing organ metabolism and function in addition to structure. PET studies are similar to other nuclear

350

medicine imaging procedures except that the isotopes that are employed are natural substances used in body metabolism—for example, oxygen, nitrogen, and glucose—rather than the synthetic pharmaceutical agents used in other nuclear medicine techniques. The imaging equipment used in PET creates slices that show the exact location in the body where these metabolic substances are being utilized. For example, PET can determine whether heart muscle is still alive after a heart attack by imaging oxygen or fatty acids that are naturally used by functioning muscle tissue, rather than by detecting injected thallium isotopes.

Scientists are now using PET to map the sites of various higher brain functions, such as speech, memory, attention, and emotion. What is particularly remarkable is that PET has applications far beyond the identification of diseased or damaged tissues; it can provide information about function in completely healthy people. For example, in 1991 a team of investigators from Washington University, St. Louis, Mo., published the findings of a study that examined brain function in learning and memory. The subjects were asked to read and then recall lists of words displayed on a computer screen. PET scans showed that two areas of the brain are especially important to this visual memory task—the frontal cortex, which is located just behind the forehead, and the hippocampus, a small but critical region of the brain that is situated near the ears. PET identified these areas of the brain by mapping the uptake of water labeled with an isotope of oxygen.

In a similar type of experiment, scientists at the University of California at Irvine used PET scans to monitor brain activity in people learning and then repeating an activity. Volunteers were monitored while they learned to play a computer game and subsequently during daily practice sessions. The researchers found that over time subjects who had scored highest on an intelligence test had the largest decrease in brain metabolism, indicating that "smart" brains may be able to conserve energy when performing a complex but already known task. Further investigations of this type will undoubtedly expand the understanding of normal brain functioning and of the devastating neurological diseases that can disrupt it.

Making "sound" diagnoses

Sonar, the use of high-frequency sound waves to identify objects, was first employed during World War I to locate submarines and other underwater hazards. It was further developed during World War II. Ultrasound imaging, like nuclear medicine, is a technique developed after World War II when wartime discoveries were turned to peacetime ends. Medical sonography is now commonly used to image the neck, heart, and various organs in the abdomen and to evaluate fetal development. The latter use has raised important

safety questions. It is always necessary to determine the potential hazards of any imaging technique before it is widely used, and this is particularly true for those methods used in pregnant women. While concerns that ultrasound might harm the developing fetus have generally been found to be groundless, there have been lingering doubts about the long-term effects of prenatal exposure. Addressing this issue, Norwegian researchers reported in early 1992 on a study of some 2,000 children who had been exposed to ultrasound prior to birth; the investigators found that the children had normal learning ability and no physical evidence of harm. In particular, they found no indication of an increased incidence of the learning disorder dyslexia in the youngsters, a phenomenon that had been observed in an earlier study.

Recently, special electronic techniques and computer software have enabled the development of sonographic techniques that can identify flowing blood and even show the direction of the flow. Highly sophisticated sonographic equipment can produce images that show the arteries as red and the veins as blue—just as they appear in anatomy books. These striking images have become very important in evaluating the liver and other organs of the abdomen. Another technical improvement in sonography has been the development of highly specialized mechanical probes, or transducers, that create the sound waves. These can be placed within the body—or even inside a blood vessel—producing very detailed images of the heart, bowel, and other organs.

Innovations in CT technology

Perhaps the most revolutionary development in medical imaging since Röntgen's time occurred in 1973 when the computer was linked to the X-ray; the result was computed tomography (CT; sometimes called computerized axial tomography, or CAT). The technique was invented by Godfrey Hounsfield of Great Britain on the basis of earlier discoveries by Allan Cormack, a U.S. physicist. For this achievement Hounsfield and Cormack shared the Nobel Prize for Physiology or Medicine in 1979, echoing the accomplishment of Röntgen, who received the very first Nobel Prize for Medicine in 1901. CT scanning uses X-rays for imaging, but a special computer produces pictures that are much more sensitive than standard radiographs for detecting disease in many parts of the body. CT images are cross-sectional views of the whole body rather than images of a particular region such as are seen in an X-ray of the chest or elbow. Hundreds of thousands of these procedures are now performed in the United States each year.

By 1991 CT was thought to be a "mature" technology from which little change could be expected in the future; however, that prediction was proved wrong with the very recent development of so-called spiral

A youngster undergoing MRI in an innovative "open" scanner is able to see and talk to her mother throughout the procedure. Instead of the cylindrical magnet used in conventional MRI— with its tunnel-like interior that many patients find distressingly confining—this machine employs two flat magnetic plates supported at the corners. Although only about 60 such MRI units were in use worldwide in 1992, the system is likely to become more widely available within a few years.

CT. Several technical breakthroughs now allow the radiologist to obtain a unique interconnected spiral slice through an entire organ, much like the peel of an orange or apple when skillfully removed in a single, continuous piece. This spiral technique shows great promise for producing extremely sharp three-dimensional images of the brain, heart, and spine that should be of great diagnostic importance to physicians. While spiral CT has been possible for only a short time, it has already proved its benefits in finding small nodules in the lung that could be missed with conventional one-dimensional CT images and in identifying multiple facial fractures after serious trauma. Because spiral CT does not require complete immobility of the body and internal organs, it may be especially useful for scanning of small infants without anesthesia. (Anesthetics sometimes must be used in other imaging techniques to control the child's breathing and stop the motion of the lungs during the exposure time.)

Magnetic resonance imaging: fulfilling its promise

If radiologists were asked to identify the single most important recent development in medical imaging, most would probably vote for magnetic resonance imaging, or MRI. This technique is dependent on the computer and the sophisticated tomographic techniques first developed for the CT scanner. Instead of X-rays, a powerful magnetic field (thousands of times more powerful than the Earth's magnetic field) and very specific radio frequency energies (radio waves) are employed. The primary piece of equipment is a huge ring-shaped magnet capable of generating a strong magnetic field. The patient is positioned so

that the part of the body being examined lies inside a tunnel-like opening within the magnet. MRI technology relies on the magnetic properties of hydrogen atoms that exist normally in virtually all body tissues. (Hydrogen is the principal component of water, H_2O, which constitutes about 60% of human body weight.) When placed in a strong magnetic field, nuclei of the hydrogen atoms within the tissue being imaged line up in an orderly fashion. When the magnetized tissue is subjected to radio waves, the magnetized nuclei tip out of alignment, generating electrical signals that are recorded and, with the aid of a computer, reconstructed into images. MRI scanners are extremely expensive, costing $1 million–$2 million each.

Although diagnostic imaging with X-rays is quite safe, MRI is even less hazardous than most imaging techniques because it uses no X-ray energies at all. However, the small risk reduction achieved could be offset by potential damage from the strong magnetic fields and the radio frequency energies that are required by MRI techniques. Several animal and human studies have been performed in recent years to test the safety of the procedure, all showing no apparent harm. The safety issues have not been completely laid to rest, however, as newer MRI techniques are using higher powered magnetic fields and more intense radio frequency signals than were previously employed.

The pictures produced by MRI are highly detailed; the procedure can capture both normal human anatomy and changes resulting from many diseases. MRI scans are often better for diagnostic purposes than those produced by CT because the distribution of water in the tissues is particularly important in specific disease processes; furthermore, the ability of MRI to create images at any level, or plane, of the body is a distinct asset. Essentially all experts agree that it has already proved to be the best imaging technique for diagnosing those diseases of the brain or spine in which water distribution is a useful diagnostic finding (brain tumors, for example), for evaluating stroke, and in preoperative assessment of the spine (where it allows the surgeon to visualize the relationship between the spinal, or vertebral, canal and the spinal cord). An important use of MRI is in the diagnosis of injuries of the knee and other joints where the damage often is not to the bone but to the surrounding soft tissues and cartilage. Common examples are sports injuries such as pitcher's elbow and football knee.

MRI technology is still very new; experimental machines became available only in the early 1980s. Development has been rapid, however, and recent improvements allow the production of high-quality images that provide substantial diagnostic information. Scanning speed is important, and newer techniques have reduced the imaging time for some procedures from more than 40 minutes to 5 minutes or less—a major advantage for imaging organs in which there is rapid movement, such as the pumping action of the heart. Shorter scanning times also make the examination easier to undergo and reduce the cost.

While MRI scanning is safe, painless, and usually well tolerated, some people find it stressful. The patient must lie for several minutes within a long, narrow tunnel, strapped to a platform and unable to move. During the imaging process, he or she is subjected to a repetitive pounding noise like the sound of someone hammering on metal. For patients who are claustrophobic or become panicky in closed-in spaces, it can be difficult to relax and lie still for the time required for producing the images. Many manufacturers of MRI equipment are evaluating methods to make the technique easier for the patient; for example, some machines now have earphones that the patient wears to listen to music during the procedure. Mild tranquilizers help some to tolerate the procedure. One solution to the problem may lie in the development of scanners that do not completely enclose the patient.

Early research suggests that MRI may be the most important medical imaging technique of the future. Technological breakthroughs will allow MRI procedures to study and diagnose disease in every organ, even in the heart with its rapid and constant motion. MRI technology may also enable physicians to identify many biochemical substances and metabolic functions by the use of magnetic resonance spectroscopy (MRS). MRS is a technique that has been used for many years in organic chemistry to determine the composition of unknown materials without destroying the material being analyzed. It is based on the principle that the magnetic frequencies of certain atomic

nuclei are affected in a small but detectable manner by their immediate atomic environment. It too involves the bombardment of atoms in a magnetic field with a series of radio pulses. The technique has only recently been applied to the analysis of human disease processes. With MRS important substances within the body—metabolites (i.e., products of metabolism) such as amino acids, high-energy phosphates, and lactate—can be measured in a completely noninvasive manner. MRS is currently experimental but most likely in the future will be used in conjunction with MRI to detect the concentration of these metabolites within specific organs. In other words, an image of a particular organ will be acquired with MRI, and then measurements of the metabolites within that organ will be obtained by means of MRS guided by the initial image.

MRS is available in the laboratory and can be used to analyze tissue samples, but it cannot yet be effectively applied to the living body. The diagnostic capabilities and precision of MRS improve when the imaging times are long (minutes to hours), the magnetic fields are strong (hundreds of thousands of times more powerful than the Earth's magnetic field), and the tissue under study can be precisely controlled. These criteria are easily satisfied when liquids or solids in test tubes are being studied but difficult or perhaps impossible to achieve in a living patient. Future research will seek to overcome this difficulty.

Electronic radiology

Since the time of Röntgen, all medical images have been recorded and viewed on radiographic film, which is much like photographic film. X-ray films have been improved over the years but have several limitations. Recent computer technology breakthroughs and the design of computer chips capable of storing great quantities of data are making it possible to record detailed medical images in computer memory and then to project them on TV screens. This new approach to making, storing, and displaying medical images is called electronic radiology. Electronic radiology has many advantages over X-ray film. For example, the technique allows immediate review and interpretation of the image, while X-ray film, like photographic film, cannot be viewed until it has been developed. Electronic radiology also makes it possible for images to be transmitted over long distances, even around the world. During the Persian Gulf war, U.S. forces used electronic radiology techniques to transmit medical images of injured soldiers via space satellites for interpretation by radiologists in U.S. military hospitals.

The high price of high tech

More than 250 million medical imaging procedures are performed annually in the U.S., an average of more than one procedure per citizen per year. These innovative techniques have improved the health of Americans but at a considerable cost—more than $20 billion annually. The U.S. system of health care is under intense criticism because of its high costs, and medical imaging has come in for its share of the blame. Radiologists and allied personnel are concerned about this issue, and considerable time and effort are being spent to determine how to provide appropriate imaging for a "reasonable" dollar amount. Does high technology have to come at high cost? So far the answer has been yes, but physicians and scientists are currently working to find ways to reduce these expenses.

—Ronald G. Evens, M.D.

Mental Health and Illness

According to the American Psychiatric Association, at any given time between 30 million and 45 million Americans suffer from clearly diagnosable mental disorders that cause some degree of incapacitation in their daily lives. These are people of all ages, races, and socioeconomic backgrounds. Indeed, the personal and social costs of mental disorders are comparable to those of major physical illnesses such as heart disease or cancer. The Institute of Medicine of the National Academy of Sciences estimates that in the United States alone the direct costs of mental illness total $23.4 billion a year and the direct costs of substance abuse disorders total $16.9 billion; the indirect costs of these disorders increase the total costs to more than $249 billion.

Yet only one in five people afflicted by a mental disorder seeks or receives appropriate help. This is unfortunate because there has been tremendous progress in understanding, diagnosing, and treating psychiatric illness, and most who suffer *can* be helped.

Controversies

Controversies, however, concerning mental health and illness are not uncommon. In the past couple of years, for example, two widely prescribed drugs have made headlines because of alleged severe psychiatric side effects. Reports of a possible association between the use of the antidepressant drug fluoxetine (Prozac) and suicide or other violent behavior prompted an investigation by the U.S. Food and Drug Administration (FDA). An FDA committee heard public testimony on the issue and also evaluated evidence from controlled research trials that had compared the effects of Prozac with those of placebos (pills with no active medication) in large numbers of patients. Mental health experts pointed out that suicidal thinking is a common symptom of depression and expressed concerns that inadequately supported warnings about suicidal tendencies in those taking Prozac or other antidepressants would compromise the effective treatment of depressive illness. After considering all the evidence, the FDA committee concluded that there was no credible evidence of a causal link between the use of antidepressant drugs, including Prozac, and suicidal or violent behavior.

The drug triazolam (Halcion) has become the most widely prescribed sleeping pill in the world, probably because its short duration of action does not lead to daytime "hangover" effects. However, critics have charged that Halcion causes more frequent and much more severe side effects than other sleeping pills, including memory loss, paranoia, and violent behavior. While such concerns led to Halcion's removal from the market in the United Kingdom in late 1991, the drug continues to be available in the United States. Halcion's manufacturer, the Upjohn Co., has defended itself against allegations of inadequate safety testing and offered to defend and indemnify physicians who are sued for alleged personal injuries resulting from Halcion use, assuming they have prescribed it properly. While still unsettled, the Halcion controversy underscores the importance of evaluating sleep disturbances, which are a common symptom of many mental and physical disorders, for their underlying cause and recognizing that sleeping pills as treatment are usually for only short-term use.

Another recent, highly publicized event had less of an impact than might have been expected—the insanity defense trial in Milwaukee, Wis., of Jeffrey Dahmer, the serial killer who admitted to having murdered and dismembered 15 young men. On Feb. 15, 1992, a jury found that Dahmer was sane when he committed his crimes. The jurors were instructed to base their ruling on two questions: Did he suffer from mental illness? And if so, did he have "the capacity to appreciate the wrongfulness" of his conduct or "the ability to conform to the law"? Since the uproar caused by the successful insanity defense in 1982 of John Hinckley, Jr., who in March 1981 had attempted to assassinate then president Ronald Reagan—and was committed to a mental hospital after his acquittal on the grounds of insanity—it appears that the press and the public have gained a better understanding of the distinction between insanity (a legal determination) and mental illness (a medical condition).

Persistence of a stigma

It is certainly to be hoped that this understanding is part of a growing public recognition and acceptance of the legitimacy of mental disorders as illnesses. For some patients and their families, seeing a psychiatrist or other mental health professional is still viewed as a source of shame or a sign of weakness. The extent of this problem was documented by a nationwide survey conducted for the National Mental Health Association, which found that only 46% of Americans surveyed considered depression to be a health problem, while

Medical Images Inc.

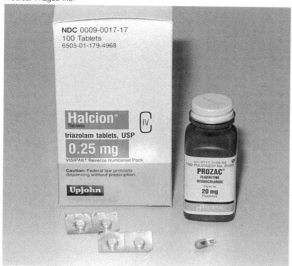

Prozac, an antidepressant, and Halcion, a short-term treatment for insomnia, have both been alleged to cause violent behavior. The claims about Prozac have not been substantiated. In 1991 Halcion was taken off the market in the U.K. In the U.S. it remains available, but the drug's labeling emphasizes that patients receiving it need to be carefully evaluated before and during treatment.

43% saw it as "a sign of personal or emotional weakness." An even higher proportion (58%) regarded alcoholism as a personal weakness. This outmoded but abiding stigma associated with mental disorders obviously adds to the pain that patients and their families already suffer from the disorders themselves. In addition, stigma serves as an obstacle to seeking and complying with treatment.

Other surveys have determined that only a fraction of persons suffering from common, treatable psychiatric disorders receive treatment. Several factors account for this: (1) a lack of recognition of the disorders, (2) insufficient numbers and maldistribution of appropriately trained mental health professionals, (3) insufficient financial resources for diagnosing and treating mental disorders, (4) a lack of third-party insurance coverage of mental health problems, and (5) stigma. Indeed, discriminatory policies regarding the coverage of mental disorders on the part of insurance plans reflect the degree to which the stigma has become institutionalized, thereby preventing persons affected by mental illness from receiving adequate treatment. Voluntary organizations and support groups such as the National Mental Health Association and the National Alliance for the Mentally Ill have made considerable progress in their efforts to put an end to this cycle and to bring mental disorders out of the shadows. Nonetheless, further educational efforts on the part of professionals and the media will be needed to eliminate persisting inaccuracies and harmful prejudices.

The importance of recognizing mental disorders as real, legitimate illnesses is well illustrated by the example of panic disorder. Recent progress in the diagnosis and treatment of this condition offers hope for millions of sufferers. In order to assess the progress, to consolidate the most enlightened thinking about the appropriate management, and to determine areas in need of further research, the U.S. National Institutes of Health (NIH) sponsored a three-day consensus-development conference on panic disorder and its treatment in late 1991. Following the conference, which brought together psychiatrists, psychologists, specialists in psychobiology and psychopharmacology, other mental health professionals, representatives from concerned voluntary organizations, patients, and the public, a "consensus-development statement" summarizing the conference deliberations was issued.

Panic disorder: common and debilitating

I'm just freaking out, and I feel like my body's freaking out. I mean the shaking and the breathing and the sweats and the heart and the pain in the chest—I feel like I'm going to have a heart attack or something. Except I never do. . . .

I went to [my family] doctor and he did a number of tests. He thought at first I had multiple sclerosis, but he ruled that out, finally, and said he wasn't sure what I had. So he sent me to a neurologist. The neurologist also did a number of tests and finally gave me a diagnosis of "nonspecific idiopathic neuropathy." I asked him what that was and he didn't give me much of an explanation. He just said that maybe I should see a psychiatrist.

Most of my attacks came on when I was on the subway, and it got to the point where I couldn't take the subway anymore and it was affecting my work because I would be out of work a lot from not being able to take the subway. But eventually, I made myself take the subway, though I still experienced the attacks.

These statements, quoted in an American Psychiatric Association pamphlet on panic disorder, suggest several important aspects of the experiences of those who suffer from this common condition. Officially recognized only in 1980, panic disorder is a debilitating illness that will affect at least one person in every 75. The hallmark of the disorder is the presence of recurrent panic attacks. The attacks are characterized by the sudden onset of feelings of severe anxiety (panic) accompanied by typical physical and mental symptoms (*see* Table, page 357). After it starts, the panicky feelings rapidly crescendo, reaching peak intensity within a few minutes. Attacks typically last about 10 minutes, but aftereffects and residual anxiety can persist for hours.

Diagnosing the disorder. A single panic attack occurring in the face of imminent danger or a life-threatening situation would probably be considered a normal reaction. Patients with specific, simple phobias can have panic attacks on exposure to the situations they fear (*e.g.,* heights, spiders, closed spaces). In

Whereas John Hinckley, Jr. (left), successfully used the insanity defense in his 1982 trial for his assassination attempt on Pres. Ronald Reagan, a decade later Jeffrey Dahmer (right), the serial killer from Milwaukee, Wisconsin, who admitted to having killed 15 young males, was convicted for his crimes and found to be sane when he committed them.

order to satisfy criteria for the diagnosis of actual panic disorder, however, at least some panic attacks must occur "out of the blue"—*i.e.,* with no apparent external trigger. In addition, the diagnostic criteria for panic disorder require either the occurrence of at least four attacks (one including at least four of the listed symptoms) during a four-week period or at least four weeks of fearful anticipation following one or more attacks. One example of the spontaneous nature of many panic attacks is the fact that over half of panic disorder patients report nocturnal attacks that awaken them from sleep. These nocturnal attacks are not a consequence of nightmares, since sleep studies show they do not occur during the rapid eye movement periods associated with dreaming.

Confusion with other illnesses. Panic attacks are devastating experiences, and persons with panic disorder usually have a vivid memory of the time and circumstances of their first attack. Because the symptoms are predominately physical, it is understandable that the initial attacks are usually thought to signify a severe and acute physical illness, adding to the patient's anxiety. In fact, patients with undiagnosed panic disorder are common among those seeking evaluations for heart disease. The sudden onset of shortness of breath, chest pain, and heart palpitations, which are typical of panic attacks, can also occur during a heart attack. Similarly, episodes of dizziness, trembling, and tingling might raise suspicions of an inner ear or cerebrovascular disorder, while rapid heart rate, trembling, sweating, and hot flushes can be caused by hyperthyroidism. Thus, initially, panic attacks often lead those experiencing them to seek evaluation and treatment at a hospital emergency room or prompt an urgent visit to their physician.

A recently published follow-up study of patients who underwent angiographic tests because of chest pain but showed no sign of heart disease found that half had panic disorder. Bernard D. Beitman, a psy-

chiatrist at the University of Missouri, who led this study (published in the *Journal of the American Medical Association,* March 27, 1991), noted that many of those patients were unnecessarily disabled by the conviction that they had heart disease.

Although its recognition as a common, specific disorder is recent, panic disorder is not a new disease. The medical literature of the past described patients with disabling attacks of anxiety and physical symptoms, referred to variously as "anxiety neurosis," "cardiac neurosis," and "phobia anxiety."

The physical nature of the symptoms underscores the importance of physicians' being able to recognize panic disorder. A careful history, physical examination, and possibly a few tests (such as an electrocardiogram and a blood test to assess thyroid hormone levels) are important under the circumstances to rule out the presence of one of the serious physical disorders that panic disorder can mimic. Too often, however, patients undergo a lengthy, expensive, and fruitless series of tests. The history should also attempt to rule out the presence of other mental disorders that can cause panic attacks, such as severe depression, simple phobias, and stimulant abuse (*e.g.,* cocaine, amphetamines).

Prevalence and course. A large community survey conducted by the U.S. National Institute of Mental Health (NIMH) found a lifetime prevalence for panic disorder of about 1.6%. The disorder may start at any time in an individual's life, although onset is most common in late adolescence and early adulthood.

The course of the illness is variable. Sometimes some mild episodes of unexplained anxiety precede the first full-blown attack. The initial attacks typically occur without specific precipitants, although often at a time when the individual is undergoing a period of stress, such as a job change or change in living arrangements. Attacks often occur several times per week. They may last for only a few months or may persist for years. The extreme discomfort and unknown source of the attacks commonly lead to increasing fear of having subsequent attacks and often to a search for a physical cause, sometimes with expanding concerns about minor bodily sensations.

There may be maladaptive attempts to control anxiety with alcohol or other drugs of abuse. This is dangerous because the panic disorder can then be complicated by the development of an alcohol or other drug abuse disorder. Demoralization or even clinical depression may develop as a consequence of the debilitating and discouraging effects of recurrent panic attacks. A recent community survey comparing the effects of various psychiatric disorders found a strong correlation between panic disorder symptoms and suicidal thoughts or attempts. In treatment settings suicide does not appear to be common among panic disorder patients, but the suicide risk may be high for persons with undiagnosed and untreated panic disorder who become despondent about their unexplained symptoms.

Many persons who experience panic attacks begin to restrict their usual activities and avoid situations where they would particularly not like to have a panic attack. The extent to which this avoidance occurs determines the two main subtypes of the disorder—*i.e.,* panic disorder with and without agoraphobia. *Agoraphobia* literally means "fear of the marketplace" but is sometimes erroneously construed as fear of open places. In effect, the fear leads to an avoidance of places or situations from which escape might be difficult or embarrassing or in which help might not be available in the event of sudden incapacitation. Such places typically include crowds, stores, public transportation, and enclosed areas without an easy means of exit. The degree of avoidance can vary considerably. Some persons with agoraphobia are willing to enter feared places or face frightening situations if accompanied by a trusted family member or friend. In extreme cases the agoraphobic individual becomes virtually housebound. Panic disorder without agoraphobia is about equally common in men and women, but panic disorder with agoraphobia is about twice as common in women.

There is some controversy among experts about whether agoraphobia is always a consequence of panic attacks. In any case, it is clear that agoraphobia can persist for years, even after panic attacks have ceased. Those who have panic disorder without agoraphobia typically experience less interference with their regular activities and less disruption of their lives. Nonetheless, they can still suffer from anticipatory anxiety related to the unpredictable nature of their attacks.

Gaining insight into the causes. The cause or causes of panic disorder remain unknown. It commonly runs in families, but genetic transmission has not been established. The clinical features of panic disorder suggest that something goes wrong with a basic "alarm" system in the brain since the symptoms of a panic attack are essentially those of a primitive "fight or flight" response to some life-threatening danger. In panic disorder the alarm goes off in the absence of a real external threat. Recent research has suggested that the norepinephrine neurotransmitter system in the brain may be abnormally overactive in panic disorder.

It has been known for years that certain chemicals—notably sodium lactate—can trigger panic attacks in patients with panic disorder but not in normal subjects or patients with other anxiety disorders. More recently, Donald F. Klein and his colleagues at the New York State Psychiatric Institute discovered that breathing higher-than-normal concentrations of carbon dioxide precipitates panic attacks in panic disorder patients. Klein has theorized that the effects of sodium lactate might result from its metabolism to carbon dioxide and that panic disorder might be due to a supersensitivity to carbon dioxide concentrations in the brain. Thus, a "suffocation alarm" might go off in persons with panic disorder when concentrations of carbon dioxide are only slightly elevated, whereas normal persons would require a severe lack of oxygen with an associated high level of carbon dioxide to trigger the biological alarm. This theory fits many of the clinical phenomena of panic attacks, including the characteristic feeling of smothering and a compelling desire for "fresh air," often accompanied by the thought "I've got to get out of here." Further research will be necessary to test this intriguing theory of a dysfunctional "suffocation alarm."

Enlightened treatment. Fortunately, even in the absence of a known cause, there is increasing information about effective treatments for panic disorder. Recognizing and diagnosing panic disorder are obviously essential prerequisites for its treatment. Patients

Panic attack symptoms	
physical	mental
shortness of breath or smothering sensations	terror, feeling of impending doom
chest pain or discomfort	fear of dying
heart pounding or palpitations	fear of losing control or going crazy
dizziness, unsteady feelings, or faintness	feelings of unreality
trembling or shaking	
sweating	
choking	
nausea or abdominal distress	
numbness or tingling sensations	
hot flushes or chills	

Adapted with permission from the *Diagnostic and Statistical Manual of Mental Disorders*, third edition, revised. Copyright 1987 American Psychiatric Association

in whom it is diagnosed should be counseled so that they know their condition is a real and treatable illness; such understanding of their problem is essential to coping with it. Any implications that the symptoms are "just nerves" or "all in the head" are both inaccurate and unhelpful. Initial counseling should advise patients to avoid caffeine, since those with panic disorder have been shown to be hypersensitive to coffee and other caffeine-containing beverages and medications. They should be aware of the hazards of attempts at "self-treatment" with alcohol or other drugs. Patients seen early in the course of panic disorder should also be advised to continue their normal activities as much as possible in order to prevent the development of agoraphobic avoidance patterns.

The NIH consensus development conference found that two types of treatment have demonstrated effectiveness for panic disorder: cognitive-behavioral therapy and pharmacological (drug) therapy.

Behavioral therapies. Gradually increasing exposure to avoided situations is a well-established and quite effective behavioral treatment for agoraphobic patients, who often need considerable support and guidance to gradually overcome well-entrenched patterns of avoidance. Similar behavioral treatments for simple phobias have also been shown to be effective.

More recently, cognitive-behavioral techniques have been developed to treat panic attacks. These include "cognitive restructuring" to change the maladaptive thought processes that lead to the interpretation of anxious symptoms as catastrophic (*e.g.,* "I'm having a heart attack," "I won't be able to control myself") and contribute to the vicious cycle of panic. In addition, so-called interoceptive exposure techniques (such as hyperventilation) can be used to desensitize the patient to the bodily sensations associated with panic attacks. Usually the therapy consists of 8 to 12 weekly counseling sessions, along with practice assignments; initial improvement is often noted 3 to 6 weeks after such treatment is begun. Unfortunately, the small number of professionals trained in these techniques limits the availability of such treatment at present.

Medications. Three classes of drugs—tricyclic antidepressants, monoamine oxidase inhibitors (MAOIs), and benzodiazepines—have been shown to reduce or eliminate the occurrence of panic attacks; each has a different profile of benefits and adverse effects. Tricyclic antidepressants (such as imipramine, desipramine, and nortriptyline) offer the convenience of once-a-day dosing, no dietary restrictions, and virtually no risk of dependence. However, they require at least three to four weeks of continuous use before they become effective and can have side effects such as dry mouth, constipation, and weight gain. In addition, panic disorder patients are often very sensitive to the initial effects of these medications, so anxiety and panic attacks may get worse for several weeks before they get better. This problem can be alleviated by the concurrent use of a benzodiazepine medication during the initial weeks of tricyclic treatment.

Like the tricyclics, MAOIs (such as phenelzine) were initially found to be effective in treating clinical depression but have also shown effectiveness in the treatment of panic disorder. Like tricyclics, they also require several weeks of treatment to become fully effective; however, the side effects of MAOIs differ. Most commonly, they include insomnia, weight gain, and delay or inhibition of orgasm. Additionally, because of a risk of a sudden rise in blood pressure that can cause cerebral bleeding or even death, patients taking MAOIs need to restrict foods with a high tyramine content: aged cheeses, pickled herring, red wine, meat and yeast extracts, fava beans, sauerkraut, and spoiled foods.

Benzodiazepines (such as alprazolam, clonazepam, and lorazepam) have the advantage of a rapid onset of action in blocking panic attacks and decreasing anticipatory anxiety. Their main side effect of sedation usually subsides after a few weeks of treatment. Physical dependence can develop after several weeks of continuous treatment. This is manifested by the occurrence of withdrawal symptoms (such as insomnia, increased anxiety, muscle cramps, tremor, and, rarely, seizures) if the drug is stopped abruptly. The severity of withdrawal symptoms varies with the dose and duration of use. However, gradual tapering of doses can minimize such withdrawal effects. Benzodiazepines should be used with caution in persons with a history of alcohol or other drug abuse, who may be at risk for excessive use or abuse of the drugs. Initial treatment with the combination of a benzodiazepine and a tricyclic or MAOI, with tapering and discontinuation of the benzodiazepine after several weeks or months, can be helpful in achieving rapid control of symptoms but avoiding the potential problems of long-term benzodiazepine use.

The combination of a drug treatment and cognitive-behavioral therapy has also been employed successfully. This makes particular sense for patients who are experiencing both frequent panic attacks and agoraphobic avoidance.

Spreading the word. Less than two months after the consensus-development conference, NIMH launched a nationwide campaign to educate the public at large about panic disorder, to provide hope to sufferers, and to ensure that doctors who are in a position to recognize and offer appropriate treatment for the debilitating illness do so.

—*Richard M. Glass, M.D.*

Further information about panic disorder may be obtained from the American Psychiatric Association, Division of Public Affairs, Dept. EB, 1400 K Street NW, Washington, DC 20005.

Special Report

Multiple Personality: Illness or Act?

by Brendan A. Maher, Ph.D., and Winifred B. Maher, Ph.D.

In 1979 Kenneth Bianchi, an accused rapist and murderer, was remanded for psychiatric examination in the state of California. The evaluation included sessions in which Bianchi was hypnotized. In the first of these, he manifested behavior suggesting that he might have the condition known as multiple personality disorder. The following excerpt from the transcript of this session is instructive.

Examiner: I've talked a bit to Ken, but I think that perhaps there might be another part of Ken that I haven't talked to. And I would like to communicate with that other part. And I would like that other part to come to talk to me. . . . Would you please come, Part, so that I can talk to you? . . . Part would you come and lift Ken's hand to indicate to me that you are here? . . . Would you talk to me, Part, by saying "I'm here"?

Bianchi: Yes.

Examiner: Part, are you the same as Ken or are you different in any way?

Bianchi: I'm not him.

Examiner: You're not him? Who are you? . . . Do you have a name I can call you by?

Bianchi: Steve. You can call me Steve.

The question raised by the above dialogue is this: Did the examiner "discover" a hidden personality? Or did the examiner create the alleged personality by suggesting that there might indeed be one? It is this pivotal question that lies at the heart of the present professional controversy surrounding the diagnosis of multiple personality.

Opinions past and present

The earliest descriptions of the condition now known as multiple personality disorder date from the latter part of the 19th century. They were reported mainly by certain French neuropsychiatrists. In 1900 Morton Prince, a Boston neuropsychiatrist and the founder of the *Journal of Abnormal and Social Psychology* (now the *Journal of Abnormal Psychology*), described the case of a Miss Sally Beauchamp, who, he reported, had "at least three" personalities. Beauchamp's basic personality was one of high moral standards—idealistic and conscientious. Her main "alternative personality" hated books, responsibility, going to church, and all the things that the basic personality represented. A third personality, whom Prince called "the Woman," was described by him as "conventionally frail and motivated by stubborn self-interest."

Prince concluded that multiple personality was a condition that arose when a patient's subconscious intruded into his or her waking behavior, manifesting itself as a new personality. Prince's explanation was based on the Freudian psychoanalytic conception of a separation of conscious and unconscious levels of awareness in the organization of individual personality. He believed that clinical examples of multiple personality were simply exaggerations of the way in which personality was organized in normal persons. "No one is wholly good or wholly bad," Prince wrote, "or wholly hard or wholly sentimental; or wholly self-centered or wholly altruistic . . . personality presents contradictory traits and conduct . . . we might say different 'selves' alternating with one another from moment to moment. But these 'selves' are plainly only different sides or phases of the same personality."

Contemporary professional opinions about the concept of multiple personality cover a broad spectrum. At one extreme is the notion that the syndrome is primarily an artifact, or artificial phenomenon, created by the therapist's suggestions to the patient; according to this viewpoint, multiple personality is simply one of many kinds of unusual behavior that can be induced by hypnotic suggestion. At the opposite end is the belief that multiple personality is a genuine psychological disorder, albeit one that is rarely diagnosed and then only by the few clinicians perceptive enough to recognize it.

Skepticism about the legitimacy of multiple personality is widespread. In one survey 80% of psychiatrists interviewed expressed strong to extreme doubt about the existence of such cases. In fact, the majority of multiple personality diagnoses come from only a small minority of practitioners. Most psychotherapists have never seen such a patient, while a few therapists have each seen more than 40 cases. Members of the latter group explain the disproportion by alleging that only a very few clinicians possess the necessary training and skill to recognize the subtle signs of the disorder.

Separate lives, separate memories

The *Diagnostic and Statistical Manual of Mental Disorders,* third edition, revised (*DSM-III-R*), of the American Psychiatric Association classifies multiple personality

Accused murderer Kenneth Bianchi claimed that "another" personality was guilty of his crimes. The growing use of multiple personality as a defense has added to the skepticism of those who doubt that it is a genuine psychiatric disorder.

as a "dissociative disorder" in which the essential feature is "a disturbance or alteration in the normally integrative functions of identity, memory, or consciousness." The specific diagnostic criteria for multiple personality are as follows:

● The existence within the person of two or more distinct personalities or personality states (each with its own relatively enduring pattern of perceiving, relating to, and thinking about the environment and self).

● At least two of these personalities or personality states recurrently take full control of the person's behavior.

Clinical descriptions of multiple personality typically include the observation that each personality is both integrated and complex, has memories unique to that personality, and displays patterns of behavior, emotional expression, and ways of interacting socially that differentiate it from the other personality or personalities. Furthermore, the transition from one to another of the multiple personalities is often sudden and associated with apparent psychosocial stress. In addition, the basic personality appears to have complete amnesia (absence of memory) for the periods of time when any of the secondary personalities is dominant. On the other hand, the secondary personalities are usually aware of each other, although they may also be cognizant of "lost" time periods. They often seem to be opposites—e.g., a quiet, retiring, highly moralistic person may on occasion behave in a manner that is promiscuous, flamboyant, or exhibitionistic.

In most accounts of multiple personality disorder by current diagnostic criteria, the age of onset is in childhood; however, cases typically do not come to clinical attention until much later. Originally the disorder was thought of as extremely rare and was most often diagnosed in late-adolescent females. However, now that the diagnosis of multiple personality has been used as a legal defense in several well-publicized criminal trials, the syndrome has come to be considered more common and is diagnosed in males as well as in females. Nonetheless, the diagnosis is still made in women more than twice as often as in men.

Not surprisingly, estimates of the incidence as well as the existence of multiple personality vary widely. Clinicians who specialize in the disorder hold that it is more common than is generally believed, whereas those who are skeptical about the diagnosis believe that it is either rare or nonexistent. The lack of any agreement about the existence of the disorder has necessarily precluded any consensus about its frequency in the general population.

Diagnostic dilemma

The diagnosis of multiple personality is complicated by the fact that several major psychiatric disorders are marked by drastic alterations in mood or behavior. Thus, borderline personality disorder and bipolar disorder—both of which are manifested by striking, intermittent behavior changes—are sometimes found in the prior medical history of multiple personality patients. The concurrent diagnosis of schizophrenia is also common. Some clinicians suggest that these disorders may exist along with multiple personality; others assert that they essentially represent errors of diagnosis on the part of therapists who are not familiar with multiple personality disorder.

Perhaps the greatest diagnostic problem, however, is the difficulty in distinguishing between multiple personality and malingering—the production of the symptoms of a physical or psychological disorder for the purpose of avoiding some unpleasant situation or securing some positive advantage. The presence of malingering behavior appears to be quite common in cases of multiple personality.

Theories about cause

Various hypotheses have been advanced to account for the emergence of multiple personalities. In order to be considered valid, however, such theoretical formulations have to fulfill two criteria: they must delineate the nature of the predisposing events that ultimately lead to the emergence of multiple personalities, and they must account for the fact that many people who have undergone similar experiences do not develop the disorder.

Dual brain, dual consciousness. Some early theories suggested that the key to understanding the phenomenon of multiple personality lay in the fact that the human brain has two distinct hemispheres. As knowledge of the anatomy of the brain progressed, physicians and philosophers became increasingly fascinated by the question of how an individual can have a single consciousness when endowed with a brain that has two separate components, each of which clearly has different functions. By the middle of the 19th century, some scientists had come to believe that one hemisphere was responsible for the impulsive, animalistic aspect of human behavior—selfishness and "evil"—while the other was responsible for the civilized aspect—altruism and "good."

Consideration of the anatomic duality of the brain and the assumed duality of human nature provides one possible basis for explaining multiple personality. Such an explanation was offered in 1886 by two French physicians, Henri Bourru and Ferdinand Burot, in their report of the case of Louis Vives, a patient who showed marked alternations of personality states. In one state he behaved "with monkeylike impudence," preached "radicalism in politics and atheism in religion," and generally acted in a violent, greedy, and quarrelsome manner. In the other he was gentle, respectful, and modest, spoke only when spoken to, and stated that he preferred to leave matters of politics and religion to heads wiser than his own.

Bourru and Burot argued that the phases of gentle, more civilized behavior occurred when the left hemisphere was dominant, while the quarrelsome and impudent behavior occurred when the right hemisphere was dominant. In normal persons, they theorized, the two hemispheres are integrated so that the dominance of left over right is essentially unchanging. Multiple personalities arise, according to this hypothesis, when some earlier stress has led to a state equivalent to an "uncoupling" of the hemispheres, thereby permitting alternating dominance—and alternating personalities. They noted, however, that their patient could be transformed from one personality to the other by suggestion, an observation consistent with the view that multiple personality may be essentially akin to the kinds of behavior that can be produced through hypnotic suggestion.

Good versus evil. As mentioned above, the notion that contradictory aspects of good and evil exist in everyone was Prince's explanation for multiple personality. Such a dualistic nature had been embodied in Robert Louis Stevenson's classic *Strange Case of Dr. Jekyll and Mr. Hyde,* published in 1886, the same year in which the case of Louis Vives was first reported. In Stevenson's tale the inner moral conflict of the protagonist, Henry Jekyll, was played out in the evil, violent, and murderous character of Edward Hyde.

A hypnotic state. As already noted, clinicians confronted with cases of multiple personality have long been struck by the similarity between the behavior that they see in these cases and the behavior that can be induced quite rapidly in normal persons who have been hypnotized. The majority of patients who display the clinical manifestations of multiple personality have been shown to be excellent hypnotic subjects. This means that these individuals are particularly

suggestible—that is, they respond readily to ideas, attitudes, or desired actions that are impressed upon them by persons of authority; they also are responsive to environmental cues. In the previously quoted case of Bianchi, the notion of another "Part," or personality, could certainly have come from the examiner's highly suggestive questions rather than spontaneously from Bianchi himself.

Childhood trauma. Most of the theories of multiple personality consider the experience of early childhood trauma—death of a parent, orphan status, physical abuse, and, most often, sexual abuse—as a predisposing condition. The latter especially is difficult to prove. If memories of apparent abuse are obtained from the patient, again the evidence may be influenced by the fact that the patient is a highly suggestible person: is what is being remembered what actually happened, or has it been fabricated because the possibility has been suggested? Corroboration through the memories of family members and friends is likely to be unreliable because, on the one hand, actual abuse does not usually occur in front of witnesses and, on the other hand, family members may deny that it has happened. Reports of the frequency of abuse in the early histories of these patients vary widely. In fact, very little exists in the way of satisfactory evidence that childhood trauma is a primary predisposing cause.

Is it "just an act"? Some years ago a prominent investigator conducted an experiment in which three groups of subjects were instructed to play the role of an accused murderer under investigation by a psychiatrist. They were told to guide their performances by using whatever cues they could glean from the situation. The first group was interviewed while under hypnosis, the interview being closely modeled on the actual one with Bianchi. The second group of subjects was also hypnotized; they were told that they *might* possess another "part" that could communicate with the examining psychiatrist but were never directly asked to produce or identify a second personality. The third ("control") group was simply told that personality is quite complex and that often there are walled-off thoughts and feelings inside a person that make it almost as if there are "different people" inside. Nothing was said to the latter group about hypnosis or about the psychiatrist trying to contact another part of them.

The outcome of this "study" was that most of the subjects in the first group and about one-third of those in the second behaved just as Bianchi had, in that they enacted multiple personalities. They also adopted different names for the secondary personality, referred to their primary personalities in the third person, and displayed amnesia for the secondary personality when the hypnosis was terminated. No member of the control group showed any manifestations of multiple personality. In short, when normal individuals are placed in a situation in which enacting multiple personality serves a purpose, most can and do act the part with relative ease.

This does not establish that all cases of multiple personality are consciously acted at all times. Some psychiatrists and psychologists propose that multiple personality commonly starts as an act, prompted by the questions of the therapist; it is initially adopted by the patient to escape the consequences of his or her antisocial behavior. The patient's behavior then confirms the hypothesis of the therapist, who believes that the disorder truly exists. Repeated interaction with the therapist subsequently convinces the patient that he or she truly does have more than one personality. A ready explanation of why the patient has no prior consciousness of the secondary personalities is that, by definition, the primary personality can have no memory of the experience of the secondary personalities.

In this respect the experience of the multiple personality patient is not unlike that of other patients in psychotherapy: the authoritative figure of the therapist offers the patient an explanation for his or her own behavior that is based on the notion that there are aspects of psychological life of which people are generally unaware. Furthermore, multiple personality patients often have active fantasy lives and vivid imaginations. As they tend to be generally dissatisfied with their actual life circumstances, they may readily turn to fantasy as a substitute.

The case against multiple personality

There are many reasons for skepticism about the existence of a true condition of multiple personality. Chief among them is the fact that the disorder so often first appears in persons who are involved in some kind of legal or other interpersonal trouble. This is especially true in male cases. One recent investigation of a group of 59 patients with diagnosed multiple personality disorder found that 62% of the males (but only 5% of the females) had a record of criminal activity. In another study 75% of males with the diagnosis had committed violent crimes, while 28% of the women patients had criminal records.

Further, the behavior of patients sometimes casts doubt on the legitimacy of their claims. Suicide attempts by multiple personality patients are frequently superficial and unconvincing. Symptoms are often exaggerated and presented in a theatrical and manipulative manner. In answering questions on objective personality tests—which have built-in checks on truthfulness—these patients often create a profile that indicates they have not been honest in their responses.

An additional reason for skepticism is that the frequency of these cases and the numbers of emerging secondary personalities (23 in one case, 100 in another) have vastly increased in the past two decades. Thus, what used to be a very rare phenomenon, in which patients exhibited at most two or three

personalities, has reached epidemic and astonishing proportions. Many authorities feel that the increase in diagnoses—and possibly the increasingly bizarre nature of reported cases—is largely due to the publicity surrounding certain cases. Prince himself publicized the Beauchamp case widely, and it provided the material for a Broadway play and an article in the *Ladies Home Journal.*

Quite a number of other cases of alleged multiple personality have captured the public imagination through popular books, motion pictures, and television dramas—and in the process have glamorized and often sensationalized the condition. Just a few examples: *The Three Faces of Eve,* a 1957 book by psychiatrists Corbett H. Thigpen and Hervey M. Cleckley, later became a widely acclaimed movie starring Joanne Woodward. *Sybil,* a 1973 best-seller by Flora Rheta Schreiber, told the story of a young woman with 16 personalities. *The Five of Me* (1977) was the autobiographical account of Henry Hawksworth, the first person to use multiple personality as a legal defense successfully. And the 1981 book by Daniel Keyes, *The Minds of Billy Milligan,* recounted the case of a convicted criminal whose multiple personality defense did not stand up in court and who was subsequently confined to a state hospital for the criminally insane.

What is "personality"?

Finally, the language employed in the official psychiatric descriptions of multiple personality is itself open to serious misunderstanding. Statements such as "The existence within the person of two or more distinct personalities" and "At least two of the personalities . . . take full control of the person's behavior" imply that some independent entity known as a personality exists "within" a person and "controls" the person's behavior. These descriptions further imply that several entities of this kind could reside within a person simultaneously. The notion of personality as something that can inhabit a person is reminiscent of ancient notions of demonology and is unacceptable to modern psychopathology.

In psychiatry, "personality" is properly defined as a complex pattern of behavior. It does not *control* a person's behavior; rather, it *is* the person's behavior. A scientific description of multiple personality can be founded only on the clinically observable behavior of the patient. Rarely, if ever, would there be reason to assert that this observable behavior is really the behavior of entities who occupy the interior of the patient or to believe that there is more than one person.

Nonetheless, the paucity of evidence that meets rigorous scientific standards makes it impossible to resolve the issue of whether multiple personality disorder is, in fact, real. What does seem clear is that the "epidemic" of alleged multiple personality cases is not likely to abate.

Special Report

An Ugly Secret: Body Dysmorphic Disorder

by Katharine A. Phillips, M.D.

Body dysmorphic disorder, or BDD, is a fascinating yet virtually unknown psychiatric disorder—one in which "normal-looking" or even attractive people are preoccupied with thoughts that they look monstrously ugly. They may, for example, think their nose is too big, their lip is crooked, their chin is receding, or their genitals are too small when in reality these "defects" are in the mind, not the body. Although these concerns may sound trivial, they are not; people with BDD are severely distressed by their preoccupations, are usually impaired in everyday functioning, and may even kill themselves as a result.

Although BDD has been described in the medical literature for more than a century and is well known in certain European countries and in Japan, it has not received much attention in the United States. BDD is probably not a rare disorder, however, only an underrecognized one. This lack of recognition may reflect the fact that people with BDD often keep their preoccupations secret; others who have the disorder believe their problem is physical rather than psychological and may even seek repetitive, unsuccessful treatment from plastic surgeons or dermatologists. The following case history is fairly representative.

Mark, a handsome 35-year-old, had worried excessively about his supposedly thinning hair since the age of 17. In reality, he had an abundance of thick, curly hair, but he nonetheless was convinced that he was "going bald." He had thought about his supposedly thinning hair "morning, noon, and night" for the past 18 years; the longest he had been free of these thoughts was only a few hours. To hide the imagined hair loss, Mark had worn a baseball cap continuously for the past three years, removing it only when alone. In desperation, he had seen five dermatologists, who had reassured him that his hair was not thinning and recommended no treatment.

In his early twenties Mark had also become preoccupied with his supposedly shrunken facial muscles and with his nose, which he thought was too long and wide. He thought he looked monstrous—likening his appearance to that of Cyrano de Bergerac, the French literary character who is remembered primarily because of his obsession with his enormous nose (although Cyrano boasted about his nose and was proud of it). When Mark consulted plastic surgeons, five of six of them refused to operate because there was no defect to correct. Finally he did undergo rhinoplasty; the surgery, however, only served to increase his fixation because he thought it had made his nose "crooked."

Mark described his preoccupations as "tormenting" and "devastating," but he was so embarrassed by them that he had kept them a secret for 18 years. He had never gone on a date because, he said, "no one would go out with someone as ugly as me." And he had been fired from his accounting job because his obsessive thoughts and frequent checking of his appearance in the mirror had made it impossible for him to concentrate on his work. He had moved back in with his parents and only rarely left the house because he thought others might be talking about his "ugliness" or laughing about it behind his back. When driving, he sometimes dangerously sped through stoplights so he would not have to sit at the intersection and be stared at by others.

On several occasions Mark's preoccupations with his "defects" had been so painful that he had tried to kill himself. He said he wished he had cancer instead because it would be easier to live with than his "ugliness."

Mark's experience is typical of that of persons with BDD. The disorder is defined in the *Diagnostic and Statistical Manual of Mental Disorders,* third edition, revised (*DSM-III-R*), as a preoccupation with an imagined defect in appearance in a normal-appearing person; in some cases where a slight physical flaw exists, the person's concern is markedly excessive (*see* Table, page 364). The preoccupation is so excessive as to cause marked emotional distress or significant impairment in the individual's work or social life.

Certainly many people—perhaps most—occasionally worry about how they look. Such concern seems a normal part of life, especially during adolescence, but BDD is different. Although it is sometimes difficult to differentiate mild cases of BDD from "normal" worries about appearance, most people with BDD clearly know that their fixation is different from and far more severe than the concern most people experience. Their intense pain and torment, the extent to which their preoccupations consume and ruin their lives, and the fact that some are driven to suicide are all clues that BDD is different from the norm. In addition, most people with BDD do not long to be beautiful—they simply want to be rid of their tormenting "ugliness." As Mark once said, "I don't need to look great; I just don't want to be as ugly as the elephant man."

Although BDD is an underresearched disorder, many cases have been described, and more studies of BDD are in progress. What follows is a synthesis of what is currently known about this disorder.

The beauty hypochondriacs

BDD was described in 1891 by Enrico Morselli, an Italian psychiatrist, who named the condition dysmorphophobia. This term comes from *dysmorfia,* a Greek word meaning "ugliness," specifically of the face, which first appeared in the writings of the historian Herodotus; it referred to the myth of the "ugliest girl in Sparta," who was taken to a shrine each day so that the gods might deliver her from her homeliness.

Dysmorphophobia was subsequently described by some of Europe's most prominent turn-of-the-century psychiatrists, among them Emil Kraepelin and Pierre Janet. And it appears that one of Freud's most celebrated patients, a Russian nobleman to whom he gave the pseudonym the Wolf Man, may have suffered from BDD. (The name referred to the patient's dreaming about wolves—not to his own appearance.) This man, whom Freud treated for obsessional neurosis, was completely engrossed in his supposedly hideous nose—its imagined scars, holes, and swelling. His entire life revolved around a pocket mirror in which he repeatedly checked the state of this offending feature.

Quite a few colorful labels have been used in the medical literature to describe BDD-like absorption in imagined ugliness and those who suffer from it. These include "beauty hypochondria" (*Schönheitshypochondrie*), "dermatologic hypochondriasis," and "one who is worried about being ugly" (*Hässlichkeitskümmerer*). Body dysmorphic disorder, however, is a relatively new name, having been used only since 1987, when the disorder was accorded separate diagnostic status in the then newly revised *DSM-III.*

BDD usually begins during adolescence but can have its onset in childhood or adulthood. Although long-term studies are lacking, it appears that it is usually a chronic condition lasting for years, if not decades. Some people with BDD have one unchanging concern or set of concerns over time, whereas others add new ones. Still others add and subtract different preoccupations; thus, one complaint disappears, only to be replaced by another.

The prevalence of BDD is unknown but, as already noted, it is far more common than has been recognized. Sufferers often keep their affliction secret even from family members and close friends because they are afraid their concerns will be considered "silly" or "vain" or will be dismissed as "normal." If they do seek psychiatric treatment, they may tell the therapist only about the depression or other problems associated with the condition and not about the obsession itself. Furthermore, because many pursue unnecessary plastic surgery and dermatologic treatment rather than psychological help, their problem is never identified as psychiatric in nature. BDD's precise gender ratio is also unknown, but it clearly affects both women and men—not only women, as is often assumed. In fact, the largest BDD study that has been conducted to date had more male than female subjects.

Another reason why BDD often goes unrecognized is that it is frequently associated with other psychiatric conditions, most commonly depression. Other coexisting mental disorders may include obsessive compulsive disorder (OCD) and social phobia (extreme humiliation or embarrassment when talking to other people or when doing certain things, such as eating, in front of others). Although the characteristic personality traits of BDD sufferers have yet to be systematically evaluated, people with this disorder often describe themselves as shy, sensitive to rejection, and having low self-esteem.

A tormenting obsession

BDD preoccupations are intensely tormenting, frightening, and shameful. They are also time-consuming, occupying hours a day and sometimes virtually every minute. Like Mark, people with BDD often have more than one imagined defect. Their imaginary deformities usually involve the face or head (most commonly the nose, skin, and hair) but may involve other body parts as well (such as the breasts, genitals, shoulders, or stomach). Whether excessive preoccupation with weight is a form of BDD is unclear. While most concerns are specific and straightforward (*e.g.,* a receding chin or thinning hair), others are mysteriously vague—for example, a patient complains of "devious-looking eyebrows" or states, "My eyes aren't firm enough."

People with BDD generally think that except for these bizarre features, other aspects of their appearance are acceptable. Occasionally an individual has a real physical defect but is concerned instead with an imagined one. A patient whose arms and legs were covered with an unsightly red, scaling eczema was tormented not by this but by her attractive eyes, which she thought were sunken and "dull," and by her chin and jaw, described by her as "off center."

Although the official definition of BDD suggests that patients always have good insight into the absurdity of their preoccupations, this frequently does not seem to be the case. BDD, in fact, seems to span a spectrum ranging, in psychiatric terms, from fairly good insight (*i.e.*, the patient recognizes that the defect is imagined or only minimal) to overvalued ideas (the patient has only limited understanding that the defect is not real or is very minor) to delusional thinking (the patient is 100% convinced that the defect is real). It appears that most lie somewhere between the extremes of having good insight and having no insight whatsoever. Most, then, often wonder if their "deformity" is real but are not totally convinced that it is.

Rituals and compulsions

Imagined ugliness is often associated with compulsive thoughts and behaviors that can cause as much distress and impairment as the preoccupation itself.

Fear of attracting attention. People with BDD typically think that others can clearly see their "defect," and they may have bizarre thoughts in this regard—for example, that a "facial scar" is visible two blocks away. Many BDD sufferers think that others also take particular notice of their "flawed" feature—that they are staring at it, talking about it, or surreptitiously making fun of it—a belief that can lead to significant social withdrawal.

Mirror checking and mirror avoidance. Most people with BDD compulsively check not only mirrors but virtually any reflecting surface, such as store windows, car bumpers, and watch crystals. This ritualistic behavior can consume many hours a day, leaving little time for other things. Although people check to reassure themselves that they look acceptable, the mirror usually confirms their worst fear—that they really appear as ugly as they think they do. This can have devastating consequences, causing severe anxiety or, sometimes, inability to work or function for the rest of the day. Because looking in mirrors makes so many BDD sufferers feel worse, some avoid mirrors altogether. They may comb their hair, apply makeup, or shave in the dark. Some alternate between avoidance and excessive checking.

Avoidance of photographs. Some people with BDD allow no photographs to be taken of them. They may be missing from their high school yearbook and from family photos. Some destroy existing photos of themselves or cut themselves out of group pictures.

Face picking, hair combing, and other grooming rituals. Face picking, hair combing, and other grooming rituals are—like mirror checking—repetitive behaviors that some patients feel compelled to perform in an attempt to diminish their anxiety about the "defect." They may spend hours a day picking at imagined or minimal acne, sometimes creating actual scars in the process. Or they may comb and recomb their hair, trying to get it to look "just right." However, these behaviors do little to diminish their anxiety and sometimes make it worse.

"Girl Before a Mirror" by Pablo Picasso, 1932, oil on canvas, 64 × 51¼ inches. Collection, The Museum of Modern Art, New York, gift of Mrs. Simon Guggenheim

Most people occasionally worry about how they look. In those with body dysmorphic disorder, however, this normal concern with appearance becomes a preoccupation that dominates—indeed, can ruin—the individual's life.

Persistent questioning. Some people persistently question others, sometimes hundreds of times a day, about their flawed feature—for example, "Dad, does my hair look okay? Are you sure?" This behavior can be extremely distressing to family members and friends because no matter how they answer, the questioning and distress persist.

Constant comparison. People with BDD may continually compare themselves with others, thinking such things as "Do I look okay compared with him?" or "He doesn't have much hair, but he seems pretty happy; why can't I be happy, too?" This behavior, too, does not make them feel much better.

Tactile sensations. BDD preoccupations may be associated with subtle tactile sensations in the area of the imagined defect. For example, one may feel itching in the area of imagined vascular markings; another may have the impression of "too much air" touching the scalp in the area of imagined hair loss.

Fears about fragility and malfunctioning. Occasionally patients have prominent concerns that the "ugly" body part is unusually fragile and in constant danger of being damaged. The "defect" in appearance—for example, a pigmented spot on the nose—may be seen as confirming this special vulnerability to destruction or constituting evidence of new "damage." Others are concerned that the "abnormal" body part does not

The person who suffers from an obsession with imagined ugliness may go to great lengths to avoid being photographed—or may even cut his or her own image out of a group photo.

function correctly—*e.g.,* that a "crooked" lip makes them unable to talk clearly. These problems are often attributed to what they consider unsatisfactory results of cosmetic surgery.

Camouflaging. People with BDD may try a variety of methods to hide their imagined ugliness—wearing a baseball cap, even in an elegant restaurant, or long-sleeved shirts, even in the heat of summer. A man may cover his face with makeup, grow a beard to disguise "large" pores, or stuff his shorts to enhance a "small" penis. People may cover the "defect" with a hand or by adopting certain postures—for example, by always turning the "ugly" body part away from others. Camouflaging sometimes diminishes the torment, but the solution is often no better than the problem. For example, one man felt comfortable only on Halloween, when he covered his imagined facial scars with a Zorro mask.

Devastating consequences

BDD often has disastrous effects on people's lives. Although some individuals, despite their suffering, manage to function relatively well, most find that their illness significantly interferes with their functioning. They may be unable to go to school or work because their preoccupations interfere with their concentration and because they do not want their "ugliness" seen by others. They often avoid parties, other social events, and sex. They may stop dating or never date at all. Girlfriends, boyfriends, or spouses may leave them because of their inability to socialize, their persistent questioning or mirror checking, or their depression.

Some even become housebound, unable to leave their home for days, months, or years. One young woman stayed in her house for five years because of her preoccupation with imagined facial hair; she missed all family get-togethers and did not see some of her own family members who lived in the same house with her for years. People with BDD may buy their clothes through catalogs, get others to buy their food, or fail to seek needed medical care—all because they cannot muster up the courage to go out and be seen.

Depression is a common complication of BDD. The depression can be persistent and severe and can become an important problem in its own right. Some people with BDD require psychiatric hospitalization because of the BDD itself, their depression, or the desperation that follows the failure of a dermatologic treatment or surgical procedure to eradicate the imagined defect. Even in the hospital, however, many patients never discuss their BDD because they are too embarrassed to do so.

BDD can also cause accidents. Patients may fall off a ladder while checking their "defects" in a window or have a car accident while looking at their "flaws" in the rearview mirror.

Eventually, some people with this disorder are so tormented that they feel their lives are not worth living. Some try to kill themselves, and some succeed. Suicide is BDD's ultimate and most devastating effect.

The quest for treatment

As noted above, it appears that most people with BDD seek nonpsychiatric solutions. Persisting in the belief that their problem is physical, not psychiatric, they may see doctor after doctor, looking for a cure. Many consult plastic surgeons and dermatologists, requesting nose jobs, chin implants, eyebrow elevation, jaw straightening, or acne medications. They may go to endocrinologists to determine the cause of their "excessive" facial hair, to ophthalmologists for evaluation of their "crossed" eyes, or to urologists for a penile implant. Some spend hundreds of dollars a month on useless hair-restoring potions.

Many who request such treatments are refused them—because there is no defect to treat or because the problem is so minor or unnoticeable that surgery is not worth the risk. Still, some people persist in their quest and eventually do get medical or surgical treatment. Some go so far as to have surgery on a body part they consider attractive to make it look even better and thereby distract people's attention from the "ugly" body part. One young woman, for example, had breast augmentation so that others would look at her breasts instead of her "crooked" lips.

It appears that surgery and nonpsychiatric medical treatments usually fail to diminish BDD preoccupations. In fact, many patients think they look worse after such treatment and may even blame the surgeon for the supposed deterioration in their appearance. Their dissatisfaction with the results sometimes fuels a desire for even more surgery, leading to procedure after procedure. One young man dropped out of college to get nose and chin operations—six of them over a three-year period—becoming only more depressed and, he thought, "uglier" after each. Others become preoccupied with a new "defect," as did one woman who, after a tooth was filed down to make it shorter, became obsessed with her supposedly large nostrils.

BDD is a serious psychiatric disorder that requires psychiatric treatment. Although controlled treatment studies are lacking, it appears that many patients improve partially or completely with the antidepressant drugs fluoxetine (Prozac) or clomipramine (Anafranil)—and perhaps others in the category of serotonergic drugs (those affecting the neurotransmitter serotonin). Although it may take months for the drugs to become effective, patients who do respond spend far less time obsessing about the "defect," can more easily resist their compulsive thoughts, and are less tormented by them. They can also better resist the mirror checking, persistent questioning, and other BDD-related behaviors. Their functioning may also significantly improve, enabling them to leave their house, go back to work or school, start socializing again, and repair wounded relationships.

Other psychiatric medications do not appear to help BDD sufferers. People who are absolutely convinced that their defect is real are often unsuccessfully treated with antipsychotic medications; they, too, seem to respond to the serotonergic antidepressants mentioned above. And it appears that electroconvulsive therapy (ECT; shock treatment) sometimes alleviates accompanying depression, although it does not treat the BDD itself.

Although empirical study of behavior therapy for BDD is just beginning, preliminary evidence suggests that certain behavioral approaches may be helpful, especially for the ritualistic behaviors, such as mirror checking, and the social avoidance. For example, some mirror checkers find it helpful to cover mirrors, and patients sometimes benefit when those around them refrain from participating in their rituals, such as refusing to answer their persistent questions about their appearance.

The effectiveness of psychotherapy ("talking therapy") in the treatment of BDD is unknown. It appears that psychotherapy generally does not diminish the obsessions or rituals themselves but can be useful—if not essential—in helping people cope with the devastating consequence of BDD on their lives. Although the efficacy of such treatment requires further validation, it is clear that BDD is serious and requires psychiatric attention. It does not respond to reassurance alone or to encouragement to try harder. Although some people with this disorder resist psychiatric evaluation and treatment, this is what they need. When it works, it can be lifesaving.

Unanswered question: what causes BDD?

There is more speculation than fact about the cause of BDD. It has been proposed that BDD symptoms have psychological meaning—for example, that BDD preoccupations arise from the unconscious displacement of more profound and emotionally threatening problems into the more manageable arena of appearance. According to this theory, sexual or emotional conflict, feelings of inferiority or guilt, or a poor self-image may be easier to cope with if one explains all these problems as simply an appearance problem. Or BDD symptoms may unconsciously be used to explain dissatisfying relationships or one's own failings—"It's not my fault; it's because of my nose!" It has also been suggested that the chosen body part may be symbolic of another body part; the psychoanalyst who treated the Wolf Man after Freud surmised that the nose may represent the phallus. Although such theories may have some validity, they are unlikely to entirely explain why people suffer from BDD.

It appears that in some cases stressful events may contribute to or acutely trigger the onset of BDD—for example, divorce, chronic teasing about appearance, or even a single negative comment about the body part of concern, such as "Why is your skin so pale?" While people with BDD are often shy, insecure, and hypersensitive to rejection and criticism, it is difficult to determine whether these traits predate the onset of BDD and actually predispose people to develop it or whether they are the result of BDD.

Although cultural or societal explanations have an obvious appeal, society's emphasis on appearance is probably not the primary cause of BDD—although it sometimes exacerbates BDD concerns. It appears that just as many men as women have BDD, which would not be expected if this were a sociologically based disorder. In addition, BDD has been described for more than 100 years and in a variety of cultures. The fact that it appears to respond to medications indicates that biological factors are probably important in its etiology.

In fact, biological explanations may ultimately prove the most valid. Because BDD often appears to respond to serotonergic antidepressant medications, it seems likely that disturbed brain chemistry—probably involving dysregulation of the neurotransmitter serotonin—plays a part in its etiology. Also, BDD has many similarities with OCD (discussed below), which appears to have a neurochemical basis. Thus, at this time it seems likely that BDD is a biologically driven disorder but that its symptoms may perhaps also be triggered, influenced, or shaped by various psychological or cultural factors.

OCD and anorexia nervosa—relatives of BDD?

Is BDD a separate disorder, or is it instead a non-specific symptom of other psychiatric illnesses? Al-

Body dysmorphic disorder has been recognized for more than 100 years and observed in a number of cultures. While social pressure to conform to an unrealistic standard of appearance may exacerbate the disorder, it is not its primary cause.

Barbara Whitney

though concerns about physical appearance sometimes accompany other mental disorders (such as severe depression), BDD's symptoms seem unique, and available data suggest that BDD is a disorder in its own right. A related question is whether BDD—even if a discrete disorder—might nonetheless be related to another specific psychiatric disorder. Although many earlier authorities considered BDD to be related to or a variant of schizophrenia, available data do not support this hypothesis. The Japanese theory that BDD is a type of social phobia is more compelling, but it lacks adequate empirical validation.

While BDD and anorexia nervosa share a disturbance of body image, they differ in that BDD patients focus on particular aspects of their appearance rather than on their weight or overall shape or size; furthermore, they actually look normal, whereas anorexics do not. In addition, BDD does not involve disturbed eating behavior.

Perhaps most compelling is the possibility that BDD may be related to or is a variant of OCD. BDD symptoms are similar to those of OCD in that they consist of persistent, unpleasant thoughts that are difficult to resist, as well as compulsive, ritualistic behaviors, such as frequent mirror checking. Both disorders also have a similar early age of onset, an often chronic course, and substantial functional impairment and apparently respond positively to serotonergic antidepressants. However, BDD and OCD seem to differ in that the person with OCD typically recognizes the absurdity of his or her behaviors. BDD preoccupations, on the other hand, are more often closer to overvalued ideas than to obsessions: the thoughts seem more natural than intrusive, are more often acquiesced to without a lot of resistance, and often are not regarded as senseless. In addition, in this author's experience, BDD rituals are less likely than those of OCD to temporarily relieve anxiety, and BDD tends to be more socially impairing. However, large-scale controlled studies are needed to confirm the apparent similarities and differences of BDD and OCD and to determine whether they are, indeed, related disorders.

Future outlook

Clearly, there is still much to be learned about this fascinating and underrecognized disorder. Continued research is essential to a better understanding of its symptoms, treatment, and cause.

In the meantime, many people have obtained some relief simply by recognizing that they have an identifiable psychiatric disorder and that they are not alone in their suffering. And many have benefited from drug treatment, behavior therapy, and psychotherapy. It is hoped that ongoing research will continue to shed light on this baffling disorder and benefit those who suffer from the secret preoccupation with imagined ugliness.

Obstetrics

The specialty of obstetrics is not immune to change. Many of the recent positive changes have occurred in the management of labor (helping to shorten it and decrease the likelihood of cesarean delivery), in the declining length of hospital stays for women who have had normal deliveries, and in the increasing acceptance of the midwife as a professional who is trained to provide high-quality care to pregnant women.

At the same time, apprehension is growing regarding the increasing number of obstetric patients who either are HIV positive (infected by the human immunodeficiency virus, the virus that causes AIDS) or have overt AIDS and are at risk of transmitting the virus to their infants. At present, although the total number of AIDS patients who deliver babies is small, the number of pregnant women who are HIV positive is not insignificant. The exact size of this group is not presently known and will remain unknown in the absence of universal screening for the virus.

Active management of labor

During the last two decades, the rate of cesarean births in the United States has risen dramatically—from 5% in 1970 to 24.4% in 1989. The country now has the highest rate of cesarean deliveries of all developed countries. In fact, cesarean section is now the most common operation performed in the U.S.

Many factors have contributed to this circumstance. First, the operation itself has become much less risky than was the case in the first half of the century. For example, advances in surgical technique, anesthesia, and infection control now make cesarean birth a safer option than certain alternatives such as some types of forceps deliveries, which involve significantly higher risk. Second, electronic fetal heart rate monitoring, which contributes to fetal safety, has become commonplace in the past 15 years, creating situations in which immediate delivery will usually result in improved newborn outcome. Third, more patients undergoing vaginal delivery receive epidural anesthesia for pain relief in labor. Some investigators believe that this type of anesthesia leads to slower and prolonged labor, increasing the chance that a cesarean will be performed. Finally, fears of malpractice liability may influence physicians to intervene in the labor process; by providing cesarean delivery, obstetricians decrease the potential risks of the relatively unpredictable labor process, avoiding potential litigation.

Despite the increase in number of surgical interventions in women who would have delivered vaginally years ago, adverse infant outcomes (infants harmed during labor or delivery) have remained relatively stable. Recently the National Institute of Child Health and Human Development of the U.S. National Institutes of Health (NIH) convened a consensus-

Joel Levine—The New York Times

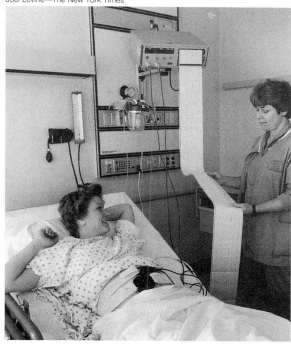

Electronic fetal heart rate monitoring has become commonplace in the past 15 years. Because it can indicate situations in which immediate delivery might result in improved newborn outcome, it has also led to high rates of cesarean delivery. Active management of labor is a strategy that increases the likelihood of an uncomplicated vaginal birth.

development conference to address issues related to cesarean childbirth. Experts attending the conference concluded that several external forces contribute to the high U.S. cesarean rate. The leading causes of the increased number of operative deliveries observed in recent years are the lack or arrest of progress during labor (labor dystocia) and a previous cesarean birth. Causes of labor dystocia include inadequate uterine contractions, a contracted maternal pelvis, excessive fetal size for a given mother's bony pelvis, and an abnormal position of the fetal head. Approximately 30% of all cesareans are presently performed for failure to progress in labor, with another one-third performed because of cesarean birth in a prior pregnancy. Under these circumstances, strategies designed to decrease the incidence of inadequate progress in labor have great potential for significantly reducing the rate of cesarean delivery.

A concept called the active management of labor (AMOL) has been proposed as one approach to achieving better progress in labor. The concept involves focusing on vaginal delivery in a subset of eligible patients—women in their first pregnancy who go into spontaneous labor. This approach was first implemented more than 20 years ago at the National Maternity Hospital in Dublin, where the rate of cesarean

New parents get ready to take their one-day-old home from the hospital. Hospital stays of just a day or two after a normal delivery are increasingly common today—in part for economic reasons but also because it is safe from a medical standpoint. This also means that parents must be exceptionally well prepared to cope with the enormously demanding and often exhausting job of caring for a newborn.

births has remained stable at approximately 6% over the years. Because the success of the Dublin program has been maintained for more than two decades, this approach has now been introduced successfully in many other centers in Europe and the U.S. Two initial reports described reductions in the rates of cesarean section from 12 and 13% in years prior to the use of AMOL to 6 and 4%, respectively, subsequent to initiation of a program of active management of labor. A more recent study in the U.S. compared AMOL side-by-side with a more conventional labor-management plan over a 13-month period in 1990–91 and found a 26% lower cesarean delivery rate in the AMOL group. Of equal or greater importance, infant outcomes were no different in the two groups, and mothers undergoing AMOL had not only shorter labors but fewer infections. This study is important because it demonstrated the safety as well as efficacy of AMOL.

As initially described, AMOL has two major components—organizational and medical. The organizational component consists of patient education, a uniform approach to labor management, close observation of the labor process by the senior obstetrician, one-on-one nurse-midwife companionship throughout labor, and rigorous review of all outcomes by hospital committees to ensure adherence to program principles. The medical component consists of an accurate diagnosis of labor, early release of the amniotic fluid (the "water" that surrounds the baby), infrequent use of epidural anesthesia, early recognition of abnormally slow labor progress, and rapid treatment of abnormal labor with the uterine stimulant oxytocin in doses higher than are usually used in current practice.

Exactly why or how the AMOL approach to labor is effective is not entirely understood. At least five potential explanations are possible. First, it is widely believed that patient anxiety contributes to labor difficulties and that education, along with constant companionship during labor, has the potential to decrease anxiety

in the mother. Second, a uniform approach to labor decreases the influence that time of day might have on physician management decisions. Third, close attention to establishing an accurate diagnosis of labor (which is difficult in many circumstances) may avoid interventions in patients whose labor is not yet well established; such interventions might predispose patients to abnormalities in the normal progression of labor. Fourth, the early release of amniotic fluid stimulates labor. And, finally, the early recognition and aggressive treatment of labor abnormalities corrects them before the uterine muscle becomes tired and less responsive to medical therapy.

Widespread application of the AMOL protocol would have numerous positive implications. First, long labors would be virtually eliminated; 95% of patients deliver within 12 hours of the diagnosis of labor. Second, delivery-related infections would be reduced by 50%. Most importantly, however, the rate of cesarean section would be significantly decreased. Such a decrease would result in fewer operative complications, shorter hospital stays, and lower hospitalization costs. Furthermore, where cesarean births could be averted, the need for repeat cesarean births in subsequent pregnancies would be virtually eliminated.

Other methods for labor management may achieve cesarean section rates as low as or lower than those of the AMOL approach. Some of these share many of the components used in AMOL, but AMOL is one approach that has an established record and that may be applicable to a wide range of practice settings. Consequently, it is likely to be used increasingly in the United States as efforts to lower the present high and costly cesarean section rates expand.

Home within two days of delivery

As recently as 1977 some women remained in the hospital two weeks after delivering their babies. Today most women return home in 24 to 48 hours after a normal delivery. Although the current practice stems primarily from economic constraints, early release from the hospital is medically safe for the mother and baby. Moreover, the psychological impact of an early discharge is generally satisfying.

The shortened postpartum stay (period after a woman has her baby) affects women in many ways. Most importantly, they may be physically and emotionally exhausted. The demands of a new baby cannot wait until the new mom and dad are "ready." Sleep deprivation and physical exhaustion often make it difficult to cope with parenting. There is an enormous amount of work (and fun) involved in caring for a newborn—feeding, changing diapers, washing clothes, and cleaning up messes. Most parents find that they are more anxious than usual the first few weeks at home. They worry about whether the baby is getting adequate nourishment, how often it sneezes, and what the different stool colors in the diaper mean. The sooner the mother and newborn are home, the sooner the new parents can adapt to their new situation.

Clearly, however, an early release puts more responsibility on the parents to be prepared; the potential adverse impact of an early hospital release can be reduced considerably with adequate education and guidance. Initially, information can be provided through the prenatal childbirth education classes, and after delivery further postpartum instruction is provided by nurses and other care providers.

Preparation of the mother for an early hospital release should include instruction about the following: warning signs of maternal infection; breast- or bottle-feeding and breast care; proper care of episiotomy stitches; the normal amount of postpartum bleeding; birth control options; diet and exercise for the mother; and any restrictions regarding sexual relations and other activities. Instructions concerning the newborn should cover care of the umbilical cord; breast-feeding or formula preparation; normal bowel and bladder functions; bathing; normal crying (and soothing techniques); infant safety—appropriate toys, prevention of falls, use of car seats, and first aid; and signs of infection and illness. Parents should leave the hospital with phone numbers of medical care providers they can contact day or night to answer their questions or advise about any unanticipated situations that arise. Parents may also benefit from assistance of family and friends, and some may wish to engage the help of a qualified home baby nurse.

Because controlling exorbitant and escalating health care costs has become everyone's responsibility, early postpartum hospital release has become an imperative. Although this puts an increased burden on the new parents, programs that thoroughly prepare them for all eventualities can help to curtail the high costs of hospitalization without compromising the health or well-being of either the mother or the baby.

Midwifery in the 1990s

More and more women in the United States are turning to certified nurse-midwives (CNMs) for prenatal care and advice during their pregnancies, to deliver their babies and help care for them after childbirth, and to provide ongoing gynecologic services. A CNM is a registered nurse with specialized training to care for women during the childbearing years. Although CNMs independently manage the care of healthy women and newborns, they do so in affiliation with a physician, who is available for consultation or referral as needed. Between 1975 and 1987 there was a fourfold increase in the number of babies delivered by certified nurse-midwives. Recent figures indicate that 2.6% of all births in the U.S. are now performed by midwives each year. (In several European countries with very low infant mortality rates, almost half of all deliveries are handled outside hospitals by midwives.)

Unfortunately, the title "midwife" is used quite loosely, and CNMs are often confused with "granny," or lay, midwives. To a great extent this confusion is a holdover from times when midwifery was not a true specialty in the eyes of the medical profession. Today all CNMs must complete a course of study in an accredited university or institution of higher education and pass a rigorous examination administered by the American College of Nurse-Midwives. State requirements for nurse-midwifery must also be met before licensure. In contrast, lay midwives (some are nurses and some are not) generally have no advanced medical education in obstetrics but have learned from experience or apprenticeship to other midwives. There are no standardized qualifications for their practice and no written or clinical criteria for assurance of competence or skills.

A certified nurse-midwife measures her patient's abdomen to check fetal growth during a routine prenatal exam. As highly trained professionals, CNMs provide complete obstetric care, including delivering babies in hospitals.

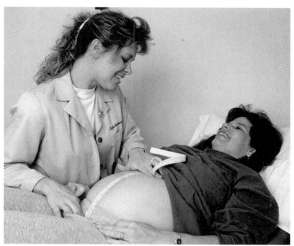

Northwestern Memorial Hospital

Women have turned to midwives to assist in childbirth for centuries. A German woodcut (c. 1580) depicts a midwife delivering a baby while an astrologer consults the stars to divine the newborn's future.

About 4,000 CNMs presently practice in the United States. As professionals, they are committed to close patient rapport, ongoing patient and family education, and promotion of individual responsibility for health. Nurse-midwives are preferred by many women who view childbirth as a natural process and believe that doctors are too impersonal and that in many hospitals childbirth is treated more like an illness. A recent review of the transformation of American midwifery in the past decade and a half, published in the *American Journal of Public Health,* concluded that midwives could be a "national solution" to the problems of escalating costs and limited access to obstetric care, particularly for poor and minority mothers.

Not only are CNMs qualified to deliver babies, they also provide prenatal and postpartum care, advise women about their reproductive health before and after pregnancy, and offer family-planning services and counseling. In many instances the nurse-midwife will fit a woman for a diaphragm, insert an intrauterine device, or, working under a physician's standing orders, prescribe birth control pills and perform follow-up examinations that are required for patients using those medications. CNMs are also qualified to provide regular gynecologic services, such as yearly pelvic and breast exams and Pap smears. Increasingly, nurse-midwives are providing gynecologic care and services for postmenopausal women. Situations in which nurse-midwives should not, as a rule, take charge of prenatal care and delivery include those in which the

mother has a multiple pregnancy, toxemia, kidney or heart disease, diabetes, or a history of repeat miscarriage or high-risk pregnancy.

Nurse-midwives typically work in hospitals, clinics, birthing centers, health maintenance organizations, or public health departments. They may also work in private practices of obstetricians. Usually, nurse-midwives deliver babies in hospitals, although a very small proportion deliver babies in the home if certain safety criteria are met. Lay midwives, on the other hand, usually deliver babies at home, and because they are not licensed to practice in many states, they may not have hospital backup arrangements should such arrangements become necessary.

For centuries, women have looked to midwives to advise and assist them in childbirth. Today's certified nurse-midwife carries on this tradition of personal, family-centered, understanding care while offering the highest level of competence and the best resources of modern medicine.

HIV infection and pregnancy

The face of the AIDS/HIV epidemic is changing and is reflected in the growing population of infected women. No longer a disease confined to adult homosexual men, AIDS is now the fifth leading cause of death for women of reproductive age. Minority women constitute the largest group infected with the AIDS virus (HIV); 50% of these patients are African-American or Hispanic. Initially, most women acquired the infection through intravenous drug use, but heterosexual transmission is now emerging as a major source of HIV infection.

Since most women currently infected with the virus are in the early stages of their infection, the course of pregnancy is generally unremarkable, and the rate of spontaneous miscarriage appears to be no higher for HIV-infected women. Infected women tend to have babies that are delivered at full term, are of normal birth weight, and have no birth defects. These circumstances suggest that the virus apparently has no direct effect on the intrauterine environment, fetal development, or growth potential of the fetus.

By far the most devastating and important consequence of HIV infection in a pregnant woman is the possibility of passing the virus to her fetus. That perinatal transmission (around the time of birth) occurs is certain; when, how, and why the virus is transmitted from some mothers to their offspring are all still unknown. However, important clues are emerging.

Transmission from a mother to her offspring (known as vertical transmission) occurs approximately 30% of the time, and for unexplained reasons, transmission rates vary by geographic location, ranging from 13% in Europe to 40% in Africa. While the exact timing of viral transmission is unclear, a few studies have shown that the virus can pass across the placenta as early as eight weeks' gestation. Nevertheless, the prevailing opinion of neonatalogists is that in perhaps 50% or more cases transmission occurs at the time of birth. For reasons that are not entirely clear, infants born prematurely are more likely to be infected than full-term babies. Unfortunately, prenatal diagnosis of HIV infection is impossible because of the risk of infecting a fetus by the invasive diagnostic procedure itself.

The mechanism by which the virus infects the baby is also not known. Possibilities include direct passage of blood-borne viral particles across the placenta into the baby's circulation sometime during pregnancy, exposure of the baby to infected maternal blood and secretions at the time of delivery, and secondary infection of the baby through exposure to infected amniotic fluid. Currently, predicting which mothers will transmit the virus is impossible, but it appears that women in the most advanced stages of the disease are the ones who transmit the virus most frequently. The study of women who have had more than one pregnancy during the course of their infection has shown that transmission is not consistent; women often have an infected infant in one pregnancy followed by an uninfected offspring in a subsequent pregnancy. The method of delivery—either by cesarean section or vaginal birth—does not appear to influence the rate of HIV transmission. Because viral transmission is pos-

As the AIDS epidemic has grown, so has the number of women who are HIV positive and at risk of passing the virus to their infants. It is still not known precisely when or by what mechanism perinatal transmission is most likely to occur.

National Library of Medicine, Bethesda, Maryland

sible during breast-feeding, it is advisable that infants born to HIV-positive mothers be fed with bottles and formula in preference to breast milk.

Primary prevention of infection in women is obviously the most effective means of reducing HIV infection in newborns. Interventions aimed at interrupting transmission from women already infected with the virus are much less likely to be successful, given the lack of specific knowledge regarding prenatal transmission. The NIH is currently investigating the efficacy of various treatment regimens in decreasing the passage of virus from mothers to their offspring. For a number of years the drug zidovudine (or AZT), the primary antiretroviral agent used to treat HIV-positive individuals, has been given to infected pregnant women in an attempt to decrease the amount of circulating virus in the mother and thereby minimize the likelihood of infection of the infant. Preliminary results show that the drug is safe for women and their newborns, but it remains to be determined whether AZT improves the mother's prognosis, whether pregnancy itself is associated with the progression of HIV infection, or whether the drug prevents vertical transmission.

Other strategies for blocking mother-to-infant HIV transmission that are planned for the near future include the use of immune system modulators that would either increase the clearance of the virus from the circulation (passive immunization with HIV specific immune globulin) or block the virus from entering susceptible cells (so-called recombinant CD4 immunoglobulin). As preventive strategies, the development of monoclonal antibodies directed against the virus and/or active immunization with an HIV specific vaccine appear to hold great promise for the future.

—*Louis Keith, M.D.*

Pediatrics

The 1991 preliminary infant mortality statistics for the United States showed that infant deaths had declined to the lowest rate ever recorded for the country—8.9 per 1,000 live births. Even so, the rate was still higher than that of almost all industrialized countries, and U.S. black infants were more than twice as likely to die before their first birthday as white babies. It did not appear likely that the federal government's goal of lowering infant mortality to 7 deaths per 1,000 live births—with the black rate no higher than 11—by the year 2000 would be met.

Increased access to prenatal care would probably have a great impact on the infant death rate and on the number of low-birth-weight babies. (Low-birth-weight babies, those under 2,500 g [5.5 lb], have a 40 times greater chance of dying in infancy than do normal-weight babies, and those who survive are at risk for lasting disabilities.) Universal access to prenatal care would result not only in healthier newborns with an improved quality of life but also in substantial savings in health care resources that are now used to care for high-risk infants.

In April 1992 the American Academy of Pediatrics recommended that infants sleep on their sides or backs instead of their stomachs. (About 80% of U.S. babies are placed on the stomach so they will not choke if they spit up.) Studies from other developed nations, many of which had considerably higher rates of death from sudden infant death syndrome (SIDS) than the U.S., found that placing babies on their sides or backs resulted in a decreased incidence of SIDS. The academy's recommendation applied only to healthy, full-term infants; those who have breathing problems or vomit excessively should still be placed on the stomach. The cause of most SIDS deaths is still unknown.

It was also recommended that babies not be placed on beanbag-type cushions. These cushions were known to have suffocated at least 35 infants, a number of whose deaths were at first attributed to SIDS. Consumers who had these cushions were asked to destroy them or to return them to the retailer or manufacturer.

Several of the child-health issues that have been the focus of recent research are discussed in more detail below.

Breast-feeding—still best

Relatively little is known about why breast-feeding protects infants against disease, but evidence that it does continues to accumulate. A U.S. government task force reported in 1981 that breast-feeding prevents gastrointestinal infections, and more recent studies show that breast-fed infants also have fewer infections of other types, including those of the respiratory system (wheezing, bronchitis, bronchiolitis, pneumonia), urinary tract, ear, bloodstream (blood poisoning), and

brain (meningitis). Breast-feeding is now being studied for its effects on the long-term health of the child. For example, breast-feeding has been shown to delay the development of eczema, particularly in families with a history of allergy. Further, breast-feeding is credited with a number of less tangible benefits—*e.g.,* low cost, enhanced mother-infant interaction, and an increase in the mother's confidence in herself as a capable parent.

The decline in breast-feeding that dominated the 1940s, '50s, and '60s was followed by an increase that reached a peak in 1982. Despite continuing efforts by advocates of breast-feeding—including most but not all physicians—survey results published in 1991 showed that between 1984 and 1989 the number of U.S. women who breast-fed steadily dropped. The greatest decline was among high-risk mothers, precisely those whose infants stand to gain the most from being breast-fed. Ironically, the popularity of breast-feeding is declining during a period of rapidly increasing knowledge about breast milk itself. Recent studies show that breast-fed infants react with measurable changes in feeding behavior when the taste and odor of breast milk are altered by manipulation of the mother's diet—for example, by the controlled introduction of garlic or alcohol—or by changes in the mother's exercise level. In the latter instance, infants may be reacting to the taste of lactic acid, the level of which increases in breast milk as a woman exercises.

British investigators reported recently that prematurely born children who were fed breast milk during the early weeks of life had significantly higher IQs at 7½ to 8 years of age than prematurely born children who were not fed breast milk. This was true even when the IQ scores were adjusted to take into account the education and social class of mothers and even when infants had been fed breast milk by tube. The researchers speculated that certain hormones and fats

Pregnant women and new mothers wait to be seen at a North Carolina clinic that is participating in a government-sponsored program to reduce infant mortality. Experts agree that universal access to prenatal care would reduce the incidence of low-birth-weight babies and lower the needlessly high U.S. infant death rate.

Nancy Pierce—The New York Times

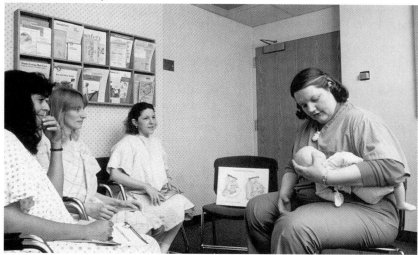

New mothers receive some practical tips about breast-feeding from a nurse clinician who has special certification as a lactation consultant. Growing evidence supports the view that babies who are fed breast milk derive both short- and long-term health benefits.

that are present in breast milk but not in infant formula might be important for the structural development of the nervous system.

Formula feeding is sometimes associated with subtle, unrecognized intestinal bleeding that may lead to anemia. In a study of five-year-old Costa Rican children, those who had been moderately anemic in infancy and had been weaned earlier scored lower on tests of mental and motor functioning at age five than did children who had not been anemic. The study did not determine whether the anemia in the formula-fed children was responsible for the poorer functioning, however.

While many physicians favor breast-feeding, it is not always the best choice. Recent studies have indicated that the human immunodeficiency virus (HIV)—the virus that causes AIDS—occasionally can be transmitted through breast milk; in areas of the world where sanitation standards are high, HIV-infected women are advised not to breast-feed. Many drugs can also be transmitted from mother to infant via breast milk. The transmissibility of any medication being taken—including prescription, nonprescription, and illicit drugs as well as alcohol—should be reviewed carefully by a prospective nursing mother with her physician.

Surfactant replacement: saving lives

Surfactant, a complex combination of fats and proteins secreted by cells in the lungs, contributes to the elasticity of lung tissue by affecting the surface tension of normal fluids in the air sacs of the lung. This action is similar to the effect of detergent on the surface tension of an oily liquid. In most fetuses, surfactant reaches levels sufficient to keep the lungs inflated by the last month of pregnancy. A deficiency of surfactant in the infant lung, which may cause the air sacs to collapse, is a leading cause of the serious breathing difficulty respiratory distress syndrome (RDS).

In the 1979 edition of one widely used pediatric textbook, RDS was identified as the cause of half the deaths occurring in the early newborn period, particularly among small premature infants, who are the most likely to lack surfactant at birth. Surfactant deficiency was listed first among the several causes of RDS, but nowhere in a long and detailed discussion of treatment was surfactant replacement mentioned. Instead, this text outlined how to support infants with RDS through the days until their own surfactant production increased to normal levels. Many did not survive that long, however, and a number of those who did were left with chronic lung disease. The importance of preventing RDS by preventing premature birth itself was emphasized, as was the importance of treating these children in a specially designed hospital unit with skilled personnel and sophisticated equipment.

Prevention of prematurity and expert care in well-equipped neonatal intensive care units are no less important today than before, but physicians now have a new tool for treating many newborns who have RDS. During the 1980s, in carefully conducted clinical trials involving thousands of low-birth-weight infants, surfactant-replacement therapy was shown to save lives and to reduce the severity of illness in infants with proven RDS. Newborn deaths in the United States declined by 8.5% between 1988 and 1989 and another 6.3% between 1989 and 1990. Many believe that surfactant-replacement therapy was responsible for much of this decrease. This treatment appears to be cost-effective, and there is no evidence that saving premature babies by the use of surfactant increases the number who are developmentally or physically handicapped at one year of age.

The U.S. Food and Drug Administration (FDA) recently approved the use of both natural surfactant, which comes from calf lung tissue, and synthetic surfactant. Many questions about surfactant use are

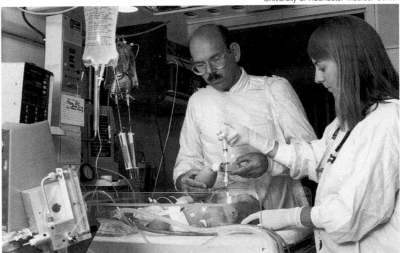

Doctors in the neonatal intensive care unit of Strong Memorial Hospital, Rochester, New York, administer surfactant to a premature infant suffering from respiratory distress syndrome. Surfactant, a substance that is normally secreted by the mature lungs, facilitates inflation and deflation of the lungs' air sacs during breathing. Surfactant treatment is now credited with saving the lives of many of these infants.

still to be answered: Is it better to give surfactant prophylactically to a premature baby who may be at risk or to wait until RDS is diagnosed? Is a single dose effective, or should several doses be given over the first few days of life? Does surfactant-replacement therapy reduce the common complications of RDS as well as ameliorating RDS itself? The answers to these questions will come with refinements in the use of surfactant.

Immunization: bad news and good

Vaccines are available for prevention of a number of serious childhood diseases, but many U.S. children are not being immunized until legally required when they enter school. In the U.S. the immunization rate for children two years old and under is worse than that in most other developed nations. One result of this low

A youngster in Pittsburgh, Pennsylvania, is vaccinated before she can start kindergarten. Compared with other developed countries, the U.S. has one of the worst records for immunization of children under school age.

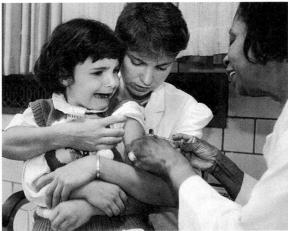

Scott Goldsmith—The New York Times

immunization rate was a major resurgence in measles cases in 1989 and 1990, especially in children under five. Although the number of cases has declined since then, epidemics continue to occur, especially in large inner-city areas.

Hepatitis B. Many thousands of cases of acute hepatitis B infection occur every year in the United States, and several thousand people die of this type of liver infection. The virus is transmitted through exposure to blood and blood products, through sexual contact, and from mothers to infants, primarily during birth. A vaccine against the hepatitis B virus has been available for some time, but initially it was not widely used, partly because its source—human blood—raised concern about transmission of other blood-borne viruses, including HIV. In general, vaccination was selective; high-risk populations such as health care professionals and Asian immigrants were vaccinated, as were some infants of mothers known to carry the virus.

However, vaccination is now recommended for all U.S. infants and, when resources allow, for all adolescents. This change has come about for two reasons: selective vaccination was not preventing the spread of this disease, and large supplies of genetically engineered vaccine, which has no connection with human blood, are now available.

Pertussis. DTP—in which P stands for pertussis, commonly known as whooping cough—is a vaccine given to infants three times during the first six months of life. Local reactions at the site of injection (redness, swelling) and more widespread reactions, including fever with associated convulsions, sometimes occur after administration of DTP vaccine. In extremely rare instances, whether or not the child had convulsions at the time of vaccination, signs of brain damage and subsequent retardation have been reported. Evidence continues to grow that such brain damage is coincidental, that it is not caused by the pertussis vaccine, and that it would have occurred in a particular child with or without pertussis vaccination.

The dangers of whooping cough far outweigh the discomforts that children may experience at the time of vaccination, but there is nothing desirable about these discomforts. The vaccine that has been in use for many years is made from killed whole-cell pertussis organisms. A new vaccine recently approved by the FDA does not contain whole-cell organisms; it contains specific proteins present in the pertussis bacterium. This vaccine is also given by injection but, while the discomfort of the shot itself remains, local reactions and fever are reduced. It is recommended only for booster doses at 18 months and 5 years of age. When its effectiveness is well-enough established, the new vaccine may be used for the first three doses.

Haemophilus influenzae type B. Because of the *influenzae* that is part of its name and the resemblance of this word to *influenza* (the viral respiratory infection that periodically affects thousands of people worldwide), *H. influenzae* type B is sometimes mistakenly associated with influenza. Actually, it is a bacterium that causes major body tissue infections, especially a serious form of meningitis in infants and young children.

Even though *H. influenzae* type B is the most common cause of bloodstream infection and meningitis during the first year of life, until recently the available vaccines were not effective in very young children. Therefore, vaccination was not recommended before 15 months of age, and the majority of serious childhood infections caused by this organism continued to occur. With the development of improved vaccines that provide protection in infancy have come new recommendations calling for a series of doses starting at two months of age. Thus, the incidence of meningitis and the other serious infections caused by *H. influenzae* type B in infants and children is rapidly decreasing.

Childhood cholesterol screening: current opinion

Currently a matter of lively controversy is whether to measure cholesterol levels in all children so as to identify those who in later life may be at high risk for coronary artery disease (CAD), the type of heart disease associated with high blood cholesterol levels. Whenever decisions are made about whether to start any kind of screening program, certain questions must be answered. In a recent issue of the *Journal of Pediatrics,* Steven R. Daniels and colleagues at the University of Cincinnati, Ohio, addressed the following important questions:

Is the disease that will be prevented severe enough to warrant screening? Unquestionably, coronary artery disease in a country like the U.S. is a major health problem. Moreover, the prevention that might grow out of a successful cholesterol screening program would be particularly important in reducing CAD because treatment often has nothing to offer: 25% of new cases are first manifested by sudden death.

Can the presence or absence of disease or factors strongly associated with disease—in this case, cholesterol levels—be determined accurately? And does the test reliably predict who will have health problems in the future? In general, studies have shown that children with elevated blood cholesterol are more likely to have high cholesterol levels later in life. High adult blood cholesterol levels increase the risk for CAD. Nevertheless, there are important exceptions. Some people with high blood cholesterol in adulthood had normal levels as children, and—conversely—one study showed that only 30% of those who had high levels as adolescents still had high levels about 10 years

Some of these San Francisco youngsters may have elevated cholesterol levels—a factor that puts them at risk of developing coronary artery disease in adulthood. But should all of them undergo cholesterol tests so that those at risk can be identified? At present, most pediatricians would say no. Screening is warranted, however, for those with a parent who has high cholesterol and those from families with a history of early cardiovascular disease.

Richard Choy—Peter Arnold

later. The reliability of childhood cholesterol screening in predicting CAD in adulthood is diminished by such exceptions.

If screening shows abnormal results, is effective treatment available? An abnormal test result has little value if it does not lead to treatment. Treatment with diet, medication, or a combination of both can lower cholesterol levels in children, but diet modification in children under two years of age, particularly when it is not supervised by a physician, can have adverse effects on growth and development. Studies have shown that older children often do not follow a program of diet and exercise consistently. There has been only limited study of medications to lower childhood cholesterol levels, and thus far no cholesterol-lowering drug has been approved specifically for children.

Is the screening test safe and cost effective, and what is the impact when a child who was formerly thought of as well is labeled as being at risk? Drawing the small amount of blood that is required for measuring cholesterol levels poses no threat, and the test is not particularly expensive. Participation in a cholesterol-lowering program does have costs, which may or may not be covered by third-party payers. Labeling a person as being at high risk for CAD may cause insurance premiums to be high throughout life. There are other issues to be considered, however, when addressing "cost" and "safety"; among them are the possible psychological effects of such labeling. Studies of children whose lives were believed to be endangered because they had a heart murmur, for example—even though the murmur had no clinical importance—found that the youngsters had developed emotional problems.

Does the available screening test do a good job of identifying problems in children who have them and in not identifying problems in those who do not? Under the best of conditions, cholesterol measurements are reasonably accurate, and their accuracy is improving. False-positive and false-negative results do occur, however, particularly when screening is universal and not limited to children known to be at risk. A false-negative test gives reassurance when such reassurance is unwarranted, while a false-positive test may lead to an expensive but unnecessary workup and much needless worry.

Whereas many cardiologists would like to see cholesterol screening for all children, probably most pediatricians are less sure that universal screening is appropriate. To provide guidance on the subject, a panel of experts assembled by the U.S. National Institutes of Health issued recommendations in 1992, as did the American Academy of Pediatrics. Both groups recommended screening only for those children who have a parent with high blood cholesterol or for those from families with a history of cardiovascular disease before age 55.

Lead: subtle hazard
In the past a certain level of lead in a child's body was considered a cutoff point; children with lead levels above that point were of concern, and they often did show clear evidence—convulsions, anemia, and brain damage—of lead poisoning. During the past few years more subtle evidence of lead poisoning has been detected in children with lower lead levels. When large populations of children are tested for both lead and intelligence, slightly lower average intelligence scores are found among the children with higher lead levels even when they do not have lead levels anywhere near high enough to cause symptoms.

It now appears, therefore, that there is no "danger" level of lead poisoning. Consequently, the CDC has set much lower limits for lead toxicity, a logical decision but one that has brought its own problems. The test that has been used for years was simple and inexpensive, but it is not able to detect low levels of lead. Use of newer tests requires blood from a child's vein instead of fingertip. These tests are much more expensive, but—more important—the facilities do not exist for performing them on large numbers of children. Moreover, there is no treatment for children with low-level lead poisoning other than to try to figure out the source of the poisoning, and even that has become more complicated. Peeling, chipping, and deteriorating paint and exhaust from leaded gasoline were primary causes of exposure to environmental lead; now, in addition to leaded paint, lead on the soil surface and in household water pipes has assumed increasing importance. Some studies have shown that the process of "deleading" a house has actually raised the exposure of children to lead. Lead exposure is without a doubt a serious problem in the U.S., one with many dilemmas at this time.

—*Birt Harvey, M.D.*

Pharmaceuticals

Having undergone an extended period of regulatory, legislative, and scientific adjustments throughout the 1980s, the pharmaceutical industry and the marketing of drugs in the United States continue to change in the 1990s. Indications are that further transformations are likely in the not-too-distant future.

A greater role for pharmacists
Among the developments in 1991 was a change in the way pharmaceuticals are reimbursed under Medicaid. A program for providing health care to the poor using both federal and state funds, Medicaid is contributing to modifications in the practice of pharmacy and changes in the educational requirements for pharmacists. Because government programs that provide prescription drugs to patients must reimburse the pharmacies that dispense them, pharmacists have

After filling a prescription for pediatric eye drops, a pharmacist explains how to use them correctly to the young patient's father. Professional pharmacy groups are increasingly advocating a broader role for pharmacists— one that would emphasize their responsibilities for counseling clients about appropriate use of medications and alerting them to possible side effects and potential drug interactions.

lobbied for the inclusion of greater pharmacy responsibilities and authority in such programs. For example, legislation pertaining to Medicaid that was enacted in 1990 requires pharmacists who wish to be eligible for participation in the program to provide such services as counseling patients about how to take their prescription drugs, keeping patient medication records, and checking physicians' prescription orders for potential medication errors. (Similar legislation pertaining to Medicare, enacted in 1988, was repealed the following year.)

At the same time, pharmacy groups have advocated giving pharmacists broader responsibilities under state pharmacy practice acts and requiring all pharmacy students to obtain a doctor of pharmacy (PharmD) degree as a minimum educational credential for entering general pharmacy practice. Many pharmacy schools now award PharmD degrees upon completion of a six- or seven-year course of study (beyond high school), but a number of institutions confer baccalaureate degrees after a five-year program. The majority of national pharmacy associations have embraced a shift to the PharmD as the sole "entry-level" degree. One notable exception is the National Association of Chain Drug Stores, which has argued that there currently is a shortage of pharmacists, which would be exacerbated by the move to the PharmD requirement.

Drugs by mail

Mail-order pharmacy is another growing form of professional practice. Health insurance programs that provide prescription drug benefits often require or encourage beneficiaries to obtain their medications for chronic illnesses through a mail-service provider on the expectation that such pharmacies can dispense prescriptions at lower cost. Mail-service pharmacies claim that they can reduce operating costs through automated, assembly-line operations and high-volume dispensing, thus allowing them to offer savings to consumers. These enterprises also provide the convenience of mail delivery, although in many cases patients will prefer to use local pharmacies when filling prescriptions for acute illnesses requiring immediate treatment. A number of commercial mail-order pharmacy companies now operate regional distribution centers throughout the United States, the largest being the private pharmacy firm Medco Containment Services, Inc. In addition, mail-order pharmacy services have been offered for decades by the American Association of Retired Persons and the U.S. Veterans Affairs Department.

A number of leaders in the profession question whether pharmacists working in mail-service settings can provide high-quality, "personal" service to patients. Mail-service pharmacies contend that they can counsel their clients effectively by enclosing drug-information leaflets with each prescription and by offering toll-free telephone numbers patients can call to speak to pharmacists when they have questions or concerns about their prescription drugs. Despite reservations on the part of educators and others, there is no doubt

Mail order versus drugstore: comparing costs*			
drug (100 pills)	selected mail-order services		Chicago-area drugstore
	AARP	Sears	Medi-Mail	Walgreens
Premarin 0.625 mg	$29.60	$39.21	$26.95	$31.99
Lasix 40 mg	$16.95	$22.49	$16.95	$16.99
Dyazide 50/25 mg	$28.95	$32.97	$28.95	$31.99
Cardizem 60 mg	$51.40	$61.44	$51.50	$55.99
Persantine 50 mg	$42.90	$48.62	$46.95	$45.99
postage/handling	$1.00	$3.00	$1.48	—

*as of July 1992
Source: *Chicago Sun-Times*, Aug. 3, 1992

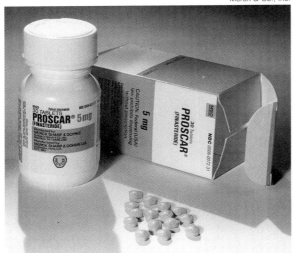

Finasteride (Proscar), which was approved for use in the U.S. in June 1992, is the first drug to be licensed for treatment of benign enlargement of the prostate gland, a condition that affects an estimated 10 million American men over age 50.

that this segment of the profession is growing. It has been estimated that mail-order pharmacy companies reached $3 billion in total sales in 1991, accounting for 8.9% of the pharmaceuticals market (compared with $2.3 billion in 1990, or 7.3%).

New pharmaceuticals

One constant in the 1990s has been the ongoing effort by the U.S. Food and Drug Administration (FDA)—the federal agency authorized to review and approve new drugs before they are marketed—to approve as many new compounds as possible. As part of this initiative, the FDA, under the leadership of Commissioner David A. Kessler and the administration of Pres. George Bush, proposed new procedures for speeding drug approvals (*see* below).

In 1991 the FDA approved 30 new chemical compounds for marketing in the U.S. The total tied a record for new approvals that had been set in 1985; by comparison, in 1989 and again in 1990, 23 new compounds were approved.

1A approvals. Five of the prescription drug products approved in 1991 were given 1A ratings under the FDA's priority review system. The "1" indicates that the drug is a new chemical compound that has never previously been marketed in the U.S.; the "A" indicates that the FDA considers the product to be a major therapeutic advance over other drugs on the market. Those new drugs were: alglucerase (Ceredase), an enzyme-replacement therapy for type I Gaucher's disease; fludarabine (Fludara), an agent for the palliative treatment of chronic lymphocytic leukemia in patients who are not helped by other therapies; dideoxyinosine, also called didanosine (ddl; Videx), a drug for

adults and children with advanced HIV (human immunodeficiency virus) infection who are intolerant of or unresponsive to zidovudine (AZT; Retrovir); pentostatin (Nipent), a treatment for hairy cell leukemia in adults unresponsive to alpha interferon; and histrelin (Supprelin), for use in controlling the symptoms of central precocious puberty.

Drugs given the 1A rating during the first several months of 1992 included: finasteride (Proscar), a drug treatment for benign enlargement of the prostate gland, and zalcitabine (ddC; Hivid), another anti-HIV drug. Early in 1992 the 1A "orphan" drug interleukin-2 was approved. (An "orphan" drug is defined as a new compound for which the patient population totals less than 200,000. The Orphan Drug Act of 1983 grants such products freedom from market competition for seven years after approval.) Being marketed under the name Proleukin, the human recombinant interleukin-2 product is indicated for treatment of metastatic renal cell carcinoma, which is generally fatal. The manufacturer, Cetus Corp., a subsidiary of Chiron Corp., estimates that approximately 10,000 cases of metastatic kidney cancer are diagnosed in the United States annually; average patient survival after diagnosis is 12 months. Clinical trials, which were headed by Steven A. Rosenberg of the National Cancer Institute and included 255 patients, showed that interleukin-2 reduced the size of tumors in 15% of patients and eliminated tumors entirely in 4%. On average, tumors reverted to pretreatment status within 23.2 months. However, the therapy is highly toxic; nearly all patients suffered severe or life-threatening side effects, and 4% died from drug-related causes. Initially Chiron said that a three-week course of treatment, involving 30 to 35 vials per regimen, would cost $6,000 to $8,000.

1B approvals. Nine new chemical entities approved in 1991 were given "B" ratings, meaning that they offer modest therapeutic gains over products already marketed for the same uses. They included: ondansetron hydrochloride (Zofran), for prevention of nausea and vomiting associated with cancer chemotherapy; gallium nitrate (Ganite), to treat cancer-related hypercalcemia (elevated levels of calcium in the blood) in patients who do not respond to hydration (use of fluids to flush excess calcium from the body); dimercaptosuccinic acid (Chemet), for treatment of severe lead poisoning in children; foscarnet sodium (Foscavir), for treatment of cytomegalovirus retinitis in patients with AIDS; clarithromycin (Biaxin), an antibiotic used to treat mild to moderate infections of the upper and lower respiratory tracts and the skin; pamidronate (Aredia), for moderate to severe hypercalcemia associated with cancer; ticlopidine (Ticlid), a platelet-aggregation inhibitor approved to reduce stroke risk in those who have had a stroke or have experienced stroke "precursors"; and the antibiotic azithromycin (Zithromax), for treatment of adult upper and lower

Now, dermatologists have a product proven to regrow hair for women: *Rogaine*.

"Finally, I can do a lot more about my hair loss than just sit back and take it."

Minoxidil (Rogaine), which has been marketed in the U.S. for several years as a treatment for male pattern baldness, was approved in 1991 for treatment of female androgenetic alopecia, the most common cause of hair loss in women. In both sexes therapy must be continued indefinitely in order to maintain hair regrowth achieved with the drug.

respiratory tract infections, skin infections, and sexually transmitted infections of the urethra and cervix.

1C approvals. Other 1991 approvals include 16 new 1C compounds, considered by the FDA to represent little or no therapeutic gain over already marketed products. They included: ramipril (Altace), for treatment of hypertension; the anti-inflammatory etodolac (Lodine), for management of pain and osteoarthritis symptoms; and doxacurium (Nuromax), a skeletal muscle relaxant used as an adjunct to general anesthesia during surgery. Three angiotensin-converting enzyme (ACE) inhibitors were approved for reducing blood pressure: fosinopril (Monopril), benazepril (Lotensin), and quinapril (Accupril). The FDA also approved beractant (Survanta), a synthetic pulmonary surfactant for prevention and treatment of respiratory distress syndrome in premature infants; an antihypertensive, felodipine (Plendil); and pravastatin (Pravachol), a cholesterol-lowering drug. Included in the 1C drugs approved just before year's end were: the antibiotic cefprozil (Cefzil); simvastatin (Zocor), an anticholesterol drug; nabumetone (Relafen), an antiarthritic; sertraline (Zoloft), for the treatment of depression; isosorbide mononitrate (ISMO), for prevention of chest pain due to coronary artery disease; and the antibiotics loracarbef (Lorabid) and enoxacin (Penetrex).

New indication for an existing drug. Another noteworthy approval in 1991—Rogaine for women—involved a new indication for an already-marketed product. Rogaine (minoxidil 2% topical solution), which has been marketed since August 1988 for male pattern baldness (loss of hair at the vertex, or back, of the scalp) in men is now approved for treatment of female androgenetic alopecia, the most prevalent type of diffuse hair thinning or loss in women. Sales of minoxidil, the only FDA-approved hair-regrowth treatment, were estimated at more than $100 million in 1991. As a remedy for baldness, however, the drug has several drawbacks: fewer than half of the patients respond to treatment; Rogaine is ineffective in restoring growth to

a receding hairline; and it must be used for life to retain any regrowth. Sales of the product have therefore been somewhat disappointing compared with projections made before it was initially approved.

New formulation. Nicotine patches, introduced in 1991, constituted a new formulation of a previously existing product. Adhesive patches worn on the skin, they provide continuous controlled release of nicotine to help cigarette smokers break their addiction. Similar patches have been used to provide extended release of such agents as nitroglycerine for angina, scopolamine for motion sickness, and estrogen in hormone replacement therapy. Four brands of nicotine patch are now available in the U.S.: Nicoderm, Habitrol, ProStep, and Nicotrol. Marion Merrell Dow became the first company to market a smoking-cessation product when it launched Nicorette, a nicotine-containing gum, in 1984. The nicotine patches quickly began to outsell gum products; in fact, several manufacturers reported difficulty in keeping up with demand.

Studies of the effectiveness of nicotine patches indicate that smokers who use them successfully have about the same relapse rate as those who try other methods of quitting. Since patches treat only the physiological effects of withdrawal from nicotine addiction (cravings, irritability, problems with concentration), wearers still must contend with the psychological aspects of addiction. According to the manufacturers' research, the best results were obtained by those who combined patch treatment with a program of behavioral therapy. While all of the products on the market contain 100% nicotine, they vary in the amount released into the blood. Some may be too potent for people who are only light smokers. Warner-Lambert's Nicotrol patch, the last to be approved, is meant to be worn only during the daytime (the others stay on for 24 hours), which could lower the incidence of sleeplessness, one of the unpleasant side effects of patch therapy. Other side effects range from minor problems such as local burning or itching to sweat-

A widely advertised new pharmaceutical product is the nicotine patch. Available only by prescription, the patch delivers a constant dose of nicotine through the skin to reduce the smoker's physiological craving for cigarettes.

ing, dry mouth, and nervousness. The FDA was also investigating reports of heart attacks suffered by some who smoked while wearing patches.

Biologics. The FDA also approved several important new biological products in 1991. "Biological products" are defined by the Public Health Service Act as "any virus; therapeutic serum; toxin, antitoxin; vaccine; blood, blood component, or derivative; allergenic product or analogous product; or arsphenamine or its derivatives (or any other trivalent organic arsenic compound) applicable to the prevention, treatment, or cure of diseases or injuries of man." The FDA distinguishes drugs from biological products before they are tested in clinical studies. Thus, when a company presents data from laboratory (*in vitro*), animal, and other preclinical studies and requests permission to begin study in humans, the agency at that point determines whether the compound is a drug or a biological product and forwards the application either to the Center for Drug Evaluation and Research or to the Center for Biologics Evaluation and Research.

The new biologics included white blood cell growth factors filgrastim, or granulocyte colony-stimulating factor (Neupogen), and sargramostim, or granulocyte macrophage colony-stimulating factor (Leukine; Prokine). Filgrastim is indicated for treatment of a blood condition (neutropenia) associated with cancer chemotherapy; sargramostim was initially approved for use in patients undergoing bone grafts and later in the year was granted a second use for treatment of cancer patients in whom bone marrow transplants fail. Another biologic, interferon alpha-2b (Intron A), was approved for treatment of hepatitis C.

A significant vaccine approval was Acel-Imune, a new diphtheria-tetanus-pertussis vaccine that includes an acellular pertussis component developed by the Japanese manufacturer Takeda. Pertussis vaccines made from killed whole cells of the pertussis bacterium have been associated with cases of the disease itself (whooping cough), neurological complications, brain damage, and even death. The acellular vaccine uses only bacterial particles to trigger an immune reaction. Although there is some concern that the acellular vaccine will not be quite as effective as whole-cell products (which are 90% effective), it is expected to be less toxic.

Treatments for HIV infection: work in progress

Some important breakthroughs were made in the fight against HIV during the year. DdI and ddC, mentioned above, were the second and third drugs (respectively) to be approved for halting progression of the AIDS virus (the first being AZT). The FDA's antiviral drugs advisory panel reviewed data on ddC in April 1992 and recommended that the product be approved as an adjunct to treatment with AZT. The panel said the data did not support the use of ddC as a single-agent AIDS therapy, but it concluded that studies to date had demonstrated ddC's ability to enhance the effectiveness and reduce the toxic effects of AZT.

At the same time, the panel agreed that data on ddI from a study sponsored by the National Institutes of Health (NIH) did demonstrate the benefits of this drug as an alternative treatment to AZT. The NIH study, which included patients who previously had been treated with AZT for 16 weeks, suggested that after being switched to ddI, HIV-infected persons with no symptoms and those with AIDS-related complex (pre-AIDS) were less likely to develop one of the opportunistic infections listed in the official case definition of AIDS. Researchers noted, however, that there was no significant difference in survival rates between patients switched to ddI and those who remained on AZT. DdI's approval had been based on preliminary data that showed an increase in the number of CD4 cells (infection-fighting white blood cells that are targets of HIV) in AIDS patients treated with the drug. The FDA considers the CD4 count a "surrogate marker" (or "surrogate endpoint") of AIDS progression because although CD4 counts decline in AIDS patients as the disease progresses, no data have been developed to show definitively that raising CD4 counts either extends survival or improves quality of life.

Recent AIDS research generated significant new—and sometimes conflicting—information about therapies already on the market. In a study published in April 1992, for example, early treatment with AZT of HIV-positive individuals was shown to reduce the death rate in this population. The report, which appeared in the *New England Journal of Medicine,* de-

Lenny Kaplan's underground dispensary in Florida imports AIDS drugs not approved in the U.S. Despite new regulations to speed drug approvals, many people with AIDS are demanding immediate access to any therapy that might curtail the progress of their disease.

scribed the results of a clinical trial involving 2,568 HIV-infected men who had not yet experienced any of the symptoms considered to be an "AIDS-defining event." The study showed that the risk of death in those patients treated with AZT prior to development of AIDS was reduced by 57% after six months and 33% after two years. Those findings support the use of AZT early in the progress of the infection, when tolerance of the drug's potentially toxic effects is high. They seem to conflict with research published only a few months earlier in the same journal, reporting on a Veterans Affairs Department study of 338 HIV-infected individuals who were symptomatic but judged to be "pre-AIDS." This study found that early AZT treatment slowed the progression to AIDS but afforded no survival advantage over patients who were not given the drug until after AIDS was diagnosed. The NIH, sponsor of the later study, suggested that its investigation, owing in part to its larger size, may be more indicative of the value of early AZT treatment than the Veterans Affairs Department study. Despite the apparent reduced death risk with early AZT, the authors of the April report called for further research to clarify the benefit of the therapy.

Other AIDS research is focusing on infants who inherit the virus from HIV-positive mothers. The NIH has disclosed plans to begin testing of a pediatric AIDS vaccine by late 1992. The study, which is expected to include 50 to 100 HIV-infected infants, would be the first clinical trial of a pediatric AIDS vaccine; approx-

imately a dozen trials are under way in adults. The agency has not yet determined which vaccine it will test but is expected to select a combination of active and passive immune therapies involving a large initial dose of HIV immune globulin, a blood product containing antibodies to HIV, followed by administration of the vaccine over a six-month period. The therapeutic strategy is to neutralize the virus with the immune globulin until the vaccine is able to induce the infant's own immune system to produce antibodies.

The NIH also plans to study HIV immune globulin in HIV-positive pregnant women to test its efficacy in reducing perinatal transmission of the virus. The clinical trial will involve 400 women with either CD4 counts below a certain threshold or opportunistic infections. They will receive AZT and monthly infusions of either immune globulin or HIV immune globulin from the late second or early third trimester to delivery; in addition, they will be given intravenous AZT during labor. Within six hours after birth and regularly for the first six months of life, infants will receive AZT and the same immune globulin given to their mothers.

The HIV immune globulin, produced by Abbott Laboratories, is manufactured from the blood of asymptomatic HIV-positive individuals, which has high concentrations of HIV antibodies. Immune globulin has been shown to reduce HIV transmission in animals. A Swedish study published in *Nature* in 1991 reported that five of seven chimpanzees that were pretreated with serum containing antibodies to an immune deficiency virus resisted infection when injected with live virus. In contrast, all of the control animals (those

Alfred M. Prince of the New York Blood Center has used HIV immune globulin to prevent infection in chimpanzees subsequently exposed to the AIDS virus. A similar approach may someday inhibit virus transmission from HIV-positive women to their newborns.

At a Nov. 13, 1991, press conference, FDA Commissioner David Kessler (left) and Vice Pres. Dan Quayle announce a program to speed the approval of new drugs marketed in the United States.

not pretreated with the serum) became infected when challenged with the virus.

Changes in the drug-approval process

On April 15, 1992, the FDA formally proposed a new regulation for speeding approvals of drug products for serious or life-threatening illnesses—such as AIDS, cancer, and Alzheimer's disease—for which there is no cure. The so-called accelerated approval proposal had long been anticipated; it represents an effort to codify a practice that dates as far back as 1986 and the initial marketing approval of AZT.

Under the proposal, the FDA sheds its "gatekeeper" role and actively seeks out data from manufacturers developing promising therapies; it also meets with them to design study protocols. Further, the agency agrees to reduce the size and number of clinical trials required prior to approval and to establish surrogate markers or endpoints (criteria that serve as arbitrary indicators of the status of a disease process, such as CD4 count in AIDS) as determinants of drug efficacy. In exchange for quicker approval, the proposal requires manufacturers to continue to develop full, standard efficacy data after approval and provides for expedited withdrawal of a drug from the market if the studies ultimately do not confirm its efficacy and safety. It also permits the agency to limit distribution to appropriate health care settings in cases involving particularly toxic therapies. In addition, the FDA has the authority to review all promotional materials prepared by the manufacturer for a product approved under accelerated procedures. DdC was the first drug to receive approval in this manner.

Accelerated approval procedures were a prominent feature of a series of FDA reforms developed by the President's Council on Competitiveness and intro-

duced on Nov. 13, 1991. Headed by Vice Pres. Dan Quayle, the council was formed to explore ways to make various U.S. industries more competitive internationally by reducing domestic regulatory burdens. Reducing FDA drug-review time for appropriate products from an average of 30 months to only 6 was seen by the council as a move that would strengthen the competitiveness of the U.S. pharmaceuticals industry. However, several key Democratic congressmen expressed reservations about the council's recommendations and asked the FDA commissioner not to implement them until they could be examined in open hearings. The legislators were particularly concerned that the recommendations were based on requests made by the industry in closed-door meetings. Although in favor of the concept of accelerated approval, they were afraid that the council, whose members include top officials in the Bush administration, would pressure the FDA into applying the proposal to therapies for diseases that are not life-threatening or serious. Even if adequate therapies do not already exist, they argued, it would be inappropriate for the agency to reduce data requirements for drugs to treat less-than-serious illnesses.

The lawmakers also took issue with three council recommendations that would reduce the extent to which the FDA would review data in marketing applications. One of these reforms called for independent institutional review boards (IRBs) in hospitals to review preclinical data for purposes of authorizing drug studies in humans. The FDA currently must approve investigational new drug applications, and the congressmen feared that permitting hospital IRBs to do so could unnecessarily endanger study subjects. The IRB concept had been proposed in the early 1980s, but hospitals almost unanimously were reluctant to accept the responsibility for approving drug applications.

Another of the council's recommendations called for the FDA to base its new drug approvals on approval in certain European countries and Japan. Although officials within the FDA and other governmental agencies are working to bring study-quality standards overseas in line with U.S. requirements, no one expects the uniformity of standards to lead to reciprocity of approval between the U.S. and other countries any time soon.

Under still another council recommendation, the FDA would contract with outside scientific consultants to review the safety and efficacy data contained in marketing applications from drug manufacturers. Under existing procedures, such review is a responsibility of the agency itself. The agency has begun to interview independent scientific consulting firms for potential participation in a pilot program in which the FDA will contract for reviews of data on a number of drug applications. Congress is concerned that contracting out the review process will prove more expensive than agency review, will actually lengthen the process by adding another layer of review to the approval procedure, and will circumvent the FDA's statutory mandate to review drugs for marketing. The extent to which the council's recommendations will be implemented remains to be seen.

Medicaid drug rebates

The reimbursement process for prescription drugs dispensed under Medicaid changed significantly in 1991. In an effort to help stem the upward spiral of health care costs, Congress passed legislation in October 1990 that requires pharmaceutical manufacturers to pay rebates to state Medicaid programs. Enactment of the law followed a decade in which increases in the prices of prescription drugs approximately tripled the general inflation rate.

The rebate requirements became effective in January 1991; during the year, companies had to pay each state at least a 12.5% rebate on sales of each of its products purchased within the state for Medicaid beneficiaries. Furthermore, if the company sold the product to any other customer at a discount greater than 12.5%, the rebate paid to Medicaid had to match the greater discount, up to a cap of 25%. In 1992 the cap rose to 50%; in 1993 and subsequent years, the cap will be removed, and the minimum discount increases to 15%. In return for the price rebates, states are generally prohibited from establishing lists of more expensive drugs that cannot be prescribed for Medicaid patients. On the other hand, a product cannot be purchased under state Medicaid programs unless its manufacturer provides price rebates to the state. Generic drug companies must pay states a flat 10% rebate on Medicaid prescription drug sales.

Many companies that historically have provided deep discounts to certain customers have responded to the rebate requirements by raising their "best" (i.e., lowest) prices. In the past these manufacturers offered extremely low prices to hospitals, health maintenance organizations, and government purchasers, such as the Veterans Affairs Department and Defense Department hospitals and clinics funded by the Public Health Service. Such purchasers represented less than 10% of companies' markets, and the reduced revenues were more than balanced by the promotional benefits of inducing doctors and hospitals to use the products. However, many manufacturers determined that the cost of providing significant discounts to these markets is too high if these same low prices must be offered to the Medicaid market, which represents up to an additional 15% of sales.

Predictably, when the "best" prices were raised, there were protests from those who had formerly received discounts. In 1991 Congress was besieged with letters from hospitals, the Veterans Affairs Department, and other affected purchasers demanding a repeal of the 1990 law. A provision authored by

Sen. Barbara Mikulski (Dem., Md.) and included in the 1992 VA appropriations specifically exempted prices offered by manufacturers to the department from January to June 1992 from being factored into "best" price calculations under Medicaid—so that price discounts offered to veterans department facilities need not also be extended to Medicaid. The House Veterans Affairs Committee passed legislation to roll back prescription drug prices charged to the department to October 1990 levels. Sen. John Chafee (Rep., R.I.) and Rep. Mike Synar (Dem., Okla.) and James Slattery (Dem., Kan.) drafted bills to change the 1990 Medicaid law so that all manufacturers would be required to pay Medicaid a fixed-percentage rebate (one proposal set the level at 18%) across the board.

The issue has yet to be resolved, and it has split the industry. Many companies that offer price discounts have pushed for a change to the flat percentage rebate. They include Glaxo, Upjohn, and Johnson & Johnson. Glaxo, which is based in the U.K. and has made inroads into the U.S. market only in recent years, largely with its antiulcer product Zantac (ranitidine) and the asthma drug Ventolin (albuterol), accounted for a disproportionately high share of all rebate revenues for state Medicaid programs. Glaxo reported paying $60 million in rebates in the second half of 1991. Total rebates paid by the entire industry for the year have been estimated at $570 million. Merck reportedly paid about $30 million in rebates for all of 1991, based on far greater drug volume than Glaxo's; Bristol-Myers Squibb paid $55 million and Pfizer $44 million. Other firms that historically have not discounted their prices have lobbied against any change in the law. These companies—which include Merck, Burroughs Wellcome, Pfizer, and Bristol-Myers Squibb—argue that flat percentage discounts would necessarily be set at a higher rate than the minimum established under current law. Congress was expected to take up the issue during 1992.

—Louis A. LaMarca

Physical Fitness

Americans' awareness of the importance of physical fitness has been growing over the past 40 years. The current interest in fitness may have its roots in research reports from the 1950s suggesting that U.S. children were less fit than their European peers. Those reports provided the impetus for a variety of programs to improve the fitness of American youth and for the establishment of the President's Council on Youth Fitness in 1956 by Pres. Dwight D. Eisenhower (which later became the President's Council on Physical Fitness and Sports). At the same time, the pervasive cold war mentality aroused concern about the abilities of young men to defend the country in time of war. The reported lack of fitness of many potential military

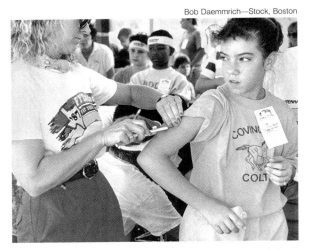

Gym students are measured for body fatness. Because of the health risks associated with being overweight later in life, the prevalence of obesity and "superobesity" among U.S. children is cause for concern.

inductees, who had failed physical examinations during World War II, led to widespread interest in raising the fitness levels of youth. (Ironically, the perception that men were unfit was not really accurate, as many candidates for the military were disqualified owing to poor eyesight, flatfeet, or syphilis.) Regardless, an outgrowth of that perception was the national development of youth physical fitness tests and programs.

Youth fitness today

The present attention being paid to the fitness status of U.S. youth is evidenced by the number of studies that have been conducted in recent years, not only by the President's Council but by the Institute for Aerobics Research (Dallas, Texas), the Chrysler Fund and the Amateur Athletic Union, and the federal government (the U.S. Public Health Service and the National Institutes of Health). While it has been widely assumed for three decades that children in the U.S. are *not* fit and that levels of fitness are declining yearly, such assumptions are now being questioned.

National studies comparing fitness trends across years are difficult to interpret for a number of reasons—among them: selection of subjects is nonrandom, the training levels of those conducting the studies differ, "sufficient fitness level" is defined differently by different researchers, and different tests and test items are used in different studies. The items that have been used to evaluate the fitness levels of youth are aerobic endurance, strength, flexibility, speed, agility, power, and body composition. Researchers disagree as to whether test items that are modifiable through training and thus not simply a function of the individual's genetic makeup are valid. Yet it is well understood that genetics may ultimately be an important limiting factor associated with all physical performance.

While some researchers have suggested a drastic decline in youth fitness levels, others point to evidence suggesting that young people are in fact the most active segment of society and that they do meet minimum physical fitness standards. In 1986 national research conducted by the President's Council concluded that "data show there is still a low level of performance in important components of physical fitness by millions of our youth." However, Charles Corbin and Robert Pangrazi of Arizona State University reanalyzed the same data and reported in 1992 that "far fewer children are lacking in fitness than previous reports have implied." Further, they found that "decade to decade comparisons of fitness produced evidence that questions the idea that youth are less fit now than in previous years." Evidence supporting the notion that youth today *are* fit comes from a survey conducted by Steven N. Blair of the Institute for Aerobics Research. He reported that 77% or more of boys and girls meet a high standard for energy expenditure in a day; moreover, in the past several years Blair and other internationally recognized fitness researchers have shown that daily energy expenditure is directly related to physical fitness and health in adults.

While various studies report different trends in children's fitness levels depending on the measures used, there is little debate that one measure clearly shows a negative change over the past quarter century. That change is in body composition (or body fatness). Children today tend to have more body fat than their age-matched peers of a generation ago. There is also evidence that the number of *excessively* fat children has increased during this period. The latest available data, from 1976–80 (published in 1987), show a 39% increase in the incidence of obesity and a 64% increase in the incidence of superobesity in children aged 12 to 17 when compared with data from 1963–70. (Obesity was defined as having a skinfold thickness above the 85th percentile and superobesity as above the 95th percentile.) In younger children—those aged 6 to 11—those percentages were even higher: 54 and 98%, respectively.

Reasons suggested for this alarming rise in childhood obesity include increasing dependence on automobiles and other forms of transportation, urban living, less time spent in outdoor activities, increasing popularity of video games and similar nonphysically active pastimes, and, perhaps most important, television watching. It is reported that U.S. children aged 6 to 11 watch approximately 23 hours of television per week, which on a yearly basis is equivalent to the number of hours children spend in school. Childhood obesity is cause for concern because overweight, inactive children are likely to become overweight, inactive adults. The diseases associated with excess weight in adulthood are heart disease, hypertension, gallbladder disease, diabetes, and certain types of cancer.

The alarming rise in obesity among U.S. children is attributed largely to inactivity. Excessive television watching and snacking on junk food are typical of the sedentary way of life that all too many U.S. children have adopted.

The fitness-health connection

Much of the present interest in childhood fitness comes from evidence that lack of physical activity is directly related to high rates of coronary heart disease (CHD) in adults and, conversely, that moderate to vigorous activity on a regular basis is associated with a decreased adult CHD risk. Research conducted by Blair and colleagues in the late 1980s, for example, found that physically active people tend to have death rates that are markedly lower than do those who are less fit. A rapid drop in deaths from all causes was seen when subjects moved from the lowest fitness category to the next higher fitness level. This pattern is observed in both men and women, and it seems to indicate that one does not have to be "super fit" to have some protection from all causes of death. In other words, even moderate levels of physical activity afford important health benefits.

As a result of such findings, most scientists and health professionals and the American Heart Association now view physical inactivity as a major risk factor leading to CHD and other adverse health consequences. More importantly, however, it is a risk factor that is behaviorally oriented and can be modified. But national surveys indicate that less than 10% of the adult population is active at a frequency, intensity, and duration sufficient for a health benefit, and less than 50% of the adult population exercises three times per week for 20 minutes regardless of the intensity. Thus, the total effect of inactivity on the public health may be as great as that of all other risk factors combined. Encouraging activity is therefore important from a public health perspective.

The fact that physical activity is related to health in adults does not necessarily mean that children who are physically active are healthier. Nonetheless, the limited evidence that exists suggests that if children become physically active in their formative years,

they can reduce chronic disease risk factors such as obesity and elevated cholesterol and blood pressure. Moreover, the *habit* of exercising is likely to carry over into adulthood and, in turn, affect adult health and mortality.

The failure of physical education

In January 1992 the U.S. Centers for Disease Control reported that fewer than 40% of high school students get sufficient vigorous exercise three times per week. Moreover, the number of students exercising progressively drops between grades 9 and 12, and female students are less active than males, while black students exercise less than Hispanic or white students.

Aerobics classes for 9-to-12-year-olds at a New York City YMCA are rarely full. Fitness experts emphasize that greater efforts need to be made not only to motivate children to exercise but to ensure that they stick with it.

Healthy People 2000: physical fitness goals

- increase to at least 30% the proportion of people aged six and older who engage regularly, preferably daily, in light to moderate physical activity for at least 30 minutes
- increase to at least 20% the proportion of people aged 18 and older and to at least 75% the proportion of children and adolescents aged 6 through 17 who engage in vigorous physical activity that promotes the development and maintenance of cardiorespiratory fitness three or more days per week for 20 or more minutes per occasion
- reduce to no more than 15% the proportion of people aged six and older who engage in no leisure-time physical activity
- increase to at least 40% the proportion of people aged six and older who regularly perform physical activities that enhance and maintain muscular strength, muscular endurance, and flexibility
- increase to at least 50% the proportion of overweight people aged 12 and older who have adopted sound dietary practices combined with regular physical activity to attain an appropriate body weight
- increase to at least 50% the proportion of children and adolescents in the first through the 12th grade who participate in daily school physical education
- increase to at least 50% the proportion of school physical education class time that students spend being physically active, preferably engaged in lifetime physical activities
- increase the proportion of work sites offering employer-sponsored physical activity and fitness programs
- increase community availability and accessibility of physical activity and fitness facilities
- increase to at least 50% the proportion of primary care providers who routinely assess and counsel their patients regarding the frequency, duration, type, and intensity of each patient's physical activity practice

In 1990 the U.S. Public Health Service established health goals for the nation, set forth in the document *Healthy People 2000: National Health Promotion and Disease Prevention Objectives.* This broad strategy is aimed at moving all levels of American society toward a healthier future. A total of 298 specific objectives were identified in 22 priority areas. On the basis of the apparent close connection between physical activity and public health, a number of physical fitness objectives were included (*see* Table). Schools could play an important part in meeting these fitness and health objectives because of their presumed ability to have an impact on the life-styles of young people.

Writing about the potential role of physical education in achieving the *Healthy People 2000* fitness objectives, James M. McGinnis, director of the Office of Disease Prevention and Health Promotion of the U.S. Department of Health and Human Services, said: "Of utmost importance is the need for research on the determinants of regular physical activity to identify the knowledge, attitudes, and behavioral and social skills associated with a high probability of adopting and maintaining a regular exercise program." He has also emphasized that *Healthy People 2000* "does not stop with setting objectives. Built into each priority area is the recognition that achieving many of the goals requires an expanded research agenda, new surveillance systems, and attention to various personnel needs."

Are school physical education programs doing their job? Approximately 97% of children in grades one through six are enrolled in physical education; by the 12th grade, however, only 50% are enrolled. Although schools are viewed as an ideal setting in which to develop the fitness habits that millions of students will carry with them throughout adulthood, research conducted at the University of Houston and the University of Texas Health Science Center at Houston School of Public Health indicates that children get relatively little physical activity in typical physical education classes. The average amount of time of observed moderate to vigorous physical activity in a 30-minute physical education class for elementary school children reportedly varies from two to six minutes. High school students were observed to be active for approximately 20 minutes of a 55-minute physical education period. However, not all of the active minutes are of sufficient intensity for a training effect.

One important reason that children may not be sufficiently active in these classes is the lack of properly trained physical education instructors. Across the U.S. student-to-teacher ratios are reported to be over 600 students per teacher per week in elementary schools and nearly 200 students per teacher per week in secondary schools. In 8 of 37 states responding to a recent survey, weekly student-to-teacher ratios were greater than 1,000 to one. Furthermore, many elementary grade programs are conducted by regular classroom teachers rather than by physical education specialists. Given these large student-to-teacher ratios and the lack of specialists, it may be difficult for typical physical education classes to provide effective instruction.

Additionally, recent evidence indicates that children (particularly those under 13) may benefit aerobically only moderately or not at all from typical school programs. Therefore, it is viewed as important to offer exercise programs that provide opportunities to have fun yet are conducive to instilling those behaviors that will last a lifetime. Many experts now agree that these activities need not be extremely vigorous and that children should be encouraged to engage in activities

George W. Gardner—Stock, Boston

Children who are introduced to enjoyable forms of exercise at an early age are likely to become accustomed to an active life-style and to engage in exercise that promotes lifetime cardiovascular health.

that they enjoy (*e.g.,* walking, running, playing tag, bicycling, swimming, and playing running games) and that will also provide a good cardiovascular workout by exercising large muscle groups.

Perhaps the most important reason for the lack of adequate exercise instruction in schools is that it has not been established as a priority. Increasingly, physical education programs are regarded as superfluous. Some states limit the number of physical education credits that a student may use toward graduation requirements. Nationwide the minimum requirements for physical education are typically less than 10 minutes per day across all grade levels. A recent survey of 120 large school districts (comprising 9,137 elementary, 2,274 middle/junior, and 1,644 high schools and representing nearly 10 million school-age children— approximately 20% of the total U.S. public school enrollment), conducted by the American Health and Fitness Foundation, Austin, Texas, and this author at the University of Houston, indicated that only 37% of the districts require daily physical education for elementary students and only 29% require daily physical education in middle or junior high schools. Only 8% of high schools require more than two years of physical education, 21% require two years, and 71% require less than two years.

As has been mentioned above, American culture is overly reliant on automobiles and other modes of transportation. Whereas in many other countries children bicycle or walk reasonable distances to school, children in the United States typically travel in a vehicle or have a relatively short distance to walk. U.S. youngsters thus miss out on an important source of

regular physical activity during the normal course of a day in addition to not getting it at school, where physical education programs may not be sufficient for a health benefit.

The federal government now has begun more than 100 different programs involving health promotion in schools through the development of physical activity behaviors in children. Representative programs include Sport, Play, and Active Recreation for Kids (SPARK) and Child and Adolescent Trial for Cardiovascular Health (CATCH).

Seeking remedies

Donald L. Cooper at Oklahoma State University considers it ironic that at the same time public health officials are "talking about health and encouraging disease prevention . . . we're letting our school physical education programs go down the drain." He has described this situation as "really tragic"; he is not alone in his concern.

The decline of school programs and the fitness status of American children are very much on the minds of parents, educators, school administrators, physicians, public health officials, and researchers alike. McGinnis has pointed out that an expanded research agenda is needed to meet the fitness goals of *Healthy People 2000.* Because of these widespread concerns about the quality of American physical education, the *Research Quarterly for Exercise and Sport* (a research-oriented publication of the American Alliance for Health, Physical Education, Recreation and

Arnold Schwarzenegger, center, accompanied by Georgia Gov. Zell Miller, touts the benefits of fitness to grade-schoolers in Atlanta. As chairman of the President's Council on Physical Fitness and Sports, the Austrian-born film star has made it his mission to inspire children nationwide to exercise.

AP/Wide World

When the U.S. Public Health Service established 298 health objectives for the nation, it included specific physical fitness goals. One is to increase the proportion of people who regularly engage in light to moderate physical activity for at least 30 minutes. Another is to increase the proportion of children and adults who regularly perform exercise that enhances flexibility and muscular strength and endurance. Walking is such an activity—one that almost anyone can do—and, because it is enjoyable, the kind of exercise that people are likely to continue doing on a regular basis.

Dance) devoted three recent issues to the subject. The September 1987 issue focused on children and fitness from a public health perspective; the June 1991 issue was a forum on "Physical education's role in the public health"; and the June 1992 issue addressed the question "Are American children and youth fit?" In each of these publications, nationally recognized leaders examined the American physical education system and its failings and offered proposals for enhancing fitness-related behaviors in young people in ways that are likely to have important implications for their health status as adults.

The challenge ahead

It is well recognized that a multidimensional approach to improving health through diet, education, and physical activity is necessary. The American Academy of Pediatrics, the International Federation of Sports Medicine, the American College of Sports Medicine, and the American Heart Association are among the groups that have issued recommendations for the enhancement of physical activity programs for young people. All of those groups are in agreement that fitness is essential to health and that physical activity habits need to be developed in the formative years.

The American Academy of Pediatrics suggests that "school programs should emphasize the so-called lifetime athletic activities such as cycling, swimming, and tennis. . . . Physical fitness activities at school should promote a lifelong habit of aerobic exercise." The International Federation of Sports Medicine emphasizes that "although physical health, as appraised by morbidity and mortality rates, has been steadily improving throughout the world, epidemiological and experimental evidence indicates that it is important for a person to engage in a program of regular physical exercise as a part of a healthy life style." The American College of Sports Medicine recommends that "fitness programs for children and youth should be developed with the primary goal of encouraging the adoption of appropriate lifelong exercise behavior in order to develop and maintain sufficient physical fitness for adequate functional capacity and health enhancement . . . school programs also must focus on education and behavior change to encourage engagement in appropriate activities outside of class. Recreational and fun aspects of exercise should be emphasized." The American Heart Association suggests that "if regular exercise is beneficial for adults and if habits are formed in childhood, then regular physical activity in childhood should be encouraged. . . . The major goal is to develop in the child a desire to be physically active that will persist through adolescent and adult years. . . . In the home, parents and siblings serve as major role models. Exercise habits should be present in the entire family."

These statements recognize that in order to affect the fitness levels and life-style behaviors of millions of children and adults, physical education must become a public health priority. Kathleen M. Haywood, professor of physical education at the University of Missouri—St. Louis and an expert on motor development in children, sees the task ahead for school physical education programs as "a dual challenge." She believes they must provide students with (1) "opportunities to be active" and (2) "an ordered sequence of educational experiences that lead them to choose active lifestyles as adults."

With these challenges in mind, each state and many governmental agencies have begun to develop specific action plans and programs to meet the national health-promotion and disease-prevention objectives of *Healthy People 2000.* James F. Sallis, associate professor of psychology at San Diego (Calif.) State University, believes that if these programs are supported, "the next century will see a healthier generation of Americans."

—*James R. Morrow, Jr., Ph.D.*

Special Report
Intriguing Insights into Longevity
by William B. Ershler, M.D.

The average life-span of people in industrialized societies now exceeds 75 years, and there are indications that this number will continue to increase. Remarkably, only a century ago the average age at death was just 47 years. The reasons for this dramatic increase are plentiful and complex but no doubt reflect advances in medicine and surgery and improvements in sanitation, education, and public health strategies. One thing that the increase in average life-span does not reflect, however, is a change in the rate at which people age or, for that matter, the maximum life-span that the human species could achieve. The best way to study the latter is to look at the age at death of the very oldest individuals. For human beings the record life-span is 114 years 296 days, achieved by a Welsh woman who, before her death in 1987, attributed her longevity to a simple life, plenty of vegetables, and a nip of sherry on her birthdays. Authenticated prior records had indicated a maximum human life-span of about 110 years. Thus, whereas average survival has increased markedly, maximum survival is unchanged. But what about life-spans before official records were kept—Methuselah, for example?

Gerontologists are quick to make two points. First, either there was some problem with record keeping during biblical times or a major change in human biology must have occurred at about the time of the Flood. Recent life-span records pale when compared with Adam's 930 years or Methuselah's 969 years. Age at death seems to have dropped precipitously after the Flood—Isaac lived to be only 180 years old, Jacob a mere 147. Scientists now believe that the antediluvian records may have been based on a different calendar.

The second point concerns the fabled longevity attributed to yogurt-eating monks in the country of Georgia and hardy villagers in the Andes Mountains of South America. Some of these individuals have been reported to live 150 years or more in modern times. It now is apparent, however, that in each case where such claims have been made, the records are either incomplete or grossly inaccurate. Social scientists studying these peoples discovered that in some of these cultures, advanced age is accorded great prestige. In one investigation in which accurate records were maintained over five years by the scientists, subjects reported age changes of 10 years and more.

If humans cannot realistically hope to extend their life-span beyond 110–115 years, can they look forward to the discovery of something that will at least slow the rate of aging? The fountain of youth, sought for centuries, has been elusive. Today, however, the quest is being vigorously pursued by scientists and, on the basis of their findings thus far, there is some reason for optimism. In animal experiments maximum life-span clearly *has* been prolonged. Also promising are human studies of the effects of hormones on aging; medical scientists have demonstrated that the replacement of certain vital hormones that decline with age is associated with an increase in vigor and, presumably, a slowing of the aging process. While all of these studies are encouraging, the results must still be considered preliminary.

The immunologic clock
Scientists have long considered the immune system as integral to aging. In fact, some have gone so far as to propose that the central organ of the immune system, the thymus gland, is the so-called biological clock. The thymus is a pyramid-shaped structure located immediately under the breastbone. It reaches its maximum size relative to the rest of the body in the first years of life but at puberty begins slowly and inexorably to shrink. By age 40 the gland is so small that it is difficult to find by standard imaging procedures. Researchers now have evidence that the thymus is, in fact, the first organ to show signs of age-related regression (involution)—long before the heart, lungs, or others. Furthermore, shortly after the initial changes in the thymus, there is an observable decrease in immune function, termed immune senescence, and this process of decline gradually continues throughout the individual's life. The response to antigens (foreign substances capable of triggering an immune reaction) becomes less robust and also less well controlled. In fact, with age the body often begins to produce antibodies (protein molecules that recognize and react to antigens) to its own tissues, or autoantibodies. This self-reactive response is termed autoimmunity, and its appearance is a hallmark of aging.

Scientists who subscribe to this "immune hypothesis" of aging point out that in experimental animals there is a direct correlation between the process of thymic involution and the appearance of autoanti-

"Our reputation for longevity is based on several factors: hard work, simple food, lack of stress, and the inability to count correctly."

bodies and other manifestations of aging. Moreover, within a given species (such as mice), inbred strains that have larger thymus glands and undergo later thymic involution have longer life-spans than other strains. There is additional experimental evidence of a close association between thymic decline and the aging process. For example, laboratory animals that are fed calorie-restricted diets tend to develop larger thymus glands than their contemporaries on unrestricted diets, and they also live longer. Nevertheless, the transplantation of mouse fetal thymic tissue into middle-aged mice has not resulted in prolonged survival. To some authorities this indicates that regulation of the aging process involves more than just thymic involution. Thus, many experts now consider the immune system to be a marker of aging rather than its primary cause.

The gradual decline in immunocompetence that occurs with age is manifested by a decreased ability to respond to disease-causing agents and consequently a greater incidence of certain illnesses. As noted above, the process seems to be directly associated with the gradual involution of the thymus gland. Indeed, of the various components of the immune response, it is thymic-related (or T-cell) functions that are most characteristically altered by the aging process. Other components also are affected but to a lesser degree. Nevertheless, the overall immune function of elderly persons is compromised sufficiently to render them susceptible to certain disease processes.

The role of the thymus gland

Several experimental observations support the hypothesis that the thymus gland is intimately related to the "biological clock." As noted above, in long-lived strains of mice, thymic involution occurs significantly later than in shorter-lived strains. Furthermore, in laboratory animals interventions that are associated with maintenance of thymic tissue mass are also associated with both high levels of immunocompetence and extended life-spans. One such intervention consists of a strictly controlled low-calorie dietary regimen. Thus, mice fed special diets that are reduced in calories but contain sufficient nutrients, minerals, and vitamins have sustained immune function, develop fewer spontaneous tumors, and live longer than similar animals fed a regular diet. The introduction of calorie-reduced diets at mid-life also results in prolonged survival of the animals (albeit to a lesser degree) and fewer age-related diseases.

Additional evidence for the importance of the thymus in aging comes from studies of so-called heterochronic transplantation in inbred strains of laboratory animals. In this type of experiment, middle-aged or old animals receive bone marrow transplants from genetically identical young donor animals. Recipients have enhanced immune function that can be further improved if the animals also receive transplanted thymus tissue from young or newborn (but not old) animals. These models offer functional correlates for what anatomists have known for close to 100 years— that the thymus gland is relatively large at birth, continues to grow until puberty, and thereafter undergoes gradual involution. Other lymphatic system structures, such as the spleen and lymph nodes, do not undergo a similar involution with aging, although the relative proportions of their component parts may alter.

What T cells and B cells do

The human immune response has two different arms, or branches—humoral immunity and cellular immunity. Each consists of subpopulations of highly specialized cells. Antibodies—the immune system component most familiar to nonscientists—are part of the humoral immune response. They recognize invading pathogens and target them for destruction by other immune system components. Cellular immunity comprises the lymphocytes (or white blood cells), which include both T cells and B cells, and accessory cells such as macrophages. Both B cells and T cells originate in the bone marrow. T cells are processed in the thymus and differentiate into several subcategories, each with its own functions. B cells eventually produce antibodies. The aging process has markedly different effects on the functioning of these various components of cellular immunity.

T cells. With the gradual involution of the thymus, there is an overall reduction in T-cell function, but— despite the occasional article in the scientific literature to the contrary—there is no striking aberration in the number, either relative or absolute, of any of the vari-

392

ous kinds of T cells. The function of T lymphocytes is consistently found to be reduced with age. Thus, when grown in culture with substances that stimulate cell division, lymphocytes from old experimental animals or people proliferate less than those obtained from younger individuals. In a living animal, the correlate of this test-tube reaction is the rejection of a tumor or a transplanted organ, a function that has been shown to be reduced in older experimental animals and in people of advanced age.

There is also a decline in the function of the subsets called helper T and suppressor T cells, which work together to regulate the immune response. Helper T cells coordinate the sequence of events in the immune response and secrete a variety of substances called lymphokines, which include, among other things, the interleukins. Suppressor T cells, as the name indicates, act to turn off or limit the immune response. In fact, this loss of immunoregulatory function may be the explanation for most immune senescence. This is particularly true for helper T cells, the activities of which are most consistently compromised by aging. For example, the production of interleukin-2, a vital modulator of immunity, by helper T cells from older individuals is invariably reduced, and this alone can account for a diminished response to various pathogens.

The diminished activity of suppressor T cells is probably less important in the context of immunodeficiency but may well account for the clinically recognized age-associated phenomenon of increased production of autoantibodies. Blood tests reveal that as many as 25% of octogenarians have circulating antibodies to self antigens (compared with only about 5% of persons under the age of 40), and experiments with laboratory animals have confirmed a relationship between the aging thymus and increased production of autoantibodies.

Thus, all aspects of T-cell immunity, as it is currently understood, are affected by the aging process. The resultant impaired cellular immunity can account for many aspects of age-associated immunodeficiency and may, in fact, be responsible for other, seemingly unrelated age-associated disease processes such as the development of atherosclerosis, Alzheimer's disease, and non-insulin-dependent diabetes mellitus.

B cells. As is the case for T cells, there are conflicting reports of the effect of age on absolute or relative numbers of B cells. There is agreement, however, on certain changes in antibody levels and in the body's ability to respond to immunologic challenges by producing specific antibodies. Careful evaluation of this latter function reveals that it is the antibody response to large or complex antigens that declines with age. Response to these antigens requires assistance from T cells, and it is the current belief that the diminished response reflects T-cell rather than B-cell

changes. Indeed, the antibody response to T-independent antigens (such as those of pneumococcal organisms) is found to be vigorous throughout the lifespan, whereas the response to T-dependent antigens (such as tetanus toxoid or protein from the influenza virus) are reduced with advanced age. It is possible that as many as one-third of elderly individuals inoculated with the influenza vaccine do not experience a satisfactory antibody response and are therefore not protected by the vaccine. This may explain why some elderly people develop influenza despite the fact that they have received flu vaccine.

Other cells. Minor age-related deficiencies in the functions of macrophages and natural killer cells—immune system components that engulf and destroy pathogens—have been reported, but it is generally believed that these cell populations do not decline significantly with age.

Cancer: a failure of immunity?

The theory that declining immunocompetence is an underlying factor in the causation of both aging and cancer is appealing but raises some knotty issues. The concept is based on several assumptions: that tumor cells carry specific antigens; that competent immune systems recognize these antigens and destroy tumor cells; and that cancer will develop only if the immune response to antigens on tumor cells is somehow muted or the individual is immunodeficient. Proponents of this theory claim that the increased incidence of cancer in older people can be explained by age-associated immunodeficiency. There are, however, persistent problems with this concept, especially in the context of age-associated tumors. Unlike tumors that are induced in experimental animals by chemicals or viral agents, most human tumors have weak or no demonstrable tumor antigens. Furthermore, when

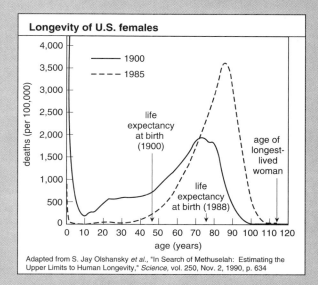

Longevity of U.S. females

— 1900
- - - 1985

deaths (per 100,000)

life expectancy at birth (1900)

life expectancy at birth (1988)

age of longest-lived woman

age (years)

Adapted from S. Jay Olshansky *et al.,* "In Search of Methuselah: Estimating the Upper Limits to Human Longevity," *Science,* vol. 250, Nov. 2, 1990, p. 634

patients are profoundly immunocompromised, as in infection with HIV (human immunodeficiency virus, the virus that causes AIDS) or after corticosteroid therapy to prevent organ transplant rejection, the tumors that arise are usually lymphomas (cancer of the lymphatic system) or the form of skin cancer called Kaposi's sarcoma rather than the broad spectrum of tumors—e.g., lung, colon, breast, prostate—observed in older people. If immune senescence accounted for the increasing incidence of cancer with age, it would be expected that elderly people would have primarily tumors of types similar to those seen in other immunodeficiency states, which simply is not the case.

Paradoxically, although tumors occur more frequently in older people, they generally grow more slowly and metastasize less frequently than similar tumors developing in young people. Thus, it seems that tumors growing in these older, immunodeficient individuals are less—rather than more—aggressive. It may be that older tissues produce smaller amounts of growth factors needed for cell proliferation.

Why, then, do older people have more cancer? Although there is no single explanation, several contributing factors have been identified. Perhaps the most important of these is time. The process of carcinogenesis (the initiation and progression of cancer) is complex and has many steps. It is only now being elucidated at the genetic level. In humans the sequence of events in carcinogenesis is best understood for colon cancer, primarily as a result of the work of Bert Vogelstein and his colleagues at Johns Hopkins University, Baltimore, Md. They have identified a series of five to seven genetic events that occur over time and a series of clinical stages (from benign polyp to adenoma to local carcinoma to invasive and metastatic carcinomas) in the development of colon cancer. Other easily biopsied cancers (such as cervical, lung, skin, prostate, and breast) may soon be shown to have similar sequential pathogeneses. This research implies that tumor progression takes time, and this fact alone might explain the increased prevalence of cancer in older populations.

There are, however, tumors that may occur because of age-associated changes in susceptible tissues. This may be the case for ovarian carcinoma, for example, which increases in incidence with the decline in ovarian function that occurs with age, and it could be true for other hormonally associated tumors (e.g., prostate and breast cancers). Lymphoma is another tumor that may be related to age-associated changes. Coincident with the mild immunodeficiency that accompanies aging, there develops a decline in the immune system's ability to regulate itself. When this happens, a constellation of age-related immune changes occurs, marked by the appearance of autoantibodies and antibodies in the blood and, occasionally, generalized swelling and tenderness of the lymph nodes. In certain strains of

mice, these manifestations precede the development of a form of lymphoma that is seen in as many as 60% of animals who reach the last tenth of the strain's life-span. A similar process might explain the increase in certain lymphomas observed in elderly people.

Infections and the elderly

While age-associated failure of immune function may not account for the increased incidence of cancer with age, there seems to be a more certain connection between age-acquired immunodeficiency and infection. There is, first of all, overwhelming evidence that infections occur more frequently in the elderly, including the "healthy" elderly, who have no known underlying disease. Furthermore, common infections tend to be more severe in older people. For example, although influenza also occurs widely in children and young adults, serious illness and death from flu are uncommon among them. This is not true of the elderly. In fact, it is the severity of infection in older people and not the increased incidence that is the best argument for vaccinating them against the flu virus.

A further point is worthy of note. Despite the sometimes striking immune defects demonstrated in elderly individuals by tests of their immune function, the infections that are common in older people are not the so-called opportunistic infections usually associated with AIDS and other immunodeficiency disorders. This fact may reflect a more modest degree of immunodeficiency than would have been predicted by the laboratory tests. The mild to moderate immunodeficiency that accompanies aging is apparently sufficient to render people susceptible to certain infections, including influenza, but not to others.

What is particularly intriguing about flu is that it is a disease that can be safely, effectively, and inexpensively prevented. Nevertheless, only about 20% of elderly people get flu shots, to a large extent because of the widespread but erroneous perception that the vaccine does not work. In fact, the vaccine is highly effective in young, immunocompetent individuals, who develop a robust and protective antibody response. In contrast, a large percentage of otherwise healthy elderly people who are vaccinated fail to achieve the level of response that is considered protective. The advantage to the elderly is that although they are not absolutely protected by the vaccine, when they do get the flu, their infection is less severe. Moreover, in these older vaccine recipients, compared with their unvaccinated counterparts, flu is associated with fewer cases of pneumonia, fewer hospitalizations, and fewer influenza-related deaths.

Rejuvenating the immune system: a possibility?

Efforts to restore age-associated losses in immunocompetence have been much more successful in the test tube or culture dish than in experimental animals or

After receiving a form of the hormone dehydroepiandrosterone (DHEA), Bandit, a canine senior citizen at age 16, looks as frisky as a pup. In addition to restoring vigor in experimental animals, DHEA has been shown to boost immune function.

in studies on humans. Several agents—e.g., interleukin-2, gamma interferon, growth hormone, prolactin, and various growth factors—have shown promise in the laboratory but are of little clinical use in restoring immune function that has declined owing to age. Given the complex interactions involved in immunity and immune senescence, this is not surprising. Further, it is unlikely that a single pharmacological agent will prove effective in enhancing overall immune function. Thus, it seems more realistic for medical science to seek more specific strategies with limited goals.

In this light, enhancing the immune response to vaccine might be of great clinical value. For example, the administration of thymosin alpha-1 (Tα1), a peptide produced by the thymus that is known to enhance certain age-reduced immune functions, has been shown to increase antibody responses to influenza vaccine in elderly individuals. A study by researchers at the University of Wisconsin demonstrated that such higher antibody levels correlated with better protection during an influenza outbreak among nursing-home residents. There were fewer cases of flu, less severe cases, and fewer deaths in those who had received the thymic peptide. In that trial residents received subcutaneous injections of Tα1 twice weekly—some receiving a total of four injections, some a total of eight. The optimal responses were seen only in those who had received the longer course of therapy. Thus, although a positive result was achieved, the fact that multiple injections

were needed has reduced the enthusiasm for Tα1 as an adjunct to influenza vaccination. However, research is now under way to develop a form of Tα1 that could be taken orally on a regular basis.

Another candidate for use in bolstering aging immune systems is dehydroepiandrosterone (DHEA), a steroid hormone that has become the focus of much gerontological investigation. DHEA production decreases with advancing age in all kinds of mammals; in humans the first signs of decline are found in the third or fourth decade of life. The lowest blood levels of DHEA are found in elderly patients with the greatest physiological evidence of senescence (*i.e.*, those who are most frail and have the most readily apparent impairment of heart, lung, kidney, or other major organs). Some investigators have proposed that DHEA has a regulatory influence on the immune system. A research team at the University of Utah recently demonstrated that administration of DHEAS, a modified form of the natural hormone, restored the ability of T cells to produce their normal patterns of interleukins and other immune-modulating substances following activation. Furthermore, old animals that were treated with DHEAS were found to generate exuberant antibody responses after vaccination. It is apparent that this modified form of DHEA has excellent potential for clinical use in the enhancement of age-reduced immune functions. Of course, this research is still at a very early stage, and there is much to be learned about both safety and efficacy.

Current conclusions about the aging process

There is probably not a single underlying process of aging. Rather, aging is the net result of several processes affecting various organs and tissues at different rates. Reflected among these changes are many that are ascribed to alterations in the immune system. These alterations are most profound in the T-cell component of the immune response and are temporally associated with involution of the thymus gland.

The clinical consequences of these age-related changes in immunity have not been fully established, but probably the most important result of immune senescence is the predisposition to infection. And of all the infections to which elderly people are more susceptible, influenza is the most important, as it remains a major cause of illness and death in older populations. At present, the only-sketchy understanding of the complexities of immune senescence does not allow medical scientists to effectively repair age-damaged immune systems. Nevertheless, in certain circumstances immune function can transiently be enhanced, and this may be of significant benefit in enhancing the efficacy of vaccines, especially influenza vaccine. Such a development could certainly extend the lives of elderly individuals who might otherwise succumb to this very common infection.

Stroke

Over the past two decades, medical science has gradually reached a consensus about what it takes to help prevent strokes. In recent years the most intensive research and clinical efforts have focused on developing specific preventive strategies. In the 1990s, designated by the U.S. Congress as the "decade of the brain," neuroscientists will concentrate a major portion of their attention on finding ways to protect the brain during stroke and to promote regeneration of stroke-damaged brain tissue.

A terrible toll

Stroke is the sudden onset of damage to brain cells and their connections caused by derangement of their normal blood supply. It is the third most frequent cause of death in U.S. adults and the most common cause of neurological disability. Cerebrovascular disease, including stroke, disables about a half million Americans a year, more than two-thirds of them over the age of 65. The rate of stroke doubles with every decade of life after age 55 until by age 85 one in 50 people suffers a stroke each year.

Over the past 30 years, the death rate from stroke in the U.S. has gradually fallen from 89 per 100,000 people to 30, in part because of more aggressive and successful treatment of hypertension (high blood pressure) and heart disease. Nonetheless, one in four stroke victims still dies within a month of the brain injury. The rate of death from stroke is 93% higher among black men and 82% higher among black women than among their white counterparts. Death is not what stroke victims fear most, however. They dread the complications of stroke—the profound sensory and motor deficits—*e.g.,* possible paralysis of one side of the body, loss or impairment of speech, or the impaired ability to understand others. They fear being unable to walk, do errands, and take care of their own basic needs—dressing, grooming, bathing, and eating. Ultimately, they fear becoming a burden on their families, no longer in control of their own lives.

Types and causes

The brain cell damage characteristic of stroke can arise either from deprivation of blood flow (ischemia)—caused by blockage of the arteries—or from bleeding within or around the brain; *i.e.,* hemorrhage.

Stroke due to obstruction. The most common cause of a stroke is atherothrombosis—buildup of atherosclerotic material containing fatty deposits, platelets, and clotted blood—causing narrowing of the artery. Atherothrombosis affects the larger arteries, ranging from the 10-mm-wide carotids in the neck to the 1–5-mm-wide branches on the surface of the brain (1 mm = 0.039 in). About as frequent as atherothrombosis is the embolic stroke, in which a blood clot travels from the heart's chambers or valves upward through a large artery in the neck and into the brain's circulation until it lodges at a point beyond which it is too big to pass. An irregular quivering of one of the heart's chambers (atrial fibrillation), heart valve damage from prior rheumatic fever, and damage to the heart muscle from coronary artery disease all predispose to the formation of a clot, or embolus. Somewhat less often, strokes arise from small-vessel disease, in which narrow arteries that penetrate deep into the brain become obstructed. These strokes cause small holes in the brain called lacunae, and in particularly vulnerable areas of the brain, they can result in paralysis of the opposite side of the body. These tiny holes, often referred to as "little strokes," can add up and cause memory loss that mimics the dementia of Alzheimer's disease.

These three types of stroke due to obstruction can be very difficult to distinguish from one another. In several large studies experienced researchers using the most up-to-date diagnostic technology were unable to state which of the three was the clear-cut cause of a stroke in 10–20% of cases. Proper treatment during the acute phase of the stroke and prevention of a subsequent stroke are more likely when the exact cause can be determined; it is therefore essential that more accurate diagnostic tools be developed.

Stroke due to bleeding. Cerebral hemorrhages account for another 20% of strokes. A conglomeration of thin-walled blood vessels, called an arteriovenous malformation, may allow blood to ooze into and around the brain. Or an aneurysm—a ballooning out of the wall of an artery—may arise at a thinning, weakened spot in the artery. In many instances the development of the aneurysm is due to a congenital defect in the arterial wall. Hypertension is especially likely to enlarge and pop the "balloon." Physical exertion often just precedes the bleeding episode, but the aneurysm can erupt at a moment of calm or even during sleep.

The first symptom is almost always an unusually severe headache that seems to strike out of the blue. One in five of the 25,000 people diagnosed yearly with cerebral aneurysm has a minor blood leak prior to the incident, signaled by a headache that the patient has ignored. If a clot quickly forms and plugs the rupture in the aneurysm, the blood flow ceases without doing any damage, but often the clot has an effect comparable to that of a finger plugging a hole in a dike. Moreover, natural chemical forces tend to dissolve clots. Unless the aneurysm is surgically eliminated, the probability is high that people who experience a warning leak will suffer a subarachnoid hemorrhage (bleeding between the brain and skull). When this occurs, no matter what physicians do, half of the victims will die from the bleeding, and half of the survivors will sustain disabilities that drastically alter their way of life. Part of the reason for this dim prognosis is

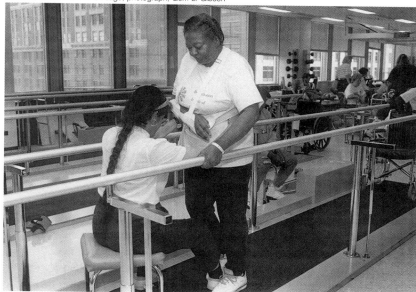

A rehabilitation therapist helps a stroke patient support herself on the parallel bars as she begins to walk again. Even stronger than the fear of death for most stroke victims is the dread of the disability and loss of independence that often follow injury to the brain. Rehabilitation may not be able to restore lost function, but it can teach patients how to compensate.

that arteries bathed in the blood that lingers over the surface of the brain after subarachnoid hemorrhage often go into spasm for a number of days. The spasm may become so severe that blood flow to a region of the brain falls to a trickle. A stroke then ensues. Drugs called calcium channel blockers were recently shown to reduce—but not to eliminate—the risk of spasm leading to brain damage.

Hypertension is the most common cause of cerebral hemorrhage (bleeding within the brain); it progressively weakens the walls of the long, fine arteries that penetrate deep into the brain until eventually one of these vessels begins to leak. The flow of blood passes through the brain tissue, pushing aside all in its path. The sheer mass of blood may cause the pressure within the skull to rise rapidly. Because the skull is incapable of expanding, the brain swells through its only outlet, which is at the base of the skull. In the process, vital centers that control consciousness and breathing are compressed and destroyed. Up to 50% of those who suffer cerebral hemorrhages die within 30 days.

Risk factors

The hereditary, environmental, and physiological factors that increase the risk for stroke include hypertension, heart disease, diabetes mellitus, smoking, a high cholesterol level and imbalances in the components of blood lipids, a high level of certain blood cells (polycythemia), use of high-dose oral contraceptives in the presence of hypertension or smoking, and alcohol and substance abuse (cocaine use in particular). Less common predisposing factors include AIDS, autoimmune diseases (for example, systemic lupus erythematosus), trauma to the carotid arteries of the neck, sickle-cell anemia, and, on occasion, migraine headache.

Two recent large-scale studies demonstrated that it is never too late to treat hypertension. The Hypertension Detection and Follow-up Program monitored the progress of almost 11,000 people who had a high diastolic blood pressure, over 90 mm of mercury (mm Hg). (There are two numbers in a blood pressure reading; the upper number, representing systolic pressure, is a measure of the peak pressure on the arteries when the heart is contracting, whereas the lower number, or diastolic pressure, is a measure of arterial pressure when the heart is resting between beats.) Hypertension patients in the study were randomly assigned to either a specific management program or the care of their physicians. The physician-referred group, it was later found, was treated in a less intensive fashion. The investigators found that patients in the management program were more likely than the others to bring their blood pressure into the normal range. Further, the subsequent five-year risk for stroke and heart attack—among men, women, blacks, and whites—was sharply reduced in those who received the more aggressive treatment.

The Systolic Hypertension in the Elderly Program followed older people with elevated systolic pressures (average 170 mm Hg). Half were assigned to a placebo, and half were treated with a diuretic plus other antihypertensive medication if needed. After five years the treated group had an average systolic pressure of 143 mm Hg and 36% fewer strokes than the placebo group, whose pressure had not changed. There is now a growing consensus that blood pressure should be lowered when it exceeds a systolic pressure of 140–150 and a diastolic pressure of 85–

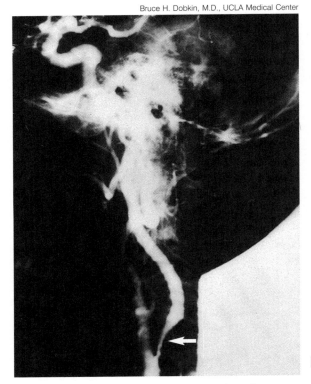

An X-ray of the carotid artery, one of a pair of vessels on either side of the neck that supply blood to the brain, reveals a point of extreme narrowing (arrow) due to the buildup of fatty deposits inside the artery.

90. It is also critical to manage the other predisposing factors—*e.g.,* to control diabetes, quit smoking, lower cholesterol levels—as best as possible to help slow or perhaps even partially reverse the atherosclerotic process.

The presence of a bruit, a whooshing sound that can be heard with a stethoscope at a point on either side of the neck just below the jaw, is another risk factor. The bruit may be a signal of a partial atherosclerotic blockage in one of the carotid arteries, the major vessels that supply blood to two-thirds of the brain. The extent of obstruction can be assessed by means of a type of ultrasound test called a duplex scan, a painless procedure in which sound waves are bounced off circulating red blood cells within the carotids. The scan provides an outline of the buildup of fatty deposits within these arteries, allowing the physician to determine whether a bruit is caused by a severe blockage (stenosis). Several clinical trials currently in progress are exploring the best intervention for potentially serious blockages, those that range from 70 to 99% of the carotid's diameter. The options under consideration are surgical removal of the obstruction, called endarterectomy, or aspirin therapy and aggressive management of risk factors (*e.g.,* stopping smoking, lowering blood pressure, getting dia-

betes under good control). Recently, researchers for the Rand Corporation estimated that over 30% of the roughly 100,000 endarterectomies performed annually in the U.S. are unnecessary. Whether the procedure is indeed effective—and under what circumstances—has been the subject of intense scrutiny (*see* below).

Of all the risk factors, however, the two greatest are a history of prior stroke and the occurrence of short-lived, transient symptoms that warn of a possible stroke. These warning symptoms include weakness or numbness on one side of the body, slurred speech, double vision, loss of balance, difficulty in verbalizing or in comprehending language (aphasia), and loss of vision in one eye or in each eye peripherally. These spells, called transient ischemic attacks (TIAs), occur when a portion of the brain briefly loses its supply of blood. Attacks typically last less than an hour, and most persist for less than 15 minutes, though they can go on for up to a day before doctors define them as permanent ischemic tissue damage—a stroke. A TIA is a medical emergency, as important an early warning signal as the crushing chest pain that indicates a possible heart attack. Unfortunately, less than one in four of those who suffer a stroke has such warnings.

Remarkably, only about 10% of those with a TIA caused by a plug of atherosclerotic debris will suffer a stroke in the six months following the episode. After that the risk falls to about 4–7% per year for the next several years. Although stroke after a TIA is not inevitable, recent studies have shown that under appropriate circumstances, medication or surgery can substantially reduce the risk.

Prevention: results of recent studies

From 1987 to 1991 researchers at 50 U.S. and Canadian centers followed the progress of 1,500 patients with symptoms of stroke. The results of this large-scale study, the North American Symptomatic Carotid Endarterectomy Trial, and those of the European Carotid Surgery Trial definitively showed that surgical removal of a stenosis that compromises the carotid artery by at least 70% reduces the risk of stroke (on the corresponding side of the brain) after a TIA by 17% compared with treatment using aspirin alone. Further studies are under way to determine whether endarterectomy is as effective in people who have less extensive (less than 60%) stenosis. Unfortunately, in some centers with less experience in performing endarterectomies, as many as 5–15% of patients suffer complications—including stroke—from the surgery, making the treatment sometimes worse than the disease.

A number of major stroke-prevention studies have been conducted over the past decade to assess the effectiveness of aspirin as a preventive. This common but potent household drug decreases the stickiness of the blood cells called platelets, thus preventing them from adhering to the inner wall of the arteries. Enrolled in these investigations were more than 29,000 people with symptomatic atherosclerosis of the cardiac and cerebral arteries. The subjects were assigned to treatment with aspirin in various doses or placebo. The results showed that at least one 325-mg tablet of aspirin (but possibly a lower dose) daily reduced the risk of stroke, heart attack, and death from vascular disease by 20–25% in men. Aspirin also probably reduced risk in women. Dipyridamole (Persantine) and sulfinpyrazone (Anturane), two other platelet-inhibiting drugs that have been studied, have failed to reduce the risk of stroke in clinical trials. Interestingly, aspirin in doses of 80 mg to 2 g per day has not been clearly shown to reduce the risk of stroke in people who have no symptoms of cerebrovascular disease and who use it for primary prevention of stroke, whereas in two large epidemiological studies, Framingham and the Physicians' Health Study, aspirin taken for several years reduced the subsequent frequency of cardiovascular symptoms in men and women who were initially symptom free.

In 1989 U.S. and Canadian researchers published the results of a study of 3,000 patients who had experienced TIAs due to atherosclerosis of the carotid and other cerebral arteries. They compared aspirin with ticlopidine (Ticlid), a drug that was not approved for use in the U.S. until 1992. Men and women given ticlopidine had 24% fewer fatal and nonfatal strokes than those who took aspirin. The reduction was 47% in the first year after the TIA. A related trial concluded that in those who had recently suffered a stroke, ticlopidine reduced the risk of a subsequent stroke by 25% compared with a placebo. Ticlopidine has occasional side effects, including a very slight risk of lowering the white blood cell count; patients must therefore be monitored by a physician for the first three months they take the drug.

Even with the development of this newer platelet-inhibiting drug, however, stroke will not disappear. For one thing, platelets do not play a major role in all types of stroke. Further, where they do participate, either other complex interactions in the circulation and within the cerebral arterial wall seem to overwhelm the effectiveness of aspirin and ticlopidine or some people have disease of the arteries that has progressed too far to be influenced by drugs that inhibit platelet stickiness.

The anticoagulant medications heparin and warfarin (Coumadin, Panwarfin), which interfere with the process of blood clotting, appear to have an equivocal effect in preventing a stroke related to atherosclerosis. However, in patients who have had a TIA or a prior stroke from a blood clot that formed in the valves or chambers of the heart, these drugs are generally more effective. Recently completed clinical trials have shown warfarin to be 50–85% more effective than placebo in preventing stroke in patients who have no stroke symptoms but have the irregular heart rhythm of atrial fibrillation. Aspirin is still being studied for its effectiveness in this situation in the Stroke Prevention in Atrial Fibrillation (SPAF) Study, but clinicians presently consider it to be significantly less useful than warfarin. The SPAF Study has also shown that the risk of stroke in persons with atrial fibrillation is about 7% per year in those who have a single additional risk factor but jumps to 17% per year when fibrillation is accompanied by the combination of a history of prior blood clot, hypertension, and congestive heart failure.

Strategies for treating acute stroke

To help the fledgling circulation to the brain in the aftermath of a stroke, intravenous fluids are given to augment blood flow into the margins around the injured tissue. Drugs are also given to optimize the heart's output of blood. Many physicians routinely infuse the anticoagulant heparin into the patient's circulation in the case of relatively small thrombotic or embolic strokes. While the drug does not break down an obstruction, it may help keep a partially blocked artery open after a TIA or partial stroke. Unfortunately, heparin can cause dangerous bleeding and, in rare cases, it leads to a paradoxical clotting. Efforts are also made to limit the medical complications that can arise in stroke victims, such as the development of pneumonia and other infections, worsening of heart disease, formation of clots in the veins of the legs, and onset of biochemical problems that often occur in the early days after stroke (see below).

Even with the above-listed treatments, about one in five stroke patients suffers continuing brain tissue damage after hospitalization. Thus, a major focus of current research is the development of strategies to protect patients from a progressing stroke and to reverse the dire consequences of too little oxygen and too few nutrients reaching the brain cells.

A major clinical research effort now under way is aimed at demonstrating whether occlusion in a carotid or one of its main branches can be melted away with an infusion of a thrombolytic agent, a substance that dissolves blood clots. One such agent that has been tried is tissue plasminogen activator (t-PA), a genetically engineered version of a natural enzyme, which is sometimes used during heart attacks to open narrowed coronary arteries. Urokinase and streptokinase are similar agents that can produce similar clot dissolution, although clinical enthusiasm for their use has been less than for the use of t-PA. While it might be expected that these clot dissolvers would quickly clear a blockage, thus restoring nutrients to starving brain tissue, they are, in fact, of limited effectiveness. For one thing, some or all of the material in a blockage may not be dissolved by thrombolytic agents. In addition, they carry the risk of a potentially seri-

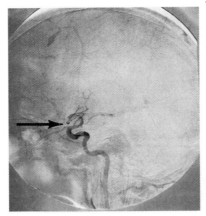

An obstruction (arrow) in the middle cerebral artery of a stroke victim's brain is revealed in the X-ray at right; the image at far right, taken after the administration of tissue plasminogen activator, or t-PA, illustrates the potential of such therapy to restore blood flow, which may reduce brain injury. Presently, the use of t-PA in the treatment of stroke is still experimental and is not without risks.

ous side effect, bleeding into the brain. In the next two years, as clinical trials with t-PA are completed, it should become clear whether this agent, which probably needs to be given within three hours of the stroke to be effective, can reduce the amount of brain injury. If it can, medicine may have its first emergency therapy for stroke.

Limiting stroke damage: future prospects

A number of experimental therapies may be available by the end of the 1990s. Physicians may be able to control biochemical reactions in stroke-damaged brain cells and in the complex, watery environment that bathes them. For example, when deprived of blood—and the oxygen and glucose it carries—neurons (brain cells) are stimulated to release massive amounts of the neurotransmitter glutamate. Although glutamate is normally present in the brain, in large amounts it produces a toxic reaction. The excess glutamate induces abnormal movement of calcium into the cells. Buildup of calcium, in turn, sets off a cascade of events that leads the cells to destroy themselves. Thus, too much glutamate, and not simply a lack of blood, appears to be a factor in triggering the death of brain cells. Experiments on laboratory animals have demonstrated that certain drugs can block the release of glutamate or prevent glutamate from opening the cells' calcium channels, thereby greatly reducing brain damage. Some of these agents are now in preliminary stages of testing in humans.

Other experimental drugs act by fortifying neurons; gangliosides, for example, which are natural to the brain, might protect cell walls, while 21-aminosteroids (lazaroids) and free-radical scavengers could neutralize toxins that poke holes in cells. Each may find a place in the therapy of acute brain injury.

Another future therapy aims to restore brain functions by promoting regeneration of the nervous system. Until very recently, scientific dogma had held this to be impossible. However, exciting new research indicates that natural growth factors, substances that are

critical in the early development of the brain, can entice the adult brain to produce new connections where a hole in the brain tissue has severed one group of neurons from another. Some of these growth factors initiate the development of the elongated appendages of the neuron, called axons, while others guide the direction in which the axon will travel. Others control the linking of two neighboring neurons to create the far-flung networks that transmit the nerve impulses necessary for thought and physical movement.

It is conceivable that a combination therapy using natural substances—growth factors and neurotransmitters—and transplantation of healthy tissue into the damaged brain might succeed in restoring some functional connections. The inherent plasticity of the nervous system—the property of nerve cells that enables them to maintain their usual interactions—offers tremendous potential for recovery from stroke. What remains is for medical science to learn how to manipulate and fine-tune these natural processes.

Rehabilitation

About 20% of stroke survivors require inpatient neurological rehabilitation. A team of therapists and nurses, under the supervision of a physician specialist, works to get patients functioning as independently as possible—at the same time providing emotional and social support to both patient and family. Much attention is given to developing alternate strategies to compensate for a lost function. For example, when an arm and hand do not recover useful movement, the patient trains to make better use of the opposite arm. Much more research needs to be undertaken to devise scientifically sound physical and drug therapies.

Inpatient therapy generally lasts an average of four to six weeks; outpatient therapies, as necessary, may continue for another one to 12 months. As long as motivation is high, more than 80% of stroke survivors will be able to walk, sometimes with the aid of braces and canes, and about two-thirds will be capable of meeting their own basic needs. Indeed, only about

400

half have any weakness six months after the stroke, but balance, vision, language, and other skills may still falter. Despite how well many compensate, the majority of stroke survivors unfortunately are not able to return to their prior level of work or socialize as they did before the stroke.

A common problem following stroke is depression, which has traditionally been viewed as a reaction to the emotional burden of disability. More recently, biochemical changes in the brain from the stroke itself have been credited with contributing to depressed mood. Such depression often responds to medication. A brain injury may also loosen the controls over the emotions; thus, at an emotional moment tears may overflow, much to the patient's embarrassment.

A number of organizations can provide reliable information about therapy for stroke patients. These include local support groups, the National Institute of Neurological Diseases and Stroke, and the National Stroke Association.

—*Bruce H. Dobkin, M.D.*

Taste and Smell Disorders

Losses in the ability to taste and smell can be extremely distressing. Impairment of these senses robs food of its flavor and palatability and interferes with the ability to detect such hazards as toxic vapors, fire, and spoiled foods. The decrease in olfactory (smell) ability that accompanies aging is a major reason why the elderly succumb more often than younger people to accidental natural gas poisoning; it also accounts for the common complaint among the elderly that their food lacks flavor.

Although many disorders of taste and smell remain an enigma, the past decade has seen considerable progress in the understanding of their causes and the appreciation of their impact on the patient's well-being. Furthermore, there have been major advances in the understanding of how the olfactory system recognizes odorant (odor-stimulant) molecules. And as a result of investigations conducted at special centers devoted to chemosensory research—located in Cincinnati, Ohio; Denver, Colo.; Farmington, Conn.; Philadelphia, Pa.; Syracuse, N.Y.; Richmond, Va.; and San Diego, Calif.—there has been an increased general awareness of these disorders. These centers were established in the 1980s with support from the U.S. National Institute on Deafness and Other Communication Disorders.

Chemosensory loss: facts and figures

Several major surveys conducted during the past half decade have suggested that permanent olfactory dysfunction is present in 1–2% of the general population. These surveys were based largely on voluntary responses from subscribers to such magazines as

Omni and *National Geographic* and therefore are not representative of the general population. However, a recent study of the olfactory function of employees at a major Philadelphia manufacturing company found a similar percentage with self-reported chemosensory dysfunction, implying that the 1–2% figure may be reliable. Still, there can be no solid estimates of the frequency of chemosensory disorders in the general population until medical scientists conduct large-scale epidemiological studies that are specifically designed to address this problem.

The question of which is more common, taste loss or smell loss, was addressed in a recently published report that was based on a study of 750 consecutive patients who sought treatment at the University of Pennsylvania Smell and Taste Center in Philadelphia between 1980 and 1986. The findings showed that most patients complained of loss of olfactory function, either alone (20.4%) or in combination with loss of gustatory (taste) function (57.7%). Only 8.7% complained of taste loss alone. Total, persistent loss of the sense of smell was the major complaint of about half of those who reported decreased ability to smell. Thirty-four percent of the patients complained of distorted taste sensations (so-called dysgeusias or parageusias), a complaint that is akin to one of pain in that it is highly subjective and cannot be independently verified. Slightly more than 29% of these individuals reported that the strange taste sensation required stimulation from food or drink in the mouth, whereas close to 40% indicated that no such stimulation was needed.

Although a majority of the patients in the Philadelphia study complained of taste loss alone or in combination with olfactory loss, objective testing revealed that fewer than 4% had a demonstrable gustatory deficit; most, however, suffered from demonstrable olfactory dysfunction. This finding largely reflects the fact that the sense of smell plays a critical role in the appreciation of flavor. Most flavors commonly referred to as taste—for example, the "tastes" of chocolate, strawberries, mushrooms, mint, and bananas—actually result from the stimulation of the olfactory receptors by odor-laden air that is forced during chewing and swallowing from the rear of the oral cavity to the higher recesses of the nose. Taste, per se, as detected by the taste buds, reflects mainly sensations classified as either sweet, sour, bitter, or salty.

Causes and connections

More than 20 causes of chemosensory dysfunction were identified among the patients in the Philadelphia study, although no single cause accounted for more than 26% of the cases. Three causative conditions—upper respiratory infection, head trauma, and nasal or paranasal sinus disease—accounted for about 60%. In general, chemosensory deficits following head trauma

Taste and smell disorders

were more severe than those resulting from upper respiratory infections or sinus disease. More than 300 of the patients in the study underwent a subsequent olfactory test at intervals ranging from 5 months to 6.4 years; this follow-up testing revealed little change in their olfactory function over time. Among the patients from the three above-mentioned etiologic categories, only those with sinus disease evidenced improvement over time, although the degree of improvement was slight.

Other studies conducted during the past five years have revealed that decreased olfactory function is among the first signs of Alzheimer's and Parkinson's diseases and is present in a wide variety of neurological disorders, including Huntington's disease, Pick's disease (a form of progressive dementia), and multi-infarct dementia (*i.e.,* dementia due to multiple, small strokes), and in the psychiatric disorder schizophrenia. As the magnitude of the smell deficit varies from disorder to disorder, and as some syndromes with parkinsonian features (*e.g.,* slowed movement, muscular rigidity) are not accompanied by major alterations in the sense of smell, olfactory testing may be of value in the differential diagnosis of some neurological and psychiatric conditions.

Until recently, considerable controversy existed as to whether cigarette smoking significantly impairs the sense of smell. A 1990 study of 638 persons for whom complete smoking histories were available clarified this issue, demonstrating conclusively the adverse effects of smoking in both current and previous smokers. The effect was dose related—*i.e.,* the more the individual smoked, the worse the olfactory loss. Among previous smokers, improvement in olfactory function was related to the time elapsed since the cessation of smoking. Current smokers were nearly twice as likely to suffer from an olfactory deficit as persons who had never smoked.

Impact on functioning

In general, there is considerable individual variation as to the importance of chemosensory disturbance for everyday functioning. Thus, smell and taste disorders are of particular consequence to persons whose

Characteristics of patients with chemosensory disorders*					
				complaint[†]	
cause or diagnosis	number of patients (%)	male/female	smell loss	taste loss	burning mouth
upper respiratory infection/cold	192 (26)	70/122	68	59	17
unknown	167 (22)	71/96	55	71	22
head trauma	132 (18)	72/60	53	46	5
nasal and paranasal sinus disease	109 (15)	55/54	30	21	3
congenital	29 (4)	15/14	0	1	0
chemical exposure	18 (2)	13/5	5	10	2
oral infection	6 (0.8)	2/4	0	3	2
other infection	4 (0.5)	1/3	1	2	2
psychiatric	4 (0.5)	2/2	2	2	1
pregnancy related	3 (0.4)	0/3	2	2	0
seizure related	3 (0.4)	1/2	1	1	0
sarcoidosis	2 (0.3)	0/2	1	1	1
lupus	2 (0.3)	0/2	0	2	0
multiple chemical sensitivities	2 (0.3)	0/2	2	0	0
brain tumor	2 (0.3)	0/2	0	0	0
other	22 (3)	10/12	6	3	0
treatment related					
dental procedures	15 (2)	8/7	1	10	4
medication induced	15 (2)	4/11	4	11	6
nasal operation	8 (1)	7/1	3	4	0
neurosurgery	5 (0.7)	2/3	5	2	0
radiation therapy	4 (0.5)	1/3	1	3	1
ear operation	2 (0.3)	0/2	0	2	2
other operation	4 (0.5)	2/2	1	1	1
total	750 (100)	336/414	241	257	69

*all patients evaluated at the University of Pennsylvania Smell and Taste Center, Philadelphia
[†]some patients had multiple complaints; others had complaints of distortions (*e.g.,* dysgeusia, dysomia)

livelihood or immediate safety depends on the normal functioning of these senses—for example, cooks, fire fighters, plumbers, professional food and beverage tasters, employees of natural gas works, chemists, and numerous industrial workers. Gastronomists and those who appreciate fine wine and food generally consider themselves more impaired as a result of these deficits than do other people.

In the Pennsylvania study 68% of the patients said they viewed their chemosensory dysfunction as affecting their quality of life. Fifty-six percent indicated that the problem had altered their daily lives or psychological well-being, and 46% reported that the problem had changed either their body weight or appetite. On average, however, the body weight changes were not marked; statistically significant deviations from expected normal body weight (based on the Metropolitan Life Insurance Co.'s body weight tables) were not observed.

Rationale for treatment and prevention

Recent investigations have led to better understanding of chemosensory disorders as well as better treatments and, in some cases, methods of prevention. Disorders of the sense of smell arise from one of three basic causes: (1) obstruction of airflow to the olfactory receptors (as a result of nasal inflammation due to allergy or bacterial infection, inflammation of the sinuses, nasal polyps, tumors, or structural abnormalities in the nasal cavities); (2) damage to the olfactory receptors (due to viral or bacterial infection, inflammatory processes, head trauma, or various airborne toxins); and (3) injury to central olfactory pathways (due to head trauma or neurological disease). Medical or surgical intervention can frequently correct, at least to some degree, olfactory loss due to the blockage of airflow. However, when diminished sense of smell is a result of extensive damage to the olfactory receptors or to the central olfactory pathways, it is not treatable in most cases. There are two notable exceptions: first, the smell hallucinations associated with some types of epileptic seizures can often be eliminated by appropriate doses of anticonvulsant medications and, second, some cases of persistent and debilitating phantom odors (termed parosmia or dysosmia) can be treated by surgical removal of one or both olfactory bulbs or by selective destruction of small regions of the olfactory membrane.

Since the majority of common olfactory disorders arise from damage to the receptors of the olfactory membrane by viruses, bacteria, and various airborne toxins, minimizing or eliminating exposure to the offending agents should prevent such losses. Unfortunately, this usually is not practical. Further, in many cases it is likely that decreased resistance of the olfactory nerves to damage from the agents also contributes to the smell loss. Interestingly, evidence pre-

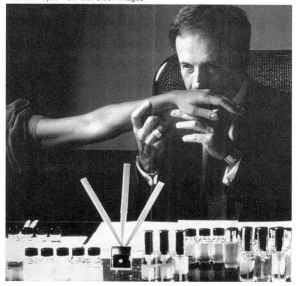

For most people, disorders that affect the senses of taste and smell are distressing. For one whose ability to earn a living depends on keen olfactory function, such as this perfume tester, the impact is likely to be devastating.

sented in the previously mentioned Philadelphia study indicated that conjugated estrogens taken by postmenopausal women may partially protect the olfactory membrane from destruction by foreign agents. Thus, postmenopausal women taking such hormone preparations were disproportionately underrepresented in the patient population, and those patients with olfactory deficits who were taking estrogens performed significantly better on olfactory odor identification tests than did those who were not taking estrogens.

Although the physical basis for most taste disorders, including lessened taste sensitivity (hypogeusia) and distorted taste sensation, are poorly understood, there are established treatments for some taste problems. First, vitamin and mineral deficiencies, as well as certain medications (*e.g.,* antibiotics, cancer chemotherapy agents, and antidepressants), can result in disturbances to the surface of the tongue and, in some cases, central nervous system changes that can lead to distortions in the ability to taste. These problems are usually reversed by vitamin therapy or by discontinuation or change of the medication in question. Second, when dental fillings and prostheses are made of several different types of metals, electric currents can be set up in the mouth, which produce metallic tastes. Replacement of the fillings or prostheses with ones composed of only a single type of metal or of a nonmetallic substance will correct this problem. Taste dysfunction occurring during radiation treatment for head and neck cancer usually subsides a few months after the completion of the treatment. Lessened taste function associated with smoking or

403

Taste and smell disorders

poor oral hygiene can be reduced to some degree by cessation of smoking and improved hygienic measures. Lessened or altered taste function due to fungal or other infections in the mouth can be reversed by appropriate treatment of the infection.

Future research: many avenues

Scientists studying chemosensory function and dysfunction represent a wide variety of disciplines. For this reason, advances in the understanding of taste and smell disorders can be expected on many fronts.

Better diagnostic tests for assessing chemosensory function are likely to become available in the near future. Most notably, the techniques of evoked response olfactometry and gustometry will be further developed. In these procedures electrical responses are recorded from various regions of the scalp following presentations of taste and odor stimuli. Such tests will provide a means of assessing chemosensory function in people with limited language or cognitive function.

Future studies will also address how, following head injury, scar tissue forms in the area of the cribriform plate (the bone separating the nasal cavity from the brain cavity) and how it can be removed or prevented from forming. Although new olfactory nerves continue to develop within the olfactory membrane in many head injury cases, a buildup of scar tissue prevents nerve cell projections called axons from making their way into the brain cavity through holes in the cribriform plate.

Although the manner in which the olfactory system works continues to be enigmatic—at least when compared with the scientific understanding of how other sensory systems work—recent findings have set the stage for significant advances in this field. For example, the specific sets of biochemical pathways involved in initiating nerve impulses are expected to be precisely delineated for a number of odorants. Odorants are now known to bind to receptors on fine hairlike structures (cilia) extending from the olfactory nerves into the mucus overlying the olfactory membrane. Some, but not all, odorants activate receptors that stimulate an enzyme called adenylate cyclase via a class of proteins called G_s proteins. This process results in the opening of small holes (ion channels), in the membrane surrounding the cilia. The opening of these channels ultimately results in the influx of positively charged ions into the cell, thereby changing its electrical properties and resulting in the propagation of nerve impulses. The cells that are fired off as a result interact in complex ways with other cells higher in the nervous system to ultimately produce the experience of smell. It is of interest that individuals with G_s-protein-deficient conditions, such as persons with some forms of the rare disease pseudohypoparathyroidism, have a corresponding deficiency in the ability to perceive odors.

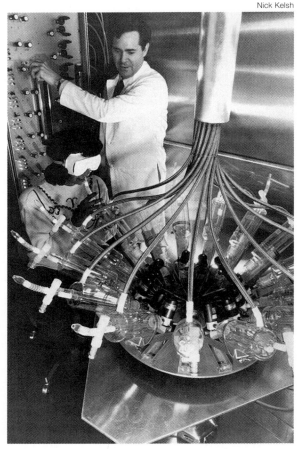

At the University of Pennsylvania Taste and Smell Center, an air-dilution olfactometer is used to test a woman's sense of smell. The instrument presents different concentrations of odors to the subject, who is blindfolded.

One line of research continues to focus on expanding the understanding of the number of different types of receptors located on the cilia of the olfactory receptor cells. A recent study conducted at Columbia University College of Physicians and Surgeons, New York City, suggested that the cilia may contain hundreds of types of odorant receptors. How such a large number of receptors interact with specific aspects of odorant molecules to code the thousands of possible different smell experiences will constitute an exciting area of future study.

Studies also will attempt to determine whether the microvillar cells—a class of cells found in the olfactory membrane that are morphologically distinct from the receptor cells—are themselves chemical receptors. Recent data indicate that these cells also have axons that project into the olfactory bulb. Traditionally it has been assumed that all olfactory transduction occurs via the ciliated bipolar receptor cells—cells that have been defined as making up the olfactory, or first cranial, nerve of the brain. If future studies demonstrate that microvillar cells are responsive to odorants, scientists may have to rethink entirely their conception of how the olfactory system operates.

A better understanding of the neurotransmitters (the chemicals that transmit nerve impulses) of the olfactory pathways is also likely in the not-too-distant future. Such knowledge may eventually make possible the development of drugs that selectively enhance olfactory function. Already, classes of drugs have been found that improve the odor-detection performances of rats. It remains to be seen whether such drugs can be used to improve the olfactory function of humans with chemosensory disorders.

Additional studies of the composition of human nasal mucus, including mucus derived from the specialized Bowman's glands located underneath the olfactory membrane, will provide insight into how odorants and toxins are deactivated within the nose. Such information may also prove of value in the understanding of some forms of olfactory dysfunction. The ability of the olfactory mucosa to protect against viral invasion is also under investigation.

It is well documented that many viruses that cause neurological disorders enter the central nervous system via the primary olfactory pathways; for example, it has long been known that the polio, rabies, and St. Louis encephalitis viruses all can enter the brain via this route. Future studies will determine more precisely the process by which viruses enter into the olfactory neurons.

Finally, as already noted, epidemiological studies, including case control studies (comparing subjects with and without olfactory dysfunction), will attempt to establish conclusively the prevalence of olfactory disorders. Such studies also will determine risk factors associated with at least some forms of smell loss.

—*Richard L. Doty, Ph.D.*

Women's Health

If the increasing visibility of women's health issues is any indicator, the 1990s may well prove to be the "decade of women's health." In December 1989 the Congressional Caucus for Women's Issues requested a study of whether the U.S. National Institutes of Health (NIH) was implementing a 1986 policy statement requiring that women be included in medical research. In June 1990 the General Accounting Office reported to a House of Representatives panel that the NIH had failed to monitor compliance with the policy. Rep. Patricia Schroeder (Dem., Colo.), chairperson of the caucus, concluded, "American women have been put at risk by medical research practices that fail to include women in research studies."

Women's groups argued that the effect of the NIH's failure to act was that researchers were being allowed to treat women as biological and psychosocial anomalies. Further, they contended that the logic of excluding female subjects from clinical research because their menstrual cycles interfere with research results is flawed; in fact, they asserted, because 52% of the population is female, the potential of women's hormonal differences to affect research results is precisely the reason it is crucial that women be included in research protocols whenever possible.

Steps in the right direction

In 1990, in response to these arguments, the NIH established a separate Office of Research on Women's Health. The following year Bernadine Healy, who had recently assumed the title of director of the NIH—the first woman to serve in this post—appointed Vivian Pinn, a pathologist at Howard University College of Medicine, Washington, D.C., as director of the new office. At the same time, the launch of the Women's Health Initiative, a $500 million NIH-sponsored program for women's health research, was announced.

The initiative is to be the largest community-based clinical intervention and prevention trial ever conducted. It has two major parts. One of these will evaluate the effectiveness of three preventive approaches—hormone replacement therapy, vitamin D-calcium supplementation, and a low-fat diet—on the incidence of cardiovascular disease, fractures resulting from osteoporosis, and breast cancer. This component of the study is expected to enroll over 150,000 postmenopausal women, aged 50–79, in a randomized clinical trial and an associated observational study to be conducted at 45 clinical centers around the U.S.; participants will include minority and low-income as well as middle-class white women.

A second part of the initiative will evaluate strategies aimed at helping women achieve healthful life-styles—including stopping smoking, improving diet, achieving and maintaining optimal weight, becoming physically active, and having regular cancer-screening tests. Selected communities will be study sites for programs designed to achieve these goals.

The Women's Health Initiative is only one of many efforts, public and private, to resolve inequities in health knowledge about and health care for women. The Office of Research on Women's Health recently sponsored two conferences—the first to set an agenda for women's health research and the second to develop strategies for increasing the number of women entering into biomedical research careers. Other organizations—most notably the Society for the Advancement of Women's Health Research—have also held hearings and conferences to publicize the gaps in research on and services for women.

Achieving a broader perspective

Despite these positive steps, there remains a larger and ongoing struggle over who can—and should—

Women's health is inextricably linked to their position in society. Today the roles of women extend far beyond the domestic; women function in multiple social contexts that affect their health status and their health care needs.

legitimately define women's health issues. From the point of view of the women's health movement, a biomedical approach can provide only partial, and sometimes inappropriate or even harmful, answers. A broader understanding of women's health has been flourishing since the late 1960s and has exerted considerable influence in the health professions. As the field has developed, it has broadened its concerns to include the roles of women within the formal and informal health care systems. This eclectic perspective on women's health has three main elements, or viewpoints: totality, centrality, and diversity.

Totality: women's many roles and contexts. In 1992 Helen Rodriguez-Trias, then president-elect of the American Public Health Association, wrote that the concept of totality "defines the health problems of women as deeply implanted in the statuses that derive from their multiple social relations." Thus, totality requires that women be seen as inextricably linked with their families and communities; their various roles—as worker, caretaker, mother, sister, and wife—cannot be separated. Clearly, from this perspective, health cannot be defined solely as "biomedical."

Under the principle of totality, mental and physical health cannot be seen as separate issues. For example, low self-esteem, although not exclusively a problem of women, has a close association with gender. Women who struggle with low self-esteem may be more likely than others to be in a relationship where they are battered or otherwise abused. Thus, a woman's mental and emotional state can contribute to behaviors that endanger her physical health.

Although access to medical care is critical, the provision of care does not in itself guarantee a woman's health. Many other, nonmedical factors influence her well-being and longevity, the starkest examples being violence against and abuse of women. Violence is now a major threat to women's lives, yet recognition of this social problem as a health issue has been slow in coming. In 1990 the National Women's Study, funded by the National Institute on Drug Abuse, found that 12.1 million U.S. women—one in eight—have been raped at least once. Of the perpetrators, 48% were known to the victim; 19% were husbands, ex-husbands, or boyfriends. In fact, assaults by husbands, ex-husbands, and lovers cause more injuries to U.S. women than motor vehicle accidents, other reported rapes, and muggings combined.

Other forms of violence, such as sociopolitical unrest, also affect women's health. In Chile bomb threats, military presence, undercover surveillance, and political demonstrations were frequent occurrences between 1973 and 1990. One study found that Chilean women who lived in high-violence neighborhoods faced a fivefold increase in the risk of pregnancy complications such as miscarriage, preterm labor, and stillbirth. Further research may illuminate similar health effects of violence in countries torn by civil strife and in high-crime, gang-ridden neighborhoods of cities in the U.S.

Sexual harassment on the job is another, more subtle form of violence against women. It involves physical contact or the threat of contact, as well as the implicit threat of loss of employment. The ground swell of women's anger against those on the Senate Judiciary Committee who trivialized Anita Hill's accusations of sexual harassment against Supreme Court nominee Clarence Thomas attests to the importance of social context—specifically workplace security—in defining women's well-being.

The legal milieu is another component of social context, and recent legislation affecting reproductive rights illustrates the impact of the law on women's health. The enactment of the Hyde Amendment in 1980 forbidding Medicaid to pay for abortions for poor women signaled the beginning of an era hostile to reproductive rights. In particular, the right of poor women to choose abortion as an alternative to unwanted pregnancy has been eroded by a succession of Supreme Court decisions, and it appears that the process has begun to curtail the rights of affluent women as well.

Finally, in contrast to men's rather clearly demarcated work and family roles, women's roles are not easily compartmentalized. Rather, women tend to enact multiple roles simultaneously. Moreover, in addition to being influenced by many social contexts and conditions, women's health is also influenced by their multiple health-related roles. For example, not only are they the majority of health care consumers, spending two-thirds of all health care dollars, they also serve as the majority of care providers—nurses, technicians, dietitians, home care givers, and others—in both professional and nonprofessional roles.

Centrality: health care that is "woman centered." Centrality, according to Rodriguez-Trias, "defines health problems as women themselves experience those problems." The centrality viewpoint "casts women as active decision makers in their own lives" and seeks to reshape the "'all too common view of women as passive recipients of health care and public health action." In a key paper on the theoretical underpinnings of women's health, Angela B. McBride of Indiana University and William L. McBride of Purdue University, West Lafayette, Ind., argue that health practitioners must take seriously the experience of women as women themselves describe it, not as the practitioners imagine that it must be.

The U.S. Public Health Service's Office on Women's Health uses a definition of women's health based on a male norm—specifically one that focuses on:

diseases or conditions unique to women or some subgroup of women; diseases or conditions more prevalent in women or some subgroup of women; diseases or conditions more serious among women or some subgroup of women; diseases or conditions for which the risk factors are different for women or some subgroup of women; or diseases or conditions for which the interventions are different for women or some subgroup of women.

By limiting women's health to a consideration of ways that women are different from men, this definition not only defines women's health incompletely—to the detriment of women—but also ensures that no beneficial effects can accrue to men, because only women's differences from men are legitimate areas of concern. A woman-centered definition devoted to meeting all of women's needs, on the other hand, promotes broader social changes that benefit everyone in society.

Also absent from this narrow biomedical definition of women's health is the recognition that health care relationships are reciprocal. This principle is especially important to engendering better self-care among women. Each health care encounter should leave a woman feeling more empowered to care for herself and her family, rather than fostering a sense of dependence on an expert. In order to achieve this goal, health care providers must demystify the scientific knowledge they impart to patients, respect the information contributed by patients, and share with patients the responsibility for clinical decision making.

If health care professionals start from women's experience, they will be able to define and promote women's health in a "woman-centered" way. For example, the postgraduate medical training program in women's health at Queen's University at Kingston, Ont., defines women's health in terms of women's life experiences and their own beliefs about and experiences of health. The graduate program in women's health at the University of Illinois at Chicago is another example of a gradually increasing number of programs using the principle of centrality to define women's health.

Diversity: meeting the needs of all *women.* Diversity requires recognizing not only women's different social roles but also their different races, economic

Grieving family members attend the funeral of a relative killed in the civil war in Croatia. Violence in everyday life takes many forms and has been shown to affect the general and reproductive health of women.

Alexander Boulat—Sipa

conditions, sexual orientations, and cultures and how these are related to health. Diversity manifests itself not only in varying rates of disease among different ethnic groups but also in different understandings of what health is and what health needs are, as they are shaped by socioeconomic status and social roles. Because women's lives are so varied, understanding the principle of totality requires an understanding of the principle of diversity.

As a discipline, women's health is necessarily global in scope. It cannot respond to the needs of middle-class white women alone, nor can it focus solely on the needs of American women. Decisions made in the United States have the potential to affect the health and well-being of women around the world. For example, decisions made by the U.S. Food and Drug Administration (FDA) often have a major impact throughout the world. Many countries, especially less developed ones, rely on the FDA for approval of pharmaceutical products, which are then distributed through the U.S. Agency for International Development. For many years, however, the FDA has not accepted responsibility for the impact of its decisions on other countries. The failure of the FDA to approve many forms of birth control has limited the contraceptive options for women worldwide. At the same time, contraceptive devices banned or not approved in the U.S. are sometimes marketed in countries that lack the resources for strict regulation. A case in point is Depo-Provera, an injectable contraceptive that has been sold widely outside the United States for decades, even though questions about its safety continue to be debated and FDA approval for marketing in the U.S. has been repeatedly denied.

If women do not become a focus for world health policy makers, efforts to address global health problems will surely fail. For example, the World Health Organization has proposed a community-based primary health care approach to reaching the goal of "Health for All by the Year 2000." Integrating women and women's health concerns into primary health care must occur worldwide if that ambitious goal is to be attained.

While it is necessary that women have access to the health care system, they must also have adequate information about their health needs and where and how to meet them; otherwise, access to even the most comprehensive system of care is of limited value. Achieving women's health is a multifaceted effort encompassing medical care improvement and reform, health education, improved access to care, expanded research on the social and biomedical determinants of women's health, and basic political and social changes.

A striking example of the diversity of women's health concerns can be seen in the list of high-priority issues drawn up by a group of 80 ethnically diverse urban community health advocates in Chicago in February 1992. Just a few of the important women's health problems cited were low self-esteem, violence of all types, poverty, and lack of economic opportunity. The group also saw lack of male involvement in addressing these issues as a basic problem. The list exemplifies the principles of totality, centrality, and diversity in that it expands the definition of women's health needs far beyond biology to encompass the broader concerns of women, their families, and the community.

An elderly nursing-home patient recovering from a broken hip receives a helping hand from a nurse. Throughout their lives, women are both the major consumers and the major providers of health care.

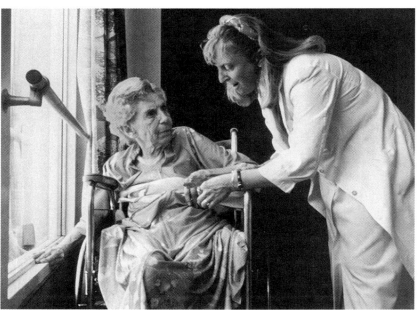

A basic tenet of the women's health movement is that those who provide care for women must have an appreciation of their tremendous diversity— ethnic, racial, social, cultural, and economic. Appropriate family-planning services and methods are a universal need.

Current women's health issues

In addition to the ongoing attempt to extend the boundaries of women's health as a discipline, a number of specific health-related issues are subjects of current concern to U.S. women. Three of them are addressed below: the effect of the AIDS epidemic, the risks and benefits of hormone replacement therapy, and the proposed use of the drug tamoxifen to prevent breast cancer.

Women and AIDS. The true number of U.S. women with AIDS is hugely undercounted in the official statistics. Because the case definition of AIDS formulated by the Centers for Disease Control was based on male symptoms, the early symptoms that occur in women, which differ from those in men, were excluded. Consequently, women have been less aware of their risk for the disease, and AIDS cases in women have tended to be underdiagnosed by health practitioners. Furthermore, given a false sense of security that AIDS is a predominantly male problem, many women delay seeking health care and thus are first diagnosed and treated at later—and more advanced—stages of the disease. Moreover, even with the official undercount, women are still the fastest growing segment of the AIDS population. In New York and New Jersey, AIDS is now the leading cause of death among premenopausal African-American women.

This demographic shift to a larger proportion of women in the patient population requires that a special effort be made to prevent more women from contracting HIV (human immunodeficiency virus, the virus that causes AIDS) and to treat the special needs of women with AIDS. For example, it is important for women to know that the rate of HIV transmission is as much as 17.5 times higher from men to women than from women to men and to understand that the risk of HIV infection increases greatly if the woman has another sexually transmitted disease. Most importantly, women must be made aware that they are not invulnerable to HIV infection.

Hormone replacement therapy. The benefits of estrogen replacement therapy for postmenopausal women have been widely reported. Epidemiological studies have demonstrated that it significantly reduces the risk of heart disease and osteoporosis. The Nurses' Health Study has followed nearly 50,000 postmenopausal women with no previous heart disease and has shown that the risk of coronary heart disease in women who take estrogen is about half that of women who have never used estrogen, and the former have a 50% lower rate of death from cardiovascular disorders. As a result of this and other studies, the medical establishment strongly promotes estrogen replacement therapy.

Nonetheless, some important questions about the safety and efficacy of hormone replacement remain unanswered. The epidemiological data from the Nurses' Health Study are based on women who have elected to use hormone therapy. As noted by those who conducted the study, these women are disproportionately white, nonobese, and middle class and have wide access to health care; they therefore are at lower risk of heart disease than the general female population. This selection bias could have a strong effect on study results. Furthermore, although most of the findings reported to date involve hormone therapy using only estrogen, many women are now being treated with combinations of estrogen and progestin, and the effects of adding progestin to the regimen are not well known. Progestin protects against the increased risks of endometrial and perhaps breast cancer that have been associated with estrogen therapy, but it may counter the other beneficial effects of estrogen, such as the reduced risk of heart disease and osteoporosis.

YOU CAN GET AIDS

For Information About AIDS Contact
The Urban League
or call 1-800-332-AIDS

AIDS Does Not Discriminate

The NIH is addressing both of these questions with the first large-scale clinical trials of hormone replacement therapy, called PEPI (Postmenopausal Estrogen-Progestin Interventions), now under way. In this study over 800 women aged 45 to 64 have been randomly assigned to treatment with either estrogen alone, estrogen and progestin in three different dosage regimens, or a placebo. These women will be medically followed for three years to assess the effect on cholesterol levels, blood pressure, bone density, and cancer of the breast and uterus. An important limitation of the study is that it will not follow the women long enough to definitively assess any differences in death rates among the various groups.

Despite the fact that many physicians recommend hormone replacement therapy, many women reject this alternative. A Massachusetts survey found that a third of women who are given prescriptions for hormones do not fill them. They may be willing to tolerate the short-term discomforts of menopause; they may have a greater fear of breast cancer than heart disease; or they may resist the prospect of prolonged hormone usage and instead opt for less invasive measures of health promotion, such as a low-fat diet and regular exercise. Clearly, hormone replacement therapy is not for everyone. It should be prescribed only for those women in whom the benefits clearly outweigh the risks. Recognition of the diversity among women, combined with results from the PEPI trials, may bring about a more selective, individualized approach to hormone replacement.

Tamoxifen as a breast cancer preventive. Clinical trials of the drug tamoxifen, sponsored by the National Cancer Institute (NCI), began in April 1992. Of all cancers, breast cancer is second only to lung cancer in claiming women's lives and is the leading cause of death of women aged 40–45. It was predicted that in 1992 alone 181,000 U.S. women would be diagnosed with breast cancer, and 46,000 would die from it. Prevention is a key to stopping this epidemic.

In the NCI trials, 16,000 healthy women at high risk of developing breast cancer will be randomly assigned to a five-year protocol of treatment with either tamoxifen or a placebo and studied to assess whether tamoxifen, which has been used to treat breast cancer, can also prevent the development of the disease in high-risk women. The effect of tamoxifen on heart disease and osteoporosis will also be studied. Tamoxifen, a synthetic hormone that blocks the effect of estrogens, has been used successfully to treat tumors that use estrogen to grow. However, in some tissues it has an estrogen-like effect, which some researchers claim will have the additional benefits of decreasing osteoporosis and lowering blood cholesterol.

Critics of the trials argue that tamoxifen is too powerful and dangerous a substance to give to healthy women. The study includes only women defined as having a high risk of developing breast cancer, but the definition of high risk used in this trial is a broad one. Potential participants include all women aged 60 or older. Also included are women aged 35–59 whose combined risk factors for breast cancer predict that they are as likely as a 60-year-old woman to develop the disease within five years; such risk factors include having at least one first-degree relative with breast cancer, nulliparity (never having had children) or late age at first birth, early onset of menstruation, and having had two or more biopsies of breast tumors that proved to be benign.

Despite the fact that they are at increased risk, the women in these groups do not have breast cancer, and the ratio of risks to benefits of tamoxifen therapy for them is very different from that for women who have already had breast cancer. Risks tolerable to a woman battling invasive breast cancer may not be tolerable to a woman facing an increased risk of breast cancer but with no existing disease. Tamoxifen's risks and side effects include an increase in the rate of endometrial cancer and vessel-blocking blood clots, irreversible damage to the retina of the eye, menopausal symptoms in premenopausal women, and a potential but as yet unknown risk of liver cancer (experimental animals given high doses of tamoxifen have an increased incidence of liver cancer). For many advocates of improved women's health research, this is not the kind of progress hoped for.

—*Alice J. Dan, Ph.D.,*
and Sarah T. Hemphill, M.S.

410

Special Report

Silicone Breast Implants: The Continuing Saga

by Elizabeth B. Connell, M.D.

After a number of years of debate over safety questions concerning silicone-gel-filled breast implants, on April 16, 1992, the U.S. Food and Drug Administration (FDA) ordered sharp restrictions in their use pending intensive studies. The decision followed two major hearings on the matter—in November 1991 and February 1992—by the FDA's General and Plastic Surgery Devices Panel.

To put these events into perspective, it is useful to look at the history of medical device regulation in the United States. Although the FDA had had jurisdiction over foods, drugs, and cosmetics since 1938, when the Federal Food, Drug, and Cosmetic Act was signed into law by Pres. Franklin D. Roosevelt, it was not until 1976 that Congress passed legislation giving the federal agency the additional responsibility of regulating all types of medical devices. When the act was passed, the devices that were already on the market were "grandfathered"—*i.e.,* when they came under the jurisdiction of the FDA, their manufacturers were not required immediately or routinely to produce safety and efficacy data. Among these devices were silicone breast implants—flexible silicone-gel-containing bags that are inserted through a small incision into the breast beneath the skin or, less often, behind the chest muscle. The implants were first used in women in 1962 for reconstructive purposes following breast surgery; subsequently they became popular for cosmetic breast augmentation.

When the FDA took initial steps toward the evaluation of the more than 130 "high-risk" pre-1976 products, it first developed a three-level classification system. Class I devices included those found to meet general safety and efficacy requirements and for which no additional studies were deemed necessary. Class II devices had to meet class I requirements, but additional data (*i.e.,* performance standards) needed to be submitted to the FDA. Class III, the most stringent category, included devices for which there was inadequate information available to allow the products to remain on the market. A manufacturer of a class III device was therefore required to submit data on its safety and efficacy identical to those needed for the premarket approval (PMA) of a new (after 1976) device.

In 1989 the FDA estimated that 445 products manufactured by 235 companies might come under scrutiny during its stepped-up review of the pre-1976 grandfathered devices; at that time the agency established a "priority list" of 30 products—silicone-gel-filled breast implants being among them. In addition, Congress passed the 1990 Safe Medical Devices Act, requiring the FDA to increase its surveillance of all marketed medical devices. The act requires manufacturers of medical devices to "track" all products that are permanently implanted or that have a life-sustaining or life-supporting function. The purpose of tracking is to ensure that manufacturers can promptly locate patients if there is a product malfunction. Tracking also allows careful records to be kept of the functioning and possible adverse side effects of devices over a long period.

Implants under scrutiny

Questions that had been raised regarding the safety of the various breast implants (including silicone- and saline-filled implants and inflatable breast prostheses) were first addressed in the early 1980s. An FDA-appointed group of experts reviewed the situation and recommended that the devices be given a class II status. The FDA, however, decided that the silicone-gel-filled implants should be required to meet the more stringent class III criteria. Then in 1988 a notice was placed in the *Federal Register* announcing that manufacturers of silicone breast implants were required to submit complete safety and efficacy data on their devices to the FDA by July 9, 1991. Four manufacturers—Dow Corning Wright, McGhan Medical Corp., Mentor Corp., and Bioplasty Inc.—submitted the equivalent of PMA data on a total of seven devices. (There were other manufacturers of silicone-gel-filled breast implants that did not submit data.)

Round one. After reviewing the data that had been submitted, the FDA convened a three-day meeting of its advisory panel—comprising physicians, scientists, and health care and health law experts—on Nov. 12, 1991. At that time the panel heard presentations by many private individuals, professional groups, the four manufacturers, and FDA staff. The panel was charged with recommending to the FDA whether the implants should be approved for continued use on the basis of the submitted data. Its nonbinding recommendation would be carefully considered before FDA Commissioner David A. Kessler reached a final decision.

Members of the FDA's General and Plastic Surgery Devices Panel heard a second round of testimony on silicone-gel-filled breast implants in February 1992 after new information concerning the devices' safety had come to light.

At the conclusion of the three days of hearings, the General and Plastic Surgery Devices Panel made several recommendations. First, it did not find that data presented by any of the four companies were sufficient to provide reasonable assurance of safety and efficacy of their breast-implant products, but neither did it find that the implants were unsafe. Second, certain local side effects were described that were associated with the implants; the panel found, however, that neither the exact incidence nor the significance of those findings was clear. Third, although information was presented regarding several possible adverse systemic effects in women who had silicone implants, the panel could find no reliable evidence of a cause-and-effect relationship. Fourth, the panel recommended that the period of review be extended and that the products continue to remain available pending further study, stating that they (the members of the panel) believed that the implants served a "public health necessity," not only for women who use them for reconstruction following breast cancer surgery but also for individuals who use them for cosmetic augmentation. Finally, the panel recommended that a number of short-, medium-, and long-term studies be carried out—including chemical, mechanical, toxicological, clinical, and epidemiological investigations that would help to answer the many unresolved safety questions. After those recommendations were issued, Kessler, by law, had until Jan. 6, 1992, to weigh the panel's findings and then respond to the four silicone-breast-implant manufacturers.

Call for a moratorium. Just prior to the beginning of the year, the FDA received new information pertaining to the implants, so on January 6, rather than accepting the panel's recommendation that the devices continue to be available to women who wanted them, Kessler called for a voluntary moratorium—asking all doctors to stop inserting all silicone-gel-filled implants and all manufacturers to stop supplying them—until the General and Plastic Surgery Devices Panel could be reconvened to consider its previous recommendations in light of the new data. At a press conference Kessler explained that the FDA had obtained information that had previously been withheld by Dow Corning Wright, the largest producer of silicone implants. The new reports regarding the implants' safety were part of a sealed court record in a product-liability case against the manufacturer.

Meanwhile, the commissioner stated that there was no reason for asymptomatic women to have their implants removed, though he recommended that women who have them have periodic breast examinations—like all women. He also indicated that for the roughly 10,000 women already scheduled to have implant surgery, saline breast implants, which are filled with salt water instead of silicone gel, were still available and thus a possible alternative.

Round two. The new information was sent to the General and Plastic Surgery Devices Panel for review, and on Feb. 18, 1992, it met again for another three days of hearings. Once again the panel reviewed all of the safety issues, following which it reached three major conclusions. First, the new information still did not show a clear cause-and-effect relationship between the use of breast implants and certain clinical findings related to systemic illnesses. Second, there still was no indication for the total banning of the use of the devices. And third, as it had done in the November deliberations, the panel again emphasized the need for studies to evaluate the many unsettled safety issues. (At that time Dow Corning Wright made a commitment to carry out such studies, regardless of its ultimate decision about whether to remain in the implant field.)

The panel additionally recommended that all future procedures in which silicone-gel breast implants are inserted be carried out under carefully controlled clinical investigative protocols that would be developed mutually by the manufacturers and the FDA. It specified that all reconstruction patients and as many augmentation patients as were needed to meet the requirements for the new protocols should have access to the devices. Finally, the panel felt that all women who either had implants or were contemplating them should be given the following information:

• Women who are not experiencing any problems with their devices need not have them removed. However, they should know that the implants are not lifetime devices and that it might be necessary to have them replaced periodically, although it is not clear how much time might elapse before replacement becomes necessary.

• The implants are known to rupture. The rate of rupture was reported by the manufacturers and plastic surgeons to be less than one in 100; the panel, however, felt that the rate is probably higher.

• Even when the implants do not rupture, they can "bleed," or leak, a small amount of silicone into the body. The frequency of leakage and precisely what effects such leakage may have are still unknown. The gel has been found in breast tissue and in the lymph nodes draining the breast; it has also been known to migrate to distant locations in the body.

• Because implants can mask or prevent detection of tumors in routine mammography examinations, women who have the devices should have mammograms done only by trained individuals at facilities with experience in the special techniques that increase the likelihood of an accurate evaluation.

Limited access. Eight weeks after the panel issued its recommendations, the FDA announced its final decision—a decision that generally followed the experts' advice. Women would still be able to receive silicone-gel implants after cancer surgery, but probably only a small number would be allowed to have them for cosmetic augmentation. All women who underwent the implant procedures would have to agree to take part in tightly controlled clinical protocols. When Commissioner Kessler made the announcement, he emphasized that "no one should think we are resuming business as usual. These are not approved devices. . . . We still want to make these available to women who have suffered, especially from breast cancer." But no woman, he said, should "jump to silicone breast implants without spending a lot of time thinking about what is right."

The unanswered questions

A number of issues remained unclear at the conclusion of both the November and February meetings. For one thing, the actual number of women who had silicone breast implants was not known; estimates ranged from as few as 300,000 to as many as two million U.S. women. Because women had received the devices since the early 1960s, and no records were kept, the actual number would never be known. In general, however, it was believed that about 20% received their implants following surgery for breast cancer or other deforming breast conditions and about 80% received them as augmentation for cosmetic reasons.

Under the new restricted protocols, careful records will be kept of all women who receive silicone-gel implants, and the Safe Medical Devices Act now requires tracking of all implants through the entire distribution chain—from manufacturer to patient. In addition, an independent, nonprofit registry was established by the Medic Alert Foundation International in January 1992. The registry will link women who have breast implants, plastic surgeons, and hospitals with information that is made available by the FDA and the implant manufacturers. It will also enable women to record and update any symptoms that may be related to their silicone implants.

The escape of the silicone and its possible role in the development of autoimmune diseases posed the most serious concerns. Although there was anecdotal evidence of diseases such as scleroderma, rheumatoid arthritis, and systemic lupus erythematosus occurring in women with implants, the consensus of the panel at both meetings was that the evidence presented did not allow the conclusion of a causal association with any specific disease or disorder. That conclusion was supported in a statement issued by the American College of Rheumatology (ACR):

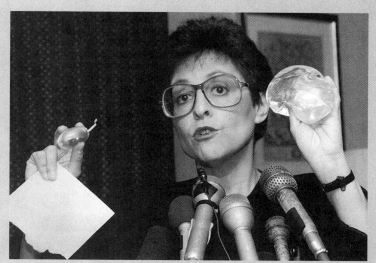

Holding a silicone-gel-filled breast implant in her left hand, a woman testifies before the FDA's expert committee in November 1991 in the first round of hearings on the devices' safety.

Reuters/Bettmann Newsphotos

All of the present evidence claiming an association between the implants and various rheumatic diseases, such as scleroderma and systemic lupus erythematosus, is hypothetical, circumstantial, or based on limited individual experiences. . . . The ACR strongly endorses the FDA Advisory Panel's recommendation for further research as well as their ruling to limit silicone gel breast implants for augmentation mammoplasty.

One of the common complications seen with breast implants is the development of a capsule of fibrous tissue around the implant envelope, known as capsular contracture. This can lead to deformity, hardening, or asymmetry of the breast as well as to pain and discomfort. It remains unknown, however, why this occurs in some recipients but not in others. In the past, capsular contracture had been treated by massage in an attempt to rupture the capsule nonsurgically. Now, however, if significant problems develop with encapsulation, it is recommended that the device be removed in an open surgical procedure.

A final question that remains unresolved is whether the implants can increase a woman's chances of developing a malignancy. No data indicating such a risk were presented to the panel. In fact, a study reported in April 1992, carried out at the University of Southern California, showed a one-third lower incidence of breast cancer in a group of women who had augmentation procedures and were followed for 10 years. In June 1992 the largest and best controlled study to date was reported from Canada; it also showed a lower risk of breast cancer in women with implants as compared with the general population. The reasons for the lower incidence of malignancies are unknown, but these studies should help to dispel one of the major sources of concern.

Impact: U.S. and abroad

It appears that the FDA's evaluation of the silicone breast implants may well be typical of future activities with regard to other medical devices. In late March 1992 the agency announced its intention to begin investigations into five other devices within the year, and many additional products were to be scrutinized by Dec. 1, 1995, the date established by Congress for the FDA to complete its review of pre-1976 devices. A number of device manufacturers have expressed concern that meeting the demands of the review process will involve considerable expense; carrying out safety tests can cost millions of dollars. It is possible that a number of smaller companies, like small pharmaceutical manufacturers that have come under intensive scrutiny by the FDA in recent years, will simply retire their products from the marketplace.

Saline breast implants, which were first marketed in 1969, were among those to be reviewed next. An estimated 6,000 women a year receive this type of breast implant. Many plastic surgeons believe they are a good alternative to silicone and are probably safer. The known problems with saline-filled implants are capsular contraction, leakage, and deflation of the devices. Doctors believe that when the salt-water-filled sacks leak, it is not harmful to the body. But since the devices have never been subjected to intensive review, the safety questions remain to be answered.

Another surgical alternative to breast implants is reconstructive surgery. There are several different approaches, which use the patient's own tissue, taken from the abdomen, back, or buttocks. The most popular of these is the TRAM technique, named for the abdominal muscle (transverse rectus abdominis myocutaneous). While these approaches avoid the use of foreign materials, they have significant problems of their own. They require extensive surgical procedures and are available only at major medical centers. In TRAM surgery the abdominal wall is left weakened, and recovery takes almost two months. Moreover, in approximately one-quarter of the cases, part or all of the transplanted tissue will die.

Despite reassurances, many women who had received silicone implants before the recent intensive investigations have been understandably alarmed. The same week in February that the General and Plastic Surgery Devices Panel held its second meeting, the FDA established a toll-free hot line for women who had concerns about their implants (1-800-532-4440); during its first days of operation, more than 4,000 calls from women seeking advice and information were received. An issue of considerable concern to both current and potential recipients of silicone implants— and all women having surgery for breast disease—is how medical insurance coverage will be affected by the recent revelations and decisions.

As a result of the controversy, both Dow Corning Wright and Bioplasty Inc. have discontinued making the devices. As was anticipated, there has been a dramatic increase in the number of lawsuits involving the implants. A particularly tragic outcome of the situation was the apparent suicide in May 1992 of a New York plastic surgeon who was reportedly severely depressed about lawsuits pending against him involving breast implants.

Not surprisingly, media coverage of the FDA activities has produced fear in women in other countries and stimulated reactions from international medical groups. In April plastic surgeons from 11 European countries met in Amsterdam and generally found no evidence to support a ban. However, the use of implants has been discouraged or actually banned in France, Germany, and Spain. On the other hand, the U.K. and The Netherlands are allowing the procedures to continue. Meanwhile, safety studies continue in the U.S. and other countries that should resolve the questions that currently are causing continued fear and anxiety for millions of women worldwide and their doctors.

Contributors to the World of Medicine

George J. Annas, J.D., M.P.H.
Special Report The Gag Rule: Who Shall Be Silenced?
Edward R. Utley Professor of Health Law, Boston University
Schools of Medicine and Public Health

Nancy H. Arden, M.N.
Influenza
Senior Research Associate, University of Michigan School
of Public Health, Ann Arbor

Susan P. Baker, M.P.H.
Injury Prevention
Codirector, Johns Hopkins Injury Prevention Center, and
Professor, Johns Hopkins School of Public Health, Balti-
more, Md.

Patrick G. Beatty, M.D., Ph.D.
Bone Marrow Transplantation
Professor of Medicine and Director, Bone Marrow Transplant
Program, Hematology-Oncology Division, University of Utah
School of Medicine, Salt Lake City

Edward P. Cohen, M.D.
Special Report "Vaccines" for Cancer—Can They Succeed?
Professor, Department of Microbiology and Immunology,
University of Illinois College of Medicine, Chicago

Elizabeth B. Connell, M.D.
AIDS
Special Report Silicone Breast Implants: The Continuing
Saga
Professor, Gynecology and Obstetrics, Emory University
School of Medicine, Atlanta, Ga.

William J. Cromie
Cancer
Science Writer, Harvard University, Cambridge, Mass.

Alice J. Dan, Ph.D.
Women's Health (coauthor)
Professor and Acting Director, Center for Research on
Women and Gender, University of Illinois at Chicago

Edwin A. Deitch, M.D.
Burns
Professor of Surgery, Louisiana State University School
of Medicine, and Director, Division of Burns and Trauma,
Louisiana State Medical Center, Shreveport

Bruce H. Dobkin, M.D.
Stroke
Professor of Neurology, University of California at Los Ange-
les School of Medicine

Richard L. Doty, Ph.D.
Taste and Smell Disorders
Director, Smell and Taste Center, and Associate Profes-
sor, Department of Otorhinolaryngology: Head and Neck
Surgery, University of Pennsylvania School of Medicine,
Philadelphia

Stephen E. Epstein, M.D.
Heart and Blood Vessels (coauthor)
Chief, Cardiology Branch, National Heart, Lung, and Blood
Institute, National Institutes of Health, Bethesda, Md.

William B. Ershler, M.D.
Special Report Intriguing Insights into Longevity
Professor of Medicine and Director, University of Wisconsin
Institute on Aging, Madison

Ronald G. Evens, M.D.
Medical Imaging
Elizabeth Mallinckrodt Professor and Head, Mallinckrodt
Institute of Radiology, Washington University School of
Medicine, St. Louis, Mo.

Richard M. Glass, M.D.
Mental Health and Illness
Clinical Associate Professor of Psychiatry, University of
Chicago; Deputy Editor, *Journal of the American Medical
Association*

Walter J. Gunn, Ph.D.
Chronic Fatigue Syndrome (coauthor)
President, Arlington Associates, Inc., Lilburn, Ga.; former
Senior Research Psychologist, Centers for Disease Control,
Atlanta, Ga.

Birt Harvey, M.D.
Pediatrics
Professor of Pediatrics, Stanford University School of
Medicine, Stanford, Calif.; Director, Medical Outreach, Lucile
Packard Children's Hospital, Palo Alto, Calif.

Sarah T. Hemphill, M.S.
Women's Health (coauthor)
Research Specialist, Center for Research on Women and
Gender, University of Illinois at Chicago

Michael D. Iseman, M.D.
Special Report TB: The Captain of All These Men of Death
Returns (coauthor)
Professor of Medicine, University of Colorado School of
Medicine; Chief, Mycobacterial Diseases Service, National
Jewish Center for Immunology and Respiratory Medicine,
Denver

Louis Keith, M.D.
Obstetrics
Professor, Obstetrics and Gynecology, Northwestern Uni-
versity Medical School, Chicago

Anthony L. Komaroff, M.D.
Chronic Fatigue Syndrome (coauthor)
Director, Division of General Medicine and Primary Care,
Brigham and Women's Hospital; Associate Professor of
Medicine, Harvard Medical School, Boston

Louis A. LaMarca
Pharmaceuticals
Capitol Hill Editor, *F-D-C Reports: "The Pink Sheet,"* and Se-
nior Editor, *Weekly Pharmacy Reports: "The Green Sheet,"*
F-D-C Reports, Inc., Chevy Chase, Md.

Brendan A. Maher, Ph.D.
Special Report Multiple Personality: Illness or Act? (coauthor)
Henderson Professor of the Psychology of Personality, and
Dean, Graduate School of Arts and Sciences, Harvard Uni-
versity, Cambridge, Mass.

Winifred B. Maher, Ph.D.
Special Report Multiple Personality: Illness or Act? (coauthor)
Lecturer in Extension Studies at Harvard University, Cambridge, Mass.

Artin Mahmoudi, M.D.
Special Report *TB: The Captain of All These Men of Death Returns* (coauthor)
Staff Physician, National Jewish Center for Immunology and Respiratory Medicine; Instructor in Medicine, University of Colorado School of Medicine, Denver

Linda G. Martin, Ph.D.
Special Report Japan's "Golden Plan"
Director, Committee on Population, National Academy of Sciences; Senior Research Scholar, Department of Demography, Georgetown University, Washington, D.C.

Charles-Gene McDaniel, M.S.J.
Special Report Once Stung, Twice Shy?
Professor and Chair, Department of Journalism, Roosevelt University, Chicago

Beverly Merz
Genetics
Free-Lance Medical Writer, Chicago

James R. Morrow, Jr., Ph.D.
Physical Fitness
Professor, Department of Health and Human Performance, University of Houston, Texas

Thomas H. Murray, Ph.D.
Death and Dying
Professor and Director, Center for Biomedical Ethics, Case Western Reserve University School of Medicine, Cleveland, Ohio; Editor, *Medical Humanities Review*

Kevan H. Namazi, Ph.D.
Special Report Caring for Patients with Alzheimer's Disease: An Innovative Approach
Director of Research, Corinne Dolan Alzheimer Center, Chardon, Ohio; Faculty Member, Departments of Psychiatric-Mental Health and Sociology, Case Western Reserve University, Cleveland, Ohio

Arnauld E. Nicogossian, M.D.
Aerospace Medicine (coauthor)
Chief Medical Officer, Office of Space Flight, National Aeronautics and Space Administration, Washington, D.C.; Assistant Professor, Uniformed Services University of the Health Sciences/F. Edward Hébert School of Medicine, Bethesda, Md.

Robert B. Nussenblatt, M.D.
Eye Diseases and Visual Disorders
Clinical Director and Chief, Laboratory of Immunology, National Eye Institute, National Institutes of Health, Bethesda, Md.

Julio A. Panza, M.D.
Heart and Blood Vessels (coauthor)
Senior Investigator and Head, Echocardiography Laboratory, Cardiology Branch, National Heart, Lung, and Blood Institute, National Institutes of Health, Bethesda, Md.

Sandra Swift Parrino
Disability
Chairperson, National Council on Disability, Washington, D.C.

Robert G. Petersdorf, M.D.
Medical Education (coauthor)
President, Association of American Medical Colleges, Washington, D.C.

Katharine A. Phillips, M.D.
Special Report An Ugly Secret: Body Dysmorphic Disorder
Instructor in Psychiatry, Harvard Medical School, Boston, Mass.; Assistant in Psychiatry, McLean Hospital, Belmont, Mass.

Howard Schneider, Ph.D.
Aerospace Medicine (coauthor)
Mission Scientist, Space and Life Sciences Directorate, Johnson Space Center, National Aeronautics and Space Administration, Houston, Texas

Albert L. Sheffer, M.D.
Asthma (coauthor)
Clinical Professor of Medicine, Harvard Medical School, Boston, Mass.

Virginia S. Taggert, M.P.H.
Asthma (coauthor)
Health Program Specialist, National Heart, Lung, and Blood Institute, National Institutes of Health, Bethesda, Md.

Kathleen S. Turner, M.P.A.
Medical Education (coauthor)
Vice President for Special Projects, Association of American Medical Colleges, Washington, D.C.

David Whiteis, Ph.D.
Health Policy
Adjunct Assistant Professor, College of Pharmacy, University of Illinois at Chicago; Director of Health Services Research, Travelers and Immigrants Aid, Chicago

Focus on Eyeglasses

by Weylin G. Eng, O.D., and Robert C. Yeager

No one knows who invented eyeglasses. Ancient peoples are believed to have worn slit disks that were made from ivory or bone over their eyes; the devices shielded them from the blinding effects of the desert sun. The Chinese as well as early Europeans used magnifying lenses, worn over the eyes in frames, as aids to reading. Probably the first portrait painting that revealed its subject wearing spectacles is from Italy (c. 1350). A full four centuries later, in 1784, Benjamin Franklin invented bifocal lenses. In a letter written from Paris, America's celebrated patriot expressed his delight with the "double spectacles" for making "my eyes as useful to me as ever they were."

Eyeglasses' slow evolution should not seem surprising; even the great Greek geometrician Euclid believed that visual rays emanated from a point within the eye, expanding outward in a "visual cone" to include the object of sight. It took another 13 centuries to demonstrate that light rays actually reflected *from* objects to the eye, and only in 1621 did the Dutch mathematician Willebrord van Roijen Snell discover the law of refraction, according to which objects are deflected from a straight path by light rays.

Today Snell's principles are embodied in corrective lenses worn by some 100 million people in the United States alone, or one of every two Americans. Though contact lenses, particularly soft-surface contacts, have grown dramatically in popularity, spectacles, or glasses, still account for more than 80% of the corrective lenses prescribed by eye-care practitioners. In recent years these traditional devices for improving vision have shown a surprising capacity for innovation and technological change. Glasses that darken automatically in sunlight; "no-line" multifocal lenses; eyeglasses specially designed for people who work with computers; spectacles for pilots, mail carriers, dentists, golfers, carpet layers, and racquetball players; lenses tinted to screen out harmful ultraviolet (UV) rays, to cut glare, or to pierce through smoky skies—these are just a few of the options available to today's eyeglasses consumers.

The importance of clear sight

The burgeoning supply of optical options is indicative of the great value people place on their sight. If anything, in an information age, that value has grown to new heights. According to a recent Gallup Poll, Americans today fear blindness more than any other disability.

418

How important is sight? "We are creatures of our vision," says George Weinstein, chairman of the department of ophthalmology at West Virginia University School of Medicine and the 1991 president of the American Academy of Ophthalmology. "Our eyes help us locate food, survive attackers, and find mates. They permit us to perform complex tasks, and to enjoy the arts, theater, and the world's beauty." Arol Augsberger of Ohio State University's College of Optometry has said: "Sight allows us to achieve our highest potential. From our TVs at home to our CRTs at work, we're a visual, data-gathering and using society. We depend on eyesight not just for niceties, but to function in a sophisticated culture."

The eye: an extraordinary organ

Indeed, the organ that powers the machinery of sight is one of the body's most remarkable organs. Poets call the human eye a window to the soul. To the physician the eye offers an unparalleled glimpse of systemic health; staring into the eye's interior, the practitioner can detect signs of hardening of the arteries, diabetes, heart disease, and other maladies.

After the brain, the eye is the body's most complex organ. It contains multiple types and layers of cells, a variety of fluids, and a central gel. The anatomic parts of the eye include the sclera, the fibrous, white outer coating; the cornea, a clear frontal sheath that allows light to enter the eye; the pupil, an adjustable opening in the center of the iris, which is the colored portion of the eye and regulates the passage of light; the lens, a tough, biconvex structure filled with fibrous tissue; the ciliary body, a structure directly behind the iris that contains the ciliary muscle, which suspends and alters the shape of the lens; the vitreous, a structure behind the lens containing vitreous humor, a clear jellylike material; and the all-important retina, located at the back of the eye and containing light-sensitive nerve cells (the rods and cones).

More than two-thirds of the brain's nerve fibers function in concert with the eye, and the retina, which can be called "the essence of the eye," is a direct extension of the brain. In a sense, the whole eyeball is designed to serve the retina. This photosensitive nerve membrane that lines the back of the eyeball acts as the "film" in the eye's camera. When light strikes the retina, the eye's rods and cones discharge chemical energy that sends messages along the optic nerve to the brain.

In order for seeing to be possible, light rays must pass successively through the cornea, lens, and the eye's gelatinous filling, the vitreous. Each of these structures bends the rays toward their point of focus at the back of the eye. The eye fine-tunes the focus by means of the lens, attached by tiny bands to an encircling muscle. As the muscle relaxes and contracts, the lens changes shape; it becomes thicker to focus on near objects, thinner to focus on distant objects.

In a normal eye light rays focus most clearly at the fovea, or center of the retina, stimulating the rods and cones. The cones provide color vision and fine detail in daylight. Rods work to give clarity at low light and to sharpen night vision.

When vision is not 20/20

However, because of variations in its shape and the stiffening with age of its lens, the eye falls prey to a number of common refractive errors. Indeed, even a fraction of a millimeter's variation in the shape of the eye's retina can tip the balance between normal and abnormal sight. A slight elongation of the eyeball causes *myopia,* or nearsightedness, because light rays converge to a focal point before reaching the retina. If the eye is a bit too short, the rays' point of focus falls behind the retina, causing *hyperopia,* or farsightedness. In *astigmatism* an irregular curvature of the cornea prevents the rays from focusing at any single point, distorting distance vision as well as near vision.

These problems are commonly corrected with lenses. A prescription lens's function is to bend light before it reaches the cornea, causing the rays to focus on the retina. Lenses for nearsightedness refract light rays slightly away from each other as they pass through the glasses. Lenses for farsightedness bend the rays toward each other. In each case the eyeglasses correct the path that otherwise would cause the rays to focus in front of or behind the retina.

Those who in their younger years manage to escape the need for corrective lenses usually develop another refractive defect about the time they turn 40—difficulty in close-up focusing. A child of 10 can focus on a book held as close as the tip of the nose. With aging, however, the eye's crystalline lens grows harder and less flexible, making it more difficult for the ciliary muscles to accommodate for close objects by changing the curvature of the lens—the impairment known as *presbyopia* (literally, "old eyes"). With the first signs of presbyopia, people typically begin to hold reading material or fine work farther from their eyes. (Normal reading distance is about 40 cm [16 in], but presbyopics are likely to hold a book at full arm's length.) They may also experience eye fatigue and headaches from doing close work. Generally presbyopia has stabilized by age 50 or so, but by then most adults—indeed 90–95%—require corrective lenses for near focusing. For those who previously did not need any correction, this will usually mean prescription reading glasses. For others it means that multifocal correction is needed; *i.e.,* bifocals for near and far distances or trifocals for near, far, and intermediate distances.

Presbyopia is like gray hair and wrinkles. It happens to everybody—or *almost* everybody. Actually, this is one time when myopia may confer an advantage. Because their focused world has always been up close, the nearsighted tend to be less troubled by presbyopia than those who are farsighted. They also are likely to be affected later than others. At first people who are normally nearsighted may compensate by removing their glasses to read. Eventually, however, they too may need reading as well as distance correction. Ironically, nearsighted people near age 40 who undergo radial keratotomy, a relatively new surgical technique to correct myopia without corrective lenses, often develop presbyopia and need reading glasses.

The right prescription

On the basis of the particular needs of the patient, an eye-care practitioner specifies the type and dimensions of lens that will best correct the vision. Eye-care practitioners include ophthalmologists, physicians who perform surgery, treat eye diseases, and prescribe corrective lenses; optometrists, who also perform comprehensive eye exams, prescribe lenses, and in some states treat eye conditions; and opticians, who fabricate and fit corrective spectacles that have been prescribed by either an optometrist or an ophthalmologist.

The lenses. Every lens has separate and specific curvatures, both front (anterior) and back (posterior), depending on the individual's needs. The interplay of the two surfaces refracts, or bends, light in such a way as to offset the effects of nearsightedness, farsightedness, astigmatism, etc. Generally, those with myopia require lenses of concave shape—thinner at

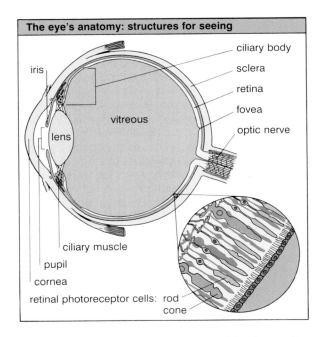

The eye's anatomy: structures for seeing

iris

ciliary body

sclera

retina

fovea

vitreous

lens

optic nerve

ciliary muscle

pupil

cornea

retinal photoreceptor cells: rod
cone

the center and thicker at the edge—while those who are hyperopic need convex lenses, in which these characteristics are reversed.

Lenses may be made of glass or plastic. Glass is the hardest surface and least likely to scratch. However, it is much heavier than plastic and has declined in popularity since large frames became fashionable.

Plastic is both lighter and more impact-resistant, but it is also quite vulnerable to scratching. Another advantage of plastic is that it does not fog up as easily; those who work in kitchens or outdoors in a cold climate may want this quality. New "high-index" plastic or superstrength polycarbonate materials are even tougher and lighter in weight, and they allow lenses to be 25–30% thinner than glass or regular plastic while retaining the same focusing power. These lenses are particularly favored by those who need extratough eyeglasses—people who play contact sports and those whose prescriptions would otherwise require a thick lens. Thinner lenses have the advantage of being more cosmetically appealing as well as more comfortable to wear because they are lighter.

Because plastic lenses are easily scratched, it is generally recommended that they be treated with a scratch-resistant coating. Such coatings will not protect from extreme abuse; care must still be taken when the glasses are cleaned and handled.

All lens materials can be tinted or coated, depending on the needs or desires of the individual. For example, a yellow tint can help pilots see through hazy or smoky skies. Brown, green, and gray tints can give clearer vision in sunlight. Tints are available in dozens of shades, including gradients of hue within a single lens, which some people choose simply

for fashion. Self-darkening photochromic lenses, now available in plastic as well as glass, change automatically from clear to dark indoors and out to shield the user from sunlight without requiring that he or she change glasses. These glasses are not recommended for driving because in order to darken, the lenses require ultraviolet light, which the automobile's windshield blocks.

Antireflective coatings are also available to block out glare. Television personalities often wear lenses with antireflective coatings so that the bright studio lights do not cause glare off their glasses, which would appear on viewers' screens. Night drivers may choose this option, too, in order to protect against the glare of oncoming headlights.

Prescription lenses are divided into single-vision or multifocal lenses, with the latter category including bi-, tri-, and occasionally quadrifocal lenses. Single-vision lenses are prescription lenses with the same focusing power throughout the entire lens. These are the most commonly prescribed eyeglasses and the simplest to use. Single-vision lenses are prescribed for distance or near vision and as a first response to declining close-up vision due to age. As an alternative to bifocal or multifocal lenses, single-vision "half-eye," or "grannie," glasses are often worn when needed for close-up work by those who require no distance correction. The refractive power of a prescription lens is designated by "diopter" (D) units, which indicate the reciprocal of the focal power of the lens in meters. The higher the diopter, the more powerful the lens.

"Drugstore," or ready-to-wear, glasses are an alternative to reading glasses obtained by professional prescription. They are sold in a range of magnifications—from one diopter to four diopters. Nothing is inherently harmful about these glasses—essentially they are magnifiers in frames that cost about $10 to $15—a considerable savings over prescription glasses. However, because they are usually not corrected for distortion, the user may develop eye strain or headaches from them, especially if his or her line of sight does not coincide with the lenses' optical center. While they may do the job quite adequately for some people, these self-prescribed glasses may give their purchasers an unwarranted sense of security, leading to skipped professional eye exams and the risk of undiscovered, potentially serious eye problems.

I imagine it will be found pretty generally true, that the same Convexity of Glass, through which a Man sees clearest and best at the distance proper for reading, is not the best for greater distances. I therefore had formerly two Pair of Spectacles, which I shifted occasionally. . . . Finding the Change troublesome, and not always sufficiently ready, I had the Glasses cut and half of each kind associated in the same Circle. . . . By this means, as I wear my Spectacles constantly, I have only to move my Eyes up or down, as I want to see distinctly far or near, the proper Glass being always ready.

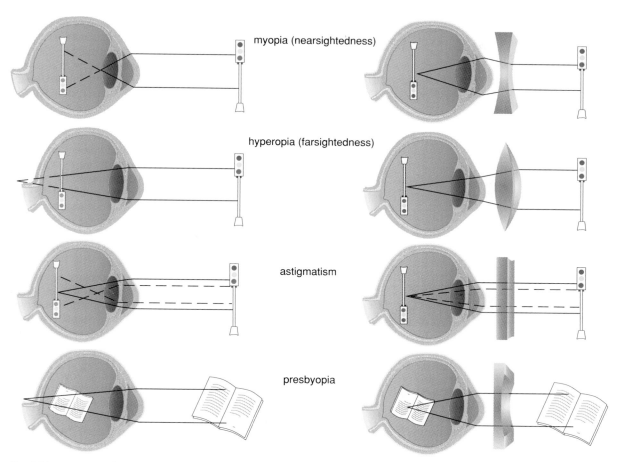

myopia (nearsightedness)

hyperopia (farsightedness)

astigmatism

presbyopia

Special lenses correct the most common refractive errors. Myopia *causes the focal point of light rays to fall before the retina; a concave lens spreads rays slightly before they reach the cornea. With* hyperopia *the focal point of light rays is behind the retina; a convex lens bends rays inward before they reach the eye. The irregular curvature of the cornea in the* astigmatic *eye prevents light from focusing at any single point; a cylindrical lens bends only certain rays to compensate for the corneal irregularity. As the eye ages,* presbyopia *causes the lens to be less flexible and thus unable to accommodate for near vision; bifocals bend light inward and help the eye focus on near objects, such as the print on a page.*

This is how Franklin described his brilliant invention in a letter to his friend George Whately. Bifocal lenses are almost always prescribed as a result of presbyopia, although occasionally they are worn by younger individuals (such as college students who spend long hours doing close work) to correct for extreme farsightedness or overconvergence of the eye muscles. In traditional bifocals the top segment is for far distances, the lower for near, and a distinct line divides the two. Now, however, there are blended-line, or line-free, lenses, which offer a cosmetic advantage; however, the user sees a distortion at the "invisible" line.

In bifocals, the size of each lens segment, or "window," is determined according to need. The wide work surface viewed by a draftsman might well call for a broad close-vision segment occupying most of the lower half of the lens. A truck driver who needs to focus on the road for hours at a time but has trouble

reading his dashboard instruments, might wish to preserve the largest lens area for distance viewing and therefore opt for a small round or half-moon-shaped close-up viewing segment.

Trifocals, which offer mid-range as well as near- and far-focus correction, are typically prescribed as presbyopia progresses and stronger bifocals are needed. The stronger power of the close-focusing segment creates a prescription "gap" between it and the distance-correcting portion of the lens. A trifocal segment bridges that gap and allows for clearer middle-distance vision—especially in the half-meter to meter-and-a-half (2–5-ft) range, the distance, say, a shopper encounters when selecting items from a grocery store shelf.

A quadrifocal lens is either a "double bifocal" or, more commonly, a trifocal with a fourth segment that repeats the close-up lens component at the top of the

421

Because Benjamin Franklin found that he could not see "clearest and best at the distance proper for reading" through the same lenses that were "best for greater distances," he devised an ingenious pair of "double spectacles," or bifocals. He expressed his great delight with this invention in a letter to a friend in 1785.

lens, usually for occupational reasons. Electricians, for example, must often work in close quarters on ceiling wiring. Thus, they may desire near-focus capability both above and below a lens's mid- and distance-focusing segments.

Perhaps the most natural correction is offered by progressive, or progressive-addition, lenses, which are designed to correct vision continuously, from distance through mid-focus to close-up reading range. Essentially a line-free trifocal, the progressive lens attempts to replicate vision as it was before the eyes became presbyopic. Although progressive lenses offer the cosmetic advantage of being line-free, the wearer may have considerable difficulty adjusting if the glasses are not properly fitted or used. The experience of wearing progressive lenses is sometimes compared to being on the deck of ship in a storm. Because of inherent properties of the lens's design, wearers of these glasses often experience peripheral distortion and blurring. The lens design requires that the user learn to focus through its central vertical area and turn the head, rather than the eyes, to look at something to the side. Thus, one has to be highly motivated to make the adjustment to progressives.

Increasingly, lens prescriptions are being designed to protect or enhance visual performance during special work or recreational activities. Many occupations that employ laser technology require lenses that block out UV and other potentially harmful light rays. Near-to mid-focus lenses are often prescribed for those whose jobs are at computer workstations. "Golfer's glasses" include a small, circular window in a corner of one lens, prefocused for belt-high scorecard reading. There are endless other "special purpose" lenses.

The frame. Eyeglass frames consist of a mounting to hold the lenses before the eyes and two temples that pass over or around the ears and keep the entire structure in place. Manufacturers offer several types of temples. "Library" temples are perfectly straight and are often favored by those who frequently remove their glasses. "Cable" temples are made of flexible wire and curve securely around the ears; these are commonly worn by athletes and may be preferred by people who leave their glasses on all day and want a good fit. The most common "spatula" temples are flat and partially curve around the ear.

The frame rests on the nose by means of either a "saddle" or a "keyhole" bridge (names that describe their distinctive shapes). For comfort and proper fit, the bridge features either fixed or adjustable nosepads.

Most frames are made of plastic or metal. In recent years more frames have been constructed of cellulose acetate (a nonflammable plastic) or of nylon, whose flexibility is ideal for sports. The latest carbonate frames are manufactured from the same materials as tennis rackets, golf clubs, and cameras; the carbon derivatives can be finished with bonded enamel and offer greater strength than metal. These frames possess the lightness of plastic but without the tendency to stretch or lose shape.

Rimless and semirimless frames are popular and lightweight but can be quite fragile and can easily bend out of shape. In rimless mountings the lenses are attached by screws at the bridge and temples. Because holes are drilled in the lens itself, chipping or breakage can occur if the glasses are not handled very carefully. The screws can also loosen easily, and in rescrewing them it is easy to scratch the lens. So-called rimlon glasses are secured by strips of invisible nylon that circle under the lenses, which make the glasses more durable while retaining the "rimless" look. When not being worn, rimless and semirimless glasses should be kept in a hard, impact-resistant case to protect them.

To a considerable extent, frame selection is driven by the lens prescription. For example, bifocal capability often necessitates a greater vertical frame dimension to allow for the additional lens segment. Similarly, thick lenses impose requirements on materials. Because of their inherent thinness, metal frames are not the best choice for these lenses. Frame selection must also ensure that the lens's optical center is placed directly before the pupil and thus in the wearer's direct line of sight. For this reason it is important to purchase glasses from a reputable professional.

422

Tips on selecting and wearing eyeglasses

One's eye-care practitioner remains the best judge of unique lens requirements, but there are some characteristics of a successful lens prescription that the consumer should be aware of.

One should ask about special coatings and tints. If one tends to be hard on glasses and chooses plastic lenses, a scratch-resistant coating is a good idea. One who does a lot of night driving or is troubled by excessive glare should consider an antireflection coating. One who works at a computer under harsh fluorescent lighting should consider a slight pink or neutral gray tint, which can soften the light and reduce reflections. One who takes a photosensitizing medication on a regular basis may need extra protection from sunlight and should therefore consider a UV coating. (Such medications include many antihypertensives, diuretics, tranquilizers, antibiotics, and oral contraceptives.) One whose eyes are especially light-sensitive should consider photochromic lenses.

One who is extremely nearsighted should stay away from large lenses. Smaller lenses will reduce distortion, weight, and edge thickness.

A person who is wearing bifocals for the first time needs to be patient during the adjustment period. Opticians recommend putting away all other glasses and wearing the new glasses almost constantly for a week or two. When walking, one should not look down at the feet. When going up or down stairs, one should tilt the head downward to look though the top part of the lenses. One should hold reading matter close, lowering the eyes, not the head. A newspaper should be folded in half or in quarters, and the paper, not the head, should be raised or lowered. If the glasses feel as if they are slipping on the face, one should check with the optician to see that they are properly adjusted.

If one has been wearing bifocals or trifocals and is selecting a new pair of glasses, it is not a good idea to make a drastic change in the size, and particularly the height, of a multifocal segment.

No matter what kind of lenses one has, one should keep them clean! The best way is to clean them with soapy water and then dry them with a soft cloth. Bar soaps can leave a film on lenses, and wiping them with a dry cloth can scratch them.

Part of any eyeglass prescription is a properly fitted frame whose design and material are appropriate to the individual's intended use. In addition to practical and optical considerations, however, nearly every frame is also chosen in part for its cosmetic appeal. Like clothing, frames frequently swing through cycles of fashion in terms of shapes, sizes, colors, and materials. Nonetheless, following certain basic guidelines can ensure the selection of a frame that has both a proper fit and an attractive appearance.

The top of the frame should bisect the eyebrows. The widest part of the frame should equal or exceed the widest part of the head. The pupils should be slightly above the center of the frame. One should make sure that the frame is properly aligned—that it does not tilt—especially if one has chosen progressive lenses.

A low temple attachment often looks best on faces whose features are long and thin. High temple attachments and a more vertical frame shape may look better with round, full faces. Oval faces generally accept the widest range of frame shapes.

Those with high cheekbones and flat noses may benefit from keyhole bridge designs or adjustable nosepads (to lift the frame away from the face). Persons with large noses may appreciate the "slimming effect" of frames with a saddle bridge. Similarly, a long nose may appear shorter in a frame fitted with a saddle bridge.

A frame should be comfortable and should fit one's personality and be appropriate for the intended use. One should choose a sturdy frame with "cable" temples if glasses are used for active sports; a frame that allows a wide field of vision if one does a lot of driving or is an aviator; a heavy-duty plastic frame if the prescription calls for thick, high-correction lenses; and a wire or rimless frame if weight on the face is a concern.

Finally, even after getting glasses, one should visit one's eye-care practitioner regularly. With a proper prescription, there is no reason that one's eyes, like Ben Franklin's, cannot remain as useful as they have ever been.

Nearly half of all Americans use corrective lenses of some sort. Despite the growing popularity of contact lenses, more then half of those who require vision correction wear eyeglasses. Today's eyeglasses consumers have a remarkable range of options in both lenses and frame styles.

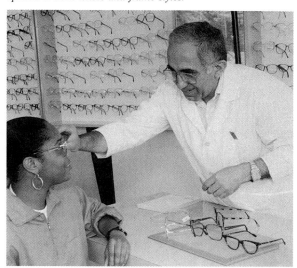

Rhoda Sidney—Stock, Boston

Appendicitis

by Donald J. Ferguson,
M.D., Ph.D.

One of the more enigmatic causes of death throughout human existence—and up to about only 100 years ago—was the disease now called acute appendicitis. Commonly, people in the prime of life were affected, without a clue as to the origin of the illness, although some astute medical scientists did put forth theories. In the 16th century, for example, the French physician Jean Fernel proposed that the perforated appendix was a source of peritonitis (infection within the abdominal cavity), and in 1827 another French practitioner reached a similar conclusion. Their findings, however, were disregarded or disputed. Thus, the cause of appendicitis remained obscure.

Beginning over 150 years ago, clinicians began to record cases of pain and swelling at a characteristic site in the right lower abdomen due to an abscess surrounding the cecum (the blind, or closed, end of the large bowel), the structure from which the appendix arises. During the 19th century it was learned that patients' lives could be saved if the abscess drained spontaneously or was surgically drained. At the same time, surgery advanced remarkably with the discovery of anesthesia (1842) and techniques to prevent infection. An 1882 study reported a death rate of only 15% in patients who had undergone surgical drainage of abdominal abscess, quite an accomplishment at that time. Finally, in 1886 Reginald Fitz of Boston established that a perforated appendix was the cause of such abscesses. In 1889 the modern era in appendicitis treatment began with New York surgeon Charles McBurney's report of the complete recovery of 10 of 11 patients who underwent appendectomy before perforation had occurred. Treatment since then has been simple: surgical removal of the inflamed appendix. The persisting problem is how to make an early diagnosis in every patient.

The disease process

The appendix is a blind tube that extends from the side of the cecum, which is located in the right lower quadrant of the abdomen. The appendix averages 8–10 cm (3.1–3.9 in) in length and 4–6 mm (0.16–0.24 in) in diameter. The body and tip may be freely movable or attached to other tissues behind the cecum. In rare instances the cecum and appendix are found in other quadrants of the abdomen. Anatomically, the appendix is intestinal, consisting of three layers of tissue: epithelium (lining tissue), muscle, and a peritoneal cover. As in the intestine, these tissues surround a lumen, or hollow cavity. Although it performs digestive functions in some mammals, the appendix has no known function in human beings.

Acute appendicitis is seen initially as a microscopic infiltration of the tissues by white blood cells—the hallmark of inflammation. Visible changes follow, including swelling, redness or other discoloration, and the presence on the surface of the appendix of a puslike exudate. The inflammatory process is usually associated with obstruction of the lumen, commonly due to compacted, sometimes calcified feces; obstruction may also be caused by swallowed seeds or other foreign bodies that become lodged in the appendix or by gallstones, tumors, or overgrowth of lymph tissue—perhaps related to a viral infection. Following obstruction, increased secretions and the proliferation of bacteria cause pressure to build within the appendix, which in turn produces pain and interferes with blood supply. Impaired circulation results in the destruction of tissue and, eventually, the formation of holes—perforation. These effects of obstruction were experimentally demonstrated in 1939 by O.H. Wangensteen, a surgeon at the University of Minnesota. When the obstructed area is walled off by adjacent intestine or by the omentum (a fatty apron that hangs down from the colon), an abscess forms. When the obstruction is not walled off or when the abscess ruptures internally, peritonitis develops.

Probably some appendiceal obstructions are temporary, accounting for the occasional case in which the typical clinical and ultrasonic findings of appendicitis resolve on their own without surgery. An alternative explanation of such a case is that the inflammation was due to a microbial infection in the absence of obstruction; however, no particular bacterium or virus has been consistently linked with appendicitis. Diets high in fiber, bran, or leafy vegetables and tomatoes have been reported to lower the incidence of appendicitis, but these reports have not been confirmed by extensive scientific study. Diet presumably could influence the likelihood of appendiceal obstruction by affecting the consistency of the bowel contents; likewise, food intake could affect the assortment of microbes living in the intestine.

Incidence and mortality

The lifetime risk of appendicitis is around 7%. It occurs in all age groups but reaches a peak incidence between ages 15 and 20. It is less likely to occur among the elderly because in most people fibrous tissue forms in the appendix with age, making it less susceptible to obstruction. Men of all ages have slightly higher rates of appendicitis than their female counterparts. One U.S. study found the incidence of appendicitis to be 1.5 times higher in whites than in other races. There is no seasonal variation in incidence.

Approximately 500,000 appendectomies are performed annually in the U.S. Of these, about half are for a preoperative diagnosis of acute appendicitis (*i.e.,* appendicitis is suspected; the diagnosis is confirmed pathologically in 90% of males and 80% of females). The other half are incidental to other surgery.

The number of deaths due to appendicitis has declined greatly in recent decades. In the U.S. the death rate from appendicitis was 11.4 per 100,000 people in 1910. Peak rates of about 15 per 100,000 were recorded in 1929 and 1931. Thereafter mortality fell rapidly, to 0.2 per 100,000 in 1987. This amounted to about 490 deaths in a population of 245 million, compared with 19,125 appendicitis deaths in a population of 125 million in 1931. (There were, by comparison, about 483,000 U.S. deaths from cancer in 1987.) Three reasons for the decline are apparent: a sharp but unexplained fall in the incidence of appendicitis since the 1930s (an 80% drop was recorded in New Jersey, for example); earlier diagnosis; and the advent of antibiotics (in the mid-1940s). Mortality remains highest in young children and the elderly, the two age groups in which incidence is lowest. On a worldwide basis, deaths attributed to appendicitis in recent years ranged from 0.1 per 100,000 in Australia, Egypt, Israel, Japan, New Zealand, and Portugal to 0.8 per 100,000 in Cuba, Russia, and rural China.

Symptoms and diagnosis

In older children and adults the symptoms of appendicitis typically begin with abdominal pain in the area around the navel. The onset may be either gradual or sudden. Loss of appetite, nausea, and one or two attacks of vomiting follow. Most patients are constipated, but some have diarrhea. The pain may be crampy or steady and may vary from mild to excruciating, but it generally tends to increase with time. Gradually the pain shifts from the central abdomen to the right lower quadrant.

The most important manifestation of appendicitis is soreness in the right lower quadrant. There is usually also rebound tenderness—pain elicited by the quick release of pressure slowly applied to the abdomen. The abdominal wall in the right lower quadrant may be in spasm. In persons whose appendix hangs down lower in the pelvis, the right-sided soreness may be more evident on pelvic or rectal examination. Typically, patients will have a low-grade fever, up to 39° C (102.2° F). Blood tests usually show an increased white blood cell (WBC) count. Observations that suggest rupture of the appendix include a duration of symptoms longer than 24 hours, prostration, generalized abdominal pain and tenderness, distension of the abdomen, and a further elevation of fever and WBC. The examining physician may be able to feel an abscess in the cecal area, the pelvis, or posteriorly (*i.e.,* in the back near the right kidney).

Patients whose symptoms are mild and of short duration can usually be observed safely in the clinic or hospital emergency room for several hours; in the absence of worsening symptoms, it is unlikely that the appendix will perforate within 24 hours after onset. Often the symptoms will regress, and the expense of additional tests or hospital admission can be avoided. On the other hand, if the patient returns home but becomes worse, appropriate treatment may be dangerously delayed.

In making a diagnosis of appendicitis, the physician will consider and rule out other possible conditions, including gastroenteritis (usually accompanied by more vomiting and diarrhea than appendicitis, without localized soreness), pelvic inflammatory disease (characterized by chronic bilateral pain that becomes worse during menstruation), ovulation (associated with pain that rapidly regresses at the midpoint of the menstrual cycle), gallstones (marked by food intolerance, a history of previous attacks, and pain in the upper rather than lower abdomen), and kidney stones (producing pain in the back). In children especially, pneumonia, which sometimes causes abdominal pain but is usually distinguished by acute respiratory symptoms, cough, and a high fever, must be ruled out.

So-called computer decision aids—data-based systems for diagnosing acute abdominal disease—have been available for about two decades. These aids can help in arriving at an accurate diagnosis—complementing the physician's clinical acumen. However, they are not yet the equal of a discerning clinician, and they are not widely used in the U.S.

In addition to the physical exam and blood count, several special diagnostic techniques are used to identify appendicitis.

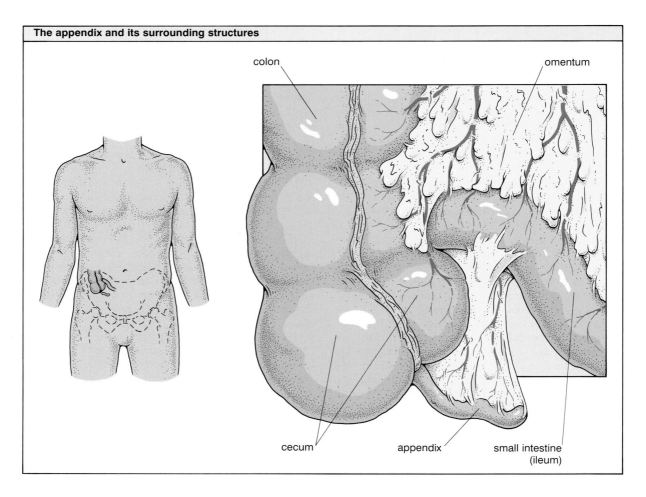

colon

omentum

cecum

appendix

small intestine (ileum)

Ultrasonography. Diagnostic imaging by means of high-frequency sound waves produces a picture of the intra-abdominal structures that may strongly suggest the presence or absence of appendicitis. The ultrasound scan requires no preparation of the patient and is quick, noninvasive, and innocuous. In one recent study of its accuracy, scans of more than 200 patients with proven appendicitis were positive (showing appendiceal diameter greater than six millimeters) in 86%; 24 other patients who proved not to need immediate surgery also had positive scans (although their final diagnosis was "abortive" appendicitis), as did four patients who had other final diagnoses. In 155 patients who had other abdominal diseases that are often confused with appendicitis, ultrasound diagnosed 140 patients (90%) correctly. In this study only 7% of appendectomies proved to be unnecessary, compared with 32% before the advent of ultrasound.

Laparoscopy. A more radical procedure than ultrasound, laparoscopy involves the insertion of a fiberoptic tube into the peritoneal cavity through a small incision, along with a probe that is inserted through another incision. In one study of the accuracy of la-

paroscopy, all cases of appendicitis were recognized, but 15% of patients undergoing the procedure were incorrectly diagnosed as having appendicitis. Incorrect diagnoses may occur because the outside of the appendix is inflamed as a result of disease of other organs (for example, the colon or the fallopian tubes); such conditions cannot always be recognized through the instrument. Laparoscopy usually requires general anesthesia and is difficult or impossible in the presence of obesity or abdominal distension; it is not performed in late pregnancy.

X-rays. An X-ray study of the colon may demonstrate perforation or other signs of appendicitis or the presence of other colonic disease. It may be useful when the methods described above are not available. The process requires a contrast medium, either swallowed or administered via an enema, but is noninvasive. The dose of radiation received is appreciable.

CT scanning. Computed tomography (CT), which produces a cross-sectional X-ray of any part of the body, also with the administration of a contrast medium to fill the bowel, can be used to recognize appendicitis. Studies indicate that CT scanning is a sensitive tool

426

for this purpose, but it is more time-consuming and expensive than ultrasound and may not be available on a 24-hour emergency basis. CT and ultrasound need to be compared directly in large studies before the superiority of one or the other of these diagnostic techniques in appendicitis can be confirmed.

Infants and children: diagnostic difficulties

Appendicitis is rare in the first year of life, is uncommon in the second, and increases rapidly in incidence thereafter up to age 20. It has been thought to run a more rapid course in the very young, but this is difficult to judge because the time of onset is often unknown in these young patients. The appendix has a thinner wall in infancy, so perforation may occur more quickly; further, the infant's omentum is too small to afford any protection against the spread of inflammation within the abdomen. Diagnosis is especially difficult for two reasons: children are generally unable to clearly describe their symptoms, and infants and young children tend to respond similarly to many different kinds of discomfort.

The initial responsibility for diagnosing a child's abdominal pain necessarily rests with the parent, who is the person best able to recognize when the child's distress is beyond the ordinary. One simple test a parent can perform consists of very gently pressing the child's abdomen, beginning on the left side, and comparing the youngster's reaction to pressure in other areas with that in the right lower quadrant. In one study of this technique, pain and tenderness were localized at an early stage of disease in 95% of young children. When a parent does elicit signs of tenderness in the right lower quadrant, this finding alone means that appendicitis must be considered. Vomiting and a degree or two of fever are also usual in children with appendicitis. Poor appetite and lethargy or irritability may also be early signs.

The differential diagnosis in this age group includes (besides the conditions mentioned above in the case of adults) mesenteric adenitis (inflammation of lymph nodes of the mesentery, an abdominal membrane, which can be detected by ultrasonography), intussusception (infolding of a segment of bowel into the adjacent segment, causing violent cramps for 10–15 seconds every few minutes along with vomiting and a palpable mass), volvulus (twisting of the bowel, characterized by vomiting and abdominal distension), and constipation. In the latter case a small enema is permissible to judge whether constipation is the cause of the symptoms. However, laxatives should not be given to a child who is suspected of having appendicitis.

Another source of diagnostic confusion is that children with appendicitis frequently have a concurrent illness—*e.g.,* respiratory infection, gastroenteritis, urinary infection—often one that involves fever and increased WBC. In many cases these coexisting conditions have been thought—by both parents and doctors—to explain the child's symptoms. As a consequence of these diagnostic problems, rates of appendiceal perforation are significantly higher in young children than in adults—having ranged from 37% to twice that, without much decline in recent years.

Diagnosis during pregnancy

The incidence of appendicitis related to pregnancy is about one in 1,400, similar to that in nonpregnant women of the same age. It is the most common surgical emergency during pregnancy. There is no significant variation in incidence with the trimester. Gestational changes increase the difficulty of clinical diagnosis: loss of appetite, nausea, and abdominal pains occur in normal pregnancy; urinary tract infections are found in one-quarter of pregnant patients who also have appendicitis; and there is a normal increase in WBC during pregnancy. While abdominal tenderness is localized in the right lower quadrant in 75% of pregnant women with appendicitis, the appendix begins to be displaced upward at four months and at term may be several centimeters above the bony pelvis. Typically, therefore, the diagnosis of appendicitis is delayed in pregnancy. In one study the incidence of perforation was 43%; it did not increase the incidence of maternal deaths, although the rate of fetal deaths was higher than normal. Appendectomy has contributed to premature birth when performed after 23 weeks but is not associated with an increased incidence of birth defects.

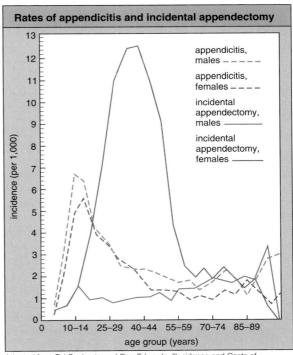

Rates of appendicitis and incidental appendectomy

appendicitis, males -----

appendicitis, females ----

incidental appendectomy, males ———

incidental appendectomy, females ———

incidence (per 1,000)

age group (years)

Adapted from Tai Sugimoto and Don Edwards, "Incidence and Costs of Incidental Appendectomy as a Preventive Measure," *American Journal of Public Health,* vol. 77, no. 4 (April 1987), pp. 471–475

Elderly patients: special considerations

The clinical picture described above as "typical" has been found in only 20% of patients with proven appendicitis who are over age 60. In one study, for example, 40% of these patients had no right lower quadrant pain, and one-third did not experience nausea or vomiting. Only half of them had a correct diagnosis on admission to the hospital, and only 70% had one by the time the surgery was performed.

For various reasons, including poverty and fear of doctors, these patients commonly had not sought medical attention until one or more days after their illness began. There was then a further delay for diagnostic tests and consultations, the results of which were not quickly acted upon because there was no single supervising physician, a common situation in emergency cases. As a consequence of these delays, 72% of elderly patients in a recent study were found upon surgery to have perforation. About 5% of them died.

Treatment

Appendectomy—surgical removal of the appendix—is the main treatment for appendicitis. The procedure may be performed through a small conventional incision or, in suitable circumstances, by means of a laparoscope, using a very short incision for the laparoscope itself and additional small openings for surgical instruments. General anesthesia is usual for either procedure, although a local block can be used instead. Antibiotics are begun preoperatively and continued one or two days after the surgery. The operative risk of appendectomy is extremely small. Patients usually stay in the hospital for one to three days, and most have no aftereffects from the surgery. They can usually resume full activity after one week.

Once perforation has occurred, treatment requires expert use of antibiotics and other supportive measures. Thanks mainly to the availability of antibiotics, perforation is now very rarely fatal, but complications are more likely than in cases where the appendix is removed earlier. Patients may have to undergo surgical drainage of the wound in addition to appendectomy. Thus, the surgical wound may be left partly open, and convalescence can be further delayed by the development of secondary abscesses requiring subsequent drainage operations. In women with appendiceal perforation, peritonitis may cause sterility by obstructing the fallopian tubes. Hospital stays for patients with perforation usually last from one to several weeks. A further postsurgical complication for these patients is the formation of adhesions—a sticking together of normally separate tissues—which may cause chronic pain and recurrent bowel obstructions, requiring additional surgery, often many years later. The extent of adhesion tends to be proportional to the degree of peritoneal inflammation and its surgical drainage.

None of the diagnostic methods described above, nor any combination of them, is infallible. Because of the risks involved in delaying appendectomy, even the most careful surgeon occasionally performs an operation that turns out to have been unnecessary. It is unlikely that such a surgeon would find more than 10% of his or her operations to have been needless, and the percentage of needless operations should approach zero among patients who are seen early and evaluated with all of the various diagnostic means available.

Incidental appendectomy

A normal, uninflamed appendix sometimes can be safely removed—thereby preventing any possibility of appendicitis—through an abdominal incision that has been made for another reason. The procedure adds no more than 15 minutes to the operating time. There are some contraindications, however. Incidental appendectomy is most often done in women because they have more abdominal surgery than men. While the risk of appendicitis declines after age 20, the opportunity to perform incidental appendectomy is comparatively rare under the age of 25.

There is considerable disagreement in the medical community about the cost-effectiveness of this procedure. It has been estimated, for example, that 59 incidental appendectomies in 35-year-old patients prevent one case of appendicitis, while 166 such operations in persons aged 60 prevent a single case. The costs of the procedure depend partly on whether the surgeon charges an additional sum for this service. In any case, even 15 minutes of time in the operating room is expensive. Given these facts, it is not surprising that there is no consensus on policy toward incidental appendectomy.

A serious—but not fatal—condition

Advances in medical knowledge during the past century have transformed appendicitis from a fatal to a curable disease. Ultrasonography and laparoscopy have made possible earlier and more accurate diagnosis, thus reducing both the incidence of perforation and the proportion of unnecessary operations. Appendicitis is nonetheless a serious condition and must be treated as such, especially in the case of the very young and the elderly. The importance of early diagnosis in young children puts a special responsibility on parents and physicians.

While the incidence of appendicitis appears to be decreasing—in the U.S., for example, it has declined by 50% over the past 60 years—it will undoubtedly remain a reason for emergency surgery. A delay in diagnosis will sometimes cause serious complications, although with modern treatment there is now little risk of death.

Aquatic Exercise: Take the Plunge

by Jane Katz, Ed.D.

Water sports have long been the favorite recreational exercise for millions of people. The physical and psychological benefits of exercising in water have been known for centuries. The motto in ancient Rome was *Mens sana in corpora sana* ("A healthy mind in a healthy body"), and training of young men for leadership and the military included swimming. In the 1st century BC the Roman statesman Maecenas is said to have built the first heated swimming pool. In 1595 Christopher Middleton wrote the first instruction book on swimming, published in England, *A Short Introduction to Learne to Swimme.* In 1726 the American statesman and scientist Benjamin Franklin published *The Art of Swimming Made Safe, Easy, Pleasant and Healthful by the Instructions Set Forth Herein,* which included a scientific explanation as to why the human body floats. In London, Franklin demonstrated his own considerable expertise in the sport by swimming five kilometers (three miles) down the River Thames, performing elaborate stunts and exercises.

By the late 1800s the role of exercising in water to improve and maintain health was beginning to be widely accepted. In 1912 the American educator Frank Eugen Dalton wrote in *Swimming Scientifically Taught* that swimming "reduces corpulency [obesity], improves the figure, expands the lungs, improves the circulation of the blood, builds up general health," and has special benefits for "nervous people."

Water exercise for therapeutic purposes has roots in the elegant "water-cure" spas of the 19th century, where hydropathy (the taking of hot or cold mineral baths) was prescribed for any number of ailments. In the 1930s U.S. Pres. Franklin D. Roosevelt was a prominent believer in the benefits of thermal waters, and he sought exercise and rehabilitation for his own polio at Warm Springs, Ga. Today water-based exercises are incorporated into many physical therapy and rehabilitation programs.

That supreme physical coordination and grace can be achieved through water workouts is evidenced in the figures and movements of synchronized swimming, which became an official Olympic sport in 1984. Well before that, in the 1940s, the glamorous Esther Williams captivated the public in lavish Hollywood aquatic extravaganzas with her stunning performances of water ballet.

The burgeoning of water exercise

In the late 1960s cardiologist and fitness expert Kenneth H. Cooper introduced the American public to "aerobics," a concept of physical conditioning in which sustained exercise promotes cardiovascular health. Since that time, numerous medical studies have attested to the many positive effects of exercise on general health and psychological well-being. This body of research has confirmed that physical fitness should be a way of life for everyone.

The exercise boom that took hold in the United States in the 1970s and peaked in the '80s as the "baby boom" generation matured gave way to a growing demand for moderation in fitness choices—due in part to the frequency of injuries incurred from high-impact exercises, such as jogging and aerobic dance. What was needed was a fitness activity that would combine stretching, aerobic conditioning, strength training, and flexibility.

For many, water exercise has provided the answer. This includes people who do not like to swim or never learned how, who have found that they can devise their own workouts, transferring to the water the exercises they had found too strenuous on land. In the past decade water exercise classes, often called hydrocalisthenics, hydroslimnastics, aquarobics, or aquacise, have been more and more in demand. An estimated five million people in the U.S. today participate in some form of aquatic exercise.

Aquatic exercise: take the plunge

Benefits galore

Water provides a superior environment for exercise. The hydrostatic support of the water allows movement to take place without stress on or jarring of joints, muscles, and organs. This effect also improves circulation because the water is putting constant pressure on every part of the body.

Water's buoyancy causes the body's apparent weight in neck-deep water to be one-tenth of what it is on land. This is especially beneficial for individuals who are overweight, out of shape, or pregnant or who have back, joint, or arthritic problems.

Water offers 12 times the resistance of air. In order to move through the water, one must displace it vertically, horizontally, or circularly. This multidirectional movement strengthens and tones muscles, helps to condition the heart and lungs, and contributes to the body's ability to utilize oxygen efficiently.

Exercising in a wet environment has an "air-conditioning" effect on the body. This permits the participant to sustain a longer period of exercise, which does more to promote cardiovascular fitness and "feeling good" than shorter and more tiring and strenuous workouts out of the water. Those who exercise in water also are more likely to emerge from their workout invigorated.

Water exercise feels good because it is done in a refreshing, "no sweat" environment. It also induces both physiological and psychological feelings of exhilaration because as the workout proceeds, endorphins—natural opiate-like hormones manufactured by the body—are released. Some experts believe that these natural mood boosters are responsible for the "exercise high" that many devoted exercisers experience.

In the cradling environment of water, the body's range of motion, flexibility, energy expenditure, and coordination are all enhanced. Aquatic exercise utilizes the large muscle groups of each area of the body: upper body (triceps, biceps, deltoids, and trapezius), middle body (abdominal, intercostal, pelvic, and back muscles), and the lower body (quadriceps, hamstrings, and calf muscles).

On average, a 68-kg (150-lb) man exercising in water for 30 minutes burns approximately 250 calories. The number of actual calories burned depends on several variables—the individual's weight, height, and level of exertion during exercise, vertical or horizontal position, water temperature and depth, and resistance equipment used in the workout. The bottom line is that water exercise done consistently, three times a week on alternate days, helps to promote general fitness.

Tips for getting started

Water exercise is a lifelong fitness activity available to virtually everyone; no special skills are required, and there are no age limits. The following are some useful guidelines for beginning an aquatic exercise program.

- Get a medical checkup before beginning any exercise program.
- Never exercise alone! Safety comes first. Exercise with supervision.
- Check the depth of the water before going in. This is a safety *must!* Enter a pool at the shallow end.
- Start slowly and listen to your body. Workouts should be paced and rest taken when needed.
- Breathe rhythmically and continuously. Never hold your breath.
- Wear comfortable swim gear that allows for freedom of movement.
- When exercising in an outdoor pool or lake, protect yourself against the Sun's ultraviolet rays, which reflect off water, increasing the potential for burning. Apply a waterproof sunscreen, with a sun protection factor (SPF) of at least 15. Out of the pool, wear sunglasses and a hat or visor for protection.
- Drink fluids both before and after exercising to prevent dehydration. Water does the best job of replenishing fluids and quenching thirst.
- If pain, shortness of breath, dizziness, or disorientation occurs during exercise, stop immediately and ask for help.

Gearing up

A wide range of aquatic facilities are suitable for water exercise. A backyard or a neighborhood pool can be just as good for a workout as the most exclusive health spa or Olympic-size pool. Waist- to chest-deep water is ideal; a water temperature about 28°–30° C (82°–86° F) is usually best.

A comfortable, lightweight swimsuit made of Lycra, nylon, or some combination of both is recommended. Some people may choose to wear a swim cap. Those

Warm-up

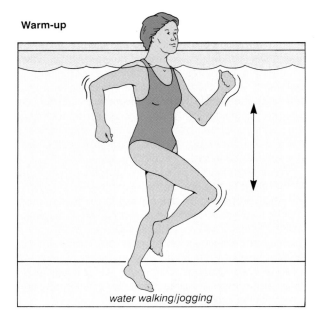

water walking/jogging

430

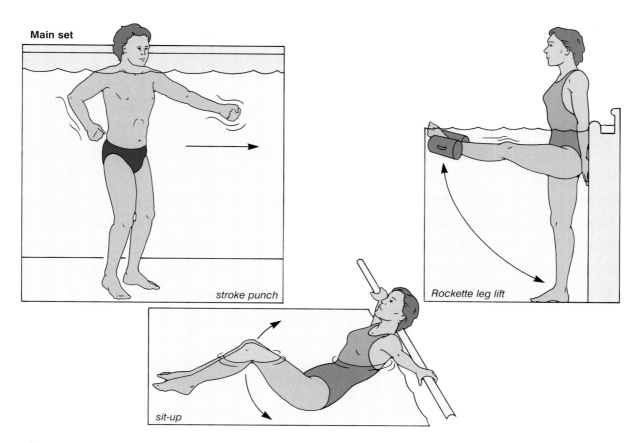

Main set

stroke punch

Rockette leg lift

sit-up

who wear contact lenses or whose eyes are especially sensitive to chlorine may chose to wear goggles. (Some eyeglass wearers choose to have prescription goggles made.)

Many aquatic facilities are equipped with a pace-clock or a wall clock for timing workouts. If these are not available, one can wear a waterproof wristwatch with a second hand.

Kickboards and pull buoys are easily adaptable for water exercises and are usually found at pool-side. If not, they can be purchased at most sporting goods outlets. Swim fins provide added resistance for thigh, calf, and abdominal muscles; their use im-proves cardiovascular capacity and flexibility of feet and ankles. Hand paddles and gloves help increase resistance during arm and shoulder exercises. Safety equipment such as flotation vests or belts is often used in deep water to simulate jogging, regardless of the participants' swimming ability. With the ever increasing popularity of aquatic exercise, many sports equipment manufacturers are now designing products that add buoyancy and/or resistance in the water, thus maximizing the effectiveness of exercising in water.

Anatomy of a workout

A water exercise workout should include the key ele-ments of any workout: a warm-up, the main set, and a cool-down, for a total workout time of 30–45 minutes.

The warm-up is a 5- to 10-minute period during which the aquatic exerciser prepares the muscles and the cardiovascular system for work by slowly loosen-ing and stretching the muscles and elevating the heart rate. This period enables the exerciser to adjust men-tally and physically from a land environment to water.

The main set is the aerobic part of the workout, consisting of 20–30 minutes of continuous movement in the water, which is designed to exercise all areas of the body while accelerating the pulse to its target heart rate (THR). The THR is a percentage of one's maximum heart rate (MHR), which is calculated by subtracting one's age from 220. Depending on one's fitness level, one should exercise strenuously enough to reach 60–80% of the MHR figure, starting at a lower THR and working up gradually. To achieve an aerobic training effect, one should work to progres-sively increase the *frequency, intensity,* and *time* of the workout. The main set is the central part of the workout where this "fit" principle is applied, exercising the upper, middle, lower, and total body.

(Opposite page, above left, and overleaf) Adapted from illustra-tions by Michael Brown in Swim 30 Laps in 30 Days *by Jane Katz: (above right and center) adapted from illustrations by Ann Jasperson in* The W.E.T. Workout *by Jane Katz*

431

Aquatic exercise: take the plunge

The cool-down concludes the workout with approximately five minutes of easy stretches and relaxation exercises to gradually return the body to its preexercise state and resting heart rate.

A sample workout

In the following workout it is suggested that each exercise be done for one minute at a time, regardless of number of repetitions. The arms should be kept under the water for maximum resistance. In between workout segments, one should "shake out" or bob to loosen and relax muscles.

Warm-up (5–10 minutes). Two types of warm-up exercise will prepare the body for the workout.

Water walking/jogging. First walk, then jog forward, backward, sideways, diagonally, in circles, and so forth. Use the deck for support if necessary.

Tricep stretch. Extend left arm over head, palm facing in. Grasp left elbow from the front with right hand, bending the left arm and guiding it to reach behind the head, resting hand at the base of neck. Gently pull on left elbow for additional stretch. Release and reverse arms.

Main set (20–30 minutes). The routine begins with exercises for the upper body.

Push-up. Face the wall of the pool and place hands on the edge so that they are shoulder-width apart and arms are extended forward. Bend elbows outward to bring chest to the wall, then straighten arms back to the starting position. To develop upper-body strength, one increases the intensity of the push-ups: straighten elbows and push body up out of the water.

Stroke punch. Make fists and alternately punch the arms forward underwater, allowing shoulders to follow the full extension of arm. This simulates the arm motions of the crawl stroke.

Arm circle. Extend arms to the side underwater and rotate them forward in circles. Then circle arms backward, alternately pulling under the water and recovering above the water. This simulates the "windmill" backstroke.

Next come exercises for the middle body.

Trunk turn. Place hands on hips. Turn torso from the waist to the right, then back to starting position. Repeat, turning to the left side. For added resistance, extend arms sideways underwater and use the hands as paddles.

Sit-up. Place back against the pool wall with arms stretched out and hands on pool edge to support body in a back float position. Bend the knees and bring them toward the chest. Then extend legs and straighten them.

Next come lower-body exercises.

Rockette leg lift. Place back against the pool wall with arms extended on the pool edge for support. Raise one leg at a time as close as possible to the water's surface, keeping leg straight. A pull buoy or fins

Cool-down

aqua lunge

can be used under the lifted heel for extra resistance.

Leg crossover. Place back against corner of pool with arms extended on deck for support. Keeping back against the wall, lift legs to a 90° angle from body, keeping them straight and together. Separate legs into a V position, then bring them together, crossing at ankles.

The final portion of the main set is devoted to total body exercises.

Aqua jumping jack. Stand with arms at sides, palms touching legs. Extend arms to the side with palms upward, and bring them to the water's surface, simultaneously separating legs by jumping into a V position. Return to the starting position by turning palms downward and bringing arms back to sides, jumping the legs together.

"Rope jump." Simulate holding the handles of a jump rope in each hand at shoulder level with elbows touching waist. As arms circle the rope forward, bend knees and jump to clear the rope.

Cool-down (5 minutes). The following exercises are used to relax the body and allow the pulse to return to a resting rate.

Side hip touch. Stand at arm's distance from and perpendicular to the pool wall. Keep feet together and grasp the edge with right hand. Touch right hip to the wall, then stretch the left hip as far as possible away from the wall. Repeat to left side.

Aqua lunge. Facing the pool wall, grasp the edge with both hands, shoulder width apart. Place feet on the wall in a wide straddle position at approximately hip height. Shift weight to the right side by bending the right knee, and then return to center. Repeat to the left side.

Arm and leg stretch. Grasp the pool edge with right hand. Raise the right leg in as comfortable an extension to the wall as possible. Reach with left arm

432

overhead in an arc toward the right side. Hold the stretch, return to starting position, and reverse.

Beyond fitness

Water exercise not only offers an excellent lifetime fitness activity for the average person but has many special applications. Water exercise helps to achieve goals such as toning specific body parts, conditioning for a number of specific sports, and maintaining fitness throughout pregnancy.

Physicians and sports medicine specialists often prescribe hydrotherapy for arthritis sufferers—routines that emphasize flexibility and range of motion exercises—and as rehabilitation for individuals with specific injuries as well as those recovering from orthopedic surgery, including joint replacements.

Deep-water running attracts a wide range of serious athletes and others who want to maintain fitness. It meets the training needs of marathoners, triathletes, and those who seek variety and a multidisciplinary approach to fitness through cross-training.

Wave of the future

Given its many benefits, water exercise is fast becoming the lifetime fitness activity of choice and moderation for the mainstream population. It is the ideal exercise for individuals, families, and especially the ever growing aging population. The life expectancy of the average American born in 1900 was 47 years; in the 21st century, it is expected to approach 80. Water exercise can help people stay fit into their later years.

At the beginning of the decade, the U.S. Public Health Service established "national health promotion and disease prevention objectives" for the 1990s, set forth in the document *Healthy People 2000*. Among the goals are the reduction of health disparities and the improvement of the quality of life for all Americans by the turn of the century. Because water exercise is a healthful fitness activity for virtually everyone, it can be an important part of this strategy. Professional aquatic and fitness associations are sensitive to this expanding market and are developing programs and guidelines for instructor training and certification, product research, and safety.

Choosing a program

Aquatic exercise programs go by a variety of names. How does one choose among them? The choice should be made on the basis of one's own fitness level and goals, the training of the instructor, the aquatic facility and its amenities, costs, and convenience of location. Types of facilities range from public pools, Y's, recreation and community centers, schools, col-

leges, private health clubs, workplace fitness centers, sports medicine centers and hospitals (for medically supervised physical therapy), and exclusive spas that offer fitness vacation "packages"—a wide range of fitness programs including individually tailored aquatic instruction.

For further information, one can consult the following:

Organizations
American National Red Cross
431 18th Street NW
Washington, DC 20006
(202) 737-8300

Aquatic Exercise Association
P.O. Box 497
Port Washington, WI 53074
(414) 284-3416

Arthritis Foundation
P.O. Box 19000
Atlanta, GA 30326
1-800-283-7800

International Swimming Hall of Fame
1 Hall of Fame Drive
Fort Lauderdale, FL 33316
(305) 462-6536

United States Water Fitness Association
P.O. Box 3601333
9851D Military Trail
Boynton Beach, FL 33436
(407) 732-9908

YMCA of the United States
101 N. Wacker Drive
Chicago, IL 60606
1-800-USA-YMCA

Books
American Red Cross. *Swimming and Aquatics Safety.* Washington, D.C.: The Red Cross, 1981.

Katz, Jane, Ed.D. *Swim 30 Laps in 30 Days.* New York: Putnam Publishing Group, 1991.

Katz, Jane, Ed.D. *The W.E.T. Workout™: Water Exercise Techniques to Help You Tone Up and Slim Down, Aerobically.* New York: Facts on File, 1985.

Lasko, Peggy M., and Knopf, Karl G. *Adapted Exercises for the Disabled Adult.* Dubuque, Iowa: Eddie Bowers, 1988.

YMCA of the USA. *Aquatics for Special Populations.* Champaign, Ill.: Human Kinetics Publishers, 1987.

Children and Medicines

by Stephen J. Ackerman

Nothing is more distressing than the anguish of a sick child. A painful, bewildering ailment can seize young systems suddenly, producing frantic cries for immediate relief. On the spur of the moment, parents may rush to the medicine cabinet in search of that relief. The most important thing that parents should remember when children become ill is that children *are* children—qualitatively different beings, not just proportionally smaller adults. More often than not, however, parents medicate children after infancy as if they were smaller versions of themselves.

In fact, children's bodies differ from adults' in several important ways. Their illnesses may appear and disappear more abruptly than those of adults, often without need for medication. Children's energy production is disproportional to their food intake. Their livers and kidneys function differently in proportion to their size; these organs have not fully matured and cannot detoxify and eliminate drugs as readily as those of an adult. Children's systems may even react differently to stress. Most important, children metabolize drugs differently into their systems. The metabolism of drugs depends on the body's relative amounts of fat and water. The proportion of fat and water and the distribution of fat differ with age—water constitutes about 70% of an infant's body weight and only 55% of an adult's—and absorption of drugs thus varies.

Pediatric drugs: a brief history

The practice of giving medicines to children has come a long way in a relatively short time. Hippocrates (*c.* 460–*c.* 377 BC) recognized the need to dilute medicinal wines to accommodate children, but knowledge of pediatric medicines lagged far behind that of adult remedies. Although the 2nd-century AD Greek physician Soranus of Ephesus, often called the father of obstetrics and gynecology, extended his interest to child care, pediatrics as a discipline did not really take form until the 18th century.

Children's remedies of the distant and not-so-distant past sought to quiet if not cure ailing infants. An ancient Egyptian papyrus recommends a mixture of beer with berries to curb bed-wetting and prescribes poppies strained with wasp excrement to stop a child's crying. Under such labels as Godfrey's Cordial and Mother's Blessing, narcotic concoctions of alcohol, opium, morphine, codeine, and cocaine were marketed right up to the 20th century to "fortify" children into docile well-being. Many patent medicine proprietors boosted their sales by recommending high daily dosages. Since these products came on the market before the enactment of modern food and drug laws, some were never tested for safety and efficacy. In the U.S. one traditional product for reducing fever and relieving colic remained on the market until 1980 and was removed only after a one-teaspoon dose killed a four-month-old infant; Sweet Spirits of Nitre turned out to be a solution of ethyl nitrite in alcohol, far too potent for young systems.

The tragic deaths of scores of children became the catalyst for modern drug regulation in the United States. In 1937 a liquid form of a popular adult "wonder drug" was put on the market, prescribed, among other things, for children's infections. Elixir Sulfanilamide was tested to ensure that it smelled, tasted, and looked good but was never analyzed for toxicity. At the recommended dosages, this diethylene glycol product attacked the kidneys, causing the long, agonizing deaths of over 100 people, mostly children. The public demanded action, and the consequent Federal Food, Drug, and Cosmetic Act of 1938 was enacted, giving the Food and Drug Administration (FDA) authority to evaluate the safety and efficacy of drugs.

Careless dispensing

Special care is required in the administration of medicines to children. Unfortunately, such care seems to be unusual. A 1989 study determined that in any two-week period, almost half of 13 million young people in the U.S. required to take prescription medicines took them incorrectly. This confirmed previous findings. Especially curious is the fact that parents seem to give potent prescription drugs for serious conditions as haphazardly as they do milder over-the-counter (OTC) products. In some cases parents may not understand the pediatrician's instructions or appreciate the importance of giving the child the medication as prescribed—at the correct dosages and intervals and for the proper period of time. (Antibiotics, in particular, must be taken for the exact duration prescribed even if symptoms have disappeared and the infection being treated has apparently cleared.)

Research involving 500 mothers of varying socioeconomic status led a panel of experts to award only "minimal approval" to the treatment decisions they made for their children. The mothers did almost as much harm as good in dispensing medications, too often giving the wrong products in the wrong dosages at the wrong intervals. Some decisions were even deemed hazardous, such as giving laxatives to ward off constipation.

One commonly abused OTC product is aspirin, which is a derivative of salicylic acid. Even children's aspirin should never be used to relieve fevers of unknown origin because of its possible relation to Reye's syndrome. Reye's syndrome is a condition characterized by severe brain and liver damage and can develop in children and teenagers who are recovering from a viral infection, such as chicken pox, flu, or an upper respiratory illness. Pepto-Bismol, a nonaspirin salicylate-containing product, is often taken for nausea, which can be an early symptom of Reye's syndrome; so that the diagnosis of the potentially fatal syndrome will not be delayed, the product now carries a warning that cautions consumers not to give the medicine to children and teenagers who have or have recently had chicken pox or flu.

The overstocked medicine chest

Until adolescence, children are not likely to take medicines on their own. Unfortunately, even well-meaning parents may medicate their children haphazardly at best. And surveys show that they apparently have a number of medications on hand with which to do so. Two-thirds of families store four to eight OTC products for children's complaints. Over 98% of families have analgesics such as children's aspirin, and nearly 75% have cough medicines intended for the child's use. Around 60% keep cold products and skin ointments. Allergy products are in more than 56% of medicine cabinets. Less common but still notable in 20–50% of homes are antirash creams, disinfectant creams, ipecac to induce vomiting in case of accidental poisoning, antinauseants, antidiarrheal products, laxatives, and antihistamines. Except for the ipecac, most of these children's products are used. Furthermore, over 43% of parents keep and dispense vitamins to their children. Stored with this array are an even larger variety of medications meant for adults, which, too often, may be pressed into service—the parents guessing at the proper dosage for a child.

Some of these medications should not be taken by anyone. This is especially true of old prescriptions for an illness long since cured (and which, at any rate, should be taken only by the person for whom they were prescribed). Seemingly inexhaustible large "economy size" bottles of OTC medicines often are useless because their active ingredients have ceased to be effective. In addition, the bathroom medicine cabinet itself may pose a threat if medicines require a "cool, dry place" for storage. A study in 1990 found that carbamazepine, for preventing epileptic seizures, was found to lose one-third of its effectiveness when stored under the hot, humid conditions that are typical of most bathrooms.

Despite these perils, parents seemingly rush to the bathroom medicine chest at their child's first complaint. Too often they select a product inappropriate for the ailment, or they administer the wrong dose, stop it too soon, or continue it too long. On the other hand, sometimes a child resists taking a prescribed medicine so vehemently that parents simply give up, even though it is needed. It must also be remembered that OTC medications do not cure illnesses; they merely provide relief for symptoms. Often indications that an illness is worsening are masked by these drugs.

Fortunately, most OTC products have such a high margin of safety that the seemingly benign practice of giving a child an adult-dosage tablet cut in half usually will not do harm. Still, one cannot be sure. The time-release mechanism in many of today's products may not be evenly distributed through a tablet, so breaking it in half may not reduce its strength. Liquid products must be shaken to ensure thorough mixing of the ingredients. The increasing complexity of medications demands that strict attention be paid to product instructions.

Adverse consequences of medicine misuse include stomach ailments, rashes, and nervous system disorders. Such misuse can be costly. Studies indicate that almost 5% of children taken to hospitals are

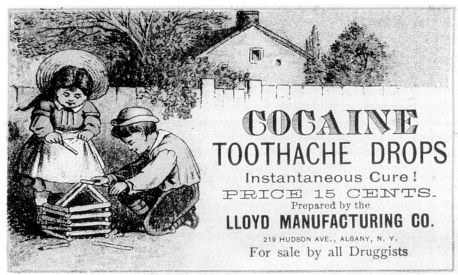

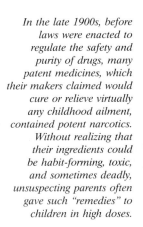

In the late 1900s, before laws were enacted to regulate the safety and purity of drugs, many patent medicines, which their makers claimed would cure or relieve virtually any childhood ailment, contained potent narcotics. Without realizing that their ingredients could be habit-forming, toxic, and sometimes deadly, unsuspecting parents often gave such "remedies" to children in high doses.

there because of a problem with medicines, and these problems are severe or fatal over 44% of the time.

Determining dosages

Indiscriminate administration of medicines by parents is not the only, or necessarily the major, obstacle to effective and safe medication of children. It is often difficult to determine the right dose for a particular child. Even pediatricians vary widely in their means of determining proper dosages. Some consult the indications in the *Physicians' Desk Reference;* others rely on experience. Hospitals can be nonchalant in their medication practices when it comes to children; a 1988 survey of 80 hospitals conducted for the FDA revealed that 70% of the drugs used for children had not been evaluated for pediatric use, and 25% of the products carried on their labeling disclaimers stating that safety and effectiveness had not been established for use in children or had specific restrictions regarding pediatric use.

For proper use of medications, the label instructions must be followed. Adults typically do not read the label when they take medicines themselves, so it is not surprising that they may not do so when giving medicines to their children. The omission is not solely due to carelessness. Instructions may be poorly written and hard to follow or so overly cautious as to invite experimentation. In addition, most medicines give a single dosage for children aged 6 to 12, seemingly ignoring the tremendous growth and physiological changes a child undergoes during this period.

Furthermore, few pediatric medicines have been tested in children. Until recently, new drugs were tested almost exclusively in healthy adult male volunteers, their dosage and applicability to children estimated by inference. Most OTC package instructions

for children are simply based on experience with products already on the market. Recommended dosages for children may, in fact, not be adequate. In 1988 an FDA advisory review panel specifically found that pediatric dosages described in the labeling of oral analgesic-antipyretic drug products (pain and fever-reducing agents) were too low to be fully effective.

Recent initiatives promise more useful guidelines. The FDA is now encouraging testing in children to determine the dosages and effects of new medications and others that are already on the market. Unfortunately, however, there are major obstacles to this initiative. Except in the case of new products for life-threatening illnesses (such as pulmonary surfactants for newborns with respiratory distress syndrome), parents are naturally reluctant to consent to experimentation on their children, and pharmaceutical manufacturers do not want the liability risk.

More advanced is the campaign to develop more precise dosage instructions for pediatric medicines. The basic question in evaluating alternatives is how best to measure the effects of drugs on a child's rapidly growing body. Age, the traditional basis for package instructions, is just one criterion. The advantage of using a child's age to determine dosage is that parents know exactly what it is. The fact that weight and age become less closely related as a child grows complicates matters, however. In particular, the wide variety of children's body types makes age the roughest measure of all.

Weight, height, and body surface area are other means that can be used. The problem with using body surface area, which is probably the most accurate means of determining the best dosage for a given child, is that few parents know how to calculate this figure. Weight and height are cruder standards but can serve as substitutes. Height (or body length for infants) is a good standard for medicines that permeate the system through body water rather than fat, since this avoids the risk of overdosing obese children. Moreover, it is a quick gauge to use in an emergency.

As the FDA found when it surveyed experts on various classes of drugs, there were wide differences in the best means of dosage determination. Lacking much reliable test data, the OTC cough-cold panel stuck with the old divisions of ages 2–6 and 6–12. Conceding the many subtleties of age, weight, drug tolerance, and metabolism, the experts concluded that the simplest standard was most practical for products with such a wide margin of safety. In contrast, the anthelmintics used to treat parasitic worm infestations (*e.g.,* pinworms) are dosed directly according to weight. Patients two years old weighing 25–37 lb (1 lb = about 0.45 kg) take 125-mg tablets or teaspoonfuls. Every additional 22 lb means an additional unit, to a maximum of 1,000 mg for adults weighing 188 lb or more. Analgesics (painkillers like aspirin and acetaminophen) seem to require six age gradations, distinguishing adult from pediatric products, with a standard proposed dosage unit of 325 mg for adult products and 80 mg for children's products.

In 1988 the pharmaceutical industry proposed a way of refining instructions for several classes of OTC products for children under the age of 12 (*see* Table). While ideal standards are still being debated, some manufacturers presently offer alternatives. With directions written in plain English, one children's acetaminophen product comes in two strengths (chil-

Proposed standard age- and weight-based pediatric dosages*		
age†	weight in pounds‡	number of dosing units
4 months to under 1 year	12–17	1
1 to under 2	18–23	1.5
2 to under 4	24–35	2
4 to under 6	36–47	3
6 to under 9	48–59	4
9 to under 11	60–71	5
11 to under 12	72–95	6
12 and over	96 and over	8

*Applicable to various classes of drugs.
†Use "age" column only if child's weight not known.
‡One pound is about 0.45 kg.

Source: *FDA Consumer,* March 1989

dren's and junior) and two forms: "Sprinkle Caps," which are taste-free capsules whose powder is sprinkled into a spoon and mixed with liquid, and suppositories. Two age ranges for children's suppositories and seven age and weight ranges for the children's "Sprinkle Caps" allow parents to calculate precisely how much to give their children.

Accurate measurement

Determining the appropriate dosage for a child is useless if that dosage is not dispensed precisely. The teaspoon so often cited in traditional instructions for liquid medications is a poor instrument for accurate dosing because most people will use a tableware

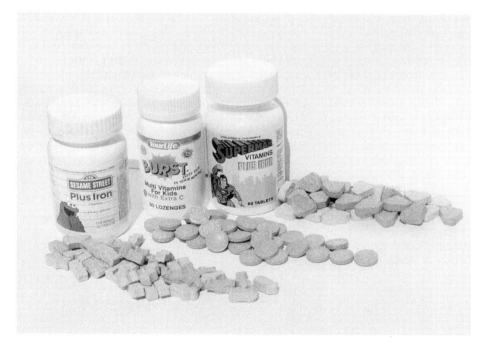

Like other medicines, vitamins should be stored and dispensed to children with care. Many children's vitamin products both look and taste like candy, contributing to the mistaken impression that they are innocuous. In fact, certain vitamins, especially those that are stored in the body's fatty tissues and in the liver, can be toxic, and overdoses are both a common and serious hazard.

"teaspoon," and these can vary widely in actual size. The calibrated plastic dosage cups now capping some cough-cold remedies might be further developed for pediatric uses; for instance, a device might be designed in terms of height, weight, or body surface ranges. Careful design of such devices is critical, however. Early in 1992 the FDA had to warn parents against the inadvertent overdosing of children with nonprescription cold and flu liquids. Marks on some of the plastic cups were found to be simply too obscure for parents to read. The grading of other dose cups was incompatible with the package instructions, and some cups were of inferior quality. The FDA has begun surveying these medicines to ensure that cups are correctly labeled. Two manufacturers voluntarily recalled products and undertook a review of dosage cup design.

The development of pills that are in units one-eighth the size of adult tablets or capsules would allow considerably more accuracy in measurement than there is at present. It has also been suggested that the precision-dosage dispensers now used for corticosteroid nasal sprays could find application for a number of pediatric medications.

Vitamins: not candy!

In addition to prescription and OTC medicines, vitamins must be dispensed to children with special care. Designed to be attractive to youthful consumers, some children's vitamin products come in colorful, flavored shapes of animals or cartoon characters. Parents must make clear that such products—as well as other chewable or sugarcoated medicines for child consumption—are *not* candy. Over 30,000 cases of vitamin overdoses are reported every year. In the last decade overdoses of iron supplements caused more deaths of children than any other medication and nearly a third of all child deaths due to poisoning.

Most children in the U.S. are able to obtain most or all of needed vitamins from eating a variety of common foods. It goes without saying that parents should give their children vitamin supplements only in doses recommended by the pediatrician. There are two categories of vitamins: water-soluble and fat-soluble. The former are excreted in the urine and thus are rapidly depleted and must be replaced daily. Fat-soluble vitamins are stored in the fatty tissue and in the liver; overdoses rather than deficiencies are a more common problem. In 1980 the Food and Nutrition Board of the National Academy of Sciences' National Research Council established recommended daily allowances of individual vitamins for children according to their age (under 6 months, 6–12 months, 1–3 years, 4–6, and 7–10) and weight (13, 20, 29, 44, and 62 lb), distinguishing fat-soluble from water-soluble varieties.

Wise dispensing: tips for parents

Administration of drugs to children requires both tact and skill. Four common errors occur when parents give children medicines prescribed by a doctor: (1) medication is stopped too soon, (2) a full dose is not given, (3) medicine is not taken at all or doses are skipped—often because the child refuses, and (4) an overdose is given.

The National Council on Patient Information and Education (NCPIE) has formulated widely accepted guidelines to make parents more enlightened dispensers of medicine to their children. These include: (1) cooperating and communicating with the pediatrician and pharmacist, supplying them with relevant information about their child and learning from them the purpose and correct dosing for any medications, (2) talking with children to gain their understanding and cooperation in their medical treatment, and (3) communicating with school officials about children's medication needs.

One of the most important things for parents to know is that many minor childhood ailments rapidly cure themselves without any treatment. They should also know that even OTC products are not necessarily mild. If an OTC product is used, it should be given for only a few days, as specified on the insert or packaging. These drugs are safe and effective only if taken according to the directions. If the condition does not respond in a few days, the advice of a physician should be sought.

The complexity of giving medicine to children should not obscure the marvels of the medicines themselves. Indeed, many childhood diseases, such as bacterial meningitis and ear infections, can be virtually eliminated with prompt antibiotic treatment. The severity of others—for example, childhood seizure disorders such as epilepsy—can be vastly reduced with appropriate medication taken on a regular basis. Parents today have unprecedented aids for giving their children the healthiest possible lives, but these must always be used carefully and properly if they are to do good rather than harm.

FOR FURTHER INFORMATION:
National Council on Patient Information and Education
666 11th Street NW, Suite 810
Washington, DC 20001

Travel During Pregnancy
by Bruce D. Shephard, M.D.

Whether to travel during pregnancy is a decision increasingly being faced by mothers-to-be. For many, travel is a necessity—for work or because of a family crisis. Others wish to travel simply for pleasure. For some couples a vacation during pregnancy represents a unique chance to enjoy life together before the rigors of parenthood begin. Regardless of the reason, travel can be a safe option for most pregnant women, provided certain guidelines are followed. Commonsense precautions apply, just as they do to other travelers—for example, allowing sufficient time for rest and avoiding places where infectious diseases are endemic. But pregnancy requires an even wider margin of safety, as well as contingency plans for the possibility of emergencies such as premature labor. The condition of pregnancy, too, subjects a woman to various minor inconveniences and discomforts—factors that should be considered along with the strictly medical ones. Ultimately, a woman's decision about traveling during pregnancy should be made only after she discusses her plans with her doctor.

When to travel

Most authorities consider the second trimester the best time for a pregnant woman to travel. This is the time from the 14th to the 28th week of gestation, counting from the first day of the last menstrual period. During this middle phase of pregnancy, a woman is less likely to be bothered by such pregnancy-related symptoms as nausea, which is usually worst in the first trimester, and fatigue, which often increases significantly during the third.

There are many reasons why the first trimester is not the optimum time for a trip. One is that the risk of certain early pregnancy complications that result in bleeding (*e.g.,* miscarriage, ectopic pregnancy) is greatest during this phase. Another is that travel during the first three months would entail interruption of prenatal care and could interfere with accurate determination of when conception occurred. The first trimester is also the optimum time for any necessary genetic screening and prenatal testing. Early genetic testing is particularly important for women over the age of 35, whose fetuses are at greater risk of chromosomal birth defects (responsible for such conditions as Down and fragile-X syndromes). Prenatal tests for these and other genetic disorders may be performed as early as the 9th to 12th week of pregnancy by the technique known as chorionic villus sampling. Other tests—*e.g.,*

Pap smears and blood tests to screen for various conditions such as hepatitis B, AIDS, toxoplasmosis, and another genetic disorder, Tay-Sachs disease—all should be evaluated within the first trimester. Some of these tests may require further diagnostic evaluation or specific treatment, both of which should be completed as early in pregnancy as possible.

Another aim of timing travel plans to the second trimester is to avoid encountering the many high-risk conditions that typically do not develop until the last two to three months of pregnancy. Such conditions include high blood pressure, premature rupture of the fetal membranes, premature labor, gestational diabetes, fetal growth retardation, and phlebitis (inflammation of the veins, particularly in the legs). Further, in high-risk pregnancies the third trimester is the time of the most intense fetal testing and monitoring and thus is not a good time for the expectant mother to be far from home.

There are some tests that are usually done during the second trimester, and these should be performed prior to travel, if possible. The most important of these is the ultrasound scan, or sonogram, which is typically performed at 16–18 weeks to assess the gestational age and the overall physical development of the fetus. Sonograms performed prior to this time may be less accurate in detecting fetal abnormalities, while sonograms performed after 18–20 weeks are less accurate in assessing gestational age and predicting the due date. Another important test that many women elect to have done during the second trimester is alpha-fetoprotein screening. A blood test that screens for the group of birth defects known as neural tube

439

defects (including anencephaly and spina bifida), it is usually performed during the 17th week counting from the onset of the last menstrual period. Given the need for such tests, an ideal "window" for travel would be between the 20th and 28th weeks. The only tests routinely performed for many patients during this time are a blood test for gestational diabetes, typically done at 26–28 weeks, and an RH antibody screen, performed only on RH-negative women at approximately 27 weeks.

When it is best *not* to travel

Some high-risk conditions warrant avoiding travel altogether. Although there are no absolute guidelines, in general, travel should be avoided if the pregnancy is complicated by high blood pressure, preterm labor, or bleeding problems such as placenta previa (abnormal positioning of the placenta at or near the cervix) or abruptio placentae (premature separation of the placenta from the uterine wall). A woman with a multiple pregnancy, including one who is expecting twins, is at increased risk for preterm labor and should avoid extended travel if at all possible. Also, women with a prior history of any of the above obstetric complications are at somewhat greater risk for recurrence of these conditions; the decision to travel in such cases depends on individual circumstances and should always be discussed with the doctor. A history of preterm labor usually will warrant, at the very least, avoiding extended travel or trips that involve excessive exertion. Patients who have a history of high blood pressure but must travel for business or other reasons may wish to carry a blood pressure cuff with them so that they can monitor any significant changes.

Pregnant women with conditions such as diabetes may need to take extra pains with dietary planning when traveling. Those with conditions such as intrauterine fetal growth retardation, which requires weekly fetal monitoring, should probably avoid travel altogether. Women who are bothered by excessive nausea, fatigue, abdominal cramping, or dizziness should also avoid travel when possible, as it is likely to aggravate such symptoms. Finally, travel during the last month of pregnancy is not a good idea for any woman—even one with an uneventful pregnancy—and should be avoided if at all possible.

Planning ahead

If possible, a pregnant traveler should choose a destination where there are no extremes of temperature. Pregnant women who are not used to the tropics or to frigid temperatures may find either one more difficult to adapt to than they would if not pregnant. If sight-seeing is planned, it is wise to limit the itinerary to a few cities. A centrally located hotel requiring a minimum amount of transportation to and from points of interest is desirable and may be worth the extra cost. For work-related travel, it is helpful to allow extra rest periods between appointments and to end the workday earlier than usual. It may be advantageous to allow an additional day of travel to and from the destination to better recover from jet lag and adapt to changes in time zone, climate, and diet.

In planning a vacation, it is best to avoid long flights or car trips if possible. After arrival in a new city, a woman should try to avoid crowded public transportation; taking cabs instead of buses and subways minimizes the likelihood of exposure to infectious disease and the possibility of bumps, jostling, and other discomforts of mass transit. Certainly, pregnancy is not a time for the "great adventure" vacation: trekking in the Himalayas, white-water rafting, or scuba diving in the South Pacific. (More is said below about physical activity and the risks of exertion.)

Because some medical insurance does not cover pregnancy during travel outside the United States, it is advisable to check in advance with the insurance carrier; for example, a woman's insurance may not cover hospitalization for preterm labor. When taking a trip of more than a few days' duration to a distant destination, the woman should remember to take along a copy of her prenatal record. It is also wise to keep her obstetrician's telephone number on hand, as a long-distance call to him or her may be most helpful if medical facilities are not immediately available. Ideally, the woman will have checked in advance to find out where appropriate medical facilities are located and, if possible, will have the name of an obstetrician at her destination in case an emergency arises. It is advisable that travel plans not interrupt the regular sequencing of prenatal visits, which normally take place every four weeks until approximately 30 weeks, every two weeks until 36 weeks, and weekly thereafter. If necessary, a woman should have her obstetrician contact a colleague at her destination so she can continue regular prenatal visits while she is away.

The following are some items that the well-prepared pregnant traveler will want to take with her when leaving home:
- medical records, especially the prenatal summary and copies of sonograms and other pertinent tests
- phone numbers where her obstetrician can be reached
- name, address, and telephone number of an obstetrician at the destination
- medical insurance card and policy information
- card or bracelet that identifies any medical problem that may require emergency care
- prenatal vitamin supplements
- medications approved by her physician (possibly including an analgesic for aches and pains; a remedy for vaginal yeast infections, especially if traveling to a warm climate; medication for diarrhea if traveling out of the United States)

Proper positioning of a car's seat belt is important for the pregnant woman, whether she is the driver or a passenger. The lap belt should be worn just below the bulge of the abdomen, the shoulder belt between the breasts.

- loose-fitting, layered clothing and low-heeled, comfortable walking shoes
- a small or inflatable pillow for back support in the car, plane, train, etc.

Risks of overexertion

Theoretically, one of the benefits of travel during pregnancy is that it affords the expectant mother an opportunity for added rest and sleep. In reality, travel is likely to involve increased physical exertion. While some exercise is beneficial for a woman's overall physical conditioning, she should take care to avoid strenuous activity for more than short periods of time (15 minutes), refrain from overdoing it in hot, humid climates, and always stop immediately if exercise causes cramping, shortness of breath, palpitations (rapid heartbeat), or dizziness. High-impact aerobics and activities that subject the body to twisting and jarring motions—waterskiing, horseback riding, high-speed downhill snow skiing—should be avoided. Swimming and walking, on the other hand, are safe, comfortable forms of exercise that can enhance the pleasures of travel. Activities such as golf, tennis, shuffleboard, and ballroom dancing also can be safely enjoyed.

As noted above, certain activities are not a good idea for any pregnant woman, even the healthiest. Scuba diving, in particular, is not recommended during pregnancy. One study showed an increase in birth defects among women who dived during their pregnancies. While the effect of increased barometric pressure on the fetus has not been studied extensively, some authorities believe decompression sickness could pose especially serious hazards for the fetus, making scuba diving risky at any depth.

High-altitude travel, likewise, should not be undertaken during pregnancy. Travel to elevations of more than 4,575 m (15,000 ft) usually involves visits to remote areas. Because of inaccessibility and the fetal risk posed by diminished oxygen, such travel is not advised. Brief trips to moderately high altitudes (2,135–2,745 m [7,000–9,000 ft])—characteristic of many ski resorts in the Colorado Rockies, for example—probably are not harmful to the fetus. However, as noted above, snow skiing itself may pose special hazards, especially during the second half of pregnancy, when balance is more difficult to maintain. Also, access to emergency obstetric care may be limited at some ski resorts. Some authorities discourage vacationing at altitudes over 2,135 m because the possible risks have not been clearly established. One study found that babies born prematurely at these altitudes had more complications than preterm infants in lower elevations.

Planes, trains, and automobiles

Automobile travel is both the most common form of travel and the most risky—for pregnant and non-pregnant travelers alike. Accidents—not illness—are the most frequent causes of serious disability during travel. Seat-belt use has been proved to protect the pregnant traveler and her baby. The device should include both shoulder and lap belts if possible. The lap belt should be worn just below the bulge of the abdomen, fitting against the upper thighs. The shoulder strap should be positioned between the breasts. When traveling by car, women should take frequent breaks every few hours to walk and stretch their legs. They may find it helpful to have a small pillow for extra back support.

441

Travel during pregnancy

Long-distance travel by bus has the disadvantages of narrow, hard-to-negotiate aisles, limited lavatory space, and only sporadic rest stops. Train transportation may be a better choice, as it affords greater ease of mobility and more frequent opportunities to move about.

Travel by ship, including cruise ships, may be disadvantageous during pregnancy because of the limited medical facilities and also the potential for motion sickness, especially during unpredictable weather. While medication is available for motion sickness and may pose relatively few fetal risks, it is better to avoid such drugs during pregnancy if possible. Some cruise lines do not accept pregnant women after eight months, so it is advisable to inquire about the company's policies before making the reservation. Some cruise lines require a medical certificate indicating that the woman's physician approves of shipboard travel during her pregnancy. The larger cruise lines have a primary care physician on board but not necessarily one with adequate experience in obstetrics.

Commercial flying is generally safe during pregnancy. Commercial aircraft maintain cabin pressures equivalent to an altitude of 1,525–2,440 m (5,000–8,000 ft). At these altitudes the air is thinner than at sea level, and oxygen pressure is somewhat decreased, which may cause symptoms of fatigue or palpitations if the woman's hemoglobin level is low (less than 8.5 g per deciliter). These may be an indication of the need for supplemental oxygen.

Although the medical effects of air travel in pregnancy have not been extensively studied, the fetus does not appear to be at risk in most healthy pregnant women. Moreover, women should be reassured that magnetometers, the devices used at airport security checkpoints, pose no hazard to their baby or themselves.

The discomforts of air travel in late pregnancy can be minimized by careful planning. The following are some tips for a comfortable, worry-free flight:

• Check ahead of time with the airline about any restrictions that may apply during pregnancy; some airlines require a letter of permission from the doctor after 35 weeks' gestation.

• Avoid flights at altitudes over 2,135–2,745 m in unpressurized aircraft.

• Take advantage of early boarding, which the airlines offer for passengers needing "special assistance."

• Request the nonsmoking section on international flights.

• Consider ordering a special meal—for example, a low-cholesterol or low-salt or a vegetarian meal—when booking the flight. Eat smaller-than-normal amounts to reduce the chance of air sickness.

• If meals are not included on the flight, bring a snack such as fresh fruit or carrot sticks.

• Request an aisle seat, preferably in the front of the cabin, where turbulence is less readily felt. An aisle seat also affords easier access to the lavatory and for walking around during the flight. Seats in the bulkhead usually offer maximum leg room.

• Drink plenty of fluids, as the humidity tends to be low in most commercial aircraft.

• Avoid gas-producing foods before the flight; one effect of altitude is expansion of intestinal gas, which may cause discomfort. Avoid the salty snacks served in flight, as they may predispose to swelling. It is also wise to avoid excess salt for 24 hours before the flight.

• Anticipate jet lag. Allow time for additional rest after the flight.

Foreign travel: general considerations

The health concerns of international travel are much the same for the pregnant woman as for any other tourist. They include potential exposure to infectious disease and limited access to high-quality medical care. The U.S. Centers for Disease Control (CDC) can advise travelers as to whether infections such as measles, malaria, polio, cholera, typhoid fever, and viral hepatitis are endemic in any given country or if there have been recent epidemics. The U.S. embassy or consulate is another source of information about public health matters. (Specific information about vaccinations and malaria prevention during pregnancy is given below.) Travelers in developed countries are much less likely to be exposed to most of these infections, with the important exceptions of measles, mumps, and rubella. The pregnant woman should ascertain her immune status to these diseases prior to travel. Rubella may cause birth defects in the fetuses of women who are susceptible. Likewise, mumps and measles when acquired in pregnancy may lead to fetal complications such as miscarriage.

Various factors affect the risk of contracting an infection during overseas travel, including the length of stay and the locale to be visited. Travel limited primarily to established tourist areas and major cities is less likely to involve exposure to food or water of questionable quality. The risks of motor vehicle accidents are heightened in less developed countries, where road conditions are less than optimal, and emergency medical services may be virtually nonexistent. Further, in the event of an accident, the need for blood transfusions may pose additional risks in countries where blood screening for HIV and other infectious agents is unreliable.

Concerns about cuisine

While all travelers would be well advised to make careful food choices, the pregnant traveler must pay special attention to her diet. A journey that exposes her to a novel cuisine or involves a sudden change of climate is often associated with digestive problems. Further, during pregnancy a woman may be more susceptible than usual to motion sickness. Small, frequent meals or snacks are helpful, particularly on a long car trip or flight. It is a good idea to avoid spicy foods and to sample unfamiliar dishes in small quantities at first.

In some areas of the world, as many as 50% of visitors will experience so-called traveler's diarrhea. In addition to frequent bouts of loose, watery stools, the condition may be manifested by intestinal cramps, bloating, nausea, and fever, depending upon the cause. Usually, traveler's diarrhea occurs as a result of ingestion of fecally contaminated food or water containing various bacteria, viruses, or parasites. However, nonspecific factors including fatigue, jet lag, and high altitude may contribute to the symptoms. The best preventive is avoidance of any potentially contaminated food or water. General precautions include the following:

• Do not eat fresh fruit or vegetables unless they have been cooked or can be peeled.

• Do not eat raw or undercooked meat or seafood.

• Do not drink tap water or beverages containing ice cubes; avoid using dishes or glassware that may have been washed in contaminated water.

It is wise to eat cooked food while it is still hot, as food that has cooled at room temperature may become bacterially contaminated. In areas where hygiene or sanitation is poor, the safest beverages for the pregnant traveler are canned or bottled carbonated drinks, including carbonated bottled water and caffeine-free soft drinks. Pregnant women should not use water-purification tablets containing iodides; these may be hazardous to the fetus.

To prevent infection that could cause diarrhea, many people take prophylactic antibiotics when they travel. This practice is not recommended in pregnancy. Antiperistaltic agents such as diphenoxylate (Lomotil), which help to relieve cramps, do not prevent diarrhea but may have some benefit in its treatment and can be taken if recommended by the woman's physician. Initial treatment for traveler's diarrhea includes fluid replacement through the drinking of canned fruit juice and caffeine-free bottled beverages. Kaopectate may be taken during pregnancy, but it may be effective only in mild cases of diarrhea. A widely available over-the-counter remedy for traveler's diarrhea, bismuth subsalicylate (Pepto-Bismol), should be avoided, however. Some infections—amebic dysentery and giardiasis, for example—respond to antibiotics such as ampicillin and erythromycin, which may be used in pregnancy. If travel to a less developed country during pregnancy cannot be avoided, it is advisable for the woman to discuss with her physician which medications should be taken in the event of traveler's diarrhea. If there is a possibility that the recommended remedies may not be available at the destination, a supply should be obtained beforehand.

Barbara Whitney

Sightseeing in Chicago, a woman in her fifth month of pregnancy stops to snap a picture at the Art Institute. Providing the pregnancy is uncomplicated and the trip does not interrupt prenatal care, travel at this time can be safe and enjoyable.

Malaria prevention

Malaria is a major health problem in Third World countries. The infection in humans is caused by a mosquito-borne parasitic organism. As noted above, the CDC can advise travelers of the risks of malaria in the region they are to visit. Malaria caused by *Plasmodium falciparum* is especially dangerous and may cause a severe form of the disease that is resistant to the usual drug of choice—chloroquine. Chloroquine is usually effective against other forms of malaria, however, and it may be taken during pregnancy if necessary.

Except for urgent reasons, all travelers—pregnant and nonpregnant alike—would be wise to avoid travel to countries where malaria is likely to be present, and especially so where the *P. falciparum* form of the disease is endemic. Complications of malaria, which may include severe anemia and renal failure, are more likely during pregnancy. Malaria also poses a threat to the fetus, causing higher-than-normal rates of miscarriage, stillbirth, fetal growth retardation, and preterm delivery. The pregnant woman who must travel to an area where malaria is endemic should discuss with her physician which antimalarial drug to take as a preventive. The medication should be started prior to departure. In endemic areas all sensible precau-

443

tions should be taken. These include sleeping under mosquito netting, wearing clothing that covers the arms and legs, and using insect repellent.

Immunizations

While no immunizations are needed for most western European countries, some may be required for travel to Third World countries. In the case of pregnant travelers, the possible risks of immunization must be weighed against the risk to both mother and baby of acquiring the disease in question. In most situations it is better to avoid travel to areas where diseases such as measles, polio, typhoid fever, viral hepatitis, malaria, yellow fever, or cholera are present in epidemic or endemic form. (CDC guidelines for vaccination against these infections are discussed individually below.) Most countries do not require visitors to be vaccinated against these diseases, although some require an international certificate of vaccination against cholera or yellow fever (or both) as a condition of entry. International travelers from the U.S. generally will not need additional vaccination, provided they have had the basic immunizations recommended by the Public Health Service. These include vaccination in childhood against diphtheria, tetanus, pertussis, measles, mumps, rubella, and polio.

Ideally it is best to administer any necessary vaccines after the first trimester of pregnancy, during which time fetal organs are developing rapidly. Live-virus vaccines—including vaccines against rubella, measles, and mumps—should be avoided completely during pregnancy owing to theoretical risks to the developing fetus. There is no compelling evidence that immunization during pregnancy using inactivated virus or toxoids (modified toxins) is harmful to the fetus.

Tetanus and diphtheria. Tetanus is found worldwide, and diphtheria is common in certain less developed countries. Most people have been vaccinated against these infections. However, if a tetanus toxoid booster has not been given in the 5–10 years preceding a trip or no primary immunization has been given, it may be advisable for a pregnant woman to be vaccinated before traveling to an area where tetanus is prevalent. A toxoid booster also may be indicated if there is a possibility that childbirth could occur in unsanitary conditions.

Hepatitis A. In the pregnant woman this relatively common traveler's infection may cause preterm labor and maternal liver damage. The virus is transmitted by means of contaminated water or food. When travel to endemic areas cannot be avoided during pregnancy, passive immunization with gamma globulin may be of benefit and should be discussed with the doctor.

Yellow fever. Yellow fever is an epidemic viral disease transmitted by mosquitoes. The infection is associated with significant maternal health risks (although the symptoms are not exacerbated by pregnancy); the

effects on the fetus are unknown. Certain countries, especially in Africa, require yellow fever immunization even for travelers who arrive directly from the U.S. Other countries may require it only for visitors arriving from a country where the disease is active or endemic. Since yellow fever vaccination uses a live virus, it should theoretically be avoided during pregnancy, although there is no proof that the vaccine causes birth defects. However, if travel to endemic areas cannot be avoided during pregnancy, the vaccination may be advisable. Otherwise, a letter of excuse may be necessary in a country that requires proof of immunization.

Cholera. An intestinal infection acquired through ingestion of contaminated water (or occasionally food), cholera is usually self-limited and relieved with fluid replacement. Most countries do not require vaccination. Although the infection causes significant risk to both mother and fetus in the last trimester of pregnancy, the vaccine does not protect 100% and is generally avoided during pregnancy except in situations where there are unusual outbreaks of the disease (as there have been since early 1991 in South and Central America).

Typhoid fever. Vaccination against this infection, also transmitted by contaminated food or water, is not generally recommended during pregnancy because of occasional reports of side effects such as fever that may predispose to preterm labor. Also, the vaccine is ineffective in about 20% of persons immunized.

Polio. Even individuals previously vaccinated against polio may need additional doses of vaccine before traveling to areas where there is an increased risk of exposure to "wild" poliovirus. A polio booster may be necessary for partially vaccinated pregnant women visiting areas where polio is epidemic. While no definite adverse effects have been documented in pregnant women or in developing fetuses, the vaccine should be avoided if possible.

FOR FURTHER INFORMATION:
An excellent publication by the U.S. Public Health Service entitled *Health Information for International Travel* is available for $5 from the Superintendent of Documents, U.S. Government Printing Office, Washington, DC 20402 (stock number 017-023-00189-2).

The International Association for Medical Assistance to Travellers (417 Center Street, Lewiston, NY 14092) can provide lists of English-speaking doctors and member hospitals outside the U.S.

The Centers for Disease Control in Atlanta, Ga., has a 24-hour-a-day automated telephone system that provides reports of disease outbreaks and information about immunizations for specific countries. The number is (404) 332-4559. During business hours operators are also available to answer questions.

Grains of Truth About Bread

by Darlene Dreon, Dr.P.H., M.S., R.D.

Muscovites lined up for bread yesterday, and waited more than an hour as temperatures dropped below freezing.
—*New York Times,* Jan. 14, 1992

Bread sales [in Moscow] have risen to record levels . . . as people substitute bread for meat, cheese, milk, and eggs, all of which have grown too expensive for many consumers.
—*New York Times,* Jan. 22, 1992

In 1992 the world saw just how important bread is in Russian daily life. As fears of famine mounted, the lines to buy this precious staple lengthened.

The staff of life

Bread is a primary staple not only of the Russians—for whom it constitutes as much as 50% of the diet—but of most cultures the world over (except those of the Far East, where rice is the preferred starch). Its origins can be traced back to Neolithic times. References to "the staff of life" abound in both the Old and the New Testaments. During the week-long observation of the Jewish festival of Passover, sometimes called the festival of unleavened bread, Jews eat matza (flat, unleavened bread) to commemorate the flight from Egypt, when the ancient Hebrews did not have time for bread to ferment and rise. In Christianity bread is a symbol of the body of Christ. Loaves with cross-shaped cuts on the top are eaten by many Christians during Lent, and many festivals around Easter time include hot-cross buns, symbolic of the resurrection.

In their book *Consuming Passions: The Anthropology of Eating,* Peter Farb and George Armelagos discuss the rich symbolism bread has in various cultures. The ancient Egyptians were known to make more than 50 kinds of bread, which was central in their offerings to the gods. Moreover, quantities of bread were stocked in Egyptian graves, presumably to provide food for the deceased in the afterlife.

According to Farb and Armelagos, present-day Greek peasants ascribe more symbolism to bread than perhaps any other single society. Greek Christmas breads are baked with walnuts to represent the fruits of the earth, and New Year's breads contain coins for good fortune. A Greek youth going into the Army carries a piece of bread in his knapsack to bring him strength and fortitude. Small pieces of bread are often put under the pillows of Greek children to protect them while they sleep.

The color and texture of bread have by tradition been associated with the economic and social class of those consuming it; fine-textured light-colored bread was once reserved for the wealthy, whereas the peasantry ate coarse, dark loaves. Today the reverse is likely to be true. White bread, made from highly milled flour, is usually cheaper, and it keeps longer because the milling of the grain removes the germ, which becomes rancid quite readily if not refrigerated. The darker, rougher whole grain breads, on the other hand, contain the germ, which is a major source of the nutrients in grain. These breads have a shorter shelf life and are usually more costly than white bread.

Bread in today's diet: how does it slice?

In the United States people do not have to wait in line to buy bread. Indeed, faced with the multitude of bread products in the typical American supermarket, many consumers are perplexed when it comes to deciding which products to buy. How do various breads and bread products compare nutritionally? How important is bread to the total diet? Should those who are on weight-loss diets avoid the bread aisle altogether? The current U.S. dietary guidelines suggest that people eat less fat, saturated fat, cholesterol, salt, and sugar but recommend that they increase their consumption of carbohydrates and fiber. In practical terms these recommendations translate into 6–11 servings per day of foods from the bread, cereal, rice, and pasta group, with a focus on products made from whole grains. Clearly, bread plays a key part in the so-called prudent diet Americans are now being urged to adopt.

Over the past three decades the U.S. consumption of crop products (vegetable oils and fats, fruits and vegetables, grains) has increased considerably. The U.S. Department of Agriculture's crop product index (quantities of those foods eaten per person per year) has risen about 16% since 1965, nearly twice the

Grains of truth about bread

rate of the animal products index. Grain products—a category that includes wheat flour, corn flour and meal, breakfast cereals, rice, and pasta—constitute the largest proportion of these crop products.

Americans now get a greater proportion of their food energy from carbohydrates than ever before, and almost half of the increase in carbohydrate consumption is attributed to an increased use of flour and cereal products. Further, the federal standards for the "enrichment" of white flour—the addition to highly milled flour of several nutrients, including thiamin, riboflavin, niacin, and iron, that are removed in the milling process—were raised in the 1970s and '80s. Because of these higher standards, along with the increase in consumption of flour and cereal products, this category of foods now contributes more significantly than ever before to the nutrient content of the U.S. diet.

Carbohydrates: simple versus complex

As a major source of carbohydrates, bread and other starches play an especially important role in the diets of today's active individuals. During exercise, the body's primary fuel source is glycogen, the stored form of carbohydrate. For athletes a high-carbohydrate diet—one in which at least 65% of calories are derived from carbohydrates—is essential; otherwise, glycogen stores will not be adequately replenished, and athletic performance will decline. Even for nonathletes, however, carbohydrates are a valuable energy source.

Carbohydrates exist in two forms, simple and complex. Simple carbohydrates are the sugars found in fruits, most vegetables, milk, and honey and in plants such as sugarcane and sugar beets, the sources of table sugar. Complex carbohydrates are the starches that are typically found in breads, cereals, rice, potatoes, pasta, and legumes. Both simple and complex carbohydrates supply four calories per gram, although simple carbohydrates are absorbed more readily in the bloodstream and are therefore a short-term, quickly depleted energy source. By comparison, complex carbohydrates (unless highly refined) provide sustained energy over a longer time.

Bread ranks high on the nutritional scorecard when compared with other complex carbohydrates (*see* table below). Whole wheat bread provides more nutritional value *per calorie* than rice, potatoes, pasta, and other starches. Fortified cereals are the only such foods that may rank higher. ("Fortification" is the addition of vitamins and minerals to levels above those that occur naturally in the grain.)

Dieter's demise—or delight?

Breads and related starches, once high on the list of foods forbidden to those on weight-loss diets, are now considered a cornerstone of sensible meal planning. There has, in fact, been a radical reevaluation of the part played by carbohydrate-rich foods in obesity. Several studies in recent years have shown that not only do thin people consume more calories than overweight people, they also derive a higher percentage of their calories from carbohydrates—whereas those who are overweight get more calories from fat. In one such study, for example, this author and her colleagues at the Stanford University School of Medicine examined the relationship between body composition and relative intake of carbohydrate and fat. The subjects were 155 fairly sedentary and moderately obese middle-aged men. The researchers found that the percentage of body fat in these subjects, which ranged from 18 to 40%, correlated positively with their intake of total, saturated, and monounsaturated fatty acids; there was a negative correlation with intake of carbohydrates and plant-derived protein.

Other investigators have demonstrated that people who overeat calories in the form of fat tend to get fatter than people who overconsume an equivalent number of carbohydrate-derived calories. Ethan Sims and colleagues of the University of Vermont College of Medicine overfed research subjects to promote weight gain. They found that an increase in the quantity of fat in the diet above the level required for maintenance of body weight is a more potent stimulator of adipose (fat) tissue accumulation than is a comparable increase in the quantity of dietary carbohydrate.

In fact, it is not bread and starches that widen the waistline but rather the fats that are usually eaten with them. Consider the average slice of bread, having about 70 cal. Given that the daily caloric intake of

---

How bread compares with other complex carbohydrates

	calories	protein (g)	fat (g)	carbohydrate (g)	iron (mg)	sodium (mg)	thiamin (mg)	riboflavin (mg)	niacin (mg)
whole wheat bread, 1 slice	60	3	1	12	1	132	0.06	0.03	0.7
rice, ⅓ cup, cooked, enriched	74	1	0.07	17	1	256	0.07	0.01	0.5
potato, ½ cup, cooked	50	2	0.1	12	0.4	2	0.07	0.03	1
pasta, ½ cup, cooked, enriched	100	3	1	19	0.7	3	0.1	0.07	1
wheat cereal (flakes), 1 cup, fortified	106	3	0.5	24	1.1–3.5	310	0.35	0.42	3.5

Source: U.S. Department of Agriculture

a "typical" American is about 2,500 cal, this slice of bread represents less than 3% of total energy needs. When spread with two teaspoons of butter or margarine, that same slice has about 140 cal—a 100% increase. Further, the number of calories derived from fat has soared. Each teaspoon (four grams) of butter or margarine contains between 30 and 36 cal (fat supplies 9 cal per g), so the 140-cal slice of bread and butter has more than 70 cal—or 50%—from fat.

Carbohydrate-rich foods have the additional advantage to dieters of being filling (probably because of their higher fiber content) yet not highly calorific. Because of the appetite-satisfying nature of bread, mothers typically caution youngsters not to "fill up" on it for fear they will not have room for other fat- and protein-rich foods needed by their growing bodies.

Health- and weight-conscious consumers should also be pleased to learn that by increasing their consumption of bread and related carbohydrates, they can decrease their food costs. Typically, protein-rich foods are more costly than those rich in carbohydrates. Further, the more processed the food product—*i.e.,* the more added fat, salt, and sugar it contains—the more costly it will be as compared with its unprocessed counterpart.

Finally, bread certainly fits into today's guidelines for a prudent diet. For long-term health benefits, the American Heart Association recommends that people eat fewer fats and more carbohydrate-rich foods. The American Cancer Society suggests increasing the amount of fiber in the diet to 25–30 g per day to reduce the risk of certain cancers. (Most Americans eat only about 10–15 g of fiber per day.) Certain diseases appear to be more common in populations that consume a low ratio of carbohydrate to fat in their diet. For example, coronary artery disease, cancers of the colon, breast, and prostate, and diabetes are much more prevalent in the more "westernized" countries than in less developed areas of the world.

Going with the (whole) grain

Not only does it supply an easily digestible form of energy and some protein at a relatively low cost, bread—unless made from highly milled flour—is also a good source of several vitamins and minerals. What are the best breads to buy? Nutrition-conscious consumers will choose either whole grain—*i.e.,* made with whole grains, or seeds, of wheat, rye, millet, and the like—or enriched—*i.e.,* some of the vitamins and minerals removed in milling have been restored. (*See* table, this page.)

All grains must be milled to make them fit for human consumption. It is the extent of the milling, however, that determines the amount of nutrients that are removed. Most of the vitamins, minerals, and protein in the whole grain are in the endosperm and the germ (*see* diagram). Usually in milling, the bran (the fibrous

Whole wheat versus white bread*				
bread	thiamin	riboflavin	niacin	iron
unenriched white	0.40	0.36	5.6	3.2
enriched white	1.1–1.8	0.7–1.6	10–15	8–12.5
whole wheat	1.2	0.56	12.9	10.4

*amounts in milligrams per 1-lb loaf

Sources: U.S. Food and Drug Administration and the U.S. Department of Agriculture

outer coat of the seed) and the nutrient-rich germ are removed, the bran because it is nondigestible and the germ because it can become rancid. In the refining process by which white flour (often referred to on labels as "wheat flour") is made, the outer layer of the endosperm is also removed—along with about 75% of the thiamin and a substantial amount of iron, other B vitamins, and minerals. In addition, white flour has been bleached (freshly milled flour is yellowish in color) with any of a number of oxidizing agents, a process that further destroys vitamin E. As noted above, in the U.S. the federal government sets standards for enrichment of white flour with thiamin, riboflavin, niacin, and iron. This practice was instituted in the 1940s to ensure that no segment of the population suffered from deficiencies of these nutrients.

Whole grain bread not only contains the vitamins and minerals present in the whole grain, it usually has some nutrients that are lacking even in enriched white

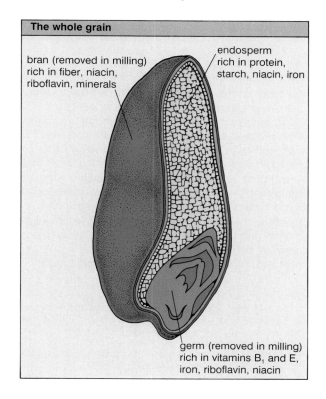

The whole grain

bran (removed in milling) rich in fiber, niacin, riboflavin, minerals

endosperm rich in protein, starch, niacin, iron

germ (removed in milling) rich in vitamins B_1 and E, iron, riboflavin, niacin

Anxious about rising food costs and the threat of shortages, Muscovites stock up on a precious staple at a state-run store in January 1992. The price of bread had recently quadrupled.

bread, as not all of the nutrients that are removed when the flour is refined are replaced by enrichment. These include vitamin B_6, zinc, copper, and chromium.

While most varieties of white bread are made with enriched flour, many bread products are not. Cakes, cookies, pastries, and croissants, for example, are not typically enriched. Some manufacturers improve the nutritional quality of white flour products by adding skim milk powder (increases content of protein, thiamin, riboflavin, and calcium), brewer's yeast (adds iron, thiamin, and niacin), or wheat germ (adds vitamin E, thiamin, niacin, and protein). Others supplement their products with vitamin D or calcium, as grains are not typically rich sources of these nutrients.

Labels: how helpful?

The label on the average loaf of "store-bought" bread often raises as many questions as it answers. What is the difference between the loaf that has a short list of ingredients and one with a long list? And which of the many items listed have no nutrient value? After all, the basic ingredients in bread are nothing more than flour, water, yeast, and salt. Fat and sugar, although not essential in bread making, are sometimes added. Some breads carry a long list of perplexing and unheard-of ingredients, many of which are additives to improve the texture of the product and, more importantly, to extend its shelf life. The following is a typical ingredient list from a loaf of enriched white bread:

wheat flour, water, corn syrup, contains 2% or less of each of the following: yeast, salt, partially hydrogenated soybean oil, soy flour, whey, lactose, dough conditioner (mono- and diglycerides, ethoxylated mono- and diglycerides, calcium and sodium stearoyl lactylates, calcium peroxide), cornstarch, malted barley flour, yeast nutrients (monocalcium phosphate, calcium sulfate, ammonium sulfate), niacin, iron, thiamine mononitrate, riboflavin.

Whey and lactose are, respectively, a protein and a sugar found in milk. The dough conditioners have emulsifying properties. Monocalcium phosphate is an acid that controls the pH of the dough; calcium sulfate is a stabilizing agent; and ammonium sulfate facilitates the growth of yeast. Finally, niacin, iron, thiamine, and riboflavin are the nutrients added to enrich the

Breads compared			
kind of bread	calories	protein (g)	fat (g)
bagel, plain	200	7	2
bran muffin, homemade	112	3	5.1
breadstick (2)	77	2.4	trace
buttermilk biscuit	165	3.5	6.6
cinnamon raisin (1-oz slice)	80	2	1
cornbread (2-in square piece)	130	3	3
cracked wheat (1-oz slice)	66	2.3	trace
croissant	235	5	12
Danish pastry	295	3	20
doughnut, cake (2 oz)	227	3	11
English muffin	140	5	1
hotdog bun	129	3.2	2.2
kaiser roll	156	4.9	1.6
oatmeal (1-oz slice)	60	2	1
Italian/French (1-oz slice)	80	3	trace
pita	165	6	1
pumpernickel (1-oz slice)	70	3	trace
rye (1-oz slice)	70	3	trace
sourdough	70	3	1
tortilla, corn, enriched (1)	67	2.1	1.1
tortilla, wheat (1)	85	2.5	2
white, enriched (1-oz slice)	75	3	1
whole wheat (1-oz slice)	70	3	1
multigrain (1-oz slice)	70	3	1

Sources: *The Wellness Encyclopedia*, the University of California at Berkeley, and the U.S. Department of Agriculture

448

flour. Of course, consumers must also know how to interpret the label. The order in which the ingredients are listed represents—in descending order—their proportions by weight in the product. Thus, on a loaf of whole wheat bread the words *whole wheat flour* will appear first in the list of ingredients. Some products list wheat flour first, followed by whole wheat flour; this means that the bread contains primarily *white* flour.

There are many other terms savvy consumers need to be familiar with when buying bread. To make sure they are getting a nutritious product, consumers who choose white bread should check to see that it is made with enriched flour. In enriched wheat flour the nutrients added are almost equal to the levels present in the grain before milling. If the label says the flour was fortified, the levels of some added nutrients are higher than those found naturally in the whole grain or, in some cases, that nutrients have been added that are not ordinarily found in substantial amounts in the whole grain (such as calcium). Bread labeled "cracked wheat" or "sprouted wheat" usually contains white flour and has no nutritional advantages.

Consumers should be aware that just because a bread is brownish in color, it is not necessarily made from whole grain. Many manufacturers add caramel coloring to white flour to make it appear more like whole grain flour. This is often true of rye, pumpernickel, and black bread, which simply have dark coloring added to make them appear hearty and healthful. In order to be able to advertise their product as high in fiber, some bread makers add wood pulp, a substance with no nutrient value, to refined white flour. Another way to increase fiber content is to add bran to refined white flour; bread made in this way may indeed be higher in fiber than whole wheat bread, but it does not provide the same level of nutrients.

Nutritional content of crackers				
kind of cracker (serving size)	calories	protein (g)	fat (g)	sodium (mg)
Cheese Nip (13)	70	1	9	130
oyster (10)	33	0.7	1	83
graham (2 squares)	60	1	1.5	66
rice cake, unsalted (1)	35	0.4	0.2	0
saltine (6)	68	1	2	183
rye crisp (3)	45	1	1	123
melba toast (4)	75	2	2	204
Wasa crisp bread (2)	136	3	4	245
matza (1)	120	3	0.5	3
wheat thin (6)	50	1	2	109
Triscuit (3)	84	2	4	118
Ritz (3)	50	1	2	109

Source: U.S. Department of Agriculture

For those who are limiting the amount of salt in their diets, there are many breads that are sodium free (*i.e.,* contain less than five milligrams of sodium per serving). Low-sodium bread contains 140 mg or less per serving. In general, if a product is lower in sodium, salt should not be listed as one of the first four ingredients.

Bread that claims to be fat free will have no added ingredient that is a fat or an oil. Low-fat bread will have three grams or less of fat per serving. With the exception of egg bread, which has about 19 mg of cholesterol per slice, the amount of cholesterol in most breads is negligible.

Some people are allergic to gluten, a protein substance found in the endosperm of the wheat and other cereal grains. The presence of gluten in flour helps

Mike Mazzaschi—Stock, Boston

Crusty, golden loaves in many shapes and sizes make an appetizing and aesthetic display in a breadshop window in the Britanny region of France. The French have a great reverence for bread, and it is a custom for them to purchase their baguettes fresh on a daily basis.

make possible the production of leavened (raised) baked goods. Those with gluten allergy should look for products labeled "gluten free."

Most commercially baked bread has preservatives (usually sodium and calcium propionates) added to prevent mold growth. Since mold is usually accompanied by other organisms, it is not a good idea simply to cut off the moldy parts of the loaf and assume that the rest is safe to eat. The term *staleness* applied to bread refers to loss of water and breakdown of the starch structure. Stale bread is not harmful to eat; it simply does not taste as good as fresh bread. Keeping bread both fresh and free of mold can be tricky. If the storage environment is warm and moist—as, for example, bread that is kept in a closed plastic bag—mold growth is hastened. Refrigeration, while the best way to retard mold formation, increases the rate of staling. Freezing both preserves freshness and prevents mold but has the disadvantage of requiring thawing before the bread can be eaten. If bread is going to be used quickly, the old-fashioned bread box is probably the best place to store it.

Making healthy choices: a mealtime guide

As with all foods, consumers must be knowledgeable and must exercise good judgment when choosing what kind of bread and related products to buy and eat. They should know, for example, that a sandwich made on a croissant can have as much as 10 g more fat than the same sandwich made with two pieces of whole wheat bread. Every meal presents its own challenge.

Breakfast. Among the many different options for breakfast are doughnuts, muffins, Danish pastries, English muffins, bagels, and toast made from a variety of breads. Since doughnuts are, by definition, cooked in fat, they are a high-fat option—having anywhere from 14 to 28 g of fat—are usually high in calories, and may have a great deal of sugar, depending on fillings and glazes. Muffins can also be packed with calories and are very high in fat, although there are many recipes for nutritious low-fat, high-fiber muffins. Buttermilk biscuits generally have about 200 cal and may have up to 9 or 10 g of fat, not counting the butter or margarine most people will spread on them; most biscuits also have between 300 and 600 mg of sodium. Better choices for breakfast, then, are bagels (often higher in protein than many breads), English muffins, or toast made from whole grain bread.

Lunch. When choosing bread for a sandwich, people watching their calorie and fat intake will do well to choose hearty, filling whole grain breads. A good alternative is pita bread, especially if made with whole wheat. A sandwich on rye bread or pumpernickel is probably no more or less nutritious than one made with enriched white bread. (Most commercial rye and pumpernickel breads use little or no whole grain flour.) A sandwich on a kaiser roll or hamburger bun is usually roughly comparable nutritionally to one on enriched white bread except when the rolls are made with whole grain. For children's school lunches, parents should look for and select breads and rolls high in protein, vitamins, and minerals; for youngsters who prefer white bread, an enriched product is the best choice.

Many dieters choose a salad as their lunchtime entree. Often this is accompanied by crackers, a food that has traditionally been viewed as low in calories and fat. In fact, many crackers are comparatively high in fat. They may also be loaded with sodium. And like many breads with names such as "hearty wheat" or "nutty wheat," most crackers with these wholesome-sounding names are made from wheat (white) flour rather than whole wheat flour. It is crucial to read the label carefully. Also important to consider is portion size: three Ritz crackers may have only 50 cal and two grams of fat, but how many people eat only three crackers? Six crackers have more calories and as much as four times the fat in a slice of bread or a bread roll. And, of course, many people eat crackers spread with butter, margarine, or cheese.

Dinner. For those who consider the arrival of the bread basket the highlight of a restaurant meal, what are the best choices? Dieters who look longingly at crusty French, Italian, and sourdough breads should know that these contain no more calories or fat per slice than most other breads—depending, of course, on the amount of butter or margarine they slather on top. Two breadsticks have about as many calories and as much fat as a slice of bread. Most dinner rolls are also comparable to a slice of bread in terms of fat, calories, fiber, and nutrients. Exceptions are whole grain rolls—a good choice because they are often high in nutrients. On the other hand, flaky, buttery crescent rolls, because they are made with large amounts of shortening, are high in fat.

What's in a name?

As is true with all foods, consumers purchasing bread should know what they are getting. They should not judge a bread by its name. Many brands have the words *earth, natural, hearty,* or *healthy* in their names, but these products may not be healthier or higher in fiber than enriched white bread, and they may cost a lot more. Only by reading—and *understanding*—the label can consumers make the best choices when it comes to bread or any other food.

Sex Education
in the Age of AIDS
by Wardell Pomeroy, Ph.D.

Children of the 1990s are growing up in a world their parents could not have envisioned, a world in which unprecedented sexual freedom is overshadowed by the specter of AIDS, a deadly disease that has reached epidemic proportions. AIDS, or acquired immune deficiency syndrome, is a viral infection that destroys the body's immune system. Since there is no known cure, the disease must be presumed to be fatal.

Today's sexual climate

Given that AIDS is an ever present risk to sexually active individuals and that 6 out of 10 U.S. teenagers will have had sexual intercourse by the time they leave high school, the task of sex education today is more formidable than ever before. Moreover, parents and educators must now compete with a flood tide of sexual information washing over children of all ages every day and virtually everywhere they turn—in books, magazines, newspapers, television, movies, and even popular music. As a result of this deluge of messages about sex, young people often feel intense pressure to engage in sexual activity. At the same time, they are particularly vulnerable to the distortions spread by these messages because they do not have adequate information and experience to put them into perspective. Urged into earlier and earlier sexual activity through peer pressure and the pervasive influence of popular culture, millions of young people are caught between impatience to experience sexual pleasure and ignorance of its consequences.

As teenagers and those even younger struggle to make their way in a social climate where sexual activity is common—even expected—the need for early and accurate sex education is more acute than ever before. The day is long past when sex education could consist simply of the basic facts about where babies come from—what used to be called "the organ recital." Today's youngsters need to understand the complexities of human sexual behavior and to know how to protect themselves from all the possible consequences of having sex.

Parents as sex educators: reluctant at best

The advent of AIDS did not mark the beginning of parents' difficulties in talking to children about sex. Parents have been dealing with this problem for centuries, and as sex educators they have never scored particularly high marks. A great many are so uncomfortable about discussing sex with their children that they avoid the subject altogether. Others are handicapped by their own ignorance, repeating the misinformation that *their* parents gave them, and they are uncomfortable with the knowledge that their children are far better informed, one way or another, than they were at the same age.

Parental reluctance and ineptitude contribute to and perpetuate the common sexual fears of children. Even in this "enlightened" era, many children still, for example, worry about masturbation, having learned, directly or indirectly, that there is something wrong or dirty about it—as the still-common term *self-abuse* affirms. The onset of menstruation remains a source of anxiety for many girls, and there are boys and girls who have erroneous ideas about how pregnancy occurs and how it can be prevented.

Now that young people must contend with the lures of alcohol and drugs and, in the new sexual climate, the threat of AIDS, it is even more imperative for parents to be able to confront sexual issues squarely and to provide their children with accurate information. And while it is true that schools can do an adequate job of teaching such matters as biology and hygiene, parents perform the more important function of imparting values.

What to say—and when

Sex therapists have known for some time that it is never too early to begin sex education and that, in fact, it begins whether or not parents are conscious that they are giving instruction. Parents are educating their children sexually through ordinary, everyday behavior simply by showing that they love and respect each other—or that they do not.

Talking to very young children about sex involves recognizing that all children are curious about and

451

want to explore their own bodies. For a great many of them, however, sex education begins with a threatening negative: "Take your hands away from there." This sort of approach results in feelings of fear, shame, guilt, and anxiety—and only discourages children from going to their parents with sexual concerns.

When children ask their first questions about sex, parents can take advantage of the opportunity to teach them the proper words for sexual activity. Before they go to school, children should know the names of the body's sexual parts and the correct words for elimination, understand the basic facts about how a baby grows in the mother's body, and be able to identify the anatomic differences between boys and girls. Those children who want to know should be told how babies are made by mothers and fathers.

Communicating with adolescents about sex presents a special challenge. Not only are teenagers at a normally rebellious stage of life, today's teens are living in an era of unprecedented sexual freedom. Parents need to take seriously the perennial cry, "You're not listening to me!" They need to listen with an open mind. They can also make clear that their willingness to discuss certain behaviors does not mean that they approve of or condone them. Openness need not be confused with permissiveness. If parents show genuine understanding of adolescents' feelings and desires, they may be able to impress upon their teenage children that certain risks, especially sexual ones, are not worth taking.

452

In sum, sex education should begin—and *does* begin, whether desired or not—before children are old enough to go to school and should continue throughout adolescence. Children want to know—and should be taught—first about their own bodies, then about the differences between male and female bodies, and finally about the uses and abuses of their own sexuality.

"Safer sex"

Since so many teenagers are involved in sexual activity and are having sexual intercourse, of primary importance is the question, When is sex "safe," and when is it not? The fact is that sex is never "safe" in the sense that prevention of pregnancy and disease can be absolutely guaranteed. "Safer sex" is perhaps a more accurate way to put it and is the preferred terminology in this age of AIDS. Certainly it can be said that intercourse without protection is the most "unsafe" kind of sex possible—and, unfortunately, this is much too often the kind of sex engaged in by adolescents. Condoms offer the most reliable means of protection, and sexually active young people should have access to them and know how to purchase and use them.

When buying condoms, teens need to know which ones to choose. Condoms made of natural materials may prevent pregnancy but do not provide adequate protection against sexually transmitted diseases (STDs). Only latex (rubber) condoms will significantly reduce the risk of transmission of the virus that causes AIDS and the organisms that cause other STDs.

Making condoms available to teenagers is only a first step, however. They must also understand how to use them properly. Explicit, easy-to-follow instructions are included in the packaging by manufacturers. For maximum safety it is crucial that the user follow these instructions; failure to do so may result in loss of protection.

Of course, a fundamental rule is that individuals should never have sex when their judgment is impaired by alcohol or other drugs. Even couples who know perfectly well how a condom is used can make a mistake if they are intoxicated.

AIDS: know the facts

Sex education today must inform children accurately about the risks and perils of AIDS. They should know that AIDS is a worldwide disease that has so far resisted any kind of cure. There is still a great deal to be learned about it. Some researchers believe that being infected with the human immunodeficiency virus (HIV) is not in itself enough to cause AIDS and that other factors, yet unknown, are necessary. Despite many years of study, scientists do not yet know what factors govern the progression of the disease. Also still unknown is the latency period—the amount of time between infection and the onset of symptoms. A further uncertainty: no one knows how many of those who are infected with HIV will eventually develop AIDS—estimates range from 50 to 90%. However, those who are infected will probably be capable of transmitting the virus to others as long as they live.

HIV is acquired by very intimate physical contact and by the exchange of bodily fluids. The virus has been found in blood, semen, vaginal secretions, mother's milk, saliva, urine, feces—even tears. However, it is generally agreed that transmission takes place only with an exchange of blood, semen, or vaginal secretions. Some researchers believe that there are actually factors in saliva that may kill HIV.

The virus can be acquired in various ways—via blood transfusions, through the sharing of unsterilized needles in intravenous (IV) drug use, and by infected blood from an open wound coming into contact with an abrasion or cut in the skin of an uninfected person. Most commonly, however, transmission occurs during intimate sexual contact, when several bodily fluids can pass between partners. This passage can occur through oral, vaginal, or anal intercourse. Whether the virus can be transmitted through deep kissing alone is not certain, but some experts believe it is possible, particularly if one individual, for example, has bleeding gums and the other is infected with HIV.

While it is crucial to alert children about the very real danger of AIDS, such education should not result in overanxiety. It is essential to point out to young people that the disease is not transmitted easily—and especially not through casual contact. People do not "catch" AIDS the way they catch colds or flu. The virus cannot travel through the air as do the agents that cause respiratory disease. Nor is it transmitted by a handshake with someone who is infected or even by hugging or "dry" kissing. Especially important, children should know that they will not get AIDS by sharing a classroom with someone who has the disease or living in the same household with an infected person.

Sex education should always emphasize that two kinds of behavior place a person at risk: sexual intercourse and the sharing of needles by IV drug users. Safer sex does not have to mean no sex, but it does mean that to ensure safety and the protection of life, one should always assume that a potential sexual partner *may* be carrying the virus. This means avoiding risky behavior before intercourse and taking appropriate precautions if intercourse occurs. Condoms are the best preventive measure, but anything that prevents the exchange of fluids must be regarded as the front line of defense. The use of spermicides in addition to condoms will make sexual contact even safer.

If they are sexually active, both boys and girls should carry condoms lubricated with the spermicide nonoxynol-9 and know their correct use. They should remember that infection can pass from male to female and vice versa but that the use of condoms will afford protection to both sexes.

AIDS: not the only risk

AIDS has so overshadowed all the other STDs that it is easy to forget about them. For centuries before AIDS, syphilis and gonorrhea were the most common such diseases, and they continue to be prevalent, although under control.

The symptoms of gonorrhea are similar for both sexes, but in girls the disease often is more difficult to detect. Boys notice burning and discomfort when they urinate, beginning 2 to 15 days after they become

Drawing by Weber; © 1991 The New Yorker Magazine, Inc.

"We teach them that the world can be an unpredictable, dangerous, and sometimes frightening place, while being careful not to spoil their lovely innocence. It's tricky."

infected. Later, pus begins to drip from the penis; the discharge has an unpleasant odor. For girls the problem begins with a painful infection in the lining of the urethra, also resulting in painful urination and the formation of pus—symptoms they may tend to dismiss as no more than a routine vaginal infection. Girls may also notice more pain during their menstrual periods or frequent cramps in the lower abdomen. Once diagnosed, uncomplicated gonorrhea can usually be cured by a single injection of penicillin. Other antibiotic regimens are also effective.

Syphilis is still a serious threat, although it is far from being the worldwide scourge of past centuries. The syphilis bacterium invades the body through any mucous membrane. It often goes undiagnosed because the first symptom is a sore—most often on the genitals—that is not painful. After the sore comes a rash, which may appear on any part of the body but lasts only a short time and also may go unnoticed. If the disease is not treated at this point, the bacterium keeps on working, silently, and no visible signs of the disease may occur for months or even years. Eventually the disease recurs, and the attack is much more virulent and is capable of doing serious, even fatal, damage to bodily organs. Death from syphilis is rare these days, as a single high-dose penicillin treatment is enough to effect a cure if the infection is diagnosed and treated at a sufficiently early stage.

Far more prevalent now than either syphilis or gonorrhea is chlamydia, a disease caused by a microscopic parasite. Chlamydia organisms are capable of causing several diseases in the human body, the most common sexually transmitted form being known as

Measuring only about 100 nanometers in diameter (a nanometer is one-billionth of a meter), HIV, the virus that causes AIDS, is 30 times smaller than the head of a human sperm. Natural membrane condoms have microscopic pores that prevent the passage of sperm—and are therefore effective in birth control—but do not stop transmission of HIV and many other STD-causing organisms. Only latex condoms can effectively reduce the risk of AIDS.

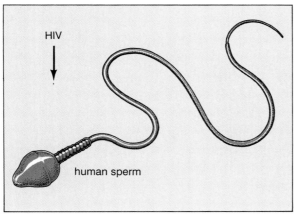

nongonococcal urethritis, or simply NGU. Chlamydial infections are now the most prevalent STDs in the U.S.—more than two million people become infected each year. The severity of these infections was not recognized until it was discovered that, if untreated, they can cause lifelong sterility in women. The disease is difficult to diagnose; girls often experience no symptoms and so become carriers without knowing it. Symptoms that may occur are painful urination and a watery, mucuslike discharge. The disease responds to antibiotics, and those who suspect that they may be infected should see a doctor at once if they notice genital pain or discharge.

Another common sexually transmitted disease is genital infection with herpes simplex type 2, a form of the virus that causes cold sores. Transmitted by sexual contact, the virus causes red, blisterlike sores on the genitals and can be extremely painful for both boys and girls. While herpes infection is neither life-threatening nor damaging to the reproductive organs, the episode is an ordeal while it lasts. Further, once acquired, the infection may recur periodically. Medication is available to ease symptoms and speed healing, but it does not eliminate the virus from the body.

Preventing teen pregnancy

Teenage pregnancy is a serious—and growing—social problem. Levels of sexual activity appear to increase with every year of age—*i.e.,* 17-year-olds are more active than 16-year-olds—and sexual activity is beginning at progressively younger ages. As a result of these trends, more than a million U.S. teenagers now become pregnant every year—that is, one in every nine girls in the 15-to-19-year-old age group. Among those who are sexually active, one in five will become pregnant. Moreover, 8 of every 10 teenage pregnancies are unintended.

What these figures mean in terms of youngsters' shattered lives is staggering, not to mention the cost to taxpayers and the dubious futures of unwanted children. Approximately half of all teenage pregnancies result in live births, and a great majority of teenage mothers keep their babies. Thus, at a very young age these girls place themselves at a socioeconomic disadvantage that, for many, persists throughout their lives. Public funds pay for at least half of all teenage births. In 1989 the U.S. government spent more than $21 billion for social, health, and welfare services for teenage mothers and their offspring.

Many teen pregnancies could be prevented by sex education that would dispel the myths and misconceptions that so many girls have about sex and pregnancy. Girls need to know that they can get pregnant even during menstrual bleeding. A girl can also become pregnant even though she has intercourse standing up, fails to have an orgasm, or urinates immediately after intercourse. Many teenage

Ira Wyman

Because she is enrolled in a special program for adolescent parents, this teenager will probably finish high school and thus may secure a more hopeful future for herself and her baby. Most teen mothers are not so fortunate.

girls mistakenly believe that they can avoid pregnancy by douching afterward—with anything from vinegar to soft drinks—just as they think that intercourse is safe if the boy pulls his penis out of the vagina before he climaxes or the girls jumps up and down afterward. Some believe—also erroneously—that they cannot get pregnant before their first period or if they are under age 12. Some think that they will not get pregnant simply because they are "too young."

Goals of today's sex education

Parents (and teachers, too) must do their best to help adolescents understand that nothing is worth the risk of acquiring AIDS, a disease that not only is fatal but also causes prolonged suffering. Keeping this harsh reality in mind, young people may be able to resist being talked into having sex. They should be aware

that the choice is their own. They must remember, too, that their sexual partners cannot be depended on to provide protection or exercise good judgment. Fostering a strong sense of personal responsibility is an important element of successful sex education. Youngsters who are ready for sexual intercourse—and who will have it with or without parental approval—can be helped through sex education to understand, among other things, that sexual activity can be pleasurable without penile penetration of the vagina and that the risks of pregnancy and all STDs can be minimized by "safer sex" practices.

Medical scientists may one day solve the puzzle of AIDS; they may find a cure for the disease or a vaccine that can prevent it. For now, it is hoped that through enlightened sex education young people—on whom the future depends—will be spared the tragedy of this devastating disease.

FOR FURTHER INFORMATION

Books:

Calderone, Mary S., and Johnson, Eric W. *The Family Book About Sexuality.* New York: Harper & Row, 1990.

Planned Parenthood Federation of America, Inc. *How to Talk with Your Child About Sexuality.* New York: Doubleday, 1986. Available from Planned Parenthood, 810 Seventh Avenue, New York, NY 10019.

Pomeroy, Wardell B. *Girls and Sex* and *Boys and Sex,* 3rd rev. ed. New York: Delacorte Press, 1991.

Videos (available for purchase or rental):

"A Conversation with Magic" (Nickelodeon), in which basketball star "Magic" Johnson answers children's questions about AIDS and talks about the problems of people who are HIV positive.

"Growing Up in the Age of AIDS" (MPI), which features newsman Peter Jennings and a panel of physicians, teachers, youngsters, and parents.

"What Kids Want to Know About Sex and Growing Up" (Pacific Arts), a program shown nationally on PBS, in which educators frankly answer children's questions.

Toll-free AIDS hot line (24 hours a day):

1-800-342-AIDS (English)
1-800-344-SIDA (Spanish)
1-800-AIDS-TTY (deaf access)

Rash Reactions: Contact Dermatitis
by Robert M. Adams, M.D.

"I have had this rash on my fingers for weeks, and I have tried everything," a distraught middle-aged woman explained to her doctor. "In fact, I think some of the stuff I put on it made it worse," she elaborated.

A familiar story, and one that dermatologists hear often. After extensive questioning the physician learned that his patient was an avid gardener and that her rash usually disappeared when she remained away from her plants for any length of time. Two months before the onset of the rash, she had planted a row of Chinese primrose along the front walkway of her home, and almost daily she pinched off a few dead leaves with her fingers. The physician asked her to bring in a leaf of the primrose and also, if possible, to obtain the botanical name of the plant. He then placed a tiny piece of the leaf on her back and covered it with nonirritating tape for 48 hours; this produced a rash with the same appearance as that on her hands, confirming the doctor's suspicion that the primrose was the culprit. The plant was found to be of the family *Primula obconica,* a well-recognized cause of allergic contact dermatitis. To make matters worse, the patient had applied rubbing alcohol to the rash in the mistaken belief that it would "cleanse" the area.

Many patients with a diagnosis of contact dermatitis are surprised when they find out the cause of their skin problem. This is especially true of the allergic variety; patients often think they have no allergies—until they develop a chronic and difficult-to-clear skin irritation that interferes significantly with their daily activities.

What is contact dermatitis? Quite simply, it is a rash caused by contact with something in the environment. That "something" can be almost anything—water (if very cold or hot), soaps, detergents, cosmetics, dyes, fabric finishes, rubber, adhesives, metals, a wide variety of industrial chemicals, and several poisonous and nonpoisonous plants. Studies show that patients with contact dermatitis account for nearly 10% of dermatologists' practices, 10% or more of all patients admitted to hospitals, and nearly half of all cases of occupational illness (excluding injuries).

Irritant dermatitis

Irritant dermatitis, the most prevalent form of contact dermatitis, is a nonallergic, inflammatory skin reaction caused by direct exposure to an irritating substance. The hands and forearms are most commonly affected, but any area of the body that is in direct contact with the provocative substance is vulnerable. The ap-

pearance of the skin following contact with an irritant ranges from faint redness, accompanied by mild sensations of burning and itching (as in "housewives' eczema"), to marked redness and swelling with blistering of the skin (resembling a burn).

The most serious form of irritant contact dermatitis develops almost immediately following a single contact with a potent irritant, particularly strong acids or caustics—lye, for instance—which eat through the skin. The dermatitis is very similar to a thermal burn. The majority of cases of irritant contact dermatitis, however, are milder, often requiring several weeks of repeated contact with the irritating substance for a significant rash to be produced. Alkaline substances (*e.g.,* soaps, detergents) have a greater tendency to cause this condition than do acidic ones. Soaps and detergents dissolve natural oils on the skin that serve to protect it. Other frequent irritants are solvents, which, by dissolving the microscopic amounts of fatty material between the skin's cells, readily permit other irritating substances to enter the deeper layers of skin.

Generally many factors work in concert to produce skin irritation. These include the chemical nature of the irritant itself—its pH (degree of acidity or alkalinity), its solubility, and whether it has a detergent action; the physical state of the substance (gases and volatile liquids tend to be more irritating than solids or semisolids); and the concentration of the irritant as well as the total amount that contacts the skin.

Certain areas of the body are more sensitive than others, especially the eyelids and face. The scalp and other hairy areas tend to be rather resistant, as are the palms of the hands and the soles of the feet. The neck, the collar and belt areas, and the insides of the elbows are especially susceptible to irritant substances found in dust. Fair-skinned persons, especially those with abnormally dry skin, are more likely to develop irritant dermatitis than persons with a greater degree of pigmentation.

Lacerations on the skin, even tiny ones, make a person highly susceptible to irritant contact dermatitis. Friction and sweating increase the potential for chemicals and other substances to cause irritation; perspiration dissolves substances present on the surface of the skin, and the irritation becomes much greater than when the skin is dry. Occlusion of the skin with gloves and other articles of clothing increases the irritancy of many substances by trapping and focusing them on the involved area. The presence of another skin disease or even the past history of one—particularly atopic dermatitis or ichthyosis (extremely dry skin with "fish scales")—is a common and important aggravating factor in irritant contact dermatitis.

Environmental factors at the time of contact contribute to the degree of irritation. Heat and high humidity cause heat rash, while cold and very low relative humidity promote dryness, leading to chapped skin. These conditions set the stage for a reaction to a contact irritant or can exacerbate an existing dermatitis.

The skin of infants and young children is more sensitive than that of adults and readily becomes irritated by contact with many different things in the environment. Diaper dermatitis is a condition that is characterized by the accumulation of alkaline urine and feces; secondary bacterial or fungal infection may be present as well. Young children frequently exhibit a beefy red dermatitis around the mouth from contact with irritating foods and certain objects such as rubber pacifiers and teething rings. Bubble bath, rough fabrics, especially wool, and certain rough-textured toys should be considered as sources of dermatitis in children. Common household products that all too frequently cause severe dermatitis and chemical burns in children include drain cleaners, bleaching agents, disinfectants, insecticides, solvents, detergents, and waxes.

Symptoms and course. The earliest change in the skin that occurs from contact with mild irritants is an area of redness limited to the area of contact. As the irritation persists, the redness gradually spreads and the skin begins to swell; tiny raised bumps or even blisters that are distributed throughout the reddened area will often appear. These changes are accompanied by tenderness and itching. After a few days, crusts and scales begin to form over the surface. If the contact with the irritant and activities that may aggravate the irritation cease at this time, the skin usually returns to normal within two to three weeks.

If, however, contact with the original irritant continues, and contact with other environmental irritants takes place, the dermatitis can become chronic. The skin fails to heal and instead begins to thicken and become quite scaly; often painful fissures develop,

which may follow even minor jars or injuries that occur during the course of daily activities. These fissures are exquisitely tender, often bleed, and are among the most uncomfortable symptoms of this chronic type of contact dermatitis. After a variable period of time, increased pigmentation of the affected area may develop, especially in darker-skinned persons.

Allergic contact dermatitis

This type of contact dermatitis is an acquired sensitivity to a specific agent that develops after one or many exposures. Allergic contact dermatitis, although less common than irritant dermatitis, can be considerably more disruptive to a person's life. When the offending irritant is identified and the contributing factors are controlled or removed, an individual with irritant dermatitis can usually resume normal daily activities without much difficulty. A person who is allergic to a substance, however, is permanently sensitive to that substance and must avoid even very minor contact in order to prevent a recurrence. This may pose considerable difficulty if the allergen is frequently encountered in the environment, especially on the job.

Individuals of any age may develop allergic contact dermatitis. Although this condition in infants and young children is unusual, the occasional case may be overlooked because patch testing is not commonly done in this age group. Poison ivy or oak dermatitis, nickel dermatitis from ear piercing, shoe dermatitis from chemicals in rubber, and dermatitis from ingredients of creams and lotions and certain medications (*e.g.,* thimerosal [Merthiolate]) account for most cases of allergic skin rashes in children.

Probably the most common source of allergic contact dermatitis in the U.S. is poison ivy. The allergen is a simple chemical possessing great potency, found in virtually all parts of the plants. Cross-sensitization to other members of this plant family may occur, so allergic people can react not only to poison ivy but also to poison sumac and oak, the oil in cashew nutshells, the peel and leaves of mango fruit, and the fruit of the gingko tree. A few of the many other plants that can be responsible for allergic contact dermatitis are the Chinese primrose, chrysanthemums, oleanders, narcissus, and tulip bulbs.

Other common examples of contact allergens are nickel (in jewelry—especially earrings—buttons, and tools); cured latex, from the milky sap of the rubber tree *Hevea brasiliensis,* which is used in gloves, balloons, condoms, rubber bands, elastic adhesives, and other products; uncured plastics (epoxy and acrylic resins, for example); and preservatives (especially those in cosmetics, certain topical medications, and many industrial formulations, such as cutting fluids).

Whereas any person can develop irritant dermatitis if the conditions are favorable, allergic contact dermatitis develops in far fewer individuals and is

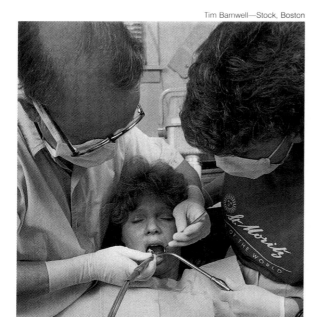

Latex rubber gloves are a frequent cause of allergic contact dermatitis and contact urticaria—a hivelike skin reaction— in health care workers. Symptoms develop almost immediately upon exposure to the rubber. Most workers in the medical and dental professions can safely wear polyvinyl gloves.

dependent upon the allergen. The allergen present in poison ivy is so potent that 50–80% of exposed individuals will develop sensitivity. Allergy to chemicals in rubber, on the other hand, is less common, especially considering that most people are exposed daily to a variety of rubber-containing materials. Of the more than 80,000 individual chemicals widely used in industry and largely present in the environment, approximately 2,000 have been documented as causes of allergic contact dermatitis. Among the many metals people encounter in their daily lives, only nickel, cobalt, chromium (hexavalent), and mercury are common sensitizers, while gold, palladium, and platinum rarely sensitize, and most other metals are probably not capable of causing allergic sensitization.

Symptoms and course. The sensitization in allergic contact dermatitis is highly specific; that is, the allergy that develops does so only to a certain chemical or chemical configuration. The dermatitis is characteristically delayed—appearing 24 to 48 hours after contact with the allergen—but then the onset of redness, blistering, and considerable itching is usually quite sudden. The rash then may spread to other body areas.

Once the dermatitis appears, if there is no further contact with the allergen and if aggravating factors are avoided, the rash should subside within 7 to 10 days. In practice, however, because frequently the offending substance is impossible to avoid (or, more commonly,

the person is not aware of the cause of the dermatitis), the rash persists or recurs repeatedly, interfering with the person's everyday activities. In children bacterial infection often develops secondarily, from rubbing or scratching. In the elderly an allergic contact dermatitis may be very slow to disappear, and the affected skin readily becomes thickened and pigmented from continued scratching and rubbing.

Photoallergic and phototoxic contact dermatitis

There are a number of chemicals that will produce dermatitis upon exposure to light—especially bright sunlight. The reactions are termed phototoxic and photoallergic—the latter requiring an acquired allergic sensitivity as well as exposure to certain wavelengths of light for the rash to be triggered. Coal tars, chemicals called furocoumarins found in certain plants (*e.g.,* parsley and figs), sunscreens, and some topical medications are among the substances that cause phototoxic reactions. Photoallergic reactions most often result from contact with soaps, drugs, fragrances, sunscreens, and the juices of numerous plants. Photoallergic and phototoxic reactions cause a dermatitis that is itchy, blisters, and affects body areas that are commonly exposed to sunlight—the face, ears, neck, tops of the hands, and forearms.

Contact urticaria

Contact urticaria is a hivelike reaction that occurs almost immediately following contact with a provocative substance and develops rapidly, with redness, itching, and swelling of the skin occurring within a few minutes following the contact. Many plants and foods can cause this condition—some of which have been known for centuries (nettles of various types, for example).

Latex rubber products, especially gloves, have frequently been associated with these hivelike reactions. The allergen is a basic chemical complex found in

Nickel is one of a handful of metals that are common allergic sensitizers. Nickel dermatitis is most often seen in earlobes from ear piercing or nickel earring posts; redness, blistering, and severe itching develop within 24 to 48 hours of exposure.

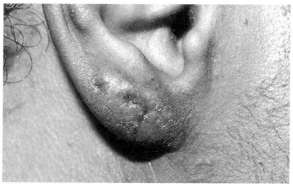

the natural latex itself, or it can be one of a number of rubber additives or the powder used in these products. For most persons the reaction is temporary and mild, but in highly sensitive persons contact with any latex article can be life-threatening, resulting in the sudden appearance of hives over widespread areas of the body, difficulty in breathing, wheezing, loss of consciousness, and even death. In the last decade many persons working in the medical and dental professions who are at risk for exposure to the AIDS virus have been wearing latex gloves as protection during most of their patient contact. Increasing numbers of these workers have developed either allergic contact dermatitis or contact urticaria to the latex or a component of the latex. Most workers who are allergically sensitive to latex can wear polyvinyl gloves safely. Several manufacturers are now making such nonlatex gloves, both sterile and unsterile, for use by those in the medical and dental professions.

Such a reaction can occur in patients, too, during dental procedures—from materials such as a rubber dam placed in the mouth that presses on the insides of the cheeks, from elastic adhesives, or from the dentist's or dental assistant's rubber gloves. Rubber instruments used during various types of medical exams and surgical procedures—catheters, ileostomy bags, tips of enema devices, etc.—are other potential causes of severe contact urticaria in patients.

Rubber condoms may also cause these reactions. Moreover, the incidence of such reactions may be increasing; because condoms are effective barriers against AIDS and other sexually transmitted diseases, they are in wider use today than ever before.

Medical evaluation

A thorough medical history should bring out not only the specifics concerning the current dermatitis but also the patient's previous illnesses and surgical procedures, topical medications used (including those purchased over the counter), skin contactants of all types (cosmetics, soaps, detergents, etc.), and even the medications and cosmetics used by a spouse or others living in the same household. The nature of the work the patient does and the specific chemicals contacted on the job are very important pieces of information, as are substances contacted during leisure activities.

When taking the history, the doctor will seek to learn whether there is a present or past history of atopy, such as repeated episodes of asthma, hay fever, and a characteristic type of a dry, itching dermatitis involving the bends of the elbows, knees, neck, and face. Atopic dermatitis is especially common during early childhood. This condition is inherited and is present in some form in up to 15% of the population. Persons with this inheritance may be free of dermatitis for many years but then often develop recurrent der-

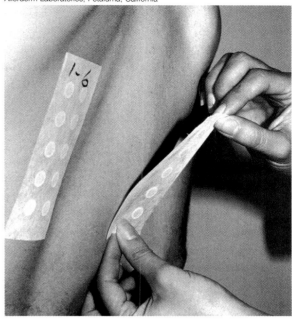

Patch testing involves the application of small amounts of allergens to the back, which are covered and left in place for 24 hours (sometimes longer) and then checked for an allergic reaction—redness and swelling at the site of the patch. In most cases the patch test is the only reliable means of determining the exact cause of allergic contact dermatitis.

matitis when they are later employed in occupations where they are in contact with numerous irritants—especially wet work (hairdressing and other jobs in cosmetology, medical and dental work, cooking and other restaurant jobs, etc.). The dermatitis then may seriously interfere with their ability to do the work.

Finding the specific cause of contact dermatitis may not be easy because there are so many possibilities to consider. For example, among the cosmetics that frequently cause allergic contact dermatitis are permanent-type hair dyes, permanent wave solutions, nail polishes and artificial nails, perfumes and fragrances, body lotions and face creams, eye makeup, lipstick, after-shave lotions, acne medications, depilatories, sunscreens, and deodorants and antiperspirants. If clothing is suspected as the culprit, the reaction may be to the formaldehyde-based finish in a fabric or to a dye. Also, various materials used in shoes—dyes, rubber compounds, and leather-tanning products—can cause a severe dermatitis on the feet or hands (from touching the shoes).

Once the source of the dermatitis has been discovered, physicians often report these cases in the medical literature. In this way, other physicians become alert to potential causes of contact dermatitis, and manufacturers can utilize the information to reformulate products.

Patch testing

When the contact dermatitis is suspected to be of the allergic variety, the goal is to find the specific agent or agents responsible. To accomplish this, dermatologists rely on patch testing, a method that has been used for nearly a century and is one of the most direct forms of diagnostic testing in all of medicine—the procedure involves the same substances presumed to be responsible for the condition and the same organ of the body (the skin).

Small, nonirritating amounts of allergens diluted in a petrolatum or water vehicle are placed on the skin of the patient's back and covered with nonabsorbent adhesive patches that are left in place for 48 hours. They are then removed and the reactions noted. Redness, swelling, and the presence of small vesicles at the site of the patch indicate a positive reaction. Because a reaction sometimes takes longer to occur, the patch area may be observed again at 72 or 96 hours.

Photopatch testing to test for photoallergy is similar except that two sets of identical patches are applied to the back and one is left covered while the other is exposed to light after 24 hours. A positive reaction on the light-exposed side signifies photoallergic sensitivity; if the reaction on the covered side is negative, the test will have shown that exposure to sunlight is required for the reaction to be elicited.

In both types of patch testing, a positive result does not always indicate that the agent used in the test itself is the cause of the current dermatitis, as the testing reveals sensitivities that have developed over the lifetime of the patient. After a positive reaction occurs, it is then necessary for the dermatologist to attempt to associate the test findings with the current dermatitis and with the substances that the patient has had recent contact with.

It is easier to pinpoint the specific allergen with certain products than with others. Since the late 1970s cosmetics sold over the counter in the U.S. have been required to have all the ingredients listed on the product label, and most cosmetics manufacturers are cooperative with physicians—providing the ingredients that are used in their products for patch testing.

In workplaces, too, information about chemicals used on the job is readily available. Federal legislation in the U.S. requires that information sheets called Material Safety Data Sheets be at the disposal of all workers. These sheets describe the chemicals used in the workers' jobs and how they should be properly handled. Although the sheets may not contain all the important information needed to solve a problem case of contact dermatitis, physicians may obtain further data by calling a telephone number given on the sheets. Workplaces generally will provide chemicals to dermatologists for testing. The information derived from these sources is of inestimable value to the dermatologist in finding the exact cause of an allergic contact dermatitis and in helping patients avoid future recurrences, especially because as of mid-1992 only 20 patch test allergens had been approved by the U.S. Food and Drug Administration.

Treatment

If a person accidentally or inadvertently has direct contact with an irritating substance, he or she should wash the affected area right away. The cornerstone of successful treatment for contact dermatitis is removal of the offending irritants or allergens from the person's environment whenever possible. If this cannot be done—for example, on the job—wearing gloves, goggles, face masks, aprons, coveralls, boots, and other protective clothing may sometimes be helpful. In certain situations, however, gloves—the most widely used protective garment—are of no value. For example, a chemical used in acid-type permanent wave solutions easily penetrates the glove material. Similarly, surgeons allergic to an acrylic material used to reconstruct hip and knee joints and dentists allergic to uncured acrylic denture materials are not protected by wearing rubber gloves because the acrylic ingredients readily pass through rubber. Furthermore, wearing gloves to avoid contact with a provoking substance may not be helpful because, as already noted, many workers often become allergically sensitive to the latex gloves themselves!

In the case of atopic individuals who develop a recurring dermatitis and who cannot avoid contact with workplace irritants, a job change is sometimes necessary. Unfortunately, a complete job or career change for many people, especially for highly skilled, older workers, is often impossible.

Besides searching for the cause and evaluating the multiple contributing factors, proper treatment includes alleviating the rash of acute contact dermatitis. This involves the judicious use of topical corticosteroids to reduce the inflammation, oral antihistamines to decrease itching, and sometimes a brief course (a week or so) of systemic corticosteroids. In some cases, bacterial or fungal infections can be superimposed on the contact dermatitis. If the dermatitis appears to be secondarily infected, a short course of oral antibiotics or an antifungal medication may be necessary.

Chronic contact dermatitis requires regular treatment with corticosteroid creams. If the skin becomes thickened and there is scaling, cortisone ointments can be applied at night and covered with a thin plastic wrapping. This treatment is continued for several days and is usually supplemented by oral antihistamines to decrease itching.

Finally, it is important that further contact with irritants or allergens does not occur during treatment. And excessive washing, the use of harsh soaps, and rubbing and scratching should be avoided.

Zoonoses
by Larry R. Thall

Pliny the Elder, the 1st-century AD Roman natural philosopher, called ticks "the foulest and nastiest creatures that be." While it is known today that Pliny erred in some of his theories, there are still those who agree with his pronouncement on ticks. Parasitic arthropods that live exclusively on the blood of humans and other mammals, ticks are wont to exhibit truly abominable table manners, gorging themselves until they appear ready to explode and often repaying the host animal for its hospitality by making it sick. Ticks serve as vectors (carriers of disease) between human beings and other animals and, as such, they are important transmitters of zoonoses.

Zoonoses are diseases humans can acquire from other vertebrate animals—apparently healthy, well-cared-for pets *not* excluded. Experts divide zoonoses into several different types, or categories, on the basis of their patterns of transmission. In one type the disease is passed directly from an infected animal to a human, as is the case for rabies. In another type both vertebrate and invertebrate animals are required for spread of the disease to humans—examples include tick- and mosquito-borne illnesses and schistosomiasis, a parasitic disease transmitted by snails. In still another type of zoonosis, specific environmental conditions must be met in order for humans to acquire the disease; an example is histoplasmosis, a fungal disease that develops in soil where bird droppings have been deposited. Strategies for the control or eradication of zoonoses differ according to mode of transmission.

Extent of the problem

To date, approximately 285 zoonoses have been identified; more than 40 of these are commonly associated with pet animals, primarily cats and dogs. Other rarer pets, however, such as exotic birds, reptiles, and ferrets, also can harbor and transmit zoonoses.

Statistical data concerning zoonoses are sketchy. Of the several dozen diseases known to be transmitted from pets to people, fewer than a dozen are official "notifiable diseases" that are reported on a weekly basis to the U.S. Centers for Disease Control. Also, public health experts believe that even for these illnesses, only a small percentage of cases are actually reported. Further complicating matters, many zoonotic infections in people result in flulike symptoms, and therefore incorrect diagnoses are possible. Nonetheless, it is estimated that as many as four million U.S. pet owners become ill each year from their animals.

Not all zoonoses are spread by house pets. Other domesticated animals—cattle, horses, sheep, goats, swine—may be involved, as may a variety of wild animals—rodents, rabbits, and bats, to name a few. In rare instances zoonoses may be occupational diseases. Laboratory workers, for example, are at increased risk of certain zoonoses that rarely affect the general population.

The effects of these diseases in people run the gamut from mild and self-limiting to potentially life-threatening. Some zoonotic diseases, such as Lyme disease and toxoplasmosis, may result in chronic health problems.

Transmission and risk

It is not necessary for a sick animal to scratch or bite a person in order to transmit disease. Zoonoses commonly are acquired by many other means—*e.g.,* from contact with animal feces or soil contaminated by feces and from eating undercooked meat and unwashed vegetables. Sharing bedding or plates with pets further enhances the opportunity for human infection. Small children, who are likely to put dirt, tree bark, and other organic matter in their mouths, may be at higher risk for contracting various parasitic infections, such as hookworm, tapeworm, and an especially dangerous roundworm (*Baylisascaris procyonis*), which is transmitted via raccoon feces. In addition, many zoonoses—for example, toxoplasmosis—can cause

461

potentially serious disease in humans, yet infected animals can remain completely asymptomatic.

Rabies

Rabies is probably the best known of all zoonoses and certainly one of the most feared. Fortunately, human rabies is extremely rare in the U.S., averaging only one or two cases per year. Mandatory vaccination has gone a long way toward eliminating this deadly viral disease in pet cats and dogs. Most human rabies cases reported in the U.S. in recent years have resulted from contact with bats and wild carnivores.

The bite of a rabid animal in itself is not sufficient to cause rabies; the animal must be shedding the virus in its saliva at the time of the bite, and the infected saliva must make its way into the bloodstream of the victim. Any time a person is bitten, it is crucial that the wound be irrigated as soon as possible with a large volume of soap and water so that as much saliva as possible can be removed. If the offending animal is an apparently healthy dog or cat—as is the case with most animal bites—it should be kept under close observation for 10 days. If the miscreant cannot be caught, a series of prophylactic injections may be required.

When deciding on the most prudent course of action, the victim's physician will take several factors into consideration: the absence or presence of rabies in the area; the severity of the wound; and the behavior of the animal, which may provide clues as to whether it was infected at the time it bit the patient.

Regardless of the physician's judgment, however, many bite victims elect to undergo vaccination. This is understandable, as the rate of death from rabies, even with the finest medical care, is virtually 100%. At one time perhaps only the disease itself was feared more than rabies vaccination—a series of 14 or more painful injections, often with unpleasant side effects. Fortunately, the vaccine that is used today is more potent, less toxic, and much less painful. Five injections are given over a four-week period.

Toxoplasmosis

As many as 50% of all cats in the United States become infected with toxoplasmosis at some point in their lives. The disease is caused by a protozoan parasite (*Toxoplasma gondii*) that cats usually acquire by ingesting prey that is infected with the organism. Once the parasite has established residence in the cat's intestine, it begins sexual reproduction. The fertilized eggs, called oocysts, are deposited in the cat's feces, thus creating an easy vehicle for transmission to humans.

In human adults the symptoms of toxoplasmosis—fatigue, muscle aches, sore throat, swollen lymph nodes in the neck and armpits—usually are self-limiting and relatively mild. Occasionally, chronic prob-

lems can result, causing additional symptoms such as headaches, diarrhea, muscle weakness, weight loss, and eye damage. The congenital form of the disease, however, is far more serious. When a woman becomes infected during pregnancy, the disease may cross the placenta and infect the fetus, potentially resulting in birth defects including blindness and mental retardation. Fortunately, toxoplasmosis in pregnancy is rare. Approximately two to six cases of primary maternal infection occur per 8,500 pregnancies in the U.S., according to a recent study. Of that small minority, fewer than 50% of the infants become infected, and only about 10% of infected babies are born with severe defects. However, 20% of those infected suffer minor abnormalities.

Because cats with toxoplasmosis usually exhibit no signs of illness, pregnant women and those attempting to become pregnant would be wise to consider all cats to be infected, unless proved otherwise. They should routinely wash their hands after handling a cat. Overly cautious physicians have been known to encourage pregnant women to get rid of their cats; most veterinarians feel that such drastic measures are unnecessary. Shed oocysts require at least 24 hours (some experts estimate as long as five days) to become infectious, so cleaning the litter box daily—even if done by the pregnant women herself—should prevent infection. As a precaution such women should wear rubber gloves when performing this chore. Even better is to enlist a family member or friend to do the cleaning. Pregnant women also should wear gloves when working in the garden—or anywhere else that is conceivably contaminated with cat feces—and should wash their hands thoroughly afterward. It should be noted that despite the understandable emphasis on proper litter-box hygiene, veterinarians agree that more cases of toxoplasmosis in pregnancy are caused by the eating of undercooked meat and unwashed vegetables than from contact with a pet's feces.

Cat scratch disease

Cat scratch disease, also called cat scratch fever, originally was thought to be a viral infection. In 1983, however, researchers at the Armed Forces Institute of Pathology, Washington, D.C., discovered the bacterium that actually causes the illness. Cats infected with the organism remain unaffected.

Despite its name, cat scratch disease can be transmitted through cat bites as well as scratches. Cats, therefore, should never be allowed to lick open wounds or skin abrasions on people. Any cat scratches or bites should be washed well and disinfected with alcohol. Physicians will generally prescribe antibiotics for any deep scratches or bites to protect against pasteurella, another zoonotic infection caused by a bacterium (*Pasteurella multocida*) that is often present in the mouths of healthy cats and dogs.

In the vast majority of cases, cat scratch disease produces mild and self-limiting symptoms; a pimple appears near the site of the wound and may be followed about two weeks later by swollen lymph nodes, headaches, malaise, fever, and loss of appetite. Occasionally, more serious problems occur, such as severe rashes, liver abnormalities, bone damage, and brain inflammation. Standard antibiotics are not effective in treating acute manifestations of the disease. Gentamicin, an extremely powerful antibiotic that can have serious side effects, has been used successfully in severe cases.

Tick-borne diseases

As noted above, ticks often act as carriers of zoonotic diseases. Two of the most important such maladies are Lyme disease and Rocky Mountain spotted fever.

Lyme disease. The tick-borne arthritic disorder called Lyme disease has received much press coverage since its discovery in the mid-1970s. Although first detected in Lyme, Conn., the disease now has infected persons in 46 states and is reported to be one of the fastest-growing communicable diseases in the United States.

Certain species of ticks spread Lyme disease during the middle, or nymph, stage of their two-year life cycle. The actual disease-causing agent is not the tick but a microscopic bacterium (*Borrelia burgdorferi*), which the tick acquires during the immature, or larva, stage while feeding on white-footed mice. The organism is subsequently injected into the next animal host, usually near the end of the tick's lengthy meal, which lasts up to 12 hours.

Finding ticks on the skin before they feed is a challenge; usually they are no bigger than a poppy seed. Ironically, the gluttony of the tick may constitute a virtue in disguise, as Lyme disease can be prevented if the arthropod is removed before it reaches the stage of feeding where it deposits the bacterium. Therefore, if an embedded tick is found on the skin, it should be removed immediately.

Dogs, and to a lesser extent cats, have shouldered an unfair proportion of blame for human cases of Lyme disease. Although it is possible for a pet to transmit an infected tick to its owner, experts agree that the majority of human cases are caused by direct contact with infected deer ticks (*Ixodes dammini*) and southern blacklegged ticks (*I. scapularis*) during outdoor activities such as hiking, camping, and picnicking. The tremendous increase in Lyme disease in recent years is attributed to the dramatic growth of the deer population, deer being a preferred host of *Ixodes* species during the adult phase of the tick's life cycle.

People who live in tick-infested regions—especially those who spend time outdoors in heavily wooded areas—should do everything possible to prevent tick bites. These precautions include wearing light-colored

Although the risk of acquiring a disease from a pet is small, commonsense precautions—such as washing hands after handling an animal—should still be observed. Experts recommend that pet raccoons, like dogs, be properly wormed.

clothing (which makes the ticks easier to see) and tucking pant legs into sock tops. It is a good idea to apply a commercial tick repellent to skin and clothing. When spending time in open fields or woodlands known to harbor the parasites, people would be wise to check for ticks a couple of times a day. Taking a shower after a day spent in the woods may wash away ticks before they have a chance to attach to the skin. The scalp, armpits, and groin are particularly vulnerable areas of the body.

Close health monitoring should follow any tick bite, and medical attention should be sought immediately if symptoms appear. Untreated, Lyme disease has the potential to cause serious chronic health problems, including arthritis of the large joints, neurological disorders, and heart and liver problems. In the early stages of the infection, common antibiotics such as penicillin and tetracycline have proved to be very effective. Once the disease has progressed, however, it may not respond well to any sort of antibiotic therapy.

Dogs and cats—and other domesticated animals— also are susceptible to Lyme disease. Dogs that live in endemic areas should be brushed thoroughly to remove ticks from their coats, preferably while standing on newspaper so that ticks dislodged from the fur can

463

be easily spotted and destroyed. Some chemical tick repellents are safe for use on dogs, but those containing DEET (N,N-diethyl-meta-toluamide) are toxic to dogs and extremely dangerous to cats. Owners should carefully read warning labels before applying any such product to a pet.

Rocky Mountain spotted fever. This is another potentially serious disease transmitted to humans by ticks, primarily the dog tick (*Dermacentor variabilis*) and related species that live on cattle and sheep. The actual infectious agent, though, is *Rickettsia rickettsii*, a parasitic organism that uses the tick as its host. Despite the geographic reference in the disease's name, cases of Rocky Mountain spotted fever have been reported all across the continental United States.

Common symptoms include fever, headache, and a rash on the palms of the hands and soles of the feet that gradually extends to most of the body. As with Lyme disease, the best preventive measure is frequent checks for and removal of ticks and close health monitoring following a tick bite. Antibiotics often are effective in early treatment.

Infections caused by worms

Hookworms, tapeworms, and roundworms all are spread to people—most often, children—through direct contact with infected animal feces or contaminated soil and sand. The eggs of some parasitic worms can remain alive in soil for months. The best preventive measures are restraining children from putting dirt and sand—or dirty hands—in their mouths or near their noses. Childrens' hands should be washed after outdoor play, and cats and dogs should be kept out of sandboxes. Pets—including pet raccoons—should be properly wormed, and owners should clean up after their animals outdoors and remove animal feces from their yards on a regular basis. Some parasitic infections, such as cutaneous larva migrans, or creeping eruption, caused by the dog hookworm (*Ancylostoma caninum*), affect only the skin and clear up spontaneously after several weeks of an uncomfortable red, itchy rash. Others, such as toxocariasis, caused by the common dog roundworm (*Toxocara canis*), produce larvae that can migrate throughout the body; these infections require medical attention.

Psittacosis

Psittacosis, also called parrot fever, is the best-known of all avian zoonoses. Originally, it was thought that only birds of the psittacine (parrot) family were vulnerable to the bacteria-like organism (*Chlamydia psittaci*) that causes the illness. Today, however, experts recognize that all birds are susceptible, although parrots and parakeets are most frequently responsible for transmitting the disease to people. While many of the birds that are infected with *C. psittaci* exhibit respiratory problems and diarrhea, others just appear sluggish and sickly. Some species show no signs of infection.

Human cases of psittacosis are rather rare—between 100 and 150 cases are reported per year in the U.S. When people do become infected, it is usually as a result of inhaling contaminated dust from the bird's cage. The lung infection can cause shortness of breath and coughing, as well as headache, chills, loss of appetite, nosebleeds, fever, and enlargement of the spleen. In severe cases delirium, abdominal pain, and cyanosis (bluish discoloration of the skin) also may occur. The antibiotic tetracycline usually is effective in treating psittacosis. However, protracted illness and even death do result on occasion.

In recent years psittacine birds have become popular as pets in institutions for the elderly. Since older people are at higher risk of respiratory infections than young people, it is important that any bird taken into a facility be healthy.

Salmonellosis

Since the U.S. Food and Drug Administration banned the sale of small pet turtles (those under 10 cm [4 in] long) in the mid-1970s, salmonellosis, a bacterial infection, typically has been associated only with food poisoning. However, an estimated 40,000 Americans acquire *Salmonella* infections from animals each year—primarily from dogs, Easter chicks, and pet birds and occasionally from home aquariums, particularly those containing snails. Recently, a few cases were associated with pet iguanas. With common symptoms of abdominal pain, diarrhea, vomiting, fever, and chills, salmonellosis is often mistaken for intestinal flu. The best prevention is good hygiene; the washing of hands after handling pets and especially after cleaning aquariums or bird cages is highly recommended.

Your pet: a health hazard?

The risk of acquiring a disease from a pet animal is, in reality, extremely small. Indeed, most people are much more likely to contract an infectious illness from another human than from an animal. When cases of zoonoses involving pets do occur, they are often the result of a failure to follow commonsense hygienic practices. Children, who often neglect to wash their hands after fondling an animal and who may come into contact with animal excrement during outdoor play, are probably at greatest risk for those diseases that can be acquired from animals.

Can sick people transmit diseases to their pets? In theory, yes. *Salmonella* and the protozoan organism *Giardia lamblia,* also a cause of diarrhea, are two infections that can be transmitted easily from people to animals. In most cases, however, extraordinary circumstances are required for human-to-animal transmission to occur.

Arrhythmias
by Marc K. Effron, M.D.

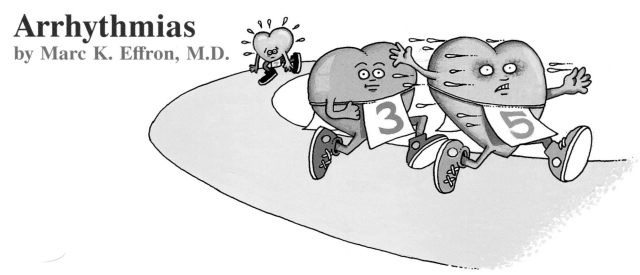

An arrhythmia is an abnormal rhythm of the heart. There is a broad clinical spectrum of arrhythmias, which range from benign to truly life-threatening. Premature (early) beats are common and often go unnoticed, but at the other end of the spectrum is ventricular fibrillation, a rapid, uncoordinated beat, which can be fatal if not corrected within minutes after it begins. In order to understand the nature and causes of rhythm disturbances, it is necessary to know something about normal electrical conduction in the heart.

Understanding the cardiac conduction system

The normal cardiac conduction system is composed of specialized nervelike tissue that conducts electrical stimuli from the natural pacemaker site to the chambers of cardiac muscle, affecting muscular contraction of the chambers. The heart's normal rhythm is known as a sinus rhythm. It is controlled by the sinoatrial, or sinus, node, situated in the wall of the right atrium (the upper right chamber of the heart) near the junction with the superior vena cava, a large vein that feeds blood to the right atrium. The sinus node functions as the body's natural pacemaker. It responds to the circulatory needs of the body by slowing when one is at rest and accelerating at times of physical or psychological stress. The electrical impulse generated by the sinus node travels through the atrial tissue to a delay station, the atrioventricular node. A fraction of a second's delay in conduction permits the atria to complete their contraction and fill the heart's lower chambers, the ventricles, before the impulse is carried down the cardiac muscle fibers (bundle of His and Purkinje fibers) into the ventricular muscle.

This system of conduction enables the regular beating of the heart. The sinus rate is controlled by nerve fibers of the autonomic nervous system, but circulating catecholamines, substances (such as epinephrine) that transmit nerve impulses, also affect the sinus node activity. A newborn's heart rate may be as high as 150 beats per minute. By age six a child has a heart rate, or pulse, of less than 100 beats per minute. A healthy adult's pulse is about 70–78 beats at rest but with exercise conditioning can drop to 50 beats per minute. Sinus tachycardia describes an abnormally fast resting heartbeat—elevation of the sinus rate to above 100 beats per minute in an adult—which can occur in response to exercise or to illness. This physiological response is not a primary disturbance of the heart rhythm.

Normal sinus rhythm is often not perfectly regular. There is typically a phasic slowing and quickening of the heartbeat in response to respirations. Some adults and many adolescents exhibit quite marked respiratory-cycle-induced variation of heart rate, which is mediated by vagal nerve tone. Although known as sinus arrhythmia, these fluctuations are simply a variant of normal.

Symptoms of arrhythmias

Palpitations are the most common symptoms of arrhythmias. An individual becomes aware of a forceful rapid or irregular heartbeat felt in the chest. Many healthy people have mild palpitations; often these are so brief that the patient describes them as lasting only one or two seconds. Such palpitations are almost always attributable to premature beats or to a brief and benign type of racing of the heart. These symptoms can, however, be disturbing—even frightening—to the individual who experiences them. Electrocardiographic documentation of the benign nature of arrhythmia, the absence of other cardiac symptoms, and an otherwise normal physical examination will usually serve to reassure the patient that the abnormality in heartbeat is not serious and that no treatment is needed. Palpitations generally do not warrant further investigation, particularly in a young and healthy patient.

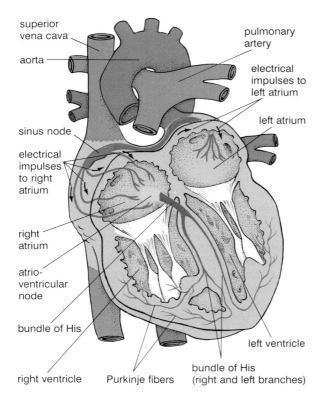

Cardiac conduction system

superior vena cava

aorta

pulmonary artery

electrical impulses to left atrium

left atrium

sinus node

electrical impulses to right atrium

right atrium

atrio-ventricular node

bundle of His

left ventricle

right ventricle

Purkinje fibers

bundle of His (right and left branches)

On the other hand, sudden awareness of a rapidly pounding heart suggests a paroxysmal tachycardia, and episodes lasting several seconds or longer should be brought to medical attention. A pathological heart rhythm is usually the cause of this symptom. However, an occasional patient with panic disorder (acute anxiety episodes) describes this very type of palpitation. In such cases the tachycardia is only sinus tachycardia induced by circulating catecholamines. It is important but often difficult to distinguish whether anxiety has been induced by actual tachycardia or an anxiety episode has triggered a benign racing of the heart. Appropriate therapy depends on knowing what the primary problem is.

Syncope is a sudden and transient loss of consciousness. Presyncope is a warning, or premonitory light-headedness, a sign that loss of consciousness may soon occur. These symptoms can be an important indication of a very slow or very rapid heart rhythm that may require testing and treatment. The setting in which a syncopal episode occurs may give clues to its underlying cause. For example, if a soldier stands at attention for a prolonged period on a hot day, his blood pressure may drop precipitously and he may faint. In this case no arrhythmia is suspected. On the other hand, if a person who is seated comfortably in a chair suddenly blacks out, an arrhythmia may certainly be the cause.

Occasionally a sustained slow or rapid heartbeat may cause symptoms of weakness or easy fatigability. In some cases arrhythmias provoke symptoms of other heart conditions. For example, actual congestive heart failure (an accumulation of fluid in the lungs) can be precipitated by prolonged extremes of the heart rate. And some patients with coronary artery disease notice the onset of angina pectoris (chest pain originating from the heart) during an episode of tachycardia.

Evaluating arrhythmias

Careful review of a patient's symptoms and past medical history is the first step in evaluating a suspected arrhythmia. Examination of the pulse can directly reveal heart rhythm abnormalities if the arrhythmia is frequent or sustained. Physical signs of cardiac enlargement, valvular or congenital heart disease, or congestive heart failure can suggest an underlying basis for potentially serious arrhythmias. Chronic lung disease or hyperthyroidism (overactivity of the thyroid gland), too, can explain the occurrence of certain tachycardias.

An electrocardiogram is the standard means of diagnosing an arrhythmia. The conventional electrocardiogram, however, is a brief recording of heart rhythm, which can miss a very intermittent abnormality. Even if the actual arrhythmia is not detected, the electrocardiogram may still reveal other abnormalities of the cardiac conduction system, defects in the heart muscle, and even cardiac changes characteristic of certain drug toxicities. When the symptoms of an arrhythmia are very brief and intermittent, documentation is better achieved with a 24-hour ambulatory monitor, commonly known as a Holter monitor. The patient wears a set of electrodes taped to the chest and carries a portable recording device that monitors the heart rhythm for a full day and night. The 24-hour recording is then analyzed with the aid of a computer to enable the physician to correlate the patient's symptoms with possible arrhythmias.

Some palpitations are severe enough to warrant documentation but are so infrequent that even a 24-hour Holter study is unlikely to capture and record the abnormalities. In such cases the patient may be asked to wear a heart rhythm recording device that can be activated at the onset of palpitations. The patient simply pushes a button to start the recording; in this way several seconds of potentially meaningful electrocardiographic tracings can be recorded for later review and diagnosis.

Another method of evaluating rhythm disturbances is the signal-averaged electrocardiogram, a modified electrocardiogram that examines more subtle aspects of ventricular muscle electrical activity. This method is gaining favor as a screening test to identify patients at high risk for life-threatening ventricular arrhythmias. Those with abnormal signal-averaged electrocardiograms may then need to undergo an invasive procedure known as an electrophysiological study (EPS).

The EPS is the most direct method for evaluating arrhythmias—one that is generally performed in a cardiac catheterization laboratory of a hospital. Electrodes attached to catheters are advanced to the right heart chambers via the right femoral vein of the groin. The state of the conduction system is measured by a series of electrode recordings. Catheter stimulation to induce tachycardia further tests the conduction system and may bring out a clinically important arrhythmia that had not occurred spontaneously during evaluation with a 24-hour Holter monitor.

Recent advances in understanding and diagnosing heart rhythm disturbances have enabled cardiologists to evolve highly effective treatments. In many cases it is now possible to prevent catastrophic consequences of arrhythmias that are life-threatening. Specific arrhythmias and their management are described below.

Sinus bradycardia

Bradyarrhythmias are abnormally slow heart rhythms, the most common being sinus bradycardia, characterized as a sinus rate below 60 beats per minute. As already noted, slowing of the sinus rate is commonly seen in athletes and is a response to increased vagal tone. Many accomplished athletes have actually trained their hearts to beat slower—the rate may drop to 50 beats per minute or less—and pump more blood with each beat. Except in rare cases, this lowered heart rate, sometimes called "runner's bradycardia," causes no symptoms and should be considered a physiological variant of normal.

Sinus bradycardia can also occur when there is an intrinsic dysfunction of the sinus node and can lead to presyncope or true syncope. A rhythm disturbance known as sick sinus syndrome encompasses severe and sustained sinus bradycardia as well as sudden pauses of the sinus node activity. Symptoms may appear if the heart rate is less than 45 beats per minute and almost always appear at rates below 40 beats during waking hours. In sick sinus syndrome, syncope occurs if sinus pauses exceed five seconds.

Slower sinus rates and true sick sinus syndrome are commonly seen in older patients. Sinus node dysfunction does not cause symptoms unless it is extreme. Holter monitoring of elderly patients may reveal a significantly reduced average daily heart rate—profound slowing to rates in the high 20s and abrupt sinus pauses of up to three seconds during sleep—yet the elderly patient usually has no symptoms.

Sinus node dysfunction can also be potentiated by certain drug therapies for hypertension and angina. Beta-adrenergic blocking drugs and some of the cal-

cium-channel-blocking drugs have this effect. If it is medically feasible, such drugs should be withdrawn when severe sinus node dysfunction occurs.

When sick sinus syndrome is causing symptoms or when the bradycardia is extreme (below 40 beats per minute) during waking hours, implantation of an electronic pacemaker is warranted. Single-chamber ventricular pacemakers, with a lead positioned in the apex of the right ventricle, and dual-chamber pacemakers, with leads positioned in the right atrium and ventricle, are available. The leads are coated wires that conduct electric stimuli from a generator to cardiac muscle. A pacemaker can have a fixed-rate pacing mode that delivers continuous impulses at a specified rate, or it can be rate-responsive—accelerating or slowing in response to the individual's activity level.

In tachycardia-bradycardia syndrome, or tachy-brady syndrome, sinus node dysfunction is interspersed with episodes of tachycardia. The heartbeat essentially varies from one extreme to the other, very slow to very fast. Tachy-brady syndrome usually requires a twofold treatment: drug therapy suppresses the tachycardia, and an implanted pacemaker prevents the extremely slow heartbeats.

Heart block

Heart block describes conditions in which the spread of cardiac electrical activity is slowed or interrupted in a part of the normal conduction pathway. One such condition is atrioventricular block; deterioration of the conduction system at or below the atrioventricular node produces a loss of impulse conduction from the top to the bottom of the heart. If heart block is brief and intermittent, a prolonged period of monitoring may be required for diagnosis of the rhythm abnormality. Sustained complete heart block, on the other hand, usually causes profound weakness or syncope and is sometimes fatal. In complete atrioventricular block, although no impulse from the sinus node reaches the ventricles, there may be a slow "escape" rhythm originating just below the atrioventricular node or in the ventricles. Thus, the ventricles are controlled by an auxiliary pacemaker. Other forms of heart block are sinoatrial block, in which impulse transmission is extremely slow out of the sinus node tissues, and intraventricular block (impulse transmission is interrupted or slowed at one of the bundle branches stemming from the bundle of His).

As with sick sinus syndrome, sometimes heart block may be caused by certain medications and may therefore improve if the drugs are withdrawn. Calcium-channel blockers and some antiarrhythmic medications, for example, can cause a reversible form of complete heart block. Heart block may also be caused by acute heart attack, infective endocarditis, sarcoidosis (a chronic inflammatory condition involving the lymph nodes, lungs, bones, and skin), and Chagas' disease (a parasitic infection endemic in South America). In such cases the healing of the myocardial tissue or early treatment of endocarditis and sarcoidosis may improve cardiac conduction and obviate the need for pacemaker implantation.

Most cases of complete heart block are attributable to a poorly understood degeneration of the heart's conduction system. The nodes and the His bundle and its branches develop fibrosis and gradually lose function. Severe calcification of the aortic valve or the base of the mitral valve can impinge upon the atrioventricular node and His bundle. Syncope is sometimes the first symptom of these valvular problems.

Unless a reversible cause of complete heart block is identified, pacemaker implantation is usually necessary. Advances in pacemaker technology over the past decade have resulted in the availability of highly refined and effective devices. Improvements include smaller generator size, longer lasting batteries, increased programmability, and the ability to mimic the physiological responsiveness of the heart's own natural pacemaker to the body's circulatory needs.

Premature atrial contractions

Premature atrial contractions (PACs) are the most common arrhythmia originating in the atrial tissue. These premature beats usually cause no symptoms, though some individuals are aware of a brief palpitation. Many healthy people have a few PACs each day; this is not considered abnormal. Less commonly PACs are very frequent, numbering thousands per day. Still, no treatment is required in the absence of more severe arrhythmias.

Supraventricular tachycardia

Supraventricular tachycardia, or paroxysmal supraventricular tachycardia (PSVT), is a rapid and regular racing of the heart that starts and ends suddenly. The usual form of PSVT emanates from the atrioventricular node. A premature beat conducts into the atrioventricular node and catches some of the nodal tissue in a refractory state. The impulse conduction travels in a so-called reentry pattern—*i.e.,* up and down different fibers in the atrioventricular node—typically at a rate between 150 and 220 beats per minute. The impulses reflect back into the atrium, the chamber of their origin, and also travel out into ventricular muscle, producing a tachycardia of a similar rapid rate.

PSVT can occur in all age groups. Most often it is not associated with any other signs of heart disease. Patients with PSVT describe a sudden racing or pounding in the chest. Very rapid rates may cause weakness, light-headedness, or even syncope. The tachycardia usually occurs randomly, but for some patients there is a clear association with vigorous exercise.

An acute episode of PSVT can be treated with physical maneuvers that interrupt conduction via the atrioventricular node and thereby evoke an increase of vagal tone. Some patients respond quite well to carotid sinus massage. Alternatively, the patient may perform a Valsalva maneuver, making a forceful attempt at expiration while holding the nostrils closed and keeping the mouth shut and by bearing down to increase pressure in the thorax. The increased vagal tone then slows conduction in the atrioventricular node and can interrupt the reentry cycle of the impulse. Patients can be taught to perform these maneuvers at the onset of PSVT.

Pharmacological treatment of an acute PSVT attack is given in the physician's office or a hospital setting. Successful conversion to a normal sinus rhythm can be achieved in over 90% of cases through administration of adenosine or verapamil intravenously. These drugs block conduction in the atrioventricular node and thereby break the reentry cycle.

If PSVT becomes frequent and the episodes are prolonged, the treatment of choice is chronic suppressive therapy in order to prevent recurrent attacks. A single daily dose of a long-acting beta-blocking drug is the simplest approach. Some patients may instead require a class I antiarrhythmic agent such as quinidine, procainamide, or disopyramide. For severe cases of recurrent PSVT that do not respond to drug therapy, a new percutaneous catheter technique of radiofrequency intracardiac ablation (discussed below) can disrupt the reentry circuit and effect a permanent cure.

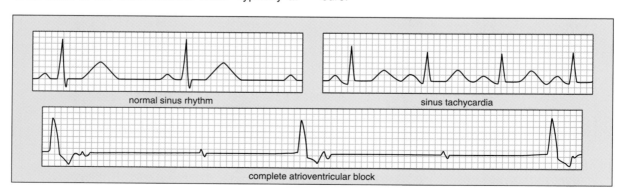

normal sinus rhythm

sinus tachycardia

complete atrioventricular block

Atrial fibrillation

Atrial fibrillation produces a rapid and quite irregular heartbeat. Within the atria there are very rapid and disorganized electrical impulse formations (depolarizations)—up to 400 per minute. As not all of these impulses can pass through the atrioventricular node, the ventricular response is usually 140 to 200 beats per minute.

Atrial fibrillation can be paroxysmal or chronic. In young and old patients, it is frequently the only identifiable cardiac abnormality. Such patients are sometimes referred to as "lone fibrillators." There are also several cardiac and noncardiac conditions that can lead to atrial fibrillation, including congestive heart failure, cardiomyopathy (heart muscle degeneration), pericarditis, valvular and congenital heart disease, hyperthyroidism, and acute or chronic lung disease.

The onset of atrial fibrillation may go unnoticed in some patients, particularly if the heart rate is not exceedingly fast. Most patients are soon aware of the arrhythmia because they experience symptoms such as palpitations, weakness, exertional fatigue, or shortness of breath. Rapid ventricular rates can provoke angina in patients with coronary disease or congestive heart failure in those with valvular heart disease or cardiomyopathy.

Sustained episodes of atrial fibrillation pose the risks of emboli and possibly stroke. Because there is minimal mechanical activity of the fibrillating atria, blood slows and clots on the atrial walls. An atrial blood clot (thrombus) can detach and float out into the systemic circulation (systemic embolus). If such an embolus lodges in an artery of an arm or leg, the extremity becomes cold and painful; the embolus can sometimes be extracted with a special balloon device (embolectomy catheter). If an embolus obstructs a cerebral artery, however, catastrophic stroke can result.

The first priority in treatment of an acute episode of atrial fibrillation is control of the ventricular rate—usually by intravenous or oral administration of digoxin (digitalis), which slows conduction in the atrioventricular node. Slowing of the ventricular rate also is facilitated by the calcium-channel antagonists verapamil and diltiazem, as well as by beta-blocking drugs.

If a patient does not convert back to sinus rhythm after control of the ventricular rate, a class I antiarrhythmic drug will facilitate conversion. Quinidine is used most often for this purpose, but several other drugs may also be effective.

Electrical cardioversion by application of a direct-current shock to the thorax is a very effective method for converting atrial fibrillation to normal sinus rhythm. It is performed while the patient is under sedation with a short-acting anesthetic. Electrical cardioversion is needed immediately if a rapid ventricular rate leads to hypotension, angina, or severe congestive heart failure. More commonly, the electrical cardioversion is performed electively after unsuccessful attempts to convert a rhythm pharmacologically. Despite its somewhat dramatic nature, the risk of complications with cardioversion is very low.

The importance of anticoagulation therapy (hindering blood clotting) in the management of atrial fibrillation is now recognized. The goal is to minimize the risk of stroke or systemic emboli. Patients with prolonged episodes are often given the anticoagulant warfarin prior to any attempt to convert to sinus rhythm. The drug is then continued for several days after correction of the heart rhythm, following which a decision must be made regarding the need for ongoing treatment to suppress the abnormal rhythm. If recurrent episodes of paroxysmal atrial fibrillation are infrequent and well tolerated, suppressive therapy is not required. Frequent or poorly tolerated attacks are best prevented by digoxin and a class I antiarrhythmic drug.

Chronic atrial fibrillation requires not only control of the ventricular rate but prevention of emboli formation. Recent studies have confirmed an annualized risk of stroke ranging from 2 to 5% in patients with chronic atrial fibrillation. The risk of bleeding complications from treatment with warfarin is less than the risk of stroke caused by emboli in patients not treated with warfarin. This applies even to older patients and thus argues in favor of anticoagulation therapy in virtually all cases of chronic atrial fibrillation. Aspirin, too, has been used to prevent clot formation. Aspirin acts as an antiplatelet agent and poses less risk of a serious hemorrhage than warfarin. Trials are currently under

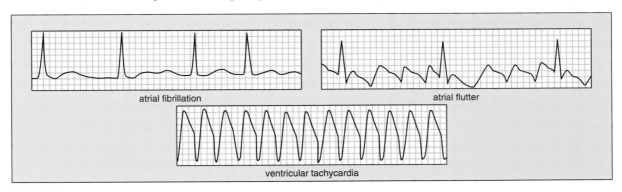

atrial fibrillation

atrial flutter

ventricular tachycardia

way directly comparing the efficacy and safety of warfarin and aspirin for atrial fibrillation.

Atrial flutter

Atrial flutter is an arrhythmia that is closely related, both electrophysiologically and clinically, to atrial fibrillation, although it is less common. Provocative factors are similar to those of atrial fibrillation, as are treatments. During atrial flutter, electrical activity within the atria is more organized and cyclic, producing an atrial rate between 280 and 320 beats per minute. Except in young children or in those with a conducting pathway that bypasses the atrioventricular node (described below), the ventricle responds at a lower rate due to atrioventricular block. Typically the patient is seen with an atrial rate of 300, ventricular rate of 150, and 2:1 atrioventricular conduction; every other atrial impulse conducts through to the ventricles. Atrial flutter is a less stable rhythm than atrial fibrillation, is usually easier to treat, and only rarely becomes chronic.

Wolff-Parkinson-White syndrome

Ventricular preexcitation describes a type of congenital abnormality of cardiac conduction. In the normal heart, conduction from the atria can reach the ventricles only through the atrioventricular node and bundle of His. In ventricular preexcitation, there is accelerated conduction to some portion of ventricular muscle. Wolff-Parkinson-White (WPW) syndrome is the best known form of preexcitation; an accessory conduction pathway is created by a muscle bridge connecting the atria and ventricles. The accessory pathway may be situated at the outer wall of the heart or within the interventricular septum (the wall between the ventricles). Faster conduction down the accessory pathway leads to activation of ventricular muscle in advance of the stimulus traveling down the atrioventricular node. The electrocardiogram in WPW thus shows a short interval between atrial and ventricular activation and a slurred and unusual pattern of ventricular depolarization (impulse formation within the ventricles).

Although most cases of WPW occur in the absence of other signs of structural heart disease, certain congenital heart conditions show a greatly increased incidence of WPW. These conditions include Ebstein's anomaly of the tricuspid valve, ventricular septal defect, and transposition of the great vessels.

Some patients displaying a WPW pattern on their electrocardiogram will never have palpitations or rhythm problems. Other patients, whose accessory pathways facilitate more rapid conduction, are confronted with a variety of arrhythmias. The importance of WPW is its association with paroxysmal tachycardias and sudden death.

Supraventricular and ventricular premature beats can precipitate so-called reciprocating tachycardia. The impulse travels down the normal atrioventricular node and the His-Purkinje system, then back up the accessory pathway from the ventricles to the atria. This sets up a sustained and reciprocating pattern of depolarization, producing a steady tachycardia at a rate between 150 and 220 beats per minute.

Premature beats can also induce atrial flutter and atrial fibrillation in patients with WPW. If the atrial impulse is conducted more readily down the accessory pathway than down the atrioventricular node, a very rapid ventricular response ensues. The usual "delay station" function of the atrioventricular node is circumvented. Ventricular rates during atrial flutter and fibrillation may thus exceed 300 beats per minute and lead to collapse of the patient and cardiac arrest.

For decades, pharmacological therapy to prevent tachycardia in WPW was the mainstay of treatment, and it is still preferred in patients who are easily controlled with medication. Drug therapy is not desirable in young patients who would face a lifetime of medication use or in those whose accessory pathways display very rapid conduction. And some drugs that are routinely used for treating various tachycardias or atrial fibrillation may worsen a tachycardia in WPW and thus be more hazardous than helpful. Digoxin, for example, can accelerate conduction down the accessory pathway and thereby accelerate the ventricular rate during atrial fibrillation.

The electrophysiological study now plays an important role in the management of patients with WPW. EPS can locate the accessory pathway, evaluate its conduction properties, clarify the mechanism of a regular tachycardia, and assess the degree of danger during atrial fibrillation. The effect of antiarrhythmic drugs on conduction in the accessory pathway can also be documented, which helps predict which drugs will be beneficial and which drugs are contraindicated.

Electrophysiological mapping of the accessory pathway now permits definitive therapy of WPW when drugs are not the treatment of choice. Surgical or catheter ablation techniques are highly effective treatments for many patients with WPW. Because the minute accessory pathway is not obvious on visual inspection of the heart's surface, electrophysiological mapping is used to identify the area to be ablated. One means that is used to selectively destroy the accessory pathway in an open-chest surgical procedure is cryoablation, the technique of locally applying a freezing probe to tissue.

Now, however, radiofrequency catheter ablation has been developed as an alternative to open-chest surgical treatment of WPW. The procedure does not require general anesthesia, and patients can usually leave the hospital after two days. Catheter ablation is becoming the procedure of choice unless cardiac surgery is also needed to correct associated congenital anomalies. Radiofrequency alternating current at low voltages of 40 to 60 v is delivered to the accessory pathway via the steerable tip of an ablating catheter, which has been inserted through a vein or artery and advanced into the precise location in the heart. The resulting tissue injury is quite controlled and localized. The contractile function of the heart is not affected, and the large majority of patients tolerate the procedure well. For the small percentage of patients who later show recurrence of preexcitation, the radiofrequency ablation can be repeated with good success.

Premature ventricular contractions

Premature ventricular contractions (PVCs) originate in the ventricular tissue. The early contraction permits less time for ventricular filling; thus, the heart does not eject as much blood as it normally would with a regular beat. The PVC is usually followed by a compensatory pause before the regular heart rhythm is resumed. This pause permits extra ventricular filling, and the post-PVC beat is more forceful. It is the post-PVC beat that is actually felt; patients may sense this as a forceful motion in the chest, variously described as a "flip-flop," "flutter," "skip," "double beat," or even "something jumping in my chest."

A few PVCs are common in healthy people, and occasional individuals without any structural heart disease have thousands every day and no awareness of the arrhythmia. The prevalence of PVCs increases in patients with cardiomyopathy, coronary heart disease, prior heart attack, and valvular heart disease.

The clinical approach to PVCs has changed considerably over the past two decades. The association between frequent PVCs and cardiac arrest has long been recognized, and aggressive pharmacological suppression of the arrhythmia was sought as a means to prevent sudden death. However, not all cases carry the same prognosis. In the absence of underlying structural heart disease, this ventricular arrhythmia generally is not dangerous and need not be treated unless symptoms are intolerable. Even in patients with significant structural pathology of the heart, simple suppression of PVCs with medication does not necessarily protect against more complex and life-threatening ventricular arrhythmias. Ironically, treatment with a class I agent can sometimes cause more serious ventricular arrhythmias to emerge. This "proarrhythmic" effect has caused physicians to reevaluate the indications for treatment. The strongest evidence against drug therapy of PVCs comes from the preliminary results of the Cardiac Arrhythmia Suppression Trial. In this study 1,727 patients with a recent heart attack were randomized to treatment with one of a variety of antiarrhythmic drugs or a placebo. Patients treated with one of two drugs, flecainide and encainide, showed an increased incidence of sudden death, despite the known efficacy of the drugs in suppressing PVCs. It was concluded that those two drugs should not be used to treat patients who have a history of heart attack and asymptomatic or mildly symptomatic ventricular arrhythmias and that the proarrhythmic effects of the drugs need further study.

Ventricular tachycardia and ventricular fibrillation

Ventricular tachycardia is a life-threatening arrhythmia. Often initiated by a PVC, ventricular tachycardia is usually a rapid and regular rhythm. Symptoms range from palpitations and weakness to full collapse and unconsciousness. The severity of symptoms during ventricular tachycardia depends in part on the heart rate and strength of the heart muscle. The heart rate is usually between 140 and 250 beats per minute. Sustained ventricular tachycardia can degenerate into ventricular fibrillation (cardiac arrest).

Ventricular fibrillation is a chaotic and mechanically ineffective depolarization of the ventricular muscle. It amounts to a fatal cardiac arrest unless resuscitative measures are immediately undertaken. Ventricular fibrillation may be preceded by ventricular tachycardia, or it may occur suddenly and without warning.

Both conditions are more prevalent in patients with severe ventricular dysfunction of various causes. The largest group comprises those patients with advanced coronary artery disease and prior heart attack. It is the acute phase of the attack in particular that poses the highest risk. Cardiomyopathy patients are another high-risk group.

A patient has a routine pacemaker check. Implantable cardiac pacemakers are highly refined devices that correct many types of arrhythmias by mimicking the physiological responsiveness of the heart's own natural pacemaker.

Illinois Masonic Medical Center; photograph, Peter Kiar

If a patient with sustained ventricular tachycardia maintains consciousness, there may be time to infuse lidocaine and other antiarrhythmic drugs intravenously. Inadequate blood flow to the brain usually leads to loss of consciousness. Electrical cardioversion (defibrillation) by direct-current shock to the chest is immediately required. Cardiopulmonary resuscitation can support the patient until cardioversion equipment arrives. If ventricular tachycardia degenerates into ventricular fibrillation or if ventricular fibrillation is the original arrhythmia, only electrical defibrillation can save the patient's life. A direct-current shock of 200 to 400 joules is delivered through paddles placed over the chest. Defibrillation is facilitated by rapid correction of acid-base and electrolyte disturbances and by intravenous delivery of drugs such as epinephrine, lidocaine, and bretylium.

Sudden death due to ventricular tachycardia and ventricular fibrillation remains a health problem of major importance in Western society. In the U.S. up to one-fifth of all deaths are sudden, and there are over 500,000 cases of death due to ventricular fibrillation each year. Only a small percentage of individuals who succumb to sudden death have warning symptoms, but the majority have severe underlying coronary artery disease (documented on postmortem examination). Although it is commonly said that a person who dies of cardiac arrest has had a "heart attack," this is true in only a minority of cases, which emphasizes the primary importance of recognizing and treating life-threatening arrhythmias.

Survivors of cardiac arrest undergo intense investigation for possible anatomic and electrophysiological abnormalities. Most, though not all, show significant coronary disease or abnormalities of ventricular function, but only a small proportion display frequent PVCs or nonsustained runs of ventricular tachycardia during in-hospital monitoring or with ambulatory monitoring.

Programmed electrical stimulation during EPS can induce ventricular tachycardia in survivors of cardiac arrest, which can be used to evaluate response to drug therapy. If a class I antiarrhythmic drug renders the patient's ventricular tachycardia "noninducible," the drug is likely to prevent spontaneous recurrences of the life-threatening arrhythmia. Although programmed stimulation serves as a good guide for drug therapy, it is not fail-safe. Some patients treated with drugs that appear to control arrhythmias still die suddenly. For others, no drug prevents programmed induction of ventricular tachycardia. Moreover, for some patients with well-documented spontaneous ventricular tachycardia or ventricular fibrillation, ventricular tachycardia cannot be reproduced by programmed stimulation.

Surgical treatment to suppress recurrent ventricular tachycardia has been developed to overcome the inadequacies of drug therapy. The arrhythmia-producing region of ventricular muscle can be mapped by means of sensing electrodes placed on the surface of the exposed heart. Surgical incision and cryoablation are used to disrupt and confine the conducting properties of the tissue responsible for the ventricular tachycardia. Such surgery is associated with some failures; moreover, abnormal ventricular function elevates the risk of surgical complications.

Automatic defibrillators: dramatic and lifesaving

Frustrated with attempts to prevent ventricular tachycardia and ventricular fibrillation, cardiologists instead sought an implantable device that could immediately correct potentially fatal arrhythmias. The automatic implantable cardioverter-defibrillator (AICD) was developed for this purpose. Nearly a decade of experience with the AICD has demonstrated its effectiveness in preventing sudden death.

During surgical implantation of the AICD, permanent electrode patches are attached directly to the surface of the heart. Wire leads are brought out to the upper abdominal wall, where an AICD generator pack is connected and positioned subcutaneously. The AICD is programmed to respond if the heart rate exceeds a specified rate or if ventricular fibrillation occurs. Energy delivery is also programmable. A low-energy shock is used initially, but if the device detects persistent ventricular tachycardia or ventricular fibrillation, higher-energy shocks then follow. The AICD stores information about each tachycardia episode, including the number of shocks delivered. This information and the remaining battery charge are easily transmitted by radio signal to the cardiologist. The newest generation of AICD devices also includes an antitachycardia pacemaker function. Upon detection of ventricular tachycardia, the device will at first attempt to stop the arrhythmia by rapid ("override") pacing. If this attempt is unsuccessful, a conventional shock is then automatically delivered.

Most recipients adjust well to their lifesaving automatic defibrillators. The internal shocks can be uncomfortable, but the reassuring effectiveness of the device more than compensates. Defibrillation is so prompt that most patients do not lose consciousness before the corrective shock is delivered. If a dependable AICD could be implanted by a minor surgical procedure, the indications for its use in patients with a variety of potentially life-threatening arrhythmias would be liberalized, and patients who were judged to be at very high risk of ventricular tachycardia or ventricular fibrillation but who had not yet had such an event might have an automatic defibrillator implanted prophylactically. Consequently, attempts are now being made to develop an AICD system that does not require surgical opening of the chest for implantation; currently being investigated are systems that use transvenous and subcutaneous electrodes.

Stress Testing the Heart

by Marc K. Effron, M.D.

Coronary artery disease is a major source of death and disease in the Western world. Clinical manifestations include angina pectoris (recurring chest pains), acute myocardial infarction (heart attack), heart failure, abnormal heart rhythms, and sudden death. Despite the high prevalence of coronary disease, its early detection and the prevention of its complications continue to present a considerable public health challenge. The so-called exercise stress test became one of the first diagnostic tools for the evaluation of patients with suspected coronary artery disease when medical scientists discovered that a patient could display an entirely normal electrocardiogram at rest, but reproducible electrocardiographic abnormalities would appear during exercise. The basis for this finding lies in the physiology of the compromised coronary circulation; a severely narrowed coronary artery may not significantly impair delivery of oxygenated blood to the heart muscle (myocardium) at rest but limits oxygenated blood delivery at times of high oxygen demand, such as during exercise.

The prototype exercise stress test was the "step" test. While the patient walked up and down a set of two steps, an electrocardiographic reading was taken. Stress testing has evolved into standardized protocols using automated treadmills or in some cases a cycle ergometer—sometimes in conjunction with radionuclide imaging of the myocardial blood flow.

Indications for exercise testing

If a 50-year-old male who smokes cigarettes reports that when he walks rapidly a pressing chest pain radiates to his jaw and left arm, angina pectoris is so highly suspected that stress testing can add little to the patient's management. Such classic angina in an individual with accentuated risk for coronary artery disease leaves little uncertainty as to what subsequent diagnostic and therapeutic measures are needed. Un-

fortunately, most cases are less well defined. Many patients with coronary disease do not have a classic anginal pattern of symptoms. Although chest pains may be present, they may not be typical in duration, location, or time of occurrence. Also, some characteristics of cardiac chest pain mimic or overlap the characteristics of pain in the chest wall or esophageal pain. Moreover, about one-half of all heart attacks are not preceded by any warning symptoms at all.

Major goals of exercise testing are the clarification of symptoms that are not fully typical for myocardial ischemia (poor blood flow to the heart muscle) and the early detection of coronary disease in patients without symptoms. Clinical indications for exercise testing are, in practice, much more varied. These indications have been enumerated by the Subcommittee on Exercise Testing of the American College of Cardiology/American Heart Association Task Force on the Assessment of Cardiovascular Procedures and have been divided into two classes: (1) conditions for which there is general agreement that exercise testing is justified and (2) conditions for which such testing is often performed but opinion diverges with respect to its value.

Since exercise testing with electrocardiographic monitoring is more accurate in men than in women, the primary subjects are male patients with atypical symptoms. Other generally accepted indications for exercise testing are the evaluation of patients after coronary bypass surgery or balloon angioplasty and the assessment of functional capacity of patients with known coronary artery disease or who have had a recent heart attack. Less frequent indications are the evaluation of abnormal heart rhythms and the functional assessment of patients with congenital heart disease or with certain types of implanted cardiac pacemakers.

There are many more indications for exercise testing that are still subject to debate, particularly in terms of validity and cost-effectiveness. Foremost among them is the evaluation of asymptomatic male patients over the age of 40 with special risk factors for coronary disease or those in special occupations (*e.g.,* pilots, police officers, railroad engineers). Similarly, patients in need of elective surgical procedures such as peripheral vascular surgery may undergo stress testing for assessment of cardiac risk at the time of such surgery. Other situations in which exercise testing is often recommended but may or may not be appropriate include the assessment of cardiac risk in males over age 40 before they undertake a rigorous exercise program, the evaluation of women with typical or atypical symptoms, the routine follow-up of patients who have known coronary artery disease or have had a previous revascularization procedure, and the assessment of functional capacity in patients who are under treatment for heart failure or have valvular heart disease.

Who should *not* undergo exercise testing

Exercise testing is generally very safe, assuming the test is administered by a trained clinician and the patient's electrocardiogram and blood pressure are carefully monitored during physical exertion. There are, however, special circumstances when exercise testing carries an elevated risk of complications and is distinctly contraindicated. Patients who should not undergo an exercise stress test are those with unstable angina (angina at rest or rapidly progressive angina), those who have had a very recent heart attack (within six days), those with aortic valve stenosis, those with severe congestive heart failure, and those with severe hypertension.

Conventional treadmill exercise testing is not feasible in patients with arthritis, neuromuscular conditions, or advanced lung disease. In some of these cases, cycle ergometers or arm exercise can be used in place of the treadmill. The cycle ergometer may also be safer than treadmill exercise for some elderly patients and others who may be at risk of falling.

In patients with debilitating noncardiac conditions, who cannot use any form of exercise to achieve a significant increase in cardiac work load, pharmacological substances that stress the heart (described below) can be substituted. Similarly, if a patient is under treatment with a medication that prevents an adequate increase of cardiac rate, such as one of the commonly used beta-adrenergic blocking drugs, a pharmacological stress test is preferred to the treadmill.

The treadmill test: step by step

Exercise testing is usually performed in a physician's office or hospital cardiology department. A patient is instructed not to consume solid food or large amounts of liquid for a least four hours prior to the test. He or she wears rubber-soled shoes and loose-fitting cloth-

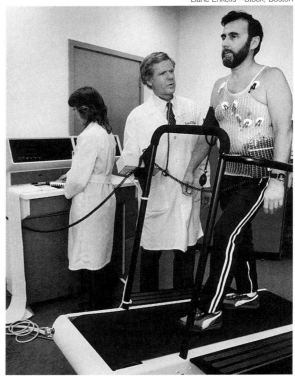

A patient undergoes a treadmill test under the supervision of a cardiologist. In the standard treadmill test, exercise is begun at a low level, then steadily increased. The higher the level of exercise that is reached, the more reliably the test can exclude the presence of coronary artery disease.

ing—shorts or pants. Adhesive electrodes for electrocardiographic monitoring are attached to the chest, and a blood pressure cuff is applied to the arm. Most often, a cardiologist or other physician specifically trained in exercise testing is present. The entire procedure, including preparation and actual performance, takes 30–45 minutes.

The most commonly performed treadmill test in the U.S. is the Bruce protocol. The patient is instructed to begin exercising at a relatively low level; the work load is then increased every three minutes with combined increases of speed and slope. For elderly patients or those with special disabilities, the Bruce protocol can be modified to provide an easier initial work load and a more moderate progression of activity. Another protocol, the Balk-Ware, begins at a very low work load and increases in slope but not in speed. There are various other protocols that are sometimes used.

Measuring exercise capacity. In all treadmill testing protocols, exercise capacity (sustained activity involving large muscle groups) is described in terms of metabolic equivalents (METs). One MET is the basal metabolic expenditure at rest. Published tables list the MET values for various speed and slope combinations. Normal exercise capacity for men aged under 30 is 13 METs; for men aged 50 to 59 years, 8 METs; and for men over age 80, 4 METs. Measurement of work performance in METs enables exercise results from various protocols to be easily compared.

The advantage of standard protocols is that of reproducibility. A similar work load can be used to compare the performance of a patient before and after one or another form of treatment. In research a standard protocol with incremental work loads can be used for large-scale comparison of exercise capacity and anginal threshold in various groups of patients.

An exercise test can exclude the presence of coronary artery disease more dependably if higher exercise levels are reached. In practice the heart rate is often used as an index of the adequacy of the level of physical exertion. Standard tables show maximum predicted heart rates according to age. A person 50 years old, for example, has a maximum heart rate of about 170 beats per minute. In treadmill testing generally a "target" heart rate of 85% of the maximum is sought. The target rate for the 50-year-old is thus 144 beats per minute. Exercise to less than this level may be insufficient to elicit symptoms or electrocardiographic changes indicative of cardiac ischemia. (The electrocardiogram comprises continuous, measurable signals that emanate from the heart during its cycles of contraction and relaxation. The primary electrocardiographic manifestation of ischemia is a deviation—depression or elevation—of one of these signals: the so-called ST segment.)

For a maximal (or symptom-limited) stress test, patients are encouraged to perform until they are limited by moderate chest pain, significant fatigue, or severe shortness of breath. Some patients may need to stop exercise because of progressive chest pain or light-headedness. Submaximal (or heart-rate limited) testing is used for patients who have had a very recent heart attack—when a lower peak work load increases the safety of the test but still permits prognostic findings. With this method the amount of exercise is based on the person's age and health; the test is concluded when a predetermined level of exercise is reached—unless symptoms occur prior to that time or there is a clear change in the electrocardiogram.

The treadmill test is, of course, an effort-dependent test. Patients will not perform up to their true capacity if they are afraid to push themselves physically. Those who have a sedentary life-style or who have had a recent heart attack may require considerable encouragement during the test. Without adequate effort the result will not be useful for diagnosis.

Following completion of the exercise, the patient lies in a supine position for at least six minutes of additional monitoring. This is known as the recovery period. If changes in the ST segment of the electrocardiogram have appeared during exercise, the amount of time it takes for the electrocardiographic pattern to resolve during recovery is of diagnostic importance. In rare cases electrocardiographic changes indicating poor blood flow to the heart muscle are first seen during recovery rather than during the actual physical stress.

Reasons to stop a treadmill test. In practice most treadmill tests are limited in duration by the patient's exercise capacity. The patient becomes fatigued to the point where the test must be stopped. Less frequently the supervising physician chooses to terminate the test before the patient asks to stop. The test should be stopped if the patient has progressively severe chest pain, especially if it is more intense than previous chest pain symptoms. If ST-segment depression surpasses three millimeters or if significant ST-segment elevation is observed, further exercise adds little to diagnostic accuracy and may pose a risk. A progressive blood pressure drop, light-headedness, pallor, or arrhythmias (disturbances in the normal pattern of heart beats) that could be life-threatening also indicate the need to stop the exercise.

Potential complications. The safety of exercise testing is well established—the mortality rate being one in 10,000. Similarly, ventricular fibrillation (the occur-

The top tracing, taken at rest, is normal. The bottom tracing, taken five minutes into an exercise stress test, is abnormal owing to the presence of ST segment depression (arrow), indicating that the heart muscle is not receiving adequate blood flow. (Images enlarged)

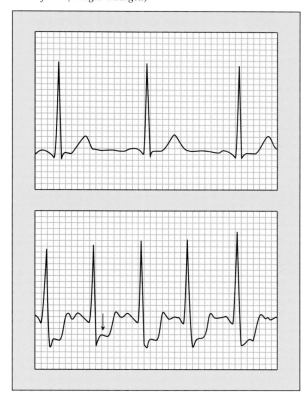

rence of very rapid, uncoordinated contractions of the ventricles of the heart) necessitating cardiopulmonary resuscitation may occur once in every several thousand cases. The other rare but serious complications are prolonged angina and true myocardial infarction.

Appropriate screening of patients prior to testing can help to minimize such complications. The most common high-risk and inappropriate referral for exercise testing is the patient whose history indicates unstable angina. Such patients have prolonged episodes of angina, angina at rest, or very recent onset of exertional angina. In some cases the supervising physician will need to review the patient's history and results of pertinent tests and physical examination to be sure that a major contraindication is not present before proceeding with the treadmill testing.

Diagnostic criteria: accuracy and limitations

As already noted, the hallmark indication of ischemia on an exercise test is deviation of the ST segment. One millimeter of flat ST segment or downsloping ST-segment depression is usually taken as the minimum electrocardiographic indicator of a positive test. However, exercise testing has a limited diagnostic accuracy. There is no exact threshold for significant ST

Conventional treadmill testing is not feasible for all patients. One alternative is a cycle ergometer adapted for arm exercise. The subject turns the ergometer's wheels by grasping handgrips that are fitted over the pedals.

Barry A. Franklin, William Beaumont Hospital Rehabilitation and Health Center, Birmingham, Michigan

segment change. An occasional patient with coronary disease will develop typical angina at a stage of exercise when the ST segments are not depressed or are depressed to a depth less than one millimeter.

A diagnostic criterion such as the degree of ST-segment depression can be adjusted according to the particular clinical need. If "positive" is defined as only 0.8 mm ST-segment depression, then there will be more false-positive but fewer false-negative results; the test would falsely include some normal patients as abnormals but would be less likely to miss significant coronary artery disease in a tested group of patients. Alternatively, if "positive" is set at a more severe degree of ST-segment depression, *e.g.,* two millimeters, then there will be fewer false-positive but more false-negative test results.

In addition to the degree of ST-segment depression, other criteria may assist in the interpretation of exercise test results. Early onset of ST-segment depression suggests more extensive ischemia. ST-segment elevation can also be a sign of severe ischemia. Exercise-induced angina during the treadmill test suggests ischemia but is not very dependable in the absence of ST-segment depression. While the normal response of blood pressure during exercise is a gradual elevation of systolic pressure and more mild changes of the diastolic pressure, a patient with extensive ischemia may show an actual drop of blood pressure during exercise. This paradoxical hypotensive response to exercise can be taken as a sign of left main coronary artery or severe multiple vessel coronary artery disease, which often requires surgical treatment.

The accuracy of a diagnostic test is partly determined by the incidence of the disease in the population being tested. As described in Bayes' theorem, screening of asymptomatic and low-risk individuals for coronary disease will lead to a high rate of false positives. For example, among 1,000 military recruits aged 18 to 28 years, most would have a normal test result, but a few would show ST-segment depression to or beyond a one-millimeter depth. Of these few, all or nearly all would actually have no underlying coronary artery disease. Their test findings would be false-positive results.

If 1,000 middle-aged high-risk men with typical angina are tested, the test population has a very high pretest incidence of coronary artery disease. Most exercise test results would be true positives in this group. Some negative results would also occur, but most of these would be false negatives—*i.e.,* ischemic criteria would not be met during the test, but significant coronary artery disease is still present.

Application of Bayes' theorem and familiarity with the clinical profile of the individual patient undergoing the stress test assist the physician in interpreting test results. The treadmill exercise stress test is not always clearly positive or negative: some tests must be described as "indeterminate" or "nondiagnostic"; in other cases the absence of symptoms and prompt resolution of ST segment changes during the recovery period suggest the possibility of a false-positive test result.

With the application of Bayes' theorem, the limitations of exercise treadmill testing in certain groups of patients are more easily understood. Male patients under age 40 and even older male patients without special risk factors for coronary artery disease represent a population with a low pretest incidence of the disease. Diagnostic accuracy is thus quite limited. The rate of coronary disease is quite low in women until after the age of 50. Moreover, there is an especially high risk of false-positive ST-segment depression in women during exercise. The physiological basis for this ST-segment depression is not understood, but the practical consequence is that standard exercise testing with electrocardiographic monitoring is of limited usefulness in women of all ages. False-positive electrocardiographic results are also quite common in patients with hypertension, left ventricular hypertrophy, and valvular heart disease and in those who are being treated with the heart stimulant drug digitalis.

Conduction system disease will cause distortion of the stress test results—for example, right bundle branch block poses problems for interpretation of ST-segment depression, and left bundle branch block essentially masks any ischemic changes. If a patient's heart rhythm is controlled by an artificial ventricular pacemaker, no electrocardiographic interpretation of ischemia is possible. Other patients are not able to achieve an adequate work load owing to physical impairments or to inadequate heart rate elevation caused by a dysfunction of the sinus node—the heart's intrinsic pacemaker—or as a result of beta-blocker drug therapy. In such cases, test results are not meaningful.

Myocardial perfusion imaging

To overcome the limitations of conventional exercise testing, the technique known as myocardial perfusion imaging has been developed to supply more accurate information about myocardial ischemia. This nuclear medicine imaging method can be applied in the evaluation of women and selected other groups of patients not usually suitable for regular exercise stress testing.

Myocardial perfusion imaging has been most commonly performed with the radioisotope thallium-201. This radioactive thallium isotope is handled by the body as an analogue of potassium, a common intracellular substance. At the peak of exercise, thallium is injected intravenously into the subject's circulation. It rapidly perfuses into the heart muscle and stays there. The distribution of radioactive thallium, as detected by a scanning gamma camera, corresponds to the distribution of the blood flow to the heart muscle. Myocardium supplied by a narrowed coronary artery will not

Ami S. Iskandrian, M.D., Philadelphia Heart Institute, Presbyterian Medical Center

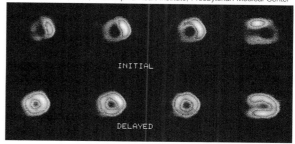

Myocardial perfusion imaging using the radioisotope thallium-201 can assess myocardial ischemia (poor blood flow to the heart muscle) more accurately than exercise testing alone. Scans taken during exercise (in the top row) show reduced blood flow (dark areas); blood flow patterns after three hours' rest (bottom row) are normal.

receive as much blood flow during exercise, and this will be revealed as diminished uptake of thallium-201. Over a few hours, the thallium redistributes into all viable (nonscarred) myocardial areas, and a second, delayed scan can be used for comparison with the initial stress scan.

In the myocardial-imaging exam an area of heart muscle that does not take up the isotope with exercise or at the delayed scan represents scarring of myocardial tissue from a prior myocardial infarction. An area that shows limited uptake with exercise but reperfuses well at rest is highly predictive of myocardial ischemia due to advanced coronary artery disease.

In a recently developed variation, which will make myocardial perfusion imaging less time consuming and probably more accurate, a resting image is obtained first, before the patient exercises. Thallium-201 is given by injection prior to the resting image; the isotope thereby immediately perfuses into all viable areas of myocardium. The patient then begins to exercise, and at peak exertion another radioisotope, technetium-99m methoxy-isobutyl-isonitrile (Tc-99m-MIBI), is injected. The Tc-99m-MIBI emits higher energy gamma photons than thallium-201. This permits scanning with special gamma cameras that will distinguish differences in the distribution of blood flow before and during exercise in a single scanning session.

Myocardial perfusion imaging overcomes many of the limitations of conventional exercise testing. False-positive and false-negative rates are greatly reduced. If, for example, on a standard treadmill test a male patient displays an ST-segment depression that is of borderline significance or if a false-positive pattern is suspected, myocardial perfusion imaging will clarify the findings. Owing to the very limited accuracy of conventional exercise testing in women, myocardial perfusion imaging has become the initial diagnostic test for many female patients.

The imaging of the myocardial blood flow distribution also permits exercise testing in other patients for whom no meaningful electrocardiographic information could be obtained. It is the procedure of choice for patients with left bundle branch block and certain other cardiac conduction system abnormalities. It is also preferred in those with rate-responsive pacemakers or dual chamber pacemakers whose sinus node function is normal.

Despite the enhanced accuracy, however, such imaging is not fully accurate for a diagnosis of coronary artery disease. Hypertensive patients will have a high rate of false-positive results. And the accuracy in women is still not as good as in men.

Pharmacological stress imaging

There remain some patients who are not eligible for either standard exercise testing or exercise testing with myocardial perfusion imaging, owing to physical limits on the ability to exercise or to heart rhythm abnormalities that prevent adequate heart rate elevation during physical stress. Such patients include those with heart rhythm conditions such as intrinsic sinus node dysfunction, those receiving beta-blocking drug therapy, and those with fixed-rate demand pacemakers. These special conditions are not uncommon among patients needing assessment for possible coronary disease in a cardiology practice.

In the patients just described, so-called pharmacological stress testing can be used in place of physical exercise. Intravenous administration of the drug dipyridamole produces marked vasodilation of the coronary arteriolar system. This drug action is mediated by the endogenous vasodilating substance adenosine. Dipyridamole inhibits cellular uptake of adenosine; the adenosine then accumulates and coronary vasodilation results. In the presence of a severe coronary artery stenosis (narrowing), myocardial blood flow is preferentially shifted to areas perfused by normal arteries and reduced in areas served by the narrowed artery. Following the administration of dipyridamole, thallium-201 myocardial perfusion imaging is promptly performed, and the differential myocardial uptake of the isotope will reveal the area of ischemia. This technique requires no physical exertion on the part of the patient other than an easy handgrip exercise, which can help to improve the quality of the study. Rare side effects that occur following intravenous dipyridamole infusion include prolonged chest pain, true myocardial infarction, and acute bronchospasm (asthma). Such complications can largely be avoided by infusion of another pharmacological agent, aminophylline, which acts as an antidote to reverse the effects of dipyridamole, soon after the test is completed.

In some cases directly infusing adenosine in place of dipyridamole will increase the safety of the procedure. Adenosine's very brief biological half-life enables it to be processed from the circulation so rapidly that prolonged side effects are not possible. Adenosine, however, can potentiate blockage of the atrioventricular node, which normally conveys the impulse from the base of the atria down into the ventricular conduction system, and should not be used in patients with certain kinds of arrhythmias or with severe conduction system disease.

Other heart-stressing techniques

Myocardial ischemia leads to decreased function of the affected heart muscle. In the presence of a critically narrowed coronary artery, the corresponding area of heart muscle usually contracts normally at rest but shows decreased contraction during exercise. This is known as an exercise-induced regional wall motion abnormality and is regarded as a sign of ischemia. Stress wall motion imaging can be performed, most often with the use of the radioisotope technetium-99 in conjunction with so-called gated blood pool scanning, a nuclear imaging technique for observing contraction of the left ventricle.

Another technique now available is stress echocardiography. This fully noninvasive imaging method uses diagnostic ultrasound to provide two-dimensional pictures of the myocardial wall motion before and after exercise or before and after infusion of a pharmacological stress agent—dipyridamole or dobutamine. It does not require any use of ionizing radiation.

Exercise testing in perspective

The ease and accuracy of stress testing have been greatly enhanced over the past two decades, mainly by refinements in the use of radiopharmaceuticals. However, the gold standard of coronary diagnosis remains the coronary arteriogram, an invasive procedure performed in a hospital, involving cardiac catheterization and injection of radio-opaque dye into the coronary arteries in order to obtain X-ray pictures of the heart. In patients with suspected coronary artery disease, the coronary arteriogram procedure is still most often required for a definitive treatment decision.

Although as a screening tool conventional exercise testing has limited usefulness, it is a relatively simple, safe, and cost-effective procedure that in many cases can help clinicians determine whether patients with suspected coronary artery disease should be referred for coronary arteriography. The myocardial perfusion imaging techniques can theoretically improve screening capability, but their costs as screening tests may be prohibitive.

Finally, because all stress test methods rely on the presence of coronary narrowings that are sufficient to limit blood flow, disease is detected at a relatively advanced state. Consequently, an inexpensive and widely applicable test for earlier detection of coronary disease remains a major need of today's health care system and of society.

Cat Allergy: Nothing to Sneeze At

by H. James Wedner, M.D.

The domestic cat (*Felis domesticus*) has become the number one household pet in the United States. Although the actual number of cats in the country is not known, it has been estimated that there are over 50 million felines living in more than 20 million U.S. homes. As more and more people are exposed to cats, increasing numbers have become sensitized to them. Thus, cat allergy has emerged as a major health problem.

Why are cats allergenic? What are the symptoms of cat allergy? What treatments are applicable for patients who suffer from cat allergy? These and other questions are addressed below.

What is an allergy?

From 25 to 30% of the people in the United States have the genetically inherited ability to develop an allergy. This predisposition is known as atopy. What atopy really represents is the likelihood that upon exposure to certain substances, the body will produce antibodies—specifically, antibodies of the immunoglobulin E (IgE) class.

Although antibodies are generally considered "good" because they are produced by the body as a means of fighting infection, the production of some antibodies, rather than helping to prevent disease, actually causes disease; the immune response represented by the production of IgE is perhaps the best example of this phenomenon. IgE antibodies originally evolved to help in the fight against certain parasitic diseases. Because the number of parasitic infections to which people in the U.S. and other industrialized countries are exposed is very low, their bodies no longer need IgE. Nonetheless, the ability to make the antibody remains, and atopic individuals now produce IgE in response to other, usually innocuous, things in their environment. Thus, people who are allergic may react to substances in the air they breathe (*e.g.,* tree, weed, and grass pollens; mold spores; and house dust), foods they eat (*e.g.,* wheat, milk, or soy protein), or materials that come in contact with their skin (*e.g.,* chemicals in paint). They may also react to household pets, such as dogs or cats. (All of these reactions are known as type I hypersensitivity reactions.)

When an allergy develops, the reaction is actually against some of the proteins in the plant, animal, or other substance. These water-soluble proteins are known as allergens. For a given plant or animal, the number of allergens may be very large, such as the 28

proteins in the pollen of the oak tree. Or the number may be very small; only a single allergenic protein is responsible for cat allergy. By international convention, the names of all allergens use the first three letters of the genus of the plant or animal, followed by the first letter of the species and then by a Roman numeral indicating the order in which the allergens were identified. Thus, the cat allergen is known as Fel dI.

The cat allergen: recent insights

Fel dI is a very interesting protein. Sophisticated molecular biology methods have made it possible for scientists to fully characterize the protein. Although Fel dI has no known biological function, it is known not to be critical to the cat.

Early studies suggested that the majority of the allergen was in the cat's saliva, which was deposited on its skin by the constant preening (licking of the fur) that is common to all felines. More recent studies have demonstrated that this is not the case. Most of the Fel dI actually comes from the sebaceous glands below the surface of the skin; the sebaceous glands open into the hair follicles and secrete an oily substance—largely composed of fat—that softens and lubricates the skin. As the hair shafts grow through the glands, Fel dI is deposited on the cat's body. And, since the cat constantly sheds dander, which is composed of fur and skin, Fel dI is constantly released into the animal's environment.

The amount of Fel dI produced by individual cats varies widely. Studies have demonstrated that some cats make as much as 12,000 milliunits or more per month, while other cats produce very little (less than 200 milliunits per month). In general, male cats produce more of the allergen than do females, although this is not always the case. There is also a great deal of variability in the amount of Fel dI that an individual cat produces from one month to another.

Some researchers have speculated that certain breeds of cat produce lesser amounts of Fel dI—notably, certain shorthair cats that have altered fur as a result of breeding. Those that have been singled out are the Rex, whose coat is fragile and lacks guard hairs; the Manx, which has a double coat—a plush, thick undercoat and a glossy topcoat; and the Sphynx, which is virtually hairless. However, many cat allergy sufferers do react to these breeds. Moreover, other studies have suggested that all of the various breeds—longhair and shorthair—produce Fel dI; therefore, any cat, whether inbred or outbred, must be considered a potential cause of cat allergy.

In contrast to many other allergens that may be found in the home, Fel dI is a very sticky protein. This is of great importance to allergy sufferers. Once a cat is in the house, it will begin to deposit Fel dI every place it goes and, as every cat owner knows, cats go everywhere! Because of the sticky nature of the protein, it stays where it is deposited. Thus, studies have demonstrated that Fel dI can be found not only on horizontal surfaces, such as floors, sofas, and beds, but also on vertical surfaces, such as walls. In addition, Fel dI is deposited on the clothing of those who reside in the home, which means that the allergen is readily transported to sites beyond the home.

Indeed, studies have discovered that Fel dI is virtually ubiquitous: it is present in petless homes; it adheres to the floors of large shopping malls; it is even found in allergists' offices. Once Fel dI is deposited in the home or anywhere else, it becomes aerosolized and then can produce symptoms in cat-allergic individuals.

Prevalence of cat allergy

As a single allergenic protein, Fel dI is one of the most potent causes of allergic disease. It is estimated that roughly 10% of the general U.S. population are allergic to cats (with females being allergic about twice as often as males). For atopic individuals the percentage is even higher; studies involving large numbers of subjects have found that 25% of all atopics are sensitive to cats.

Cat allergy is the most prevalent of the allergies to animal proteins, and there are significantly more cat allergic individuals than there are individuals allergic to dogs, horses, or pet rodents, for example. While it is possible to be allergic to cats alone, the majority of cat allergy sufferers also have allergic reactions to other common allergens; these would include various molds, pollens, and household dust.

Allergic reactions in general are more common in children than in adults; this is also true for cat allergy. It is well known that some children will lose their allergic sensitivity—including that to cats—around the time of puberty. However, well-controlled studies have demonstrated that only 50% of children will become allergy free, and a significant percentage of these children will redevelop their allergic sensitivity sometime later in life.

Symptoms: sneezing, wheezing, and more

The symptoms of cat allergy are typical of those that are seen with any allergen that can be aerosolized or deposited on the skin. Because Fel dI most commonly enters the body through the air, the major organ systems that are affected are the upper respiratory tract—the nose, mouth, and throat; the lower respiratory tract—the trachea and lungs; and the eyes.

The symptoms of allergy of the upper respiratory tract are collectively known as allergic rhinitis. Patients experience symptoms that are often associated with hay fever; *i.e.,* sneezing and an itchy, runny nose (rhinorrhea). Because of the itching, sufferers tend to rub the tip of their nose excessively, causing it to be red and to develop a distinct crease. Examination of the nose in these patients will show that the olfactory mucosa (the membrane lining the nasal cavity) is swollen, often causing nasal stuffiness.

The swelling of the mucosa may be so profound that the nasal passages are completely blocked, and secretions caused by the cat allergy then are forced to drip down the back of the throat (postnasal drip). Such swelling can also block the openings to the paranasal sinuses and may result in sinusitis. This occurs because the openings of all of the paranasal sinuses are in the nose. (There are four sets of paranasal sinuses: the maxillary sinuses in the cheek bones; the ethmoid sinuses, which are in the bones next to the eye sockets; the frontal sinuses, which are in the frontal bone above the eyes; and the sphenoid sinuses, which are behind the ethmoid sinuses.) Patients with acute sinusitis feel ill and may have a fever. Many sufferers will complain of pain or a pressure in the area of the sinus that is affected.

Another problem caused by the swelling of the nasal mucosa is that the eustachian tubes, which also open into the nasal cavity and serve to equalize the pressure between the middle ear and the outside, are affected. Some patients with cat allergy may note that sounds have become muffled, which is due to failure of the eardrum to move properly. Moreover, the blockade of the eustachian tubes may result in an infection of the middle ear called otitis media. Like sinusitis, otitis media causes pain or pressure, and occasionally there may be drainage from the affected ear.

Because humans breathe through the mouth as well as the nose, the allergen from cats will be deposited on the lining of the mouth as well. This results in an allergic inflammation that is similar to that in the nose. The symptoms may not be as profound as those of allergic rhinitis, but it is not uncommon for individuals who are allergic to cats to complain of itching of the palate or the back of the throat.

The major organ of the lower respiratory tract is the lungs; when the cat allergen is inhaled into the lungs, the patient experiences asthma. Asthma is an inflammatory reaction of the bronchial tubes that results in swelling of the lining of the bronchi and constriction of the bronchial musculature. Thus, there is an impediment to air flowing into and particularly out of the lungs. The most notable symptoms of asthma are wheezing on expiration, cough, and shortness of breath. Such symptoms may be mild or profound; in some cases asthma associated with cat allergy is life threatening. Patients with mild asthma may be asymptomatic most of the time but may note the onset of symptoms when they exercise. In patients with asthma who have a cat in their home, such symptoms tend to be chronic; these individuals will generally require treatment with antiasthma medications. Patients who do not have cats may suffer acute asthma attacks when they are in homes where there are cats or in sites where Fel dl has been heavily deposited.

Fel dl may also be deposited in the eyes and cause allergic conjunctivitis: the eyes become teary and itchy; some patients report a feeling of grittiness, as though there were sand in the eyes. There may also be crusting of the eyes, especially in the morning. In extreme cases, infection of the eyes may occur. The itching, not surprisingly, causes allergy sufferers to rub their eyes, which can lead to the appearance of circles around the eyes that have a black and blue tinge. These "allergy shiners" are most common in children but are also seen in adults.

As noted above, some people who are allergic to cats develop skin symptoms—most notably, urticaria (hives). Others may simply report that their skin itches and becomes red. These symptoms usually occur only when there is direct contact with the cat, such as petting; generally concentrations of Fel dl in the air alone are not sufficient to cause a skin reaction. In homes with many cats, however, the urticaria may be chronic and not related to touching the cat. As an example, a patient seen by this author reported that he experienced chronic urticaria in his home; he developed hives even if he studiously avoided touching any of the 27 cats that lived with him! Fortunately, the symptoms disappeared whenever he left this environment.

Diagnosing cat allergy

The diagnosis of cat allergy is generally inferred from the patient's history. In other words, patients will report that they experience symptoms such as those described above when they are or have recently been in places where cats are present. For individuals who have cats in their homes, the diagnosis may not be obvious. If their allergy to cats was present when the cat was brought into the home, they usually develop symptoms immediately. However, a patient can also develop sensitivity at some point after the cat was acquired as a pet. Since there are many potential household allergens, such as dust, molds, or other pets, it is not always clear that the cat alone is the culprit.

In patients with a history that is consistent with cat allergy, the diagnosis can be confirmed by either *in vivo* or *in vitro* testing. *In vivo* tests are the commonly performed allergy skin tests. A small amount of an extract of cat dander containing Fel dl is applied to the skin, usually of the forearm or the back, and then the skin is pricked or punctured with a needle. Alternatively, a small amount of the extract is injected into the skin (intradermal skin test). If the patient is allergic to cats, a wheal (hive) and flare (redness) will be seen in the area of the scratch or injection within 15 minutes. The size of the wheal-and-flare reaction, in general, is an indication of the degree of sensitivity of the patient to cats, although any person with a positive skin test should be considered allergic to cats.

In vitro testing involves an assay for the IgE antibodies that are directed against Fel dl. These tests are performed on a sample of the patient's blood. In contrast to the skin test, the *in vitro* test takes several hours to several days to perform, is much more expensive, and is somewhat less sensitive. In practice, the skin test is the preferred procedure, and the *in vitro* test should be performed only in those situations where a skin test is not possible. For example, patients with extensive skin disease, such as eczema, cannot be skin tested.

The best treatment: get rid of the cat

The most obvious treatment for cat allergy is for the allergic individual to avoid contact with the cat allergen, Fel dl. However, for many who are allergic to cats, this approach is unacceptable; for those with severe allergy, it may be impossible.

It may seem surprising, but a large proportion of patients with cat allergy have cats in their homes, and the majority of these individuals, despite the advice of their physicians, are unwilling to remove cats from their environment. A recent survey of patients seen in clinics of the Washington University School of Medicine, St. Louis, Mo., found that over 70% of those who indicated that they were allergic to cats had not gotten rid of their pet.

Nonetheless, the single-most-effective treatment remains removal of cats from the home and avoidance of places where cats have been present. In the majority of cases, this will obviate the need for the therapeutic methods that are outlined below. And in the

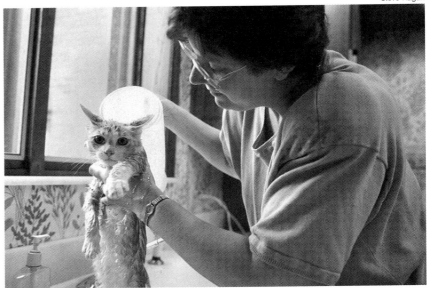

Washing cats in warm water for about 10 minutes on a monthly basis significantly reduces the amount of allergen (Fel dI) that they shed. Researchers made this discovery serendipitously in the course of trying to find a way to shut down cats' glandular activity and thereby stop their Fel dI production. Cat allergy sufferers may find that they get relief from allergic symptoms by regularly bathing their pet. Though cats are not likely to be enthusiastic about the baths, most will adapt to the routine, especially if they are introduced to it when they are kittens.

exquisitely sensitive patient who requires treatment, it will make the therapy all the more effective.

Reducing exposure to the allergen

As noted above, many allergy sufferers are so attached to their pets that they are simply unwilling to give them up. In such cases there are a number of remedies that can be tried.

Limiting the cat's domain. Many cat owners will give their pet free run of the home, including the bedroom. And over 60% of allergic patients report that they allow their cat to sleep in their bed. Quite obviously, one who sleeps for eight hours a night with a cat near his or her head is directly exposed to Fel dI for a significant portion of every day. This is the worst possible situation for an allergic individual. It is strongly recommended that those with cat allergy restrict their cat to only certain rooms; particularly, cats should not be allowed in the bedroom. For a majority of sufferers, this single change will decrease exposure to Fel dI markedly; in some cases it will decrease the symptoms of cat allergy to a manageable level.

Washing cats: a new approach. Various methods of reducing the amount of allergen that cats shed have been sought. Researchers at Washington University recently gave certain drugs to cats in an attempt to shut down gland activity and thereby decrease the amount of Fel dI that they produced. This proved to be ineffective. However, in the course of these studies, the researchers discovered that washing the cats resulted in notable decreases in their production of Fel dI.

In the laboratory, cats were placed in a basin containing one liter (about one quart) of distilled water, which had been warmed to 37° C (99° F). Prior to

the washing, cats were given a mild anesthetic. This was done to prevent them from splashing because the investigators needed to be able to collect all the water that was used for careful analysis of the amount of Fel dI removed. The water was poured over the cats, and all of the fur with the exception of the face and anogenital areas was then gently scrubbed. The procedure was repeated three or four times over a period of 10 minutes. As much water as possible was then expressed from the cats' fur, after which they were towel dried and finally thoroughly dried with a hair dryer on the lowest setting.

Overall, the decrease in Fel dI production in the 10 cats used in this study was from an average of 3,300 milliunits per month to less than 400 milliunits per month; ultimately the majority of cats stopped making Fel dI altogether. While these studies demonstrated that Fel dI production can in fact be stopped, further studies must be done to determine the extent to which this will result in a decrease in symptoms in those who are allergic. Nonetheless, many patients with cat allergy are now bathing their cats and reporting positive results.

The recommended procedure for bathing cats at home is to place them in a basin of warm water (cats do not like a cold bath any more than humans do). Although researchers used distilled water (which can be purchased at the grocery store for less than $1 a gallon [3.8 liters]—enough for four washes), probably clean tap water is just as good. The water is poured slowly over the cat, and its entire body is rubbed gently. Use of soap or pet shampoo is neither necessary nor desirable. This procedure should be repeated several times, with care taken to avoid getting water in the animal's eyes or ears (many groomers suggest placing a small piece of cotton in each ear). The entire procedure should take about 10 minutes. After the bath, as much of the water should be expressed from the fur as possible. The cat is then dried thoroughly with a towel. (Using a hair dryer is not recommended when cats are bathed at home.)

For the initial bathing, allergists suggest that a family member who is not allergic be responsible. The washing procedure should be performed once a month; the decrease in Fel dl becomes evident after three to eight months. Once the cat no longer makes Fel dl, the allergic person can take over the regular bathing.

While cats are not fans of the bathing procedure, most can adapt to it. Ideally, the process is begun with kittens, as they are easier to handle and the monthly baths readily become part of their routine. Adult cats, on the other hand, should be introduced to the washing gradually. Cat owners should be reassured that such bathing is not harmful to cats. In fact, the American Cat Fanciers' Association recommends washing cats at regular intervals.

A clean house. While a once-a-month washing regimen can clearly reduce or eliminate Fel dl production over time, researchers at the University of Virginia recently conducted a study in which cats were bathed once a week. Their regimen also included a thorough weekly cleaning of the home. This resulted in a significant decrease in the amount of cat allergen (as measured in dust that was collected in the home). Moreover, these levels were low enough to reduce the symptoms of allergic individuals.

Although a commitment to bathing a cat once a week may be more than most allergy sufferers are willing to make, this study clearly emphasizes the need for cleaning not only the cat but the home. As noted above, Fel dl is a very sticky substance that is deposited throughout the house. Thus, no matter how frequently cats are bathed to reduce their production of Fel dl, much of the allergen will still be present in the home. Thorough cleaning of the home is therefore an essential part of the strategy to reduce cat allergen in the allergic person's environment.

Other approaches. There are also a number of products on the market that purport to either decrease the amount of Fel dl shed by cats or inactivate the Fel dl once it has been shed. For example, a solution or spray containing 3% tannic acid will inactivate many allergens, including Fel dl, so that they no longer cause problems. In limited studies, tannic acid has been shown to be effective when sprayed on carpets, furniture, bedclothes, and other household materials. Tannic acid is a brownish compound that is found in oak bark, tea, coffee, and cocoa. Because it may alter the color of carpets or upholstery, one should test the solution in an unobtrusive area before using it throughout the home.

Other solutions that claim to decrease the amount of Fel dl that is shed are available; they are sprayed directly on the cat. However, many patients with cat allergy report no benefit from using them.

Immunotherapy

Immunotherapy (allergy shots), also called desensitization or hyposensitization, is an effective treatment for certain allergies—cat allergy among them. The therapy consists of injections of an extract containing Fel dl; the quantity given is initially very small and then is gradually increased. Usually injections are given every week (although some allergists administer them biweekly) until the maximum concentration is reached. The frequency of injections is then reduced to once every other week and finally once a month. The injections are generally given for two to three years; then, if there has been notable improvement, the immunotherapy is discontinued. In many patients the benefit remains indefinitely, while some patients may need continual therapy for long periods of time.

Cat-sensitive patients who contemplate immunotherapy must bear in mind that the shots work only when regular exposure to cat allergen is limited. In other words, if there is a cat in the home, the shots will not work. Thus, immunotherapy is generally reserved for those patients who do not have cats but are so sensitive that they react to Fel dl outside the home. Immunotherapy is also often used in allergic individuals whose occupations require contact with cats, such as laboratory workers and veterinarians.

Medications

There are a number of medications that are used for the treatment of cat allergy. The choice of one or more of these agents will depend on the type and the severity of the allergic symptoms. Patients with mild allergic rhinitis may be able to alleviate their symptoms with antihistamines or combined antihistamine-decongestants that are available over the counter. Some patients with upper respiratory symptoms may require prescription antihistamines such as the newer, nonsedating agents (*e.g.,* terfenadine, astemizole), corticosteroids (*e.g.,* flunisolide, beclomethasone, triamcinolone), or cromolyn sodium. The latter two medications are administered by nasal inhaler. Allergic conjunctivitis is treated with oral antihistamines or with antihistamines in eye drops. In severe cases steroid-containing eye drops may be necessary.

For patients with asthma due to cat allergy, there are a variety of medications that can be used alone or in combination. These include inhaled agents—corticosteroids, cromolyn sodium, and beta$_2$-adrenergic agonists. Some asthma patients may also need systemic medications—*e.g.,* theophylline and its derivatives, orally administered beta$_2$-adrenergic agonists, and in extreme cases oral corticosteroids.

Contributors to HealthWise

Stephen J. Ackerman
Children and Medicines
Free-Lance Writer, Washington, D.C.

Robert M. Adams, M.D.
Rash Reactions: Contact Dermatitis
Clinical Professor, Department of Dermatology, Stanford University School of Medicine, Stanford, Calif.

Darlene Dreon, Dr.P.H, M.S., R.D.
Grains of Truth About Bread
Staff Scientist, Lawrence Berkeley Laboratory, University of California at Berkeley

Marc K. Effron, M.D.
Arrhythmias; Stress Testing the Heart
Cardiologist, Scripps Memorial Hospital; Clinical Assistant Professor, University of California at San Diego School of Medicine, La Jolla

Weylin G. Eng, O.D.
Focus on Eyeglasses (coauthor)
Director of Clinics and Associate Clinical Professor, University of California at Berkeley School of Optometry

Donald J. Ferguson, M.D., Ph.D.
Appendicitis
Professor Emeritus, Department of Surgery, University of Chicago

Jane Katz, Ed.D.
Aquatic Exercise: Take the Plunge
Professor of Health, Physical Education, and Athletics, John Jay College of Criminal Justice, City University of New York; Consultant, President's Council on Physical Fitness and Sports; author, books on swimming and water exercise

Wardell Pomeroy, Ph.D.
Sex Education in the Age of AIDS
Coauthor, *Kinsey Reports;* author, *Boys and Sex* and *Girls and Sex*, Walnut Creek, Calif.

Bruce D. Shephard, M.D.
Travel During Pregnancy
Clinical Associate Professor of Obstetrics and Gynecology, University of South Florida College of Medicine, Tampa

Larry R. Thall
Zoonoses
Free-Lance Writer, Chicago

H. James Wedner, M.D.
Cat Allergy: Nothing to Sneeze At
Associate Professor of Medicine and Chief, Clinical Allergy and Immunology, Washington University School of Medicine, St. Louis, Mo.

Robert C. Yeager
Focus on Eyeglasses (coauthor)
Senior Editor, Chevron Corp; contributor to *Reader's Digest;* Oakland, Calif.

Title cartoons by Skip Williamson

Index

This is a three-year cumulative index. Index entries to World of Medicine articles in this and previous editions of the *Medical and Health Annual* are set in boldface type; *e.g.*, **AIDS.** Entries to other subjects are set in lightface type; *e.g.*, aspirin. Additional information on any of these subjects is identified with a subheading and indented under the entry heading. The numbers following headings and subheadings indicate the year (boldface) of the edition and the page number (lightface) on which the information appears. The abbreviation *il.* indicates an illustration.

AIDS, *or acquired immune deficiency syndrome* **93**–230; **92**–245; **91**–241
  Chinese medicine **93**–143
  diagnosis for women (special report) **92**–318
  drug-testing regulations **92**–364; **91**–274
  lymphoma **92**–263
  mother-to-infant transmission **93**–372
air pollution
  cancer role **91**–201
  Persian Gulf war **93**–20, 37, *il.*

All entry headings are alphabetized word by word. Hyphenated words and words separated by dashes or slashes are treated as two words. When one word differs from another only by the presence of additional characters at the end, the shorter precedes the longer. In inverted names, the words following the comma are considered only after the preceding part of the name has been alphabetized.
Examples:

> Lake
> Lake, Simon
> Lake Charles
> Lakeland

Names beginning with "Mc" and "Mac" are alphabetized as "Mac"; "St." is alphabetized as "Saint."

a

AAMI: *see* age-associated memory impairment
Abate: *see* temephos
abdomen
  appendicitis **93**–424
abdominal fat, *or* upper-body fat
  disease risks **91**–352
  middle-age spread **91**–474
Abdul-Jabbar, Kareem *il.* **92**–444
abortion
  delayed childbearing **91**–477
  Eastern European policies (special report) **92**–372
  fifth-disease association **91**–373
  multiple births **92**–72
  political controversy **91**–359
  sexual and reproductive health **92**–379, *il.* 380
  U.S. federal regulations (special report) **93**–316
  women's health **93**–406
  X-rays during pregnancy **92**–477
Abortion Act (U.K.) **92**–72
abruptio placenta
  pregnancy and older women **91**–479
  travel during pregnancy **93**–440
abscess
  appendicitis **93**–424
abstract thinking
  adult dyslexia (special report) **92**–325
Abuchowski, Abraham *il.* **92**–365
AC: *see* alternating current
Accidents and Safety 91–230
  alcohol warning labels impact (special report) **93**–170
  burns **93**–250
  housing conditions **93**–200
  injury prevention **93**–331
  Maryland death rate **93**–315
  organ transplantation **91**–409
  professional football injuries **93**–180
  taste and smell functions **93**–403
  travel during pregnancy **93**–441
ACE inhibitor, *or* angiotensin-converting enzyme inhibitor
  blood pressure reduction **93**–381
  hypertension treatment **91**–332
  ramipril **92**–367
Acel-Imune (vaccine)
  FDA approval **93**–382
acellular vaccine
  pertussis vaccination **93**–382; **91**–374
Acer, David J. **92**–247
acetohydroxamic acid (drug)
  kidney stone treatment **91**–430
acetylcholine
  Alzheimer's disease **92**–349
  hallucination role **91**–444
  Parkinson's disease **91**–235
acetylsalicylic acid: *see* aspirin
acid phosphatase
  prostate cancer detection **91**–412

acidic fibroblast growth factor, *or* aFGF
  coronary restenosis **92**–336
acitretin **92**–387
acne keloidalis, *or* dermatitis papillaris capillitii **91**–434
acoustic trauma
  hearing disorders **92**–327
acquired immune deficiency syndrome: *see* AIDS
acromegaly **91**–47, *il.* 46
act psychology: *see* intentionalism
ACTH: *see* corticotropin
Actimmune: *see* gamma interferon
actinomycin-D **91**–97
activation
  osteoporosis **91**–362
active management of labor
  obstetrics **93**–369
activin **91**–46
acupuncture **91**–108, *il.* 110
acute abdomen
  diagnostic techniques **93**–425
acute appendicitis **93**–424
acute encephalopathy
  children and lead poisoning (special report) **91**–287
acute infectious encephalitis: *see* encephalitis lethargica
acute lymphoblastic leukemia
  childhood cancer **91**–92
acute pulmonary disease
  sickle-cell disease **91**–386
acute stage of mourning
  anniversary reactions (special report) **91**–347
ADA deficiency: *see* adenosine deaminase deficiency
Adair, Robert **91**–302
Adalat: *see* nifedipine
ADAP: *see* Alzheimer's disease associated protein
ADD, *or* ADDH, *or* ADH: *see* hyperactivity
addiction
  compulsive shopping (special report) **91**–343
  see also Alcoholism; Drug Abuse
Addison's disease: *see* adrenocortical insufficiency
additive, *or* food additive
  drug-induced asthmas **91**–254
adenosine
  coronary artery disease testing **93**–478
adenosine deaminase deficiency, *or* ADA deficiency
  gene therapy **92**–303; **91**–306
  pharmaceuticals **92**–365
adenylate cyclase
  smell experience **93**–404
Ader, Robert *il.* **92**–35
Adey, W. Ross **91**–302
ADH: *see* vasopressin
adhesion
  appendicitis complication **93**–428
adipocyte
  fat accumulation **91**–473

adjuvant therapy
  cancer treatment (special report) **93**–267; **92**–262; **91**–400
Adkins, Janet **92**–277
adolescent health
  AIDS **93**–208
  alcohol warning labels (special report) **93**–168
  appendicitis **93**–425
  burns **93**–250
  influenza treatment **91**–421
  injuries **93**–336
  junk food **92**–449
  physical fitness **93**–385
  pregnancy and infant mortality **91**–355
  rhinoplasty **91**–404
  sex education **93**–451
  skateboarding and dental injuries **91**–264
  suicide **91**–84, *il.*
  U.K. efforts **93**–102
Adolescent Medicine 93–434; **92**–241
Adolph Coors Co. (U.S.)
  alcohol advertising **93**–158, 166
adoptee
  alcoholism studies **92**–158, *il.* 159
adrenal cortex
  hormone action **91**–47
  hypertension role **91**–332
adrenal gland
  Addison's disease **91**–41
adrenaline: *see* epinephrine
adrenocortical insufficiency, *or* Addison's disease
  Addison's research **91**–41
adrenocorticotropic hormone: *see* corticotropin
adult-onset diabetes: *see* non-insulin-dependent diabetes mellitus
advance directive, *or* medical directive
  right-to-die issue **92**–277
Advanced Laparoscopy Training Center (Ga., U.S.) **92**–407
adventitia layer
  coronary artery **92**–334
advertising
  alcohol **93**–152
  cigarettes **92**–399
  prescription drugs **92**–363; **91**–276
  sexually transmitted diseases **93**–114
  U.K. public health issues **93**–105
"Advertising Alcohol: This Brew's for You" (Baldwin, Jacobson and Taylor) **93**–152
aerobic exercise
  aquatic exercise **93**–429, 431
  arthritis (special report) **92**–391, *il.* 393
  children *il.* **93**–387
  fibromyalgia **92**–439
  middle-age spread treatment **91**–475
  physical fitness **91**–382
aerosol
  environmental health **92**–290
Aerospace Medicine 93–224
aFGF: *see* acidic fibroblast growth factor
Africa
  AIDS occurrence **93**–231
  cataract **93**–292
  cholera epidemic **93**–76
  guinea worm disease **93**–22
  plant-derived drugs **93**–143
  travelers' immunization **93**–444
African American: *see* black American
Africanized bee
  insect stings (special report) **93**–281
aftershock
  Loma Prieta earthquake **91**–271
agammaglobulinaemia **91**–267
age-associated memory impairment, *or* AAMI **92**–127
age spot, *or* liver spot **92**–463
Agency for Toxic Substances and Disease Registry (U.S.)
  children and lead poisoning (special report) **91**–288
  occupational health **92**–362
aggression **91**–234, *il.*
Aging 91–234
  Alzheimer's disease **92**–347
  appendicitis **93**–425
  domestic accidents **93**–201
  exercise **92**–135
  eye diseases and visual disorders **93**–293, 296, 419
  health care costs **92**–309
  hormones' role **91**–54
  Japan's demography and government plan (special report) **91**–337
  long-term care and women **91**–160
  longevity (special report) **93**–391
  memory loss **92**–127
  middle-age spread **91**–472
  olfactory ability **93**–401
  physical fitness **91**–378
  pregnancy and older women **91**–478
  Stendhal syndrome treatment **91**–188
  see also senior citizens
"Aging and Immunity" (Ershler) **93**–391

"Aging: Don't Take it Sitting Down!" (Wood) **92**–134
agoraphobia **93**–357
agranulocytosis
  clozapine causation **91**–341
  Graves' disease **92**–456
agriculture, *or* farming
  homeopathic treatment **91**–116
Agriculture, U.S. Department of, *or* USDA
  food labeling **92**–285
  harvesting Pacific yews **93**–132
AHA: *see* American Heart Association
AICD: *see* automatic implantable cardioverter-defibrillator
AIDS, *or* acquired immune deficiency syndrome **93**–230; **92**–245; **91**–241
  adolescent health and sex education **93**–208, 451
  camps for children **91**–454
  cesarean delivery **91**–358
  Chinese medicine **93**–143
  diagnosis for women (special report) **92**–318
  drug-testing regulations **92**–364; **91**–274
  drug treatments **93**–147, 382
  Eastern Europe (special report) **92**–373
  epidemiological investigations **92**–96
  eye disorders **93**–296
  fungal diseases **92**–479
  lymphoma **92**–263
  mother-to-infant transmission **93**–372
  National Library of Medicine poster collection (special report) **93**–124
  "New England Journal of Medicine" **92**–190
  "Oxford English Dictionary" inclusion (special report) **92**–267
  polymerase chain reaction **91**–305
  professional sports awareness **93**–188
  public education **93**–122
  refugees **91**–141, *il.*
  syphilis **92**–381
  tuberculosis (special report) **93**–243
  U.K. awareness efforts **93**–112
  women's health **93**–409
AIDS-related virus: *see* human immunodeficiency virus
air
  disease transmission **92**–107
  lead poisoning in children (special report) **91**–288
air bag **93**–332; **91**–230
air-conditioning system
  disease transmission **92**–107
Air-Crib *il.* **92**–378
air-dilution olfactometer *il.* **93**–404
air pollution
  asthma attack cause **91**–254
  California (special report) **92**–252
  cancer role **91**–201
  Eastern Europe (special report) **92**–371, *il.* 374
  exercise **92**–290
  Persian Gulf war **93**–20, 37, *il.*
air pressure: *see* atmospheric pressure
air temperature **91**–469
airplane
  safety seats for children **91**–230
  travel during pregnancy **93**–442
  wheelchair access **91**–154
airway hyperreactivity, *or* airway hyperresponsiveness
  asthma **93**–236; **91**–253
akathisia
  encephalitis lethargica **92**–210
Albert Einstein College of Medicine (N.Y.C., N.Y., U.S.)
  taxol research **93**–130
Albrecht, Johan Peter **92**–205
Albright's hereditary osteodystrophy **91**–46
alcohol
  advertising **93**–152
  hypertension treatment **91**–335
  Mormons' proscription **91**–194
  product warning labels (special report) **93**–168
  see also drinking, alcohol
Alcohol Concern (org., U.K.)
  public health **93**–111
alcohol industry **91**–154
Alcohol, Tobacco and Firearms, Bureau of, *or* BATF (U.S.)
  alcohol advertising interventions **93**–160, 164
  alcohol warning labels (special report) **93**–169
"Alcohol Warning Labels: Are They Working?" (Laughery and Young) **93**–168
Alcoholic Beverage Labeling Act (U.S.)
  product warning specifications (special report) **93**–168
Alcoholism
  attitudes and use
    American **93**–154; **92**–150
    British **93**–111
    French **93**–50
  hallucination occurrence **91**–443

norepinephrine
   anorexia nervosa **91**–283
   hypertension **91**–331
   stress **92**–31
norethindrone
   heart disease and women **92**–424
Norplant
   sexual and reproductive health **92**–383, *il.*
North American Symptomatic Carotid
      Endarterectomy Trial
   stroke prevention study **93**–398
North Carolina (state, U.S.) **91**–269
Northcliffe, Lord **91**–67
Norway
   alcohol advertising **93**–167
Novello, Antonia **91**–371
   advertising industry **93**–163
   AIDS and adolescent health **93**–208
"Nowhere a Promised Land: The Plight of
      the World's Refugees" (Toole and
      Waldman) **91**–124
NOx (gas)
   air pollution (special report) **92**–253
NRC (U.S.): *see* National Research Council
NREM sleep: *see* non-rapid eye movement
      sleep
NSAID: *see* nonsteroidal anti-inflammatory
      drug
NSC (U.S.): *see* National Safety Council
NST: *see* nonstress test
nuclear magnetic resonance: *see* magnetic
      resonance imaging
nuclear medicine
   medical imaging **93**–350
   X-rays during pregnancy **92**–478
nuclear power plant
   leukemia incidence **92**–293
nucleic acid hybridization
   polio research **91**–20
nucleotide
   genetic and physical mapping **91**–304
Nuromax (drug): *see* doxacurium
nurse educator
   gestational diabetes treatment **91**–426
Nursing
   Nightingale's contribution **91**–65
   patient-physician relationship **92**–474
nursing home
   Alzheimer's patients (special report)
      93–298
   Japan's aging population (special report)
      93–340
   long-term care **91**–162, 240
nutrient
   eye disease prevention **93**–295
   pregnancy requirements **91**–447
nutrition: *see* Diet and Nutrition
nutritionist
   sports medicine **93**–179
nux vomica **91**–114
nylon
   guinea worm disease *il.* **92**–24

o

Oak Ridge National Laboratory (Tenn., U.S.)
   occupational hazards **92**–362
oat bran **91**–330
Obesity 91–351
   children **93**–386; **91**–377
   diet and nutrition **92**–282
   food cravings **92**–450
   health hazards
      endometrial cancer **93**–259
      gestational diabetes **91**–424
      heart disease **92**–424
      hypertension link **91**–335
      middle-age spread **91**–474
   nutrition during pregnancy **91**–446
obsession
   body dysmorphic disorder (special
      report) **93**–363
   compulsive shopping (special report)
      91–344
obsessive compulsive disorder, *or* OCD
   body dysmorphic disorder comparison
      (special report) **93**–368
obsessive compulsive personality **92**–429
Obstetrics and Gynecology 93–369;
      91–354
   body fat increase **91**–351
   care of the elderly **91**–164
   comparison with U.S. abortion funding
      (special report) **93**–317
   gestational diabetes complications
      91–423
   laparoscopy **92**–408
   multiple births **92**–72
   nutrition during pregnancy **91**–445
   travel during pregnancy **93**–439
   see also pregnancy; Sexual and
      Reproductive Health
obstruction
   appendicitis **93**–424
   coronary artery disease **93**–320
   smell disorders **93**–403

stroke **93**–396, *il.* 400
OC: *see* oral contraceptive
occlusion
   coronary disease **93**–324
   stroke treatment **93**–399
occult blood **92**–297
Occupational Health 92–359
   alcoholism studies **92**–158
   asbestos **92**–291
   electromagnetic fields (special report)
      91–301
   medical uses of space technology
      91–158
   see also Environmental Health
Occupational Safety and Health
      Administration, *or* OSHA (U.S.)
   occupational health **92**–359
OCD: *see* obsessive compulsive disorder
ocean liner
   travel during pregnancy **93**–442
octuplets **92**–58
oculogyric crisis **92**–211
odorant
   smell experience **93**–404
oedipal phase
   compulsive shopping (special report)
      91–345
"Of Mice and Maine" (McBride) **91**–313
Office of Research on Women's Health
   establishment **93**–405
Office of Technology Assessment, *or* OTA
   electromagnetic field research (special
      report) **91**–303
ofloxacin, *or* Floxin (drug)
   FDA approval **92**–367
Ogston, Sir Alexander **92**–51
oil
   Persian Gulf war **93**–37
oil folliculitis
   hair problems of blacks **91**–433
Okinawa (is., Japan)
   diet and health **93**–45
old age: *see* Aging; senior citizens
Old Testament
   language **92**–171
Olesen, Jes **91**–323
Olestra, *or* sucrose polyester
   fat substitutes **92**–283
olfaction: *see* smell
olfactory membrane
   smell experience and disorders **93**–403
olfactory mucosa
   cat allergens **93**–480
olfactory nerve
   smell experience and disorders **93**–403
olfactory pathway
   smell disorders **93**–403
olfactory receptor cell
   taste and smell experience and disorders
      93–401
oligonucleotide mapping
   polio detection **91**–15
olive oil
   Italian cuisine **93**–47
olsalazine sodium, *or* Dipentum (drug)
   FDA approval **92**–366
omega-3 fatty acid
   diet and coronary heart disease **93**–45
omentum
   appendicitis in infants **93**–427
omeprazole, *or* Prilosec (drug)
   peptic ulcer treatment **92**–295
"On the Mode of Communication of
      Cholera" (Snow) **93**–83
"Once Stung, Twice Shy?" (McDaniel)
      93–281
ONCOCIN
   medical decision aids (special report)
      91–367
oncogene
   cancer research **92**–265; **91**–89
   genetic research **91**–307
oncology: *see* cancer
ondansetron hydrochloride, *or* Zofran (drug)
   FDA approval **93**–380; **92**–366, *il.* 364
"One Flew Over the Cuckoo's Nest" (movie)
   shock therapy *il.* **92**–93
1A rating
   pharmaceuticals **93**–380; **92**–364
1B rating
   pharmaceuticals **93**–380; **92**–365
1C rating
   pharmaceuticals **93**–381; **92**–366
only children **92**–441
onychomycosis: *see* fungal nail disease
oocyst
   toxoplasmosis transmission **93**–462
oocyte
   preimplantation genetics **92**–304
open surgery **91**–429
operant conditioning **92**–378
ophthalmologist **93**–419
   corrective procedures **93**–293
ophthalmoscope
   vision screening of children **91**–373
opioid
   anorexia nervosa role **91**–283
opium **93**–137

opportunistic infection
   AIDS association **93**–232; **92**–250;
      91–244
   HIV-related eye disorder **93**–296
   tuberculosis (special report) **93**–244
OPV: *see* orally administered poliovirus
      vaccine
oral contraceptive, *or* birth control pill,
      or OC
   heart disease and women **92**–424
   melasma association **91**–435
oral hygiene: *see* hygiene
oral literature **92**–125, *il.* 124
oral phase
   compulsive shopping (special report)
      91–345
oral rehydration salts, *or* ORS
   cholera treatment **93**–90
oral rehydration therapy, *or* ORT
   child health **92**–269
   cholera **93**–88
oral surgery
   laser dentistry **91**–262
   wisdom teeth **92**–434
orally administered poliovirus vaccine, *or*
      OPV **91**–12
orchiectomy
   prostate cancer treatment **91**–413
ordeal bean: *see* Calabar bean
Oregon (state, U.S.)
   yews **93**–130
Oregon Health Sciences University
      (Portland, Ore., U.S.)
   dietary experiment **93**–47
organ
   cancer site **92**–266
organ donation **91**–409
   bone marrow transplantation **93**–246
   heart transplantation **93**–322
   liver transplantation **93**–9
organogenesis
   X-rays during pregnancy **92**–475
Oriental flush
   alcohol reaction **92**–161
Ornidyl (drug): *see* eflornithine
      hydrochloride
ornithine decarboxylase
   electromagnetic fields (special report)
      91–302
orphan
   play (special report) **92**–299
orphan drug **93**–380; **92**–365
ORS: *see* oral rehydration salts
ORT: *see* oral rehydration therapy
orthopedic shoe **92**–468
orthopedic surgeon **92**–184
   sports medicine **93**–176
orthopedic surgery
   joints replacement (special report)
      92–272
orthostatic hypotension: *see* postural
      hypotension
orthostatic intolerance
   spaceflight biomedical research **93**–226
orthotic
   flatfeet **92**–468
OSHA (U.S.): *see* Occupational Safety and
      Health Administration
O'Shaughnessy, William Brook
   cholera research **93**–87
Osiris
   Egyptian funerary papyrus *il.* **92**–172
osteoarthritis **92**–142
osteoblast
   osteoporosis role **91**–362
osteoclast
   osteoporosis role **91**–362
osteogenic sarcoma, *or* osteosarcoma
   childhood cancer **91**–98, *il.*
osteomyelitis
   sickle-cell disease complication **91**–387
Osteoporosis 91–361
   anorexia nervosa **91**–283
   chronobiology research (special report)
      91–398
   exercise **92**–142; **91**–378
   hormone replacement therapy **91**–361
osteosarcoma: *see* osteogenic sarcoma
Ostrander, Gilbert **92**–160
ostrich meat, *or* strauss
   diet and nutrition **92**–283, *il.*
OTA: *see* Office of Technology Assessment
ovary
   anterior pituitary role **91**–42
   taxol treatment **93**–130, 263
over-the-counter drug, *or* nonprescription
      drug, *or* OTC drug
   Food and Drug Administration **92**–367
   pediatrics **93**–435
overcorrection
   visual disorder corrective procedure
      93–294
overcrowding
   unhealthy housing conditions
      93–190, 202
   U.S. public hospitals **93**–312
overeating
   middle-age spread **91**–473

overflow incontinence
   aging disorder **91**–236
overproduction theory
   alcoholism **92**–163
overvalued idea
   body dysmorphic disorder (special
      report) **93**–365, 368
overweight: *see* Obesity
ovulation
   appendicitis diagnosis **93**–425
   hormones **91**–45
   multiple births **92**–59
oxalate
   kidney stone formation **91**–427
   liver disease **93**–9
"Oxford English Dictionary, The"
   medical terms (special report) **91**–265,
      il. 267
oxidation
   visual disorders **93**–296
Oxsoralen: *see* psoralen
oxybutynin hydrochloride, *or* Cystrin, *or*
      Ditropan **91**–236
oxygen
   air travel during pregnancy **93**–442
   arteriovenous fistula (special report)
      92–286
   retinopathy of prematurity **93**–294
   stroke brain damage **93**–400
oxytocin (drug)
   induced labor **91**–481
ozone
   air pollution **92**–290
   asthma **91**–255
   cancer **93**–260
   smog (special report) **92**–253

p

p53 (protein)
   cancer role **93**–259; **92**–265; **91**–307
P300 evoked potential
   chronobiology research (special report)
      91–396
pacemaker
   cardiac conduction system **93**–465,
      il. 471
   exercise testing **93**–477
   heart rhythm disorders **91**–324
   implantable defibrillator comparison
      93–323
Pacific yew, *or* Taxus brevifolia (tree)
   taxol source **93**–130
PACs: *see* premature atrial contractions
Page, Clarence **92**–152
Paigen, Kenneth **91**–315, *il.* 318
pain
   acupuncture treatment **91**–112
   appendicitis **93**–425
   back **92**–257
   childbirth **91**–358
   computer diagnosis (special report)
      91–367
   fibromyalgia **92**–437
   headache **91**–319
   hypochondria **92**–429
   tooth sensitivity **91**–263
   wisdom teeth postoperative **92**–436
painkiller: *see* analgesic
paint
   children's risks (special report) **91**–286
painting
   liver transplantation surgeons and
      patients **93**–14
Pakistan
   guinea worm disease **92**–21
PAL: *see* Program for Advancement of
      Learning
palilalia
   encephalitis lethargica **92**–210
palmitic acid
   meat consumption **92**–420
palpitation **93**–465
pamidronate, *or* Aredia (drug)
   FDA approval **93**–380
Panama
   Africanized bee (special report) **93**–282
Panax schinseng (plant): *see* ginseng
pancreas
   Mormons cancer rate **91**–202
   transplantation **91**–409
pancreatitis **91**–244
pandemic
   cholera **93**–74
   influenza **91**–417
panic
   disorder **93**–355
   Stendhal syndrome **91**–187
Pap smear, *or* Papanicolaou smear **91**–463
   cancer detection **93**–258
Papanicolaou, George **91**–463
papaverine (drug)
   impotence treatment **91**–414
papule **91**–434
papulosa nigra, dermatosis: *see* dermatosis
      papulosa nigra